10%

BLACKWELL'S POLITICAL TEXTS

General Editors: C. H. WILSON and R. B. McCALLUM

A FRAGMENT ON GOVERNMENT
and
AN INTRODUCTION TO THE
PRINCIPLES OF MORALS
AND
LEGISLATION

A FRAGMENT
ON GOVERNMENT

AND

AN INTRODUCTION TO THE
PRINCIPLES OF MORALS
AND LEGISLATION

By JEREMY BENTHAM

Edited with an Introduction by
WILFRID HARRISON
Fellow of Queen's College, Oxford

BASIL BLACKWELL
OXFORD
1948

Printed in Great Britain for Basil Blackwell & Mott, Ltd.
by A. R. Mowbray & Co. Limited, London and Oxford

CONTENTS

THE TEXT

The text of the First Edition of the *Fragment on Government* has been followed here.

The *Introduction to the Principles of Morals and Legislation* was printed but not published in 1780. It was first published in 1789 in the form in which it had previously been printed, but with a Preface, some emendations, and some footnotes added, and further new passages added at the end. Bentham brought out a new and corrected edition in 1823, adding some further footnotes, with dates, and incorporating in the text the passages previously added at the end. This 1823 edition has been followed here.

ABBREVIATIONS

I have used the following abbreviations in the footnotes to the Introduction:—

F—*A Fragment on Government.*
P—*An Introduction to the Principles of Morals and Legislation.*
B—*The Works of Jeremy Bentham, Published under the supervision of his Executor, John Bowring* (11 Vols., 1843).

W. H.

INTRODUCTION

I

JEREMY BENTHAM was born on February 15th, 1748, into a well-to-do middle-class and Tory family of some standing in the City of London. Jeremiah Bentham, his father, was the son of a lawyer of Jacobite sympathies, the grandson of a prosperous pawnbroker, and a lawyer himself; he had interests in real property and was Clerk of the Scriveners' Company. Jeremiah Bentham went against his parents' wishes in marrying the daughter of an Andover tradesman; but he was otherwise orthodox: Jeremy was to practise law and enhance further the family's property and standing, and his education was planned accordingly. While he was still at home he was placed under masters in dancing, drawing, French and music; he went to Westminster School in 1755 and to Queen's College, Oxford, in 1760, was entered at Lincoln's Inn in 1763, and called to the Bar in 1769. Delicate, nervous, and precocious, however, he had shown from early years both intellectual and temperamental waywardness: he retained an interest in language and music, but before he was twelve he had (according to his own account) found an ideal of character in Fénelon's *Télémaque*[1], and, after reading about some protracted legal proceedings he had vowed war against the 'Daemon of Chicane.' At twelve, when he was admitted to Queen's, he had scruples about signing the Thirty-Nine Articles; while at Queen's he developed an interest in natural science. When he was in chambers he conducted scientific experiments, and, instead of preparing for legal practice, spent his time considering the defects of the existing legal system and of current legal thought. At twenty he had decided his vocation: he would provide a foundation for scientific jurisprudence and legislation.

The whole of Bentham's unusually long working life was governed by this decision. The outlines of a massive programme were already in his mind before the publication of the *Fragment on Government* in

---

[1] *Les Aventures de Télémaque* was published in 1699, a year after Fénelon had been appointed to instruct the son of the Dauphin. Telemachus is a very virtuous character. The book also sets out views on the obligations of monarchs, and by implication criticizes several features of the government of France under Louis XIV. Bentham later professed to have been interested, at the age of seven, in some of these political arguments, although he did not realise that the work was a political satire. (See B., vol. 10, p. 11.)

1776; and he had also by then begun work preliminary to the preparation of a penal code; indeed, as early as 1788 he was aware of the need for disciples to whom the detailed working out of some of his constantly expanding ideas could be entrusted. For a school of this sort he had long to wait; but from 1765 a small private income enabled him to concentrate on his chosen task. In this he was fortunate, for he was not aided by patronage although he was taken up by Lord Shelburne after the publication of the *Fragment*; and public knowledge of his theories was very slow in growing; it was retarded by the very fertility of his ideas, his apparently insuperable desire to follow out in full every consequence of every idea, his very considerable reluctance to publish work that he considered to be incomplete, and his lack of interest in publication if his mind had turned to some new topic.[1] Yet he did not wholly occupy himself with writing. In 1785, still obscure, he went to Russia to see his brother[2] and an experiment on which he was employed—the creation of a modern agricultural and industrial colony in the Ukraine. In Russia he wrote a book on political economy,[3] and he returned to England in 1788 with his project for a model prison or 'Panopticon.'[4] Attempts to secure government backing for this project occupied him intermittently until 1811; and meanwhile his main work and its derivative studies continued. In 1788 the foundations of a European reputation were laid: through Samuel Romilly he met a Swiss exile, one Étienne

[1] As a result, the writings of Bentham constitute something of a problem. During his lifetime, between thirty and forty works were published either by Bentham himself or by collaborators from his manuscripts. About twenty more were published posthumously. University College, London, has numerous boxes of manuscript material left by him, most of it still unpublished. There is more unpublished material in the British Museum. Some of the works that were published during Bentham's lifetime were written anything up to thirty years before publication. Some works are, in whole or part, re-hashes of others: some are only fragments. These writings cover legal science, political economy, education, the church, language, the poor law, local government, banking, the postal service, the census, international organization, and a considerable number of other subjects. (See bibliographical appendix in Halévy, *The Growth of Philosophical Radicalism*.) For Bentham's own remarks on his programme and his difficulties in coping with it, see *P.*, Preface, paras. 2–4 and 18–31.

[2] Samuel Bentham (1757–1831), educated at Westminster School and apprenticed at Woolwich Dockyard. He was employed in Russia by Prince Potemkin, and his plan of 'central observation' of his workshops was an early form of the Panopticon idea. He later carried out naval dockyard improvements for the British Admiralty and became one of the commissioners of the Navy. He was known as Sir Samuel Bentham, but this was apparently on the basis of his being a knight of the Russian order of St. George.

[3] The *Defence of Usury*, published 1787.

[4] *Panopticon, or the Inspection House* (1791) and *Panopticon versus New South Wales* (1812).

Dumont, who undertook the revision and French translation of parts of his manuscripts; publication in France began in the same year in Mirabeau's *Courrier de Provence*. Three years later Bentham's financial position improved as a result of his father's death; and soon afterwards it began to appear that at least part of his work might be accorded recognition in England, for in 1794 Parliament accepted the Panopticon scheme. But there were then difficulties: five years elapsed before a site was found and there were further delays in providing funds.

By 1802 over quarter of a century had passed since the publication of the *Fragment on Government*, and in the interval Bentham had published several other works in England, including some that are famous to-day, such as the *Defence of Usury* (1787), the *Introduction to the Principles of Morals and Legislation* (1789), the *Essay on Political Tactics* (1791), and *Emancipate Your Colonies* (1793). He had also written but not yet published several more works that are equally famous to-day, including *A Table of the Springs of Action*, *Principles of International Law*, *Anarchical Fallacies*, and the *Manual of Political Economy*. In addition several manuscripts were in the hands of Dumont. By 1802, then, Bentham had covered a great deal of ground, but he was still very little known in England. But in that year Dumont published in France, from Bentham's *Introduction to the Principles of Morals and Legislation* and his manuscripts, the *Traités de Législation Civile et Pénale*,[1] and this work was quickly to become known and admired in France, Russia, Spain and Latin America. Meanwhile Bentham was occupied in England with further trouble over the Panopticon. He had regarded himself hitherto as a humanitarian reformer, certainly not as a radical; he had attended the Wilkes trial as a Tory sympathiser, and he later wrote that he 'never suspected that the people in power were against reform'; he 'supposed they only wanted to know what was good in order to embrace it.'[2] But the Panopticon affair provided a lesson that coincided with new influences and the appearance at last of the long-awaited opportunity for the founding of a school: in 1808 Bentham became acquainted with James Mill. In the years immediately following, a school developed and Bentham then became known as a radical, although the transition was

---

[1] A translation by John Neal was published in Boston in 1830, and some of the material used was available in Bowring in 1843, but the first translation widely used was that of Richard Hildreth (1864). This translation is used in C. K. Ogden's edition (*The Theory of Legislation*) (1931).

[2] B., vol. 10, p. 66; cf. various comments in Bentham's own introduction to the second edition of the *Fragment on Government* (1828), B., Vol. 1, pp. 240–259.

made without any fundamental changes in his central ideas and aims. He wrote his *Catechism of Parliamentary Reform* in 1809 and his *Radicalism Not Dangerous* in 1819; but he was also continuing to follow his other interests. In 1810 he considered making a journey to Venezuela to codify legislation. In 1814 he began his *Deontology*.[1] In 1816 he published his *Chrestomathia*[2] and in 1818 his *Church of Englandism*.[3] When a committee finally decided against the Panopticon he demanded and obtained compensation to the extent of £23,000. In 1820–21 he was consulted by the Portuguese Constitutional Party. By then he was also an established influence at home: the French versions of his work and his own later writings were becoming known. In 1823 he was a member of the Greek Committee, and began work on the *Constitutional Code*, which was to be the chief occupation of the greater part of his remaining years. But this work did not exclude other activities: he supplied the funds to start the *Westminster Review*, and offered his all-comprehensive code of law for 'all nations and all governments professing liberal opinions':[4] he was one of the founders of University College, London; in 1828 he was writing to Mehemet Ali on the feasibility of a Suez Canal, and was in correspondence with Daniel O'Connell about Ireland. He died on June 6th, 1832.

Bentham had already begun to influence practical affairs before the end of his life. But the main achievements were to come: for half a century after his death *Benthamism* continued as the most potent force in English reform. Utilitarian theory was further developed by the Mills, by Austin, and by Bain and Sidgwick.[5] For a time the strict tenets of Philosophical Radicalism had their avowed representatives in

[1] *Deontology: or, the science of morality: in which the harmony and coincidence of duty and self-interest, virtue and felicity, prudence and benevolence, are explained and exemplified* (Published 1834).

[2] *Chrestomathia: a collection of papers, explanatory of the design to be set on foot, under the name of the Chrestomatic Day School, or Chrestomatic School, for the extension of the new system of instruction to the higher branches of learning, for the use of the middling and higher ranks of life.*

[3] *Church of Englandism and its catechism examined: preceded by strictures on the exclusionary system as pursued in the National Society's schools: with parallel views of the English and Scottish established and non-established Churches; and concluding with remedies proposed for abuses Indicated: and an examination of the Parliamentary system of Church Reform lately pursued and still pursuing: including the proposed new Churches.*

[4] See title of the first volume of the *Constitutional Code* published in 1830. The full work was published posthumously.

[5] And, of course, the work of economists like Ricardo, Jevons, and even Marshall, was affected both by Bentham's own thought and by Benthamism. On this, and on Bentham's originality as an economist, see W. Stark: *Jeremy Bentham as an Economist* (The Economic Journal, April 1941 and December 1946).

Parliament in Grote, Roebuck and Molesworth. But these indications in no way reveal the extent of Benthamism's political power. It would be wrong to suppose that Bentham or the Mills were widely read by the new business men, or that many of those who were enfranchised in 1832 would have called themselves Benthamites. No more would Peel or Russell or Macaulay have called themselves Benthamites; but politicians such as these none-the-less actively helped to pass a flood of Benthamist legislation. The reasons for this state of affairs I will discuss later. The briefest explanation is that the systematic social views of the Benthamites and the unexpressed and perhaps unreflective attitudes of some of the leading politicians and of their followers reinforced one another; and the Benthamites had the advantage that they energetically provided, very often from the works of the master himself, proposals for reform that were acceptable in principle, and that were practicable because they were prepared in full detail and were ready for almost immediate application. As a consequence, it would be difficult to overstate the importance of the achievements of Benthamism in England. They include two fundamental alterations in the methods of government—the establishment of legislation as the primary means of reform, and of central control and inspection as means for the direction of administration. Benthamism further gave shape to the equally fundamental reforms of the Poor Law and of Local Government; to the inception of a Public Health service; to far-reaching reforms of legal procedure and of the provisions for access to the Courts; to extensive humanitarian reforms of penal laws, and to laws for the protection of children and animals. Benthamism also vastly extended freedom of contract through such measures as the abolition of the Navigation Acts and of the laws against usury, and through divorce reform; and it had much to do with the Combination Acts of 1824–5, the acceptance of the principle of limited liability, and the removal of religious disabilities.

The magnitude of these consequences of Benthamism on legislation and administration in the nineteenth century has not been underestimated by commentators; nor, again, has there been any lack of acknowledgement of the extent to which, for a large part of the nineteenth century, English jurisprudence was dominated by ideas derived from Bentham and expressed by John Austin. And while the authority of Austin's analytical jurisprudence came to be shaken by the 'Historical School' and progressively declined when the writings of continental jurists were more widely read, the influence of Austinian

—and therefore of Benthamic—ideas has continued to be manifest. When we seek to-day to understand the British Constitution, we still make use of the interpretations of A. V. Dicey, and these to a considerable extent rest upon a combination of the methods of the Austinian and the Historical schools; while for practical purposes the general background of thought of most English lawyers has continued to be Austinian.

But in the course of the nineteenth century, while the importance of the Benthamist influence on practical reform and on legal thought was readily admitted, various legends became current about the man himself and about the value of his writings. Many of these legends were rather patronizing, and not all of them were consistent with one another: Bentham was a 'mere practical reformer'; he was an eccentric philosopher of the closet without knowledge of practical affairs; his barren qualities of mind were reflected in a turgid and humourless style; he need be heeded only as an example of muddled philosophical thinking, or as the crude forerunner of James and John Stuart Mill, or as one of the founders of the modern science of economics.

These conflicting views arose in part because of the quantity and variety of Bentham's works—which very few people bothered to read—and in part because of the constant repetition of the kind of picture of him that was drawn by John Stuart Mill.[1] They may be resolved by reading Bentham at first hand and by looking at more objective accounts of his life and character.[2] Any difficulties that arise in understanding Bentham are of a different order from those which arise in understanding Plato, Rousseau, or Hegel: there are few great puzzles of interpretation, his ideas are not intrinsically complicated and his ambiguities of expression are not impenetrable. The two works that are published here at least make it clear that he had a double interest that was far from peculiar: he was concerned with practical reform and with clarifying thought about social phenomena—so was T. H. Green, and so, indeed, was Karl Marx. Nor was he any unworldly or unpractical eccentric. Unlike John Stuart Mill, Bentham had a strong sense of the ridiculous; and he had interests as wide as the normal educated man of his time: he observed nature, he was interested in architecture, chess, music and the theatre. He remained unmarried, but not because he led a completely cloistered life: there is still in exist-

---

[1] See his essay on Bentham in *Dissertations and Discussions*, Vol. 1. Cf. the view in Hazlitt's essay in the *Spirit of the Age*.

[2] See especially C. W. Everett: *The Education of Jeremy Bentham* (1931).

ence a letter in which, as a young man, he advises his younger brother very knowledgeably on the conduct of love affairs.[1] He remained, indeed, until the end of his life a sociable, affable and kindly man. The Russian journey was an enterprising and arduous grand tour.[2] He was in many ways a simple-minded man, but he was far from being consistently unpractical: the story of his inventiveness and of the practicability of his inventions is part of the general history of the nineteenth century and it makes very impressive reading in Dicey;[3] even the Panopticon worked, for instance in Joliet Penitentiary, Illinois, in 1920, and in the 1932 Cuban Penitentiary.[4] Bentham's style could certainly be cumbersome,[5] and it became increasingly so as he got older; but there was a special reason for this in that he was very conscious of the ambiguities in ordinary language,[6] even to the extent of inventing words for the sake of ensuring clarity; and if we have never accepted 'epistemo-threptic,' we have gratefully adopted 'international,' 'codification,' and several other of his inventions. In any case, his style is not uniformly cumbersome: in both of the present works there is much very lucid writing, and there are some very telling epigrams. Again, if we approach Bentham as a would-be nineteenth-century philosopher, then we are likely to find plenty of confusion in him; but it is not in this character that we should approach him. As for his relationship to James and John Stuart Mill, he was the successor of a host of earlier thinkers as well as the forerunner of these two. On the whole, where Bentham's thought is crude (as in some of his psychological conceptions) the crudity consists in the employment of the same conceptions as were employed by the majority of English thinkers in his time; and it would be a remarkable thing if since that time no advances had been made in any of the numerous fields which Bentham touched. But his thought is in any case, on many subjects, quite the reverse of crude: there are, for instance, many sections in the *Introduction to the Principles of Morals and Legislation* in which even the most exacting of modern readers is unlikely to call for further refine-

[1] See Everett, *op. cit.*, pp. 69–70.
[2] The outward journey was *via* Nice (reached by coach, canal and the Rhone) to Smyrna (by way of Genoa and Leghorn) thence to Constantinople and through Bulgaria and Poland. The return journey took him to Warsaw, Berlin and the Hague.
[3] *Lectures on the relation between Law and Public Opinion in England in the nineteenth century* (1905). See also C. K. Ogden, *Jeremy Bentham*, 1832–2032 (1932).
[4] There is a photograph of the latter in Ogden's book referred to in the previous footnote.
[5] He was fully aware of this himself. See *P.*, Preface, paras. 3 and 16.
[6] See *P.*, Preface, para. 39, and *P.*, chap. 6, para. 6, note 1 (p. 166), and chap. 10, para. 13.

ments of analysis. He wrote about political economy, but much less than he wrote about law and government, and there are several works which are neither about political economy nor about law and government. Bentham is not one to be summed up quickly; outside the field of legal theory, his thought touched the general problems of political theory at a few points only, and we are concerned here with only certain of these contacts in two early works. If we come to know these two works thoroughly we shall do well, but we shall still have a lot to learn about Bentham.

II

We should approach the two works before us with open minds, forgetting alike the legends and the later developments of utilitarianism. These early works of Bentham state certain of his views in forms which are more or less those in which he was to continue to hold them for the rest of his life. But they are by no means definitive statements of a 'position': still less are they definitive statements of any body of utilitarian doctrine held in common by Bentham and later utilitarians. Utilitarianism is frequently thought of as a nineteenth-century doctrine; but these works were written in the earlier part of the last quarter of the eighteenth century, and they represent a stage in the development of diverse strands of eighteenth-century utilitarianism. Utilitarianism is frequently thought of as having been associated with middle-class franchise and administrative reform, and it came to be so associated; but at the time when he was writing these works Bentham was not concerned with parliamentary reform and not very greatly with administrative reform. Nor had he developed very far the notions on education which were later to be discussed in the *Chrestomathia*, although there are some views on education in the *Principles*. We are here at the foundations of Bentham's thought as a law reformer, not as a parliamentary, administrative, or educational reformer, although some of the fundamental positions involved in all of these later interests are here given first expression. At least in the first instance, then, we should not look backwards at the *Fragment* and the *Principles* in light of knowledge of later developments.

We should seek to understand these works in their settings; but relating theories to their settings is no simple matter of 'placing' them in a period or a polity, and the setting of a philosophical theory is not necessarily to be explained in the same terms that are appropriate to the explanation of the expression of an 'ideology.' Plato's *Republic* was written in the light of experience of the Greek *polis* and not of the modern nation-state, but it was not solely because of his experience of the *polis* that Plato thought systematically and conceived himself to be concerned with principles that transcended particular temporal organizations. The setting of Hegel's political theory is at least both the Prussian state of his day and the previous development of idealist philosophy. If we are to understand a theory in its setting we can never be content simply to look for an explanation in terms of one factor, although in some cases one factor may be more important than another: a study of earlier developments in formal philosophy helps us perhaps better than anything else to understand Bernard Bosanquet's *Philosophical Theory of the State*, while a study of the general politics of the period and of the débris of philosophical systems is more important if we wish to understand the views of Tom Paine. Theories, in other words, relate in different ways to their settings: they relate, indeed, in different ways to different aspects of their settings; and such aspects include not simply some general social background or historical period, but complex social traditions that are often in conflict, theories and explanations that are almost certainly in conflict, and a writer's more immediate and personal circumstances—his temperament, education, moral outlook and tastes. All of these factors influence the way in which current social institutions affect a man's thought: they play parts in determining the traditions and views to which a man has access and what he comes to make of the logic of other theories. Some men simply apply in their political thinking general techniques that they have previously developed in considering the problems of knowledge or of moral obligation; other men start in the political field and look elsewhere for convenient or plausible techniques to take over. Most men mix such methods and add a quota of acceptance of current dogma or prejudice. All men build on the basis of their own moral judgments.

When we have looked into all these questions we may begin to speak with some confidence of the setting of a man's theory; but even then we must beware of over-confidence. It is equally possible for a theory to remain a period-piece in spite of its author's desire to write not for an age but for all time; or for it to contain some universally valid truth in spite of its author's obsessions with problems typical of his own day.

We shall take the first step towards understanding the two present works in their setting if we realise that Bentham did not begin by

b

thinking of the pleasure-pain psychology and ethics and then rear a political theory on this foundation. His primary concern was with neither psychology nor ethics, nor was it with 'political theory', but with the reform of existing laws by means of a science of law. He started with his experience of the law and of the legal England of his day, with the standpoint of a practical critic. He was born in the period of the Whig ascendancy, a period when the principles of the Constitution were viewed with no little complacency; by Whigs because of their ascendancy, and by both Whigs and others because of the success with which the Constitution had survived the disorders of the previous century. Such attitudes favoured the maintenance of the status quo; and the status quo was one in which Parliament's function was conceived as lying in the supervision of administration rather than in the creation of new law by statute; while it was not considered anomalous that the Common Law and the lawyer should play leading parts in the regulation of social life. In these circumstances, systematic examination and comprehensive overhaul of laws and institutions were not notions likely to commend themselves to those whom Bentham came to describe as 'the people in power'; but Bentham considered that both the Common Law and the administration that Parliament was supposed to supervise were incoherent and antiquated, and that systematic examination and comprehensive overhaul were just precisely what were required.

Bentham's approach to these questions was very much in the general idiom of the thought of his time. His interest in law and government was not one based on an interest in man in his place in the cosmos, in his 'ontological status'. Nor was it one based on an interest in problems of moral obligation as later philosophers came to understand such problems. His quest was for reasonable solutions to social problems of a practical nature, and he viewed his task with characteristic eighteenth-century confidence and characteristic eighteenth-century narrow-mindedness. He had no doubts about the capacity of reason to furnish solutions, partly because of the evident advances of reason in scientific fields and the apparently approaching completion of geographical and ethnographical knowledge,[1] but partly also, perhaps, because to an Englishman of Bentham's day a background of increasing political security and increasing urban and domestic comfort made social problems appear to be relatively simple in their nature. The *Fragment* and the *Principles* reveal no inkling of

---

[1] See the opening sentence of *F.*, Preface.

impending turbulence in human experience as the result of political revolutions or of the quickening of technical, industrial and commercial development. Still less, of course, do they reveal any foreknowledge of the emergence of new modes of thought, of, for instance, the biological notion of evolution or the psychological notion of the positive functions of the irrational. Further, Bentham's ideas belong to an age which had scarcely conceived the possibility of the removal of whole tracts of scientific knowledge from the ken of the ordinary educated man.

But the conceptions used by Bentham are by no means such fragments of the theories of others as any man might pick up in the marketplace. The influence of study and reflection on earlier theories is most marked in his writings and is acknowledged by Bentham himself. He had been familiar with Locke's ideas from childhood, and he had found considerable sympathy with Hume and Voltaire. More specifically, while in chambers he had been reading Barrington, Hartley, Beccaria, Montesquieu, Priestley, and Helvetius.[1] Locke, said Bentham, had given him a clue to method;[2] Hume had demolished the 'chimera' of the Original Contract, and had had some perception of the true principles of morals;[3] Hartley had revealed the 'association principle . . . the bond of connection between ideas and language and between ideas and ideas';[4] Voltaire had appealed because of his generally sceptical attitude towards existing institutions,[5] and Barrington because of his criticisms of existing English law;[6] moreover, these two, together with Montesquieu, Beccaria, and Helvetius, had 'set' Bentham on the

---

[1] Daines Barrington, *Observations on the more ancient Statutes from Magna Charta to the Twenty-first of James I cap XXVII* (1766).

David Hartley: *Observations on Man, his Frame, his Duty and his Expectations* (1749).

Marquis de Beccaria: *Dei delitti e delle pene* (1764, translated into French 1766, and into English 1767).

Charles Louis de Secondat, Baron de la Brède et de Montesquieu: *De l'Esprit des Lois* (1748).

Joseph Priestley: *An Essay on the First Principles of Government, and on the Nature of Political, Civil and Religious Liberty* (1768).

Claud Arian Helvetius: *De l'esprit* (1758).

[2] *F.*, chap. 5, para 6, note 1.   [3] *F.*, chap. 1, para 36, and note (1).

[4] B., Vol. 10, p. 561.

[5] Bentham translated in 1774 one of Voltaire's lesser-known works, *Le Taureau Blanc*, and wrote a preface for it in the style of Voltaire.

[6] Barrington (1727–1800), barrister and later judge, discussed in his *Observations* the statutes indicated in his title, and added legal, historical and etymological notes. He argued for the formal repeal of obsolete statutes and the reduction to one statute of different Acts of Parliament relating to the same subject. He did not, however, consider that codification in the form proposed by Bentham was a practicable project.

Principle of Utility.[1] But in Montesquieu there was too much 'pseudo-metaphysical sophistry,'[2] and the consequences of the notion of the 'greatest good of the greatest number,' which Bentham had also hailed with delight in Priestley,[3] were most fruitfully to be considered with Helvetius in terms of legislation[4] and with Beccaria in terms of a science of punishment.[5]

There was, however, a more distinct pattern in the incidence of these influences than Bentham's own scattered references reveal. Accepting directly from Locke much of his conception of method, Bentham was at the same time accepting other lines of influence connecting with Locke, some from England and some from France. On the English side fell certain developments of Locke's ideas in the hands of Hume, Hartley and Priestley; on the French side fell different developments of Locke's ideas in the rationalism of the French Enlightenment. And from the standpoint of his interest in law, Bentham was making, with peculiar thoroughness, his own unique amalgam.

Locke's theories were as much an amalgam as Bentham's, and this is particularly true of his political and social ideas. His attack on Divine Right and his emphasis on a representative constitutional system were re-statements of a mediaeval position, and they were made in terms of the equally mediaeval notion of natural law; but Locke's thought was also affected by the Cartesian blend of empiricism and rationalism. The elements of knowledge were to be derived from the senses only, yet scientific knowledge was certain and in the moral field only the complexity of ideas and the lack of sensible representations served to prevent an appropriate science from being easy to formulate.[6] These various sides of Locke's thought pulled in

---

[1] B., Vol. 10, p. 54.   [2] F., chap. 1, para. 42, note 1.

[3] *Deontology*, Vol. 1, p. 300. But see B., Vol. 10, p. 142, 'Priestley was the first (unless it was Beccaria) who taught my lips to pronounce this sacred truth—that the greatest happiness of the greatest number is the foundation of morals and legislation.' Beccaria used the phrase 'la massima felicita divisa nel maggior numero.' But Frances Hutcheson had used a similar phrase in his *Inquiry into the Original of our ideas of Beauty and Virtue* published in 1725—'that action is best, which procures the greatest happiness for the greatest numbers' (see the Second Treatise, *Concerning Moral Good and Evil*, sect. III, par. 8, p. 177, 2nd Edit., 1726). Whoever may have originated the phrase, the general doctrine goes back, in one form or another, at least to the Stoics. And the forms vary considerably. For instance, Hutcheson makes the important qualification, in the paragraph quoted, that 'the dignity, or moral importance of Persons, may compensate numbers.'

[4] B., Vol. 10, p. 27; cf. p. 561.   [5] B., Vol. 3, pp. 286-7.

[6] Locke maintained that if definitions were carefully framed this difficulty might be overcome. If 'men would, with the same indifference, search after moral as they do after mathematical truths, they would find them to have as strong a consequence from our

different directions and led to divergent developments in the hands of his successors. Some of Locke's notions (such as his views on the powers of government which were developed by Montesquieu and repeated in the arguments of Blackstone which Bentham attacked in the *Fragment*) became vehicles for the expression of English eighteenth-century constitutional interpretation. This was, perhaps, to no little extent because Locke's general political position was a re-formulation of traditional interpretations of English institutions: in this respect there is more continuity between his ideas and those of Burke than is generally supposed. But by other men the logic of Locke's empiricism was carried much further than he himself had taken it, and in such a manner as to divorce it both from traditionalism and from rationalism. These developments were most thoroughly undertaken by Hume, following the lead given by Berkeley. If the discrete particulars of sense experience were the bases of knowledge, then the principles of their combination were subjective; and we were not aware, for instance, of objective natural laws or natural rights; neither was there any social contract: society and government must be considered to be conventions that developed out of human experience[1]—another link with Burke. But there was yet a further development from Locke's empiricism. While holding that we apprehend laws of nature by means of reason, Locke had held the ancient view that 'good and evil . . . are nothing but pleasure and pain, or that which occasions or procures pleasure and pain to us'; the will of God deciding what is to give us the one or the other.[2] This theological hedonism was destined to have a very long life in England. Gay[3] and Hartley developed theories of psychology based on pleasure-pain and association, and with a theological reference; and Priestley and Paley[4] developed social theories that used these psychological ideas and spoke in terms of greatest happiness; but they again made recourse to God as the guarantor of the identification of individual and social interest.

From Locke's own notions Bentham drew very little directly save his ideas on science and scientific method; and in the application of these 'Newtonian' ideas to social and political questions, both Locke

clear and distinct ideas and to come nearer perfect demonstration than is generally supposed' (*Essay Concerning Human Understanding*, Bk. 4, chap. 3, paras. 18–20).

[1] *Treatise of Human Nature*, Bks. 2 and 3.

[2] *Op. cit.*: Bk. 2, chap. 28, para. 4; cf. chap. 7, paras. 2–4, chap. 20, para. 2, chap. 21, para 42.

[3] John Gay: *A Dissertation concerning the Principles and Criterion of Virtue and the Origin of the Passions* (1730).

[4] William Paley: *Principles of Moral and Political Philosophy* (1785).

and Bentham were very much in line with older views; the successful
models for the development of science lay in mathematics or mathematical astronomy conceived as provinces for the deductive operations
of a naturally inerrant reason.   For Bentham and Locke, however,
the method of reason was that method for which Descartes had provided rules: problems should be resolved into their simplest elements,
nothing should be taken for granted that was not clear and distinct,
and thought should move in single steps each one no greater than the
manifest connections of the subject-matter warranted.[1] As a consequence, while on the one hand a very considerable role was accorded
to reason, on the other hand severe limitations were imposed as regards
the tractability of reason's subject-matter: certainty might be achieved,
but only in a field that permitted a first process of reduction to simple
units and a consequent process of recomposition. Hume's philosophy
had involved both processes, but it had provided a subjective account
of the second of them that was opposed both by the majority of his
contemporaries and by later thinkers. Bentham was probably not
concerned to follow all that Hume had to say, least of all those aspects
of Hume's thought in which it was held that the deficiencies of reason
were to be remedied by instinct. He was mainly impressed by Hume's
attack on contract and natural law, and he tended to retain a role for
reason that Hume would have rejected. On the other hand, he was
nearer to Hume than were some of the French descendants of Locke
to whom Voltaire and Montesquieu had brought the doctrines of the
English Revolution, and by whom these doctrines were received as a
basis for a sceptical consideration of the existing French régime.
The Philosophes, or those of them who were to influence Bentham
most, were concerned with solvents of custom and tradition in France
and the foundation of a reasonable philosophy and political theory.
Some of these men conceived that reason should enable men to free
themselves from the bonds of custom and authority: if reason operated,
as Locke had suggested, without the aid of innate ideas, then it was
possible by taking thought to undermine the sway of tradition; by
means of education and the control of the environment whole social
structures might be altered, and altered quickly. In this interconnection of reason and progress there was much common ground
with Bentham, as there was also common ground in the search for
laws or principles that reason should follow. But Bentham was not
inclined to maintain that such laws or principles were those of reason

---

[1] *Discourse on Method* (Everyman Edition, pp. 15–16).

itself; still less was he inclined to maintain, as Montesquieu still maintained, that they were in any sense natural laws.

Yet Bentham was more influenced by the utilitarian developments of Locke in their French than in their English form. Interested in certain aspects of psychology, and in particular in the psychology of language, he was insufficiently interested in the general minutiae of psychological analysis to wish to follow Hartley in detail; and his own other interests and perhaps the influence of Hume were unlikely to lead him to the theological utilitarianism of Priestley. To a considerable degree Bentham was adopting towards the legal institutions of his own country much the attitude that the rationalist Philosophes were adopting towards the whole of the social institutions of France. Bentham's adoption of a non-theological utilitarianism was thus further encouraged when he read in 1769 the *De L'Esprit* of Helvetius, who was an atheist; for that work propounded a secular science of morals which would also be a science of legislation. Maintaining that pleasure and pain were the sole springs of human action and judgment, Helvetius argued that the gap between private and public interest could be bridged by the legislator who worked from a knowledge of human nature. Such a legislator could frame a system of rewards and punishments that would serve the interest of the public, which was the same as that of the 'greatest number.' Helvetius also indicated that the 'principle of the utility of the public' was a principle which embraced the whole of 'morals and of legislation'. These ideas of Helvetius were further developed by Beccaria in his *Crimes and Punishments*, published in 1764, translated into English in 1767, and read by Bentham. Beccaria, like Paley later, classified pains and spoke of their intensity, duration, proximity and certainty. He also spoke of the 'greatest happiness of the greatest number,' and he dealt with the subject-matter with which Bentham was concerned.

At first sight, then, much of Bentham's thought in the present two works might appear to derive very directly from Helvetius and Beccaria; but the other influences on him were not less important. The shape in which he received the French utilitarian ideas and the application he made of them were affected by the employment of a method akin to Locke's, by a scepticism akin to Hume's, and by Bentham's own legal outlook and interests. Further, account must be taken of Bentham's own unusual capacity for industry, his remarkable pertinacity, his peculiar flair for side-issues, and his particular interest in language. His views are thus not merely eclectic: in his systematization alone, but also in particular developments, he brings many individual contributions, and he is certainly not to be studied simply as one through whom a mechanical blend of influences from earlier writers was passed on to his successors.

There is one final characteristic, however, which is common to Bentham and many of the writers of the French Enlightenment. Bentham was not one of the builders of a great 'system' of theory. He moved somewhat jerkily from subject to subject and by no means always within the field of politics; his mind penetrated a short distance here, a greater or lesser distance there; he was interested unevenly in different topics and followed up some ideas and not others; he could maintain a rigid scepticism in face of some accepted ideas, yet receive without examination other ideas that some of his contemporaries might question. The works we are considering here are to be regarded as the products of an unsystematic intellectual radicalism; and that is not merely another way of saying that they belong to philosophical as opposed to popular radicalism. The radicalism here is a radicalism of the intellect, and therein lies a major compensation for some of the common limitations of the period, for the incompleteness of the works as considerations of social and political problems, and for the absence of a system; particularly for the latter. We explore the ramifications of a system with decreasing interest when we have learned that it rests on a fallacy. We may consider that Bentham abounds in fallacies; but he produced no edifice on any single basis. His radical turn of mind made him turn back constantly to dig up a variety of conceptions and examine their roots. We have much to learn from such an attitude and from the results of many of his examinations. We are confronted here with something more challenging than a ready-made system—a series of possible approaches to central problems of society and politics, any one of which we may be able to utilize without committing ourselves to the others, and any or all of which may be capable of adaptation.

III

Bentham interrupted his work on punishments in 1774 to make drafting suggestions to his friend Lind[1] on a Commentary that Lind

---

[1] John Lind (1737–1781), an ex-clergyman who entered the service of the King of Poland. When Bentham knew him he was engaged in political journalism and acted as an unofficial Polish representative in London.

had begun to prepare on the *Commentaries* of Blackstone. Bentham quickly produced work that Lind so greatly preferred to his own that he agreed that he should withdraw and that Bentham should go on. Bentham did go on, and almost but not quite completed his *Comments on the Commentaries*, which for some reason he then put aside and to which he did not subsequently return. It was published from the manuscript for the first time in 1928. But before he had quite finished with his *Comments on the Commentaries*, Bentham turned back to consider a point about the nature of sovereignty that Blackstone had inserted into his discussion of municipal law. It occurred to Bentham that his own digression on this digression of Blackstone's might stand by itself, and accordingly he decided to publish it. The result was the *Fragment on Government*, which appeared anonymously in 1776.

In the preface to the *Introduction to the Principles of Morals and Legislation* Bentham gives us some account of the origin of that work. It was intended as the introduction to his penal code which would follow in the same volume. This project, says Bentham, was held up because he found himself (for what was by no means to be the last time) 'unexpectedly entangled.' The introduction was set up in type by itself and printed but not published in 1780: some of the copies got about without Bentham's authorisation. Bentham says that meanwhile he had found that the principles he had set out in this introduction were underlying his subsequent thought and that he therefore decided on an authorised publication embodying some emendations and corrections; hence the publication in 1789. This is not, however, the whole story. Bentham had in fact to be pressed by his friend Wilson[1] as late as 1788, to publish his introduction at all, and Wilson was concerned because Paley had published in 1785 his *Principles of Moral and Political Philosophy* with the consequence that the public might think that Bentham had borrowed ideas from Paley.

It is thus apparent that these two works were rather casual productions, both as regards their form and as regards the circumstances of their publication. Further, neither separately nor together do they cover all the ground that Bentham had covered by 1789. Between

---

[1] George Wilson (? – 1816), a Scottish barrister who later became leader of the Norfolk circuit. On one occasion Wilson appears to have saved Bentham from drowning. The friendship was an early and not very lasting one: the temperaments of the two men seem to have become increasingly incompatible. In the Preface to *F.*, 2nd edit. (1828) Bentham admitted that the *Principles* 'would not have come out when it did, in 1789, but for George Wilson' (Bowring, Vol. 1, p. 252).

the publication of the *Fragment* and the publication of the *Principles*, Bentham had written and published his *Defence of Usury*, a work on political economy; and the manuscripts entrusted to Dumont touched on aspects of law that are not discussed in either of the present works. It may therefore appear to be questionable whether there are any good reasons why the *Fragment* and the *Principles* should be chosen for re-publication to-day as political texts. But there are several good reasons. The most important reason is that these complementary products of the same period of Bentham's thought give fairly complete expression to Bentham's views on certain political themes. A second reason is that much that has been written about Bentham's views on these themes has drawn to a surprising extent on Dumont's edited *Theory of Legislation*, and while Dumont on the whole performed his task of editing very faithfully,[1] it is preferable to read what Bentham had to say exactly as he himself said it. A third reason is that there is still a tendency in some commentaries to speak as though Bentham had somewhere expressed a 'political theory' in a firm and final form; whereas no one of his works is definitive, and so far at least as one aspect of his political thought was concerned, there was a difference between his earlier and later views. The present two works have the advantage of revealing the earlier Bentham who wrote before there was a 'Utilitarian School.' Finally, these two works are not easily obtainable to-day in convenient form in one volume.

IV

The Argument of the Fragment on Government.

Bentham's purpose in the *Fragment*, as also in the *Comments on the Commentaries* which he did not publish, was to subject the doctrines of William Blackstone's *Commentaries on the Laws of England* to destructive criticism that would be effective in undermining their authority. What was authoritative about Blackstone's work? It was written by the first Vinerian Professor of Law at Oxford, which perhaps in itself gave it some standing. Its substance had already figured in the Professor's lectures (which Bentham had returned to Oxford to hear in 1763) and his doctrines had therefore begun to contribute to the outlook of lawyers and others in Bentham's own generation.[2] But

---

[1] See the appendix to Halévy's *Growth of Philosophical Radicalism*, and Ogden's Introduction to his edition of the *Theory of Legislation*, pp. xxxvii–l.

[2] See *F.*, Preface, paras. 28–29.

probably most important of all was the fact that the four volumes (which appeared between 1765 and 1769) were written in what Bentham himself acknowledged to be the language of 'the scholar and the gentleman':[1] in brief, the work appealed to and was received by, a wide circle of readers.[2]

What concerned Bentham in this was the further currency that was now liable to be given to ideas of whose fallacious nature he had already become convinced when he first heard them in the author's lectures. There was no novelty in panegyrics on the British Constitution since Montesquieu had written in 1748. Between the publication of the *Commentaries* and that of the *Fragment* there had appeared yet another eulogy in the shape of de Lolme's *Constitution of England*. Blackstone was in a tradition. As Bentham saw it, Blackstone, with all his learning and his elegance of diction, was no more than repeating the same inconsistent medley of clichés of which current legal thinking was composed. The law of nature was there, sometimes revealed by God, sometimes discovered by Reason; and it was accompanied by self-interest as the basic principle of action. Sovereignty was supreme and absolute authority, yet the sovereign could be spoken of as having duties; and individuals had absolute natural rights which it was the principal aim of society to protect. While previously isolated individuals did not deliberately agree to institute society, compact yet somehow represented the organized relations between individuals and society. And the virtues of the British Constitution would be found to reside in the fact that it was an almost perfect example of 'mixed government' and separated and balanced 'powers.' It was clear to Bentham what the vogue of such ideas would do if it went unchecked: it would confirm those prejudices which he was most concerned to overturn, and it would erect a barrier against the reforms he hoped to accomplish. The main purpose of the *Fragment*, therefore, is to explode these ideas; but the work is also intended to indicate other ideas that should take their place.

Bentham acknowledges that the aims of the *Fragment* are mainly negative, rather to overthrow than to set up, but he thinks that they may go some way towards helping readers to think for themselves.[3] His critical aim is to show Blackstone's inaccuracy of thought and his confusion, and how his ideas make him an enemy to 'reformation.'[4] This is to be done by means of a close examination of one

[1] *F.*, Preface, para. 46.   [2] *F.*, Preface, para. 4.   [3] *F.*, Preface, para. 69.
[4] *F.*, Preface, para. 5.

passage in the *Commentaries* in which, Bentham claims, the essential fault of the whole is exemplified.[1] This fault resides in the confusion of the functions of two quite different and separate types of jurisprudence, a descriptive jurisprudence which Bentham calls 'expositorial,' and a critical jurisprudence which Bentham calls 'censorial.' The result of such confusion is that existing laws are always justified and as a consequence reforms are always resisted.[2]

Bentham's arguments in the *Fragment* are not systematized: they follow the order of Blackstone's statements in the passage chosen for criticism, and the specific notions of Blackstone that are chosen for attack are clear enough from the five chapters following the preface and the introduction. There is little to be gained from dwelling on the details of Bentham's criticisms of Blackstone's points; some of Bentham's most telling criticisms come from Hume and much that he has to say is merely captious and should charitably be attributed to youthful exuberance. Nor did Bentham's attacks prevent the continued popularity of the *Commentaries*. But there are certain important central conceptions behind Bentham's attacks, and he advances certain positive alternative ideas. We have to search for these themes, especially in the preface and the footnotes, and we have to systematize some of them for ourselves; but when this is done they compose an impressive and consistent thesis.

In his attacks Bentham is really opposing three tendencies in legal and political thought that are still all too common even to-day. The first of these tendencies is the confusion of the *de facto* and the *de jure*. Bentham contends that the law of nature is 'nothing but a phrase,'[3] insists that what men in fact intend and what they ought to intend are by no means the same,[4] and objects to such notions as that free governments must necessarily have less power than despotic governments,[5] or that the supreme power in a society can have duties.[6] The second tendency attacked is the misuse of analogy, and Bentham criticises both the doctrine of original contract[7] and the doctrine of implied consent.[8] The third tendency attacked is the misuse of limiting concepts. 'However distinct the ideas may be that are suggested by

---

[1] The passage occurs at I *Comm.* 47 ff. and is copied almost verbatim from J. J. Burlamaqui's *Droit de la Nature* (1747) which Blackstone apparently read in a translation of 1748. Burlamaqui was influenced by Puffendorf, for Bentham's views on whom, in company with Grotius, see *F.*, Preface, para. 24, note 2. Cf. *P.*, chap. 19, para. 27, note 1.

[2] *F.*, Preface, para. 14 ff.   [3] *F.*, chap. 4, para. 19.   [4] *F.*, chap. 4, para. 10.

[5] *F.*, chap. 4, para. 23.   [6] *F.*, chap. 5, paras. 1–4.   [7] *F.*, chap. 1, para. 36.

[8] *F.*, chap. 4, para. 11.

those names, the things themselves have no determinate bounds to separate them.'[1] Actual societies, for instance, need not necessarily be either perfectly natural or perfectly political:[2] governments do not fall neatly into the classification 'monarchy, aristocracy, democracy,' with complementary virtues of 'strength, wisdom, goodness':[3] the British Constitution does not, through a 'balance' of King, Lords and Commons, represent a 'blend' of the three supposed forms of government, or of their virtues without their vices:[4] the notion of the 'powers of government' is hard to apply—where, for instance, is the 'executive' in England,[5] and how independent of it is the judiciary?[6]

Bentham rejects these currently accepted conceptions employed by Blackstone, but he suggests alternatives. He suggests that 'political society' and 'natural society' are limiting conceptions. The essential character of a political society resides in the fact that it involves 'a number of persons (whom we may style subjects) . . . supposed to be in the habit of paying obedience to a person or an assemblage of persons, of a known and certain description (whom we may call governor or governors)'.[7] The notion of a natural society is simply the negative of this: 'When a number of persons are supposed to be in the habit of conversing with each other, at the same time that they are not in any such habit as mentioned above, they are said to be in a state of natural society.'[8] When we come to actual societies, however, we may expect the habit of obedience to be neither perfectly present nor perfectly absent.[9] Indeed, the same man may be in a state of nature with some people and in a state of political society with others, or may alternate in his relations with the same people.[10] The same men may be governors in one relation and subjects in another, or may alternate.[11] And government itself may only be a temporary phenomenon.[12] In practice we can reasonably take a given society to be political when acts of obedience within it predominate over acts of disobedience.[13] Borderline cases will undoubtedly be difficult to determine; but it might be said that the authority of a society's government ceases to be effective when there is, on the part of a sufficient number of persons within the Society, more than a certain degree of conscious,

[1] *F.*, chap. 1, para. 12.   [2] *F.*, chap. 1, para. 13.   [3] *F.*, chap. 2, *passim*.
[4] *F.*, chap. 3, *passim*.   [5] *F.*, chap. 3, para. 5.   [6] *F.*, chap. 4, paras. 30–32.
[7] *F.*, chap. 1, para. 10. He suggests later (Note 1 to para. 13) that further to distinguish political society (from, e.g. a family) we should presuppose within it a considerable number of persons and an indefinite duration.
[8] *F.*, chap. 1, para. 11.   [9] *F.*, chap. 1, para. 12.   [10] *F.*, chap. 1, paras. 14, 16.
[11] *F.*, chap. 1, paras. 15–16.   [12] *F.*, chap. 1, paras. 19–20.
[13] *F.*, chap. 1, para. 12, note 1, and para. 14.

open and forcible disobedience of a type that has been recognised in the society as treason.[1]

It is clear enough what Bentham is here concerned with. He is concerned with government as a sociological fact; he is not concerned to ask on what grounds, or in what circumstances, moral authority may be claimed for government. Nor does his more detailed analysis of the notion of government as a sociological fact introduce the question of moral authority: it leads logically to the isolation of further technical and morally neutral conceptions. Thus, when a political society is functioning, then the supreme body in it is absolute: nothing it does can be illegal, except where it is limited by an express convention.[2] The expressions in words of the will of such a political superior are commands, and statute law is composed of commands. Common law consists of quasi-commands—tacit expressions of the will of the superior, 'supposed' to have been uttered. Duties are then acts that are the objects of such commands or quasi-commands. Duties and rights are correlative in the sense that my duties are what others have a right to have me made to do; but what others have a right to have me made to do can only be what I am liable according to the law to be punished for not doing.[3] Thus the notion of law as command is central, and essential to it is the notion of punishment, which is that of 'pain annexed to an act, and accruing on a certain account and from a certain source.'[4]

These are the central conceptions of expositorial or descriptive jurisprudence, the technical conceptions that Bentham conceives are necessary if we are concerned to describe a society's laws without begging any questions as to their goodness or badness. They are technical conceptions that it is logically necessary to use no matter with what legal system or what political society we may be concerned. Other technicalities may be involved in any legal system, but their existence may be accidental, and it will give rise to misunderstandings if we confuse technicalities that are non-essential with those that are essential. This is especially important when we set out to practise

[1] *F.*, chap. 1, paras. 21–28.

[2] *F.*, chap. 4, para. 26. Cf. chap. 4, para. 34 ff. This qualification of Bentham's is not always appreciated. Bentham insists that no contradiction is involved in holding that the supreme political or legal power may be limited by convention, and he points out that there are in fact instances of such limitation in the cases of the German Empire, the Dutch Provinces, and the Swiss Cantons. The fundamental point is that political power rests upon 'a habit of, and disposition to, obedience' which may be 'absent with regard to one sort of acts' while 'present with regard to other' (Chap. 4, paras. 34 and 35).

[3] *F.*, chap. 1, para. 12, note 1.   [4] *F.*, chap. 5, para. 6, note 1 (para. 3).

expositorial jurisprudence, that is, to give an exposition of any system of law. Exposition must be systematic; there must be an order of description, or, as Bentham calls it, an 'arrangement'. Bentham conceives that arrangement in any exposition should be what he calls 'natural' as opposed to 'artificial' arrangement; instead of exposition following the pattern of technicalities that have come into use from unreflective practice and may be based on all sorts of prejudices and whims, it should be concerned to arrange its subject-matter in accordance with the properties involved that are most prone to engage and to retain men's attention. Now the subject-matter of law is men's actions, and it is to the utility of actions that men naturally attend. Therefore the principle of arrangement in jurisprudence should be utility.[1]

At first sight Bentham may seem in the arguments just summarised to be speaking from a standpoint different from that adopted in the arguments summarised earlier. He produces certain technical conceptions by means of what appears to be a logical analysis of the actual phenomenon of political society. It would be natural to suppose from what he says about political society that the 'subject-matter' of law would be commands, or kinds of commands; but he says that it is actions. Further, if exposition should be 'natural' in the sense in which he uses this expression, ought not analysis to be 'natural' also? Can the analysis which indicates meanings for 'law,' 'right' and 'duties' be so described? Bentham did not stop to ask these questions, but it is unlikely that they would have perturbed him. Commands are concerned with permitting or forbidding actions: offences against laws will be punished, so that disobedient action has a determinate disutility 'annexed' to it; there is thus nothing illogical about the arrangement of laws in terms of offences created (which is at the same time an arrangement in terms of utility or disutility); it is a useful form of arrangement from the point of view of both law-makers and subjects, and this does not introduce any different standpoint, for Bentham's discussion of law always implicitly and sometimes explicitly proceeds on the pre-supposition that in some sense or other it is part of the nature of law that it has a use. Further, this notion of arrangement nowhere steps outside the range of conceptions that arises from the analysis of political society except at the point at which utility is introduced. But this is not a gratuitous addition: command and obedience, law-making and respect for the law, are implicit in

---

[1] *F.*, Preface, para. 52 ff.

the notion of political society, and in introducing utility Bentham is doing no more than turning his analysis in a psychological direction. Given the sociological nature of the phenomenon under review, this is not inappropriate.

Rightly or wrongly, however, these arguments have throughout a pragmatic character. It becomes evident at the next stage of Bentham's discussion of alternative conceptions that the basis of the pragmatism is an emphasis on the ethical significance of jurisprudence. So far we have discussed what he has to say about expositorial jurisprudence. But there is another form of jurisprudence—'censorial' jurisprudence. Whereas expositorial jurisprudence is concerned with what law *is*, censorial jurisprudence is concerned with what law *ought* to be.[1] It must use the same materials and arrangement as expositorial juris-prudence, but it must employ an objective standard to decide what law ought to be. This takes us beyond utility as such to the Principle of Utility[2]—'this fundamental axiom—it is the greatest happiness of the greatest number that is the measure of right and wrong.'[3]

These are the main conceptions that are advanced by Bentham in place of those used by Blackstone, and they, rather than the detailed discussions of separate points in Blackstone, constitute the main interest of the *Fragment* to-day. It is of importance to notice that they are developed as a doctrine of jurisprudence and not as a 'political theory', that they involve other ideas in addition to what we have come to regard as being strictly 'utilitarian' ideas, and that Bentham is in the main assuming the existence of government and is not asking how governments ought to be constituted. But there are some other discussions in the *Fragment* that are relevant to this last subject.

Kings, says Bentham, should keep within established laws and abstain from measures which tend to increase the unhappiness of their subjects; while subjects should only obey kings so long as they so conduct themselves—'so long as the probable mischiefs of obedience are less than the probable mischiefs of resistance.'[4] Each man may use the Principle of Utility to tell himself when the juncture for resistance has arisen, but there is no way in which there can be a common test for all concerned,[5] unless, perhaps, in the case in which there is a definite convention for the government to overstep.[6] It is, however, possible to characterise a 'free government,' and that without resort to the use of 'fictions.' It depends on how the supreme power is distributed

---

[1] *F.*, Preface, para. 13. [2] *F.*, Preface, paras. 55–62. [3] *F.*, Preface, para. 2.
[4] *F.*, chap. 1, para. 43. [5] *F.*, chap. 4, para. 21 ff. [6] *F.*, chap. 4, para. 36.

amongst the sharers of it, on the frequency and ease with which changes between governors and governed take place 'whereby the interests of the one class are more or less indistinguishably blended with those of the other.' on the responsibility of the governors, on the right a subject has of having public explanations given of all acts of power exercised over him, on the liberty of the press to make complaints publicly known, on the liberty of association, 'on the security with which malcontents may communicate their sentiments, concert their plans, and practise everything short of actual revolt before the executive power can be legally justified in disturbing them.'[1]

These are remarkable passages in respect both of what they say and of what they leave unsaid. It is surprising in light of what Bentham has to say about the separation of powers, to find that something very like the same notion is apparently being restored. The notion of a 'source' of titles to power is a further example of a conception that would have been the better of closer examination. Moreover, since the various forms of liberty mentioned appear to have positive functions, it would have been interesting to have been told what could be made of this suggestion in terms of utility. But the most important unanswered questions are those raised by the statements that indicate that individual subjects may pass judgments on laws by reference to the Principle of Utility. If this may occur, then a governor's view of what is in accordance with the Principle of Utility has no claim to superior validity; and Bentham himself, indeed, at least here perceives that there is an important practical problem of ensuring that governors and subjects will think alike. It should be clear from this that no censorial jurist can claim universal validity for his jurisprudence: as in the case of governors, some device is required whereby censorial jurists and subjects will think alike. But Bentham does not draw this moral.

The *Fragment* thus touches rather casually on some important questions of political theory. Bentham presumably did not consider himself called upon to develop his general suggestions because his main purpose was to discuss something else; and it is probable that he was little interested to develop them. They are in the nature of asides, improvisations on current political ideas of a fairly common and fairly simple kind. As such, they throw some light on Bentham at this stage, and they should be borne in mind when some of Bentham's later political ideas are considered. But the real concern of the *Fragment* is with the substructure of political theory, and with that sub-

---

[1] *F.*, chap. 4, para. 24.

structure as it relates to the functioning of government rather than to the constitution of government. The balance of interest is thus almost the opposite of that which is common in political theories, and so is the balance of attention. In other theories attention is concentrated on this problem—how the authority of a state's constitution may be justified; and often little is said on the other question—how the separate actions of government are to be justified. By implication, perhaps, a constitutional government's actions are justified when they in turn are constitutional; but there are serious gaps in such an explanation, and these widen to form a gulf if the framer of a constitution theory fails to indicate by what means it is to be ensured that the spirit of a constitution will inform the daily dealings of government. Bentham's attention in the *Fragment* is centred on the daily dealings of government and not on the character of a just constitution. He is not unconcerned with justification, but he is discussing the question of a test to be applied *ad hoc* to each separate action of government rather than the question of general consistency with a just constitution. At this stage, while not unaware that there is at least this further question, he is curiously indifferent to it: indeed, it is clear that he considers that the subject he is discussing is the only important subject.

V

The Argument of the Introduction to the Principles of Morals and Legislation.

The *Principles* are even less concerned than the *Fragment* with 'political theory,' although they are much more concerned with what is usually thought of as constituting the subject-matter of 'utilitarianism'. They are of interest to the political theorist because they provide an expansion of the conception of the Principle of Utility and of its relation to the conception of law that is developed in the *Fragment*. Yet the *Principles* are not a treatise on utilitarianism, but a separately published introduction to a penal code; and their main concern is again with the science of law, this time with special reference to punishment. This is evident in the main structure of the argument, which, in spite of asides and the much greater length of the book, is much more closely-knit and much less scattered than that of the *Fragment*, so that its outlines may be indicated here quite briefly.

The Principle of Utility is the only possible objective basis for legislation and morals.[1] It is therefore to be followed both by the legislator and by private individuals;[2] and Bentham is mainly concerned with the legislator. The legislator, working through compulsion, must work on the pleasures and pains of individuals.[3] Compulsion is really the supplying of motives: the sources of motives are 'sanctions'.[4] There are physical sanctions operating in the ordinary course of nature without human or divine intervention, political sanctions operating through the organs of government, moral or popular sanctions arising from general social contacts, and religious sanctions arising from the 'immediate hand of a superior invisible being, either in the present life or in a future.'[5] The sanctions other than the physical sanction can only work through the physical sanction,[6] and the political sanction differs from the other three sanctions (when these are operating without it) in that it alone can be certain in its effects whereas they are always uncertain.[7] To do his work properly, therefore, the legislator must understand the force or value of the pleasures and pains that are both his ends and the instruments he has to work with.[8] This is to be measured, in the case of a single pleasure or pain of one individual, in terms of intensity, duration, certainty or uncertainty, and propinquity or remoteness.[9] When not the isolated pleasure or pain, but the 'tendency' of the act by which pleasure or pain is produced is considered, then account must also be taken of fecundity and purity: that is, of the chance that the immediate pleasure or pain associated with the act under review will be followed by further sensations of the same kind, and the chance that it will not be followed by sensations of the opposite kind.[10] When a number of persons is considered, then the legislator must take into account all the foregoing tests and another test which Bentham calls 'extent': that is, the number of persons affected.[11] Thus a calculus of pleasures and pains may be effected: this is not strictly pursued in all moral judgments or all legal operations, but the more closely it is followed, the greater accuracy will such judgments and operations possess.[12]

[1] P., chap. 1, para. 14.   [2] P., chap. 1, paras. 1–2.   [3] P., chap. 3, para. 1.
[4] P., chap. 3, para. 2 and note. The motives in question are obligatory motives, 'capable of giving a binding force to any law or rule of conduct.'
[5] P., chap. 3, paras. 2–6.   [6] P., chap. 3, para. 11.   [7] P., chap. 14, para. 26.
[8] P., chap. 4, para. 1.   [9] P., chap. 4, para. 2.   [10] P., chap. 4, paras. 5–6.
[11] P., chap. 4, para. 7.
[12] P., chap. 4, paras. 5–6; cf. chap. 14, para. 28. See Ogden's Introduction to his edition of the Theory of Legislation (pp. xiv–xv) for the view that the calculus was merely a 'classificatory convenience' valid because it worked. This view is supported by Halévy's quotation on p. 495 of the Growth of Philosophical Radicalism of a statement in one of

So far Bentham's arguments appear to confirm all that is said in the most unsympathetic accounts of his ideas, except that these do not always make clear the emphasis laid on the legislator or the qualification noted at the end of the previous paragraph. But now Bentham proceeds to explain various refinements that must be introduced in order to apply his method more realistically, and it is important that the reader's patience should extend to this part of his argument. Pleasures and pains must be classified according to their sorts, and a distinction must be made between simple and complex pleasures and pains so that the law knows what it is dealing with.[1] Account must next be taken of the fact that in different people the quantity of pleasure or pain produced by the same cause is not uniformly in proportion to the force exerted by the cause of the pleasure or pain; and thirty-two kinds of 'circumstances affecting sensibility' are listed and examined which must be considered by legislators and judges so that the punishment designed by the one and applied by the other will have just the effect it is intended to have.[2] Then the effects of circumstances on men's acts are considered—what is meant by saying that acts are intentional, what motives are, and what is the nature of disposition.[3] Only after these enquiries does the discussion reach a point at which punishment as such can be dealt with.[4] In itself, as involving pain, punishment is a mischief: its use is justified only for the sake of excluding some greater evil,[5] and it is therefore to be avoided where there is no mischief to prevent, where it cannot effectively prevent mischief, or where it will produce more mischief than it prevents.[6] When punish-

Bentham's MSS. to the effect that the 'addibility' involved is a necessary postulate of political reasoning to be regarded as having the same sort of validity as 'the equality of chances to reality, on which the whole branch of the mathematics which is called the doctrine of chances is established.' In short, the calculus is a pragmatic conception.

There can be little doubt of Bentham's later pragmatic tendencies. See the *Rationale of Evidence*, chap. 7 (B., Vol. 6, p. 241) 'Experience is the foundation of all our knowledge and of all our reasoning—the sole guide of our conduct, the sole basis of our security.' Cf. the *Essay on Logic*, first published by Bowring. 'Logic, like every other branch of art and science, in a word, like everything else, is not any otherwise, nor any further deserving of regard, than in so far as it is capable of being of *use*. But of *use* in an intelligible sense, neither can this, nor any thing else ultimately be, any further than it has been or is capable of being conducive to the diminution of pain in some shape or other or to the increase of pleasure.' (B., Vol. 8, p. 222). But not all of Bentham's statements, particularly at this stage, will support the view that he was consistently a pragmatist: in many cases he appears to take 'addibility' literally. In other words, Bentham's position should *not* be regarded as consistent. It is partially rationalist and partially pragmatist. This is not surprising in view of the various sources on which he was drawing.

[1] *P.*, chap. 5, paras. 1 and 33.   [2] *P.*, chap. 6, especially para. 45.
[3] *P.*, chaps. 7–11.   [4] *P.*, chap. 12.   [5] *P.*, chap. 13, para. 2.
[6] *P.*, chap. 13, para. 3.

ment is worth while, it will prevent mischiefs absolutely, or if that is not possible, will induce a preference for less mischievous offences.[1] Bearing these points in mind, it becomes possible to state rules by which the apportionment of punishments to offences should be governed,[2] and from these rules may in turn be derived the properties that must be found in particular punishments.[3] Offences may then be classified in accordance with the dictate of the Principle of Utility that only such acts ought to be offences that the good of the community requires should be such.[4]   Finally, Bentham discusses the whole of the field of the legislator(which is what has already been under discussion) in its relation to the field appropriate to private ethics.[5]

At the political level, then, this discussion remains very firmly within the terms of reference of the discussions in the *Fragment*. It is concerned with the daily actions of government, and mainly with their compulsory aspect. It is a discussion of the social psychology, or sociology, of compulsion. It is partially technical, and the tyrannically minded equally with the public-spirited might value many of the considerations advanced, but it is in fact undertaken because Bentham is concerned with the problem how government ought to behave, and it is in consequence of this concern that several matters are touched upon that are not revealed in the brief general summary given above: there are discussions of the aims and methods of social sciences: the psychology is a moral psychology: the proper functions of government and the limits of governmental effectiveness are discussed. Thus the *Principles* both concentrates on one aspect of the discussions of the *Fragment* and serves to provide a wider background for those discussions as a whole.

VI

These, then, are the themes in the *Fragment* and the *Principles* that are of leading interest to the political theorist. Clearly, neither the *Fragment* nor the *Principles* constitutes separately a treatise on political theory in the usually accepted sense; nor do they do so in conjunction. Bentham's own temperament and interests, the circumstances of writing and of publication, and the particularity of the subject-matter, all combined to prevent his even contemplating any such work. The overt purpose of the *Fragment* is very specialized, and a reading of the *Principles* will quickly serve to remind the reader that especially

---

[1] *P.*, chap. 14, paras. 2–6.   [2] *P.*, chap. 14, paras. 7–25.   [3] *P.*, chap. 15.
[4] *P.*, chap. 16.   [5] *P.*, chap. 17.

when we deal with that work as a political text we are selecting themes, and that the jurist or the penologist would make quite a different selection of themes. Unfortunately, too, brief general summaries tend to make the political themes of both works appear very thin, and we are in any case disinclined to expect very much more from further reading when we remember that they belong to an early phase of Bentham's thought, to the legal side of that phase, and to one aspect only of the legal side. By 1789 Bentham already had other irons in the fire: in addition to the views expressed in the *Fragment* and the *Principles*, he had also expressed other views which were to affect the later development of his political thought. In the *Principles* he was providing an introduction to a penal code. But he had also before 1789 recorded his views on civil law. He had considered the necessary interconnection and interdependence of legal rights and duties in a practicable legal system, and he had advocated as a rational aim for the law the maintenance of security, subsistence, abundance and equality with security as the 'principal object.'[1] He had, further, already expressed himself on political economy as a disciple of Adam Smith: in the economic field the maximising of happiness depended upon the reduction of intervention by government to the unavoidable minimum.[2]

But the force of the two present works should not be under-estimated. Many of the arguments in the *Fragment* are purely negative, and, as has already been mentioned, some of the most telling of them derive from Hume, while Bentham's own arguments are often no more than captious. Yet none of the notions chosen for attack were repeated by any major writer in England after the 1770's in just the form in which Bentham had attacked them.[3] More important,

---

[1] See the *Theory of Legislation*, Principles of the Civil Code, chap. 2, chaps. 11–12. Cf. *F.*, Preface, para. 3—'If it be of importance and of use to us to know the principles of the element we breathe, surely it is not of much less use to comprehend the principles and endeavour at the improvement of those laws, by which alone we breathe it in *security*.' (My italics.) W. Stark (op cit.) argues that nonetheless Bentham's fundamental idea is really *equality*; but it is doubtful whether Bentham can be pinned down to any one fundamental idea; and his use of 'equality' is specialized and restricted.

[2] See *Defence of Usury*. Bentham's acknowledgement of what he owes to Smith comes in Letter XIII (B., Vol. 3, p. 20). The theme of the *Defence of Usury* is given in Letter I (B., Vol. III, p. 3)—'No man of ripe years and of sound mind, acting freely and with his eyes open, ought to be hindered with a view to his advantage, from making such bargains, in the way of obtaining money, as he thinks fit.' Bentham is in fact going a step beyond his master in the *Defence of Usury*, as he is attacking Smith's admission of a fixed maximum rate of interest.

[3] Bentham's own copy of the *Fragment* was inscribed by him—'This was the very first publication by which men at large were invited to break loose from the trammels of authority and ancestor-wisdom on the field of law.' (B., Vol. 1, p. 260.)

Bentham's alternative ideas in the *Fragment* have the considerable merit of clarity and consistency, and on the psychological side they are given logical development in the *Principles*, where, if the arguments are at times ponderous and at times artificial they are again undoubtedly coherent and well-sustained. And it is certain that his ideas are by no means crude. (i) He has clear if limited aims. (ii) He considers at some length the question of method. (iii) His psychological and ethical ideas are loosely expressed, but the central positions are held in common with many other thinkers of his own time and later: he is not trying to explain away morality as it is normally understood; indeed, his arguments are to a considerable extent based upon a moral postulate. (iv) The arguments against Blackstone have as their aim the disentangling of special legal senses for such words as 'law,' 'rights' and 'duties' in order that discussions of law may be so conducted as to avoid begging ethical questions; and these conceptions provide a framework for a theory of government. Moreover, as he develops these themes, Bentham uncovers other issues of considerable interest. We shall be less than just to Bentham if we go astray on these points, and for that reason it is useful to examine them at greater length.

(i) *The aims of social enquiry.*

Bentham makes it clear that his aims in social enquiry are practical. At the very beginning of the *Principles* he tells us that he is concerned with a 'system, the object of which is to rear the fabric of felicity by the hands of reason and of law.'[1] And the science of law, he explains in the Preface to the *Fragment*, is the foundation of the practice of the legal art.[2] In the same place he explains his aim as 'Reformation'. Reformation corresponds in the moral world to discovery and improvement in the natural world.[3] It must depend upon better acquaintance with the chief means of living happily, on comprehension of the principles of law, and on the improvement of laws.[4] It will not be achieved save in a critical spirit: 'if nothing is ever to be found fault with, nothing will ever be mended.'[5] In particular, the legal profession in England has been undiscriminating in its attitudes of reverence towards the laws and of obsequious respect for authority.[6]

This idea of reformation is restricted. As we shall see, it is restricted by all the deficiencies of the psychological and ethical notions that

[1] *P.*, chap. 1, para 1.   [2] *F.*, Preface, para. 13.   [3] *F.*, Preface, para. 2.
[4] *F.*, Preface., para. 3.   [5] *F.*, Preface, para. 17.   [6] *F.*, Preface, paras. 21-23.

Bentham employed, and by Bentham's lack of curiosity at this stage on the problem of ensuring that government will engage in reform. It is further restricted by the mental attitude represented in his analogy between the social reformation at which he aims and discovery and improvement in the natural world. Bentham was at times more anxious to reduce complex ideas to simple forms than to enquire whether the simple forms at which he arrived did justice to the facts. He was not deterred by the thought that the social world might not merely be more complex than the physical world but also quite different in its principles of organization; and he was not very exact in explaining the terms of his analogy.[1] Restricted in meaning, the conception is also restricted in its application. Reformation is intended to involve the removal of mainly legal obstacles to 'progress' in the eighteenth-century sense rather than to involve anything akin to 'evolution' in the nineteenth-century sense: at the same time it is not intended to involve revolution. Laws and institutions are so to be adjusted to human nature that they will make for felicity. In the pages that follow it becomes increasingly clear that what this mainly means is that existing laws and institutions should be looked at critically, then renovated rationally, whereupon they will both fit human nature better and serve better to affect it for good. There is no objective proposed for human development, no question of raising human nature to a new level; only one of raising standards when they are below the average. Bentham is either assuming that human nature as he finds it in his own time is fully developed, or that further development will occur automatically so long as laws and institutions do not hinder it. Nothing is said on the subject of what kind of people must engage in reformation, or on whether any steps require to be taken to ensure that it is the right people who do engage in it. There is no indication that any great innovations are involved; and there are no proposals for any fundamental social reorganization.

[1] When he is speaking of discovery and improvement in the natural world he gives examples of the first (exploration and the analysis of air) but not of the second. The expression 'improvement' was of course a popular one in the eighteenth century: it was used, for instance, of the introduction of new methods in agriculture. It meant something like the application of discovery, that is, the practical use of knowledge of scientific laws for the purpose of securing a domination of nature. Bentham says that reformation in the moral world corresponds to *both* discovery and improvement in the natural world— unless, as seems possible, there is still some room for discovery in the moral world. What happens in that event is not clear. Possibly reformation then corresponds simply to improvement. Discovery in the moral world would then lie in the development of the consequences of the Principle of Utility with 'method and precision', and reformation would consist of the practical application of such developments.

For some schools of thought this has implied a fatal deficiency in Bentham's views. The Hegelian has seen man derive his moral and metaphysical status from his relations with the State: even John Stuart Mill was concerned with the advance of 'Civilization';[1] but Bentham was apparently simply concerned with making people as he found them more happy. Many socialists have held an equally humanistic position, but they have insisted on the necessity of social and institutional changes that would be revolutionary in nature if not also in their mode of accomplishment before the desired state of society could be attained. For such men also Bentham says too little here; he still says too little, indeed, in his later writings. None-the-less, the standpoint from which Bentham was writing even in this first phase is not irrelevant for any political theorist, and it is perhaps one to which it is particularly necessary to draw the attention of the idealist and the socialist. Men's happiness is not a disreputable subject, and men cannot be blamed for looking askance at political theories into which concern for their happiness does not enter. Moreover, other forms of change can be desirable besides those that represent the difference between an existing state of society and a utopia. We are entitled, although some contemporary political thought would deny this, to try to make the best of society as it exists even while we try to advance it to a new level, and governments should be concerned to be efficient and to care for the public in the present as well as to prepare and to plan for the future. Even in a utopia, indeed, unless human nature were to become completely invariable, there would be some occasion for adjustments in laws and institutions to changing interests and outlooks. Bentham is not discussing utopias, but is considering what may reasonably be expected of government in a reasonable society. It is a reasonable subject of discussion.

(ii) *Science*

According to Bentham, reformation and clear thinking were allied; and in common with others before him and after his time, he thought that natural science had given a model for clear thinking about social questions. At least in the natural world, he held, knowledge could be considered to be advancing rapidly to perfection, and the essence of this success on the part of natural science would appear to lie in its use of method. Here Bentham had several points in mind.

To some extent he was concerned simply with classification as such.

[1] See his essay on that subject in *Dissertations and Discussions.*

When we enquire into anything, he tells us, we seek to become better acquainted with its qualities or properties, some of which will be common both to it and to other things, and some of which will be peculiar to it alone. As concerned with the framing of general conceptions, we must make ourselves clear both about the bases of common characteristics and about the differences between characteristics that are peculiar. We can do this only by comparing, and as only two things can ever be compared at once, we must find a method that will let us deal with objects in pairs that are suitable for comparison because they exhibit opposed or contrasting characteristics. These requirements can be fulfilled only if we take wholes and break them into 'parcels' on the system of 'bipartition', that is, if the whole to be considered is first subjected to a division into two main contrasting parts, each of these is similarly in turn divided in two, and the process is repeated until it is no longer possible to employ it because no more divisions can be made.[1]

If this is science, it is science in a very antiquated form. Bentham's device is, indeed, an ancient one known as 'logical division'. In his favourite form (in which one classifies at each stage in terms of the presence or absence of a particular characteristic) it is known as 'division by dichotomy.'[2] It is most cumbersome to use, and Bentham himself acknowledges that its use becomes tedious.[3] Moreover it certainly introduces some prolixity and artificiality into his discussions. On the whole, however, it is a harmless device as handled by Bentham. In some instances it does help him to ensure exhaustive discussion. And it has the merit of making his arguments orderly and easy to follow. To pursue such a course is naturally to make the task of a critic easier; many writers have succeeded in making the task of the critic harder by avoiding logical forms of exposition.

In his interest in classification, however, Bentham was impelled by more than intellectual honesty. In legal science, for instance, he was, quite properly, concerned with the introduction of order into legal thinking so that various improvements of legal technique could be undertaken. In the *Fragment* it is in relation to the expositorial or descriptive jurisprudence that Bentham considers the applications of

---

[1] *P.*, chap. 16, para. 1, note 1. Cf. para. 27, note 1.

[2] A discussion of its merits and limits will be found in L. S. Stebbing, *A Modern Introduction to Logic*, chap. 22. Bentham stated that he was indebted to that 'melancholy monk,' his tutor at Queen's College, for the 'Porphyrian Tree' device which provided the foundation of his logical method. (B., Vol. 10, p. 563). A systematic exposition of various uses of Division is given in the *Logic*, chap. 8 (B., Vol. 8, pp. 253–9).

[3] *P.*, chap. 16, para. 16, Note ii.

scientific method. He is mainly concerned with it when it deals with the current state of the law,[1] and in this character he calls it 'demonstration.'[2] The most important part of demonstration is 'arrangement,' in which the jurist is concerned to distribute the 'several real or supposed institutions into different masses for the purpose of a general survey,' to determine the order of presentation and to find a name for each part.[3] When this has been achieved then further operations can take place. Elsewhere in the *Fragment* Bentham indicates as functions for legal science, digestion and promulgation, which bring together the scattered materials of past legal decisions, register and publish decisions as they are made, transform the body of the law thus digested into statute law, and break down the mass of the statute law into Codes.[4] In the field of moral science he goes a step further. The full development of a moral science, he says, would require yet another form of study, a 'moral physiology,' the preparation of which would involve the study of cases drawn from history and biography. Bentham does not claim to have embarked on any such study, but he is attempting to map out some of its central points, and to indicate a method that may be useful to later enquirers.[5] Such an inductive method of study has indeed been useful: it is the chief basis of much of the sociological work that is done to-day.

Behind this concern with classification and its applications, however, lay two further attitudes. Bentham's main concern was to show how legal and moral questions could be handled objectively. This caused him sometimes to move from his classical and analytical notion of science to the more contemporary and mechanistic one that equated objectivity with the establishment of the possibility of measurement. As has been seen, in expositorial or descriptive jurisprudence, arrangement should be 'natural'. Then laws are classified in accordance with the offences they create. Offences themselves should be classified according to their degrees of mischief, which constitute the reasons why they are offences.[6] This method has the advantage, says Bentham, both that it can be applied in any country and that it shows up the badness of bad laws.[7] In the *Principles* there is added to these notions the conception of a legal science as a branch of a possible 'logic of the will.' Such a science would emanate in a body of proposed laws

---

[1] It may also deal with the history of law.   [2] F., Preface, para. 48 ff.
[3] F., Preface, para. 49.   [4] F., chap. 5, para. 11.
[5] P., chap. 6, para. 6, note 1.   [6] F., Preface, para. 59.   [7] F., Preface, paras. 56–57.

accompanied by a commentary of reasons.[1] This proposed conception is therefore on the threshold of 'legal art.'[2]

These ideas of legal science depend upon the possibility of measuring mischief and its opposite, and we have seen that it is difficult to pin down Bentham's attitude on this question. If it is true that the 'value' of pleasures and pains can be measured only approximately, then a legal science based on the notion of the possibility of exact measurement can be approximate only in its results. Furthermore, if 'addibility' in its materials is a *sine qua non* of science then legal science can be no more than approximately scientific. It is not clear whether Bentham would have been content with these positions; but they are not impossible positions. For 'economic science' at least, or for some of its practitioners, the idea does not appear to be defunct that some results of value can be obtained from the attempt to measure such intensive variables as utility and welfare. And there are some aspects of our everyday unscientific thinking which make no sense at all if no form of measurement is ever possible in the fields of pleasure and pain and good and evil: consider the conceptions involved in regulations for conscription for the armed forces or for the rationing of commodities.

But there was another side to Bentham's concern with method which did not relate to the question of measurement. It was necessary, he thought, to avoid an analytical method that would remain completely *a priori*;[3] and, above all, it was necessary to get behind language to things.[4] Failure to achieve this latter aim had produced that particular enemy to which Bentham had already devoted some attention and to which he was to give more attention later—the 'fiction', which 'poisons the sense of every instrument it comes near.'[5] Fictions are mental constructions that are not understood as such because they arise from the domination of the mind not by reason but by the sensitive or imaginative faculties.[6] We entertain fictions when we conceive that because there is a word there must be a corresponding reality; for instance, when we think that abstract qualities are real and forget that the only real things are those in which such qualities inhere. Many of the common concepts of law and politics are fictions.[7]

[1] P., Preface, paras. 35–38, cf. the views expressed in the *Logic* (B., Vol. 8).
[2] See F., Preface. para. 13: cf. P., chap. 17, paras. 5 and 21.
[3] F., chap. 5, para. 6, note 1 (para. 7).
[4] Note his criticism of Blackstone in F., Preface, para. 7—'Natural society the mother, and . . . Political society the daughter, of Law Municipal, duly begotten in the bed of Metaphor.'
[5] F., Preface, para. 41, note. Cf. chap. 1, para. 37.
[6] P., chap. 2, para. 11, note 1.   [7] F., chap. 4, para. 5.

Justice is a fiction,[1] so are powers and rights,[2] so, indeed, is jurisprudence.[3] It is therefore not surprising that Bentham should consider it
necessary to try to follow in his own thought a method which, by
reducing complex doctrines and notions to the simplest possible terms,
would aim at the thorough exposure of the fictitious.

Bentham in more than one place describes methods whereby the
snares of fiction may be avoided. He says, for instance, that the sentences in which a doctrine is expressed should be translated into other
sentences in which words are expressive of simple ideas, of substances,
simple modes, or emotions.[4] Here Bentham is fairly closely following
Descartes and Locke, the latter of whom he cites; but the special
caution about language is his own.[5] This preoccupation undoubtedly
encouraged a tendency on Bentham's part to oversimplify and to be
content to brand concepts as fictions rather than to enquire further and
seek to appreciate the element of truth they might contain; yet this
conception was of first importance. In political theory as in many other
subjects, a good deal of controversy has really centred upon the
meanings of words; and not a few controversies have been protracted
because of the persistence of traditional phraseologies: in Bentham's
time, discussions of natural rights and of contract were certainly in
this position; the same might be said to-day of much discussion of
'capitalism' and 'socialism'.

It was as a result of this last phase of Bentham's method that he
made what is perhaps his major contribution to modern social thought
—his separation of neutral or technical meanings of sovereignty, law,
rights and duties. These are central conceptions of jurisprudence and
also of an important aspect of political theory; and Bentham stated
them in the form in which most plain men to-day accept them and to
which the later criticisms of analytical legal and political theorists
have made differences by way of refinement rather than of substantive

---

[1] *P.*, chap. 10, para. 40, note 2 (pp. 240–241).   [2] *P.*, chap. 16, para. 25, note 1.
[3] *P.*, chap. 17, para. 21.   [4] *F.*, chap. 5, para. 6, note 1 (para. 6).
[5] This is not to say that Bentham's interest in words was unique or that he was entirely
original. After all, the whole of Book 3 of Locke's *Essay* is about words, and so is chap. 7 of
Hobbes's *Leviathan*. A tradition of interest in words goes back to and beyond the mediaeval
nominalists. Nor did Bentham's contemporaries neglect it: see, e.g. Horne Tooke's
Diversions of Purley (1787). The special quality in Bentham is a particularly close and
constant application of a psychological analysis of language to the field of social concepts.
See the *Logic*: 'The grand instrument of thought . . . the faculty of discourse' (B., Vol. 8,
p. 230). For a fuller examination, and an account of the later developments of Bentham's
ideas on this subject, see Ogden, *Bentham's Theory of Fictions* (1932); but Ogden rather
tends to give the impression that Bentham's ideas were almost wholly original.

alteration. Within analytical jurisprudence the main change has assumed the form of paring down the 'politico-psychological' element contained in Bentham's views, a process begun in Austin and carried further in our own day by the school of 'pure' jurisprudence.[1] But the essentials of Bentham's central ideas have remained, and in spite of the recrudescence of Natural Law theories: it is to-day appreciated that we may deal with positive law as such and that rights and duties may be studied as legal conceptions and not only as moral or political conceptions. In political theory, also, this technique has an important use, and more in the form in which Bentham left it; we employ it when we concern ourselves with states as they are. Not that Bentham invented his notions of sovereignty and law. The claim to be made for him is simply that he indicated a means of disentangling these ideas from natural law associations. Bodin and Grotius, Hobbes, Locke and Rousseau, had also taken political society to involve the relation between sovereign and subjects that Bentham indicated as essential; but they also included in their discussions considerations of various questions of justification, including constitutional justification. Bentham, while unresponsive at this stage to the question of constitutional justification was none-the-less clear that fact and justification should be discussed quite separately. Of his precursors, Hobbes was nearest to Bentham in his view of the nature of law as such, but his general view of human nature led him to a view of government that was more restricted and less flexible than that of Bentham. Locke and Rousseau, on the other hand, and in their vastly different ways, both integrated their explanations of the nature of government with explanations of human nature, and in such a manner as to discuss simultaneously the nature of government and the character of a good constitution. They meant by government as such the same as Hobbes and Bentham meant, and beneath the natural law ideas they retained were identical notions of *de facto* sovereignty, rights and duties. The same has been true of later writers, even when their aim has been to assimilate the actual state to an ideal state, or positive law to natural law, or when they have sought to assert a 'pluralist' position. Bentham himself was emphatic on the distinction between what law is and what law ought to be: his contribution was to insist that the understanding of the technically necessary attributes of law and government[2]

[1] See the discussion in J. W. Jones: *Historical Introduction to the Theory of Law*, pp. 92–97.

[2] This is not, of course, legal technicality in the sense criticised by Bentham. It is the technicality that derives from the technique of practising law and government.

must precede attempts to deal in any form with problems of the moral authority of government.

These notions of legal and moral science, then, are mixed and at times muddled. The analysis of terms is one thing. The employment of the possibility of measurement as the criterion of objectivity is another. The conception of arrangement in terms of what men are most likely to attend to is not universally plausible, although Bentham was on sound ground in maintaining that in the treatment of any subject-matter with a social reference, undue devotion to un-examined technicalities will lead to artificiality and aridity. The notion of arrangement in terms of offences created is more plausible when a penal code is under consideration than when other aspects of law are being considered; and in any case Bentham's jurisprudence is that of a social reformer rather than a lawyer. The idea of classi-fication of offences in terms of degrees of mischief depends upon the possibility of measuring mischief which may be possible in some approximate sense but on which Bentham's ideas remain obscure. Moral science as based on an inductive 'moral physiology' would be quite a different kind of study from any of the others discussed. In his attack on the fiction in legal and political thinking, however, Bentham was developing a notion whose validity rested neither upon over-simplifications of 'social science' nor upon the possibility of adding pleasures and pains, and it may be claimed that he was here indicating, however partially and inexactly, an approach whose im-portance has only fairly recently been generally appreciated, and which has remained, on the whole, to such an extent under-appreciated in political thinking, that it has yet to be thoroughly and impartially applied.[1]

(iii) *Utilitarianism*

In his concern to be scientific, Bentham moved to and fro between different conceptions of science. When he discusses human nature and obligation, he once again appears to draw upon several different types of approach and not completely to be successful either in keeping them apart or in confining each to an appropriate subject-matter. At times he is concerned with psychological analysis, at times with the

---

[1] Both the approach and the tradition have been appreciated in another field. See A. J. Ayer's statement in *Language Truth and Logic* (1936), p. 59, that the claim that the activity of philosophising is essentially analytic is made from a standpoint that has always been implicit in English empiricism. He refers to Hobbes, Hume, Bentham, and J. S. Mill.

analysis of moral obligation as ordinarily understood, at times with such analysis of responsibility as is required for the purpose of penal law, at times with the characterization of at least the externals of good citizenship. And there is a further complication in that while in some places his use of words is pedantically accurate, in other places it is very casual.

Bentham's critics have delighted to point out the inconsistencies and loose ends in his psychological ideas. They certainly abound. Bentham's language is very loose even when he sets out to say what pleasures and pains are. In one footnote we have a general account in terms of current sensationalism and associationism. All ideas, he says, are derived from the senses as the result of the operation of sensible objects on these: this is equally true of pleasurable and painful ideas, including those of the mind: the pleasures and pains of the body may arise immediately from the perceptions they accompany, but those of the mind will arise from an association operating between the action of the object of sense and the appearance of the pleasure or pain.[1] Does this mean that pleasures and pains are ideas? He says elsewhere that they are caused in men's minds, although their 'force' (or effectiveness) is also conditioned by the sensibility or disposition of the particular person.[2] But he also says that pleasures and pains are the names of 'homogeneous real entities,'[3] that they are 'perceptions,'[4] that they are 'sensations'[5] and that they are felt.[6] Nor is it clear whether they are all the same in kind or not. By implication he treats them as all the same in kind inasmuch as he considers the possibility of dealing with them arithmetically, but in one place he seems to be saying that pleasures really are of different 'sorts,' although he does not say whether this means only that their origins are different or that they really are different as pleasures.[7] He is clearer, although not entirely clear, when he deals with what pleasure and pain do. They, rather than desire, about which he has almost nothing to say,[8] are our moving forces; but whereas the opening statement of the *Principles* suggests that they are the sole determinants of behaviour, it appears later that there are other determinants also, for instance, sympathy and imagination.[9] Bentham

---

[1] P., chap. 16, para. 11, note 1.   [2] P., chap. 6, para. 1.
[3] P., chap. 6, para. 6, note 1 (p. 166).   [4] P., chap. 5, para. 1.
[5] P., chap. 5, paras. 5 and 6.   [6] P., chap. 6, para. 2.   [7] P., chap. 5.
[8] At P., chap. 5, para. 18, he seems to consider it sufficient to say of desire that it is a form of pain.
[9] P., chap. 2, para. 11, note 1. The sympathetic principle is based on the sensible faculty, the principle of caprice or 'phantastic' principle is based on the imaginative faculty.

is again no clearer on the question of the freedom of the will. The will, he says, is moved by motives.[1] (Motives are described as being either perceptions of individual lots of pleasure or pain or external events, although the immediately moving motive is always a pleasure or pain.[2]) In his accounts of the 'circumstances affecting sensibility,' (especially of 'firmness of mind,' 'steadiness,' and 'moral sensibility,')[3] and in his account of 'disposition,'[4] Bentham appears to give a determinist account of volition; but he says elsewhere that the will, when determined by a pleasurable motive is uncoerced,[5] and in general he writes as though there were no doubt of the freedom of the will of at least censorial jurists and legislators.[6] For the most part, however, Bentham prefers to leave this question on one side and to concentrate his analysis round the meaning of 'tendencies of acts'.[7]

But we should not be too quick to pass judgment. If we look at the statements on these subjects that were made by other writers of Bentham's time, or, indeed, by most other writers until close on the end of the nineteenth century, we find the same difficulties, and in particular we find this notion of passions and affections as some sort of incomplete and obscure ideas. They may arise from the 'senses' and therefore from the body, but they have also somehow or other to be 'data' for consciousness and therefore for intellect or reason. The notion of psychical phenomena independent alike of intellect and of external objects was a derivative of later developments in biological science.

Moreover, we must admit considerable ingenuity to Bentham's analysis, partly psychological and partly ethical, of the 'tendencies of acts.' He indicates as relevant to the legal consideration of action, six elements—the action itself, its consequences, the general disposition of the agent, his particular motive for acting, his particular intention in respect of the action, and the extent of his awareness of the circumstances liable to effect the consequences of the action.[8] Motive, as the perception of the aim of the action or of the impulse to perform it,[9]

Chap. 5, para. 13: Imagination imposes a different order on material supplied by memory. Later, (see Appendix A to the *Logic* in B, Vol. 8, pp. 279–81) Bentham regarded faculties other than the two basic ones 'the perceptive' and 'the appetitive' as fictitious. But his reference at *P.*, chap. 5, para. 1, to pleasures and pains as 'interesting perceptions' might have led to an even further reduction.

[1] *P.*, chap. 8, para. 2, note 1.   [2] *P.*, chap. 10, paras. 5–7.   [3] *P.*, chap. 6.
[4] *P.*, chap. 11.   [5] *P.*, chap. 8, para. 2, note 1.
[6] Cf. *F.*, Preface, para. 70: 'He that is resolved to persevere without deviation in the line of truth and utility, must have learnt to prefer the still whisper of enduring approbation to the short-lived bustle of tumultuous applause.' Cf. also *P.*, chap. 10, para. 3 and note.
[7] *P.*, chap. 8, para. 2, note 1.   [8] *P.*, chap. 7, paras. 6–7.   [9] *P.*, chap. 10, paras. 5–6.

d

is carefully distinguished from intention as the general state of volition and understanding in regard to the projected action and its attendant circumstances.[1] Motive produces intention: it is what causes us to intend; the intention is what we intend.[2] The 'goodness' or 'badness' of motives and intentions are independent of one another: the 'goodness' or 'badness' of an intention depends upon consciousness of circumstances;[3] in separate cases we may say that a 'good' motive is one giving rise to a 'good' intention,[4] but generally speaking the 'good' motives may be regarded as being those which usually have good effects.[5] What is really good or bad in a man is his disposition.[6]

But if Bentham's general psychological ideas simply reflected certain prevailing notions, so too did his general ideas on ethics. Here Bentham's views, if regarded as we should regard later nineteenth-century moral philosophy, have been so frequently discussed that no long repetition of the standard criticisms is required. If pleasure is that at which we unavoidably aim, then there is no question of what we ought to do; and it is impossible to move by the mere exercise of arithmetic, or by any other exercise, from each individual's maximum happiness as a good to him to the maximum happiness of a number of people as a good to each individual member of that number. But Bentham is here scarcely out of line with several other British moralists of the eighteenth century who in the main did little more than make varying compositions of the same ingredients. Shaftesbury argued that 'to have the natural and good affections is to have the chief means and power of self-enjoyment.'[7] Hutcheson's 'benevolence' advised that that action is best which accomplishes the greatest happiness of the greatest number.[8] Hume's 'sympathy'—the 'chief source of moral distinctions'—was the only means whereby the happiness of strangers could affect the individual and was therefore the basis of 'the sentiment of approbation which arises from the survey of all those virtues which are useful to society or to the person possessed of them.'[9] Smith's 'sympathy' imaginatively identified the pleasure and pain of other

---

[1] P., chap. 7, para. 7.   [2] P., chap. 6, para. 4, note 1 (p. 165): chap. 7, para. 5.
[3] P., chap. 9, para. 13.   [4] P., chap. 10, para. 33.
[5] P., chap. 10, paras. 12 and 29.   [6] P., chap. 11.
[7] Inquiry Concerning Virtue, Pt. 2, Sect. 1 (In Selby-Bigge: British Moralists, Vol. 1, p. 54).
[8] See note 3, page xx.
[9] Treatise, Bk. 2, Pt. 3, Sect. 6 (pp. 310–311 of Everyman Edition). There are some very close resemblances between Bentham's language in the Principles and Hume's in the Treatise; e.g. see Bk. 2, Pt. 3, Sect. 1 (p. 281 in Everyman Edition) where Hume speaks of 'extensive sympathy.'

men with one's own pleasure and pain.[1] And the final form in which the utilitarian view is developed by Bentham in the *Principles* must also not be overlooked. It involves the drawing together of analyses spread over the central chapters of the book, and it culminates in the statement that the 'dictates of utility are neither more nor less than the dictates of the most extensive and enlightened (that is, well-advised) benevolence.'[2] The pleasures of benevolence, he has earlier explained, may also be called those of good-will, sympathy, or the benevolent or social affections, and they result from the view of pleasures in others who are the objects of benevolence.[3] Extent, it will be remembered, is the special circumstance that has to be taken into account when we pass from considering the pleasures and pains of one person to considering those of a number of persons.[4] 'Sympathetic bias,' he elsewhere explains, may extend from 'certain individuals' to any subordinate class of individuals, to the 'whole nation,' to 'human kind in general' and finally to 'the whole sensitive creation.'[5] 'According as these objects of sympathy are more numerous, the affection by which the man is biased, may be said to be the more enlarged.'[6] Acts, he explains in another place, are well advised to the extent to which the actor is conscious of the circumstances upon which their consequences depend.[7] If the original statement, then, is re-phrased with the aid of these clues (some of which Bentham himself gives us in the footnotes to the paragraph in which the statement occurs) we may still conceive it technically correct to say with one of Bentham's critics that he 'repeats the selfish and hedonistic ethics of Helvetius,'[8] but we are unlikely to consider that this adequately conveys the whole of what Bentham had in mind.

It is clear that in his ethical views Bentham sat very loosely to his already loose psychological doctrines. He appears at times to regard sympathy as in itself an activating and independent principle, but if it really were such then it would not necessarily be egoistic. He tries to safeguard his usual position by characterizing sympathy as involving the individual's pleasure or pain when induced by the pleasure or pain of others. Had he followed Hartley more closely he might have argued that sympathetic feelings arose from egoistic feelings by means of association although this would simply have pushed the problem one

[1] *Theory of the Moral Sentiments* (1759), Pt. 1, Sect. 1, chap. 1 (Selby-Bigge, *op. cit.*, Vol. 1, pp. 257–263).
[2] *P.*, chap. 10, para. 36.   [3] *P.*, chap. 5, para. 10.   [4] *P.*, chap. 4, para. 7.
[5] *P.*, chap. 6, para. 21.   [6] *P.*, chap. 6, para. 21.   [7] *P.*, chap. 9, para. 2.
[8] A. Seth Pringle-Pattison: *The Philosophical Radicals*, p. 33.
d*

stage back.[1] Bentham's difficulties largely arise from his notions, first,
that morals must be dealt with scientifically; second, that this means
the introduction of measurement; and third, that pleasures and pains,
but not sympathy, can admit of the introduction of a technique of
measurement.[2] But it is evident that some of what Bentham had to say
was much closer to what Kant had to say than is generally appreciated.
The two men started from broadly the same psychological position;
Kant's attempted escape from the difficulties of this position was by
means of an elaborate conception of Pure Practical Reason; Bentham's
attempted escape was really, although more simply, in terms of a
disinterested practical reason, for it is difficult to see how otherwise
than by the disinterested exercise of reason any individual, whether
in his private life or as a legislator, can set before himself and follow
the Principle of Utility.

Curiously enough, Bentham has much less to say about the Principle
of Utility than might be supposed. What he does say is ambiguous
but interesting. Utility itself, he says in the *Principles*, is that 'property
in any object whereby it tends to produce benefit, advantages,
pleasure, good or happiness . . . or . . . to prevent the happening of
mischief, pain, evil or unhappiness.'[3] Here utility is a property of an
'object'. In the *Fragment* it is the tendency of an *act* towards happiness
as an end.[4] The Principle of Utility itself is discussed solely with
reference to acts. It is that principle 'which approves or disapproves
of every action whatsoever, according to the tendency which it
appears to have to augment or diminish the happiness of the party
whose interest is in question.'[5] If we remove the metaphor, this
presumably means that when men approve or disapprove in the way
described they are using the Principle of Utility. But notice that the
way in which the word 'interest' is used is ambiguous. Interest may be
another synonym for happiness, or it may mean a conception or view
of what will make for happiness; and if it means the latter, then it
is important to know whether it refers to the conception or view of the
party concerned himself (or themselves) or to the conception or view

[1] But at *P.*, chap. 5, para. 15, he points out that pleasures arising from association form
a separate 'sort' from others, including those of benevolence or good-will.
[2] But remember that measurement is introduced in a very general sense only (see
above, note 12, page xxxv). Bentham himself implied in his later *Codification Proposal* that he
did not hold that pleasures and pains could literally be measured—'Pleasure itself not being
ponderable or measurable . . . take the general source and thence representative of
pleasure, viz., *money*' (B., Vol. 4, p. 540).
[3] *P.*, chap. 1, para. 3.   [4] *F.*, Preface, para 54.   [5] *P.*, chap. 1, para. 2.

of some other party. Bentham does not explain, and he tends to use both senses.

Putting these ambiguities on one side, there are further difficulties about the Principle of Utility. Bentham's first concern with it was undoubtedly a concern with a scientific first principle. His 'proofs' of the validity of the Principle of Utility as such a scientific first principle are not very satisfactory. In one argument he says that it is not possible to establish the Principle by means of any direct proof:[1] we require to establish some principle that will indicate 'some external considerations as a means of warranting and guiding the internal sentiments of approbation and disapprobation,'[2] and we have to accept the Principle of Utility for this purpose because there is no alternative principle that is not founded simply on sentiment and is therefore merely subjective and anarchical.[3] The Principle of Utility is thus held to be established by a process of elimination. This in itself is scarcely adequate. But the alleged elimination of the rival standards is even less convincing: indeed the argument involved in it is circular. The Principle of Utility has to be accepted because the rival principles are subjective; but when the rival principles are considered, the Principle of Utility is taken as established, and the unsatisfactoriness of the rival principles is shown by the fact that they are contrary to the Principle of Utility.[4] A possible alternative argument is that the objectivity and validity of the Principle come from another source that is indicated at the beginning of the first chapter of the *Principles*: 'Nature has placed mankind under the governance of two sovereign masters, pain and pleasure. It is for them alone to point out what we ought to do, as well as to determine what we shall do . . . The Principle of Utility recognises this subjection.'[5] If this is the case, then the basis of the Principle lies in a pair of interlocked (and false) assumptions in psychology and ethics; and it is clear that Bentham sometimes thinks that it is thus based, although not that the assumptions are false. But whether he can establish his first principle or not, it is evident that Bentham regards it as furnishing an objective standard. In the *Fragment* he tells us that it is the 'sole and all-sufficient reason for every point of practice whatsoever.'[6] Moreover, it puts all disputes on a basis of fact, and parties to arguments can appeal to the evidence of past matters of fact that can be held to be analogous to the matters they are disputing: thus intelligible and explicit issues can be found

[1] *P.*, chap. 1, para. 11.   [2] *P.*, chap. 2, para. 12.   [3] *P.*, chap. 1, para. 14.
[4] *P.*, chap. 2, passim.   [5] *P.*, chap. 1, para. 1.   [6] *F.*, chap. 1, para. 48.

which, when explored, will lead to reconcilement; for 'men, let them but once clearly understand one another, will not be long ere they agree.'[1] This is indeed a far-reaching statement: Bentham appears to be close to indicating not simply that the Principle of Utility is a valid scientific principle, but that Truth is great and will prevail—a position well in accord with the notion of a pure practical reason.

But when Bentham moves to the Principle in its extended form, he is moving away from it as a scientific first principle, however based; and while we reach here, perhaps, a point of fundamental confusion in Bentham's thought, we none-the-less reach one major reason for maintaining that Bentham's theories do not stand or fall on the validity of his notions of psychological, ethical, or scientific methods. 'It is the greatest happiness of the greatest number that is the measure of right and wrong';[2] this is really a moral maxim—a form of summary of a moral position, the position that it is morally right to seek to secure the greatest happiness of the greatest number, morally wrong to work against it, that nothing is good that does not make for such happiness or wrong that does not work against it. No such maxim is in any way buttressed, let alone established, by the elaborate superstructure whereby individual and social ends are supposed to be linked by the operation of the two 'homogeneous entities' pleasure and pain. The superstructure is there because Bentham, like many another man, considered it essential to universalise the validity of his own moral judgments so that they became statements of scientific social laws, rules, the following of which, and only the following of which, could make for order and improvement in society. But that is neither here nor there. The maxim is not very different in essence from the fundamental maxims of many other social theorists, and of vast numbers of those for whom they have written, few of whom have considered it necessary to establish or even to examine such basic principles.

The truth of the matter is that Bentham was neither a psychologist nor a moral philosopher. He was a reforming lawyer, and he found in Hume, Hartley and Helvetius, suggestions for methods that seemed sufficient for his purpose. He did not reflect very thoroughly on these methods; he was not interested to do so: he was really concerned for the most part with moral actions viewed from the outside, with the arranging of sanctions so that self-interested action would not differ from action that was directed towards the common good. Hence his primary concern with 'intention'. None-the-less he was far from being

---

[1] F., chap. 4, para. 41.   [2] F., Preface, para. 2.

devoid of insight in at least the field of psychology, and the creaking apparatus he employed has perhaps too often misled his readers into underestimating the penetration of some of his ideas. If he failed to be bothered about the difficulties of his methods, he was particularly alert to some extravagances.[1] The notion of the calculus of pleasures and pains is not advanced in the *Principles* in anything like the simple mechanical form in which it is so often thought to have been advanced: he is not suggesting that there is nothing to consider but the application of arithmetic to easily identifiable and uniform pleasures and pains of individuals cut to the same rational pattern: he recognises that attempts to operate the calculus are liable to be approximate rather than exact.[2] Moreover, once the validity of his external standpoint is conceded for its appropriate purposes, then much of what he has to say will be recognised as a form, and by no means an inept form, of the type of enquiry that is common to-day under some name such as sociology or social psychology. In this sort of enquiry, Bentham did not by any means lose sight of the intricacies of human nature or of the differences between men's characters, nor was he unaware of non-rational elements in individual characters: see his chapters on the Circumstances Affecting Sensibility and on Human Dispositions in General. And not only is he at pains to expound the complicating factors that make the reactions of one man different from those of another, but he emphasises the problem that this raises in relation to the fact that the nature of law is to be general.[3] Again, given the end in view—the consideration of the rational use of punishment—the arguments of the later chapters on the analysis of actions and the nature of responsibility will be found to be relevant and effective, even if they are not couched in language that is fashionable to-day. The same can be said of his account of the social role of punishment. He is more open to criticism for his treatment of punishment in relation to the individual offender; but then the social role of punishment is his avowed main theme.

(iv) *Government*

We now have some inkling of the background to the phase of Bentham's views on government that is expressed in the *Fragment* and the *Principles*. The purpose of his enquiries is practical and

---

[1] See, e.g. *F.*, chap. 4, para. 10, of men 'joining their wills'—'wills will not splice and dovetail like deal boards.' In paras. 12–15 he shows himself very alert to 'rationalisation' in argument. Cf. end of Preface, para. 5, and paras. 27 and 28.

[2] See above, summary of argument of *Principles*.   [3] *P.*, chap. 17, para. 15.

limited: he is not concerned with the structure of ideal society or with the justification of constitutions but with the improvement of actual societies by means of the rational day-to-day use of the instrument of government. This is none-the-less a moral purpose. We are concerned with men's welfare, and by means of law we are to obtain from men the same co-operative behaviour that would appear without the intervention of law if only they were enlightened. The rational use of law involves reflection in several forms: we require disciplines of thought that will force analysis to be practically realistic: we obtain a reinsurance of such realism by relating our reflections on law and government to the facts of human nature. On these bases we may devise a reasoned method for the exposition of law, and when we come to consider what may be accomplished through the instrumentality of government we will also be able to estimate the limits of what can be so accomplished and to decide by what means its accomplishment may best be achieved. Such further views on political theory as are expressed in the two works are very incomplete because political theory forms an incidental rather than a central theme.

Is is clear, however, that Bentham is holding a theory of government without any allied conception of society or state. He is concerned in the *Fragment* to reject many of the previously accepted standard concepts of political thought, and to develop instead a technical view of political society. Such a society involves a 'habit' of obedience to a governor or governors whose commands are law; but the word 'habit' is not to be construed as implying any principle of integration in society that cannot be explained quite adequately in terms of individual psychology.[1] Thus, for instance, Bentham says that legislators prefer to deal with married men rather than with single men, and with people with children rather than with the childless, because the more numerous a man's connections by way of sympathy are, the stronger is the hold of the law on him. 'A wife and children are so many pledges a man gives to the world for his good behaviour.'[2] Even this type of analysis might have been carried further, but Bentham did not pursue it. Instead, he informs us that there is no such thing as a 'community'. Communities are fictitious bodies.[3] Political relations are thus conceived as consisting entirely of relations between individual governors and individual subjects, and if laws have any moral authority, it is because of their effects on the welfare of individuals.[4]

---

[1] *F*., chap. 1, para. 12, note 1. Cf. *P*., chap. 7, para. 18.
[2] *P*., chap. 6, para 26, note 1 (p. 174). [3] *P*., chap. 1, para. 4. [4] *P*., chap. 3, para. 1.

But this is the subject to which Bentham wishes to address himself. The art of government consists of legislating in such a way as to ensure the welfare of the greatest number of individuals, and it starts from the work of the censorial jurist, who uses the work of the expositor inasmuch as that has natural arrangement and gives reasons for laws. The work of the censor looks forward to political practice: he it is who tells the legislator what he ought to do; and the legislator practises the legal art or art of government. In the *Principles* Bentham says that the art of government assumes two forms. When it is concerned with the actions of non-adults it constitutes the field of education. Education may be private or public: in the latter case it is handled by 'those whose province it is to superintend the conduct of the whole community.'[1] Thus while strictly speaking the government of adults is not part of the art of education, the art of government is none-the-less a tutorial art, and Bentham's theory of government at this stage might not unsuitably be called the tutorial theory of government.[2]

This position permits considerable positive scope to government. The promotion of happiness by rewarding is rarer than its promotion by punishing,[3] but in addition to seeking to avert mischiefs, government should seek to make additions to the sum of welfare, although this is a notion of comparatively recent appearance in the history of political societies.[4] At the same time, however, there is a natural limit to what a legislator can do even when he is engaging to the best of his ability in his proper business. The legislator cannot know more than the individual does about the individual himself. He can deal successfully with broad lines of conduct in which all individuals or large and permanent classes of individuals are involved, but he cannot deal successfully with matters depending upon the individual's peculiar circumstances. Drunkenness and fornication, for instance, are not suitable fields for legislative action.[5] Thus there are separate and autonomous spheres of government and of private ethics.[6] The first is that of the political sanction, the second that of the other sanctions operating without the political sanction. In private ethics the prudence,

---

[1] *P.*, chap. 17, para. 5.

[2] 'The magistrate operating in the character of tutor' . . . his 'controlling influence, different in this respect from that of the ordinary preceptor, dwells with a man to his life's end' (*P.*, chap. 6, para. 41).

[3] *P.*, chap. 16, para. 18. Cf. chap. 7, para. 1.

[4] *P.*, chap. 16, para. 17 and note 1 (p. 323).

[5] *P.*, chap. 17, para. 15. See para. 12 ff. The 'great field for the exclusive interference of private ethics' is that of the 'cases where punishment would be unprofitable.'

[6] *P.*, chap. 17, paras. 3–4.

probity and beneficence of the individual are at work: in the political field the legislator may prompt these 'branches of duty' to work.[1] That is the essence of Bentham's political theory at this stage.

There are hints of other views. We have already considered those that are introduced in the *Fragment*. In the *Principles* Bentham introduces others; for instance, he mentions that sovereign power 'upon the Principle of Utility can never be other than fiduciary'.[2] But such notions are not developed. Bentham was not at this stage interested in questions of forms of government. Doctrinally he was neither an authoritarian nor a libertarian. Perhaps he inclined to 'free government,' but we know that he was not averse to despots if they were benevolent, and that he had entertained the possibility of interesting Catherine the Great of Russia in his suggestions for practical reforms: later he was equally ready to advise the Estates General. As we have seen, he supposed 'the people in power' 'only wanted to know what was good in order to embrace it,' and he had said that 'men, let them but once clearly understand one another, will not be long ere they agree.' His position was a blend of pessimism and optimism. Men would not by themselves follow the Principle of Utility in all matters: the political sanction was required in order to induce them to do so; but what was to make the legislator employ the political sanction properly? Apparently nothing more than the reasonable explanations of the censor. In the *Fragment* Bentham had conceded the technical possibility of conventions limiting government, and he had asserted that government should be obeyed only so long as the probable mischiefs of obedience were less than the probable mischiefs of resistance. But these conceptions dealt with limiting cases only. If a government oversteps the bounds of a convention there is a signal for resistance: when governments make bad laws the individual may justifiably decide to resist. But how are governments to be made to make good laws?

There, then, for the moment, Bentham leaves the question of government. His account may well seem very thin and unsatisfactory. Not only do social forms other than government remain unanalysed, and not only is the constitutional question disregarded, but his individualism remains barren: the notions of an autonomous sphere for individual prudence and of natural limits of government action (which might, if developed, have led to the constitutional question)

---

[1] *P.*, chap. 17, para. 6 ff. His aid is most needed in respect of probity.
[2] *P.*, chap. 16, para. 55, note 1, para. IX (p. 391).

do not begin to touch those positive aspects of individual liberty that were to be discussed by John Stuart Mill and T. H. Green. Moreover, Bentham certainly appears to lay himself open to an obvious charge which critics from Macaulay and J. S. Mill onwards have not failed to bring against him—that he ignores the possibility of drawing lessons from history.[1] Yet the *Fragment* and the *Principles* occupy a special place in political theory. They are the first major works in which a clear statement is given of the nature of government as an instrument whose value is to be judged by its effects, and in which at the same time far-reaching claims are made in regard to the potential effectiveness of government. The notion of government as a fabricated device was already old when Bentham was writing, but preoccupation with the contract theory had led to a greater concentration on the mode of fabrication than on the results of the operation of the device, other than as these served to preserve original natural rights, or to erect barriers against the evils or deficiencies of the state of nature. Bentham was unconcerned about origins, and considered that there were no such things as natural rights. He distinguished political and natural society, but analytically. The operation of his political sanction perhaps introduced into the operation of the other sanctions somewhat the same difference that others had conceived to be introduced by the move from the state of nature into political society; but Bentham was doing more than repeating old theories in a new form; he was advancing to a new standpoint in spite of the deficiencies of his logic and of his psychological ideas, and in spite of his over-reliance on reason and the mere apparatus of law. He was holding a new view of human nature. The individual of his psychology, artificial as he may appear to-day, was less of an abstraction than the possessors of natural rights who were postulated by many of his predecessors. He was an individual who might change and be changed. In consequence Bentham was holding a new view of government. His 'tutorial' theory should not read strangely to-day. It does not derive its character from the fact that Bentham in his time looked to benevolent despots as possible sponsors of his ideas. He also looked to other forms of government, and I think it is clear that he continued to think that the function of the legislator remained tutorial no matter what, on other grounds, it was considered that the form of government should be.

[1] In his essay on Coleridge in *Dissertations and Discussions* Mill criticises Bentham for not concerning himself with laws of social development or with the nature of tradition. But this type of criticism can be carried too far. It should not be forgotten that Bentham later wrote on *The Influence of Time and Place in Matters of Legislation*.

We should recognise that there is an important sense in which, in even the most democratic community, at least certain types of legislation must have the character that Bentham here tends to hold should attach to all legislation. For the same reasons that a representative rather than a direct form has become recognised as practicable for modern democratic government, legislation is liable to represent in democracies not any precise and direct expression of a 'will of the people,' or even of majorities, but some fairly complex interaction between ideas evolved in varying forms in different social groups; and in this process a leading part is played by élites at various points within society, especially élites of parliamentarians and administrators. The representative principle, party organization, and other influences, may place limits on the freedom of action of such élites: but within such limits élites frequently lead and indeed educate the 'general public,' and their legislation is even frequently and specifically designed to educate.[1] Such actions of government are tutelary in nature whether we like it or not. Bentham made less than we should of the reasons why such legislation occurs. It occurs in part because the majority of us accept the basis of government under which we live, wish to give the maximum of attention to our private lives, and are only too glad to be told what to do in the greater number of situations in which our actions and those of our fellows affect each other. It occurs in part for a reason that operates more to-day than in Bentham's day— because we are already committed to such a degree of common enterprise that detailed adaptations must be made from the centre. It also occurs in part, however, because there are some people who make it their business to be longer-sighted than others and to put themselves in positions in which they can secure the co-operation of others through legislation. Such men practise the art of government, although they no doubt require to practise other arts in order to achieve the position from which they can practise this one. It may, then, not be the whole of government, but it is an inevitable part of it, and it is by no means futile for Bentham to discuss it. Indeed it is a question the discussion of which is still very far from being at an end. Some consideration has been given by specialised sociologists to the position of élites, but those concerned with the wider problems of political theory have hitherto scarcely dealt with the question, and in particular little attention has been paid to the moral issues it involves.

It is not a matter for surprise that few have held that Bentham's

---

[1] Cf. the discussion of the Benthamites, pp. xii-xiii, lxi-lxiii.

partial and unfinished views on government in these two works stand
up to comparison with the leading views of other writers of his period.
While Bentham spoke from a moral standpoint, it would be difficult
to maintain that his moral insight equalled that of Rousseau. The
historical sense of Burke is certainly not present in Bentham's analysis.
Perhaps he also lacked the sense of justice of Paine and other popular
radicals. But considerations such as these should not lead us to lose all
sense of perspective in passing judgment on the *Fragment* and the
Principles; there were some very important and perhaps over-riding
compensations. Was reliance on reason and the law for the attainment
of the felicity of the greatest number more paradoxical or less paradoxical than the notion of forcing men to be free?[1] Was the proposition that the legislator ought to be guided by reason more helpful
or less helpful than the conclusion that 'the unerring and powerful
instincts' of Nature should be called in 'to fortify the fallible and feeble
contrivances of our reason'?[2] Has the notion of government as an
adaptable instrument been more in accordance with experience or less
in accordance with experience than the notion that at best government
can be no more than a necessary evil?[3]

Nor let us fall into the fallacy of supposing that other writers were
more in some main stream of 'the development of political theory'
than was Bentham. There has been no main stream of political theory.
(And, in particular, if there ever was a fiction, it is the idea that there
has been some objective dialectical movement of political thought
that culminated in the thesis of Hegel and the antithesis of Marx.)
The ideas underlying the various political systems of to-day are
manifold, and they are diverse in their origins. And whatever else
may be said about them, the ideas of Bentham and of his successors
have at least played a considerable role in one of the many political
traditions of the world, the tradition that has held that government is
made for man, and not man for government.

V

It will be apparent that the historical influence of Benthamism
does not mean the same as the influence of Bentham, and that it was
a selection of Bentham's ideas and not the whole of his ideas that

[1] *Social Contract*, Bk. 1, chap. 7, last para.
[2] *Reflections on the French Revolution* (World's Classics Edition, Vol. IV, p. 37).
[3] *Common Sense*, first para.

entered into Benthamism. Bentham's working life covered the period that included the American Revolution, the French Revolution and the first phases of the Industrial Revolution. The *Fragment* and the *Principles* represent, as has been said, the attack of an eighteenth-century intellectual radicalism on the traditional English eighteenth-century views of law and government. Later in the eighteenth century, and in the first few decades of the nineteenth century, these traditional views were attacked from other quarters. The French Revolution stimulated violent assertions of popular rights: economic and social changes made many industrialists and humanitarians perceive that at least to certain situations that were arising much of the existing fabric of political institutions was inadequate; urbanization, for instance, and the development of the factory system, were introducing new problems of town government, of relations between employers and employees, and of commercial law: solutions to such problems might be obtained more rapidly and more thoroughly by the interests concerned through Parliament than through the Courts, but effective action by Parliament would not be forthcoming unless the electoral system were reformed and unless legislation replaced administration as Parliament's main concern. For a considerable time these two new tendencies impeded one another: so long as there was a possibility that reform might come to mean Jacobinism and violence, the alternative was not moderate reform but no reform at all; only after 1815 did the view become common that moderate reform might be the preventive and not the encouragement of revolution. It was in these circumstances and at this point that the influence of Benthamism began.

The Benthamites were unrevolutionary reformers: their schemes were based on a knowledge of English law and provided workable means of obtaining the desired changes within the existing institutional framework and without any redistribution of social power more fundamental than the transfer of influence from the landowners to the middle class. The reasons why Bentham himself gave his name to this movement and was acknowledged as its prophet are not entirely straightforward. Not all of the Benthamites, let alone those who found in their proposals acceptable means to their ends, subscribed to the whole of Bentham's ideas or even concerned themselves to discover what these were. But, broadly speaking, Bentham became the prophet of the movement which provided objectives, programmes and methods for middle-class reform because, after sixty years of forceful statement and re-statement, he became known as a moderate middle-class man with a reasonable doctrine of moderate improvement, and ingenious and practical suggestions for devices by means of which such improvement might be accomplished.

The fuller explanation of this position takes us beyond the present two works and may be considered only briefly here. In neither the *Fragment* nor the *Principles* had Bentham anything to say about Political Economy. He expressed himself on this subject, however, in the *Defence of Usury*, in the *Manual of Political Economy*, and in other works. In these writings Bentham was influenced by Adam Smith and added to parts of private ethics another field in which, in general, action by government could not profitably be undertaken in a developed society. This was not really consistent with the doctrines of the *Principles*[1] or with the conclusions that a more sceptical reading of the *Wealth of Nations* might have suggested. If only in their private lives could men follow the Principle of Utility without being prompted thereto by the political sanction, how could their actions be counted upon to be in accordance with the Principle of Utility in their economic transactions, the consequence of which transcended the bounds of their own control? Adam Smith himself had mentioned that those who live by rent, those who live by profit, and those who live by wages might come to have different ideas of their own interests.[2] He did not conceive that government action might be introduced in order to redress such tendencies towards lack of balance, although he did conceive the necessity for certain positive services by government in the economic sphere.[3] The omission is one that Bentham rather than Smith might have been expected to remedy. The fact that Bentham went only part of the way to remedy this deficiency affected the subsequent history of both liberal and socialist theory.[4]

[1] See W. Stark (op. cit.) for the view that, in the form in which Bentham held it, it was more consistent than has been supposed.

[2] *Wealth of Nations*, Bk. 1, chap. 11, Conclusion (Everyman Edition, Vol. 1, pp. 228–232).

[3] *Wealth of Nations*, Bk. 5, chap. 2. The state is required to maintain not only defence, justice, education and religion but also certain public works; and as regards justice—'civil government, so far as it is instituted for the security of property, is in reality instituted for the defence of the rich against the poor' (Everyman Edition, Vol. 2, p. 203).

[4] See below, p. lxv, note 1. Bentham got as far as urging the employment of the 'interest junction-prescribing' principle against aristocratic predominance. And see W. Stark (op. cit.): Bentham advocated a limited amount of government interference for the reduction of economic inequality—through encouragement of thrift and regulation of testamentary provisions; and on more than one other question he would have been 'to the left' of the Manchester School.

Bentham's influence on liberalism is due to his association with James Mill and his friends and his 'conversion' to radicalism. This conversion involved the closing of a gap in Bentham's political views through the utilisation of a method which had for long lain to hand. Bentham had not enquired how legislators were to become minded to make greatest happiness their objective.[1] But others had considered a like problem. Hume had pointed out that authority was needed in society in order to overcome the tendency of most men to prefer trivial present advantage to remoter but greater interests. Authority should make 'the observance of the laws of justice our nearest interest and their violation our most remote'; and to ensure that authority does this it should be arranged that authority itself has an immediate interest in justice.[2] How this was to be done Hume did not say, but radical thinkers had suggested an answer. Priestley had argued that the best way to ensure the identification of interests of government and governed was to maintain in governors the fear that they would be turned out of office in favour of rivals if they did not consult the interests of the people and court their favour.[3] And in the same year in which Bentham published the *Fragment*, Tom Paine argued in *Common Sense* that the dangers of government could be reduced to a minimum if governments were representative in character and if elections were held as frequently as possible so that electors and elected were constantly changing places and their interests would therefore be likely to remain the same.[4] The notion of frequent exchange between governors and governed as a means whereby 'the interests of the one class are more or less indistinguishably blended with those of the other' was, as has been seen, one of the ideas in Bentham's digression on 'free government' in the *Fragment*; but it was not there linked with a view of representation. Bentham was early aware of the possibility of discussing representation in utilitarian terms: he did so in 1788 in a piece of advice designed for the Estates General; but his real concern on that occasion was with the advocacy of a utilitarian rather than a natural rights standpoint, and not with representation as such. The emergence of a genuine utilitarian view of representation came after Bentham's

[1] In the Preface to the 2nd Edition, Bentham said that when the *Fragment* was first written he saw in the imperfections of government no 'worse cause than inattention and prejudice: he saw not in them then what the experience and observations of nearly fifty years have since taught him to see in them so plainly, the elaborately organized and anxiously cherished and guarded products of sinister interest and artifice' (B., Vol. 1, p. 242).

[2] *Treatise*, Bk. 3, Pt. 2, Sect. 7 (Everyman Edition, pp. 2, Vol. 236–8).

[3] *Essay*, 1st Edit., p. 9.   [4] *Common Sense*, para. 6.

conversion to radicalism; and here Bentham was preceded by James Mill who published an article in the *Edinburgh Review* in 1809 in which he used arguments similar to those of Priestley. Bentham's *Catechism of Parliamentary Reform*, published in the same year, did not include any advocacy of franchise extension. It was not until 1817 that the *Catechism* was republished with an introduction insisting on radical as against moderate reform. In the following year Bentham drew up his *Resolutions on Parliamentary Reform* which were moved in the House of Commons by Sir Francis Burdett and which firmly stated that the basis of good government was the identity of interests between government and governed, and that the guarantee of such an identification could be forthcoming only 'in so far as the members of this House are in fact chosen, and from time to time removable by the free suffrages of the great body of the people.'[1]

Utilitarian radicalism, however, remained a very special form of radicalism, and particularly for Bentham. Before Bentham's time, English radical tradition, as far back as the Levellers, spoke mainly in terms of natural rights: Tom Paine was concerned with the *Rights of Man* as well as with the natural and artificial identification of egoistic interests. Further, this tradition frequently contrasted society and government to the detriment of government because government was taken to be associated with tyranny. Again, from the Levellers to Spence in his *Lecture to the Newcastle Philosophical Society* (1775), Ogilvie in his *Essay on the Right of Property in Land* (1781), and even to Paine in *Agrarian Justice* (1795–6) there had been a socialist or quasi-socialist strand in radicalism.[2] All three tendencies were foreign to Bentham, who attacked natural rights, saw the well-being of society as possible only through the instrumentality of government, and, in his *Radicalism Not Dangerous* (1820) defended reform proposals against the charge that they would be subversive of property.

It is unfortunate that Bentham, a leader of the attack on natural rights, could not extend his scepticism into the realm of economics.

---

[1] B., Vol. 10, p. 495. In the Preface to *F*, 2nd Edition, Bentham refers to 'those general conceptions in the development and application of which no small portion of the aggregate mass of my intervening works have been employed, namely, that no system or form of government ever had, or ever could have had, for its actual and principal end in view, the good of any other persons, than the very individuals by whom, on each occasion, the powers of it were exercised' (B., Vol. 1, p. 240). He goes on to say that the interests at present served by British government are those of the Aristocrat. The 'interest-junction-prescribing' principle must be brought into effect so that rulers' interests will come into coincidence with the universal interest (ibid., p. 245).
[2] See M. Beer: *History of British Socialism*, Pt. 2, chap. 2.

The natural identification of interests, eschewed in the political field, was accepted by him in the field of economics and the way was thus prepared for that separation of politics and economics which was nineteenth-century liberalism's greatest limitation. Other theories sought to remedy the deficiency in opposed and unsatisfactory ways. Hegelian theory subsumed the economic world in that of the state, but left the individual an abstraction: Marxism made the economic world the only social world and the state an organ of a dominant class, and again the individual was left as an abstraction. The disjunction between politics and economics has still, indeed, satisfactorily to be overcome, and there are other syntheses within political theory that are still awaited. An adequate political theory must consider political institutions as existing for flesh and blood men and women, yet must admit that there are social values that are not mere additions of individual values; it must find a place in society for reason, the non-rational and the irrational; it must retain the conception of government as an adaptable instrument that can be used for better or worse, but it must reconcile with this the fact that it is not possible to rely for good government upon political parties or any assemblages of governmental devices any more than upon the enlightenment of 'governors' or censorial jurists.

But in approaching these problems, the political theorist of to-day may do well to start with Bentham, and with some of those aspects of Bentham's ideas that entered very little into Benthamism. Like Hume, Bentham demolished some fictions, and it may be advantageous to carry further his attacks on the fictitious. He disentangled some fundamental conceptions, and a study of his methods may assist in the disentangling of more. Standing on the borderline between eighteenth-century and nineteenth-century political thought, Bentham reveals some of the merits and some of the defects of the thought of both periods; and he may even encourage a political theorist in the twentieth century to dare to think for himself: he may, to use his own words at the end of the *Fragment* 'do something to instruct, but more to undeceive, the timid and admiring student: to excite him to place more confidence in his own strength, and less in the infallibility of great names . . . to teach him to distinguish between showy language and sound sense . . . to dispose him rather to fast on ignorance than feed himself with error.'

BOOKS FOR FURTHER READING

OTHER WORKS OF BENTHAM:

See those mentioned in the Introduction.

LIVES AND COMMENTS:

Biography in Bowring.

Leslie Stephen: *The English Utilitarians*, Vol. 1 (1900).

C. W. Everett: *The Education of Jeremy Bentham* (1931).

F. C. Montague: Introduction to his edition of the *Fragment on Government* (1891).

C. W. Everett: Introduction to *Bentham's Comments on the Commentaries* (1928).

C. K. Ogden: Introduction and notes to his edition of Bentham's *Theory of Legislation* (1931).

C. K. Ogden: Introduction to *Bentham's Theory of Fictions* (1932).

E. Halèvy: *The Growth of Philosophical Radicalism* (Trans. Morris, 1928).

W. Stark: *Jeremy Bentham as an Economist* (*The Economic Journal*, April 1941 and December 1946).

A

FRAGMENT ON GOVERNMENT

BEING

AN EXAMINATION OF WHAT IS DELIVERED, ON
THE SUBJECT OF GOVERNMENT IN GENERAL,
IN THE INTRODUCTION TO
SIR WILLIAM BLACKSTONE'S *Commentaries*

WITH A

PREFACE

IN WHICH IS GIVEN

A CRITIQUE ON THE WORK AT LARGE

Rien ne recule plus le progrès des connoissances, qu'un mauvais ouvrage
d'un Auteur célèbre: parce qu'avant d'instruire, il faut commencer par
détromper.

MONTESQUIEU, Esprit des Loix, L. XXX. Ch. XV

PREFACE

1. THE age we live in is a busy age; in which knowledge is rapidly advancing towards perfection. In the natural world, in particular, every thing teems with discovery and with improvement. The most distant and recondite regions of the earth traversed and explored—the all-vivifying and subtle element of the air so recently analyzed and made known to us,—are striking evidences, were all others wanting, of this pleasing truth.

2. Correspondent to *discovery* and *improvement* in the natural world, is *reformation* in the moral; if that which seems a common notion be, indeed, a true one, that in the moral world there no longer remains any matter for *discovery*. Perhaps, however, this may not be the case: perhaps among such observations as would be best calculated to serve as grounds for reformation, are some which, being observations of matters of fact hitherto either incompletely noticed, or not at all would, when produced, appear capable of bearing the name of discoveries: with so little method and precision have the consequences of this fundamental axiom, *it is the greatest happiness of the greatest number that is the measure of right and wrong,* been as yet developed.

3. Be this as it may, if there be room for making, and if there be use in publishing, *discoveries* in the *natural* world, surely there is not much less room for making, nor much less use in proposing, *reformation* in the *moral*. If it be a matter of importance and of use to us to be made acquainted with *distant* countries, surely it is not a matter of much less importance, nor of much less use to us, to be made better and better acquainted with the chief means of living happily *in our own*. If it be of importance and of use to us to know the principles of the element we breathe, surely it is not of much less importance nor of much less use to comprehend the principles, and endeavour at the improvement of those *laws*, by which alone we breathe it in security. If to this endeavour we should fancy any Author, especially any Author of great name, to *be*, and as far

3

as could in such case be expected, to *avow himself* a determined and persevering enemy, what should we say of him? We should say that the interests of reformation, and through them the welfare of mankind, were inseparably connected with the downfall of his works: of a great part, at least, of the esteem and influence, which these works might under whatever title have acquired.

4. Such an enemy it has been my misfortune (and not mine only) to see, or fancy at least I saw, in the Author of the celebrated COMMENTARIES *on the* LAWS *of* ENGLAND; an Author whose works have had beyond comparison a more extensive circulation, have obtained a greater share of esteem, of applause, and consequently of influence (and that by a title on many grounds so indisputable) than any other writer who on that subject has ever yet appeared.

History of it.   5. It is on this account that I conceived, some time since, the design of pointing out some of what appeared to me the capital blemishes of that work, particularly this grand and fundamental one, the antipathy to reformation; or rather, indeed, of laying open and exposing the universal inaccuracy and confusion which seemed to my apprehension to pervade the whole. For, indeed, such an ungenerous antipathy seemed of itself enough to promise a general vein of obscure and crooked reasoning, from whence no clear and sterling knowledge could be derived; so intimate is the connexion between some gifts of the understanding, and some of the affections of the heart.

6. It is in this view that I took in hand that part of the first volume to which the Author has given the name of INTRO-DUCTION. It is in this part of the work that is contained whatever comes under the denomination of *general principles.* It is in this part of the work that are contained such preliminary views as it seemed proper to him to give of certain objects real or imaginary, which he found connected with his subject LAW by identity of name: two or three sorts of LAWS of *Nature,* the *revealed* LAW, and a certain LAW of *Nations.* It is in this part of the work that he has touched upon several topics which relate to all laws or institutions[1] in general, or

[1] I add here the word *institutions,* for the sake of including rules of *Common* Law, as well as portions of *Statute* Law.

at least to whole classes of institutions without relating to any one more than to another.

7. To speak more particularly, it is in this part of his work that he has given a definition, such as it is, of that whole branch of law which he had taken for his subject; that branch, which some, considering it as a main stock, would term LAW without addition; and which he, to distinguish it from those others its *condivident branches*,[1] terms law *municipal*:—an account, such as it is, of the nature and origin of *Natural* Society the mother, and of *Political* Society the daughter, of Law *municipal*, duly begotten in the bed of Metaphor:—a division, such as it is, of *a* law, individually considered, into what he fancies to be its *parts*:—an account, such as it is, of the method to be taken for *interpreting* any law that may occur.

8. In regard to the Law of England in particular, it is here that he gives an account of the division of it into its two branches (branches, however, that are no ways distinct in the purport of them, when once established, but only in respect of the source from whence their establishment took its rise) the *Statute* or *Written* law, as it is called, and the *Common* or *Unwritten*:—an account of what are called *General Customs*, or institutions in force throughout the whole empire, or at least the whole nation;—of what are called *Particular Customs*, institutions of local extent established in particular districts; and of such *adopted* institutions of a general extent, as are parcel of what are called the *Civil* and the *Canon* laws; all three in the character of so many branches of what is called the *Common Law*:—in fine, a general account of *Equity*, that capricious and incomprehensible mistress of our fortunes, whose features neither our Author, nor perhaps any one is well able to delineate;—of *Equity*, who having in the beginning been a rib of *Law*, but since in some dark age plucked from her side, when sleeping, by the hands not so much of God as of enterprizing Judges, now lords it over her parent sister:—

9. All this, I say, together with an account of the different districts of the empire over which different portions of the Law prevail, or over which the Law has different degrees of force, composes that part of our Author's work which he has

[1] *Membra condividentia.*—SAUND. Log. I. L. c. 46.

styled the INTRODUCTION. His eloquent 'Discourse on the study of the Law,' with which, as being a discourse of the rhetorical kind, rather than of the didactic, I proposed not to intermeddle, prefaces the whole.

10. It would have been in vain to have thought of travelling over the whole of so vast a work. My design, therefore, was to take such a portion of it, as might afford a fair and adequate specimen of the character and complexion of the whole. For this purpose the part here marked out would, I thought, abundantly suffice. This, however narrow in extent, was the most conspicuous, the most characteristic part of our Author's work, and that which was most his own. The rest was little more than compilation. Pursuing my examination thus far, I should pursue it, I thought, as far as was necessary for my purpose: and I had little stomach to pursue a task at once so laborious and so invidious any farther. If *Hercules*, according to the old proverb, is to be known *ex pede*: much more thought I, is he to be known *ex capite*.

11. In these views it was that I proceeded as far as the middle of the definition of the Law *municipal*. It was there, I found, not without surprise, the digression which makes the subject of the present Essay. This threw me at first into no small perplexity. To give no account of it at all;—to pass wholly *sub silentio*, so large, and in itself so material a part of the work I was examining, would seem strange: at the same time I saw no possibility of entering into an examination of a passage so anomalous, without cutting in pieces the thread of the discourse. Under this doubt I determined, at any rate for the present, to pass it by; the rather as I could not perceive any connection that it had with any thing that came before or after. I did so; and continuing my examination of the definition from which it digressed, I travelled on to the end of the Introduction. It then became necessary to come to some definitive resolution concerning this excentric part of it: and the result was, that being loth to leave the enterprise I had begun in this respect, imperfect, I sat down to give what I intended should be a very slight and general survey of it. The farther, however, I proceeded in examining it, the more confused and unsatisfactory it appeared to me: and the greater difficulty I found in knowing what to make of it,

the more words it cost me, I found, to say so. In this way, and by these means it was that the present Essay grew to the bulk in which the Reader sees it. When it was nearly completed, it occurred to me, that as the digression itself which I was examining was perfectly distinct from, and unconnected with the text from which it starts, so was, or so at least might be, the *critique* on that digression, from the *critique* on the text. The former was by much too large to be engrafted into the latter: and since if it accompanied it at all, it could only be in the shape of an Appendix, there seemed no reason why the same publication should include them both. To the former, therefore, as being the least, I determined to give that finish which I was able, and which I thought was necessary: and to publish it in this detached manner, as the first, if not the only part of a work, the principal and remaining part of which may possibly see the light some time or other, under some such title as that of 'A COMMENT *on the* COMMENTARIES.'

12. In the meantime, that I may stand more fully justified, or excused at least, in an enterprise to most perhaps so extraordinary, and to many doubtless so unacceptable, it may be of use to endeavour to state with some degree of precision, the grounds of that war which, for the interests of true science, and of liberal improvement, I think myself bound to wage against this work. I shall therefore proceed to mark out and distinguish those points of view in which it seems principally reprehensible, not forgetting those in which it seems still entitled to our approbation and applause.

13. There are two characters, one or other of which every *The business of* man who finds any thing to say on the subject of Law, may be *the* Censor *dis-* said to take upon him;—that of the *Expositor*, and that of the *tinguished from* Censor. To the province of the *Expositor* it belongs to explain *positor.* to us what, as he supposes, the Law *is*: to that of the *Censor*, to observe to us what he thinks it *ought to be*. The former, therefore, is principally occupied in stating, or in enquiring after *facts*:[1] the latter, in discussing *reasons*. The *Expositor*,

---

[1] In practice, the question of *Law* has commonly been spoken of as opposed to that of *fact*: but this distinction is an accidental one. That a Law commanding or prohibiting such a *sort* of action, has been established, is as much a *fact*, as that an *individual* action of that sort has been committed. The establishment of a Law may be spoken of as a *fact*, at least for the purpose of distinguishing it from any consideration that may be offered as a *reason* for such Law.

keeping within his sphere, has no concern with any other
faculties of the mind than the *apprehension*, the *memory*, and
the *judgment*: the latter, in virtue of those sentiments of
pleasure or displeasure which he finds occasion to annex to
the objects under his review, holds some intercourse with the
affections. That which *is* Law, is, in different countries, widely
different: while that which *ought to be*, is in all countries to a
great degree the same. The *Expositor*, therefore, is always the
citizen of this or that particular country: the *Censor* is, or
ought to be the citizen of the world. To the *Expositor* it
belongs to shew what the *Legislator* and his underworkman
the *Judge* have done *already*: to the *Censor* it belongs to suggest
what the *Legislator ought* to do *in future*. To the Censor, in
short, it belongs to *teach* that *science*, which when by change
of hands converted into an *art*, the LEGISLATOR *practises*.

*The latter alone
our Author's.*
14. Let us now return to our Author. Of these two perfectly distinguishable functions, the latter alone is that which it
fell necessarily within his province to discharge. His professed object was to explain to us what the Laws of England
were. '*Ita lex scripta est*,' was the only motto which he stood
engaged to keep in view. The work of *censure* (for to this
word, in default of any other, I find it necessary to give a
neutral sense) the work of *censure*, as it may be styled, or, in a
certain sense, of *criticism*, was to him but a *parergon*—a work of
supererogation: a work, indeed, which, if aptly executed,
could not but be of great ornament to the principal one, and
of great instruction as well as entertainment to the Reader,
but from which our Author, as well as those that had gone
before him on the same line, might, without being chargeable
with any deficiency, have stood excused: a work which, when
superadded to the principal, would lay the Author under
additional obligations, and impose on him new duties: which,
notwithstanding, whatever else it might differ in from the
principal one, agrees with it in this, that it ought to be executed
with impartiality, or not at all.

*Laws ought to
be scrutinized
with freedom.*
15. If, on the one hand, a hasty and undiscriminating con-
demner of what is established, may expose himself to contempt; on the other hand, a bigoted or corrupt defender of
the works of power, becomes guilty, in a manner, of the
abuses which he supports: the more so if, by oblique glances

and sophistical glosses, he studies to guard from reproach, or recommend to favour, what he knows not how, and dares not attempt, to justify. To a man who contents himself with simply stating an institution as he thinks it *is*, no share, it is plain, can justly be attributed (nor would any one think of attributing to him any share) of whatever reproach, any more than of whatever applause the institution may be thought to merit. But if not content with this humbler function, he takes upon him to give *reasons* in behalf of it, reasons whether *made* or found by him, it is far otherwise. Every false and sophistical reason that he contributes to circulate, he himself is chargeable with: nor ought he to be holden guiltless even of such as, in a work where *fact* not *reason* is the question, he delivers as from other writers without censure. By officiously adopting them he makes them his own, though delivered under the names of the respective Authors: not much less than if delivered under his own. For the very idea of a *reason* betokens approbation: so that to deliver a remark under that character, and that without censure, is to adopt it. A man will scarcely, therefore, without some note of disapprobation, be the instrument of introducing, in the guise of a reason, an argument which he does not really wish to see approved. Some method or other he will take to wash his hands of it: some method or other he will take to let men see that what he means to be understood to do, is merely to report the judgment of another, not to pass one of his own. Upon that other then he will lay the blame: at least he will take care to repel it from himself. If he omits to do this, the most favourable cause that can be assigned to the omission is indifference: indifference to the public welfare—that indifference which is itself a crime.

16. It is wonderful how forward some have been to look upon it as a kind of presumption and ingratitude, and rebellion, and cruelty, and I know not what besides, not to allege only, nor to own, but to suffer any one so much as to imagine, that an old-established law could in any respect be a fit object of condemnation. Whether it has been a kind of *personification* that has been the cause of this, as if the Law were a living creature, or whether it has been the mechanical

veneration for antiquity, or what other delusion of the fancy, I shall not here enquire. For my part, I know not for what good reason it is that the merit of justifying a law when right should have been thought greater, than that of censuring it when wrong. Under a government of Laws, what is the motto of a good citizen? *To obey punctually; to censure freely.*

17. Thus much is certain; that a system that is never to be censured, will never be improved: that if nothing is ever to be found fault with, nothing will ever be mended: and that a resolution to justify every thing at any rate, and to disapprove of nothing, is a resolution which, pursued in future, must stand as an effectual bar to all the *additional* happiness we can ever hope for; pursued hitherto would have robbed us of that share of happiness which we enjoy already.

18. Nor is a disposition to find 'every thing as it should be,' less at variance with itself, than with reason and utility. The common-place arguments in which it vents itself justify not what is established, in effect, any more than they condemn it: since whatever *now* is established, *once* was innovation.

19. Precipitate censure, cast on a political institution, does but recoil on the head of him who casts it. From such an attack it is not the institution itself, if well grounded, that can suffer. What a man says against it either makes impression or makes none. If none, it is just as if nothing had been said about the matter: if it *does* make an impression, it naturally calls up some one or other in defence. For if the institution is in truth a beneficial one to the community in general, it cannot but have given an interest in its preservation to a number of individuals. By their industry, then, the reasons on which it is grounded are brought to light: from the observation of which those who acquiesced in it before upon trust, now embrace it upon conviction. Censure, therefore, though ill-founded, has no other effect upon an institution than to bring it to that test, by which the value of those, indeed, on which prejudice alone has stamped a currency, is cried down, but by which the credit of those of sterling utility is confirmed.

20. Nor is it by any means from passion and ill-humour, that censure, passed upon legal institutions, is apt to take its birth. When it is from passion and ill-humour that men speak, it is with *men* that they are in ill-humour, not with

laws: it is men, not laws, that are the butt of 'arrogance.'[1]
Spleen and turbulence may indeed prompt men to quarrel
with living individuals: but when they make complaint of
the dead letter of the Law, the work of departed lawgivers,
against whom no personal antipathy can have subsisted, it is
always from the observation, or from the belief at least, of
some real grievance. The Law is no man's enemy: the Law
is no man's rival. Ask the clamorous and unruly multitude—
it is never the Law itself that is in the wrong: it is always some
wicked interpreter of the Law that has corrupted and abused
it.[2]

[1] *'Arrogance;'* our Author calls it *the utmost arrogance,*[a] 'to censure what has,
at least, a better chance to be right, than the singular notions of any particular
man:' meaning thereby certain ecclesiastical institutions. Vibrating, as it should
seem, between passion and discretion, he has thought it necessary, indeed, to
insert in the sentence that, which being inserted, turns it into nothing: After
the word 'censure,' 'with contempt' he adds, 'and rudeness:' as if there needed a
professor to inform us, that to treat any thing with contempt and rudeness is
arrogance. 'Indecency,' he had already called it, 'to set up private judgment in
opposition to public:' and this without restriction, qualification, or reserve.
This was in the first transport of a holy zeal, before discretion had come in to
his assistance. This passage the Doctors *Priestley*[b] and *Furneaux*[c], who, in
quality of Dissenting Ministers, and champions of dissenting opinions, saw
themselves particularly attacked in it, have not suffered to pass unnoticed;
any more than has the celebrated Author of the '*Remarks on the Acts of the 13th
Parliament*[d],' who found it adverse to his enterprize, for the same reason that
it is hostile to every other liberal plan of political discussion.
My edition of the Commentaries happens to be the first: since the above
paragraph was written I have been directed to a later. In this later edition the
passage about 'indecency' is, like the other about 'arrogance,' explained away
into nothing. What we are now told is, that 'to set up private judgment in
[*virulent and factious*] opposition to public *authority*' (he might have added—
or to *private* either) is 'indecency.' [See the 5th edit., 8vo, p. 50, as in the 1st.]
This we owe, I think, to Dr. Furneaux. The Doctors, Furneaux and Priestley,
under whose well-applied correction our Author has smarted so severely, have
a good deal to answer for: They have been the means of his adding a good deal
of this kind of rhetorical lumber to the plentiful stock there was of it before.
One passage, indeed, a passage deep-tinctured with religious gall, they have
been the means of clearing away entirely[e]: and in this at least, they have done
good service. They have made him sophisticate: they have made him even
expunge: but all the Doctors in the world, I doubt, would not bring him to
confession. See his answer to Dr. Priestley.
[2] There is only one way in which censure, cast upon the Laws, has a greater
tendency to do harm than good; and that is when it sets itself to contest their
validity: I mean, when abandoning the question of expediency, it sets itself to
contest the right. But this is an attack to which old-established Laws are not so

[a] 4 Comm., p. 50.   [b] See Remarks, &c.
[c] See Letters to Mr. Justice Blackstone, 1771. Second Edition.
[d] In the Preface.   [e] See Furneaux, Letter VII.

21. Thus destitute of foundation are the terrors, or pretended terrors, of those who shudder at the idea of a free censure of established institutions. So little does the peace of society require the aid of those lessons which teach men to accept of any thing as reason, and to yield the same abject and indiscriminating homage to the Laws here, which is paid to the despot elsewhere. The fruits of such tuition are visible enough in the character of that race of men who have always occupied too large a space in the circle of the profession: a passive and enervate race, ready to swallow any thing, and to acquiesce in any thing: with intellects incapable of distinguishing right from wrong, and with affections alike indifferent to either: insensible, short-sighted, obstinate: lethargic, yet liable to be driven into convulsions by false terrors: deaf to the voice of reason and public utility: obsequious only to the whisper of interest, and to the beck of power.

22. This head of mischief, perhaps, is no more than what may seem included under the former. For why is it an evil to a country that the minds of those who have the Law under their management should be thus enfeebled? It is because it finds them impotent to every enterprise of improvement.

23. Not that a race of lawyers and politicians of this enervate breed is much less dangerous to the duration of that share of felicity which the State possesses at any given period, than it is mortal to its chance of attaining to a greater. If the designs of a Minister are inimical to his country, what is the man of all others for him to make an instrument of or a dupe? Of all men, surely none so fit as that sort of man who is ever on his knees before the footstool of Authority, and who, when those *above* him, or *before* him, have pronounced, thinks it a crime to have an opinion of his own.

24. Those who duly consider upon what slight and trivial circumstances, even in the happiest times, the adoption or

liable. As this is the last though but too common resource of passion and ill-humour; and what men scarce think of betaking themselves to, unless irritated by personal competitions, it is that to which recent Laws are most exposed. I speak of what are called *written* Laws: for as to *unwritten* institutions, as there is no such thing as any certain symbol by which their authority is attested, their validity, how deeply rooted soever, is what we see challenged without remorse. A radical weakness, interwoven into the very constitution of all *un*written Law.

rejection of a Law so often turns; circumstances with which the utility of it has no imaginable connection—those who consider the desolate and abject state of the human intellect, during the periods in which so great a part of the still subsisting mass of institutions had their birth—those who consider the backwardness there is in most men, unless when spurred by personal interests or resentments, to run a-tilt against the Colossus of authority—those, I say, who give these considerations their due weight, will not be quite so zealous, perhaps, as our Author has been to terrify men from setting up what is now 'private judgment,' against what once was 'public[1]': nor to thunder down the harsh epithet of 'arrogance' on those, who, with whatever success, are occupied in bringing rude establishments to the test of polished reason. They will rather do what they can to cherish a disposition at once so useful and so rare[2]: which is so little connected with the causes that make popular discontentments dangerous, and which finds so little aliment in those propensities that govern the multitude of men. They will not be for giving such a turn to their discourses as to bespeak the whole of a man's favour for the defenders of what is established: nor all his resentment for the assailants. They will acknowledge that if there be some institutions which it is 'arrogance' to attack, there may be others which it is effrontery to defend. TOURREIL[3] has defended torture: torture established by the 'public judgment' of so many enlightened nations. BECCARIA ('indecent' and 'arrogant' Beccaria!) has condemned it. Of these two whose lot among men would one choose rather,—the Apologist's or the Censor's?

Our Author why attacked in the character of an Expositor.

25. Of a piece with the discernment which enables a man to perceive, and with the courage which enables him to avow,

[1] See note 1, p. 11.
[2] One may well say *rare*. It is a matter of fact about which there can be no dispute. The truth of it may be seen in the multitude of *Expositors* which the Jurisprudence of every nation furnished, ere it afforded a single *Censor*. When Beccaria came, he was received by the intelligent as an Angel from heaven would be by the faithful. He may be styled the father of *Censorial Jurisprudence*. Montesquieu's was a work of the mixed kind. Before Montesquieu all was unmixed barbarism. Grotius and Puffendorf were to Censorial Jurisprudence what the Schoolmen were to Natural Philosophy.
[3] A French Jurist of the last age, whose works had like celebrity, and in many respects much the same sort of merits as our Author's. He was known to most advantage by a translation of Demosthenes. He is now forgotten.

the defects of a system of institutions, is that accuracy of conception which enables him to give a clear account of it. No wonder then, in a treatise partly of the *expository* class, and partly of the *censorial*, that if the latter department is filled with imbecility, symptoms of kindred weakness should characterize the former.

26. The former department, however, of our Author's work, is what, on its own account merely, I should scarce have found myself disposed to intermeddle with. The business of simple *exposition* is a harvest in which there seemed no likelihood of there being any want of labourers: and into which therefore I had little ambition to thrust my sickle.

27. At any rate, had I sat down to make a report of it in this character alone, it would have been with feelings very different from those of which I now am conscious, and in a tone very different from that which I perceive myself to have assumed. In determining what conduct to observe respecting it, I should have considered whether the taint of error seemed to confine itself to parts, or to diffuse itself through the whole. In the latter case, the least invidious, and considering the bulk of the work, the most beneficial course would have been to have taken no notice of it at all, but to have sat down and tried to give a better. If not the whole in general, but scattered positions only had appeared exceptionable, I should have sat down to rectify those positions with the same apathy with which they were advanced. To fall in an adverse way upon a work simply *expository*, if that were all there were of it, would have been alike ungenerous and unnecessary. In the involuntary errors of the *understanding* there can be little to excite, or at least to justify, resentment. That which alone, in a manner, calls for rigid censure, is the sinister bias of the *affections*. If then I may still continue to mention as separate, parts which in the work itself are so intimately, and, indeed, undistinguishably blended, it is the *censorial* part alone that has drawn from me that sort of animadversion I have been led to bestow indiscriminately on the whole. To lay open, and if possible supply, the imperfections of the *other*, is an operation that might indeed of itself do service; but that which I thought would do still more service, was the weakening the authority of *this*.

28. Under the sanction of a great name every string of words however unmeaning, every opinion however erroneous, will have a certain currency. Reputation adds weight to sentiments from whence no part of it arose, and which had they stood alone might have drawn nothing, perhaps, but contempt. Popular fame enters not into nice distinctions. Merit in one department of letters affords a natural, and in a manner irrecusable presumption of merit in another, especially if the two departments be such between which there is apparently a close alliance.

29. Wonderful, in particular, is that influence which is gained over young minds, by the man who on account of whatever class of merit is esteemed in the character of a *preceptor*. Those who have derived, or fancy themselves to have derived knowledge from what he knows, or appears to know, will naturally be for judging as he judges: for reasoning as he reasons; for approving as he approves; for condemning as he condemns. On these accounts it is, that when the general complexion of a work is unsound, it may be of use to point an attack against the whole of it without distinction, although such parts of it as are noxious as well as unsound be only scattered here and there.

30. On these considerations then it may be of use to shew, that the work before us, in spite of the merits which recommend it so powerfully to the imagination and to the ear, has no better title on one account than on another, to that influence which, were it to pass unnoticed, it might continue to exercise over the judgment.

31. The Introduction is the part to which, for reasons that have been already stated, it was always my intention to confine myself. It is but a part even of this Introduction that is the subject of the present Essay. What determined me to begin with this small part of it is, the facility I found in separating it from every thing that precedes or follows it. This is what will be more particularly spoken to in another place.[1]

32. It is not that this part is among those which seemed most open to animadversion. It is not that stronger traces are exhibited in this part than in another of that spirit in our

---

[1] See the ensuing Introduction.

Author which seems so hostile to Reformation, and to that Liberty which is Reformation's harbinger.

33. It is not here that he tramples on the right of private judgment, that basis of every thing that an Englishman holds dear.[1] It is not here, in particular, that he insults our understandings with nugatory reasons; stands forth the professed champion of religious intolerance; or openly sets his face against civil reformation.

34. It is not here, for example, he would persuade us, that a trader who occupies a booth at a fair is a *fool* for his pains; and on that account no fit object of the Law's protection.[2]

35. It is not here that he gives the presence of *one* man at the *making* of a Law, as a *reason* why *ten thousand* others that are to *obey* it, need know nothing of the matter.[3]

36. It is not here, that after telling us, in express terms, there must be an 'actual breaking' to make burglary, he tells us, in the same breath, and in terms equally express, where burglary may be *without* actual breaking; and this *because* 'the Law will not suffer itself to be trifled with.'[4]

[1] See note 1, p. 4.

[2] 'Burglary[a],' says our Author, 'cannot be committed in a tent or a booth erected in a market fair; though the owner may lodge therein: *for* the Law regards thus highly nothing but permanent edifices; a house, or church; the wall, or gate of a town; and it is the *folly* of the owner to lodge in so fragile a tenement.' To save himself from this charge of folly, it is not altogether clear which of two things the trader ought to do: qui: his business and not go to the fair at all: or leave his goods without any body to take care of them.

[3] Speaking of an Act of Parliament[b], 'There needs,' he says, 'no formal promulgation to give it the force of a Law, as was necessary by the Civil Law with regard to the Emperor's Edicts: *because* every man in England is, *in judgment of Law*, party to the making of an Act of Parliament, being present thereat *by his representatives.*' This, for aught I know, may be good *judgment of Law*; because any thing may be called judgment of Law, that comes from a Lawyer, who has got a name: it seems, however, not much like any thing that can be called *judgment of common sense*. This notable piece of *astutia* was originally, I believe, judgment of Lord Coke: it from thence became judgment of our Author: and may have been judgment of more Lawyers than I know of before and since. What grieves me is, to find many men of the best affections to a cause which needs no sophistry, bewildered and bewildering others with the like jargon.

[4] His words are[c], '*There must be an actual breaking*, not a mere legal *clausum fregit* (by leaping over invisible ideal boundaries, which may constitute a civil trespass) but a *substantial* and *forcible irruption*.' In the next sentence but two he goes on, and says,—'But to come down a chimney *is* held a burglarious entry; for that is as much closed as the nature of things will permit. So also to

[a] 4 Comm., Ch. XVI, p. 226.   [b] 1 Comm., Ch. II, p. 178.
[c] 4 Comm., Ch. XVI, p. 226.

37. It is not here, that after relating the Laws by which peaceable Christians are made punishable for worshipping God according to their consciences, he pronounces with equal peremptoriness and complacency, that every thing, yes, 'every thing is as it should be.'[1]

38. It is not here, that he commands us to believe, and that on pain of forfeiting all pretensions to either 'sense or probity,' that the system of our jurisprudence is, in the whole and every part of it, the very quintessence of perfection.[2]

knock at a door, and upon opening it to rush in with a felonious intent; or under pretence of taking lodgings, to fall upon the landlord and rob him; or to procure a constable to gain admittance, in order to search for traitors, and then to bind the constable and rob the house; *all these entries have been adjudged burglarious, though there was no actual breaking: for* the Law will not suffer itself to be trifled with by such evasions.' . . . Can it be more egregiously trifled with than by such *reasons?*

I must own I have been ready to grow out of conceit with these useful little particles, *for, because, since,* and others of that fraternity, from seeing the drudgery they are continually put to in these Commentaries. The appearance of any of them is a sort of warning to me to prepare for some tautology, or some absurdity: for the same thing dished up over again in the shape of a reason for itself: or for a reason which, if a distinct one, is of the same stamp as those we have just seen. Other instances of the like hard treatment given to these poor particles will come under observation in the body of this Essay. As to reasons of the first-mentioned class, of them one might pick out enough to fill a volume.

[1] 'In what I have now said,' says he[a], 'I would not be understood to derogate from the rights of the national Church, or to favour a loose latitude of propagating any crude undigested sentiments in religious matters. Of *propagating*, I say; for the bare entertaining them, without an endeavour to diffuse them, seems *hardly* cognizable by any human authority. I only mean to illustrate the excellence of our present establishment, by looking back to former times. *Every thing is now as it should be;* unless, perhaps, that heresy ought to be more strictly defined, and no prosecution permitted, even in the Ecclesiastical Courts, till the tenets in question are by proper authority previously declared to be heretical. Under these restrictions it seems *necessary* for the support of the national religion,' (the national religion being such, we are to understand, as would not be able to support itself were any one at liberty to make objections to it) 'that the officers of the Church should have power to censure heretics, but not to exterminate or destroy them.'

Upon looking into a later edition (the fifth) I find this passage has undergone a modification. After '*Every thing is now as it should be,*' is added, '*with respect to the spiritual cognizance, and spiritual punishment of heresy.*' After '*the officers of the Church should have power to censure heretics,*' is added, '*but not to harass them with temporal penalties, much less to exterminate or destroy them.*'

How far the mischievousness of the original text has been cured by this amendment, may be seen from Dr. Furneaux, Lett. II, p. 30, 2nd edit.

[2] 1 Comm. 140. I would not be altogether positive, how far it was he meant this persuasion should extend itself in point of time: whether to those

[a] 4 Comm., Ch. IV, p. 49.

B

39. It is not here that he assures us in point of fact, that there never *has* been an alteration made in the Law that men have not afterwards found reason to regret.[1]

institutions only that happened to be in force at the individual instant of his writing: or whether to such opposite institutions also as, within any given distance of time from that instant, either *had* been in force, or were *about* to be.

His words are as follow: 'All these rights and liberties it is our birthright to enjoy entire; unless where the Laws of our country have laid them under necessary restraints. Restraints in themselves so gentle and moderate, as will appear upon further enquiry, that no man of *sense* or *probity* would wish to see them slackened. For *all* of us have it in our choice to do *every thing* that a *good* man would desire to do; and are restrained from nothing, but what would be pernicious either to ourselves or our fellow citizens.'

If the Reader would know what these rights and liberties are, I answer him out of the same page, they are those, 'in opposition to one or other of which *every* species of compulsive tyranny and oppression must act, having no other object upon which it can *possibly* be employed.' The liberty, for example, of worshipping God without being obliged to declare a belief in the XXXIX Articles, is a liberty that no '*good man*,'—'no man of sense or probity,' 'would wish' for.

[1] 1 Comm. 70. If no reason can be found for an institution, we are to *suppose* one; and it is upon the strength of this supposed one we are to cry it up as reasonable; It is thus that the Law *is justified of her children.*

The words are—'Not that the particular reason of every rule in the Law can, at this distance of time, be always precisely assigned; but it is sufficient that there be nothing in the rule *flatly* contradictory to reason, and then the Law will *presume* it to be well founded. And it hath been an ancient observation in the Laws of England,' (he might with as good ground have added—*and in all other Laws*) 'That whenever a standing rule of Law, of which the reason, perhaps, could not be remembered or discerned, hath been [*wantonly*] broke in upon by *statutes* or *new resolutions*, the wisdom of the rule hath in the end appeared from the inconveniences that have followed the innovation.'

When a sentiment is expressed, and whether from caution, or from confusion of ideas, a clause is put in by way of qualifying it that turns it into nothing, in this case if we would form a fair estimate of the tendency and probable effect of the whole passage, the way is, I take it, to consider it as if no such clause were there. Nor let this seem strange. Taking the qualification into the account, the sentiment would make no impression on the mind at all: if it makes any, the qualification is dropped, and the mind is affected in the same manner nearly as it would be were the sentiment to stand unqualified.

This, I think, we may conclude to be the case with the passage above mentioned. The word '*wantonly*' is, in pursuance of our Author's standing policy, put in by way of salvo. *With* it the sentiment is as much as comes to nothing. *Without* it, it would be extravagant. Yet in this extravagant form it is, probably, if in any, that it passes upon the Reader.

The pleasant part of the contrivance is, the mentioning of '*Statutes*' and '*Resolutions*' (Resolutions to wit, that is Decisions, of Courts of Justice) in the same breath; as if whether it were by the one of them or the other that a rule of Law was broke in upon, made no difference. By a *Resolution* indeed, a *new* Resolution, to break in upon a *standing* rule, is a practice that in good truth is big with mischief. But this mischief on what does it depend? Upon the rule's being a *reasonable* one? By no means: but upon its being a *standing*,

40. It is not here that he turns the Law into a Castle, for the purpose of opposing every idea of 'fundamental' reparation.[1]

41. It is not here that he turns with scorn upon those beneficent Legislators whose care it has been to pluck the mask of Mystery from the face of Jurisprudence.[2]

an established one. Reasonable or not reasonable, is what makes comparatively but a trifling difference.

A new resolution made in the teeth of an old established rule is mischievous —on what account? In that it puts men's expectations universally to a fault, and shakes whatever confidence they may have in the stability of any rules of Law, reasonable or not reasonable: that stability on which every thing that is valuable to a man depends. Beneficial be it in ever so high a degree to the part in whose favour it is made, the benefit it is of to *him* can never be so great as to outweigh the mischief it is of to the community at large. Make the best of it, it is general evil for the sake of partial good. It is what Lord Bacon calls setting the whole house on fire, in order to roast one man's eggs.

Here then the *salvo* is not wanted: a 'new resolution can never be acknowledged to be contrary to a standing rule,' but it must on that very account be acknowledged to be '*wanton*.' Let such a resolution be made, and 'inconveniences' in abundance will sure enough ensue: and then will appear—what? not by any means 'the wisdom of the rule,' but, what is a very different thing, the folly of breaking in upon it.

It were almost superfluous to remark, that nothing of all this applies in general to a statute: though particular Statutes may be conceived that would thwart the course of expectation, and by that means produce mischief in the same way in which it is produced by irregular resolutions. A new statute, it is manifest, cannot, unless it be simply a declaratory one, be made in any case, but it must break in upon some standing rule of Law. With regard to a Statute then to tell us that a 'wanton' one has produced 'inconveniences,' what is it but to tell us that a thing that has been mischievous has produced mischief?

Of this temper are the argument of all those doting politicians, who, when out of humour with a particular innovation without being able to tell why, set themselves to declaim against *all* innovation, because it is innovation. It is the nature of owls to hate the light: and it is the nature of those politicians who are wise by rote, to detest every thing that forces them either to find (what, perhaps, is impossible) reasons for a favourite persuasion, or (what is not endurable) to discard it.

[1] 3 Comm. 268, at the end of Ch. XVII which concludes with three pages against Reformation. Our Author had better, perhaps, on this occasion, have kept clear of allegories: he should have considered whether they might not be retorted on him with severe retaliation. He should have considered, that it is not easier to *him* to turn the Law into a Castle, than it is to the imaginations of impoverished suitors to people it with Harpies. He should have thought of the den of Cacus, to whose enfeebled optics, to whose habits of dark and secret rapine, nothing was so hateful, nothing so dangerous, as the light of day.

[2] 3 Comm. 322. It is from the decisions of Courts of Justice that those rules of Law are framed, on the knowledge of which depend the life, the fortune, the liberty of every man in the nation. Of these decisions the Records are, according to our Author [1 Comm. 71] the most authentic histories. These Records were, till within these five-and-forty years, in Law-Latin: a language

which, upon a high computation, about one man in a thousand used to fancy himself to understand. In this Law-Latin it is that our Author is satisfied they should have been continued, because the pyramids of Egypt have stood longer than the temples of Palmyra. He observes to us, that the Latin language could not express itself on the subject without borrowing a multitude of words from our own: which is to help to convince us that of the two the former is the fittest to be employed. He gives us to understand that, taking it altogether, there could be no room to complain of it, seeing it was not more unintelligible than the jargon of the schoolmen, some passages of which he instances; and then he goes on, 'This technical Latin continued in use from the time of its first introduction till the subversion of our ancient constitution under Cromwell; when, among many other innovations on the body of the Law, some for the better and some for the worse, the language of our Records was altered and turned into English. But at the Restoration of King Charles, this *novelty* was no longer countenanced; the practisers finding it very difficult to express themselves so concisely or significantly in any other language but the Latin. And thus it continued without any sensible inconvenience till about the year 1730, when it was again thought proper that the Proceedings at Law should be *done* into English, and it was accordingly so ordered by statute, 4 Geo. II, c. 26.

'This was done (continues our Author) in order that the common people might have knowledge and understanding of what was alleged or done for and against them in the process and pleadings, the judgment and entries in a cause. Which purpose I know not how well it has answered; but am *apt to suspect* that the people are now, after many years' experience, *altogether* as ignorant in matters of law as before.'

In this scornful passage the words *novelty*—*done* into English—*apt to suspect*—*altogether* as ignorant—sufficiently speak the affection of the mind that dictated it. It is thus that our Author chuckles over the supposed defeat of the Legislature with a fond exultation which all his discretion could not persuade him to suppress.

The case is this. A large portion of the body of the Law was, by the bigotry or the artifice of Lawyers, locked up in an illegible character, and in a foreign tongue. The statute he mentions obliged them to give up their hieroglyphics, and to restore the native language to its rights.

This was doing much; but it was not doing every thing. Fiction, tautology, technicality, circuity, irregularity, inconsistency remain. But above all the pestilential breath of Fiction poisons the sense of every instrument it comes near.

The consequence is, that the Law, and especially that part of it which comes under the topic of Procedure, *still* wants much of being generally intelligible. The fault then of the Legislature is their not having done *enough*. His quarrel with them is for having done any thing at all. In doing what they did, they set up a light, which, obscured by many remaining clouds, is still but too apt to prove an *ignis fatuus*: our Author, instead of calling for those clouds to be removed, deprecates all light, and pleads for total darkness.

Not content with representing the alteration as useless, he would persuade us to look upon it as mischievous. He speaks of 'inconveniences.' What these inconveniences are it is pleasant to observe.

In the first place, many young practisers, spoilt by the indulgence of being permitted to carry on their business in their mother-tongue, know not how to read a Record upon the old plan. 'Many Clerks and Attornies,' says our Author, 'are hardly able to read, much less to understand a Record of so modern a date as the reign of George the First.'

What the mighty evil is here, that is to outweigh the mischief of almost universal ignorance, is not altogether clear: Whether it is, that certain Lawyers,

42. If here,[1] as every where, he is eager to hold the cup of flattery to high station, he has stopped short, however, in this place, of idolatry.[2]

in a case that happens very rarely, may be obliged to get assistance: or that the business in such a case may pass from those who do *not* understand it to those who do.

In the next place, he observes to us, 'it has much enhanced the expense of all legal proceedings: for since the practisers are confined (for the sake of the stamp-duties, which are thereby considerably increased to write only a stated number of words in a sheet; and as the English language, through its multi-tudes of its particles, is much more verbose than the Latin; it follows, that the number of sheets must be very much augmented by the change.'

I would fain persuade myself, were it possible, that this unhappy sophism could have passed upon the inventor. The sum actually levied on the public on that score is, upon the whole, either a proper sum or it is not. If it *is*, why mention it as an evil? If it is *not*, what more obvious remedy than to set the duties lower?

After all, what seems to be the real evil, notwithstanding our Author's unwillingness to believe it, is, that by means of this alteration, men at large are in a somewhat better way of knowing what their Lawyers are about: and that a disinterested and enterprising Legislator, should happily such an one arise, would now with somewhat less difficulty be able to see before him.

[1] V. infra, Ch. III. par. VII, p. 187.

[2] In the Seventh Chapter of the First Book. The King has '*attributes*[a];' he possesses '*ubiquity*[b];' he is '*all-perfect* and *immortal*[c].'

These childish paradoxes, begotten upon servility by false wit, are not more adverse to manly sentiment, than to accurate apprehension. Far from con-tributing to place the institutions they are applied to in any clear point of view, they serve but to dazzle and confound, by giving to Reality the air of Fable. It is true, they are not altogether of our Author's invention: it is he, however, that has revived them, and that with improvements and additions.

One might be apt to suppose they were no more than so many transient flashes of ornament: it is quite otherwise. He dwells upon them in sober sadness. The attribute of '*ubiquity*,' in particular, he lays hold of, and makes it the basis of a chain of reasoning. He spins it out into consequences: he makes one thing '*follow*' from it, and another thing be so and so 'for the same *reason*:' and he uses emphatic terms, as if for fear he should not be thought to be in earnest. 'From the ubiquity,' says our Author [1 Comm., p. 260] 'it *follows*, that the King can never be nonsuit; *for* a nonsuit is the desertion of the suit or action by the non-appearance of the plaintiff in Court.'—'For the same reason also the King is not said to appear by his Attorney, as other men do; for he always appears in contemplation of Law in his *own proper* person.'

This is the case so soon as you come to this last sentence of the paragraph. For so long as you are at the last but two, 'it is the regal office, and *not* the royal person, that is always present.' All this is so drily and so strictly true, that it serves as the groundwork of a metaphor that is brought in to embellish and enliven it. The King, we see, *is*, that is to say is *not*, present in Court. The King's Judges are present too. So far is plain downright truth. These Judges, then, speaking metaphorically, are so many looking-glasses, which

[a] 1 Comm. 242.   [b] 1 Comm. Ch. VII, pp. 234, 238, 242, First Edition.
[c] 1 Comm. Ch. VII, p. 260, First Edition.

43. It is not then, I say, *this* part, it is not even any part of that Introduction, to which alone I have any thoughts of extending my examination, that is the principal seat of that poison, against which it was the purpose of this attempt to give an antidote. The subject handled in this part of the work is such, as admits not of much to be said in the person of the Censor. Employed, as we have seen, in settling matters of a preliminary nature—in drawing outlines, it is not in this part that there was occasion to enter into the details of any particular institution. If I chose the Introduction then in preference to any other part, it was on account of its affording the fairest specimen of the whole, and not on account of its affording the greatest scope for censure.

Its merits. 44. Let us reverse the tablet. While with this freedom I expose our Author's ill deserts, let me not be backward in acknowledging and paying homage to his various merits: a justice due, not to him alone, but to that Public, which now for so many years has been dealing out to him (it cannot be supposed altogether without title) so large a measure of its applause.

45. Correct, elegant, unembarrassed, ornamented, the *style* is such, as could scarce fail to recommend a work still more vicious in point of *matter* to the multitude of readers.

46. He it is, in short, who, first of all institutional writers, has taught Jurisprudence to speak the language of the Scholar and the Gentleman: put a polish upon that rugged science: cleansed her from the dust and cobwebs of the office: and if he has not enriched her with that precision that is drawn only from the sterling treasury of the sciences, has decked her out, however, to advantage, from the toilette of classic erudition: enlivened her with metaphors and allusions: and sent her abroad in some measure to instruct, and in still greater measure to entertain, the most miscellaneous and even the most fastidious societies.

47. The merit to which, as much perhaps as to any, the work stands indebted for its reputation, is the enchanting harmony of its numbers: a kind of merit that of itself is suffi-

have this singular property, that when a man looks at them, instead of seeing his own face in them, he sees the King's. 'His Judges,' says our Author, 'are the mirror by which the King's image is reflected.'

cient to give a certain degree of celebrity to a work devoid of every other. So much is man governed by the ear.

48. The function of the Expositor may be conceived to divide itself into two branches: that of *history*, and that of simple *demonstration*. The business of history is to represent the Law in the state it *has* been in, in past periods of its existence: the business of simple demonstration in the sense in which I will take leave to use the word, is to represent the Law in the state it *is* in for the time being.[1]

49. Again, to the head of demonstration belong the several businesses of *arrangement, narration* and *conjecture*. Matter of narration it may be called, where the Law is supposed to be explicit, clear, and settled: matter of conjecture or interpretation, where it is obscure, silent, or unsteady. It is matter of arrangement to *distribute* the several real or supposed institutions into different masses, for the purpose of a general survey; to determine the *order* in which those masses shall be brought to view; and to find for each of them a *name*.

50. The business of narration and interpretation are conversant chiefly about particular institutions. Into the details of particular institutions it has not been my purpose to descend. On these topics, then, I may say, in the language of procedure, *non sum informatus*. Viewing the work in this light, I have nothing to add to or to except against the public voice.

51. *History* is a branch of instruction which our Author, though not rigidly necessary to his design, called in, not without judgment, to cast light and ornament on the dull work of simple *demonstration*: this part he has executed with an elegance which strikes every one: with what fidelity, having not very particularly examined, I will not take upon me to pronounce.

52. Among the most difficult and the most important of the functions of the *demonstrator* is the business of *arrangement*. In this our Author has been thought, and not, I conceive,

---

[1] The word *demonstration* may seem here, at first sight, to be out of place. It will be easily perceived that the sense here put upon it is not the same with that in which it is employed by Logicians and Mathematicians. In our own language, indeed, it is not very familiar in any other sense than theirs: but on the Continent it is currently employed in many other sciences. The French, for example, have their *demonstrateurs de botanique, d'anatomie, de physique expérimentale, &c.* I use it out of necessity; not knowing of any other that will suit the purpose.

without justice, to excel; at least in comparison of any thing in that way that has hitherto appeared. 'Tis to him we owe such an arrangement of the elements of Jurisprudence, as wants little, perhaps, of being the best that a technical nomenclature will admit of. A technical nomenclature, so long as it is admitted to mark out and denominate the principal heads, stands an invincible obstacle to every other than a technical arrangement. For to *denominate* in general terms, what is it but to arrange? and to arrange under heads, what is it but to *denominate* upon a large scale? A technical arrangement, governed then in this manner, by a technical nomenclature, can never be otherwise than *confused* and *unsatisfactory*. The reason will be sufficiently apparent, when we understand what sort of an arrangement that must be which can be properly termed a *natural* one.

Idea of a natural arrangement.

53. That arrangement of the materials of any science may, I take it, be termed a *natural* one, which takes such properties to characterize them by, as men in general are, by the common constitution of man's *nature*, disposed to attend to: such, in other words, as *naturally*, that is readily, engage, and firmly fix the attention of any one to whom they are pointed out. The materials, or elements here in question, are such actions as are the objects of what we call Laws or Institutions.

54. Now then, with respect to actions in general, there is no property in them that is calculated so readily to engage, and so firmly to fix the attention of an observer, as the *tendency* that may have *to*, or *divergency* (if one may so say) *from*, that which may be styled the common *end* of all of them. The end I mean is *Happiness*:[1] and this *tendency* in any act is what we style its *utility*: as this *divergency* is that to which we give the name of *mischievousness*. With respect then to such actions in particular as are among the objects of the Law, to point out to a man the *utility* of them or the mischievousness, is the only way to make him see *clearly* that property

---

[1] Let this be taken for a truth upon the authority of *Aristotle*: I mean by those, who like the authority of Aristotle better than that of their own experience. Πᾶσα τέχνη, says that philosopher, καὶ πᾶσα μέθοδος· ὁμοίως δὲ πρᾶξίς τε καὶ προαίρεσις, ἀγαθοῦ τινος ἐφίεσθαι δοκεῖ· διὸ καλῶς ἀπεφήναντο τἀγαθὸν, οὗ πάντα ἐφίεται. Διαφορὰ δέ τις φαίνεται τῶν (understand τοιούτων) ΤΕΛΩΝ.—Arist. Eth. ad Nic. L. I. c. 1.

of them which every man is in search of; the only way, in short, to give him *satisfaction*.

55. From *utility* then we may denominate a *principle*, that may serve to preside over and govern, as it were, such arrangement as shall be made of the several institutions or combinations of institutions that compose the matter of this science: and it is this principle, that by putting its stamp upon the several names given to those combinations, can alone render *satisfactory* and *clear* any arrangement that can be made of them.

56. Governed in this manner by a principle that is recognized by all men, the same arrangement that would serve for the jurisprudence of any one country, would serve with little variation for that of any other.

57. Yet more. The mischievousness of a bad Law would be detected, at least the utility of it would be rendered suspicious, by the difficulty of finding a place for it in such an arrangement: while, on the other hand, a *technical* arrangement is a sink that with equal facility will swallow any garbage that is thrown into it.

58. That this advantage may be possessed by a natural arrangement, is not difficult to conceive. Institutions would be characterized by it in the only universal way in which they can be characterized; by the nature of the several *modes* of *conduct* which, by prohibiting, they constitute *offences*.[1]

59. These offences would be collected into classes denominated by the various modes of their *divergency* from the common *end*; that is, as we have said, by their various forms and degrees of *mischievousness*: in a word, by those properties which are *reasons* for their being made *offences*: and whether any such mode of conduct possesses any such property is a question of experience. Now, a bad Law is that which prohibits a mode of conduct that is *not* mischievous.[3] Thus would it be found impracticable to place the mode of conduct prohibited by a bad law under any denomination of offence,

---

[1] Offences, the Reader will remember, may as well be offences of *omission* as of *commission*. I would avoid the embarrassment of making separate mention of such Laws as exert themselves in *commanding*. 'Tis on this account I use the phrase '*mode of conduct*,' which includes *omissions* or *forbearances*, as well as *acts*.

[2] See note 4, p. 27.   [3] See note 1.

without asserting such a matter of fact as is contradicted by experience. Thus cultivated, in short, the soil of Jurisprudence would be found to repel in a manner every evil institution; like that country which refuses, we are told, to harbour any thing venomous in its bosom.

60. The *synopsis* of such an arrangement would at once be a compendium of *expository* and of *censorial* Jurisprudence: nor would it serve more effectually to instruct the *subject*, than it would to justify or reprove the *Legislator*.

61. Such a synopsis, in short, would be at once a map, and that an universal one, of Jurisprudence as it *is*, and a slight but comprehensive sketch of what it *ought to be*. For, the *reasons* of the several institutions comprised under it would stand expressed, we see, and that uniformly (as in our Author's synopsis they do in scattered instances) by the names given to the several classes under which those institutions are comprised. And what reasons? Not *technical* reasons, such as none but a Lawyer gives, nor any but a Lawyer would put up with[1]; but reasons, such as were they in themselves what they might and ought to be, and expressed too in the manner they might and ought to be, any man might see the force of as well as he.

62. Nor in this is there any thing that need surprise us. The consequences of any Law, or of any act which is made the object of a Law, the only consequences that men are at all interested in, what are they but *pain* and *pleasure*? By some such words then as *pain* and *pleasure*, they may be expressed: and *pain* and *pleasure* at least, are words which a man has no need, we may hope, to go to a Lawyer to know the meaning of.[2] In the synopsis then of that sort of arrangement which

[1] *Technical* reasons: so called from the Greek τέχνη, which signifies an art, science, or profession.

Utility is that standard to which men in general (except in here and there an instance where they are deterred by prejudices of the religious class, or hurried away by the force of what is called *sentiment* or *feeling*), Utility, as we have said, is the standard to which they refer a Law or institution in judging of its title to approbation or disapprobation. Men of Law, corrupted by interests, or seduced by illusions, which it is not here our business to display, have deviated from it much more frequently, and with much less reserve. Hence it is that such reasons as pass with Lawyers, and with no one else, have got the name of *technical* reasons; reasons peculiar to the *art*, peculiar to the profession.

[2] The *reason* of a Law, in short, is no other than the *good* produced by the mode of conduct which it enjoins, or (which comes to the same thing) the

alone deserves the name of a natural one, terms such as these, terms which if they can be said to belong to any science, belong rather to Ethics than to Jurisprudence, even than to universal Jurisprudence, will engross the most commanding stations.

63. What then is to be done with those names of classes that are purely technical?—With offences, for example, against prerogative, with misprisions, contempts, felonies, præmunires[1]? What relation is it that these mark out between the Laws that concern the sorts of acts they are respectively put to signify, and that *common end* we have been speaking of? Not any. In a natural arrangement what then would become of them? They would either be banished at once to the region of *quiddities* and *substantial forms*; or if, and in deference to attachments too inveterate to be all at once dissolved, they were still to be indulged a place, they would be stationed in the corners and bye-places of the Synopsis: stationed, not as now to *give* light, but to *receive* it. But more of this, perhaps, at some future time.

64. To return to our Author. Embarrassed, as a man must *Merits of the* needs be, by this blind and intractable nomenclature, he will *work resumed.* be found, I conceive, to have done as much as could reasonably be expected of a writer so circumstanced; and more and better than was ever done before by any one.

65. In one part, particularly, of his Synopsis,[2] several fragments of a sort of method which is, or at least comes near to, what may be termed a natural one,[3] are actually to be found. We there read of '*corporal injuries*'; of '*offences against peace*'; against '*health*'; against '*personal security*[4]'; '*liberty*':—

mischief produced by the mode of conduct which it prohibits. This *mischief* or this *good*, if they be real, cannot but shew themselves somewhere or other in the shape of *pain* or *pleasure*.

[1] See in the Synoptical Table prefixed to our Author's *Analysis*, the last page comprehending Book IV.

[2] It is that which comprises his IVth Book, entitled PUBLIC WRONGS.

[3] *Fragmenta methodi naturalis.*—LINNÆI *Phil. Bot.* Tit. *Systemata*, par. 77.

[4] This title affords a pertinent instance to exemplify the use that a natural arrangement may be of in repelling an incompetent institution. What I mean is the sort of filthiness that is termed *unnatural*. This our Author has ranked in his class of *Offences against 'personal security,'* and, in a subdivision of it, entitled '*Corporal injuries*.' In so doing, then, he has asserted a fact: he has asserted that the offence in question is an offence against personal security; is a corporal injury; is, in short, productive of unhappiness *in that way*. Now this is what, in the case where the act is committed *by consent*, is manifestly not

'*property*':—light is let in, though irregularly, at various places.

66. In an unequal imitation of this Synopsis that has lately been performed upon what is called the *Civil Law*, *all* is technical. All, in short, is darkness. Scarce a syllable by which a man would be led to suspect, that the affair in hand were an affair that happiness or unhappiness was at all concerned in.[1]

67. To return, once more, to our Author's Commentaries. Not even in a *censorial* view would I be understood to deem them altogether without merit. For the institutions commented on, where they are capable of good reasons, good reasons are every now and then given: in which way, so far as it goes, one-half of the Censor's task is well accomplished. Nor is the dark side of the picture left absolutely untouched. Under the head of 'Trial by Jury,' are some very just and interesting remarks on the yet-remaining imperfections of that mode of trial[2]: and under that of 'Assurances by matter of Record,' on the lying and extortious jargon of *Recoveries*.[3] So little, however, are these particular remarks of a piece with the general disposition, that shews itself so strongly throughout the work, indeed so plainly adverse to the general maxims that we have seen, that I can scarce bring

Manner in which the present Essay has been conducted.

true. *Volenti non fit injuria.* If then the Law against the offence in question had no other title to a place in the system than what was founded on this *fact*, it is plain it would have none. It would be a bad Law altogether. The mischief the offence is of to the community in this case is in truth of quite another nature, and would come under quite another class. When *against* consent, there indeed it does belong really to this class: but then it would come under another name. It would come under that of *Rape*.

[1] I think it is Selden, somewhere in his *Table-talk*, that speaks of a whimsical notion he had hit upon when a school-boy, that with regard to *Cæsar* and *Justin*, and those other personages of antiquity that gave him so much trouble, there was not a syllable of truth in any thing they said, nor in fact were there ever really any such persons; but that the whole affair was a contrivance of parents to find employment for their children. Much the same sort of notion is that which these technical arrangements are calculated to give us of Jurisprudence: which in them stands represented rather as a game at *Crambo* for Lawyers to whet their wits at, than as that Science which holds in her hand the happiness of nations.

Let us, however, do no man wrong. Where the success has been worse, the difficulty was greater. That detestable chaos of institutions which the Analyst last-mentioned had to do with is still more embarrassed with a technical nomenclature than our own.

[2] 3 Comm., Ch. XXIII, p. 387.   [3] 2 Comm., Ch. XXI, p. 360.

myself to attribute them to our Author. Not only disorder
is announced by them, but remedies, well-imagined remedies,
are pointed out. One would think some Angel had been
sowing wheat among our Author's tares.[1]

68. With regard to this Essay itself, I have not much to say.
The principal and professed purpose of it is, to expose the
errors and insufficiencies of our Author. The business of it is
therefore rather to *overthrow* than to *set up*; which latter task
can seldom be performed to any great advantage where the
former is the principal one.

69. To guard against the danger of misrepresentation, and
to make sure of doing our Author no injustice, his own words
are given all along: and, as scarce any sentence is left unnoticed,
the whole comment wears the form of what is called a
perpetual one. With regard to a discourse that is simply
institutional, and in which the writer builds upon a plan of
his own, a great part of the satisfaction it can be made to
afford depends upon the order and connection that are
established between the several parts of it. In a comment
upon the work of another, no such connection, or at least
no such order, can be established commodiously, if at all.
The order of the comment is prescribed by the order, perhaps
the disorder, of the text.

70. The chief employment of this Essay, as we have said,
has necessarily been *to overthrow*. In the little, therefore, which
has been done by it in the way of *setting up*, my view has been
not so much to think for the Reader, as to put him upon
thinking for himself. This I flatter myself with having done
on several interesting topics; and this is all that at present I
propose.

71. Among the few positions of my own which I have

[1] The difference between a generous and determined affection, and an
occasional, and as it were forced contribution, to the cause of reformation,
may be seen, I think, in these Commentaries, compared with another celebrated work on the subject of our Jurisprudence. Mr. Barrington, whose
agreeable Miscellany has done so much towards opening men's eyes upon this
subject; Mr. Barrington, like an active General in the service of the Public,
storms the strongholds of chicane, wheresoever they present themselves, and
particularly fictions, without reserve. Our Author, like an artful partizan in
the service of the profession, sacrifices a few, as if it were to save the rest.

Deplorable, indeed, would have been the student's chance for salutary
instruction, did not Mr. Barrington's work in so many instances, furnish the
antidote to our Author's poisons.

found occasion to advance, some I observe which promise to be far from popular. These it is likely may give rise to very warm objections: objections which in themselves I do not wonder at, and which in their motive I cannot but approve. The people are a set of masters whom it is not in a man's power in every instance fully to please, and at the same time faithfully to serve. He that is resolved to persevere without deviation in the line of truth and utility, must have learnt to prefer the still whisper of enduring approbation, to the short-lived bustle of tumultuous applause.

72. Other passages too there may be, of which some farther explanation may perhaps not unreasonably be demanded. But to give these explanations, and to obviate those objections, is a task which, if executed at all, must be referred to some other opportunity. Consistency forbad our expatiating so far as to lose sight of our Author: since it was the line of his course that marked the boundaries of ours.

A

FRAGMENT ON GOVERNMENT

INTRODUCTION

1. THE subject of this examination is a passage contained *Division of our* in that part of Sir W. BLACKSTONE'S COMMENTARIES on the *Author's Intro-* LAWS of ENGLAND, which the Author has styled the INTRO-*duction.* DUCTION. This Introduction of his stands divided into four Sections. The *first* contains his discourse 'On the STUDY *of the* LAW.' The *second*, entitled '*Of the* NATURE *of* LAWS *in general*,' contains his speculations concerning the various objects, real or imaginary, that are in use to be mentioned under the common name of LAW. The *third*, entitled '*Of the* LAWS *of* ENGLAND,' contains such general observations, relative to these last mentioned Laws, as seemed proper to be premised before he entered into the details of any parts of them in particular. In the *fourth*, entitled, '*Of the* COUNTRIES *subject to the* LAWS *of* ENGLAND,' is given a statement of the different territorial extents of different branches of those Laws.

2. 'Tis in the *second* of these sections, that we shall find the *What part of it* passage proposed for examination. It occupies in the edition *is here to be* I happen to have before me, which is the *first* (and all the *examined.* editions, I believe, are paged alike) the space of *seven* pages; from the 47th to the 53d, inclusive.

3. After treating of 'LAW *in general*,' of the 'LAW *of Nature*,' *His definition of* 'LAW *of Revelation*,' and 'LAW *of Nations*,' branches of that *Law municipal.* imaginary whole, our Author comes at length to what he calls 'LAW *municipal*': that sort of Law, to which men in their ordinary discourse would give the name of Law without addition; the only sort perhaps of them all (unless it be that of *Revelation*) to which the name can, with strict propriety, be applied: in a word, that sort which we see made in each nation, to express the will of that body in it which governs. On this subject of LAW *Municipal* he sets out, as a man ought, with a *definition* of the phrase itself; an important and funda-

31

mental phrase, which stood highly in need of a definition, and never so much as since our Author has defined it.

4. This definition is ushered in with no small display of accuracy. First, it is given entire: it is then taken to pieces, clause by clause; and every clause by itself, justified and explained. In the very midst of these explanations, in the very midst of the definition, he makes a sudden stand. And now it bethinks him that it is good time to give a dissertation, or rather a bundle of dissertations, upon various subjects— On the *manner* in which *Governments were* established—On the different *forms* they assume when they *are* established— On the peculiar excellence of that form which is established in *this country*—On the *right*, which he thinks it necessary to tell us, the GOVERNMENT in every country has of making LAWS—On the *duty* of making LAWS; which, he says, is also incumbent on the Government.—In stating these two last heads, I give, as near as possible, his own *words*; thinking it premature to engage in discussions, and not daring to decide without discussion on the *sense*.

5. The digression we are about to examine, is, as it happens, not at all involved with the body of the work from which it starts. No mutual references or allusions: no supports or illustrations communicated or received. It may be considered as one small work inserted into a large one; the contain*ing* and the contain*ed*, having scarce any other connection than what the operations of the press have given them. It is this disconnection that will enable us the better to bestow on the latter a separate examination, without breaking in upon any thread of reasoning, or any principle of Order.

6. A general statement of the topics touched upon in the digression we are about to examine has been given above. It will be found, I trust, a faithful one. It will not be thought, however, much of a piece, perhaps, with the following, which our Author himself has given us. 'This,' (says he,[1] meaning an explanation he had been giving of a part of the definition above spoken of) 'will naturally lead us into a short enquiry into the nature of society and civil government;[2] and

[1] 1 Comm., p. 47.
[2] To make sure of doing our Author no injustice, and to shew what it is that he thought would 'naturally lead us into' this 'enquiry,' it may be proper

the natural inherent right that belongs to the sovereignty of a state, wherever that sovereignty be lodged, of making and enforcing Laws.'

7. No very explicit mention here, we may observe, of the *Inadequate.* manner in which governments have been established, or of the different *forms* they assume when established: no very explicit intimation that these were among the topics to be discussed. None at all of the *duty* of government to make laws; none at all of the *British constitution*; though, of the four other topics we have mentioned, there is no one on which he has been near so copious as on this last. The *right* of Government to make laws, that delicate and invidious topic, as we shall find it when explained, is that which for the moment, seems to have swallowed up almost the whole of his attention.

8. Be this as it may, the contents of the dissertation before *Division of the* us, taken as I have stated them, will furnish us with the *present Essay.* matter of five chapters:—one, which I shall entitle 'FORMA-TION *of* GOVERNMENT'—a second, 'FORMS *of* GOVERNMENT'— a third, 'BRITISH CONSTITUTION'—a fourth, 'RIGHT *of the* SUPREME POWER *to make* LAWS'—a fifth, 'DUTY *of the* SUPREME POWER *to make* LAWS.'

to give the paragraph containing the explanation above mentioned. It is as follows:— 'But farther: municipal law is a rule of civil conduct, prescribed *by the supreme power in a state.*' 'For legislature, as was before observed, is the greatest act of superiority that can be exercised by one being over another. Wherefore it is requisite, to the very essence of a law, that it be made' (he might have added, *or at least supported*) 'by the supreme power. Sovereignty and legislature are indeed convertible terms; one cannot subsist without the other.' 1 Comm., p. 46.

C

CHAPTER I

FORMATION OF GOVERNMENT

Subject of the passage to be examined in the present chapter.
1. THE first object which our Author seems to have proposed to himself in the dissertation we are about to examine, is to give us an idea of the *manner* in which Governments were formed. This occupies the first paragraph, together with part of the second: for the *typographical* division does not seem to quadrate very exactly with the *intellectual*. As the examination of this passage will unavoidably turn in great measure upon the words, it will be proper the reader should have it under his eye.

The passage recited.
2. 'The only true and natural foundations of *society*,' (says our Author[1]) 'are the wants and the fears of individuals. Not that we can believe, with some theoretical writers, that there ever was a time when there was no such thing as *society*; and that, from the impulse of reason, and through a sense of their wants and weaknesses, individuals met together in a large plain, entered into an *original contract*, and chose the tallest man present to be their governor. This notion of an actually existing unconnected *state of nature*, is too wild to be seriously admitted; and besides, it is plainly contradictory to the revealed accounts of the primitive origin of mankind, and their preservation two thousand years afterwards; both which were effected by the means of single families. These formed the first *society*, among themselves; which every day extended its limits, and when it grew too large to subsist with convenience in that pastoral state, wherein the patriarchs appear to have lived, it necessarily subdivided itself by various migrations into more. Afterwards, as agriculture increased, which employs and can maintain a much greater number of hands, migrations became less frequent; and various tribes which had formerly separated, re-united again; sometimes by compulsion and conquest, sometimes by accident, and sometimes perhaps by compact. But though *society* had not its formal beginning from any convention of individuals,

[1] 1 Comm., p. 47.

34

actuated by their wants and their fears; yet it is the *sense* of their weakness and imperfection that *keeps* mankind together; that demonstrates the necessity of this union; and that therefore is the solid and natural foundation, as well as the cement of *society*: And this is what we mean by the *original contract* of *society*; which, though perhaps in no instance it has ever been formally expressed at the first institution of a state, yet in nature and reason must always be understood and implied, in the very act of associating together: namely, that the whole should protect all its parts, and that every part should pay obedience to the will of the whole; or, in other words, that the community should guard the rights of each individual member, and that (in return for this protection) each individual should submit to the laws of the community; without which submission of all it was impossible that protection could be certainly extended to any.'

'For when *society* is once formed, *government* results of course, as necessary to preserve and to keep that *society* in order. Unless some superior were constituted, whose commands and decisions all the members are bound to obey, they would still remain as in a *state of nature*, without any judge upon earth to define their several rights, and redress their several wrongs.'—This far our Author.

3. When leading terms are made to chop and change their several significations; sometimes meaning one thing, sometimes another, at the upshot perhaps nothing; and this in the compass of a paragraph; one may judge what will be the complexion of the whole context. This, we shall see, is the case with the chief of those we have been reading: for instance, with the words 'Society,'—'State of nature,'—'original contract,'—not to tire the reader with any more. '*Society*,' in one place means the same thing as '*a state of nature*' does: in another place it means the same as '*Government*.' Here, we are required to believe there *never was* such a state as a state of nature: there we are given to understand there *has been*. In like manner with respect to an *original contract* we are given to understand that such a thing never existed; that the notion of it is ridiculous: at the same time that there is no speaking nor stirring without supposing there was one. *Confusion among the leading terms of it.*

'Society' put synonymous to a state of nature— opposed to 'Government'— and spoken of as having existed.

4. 1*st*, Society means a *state of nature*. For if by 'a state of nature' a man means any thing, it is the state, I take it, men are in or supposed to be in, before they are under *government*: the state men quit when they enter into a state of government; and in which were it not for government they would remain. But by the word '*society*' it is plain at one time that he means that state. First, according to him, comes *society*; then afterwards comes *government*. 'For when society,' says our Author, 'is once formed, government results of course; as necessary to preserve and keep that society in order.'—And again, immediately afterwards,—'A state in which a superior has been constituted, whose commands and decisions all the members are bound to obey,' he puts as an explanation (nor is it an inapt one) of a state of '*government*': and 'unless' men were in a state of that description, they would still 'remain', he says, 'as in a *state of nature*.' By *society*, therefore, he means, once more, the same as by a '*state of nature*': he *opposes* it to *government*. And he speaks of it as a state which, in this sense, has actually existed.

'Society' put synonymous to 'government.'

5. 2*dly*, This is what he tells us in the beginning of the *second* of the two paragraphs: but all the time the *first* paragraph lasted, *society* meant the same as *government*. In shifting then from one paragraph to another, it has changed its nature. 'Tis 'the foundations of *society*,'[1] that he first began to speak of, and immediately he goes on to explain to us, after his manner of explaining, the foundations of *government*. 'Tis of a 'formal beginning' of 'Society,'[2] that he speaks soon after; and by this formal beginning, he tells us immediately, that he means, 'the *original contract* of *society*,'[3] which contract entered into, 'a state,'[4] he gives us to understand, is thereby 'instituted,' and men have undertaken to 'submit to Laws.'[5] So long then as this first paragraph lasts, '*society*,' I think, it is plain cannot but have been meaning the same as '*government*.'

A state of nature spoken of, as never having existed.

6. 3*dly*, All this while too, this same '*state of nature*' to which we have seen 'Society' (a state spoken of as existing) put synonymous, and in which were it not for government, men, he informs us, in the next page, would '*remain*,'[6] is a state

[1] 1 Comm., p. 47. [2] 1 Comm., p. 47. [3] 1 Comm., p. 47.
[4] 1 Comm., p. 47. [5] 1 Comm., p. 48. [6] 1 Comm., p. 48.

in which they never *were*. So he expressly tells us. This 'notion,' says he, 'of an actually existing unconnected state of nature;' (that is, as he explains himself afterwards,[1] 'a state in which men have no judge to define their rights, and redress their wrongs,) is too wild to be seriously admitted.'[2] When he admits it then himself, as he does in his next page, we are to understand, it seems, that he is bantering us: and that the next paragraph is (what one should not otherwise have taken it for) a piece of pleasantry.

7. 4*thly*, The *original contract* is a thing, we are to understand, that never had existence; perhaps not in *any* state: certainly therefore not in *all*. 'Perhaps, in no instance,' says our Author, 'has it ever been formally expressed at the first institution of a state.'[3]

Original contract, its reality denied—

8. 5*thly*, Notwithstanding all this, we must suppose, it seems, that it had in *every* state: 'yet in nature and reason,' says our Author, 'it must always be understood and implied.'[4] Growing bolder in the compass of four or five pages, where he is speaking of our own Government, he asserts roundly,[5] that such a Contract was actually made at the first formation of it. 'The legislature would be changed,' he says, 'from that which *was originally* set up by the general consent and fundamental act of the society.'

—asserted.

9. Let us try whether it be not possible for something to be done towards drawing the import of these terms out of the mist in which our Author has involved them. The word 'SOCIETY,' I think it appears, is used by him, and that without notice, in two senses that are opposite. In the one, SOCIETY, or a STATE OF SOCIETY, is put *synonymous* to a STATE OF NATURE; and stands *opposed* to GOVERNMENT, or a STATE OF GOVERNMENT: in this sense it may be styled, as it commonly is, *natural* SOCIETY. In the other, it is put *synonymous* to GOVERNMENT, or a STATE OF GOVERNMENT; and stands *opposed* to a STATE OF NATURE. In this sense it may be styled, as it commonly is, *political* SOCIETY. Of the difference between these two states, a tolerably distinct idea, I take it, may be given in a word or two.

Attempt to reconcile these contradictions— Society distinguished into natural and political.

[1] 1 Comm., p. 48.   [2] 1 Comm., p. 47.   [3] 1 Comm., p. 46.
[4] 1 Comm., p. 46.   [5] 1 Comm., p. 52.

Idea of political *society.* 10. The idea of a natural society is a *negative* one. The idea of a political society is a *positive* one. 'Tis with the latter, therefore, we should begin.

When a number of persons (whom we may style *subjects*) are supposed to be in the *habit* of paying *obedience* to a person, or an assemblage of persons, of a known and certain description (whom we may call *governor* or *governors*) such persons altogether (*subjects* and *governors*) are said to be in a state of *political* SOCIETY.[1]

Idea of natural *society.* 11. The idea of a state of *natural* SOCIETY is, as we have said, a *negative* one. When a number of persons are supposed to be in the habit of *conversing* with each other, at the same time that they are not in any such habit as mentioned above, they are said to be in a state of *natural* SOCIETY.

Difficulty of drawing the line between the two states. 12. If we reflect a little, we shall perceive, that, between these two states, there is not that explicit separation which these names, and these definitions might teach one, at first sight, to expect. It is with them as with light and darkness: however distinct the ideas may be, that are, at first mention, suggested by those *names*, the *things* themselves have no determinate bound to separate them. The circumstance that has been spoken of as constituting the difference between these two states, is the presence or absence of an *habit of obedience*. This habit, accordingly, has been spoken of simply as *present* (that is as being *perfectly* present) or, in other words, we have spoken as if there were a *perfect* habit of obedience, in the *one* case: it has been spoken of simply as *absent* (that is, as being *perfectly* absent) or, in other words, we have spoken as if there were *no* habit of obedience at all, in the *other*. But neither of these manners of speaking, perhaps, is strictly just. Few, in fact, if any, are the instances of this habit being perfectly *absent*; certainly none at all, of its being perfectly *present*. Governments accordingly, in proportion as the habit of obedience is more perfect, recede from, in proportion as it is less perfect, approach to, a state of nature: and instances may present themselves in which it shall be difficult to say

---

[1] V. infra., par. 12, note 1.

whether a habit, perfect, in the degree in which, to constitute a government, it is deemed necessary it *should* be perfect, *does* subsist or *not*.[1]

[1] 1. A *habit* is but an assemblage of *acts*: under which name I would also 1. *A habit.* include, for the present, *voluntary forbearances.*

2. A *habit of obedience* then is an assemblage of *acts of obedience.* 2. *A habit of obedience.*

3. An *act of obedience* is any act done in pursuance of an *expression of will* 3. *An act of* on the part of some *superior.* *obedience.*

4. An *act of* POLITICAL *obedience* (which is what is here meant) is any act done 4. *An act of* in pursuance of an expression of will on the part of a person governing. *political obe- dience.*

5. An *expression of will* is either *parole* or *tacit.* 5. *An expres- sion of will.*

6. A *parole expression of will* is that which is conveyed by the *signs* called 6. *A parole ex-* words. *pression of will.*

7. A *tacit expression of will* is that which is conveyed by any other *signs* 7. *A tacit ex-* whatsoever: among which none are so efficacious as *acts of punishment* annexed *pression of will.* in time past, to the non-performance of acts of the same sort with those that are the objects of the will that is in question.

8. A *parole* expression of the will of a superior is a *command.* 8. *A command.*

9. When a *tacit* expression of the will of a superior is supposed to have been 9. *A fictitious* uttered, it may be styled a *fictitious command.* *command.*

10. Were we at liberty to coin words after the manner of the Roman 10. *Commands* lawyers, we might say a *quasi*-command. *quasi-com- mands.*

11. The STATUTE LAW is composed of *commands.* The COMMON LAW, of 11. *Illustration* *quasi*-commands. *—Statute Law Common Law*

12. An act which is the object of a command actual or fictitious; such an 12. *Duty— * act, considered before it is performed, is styled a *duty*, or a *point of duty.* *point of duty.*

13. These definitions premised, we are now in a condition to give such an 13. *Use of the* idea, of what is meant by the *perfection* or *imperfection* of a *habit of obedience* *above chain of* in a society as may prove tolerably precise. *definitions.*

14. A *period* in the duration of the society; the number of *persons* it is com- 14. *Habit of* posed of during that period; and the number of *points of duty* incumbent on *obedience—* each person being given;—the habit of obedience will be more or less *perfect, measure of its* in the ratio of the number of acts of *obedience* to those of *disobedience.* *perfections.*

15. The habit of obedience in this country appears to have been more 15. *Illustration.* perfect in the time of the Saxons than in that of the Britons: unquestionably it is more so now than in the time of the Saxons. It is not yet so perfect, as well contrived and well digested laws in time, it is to be hoped, may render it. But absolutely perfect, till man ceases to be man, it never *can* be.

A very ingenious and instructive view of the progress of nations, from the

A perfect state of nature not more chimerical than a perfect state of government.

13. On these considerations, the supposition of a *perfect state of nature*, or, as it may be termed, a state of *society perfectly natural*, may, perhaps, be justly pronounced, what our Author for the moment seemed to think it, an extravagant supposition: but then that of a *government* in this sense *perfect*; or, as it may be termed, a state of society *perfectly political*, a state of *perfect political union*, a state of *perfect submission* in the *subject* of *perfect authority* in the *governor*, is no less so.[1]

least perfect states of political union to that highly perfect state of it in which we live, may be found in LORD KAIMS's *Historical Law Tracts*.

16. *Political union or connection.*

16. For the convenience and accuracy of discourse it may be of use, in this place, to settle the signification of a few other expressions relative to the same subject. Persons who, with respect to each other, are in a state of *political society*, may be said also to be in a state of *political union* or *connection*.

17. *Submission —subjection.*

17. Such of them as are *subjects* may, accordingly, be said to be in a state of *submission*, or of *subjection*, with respect to *governors*: such as are *governors* in a state of *authority* with respect to *subjects*.

18. *Submission —subjection*

18. When the subordination is considered as resulting originally from the *will*, or (it may be more proper to say) the *pleasure* of the party govern*ed*, we rather use the word '*submission*:' when from that of the party govern*ing*, the word '*subjection*.' On this account it is, that the term can scarcely be used without apology, unless with a note of disapprobation: especially in this country, where the habit of considering the *consent* of the persons governe*d* as being in some sense or other involved in the notion of all *lawful*, that is, all *commendable* government, has gained so firm a ground. It is on this account, then, that the term '*subjection*,' *ex*cluding as it does, or, at least, not *in*cluding such consent, is used commonly in what is called a BAD sense: that is, in such a sense as, together with the idea of the object in question, conveys the *accessary* idea of disapprobation. This accessary idea, however, annexed as it is to the *abstract* term 'subjection,' does not extend itself to the *concrete* term 'subjects'—a kind of inconsistency of which there are many instances in language.

It is not a family union, however perfect, that can constitute a political society—why.

[1] It is true that every person must, for some time, at least, after his birth, necessarily be in a state of subjection with respect to his parents, or those who stand in the place of parents to him; and that a perfect one, or at least as near to being a perfect one, as any that we see. But for all this, the sort of society that is constituted by a state of subjection thus circumstanced, does not come up to the idea that, I believe, is generally entertained by those who speak of a *political* society. To constitute what is meant in general by that phrase, a greater *number* of members is required, or, at least, a *duration* capable of a longer continuance. Indeed, for this purpose nothing less, I take it, than an *indefinite* duration is required. A society, to come within the notion of what is originally meant by a *political* one, must be such as, in its nature, is not incapable of continuing for ever in virtue of the principles which gave it birth. This, it is plain, is not the case with such a family society, of which a parent, or a pair of parents are at the head. In such a society, the only principle of union which is certain and uniform in its operation, is the natural weakness of those of its members that are in a state of subjection; that is, the children; a principle which has but a short and limited continuance. I question whether it be the case

14. A remark there is, which, for the more thoroughly *'State of nature'* clearing up of our notions on this subject, it may be proper *a relative ex-* here to make. To some ears, the phrases, 'state of nature,' *pression.* 'state of political society,' may carry the appearance of being *absolute* in their signification: as if the condition of a man, or a company of men, in one of these states, or in the other, were a matter that depended altogether upon themselves. But this is not the case. To the expression 'state of nature,' no more than to the expression 'state of political society,' can any precise meaning be annexed, without reference to a party different from that one who is spoken of as being in the state in question. This will readily be perceived. The difference between the two states lies, as we have observed, in the *habit of obedience.* With respect then to a habit of obedience, it can neither be understood as subsisting in any person, nor as not subsisting in any person, but with reference to some other person. For one party to *obey,* there must be another party that is obeyed. But this party who is obeyed, may at different times be different. Hence may one and the same party be conceived to obey and *not* to obey at the same time, so as it be with respect to different *persons,* or as we may say, to different *objects of obedience.* Hence it is, then, that one and the same party may be said to *be* in a state of nature, and *not* to be in a state of nature, and that at one and the same time, according as it is this or *that* party that is taken for the other object of comparison. The case is, that in common speech, when no particular object of comparison is specified, all persons in general are intended: so that when a number of persons are said simply to be in a state of nature, what is understood is, that they are so as well with reference to one another, as to all the world.

even with a family society, subsisting in virtue of *collateral* consanguinity; and that for the like reason. Not but that even in this case a habit of obedience, as perfect as any we see examples of, may subsist for a time; to wit, in virtue of the same *moral* principles which may protract a habit of *filial* obedience beyond the continuance of the *physical* ones which gave birth to it: I mean affection, gratitude, awe, the force of habit, and the like. But it is not long, even in this case, before the bond of connection must either become imperceptible, or lose its influence by being too extended.

These considerations, therefore, it will be proper to bear in mind in applying the definition of political society above given [in par. 10] and in order to reconcile it with what is said further on [in par. 17].

Different degrees of subjection among governors.

15. In the same manner we may understand, how the same man, who is *governor* with respect to one man or set of men, may be *subject* with respect to another: how among governors some may be in a *perfect* state of *nature*, with respect to each other: as the KINGS of FRANCE and SPAIN: others, again, in a state of *perfect subjection*, as the HOSPODARS of WALACHIA and MOLDAVIA with respect to the GRAND SIGNIOR: others, again, in a state of manifest but *imperfect subjection*, as the GERMAN States with respect to the EMPEROR: others, again, in such a state in which it may be difficult to determine whether they are in a state of *imperfect subjection* or in a *perfect* state of *nature*: as the KING of NAPLES with respect to the POPE.[1]

The same person alternately in a state of political and natural society with respect to different societies.

16. In the same manner, also, it may be conceived, without entering into details, how any single person, born, as all persons are, into a state of perfect subjection to his parents,[2] that is into a state of perfect political society with respect to his parents, may from thence pass into a perfect state of nature; and from thence successively into any number of different states of political society more or less perfect, by passing into different societies.

In the same political society the same persons alternately governors and subjects, with respect to the same persons.

17. In the same manner, also, it may be conceived how, in any political society, the same man may, with respect to the same individuals, be, at different periods, and on different occasions, alternately, in the state of governor and subject: to-day concurring, perhaps active, in the business of issuing a *general* command for the observance of the whole society, amongst the rest of another man in quality of *Judge*: to-morrow, punished, perhaps, by a *particular* command of that same Judge for not obeying the general command which he himself (I mean the person acting in character of governor) had issued. I need scarce remind the reader how happily this alternate state of *authority* and *submission* is exemplified among ourselves.

Hints of several topics that must be passed by.

18. Here might be a place to state the different shares which different persons may have in the issuing of the same com-

---

[1] The Kingdom of Naples is feudatory to the Papal See: and in token of fealty, the King, at his accession, presents the Holy Father with a white horse. The Royal vassal sometimes treats his Lord but cavalierly: but always sends him his white horse.

[2] V. supra, par. 13, note.

mand: to explain the nature of *corporate action*: to enumerate and distinguish half a dozen or more different modes in which *subordination* between the same parties may subsist: to distinguish and explain the different senses of the words, 'consent,' 'representation,' and others of connected import: *consent* and *representation*, those interesting but perplexing words, sources of so much debate: and sources or pretexts of so much animosity. But the limits of the present design will by no means admit of such protracted and intricate discussions.

19. In the same manner, also, it may be conceived, how *The same society* the same set of men considered *among themselves*, may at one *alternately in a* time be in a state of nature, at another time in a state of *state of nature* government. For the habit of obedience, in whatever degree *and a state of* government. For the habit of obedience, in whatever degree *government.* of perfection it be necessary it should subsist in order to constitute a government, may be conceived, it is plain, to suffer interruptions. At different junctures it may take place and cease.

20. Instances of this state of things appear not to be unfre- *Instance the* quent. The sort of society that has been observed to subsist *Aborigines of* among the AMERICAN INDIANS may afford us one. According *America.* to the accounts we have of those people, in most of their tribes, if not in all, the habit we are speaking of appears to be taken up only in time of war. It ceases again in time of peace. The necessity of acting in concert against a common enemy, subjects a whole tribe to the orders of a common Chief. On the return of peace each warrior resumes his pristine independence.

21. One difficulty there is that still sticks by us. It has been *Characteristic of* started indeed, but not solved—This is to find a note of dis- *political union.* tinction,—a characteristic mark, whereby to distinguish a society in which there *is* a habit of obedience, and that at the degree of perfection which is necessary to constitute a state of government, from a society in which there is *not*: a mark, I mean, which shall have a visible determinate commencement; insomuch that the instant of its first appearance shall be distinguishable from the last at which it had not as yet appeared. 'Tis only by the help of such a mark that we can be in a condition to determine, at any given time, whether any given society is in a state of government, or in a state of

nature. I can find no such mark, I must confess, anywhere, unless it be this; the establishment of names of office: the appearance of a certain man, or set of men, with a certain name, serving to mark them out as objects of obedience: such as King, Sachem, Cacique, Senator, Burgomaster, and the like. This, I think, may serve tolerably well to distinguish a set of men in a state of political union among *themselves* from the *same* set of men not yet in such a state.

Among persons already in a state of political union at what instant a new society can be said to be formed, by defection from a former.

22. But suppose an incontestable political society, and that a large one, formed; and from that a smaller body to break off: by this breach the smaller body ceases to be in a state of political union with respect to the larger: and has thereby placed itself, with respect to that larger body, in a state of nature—What means shall we find of ascertaining the precise juncture at which this change took place? What shall be taken for the *characteristic mark* in this case? The appointment, it may be said, of new governors with new names. But no such appointment, suppose, takes place. The subordinate governors, from whom alone the people at large were in use to receive their commands under the old government, are the same from whom they receive them under the new one. The habit of obedience which these subordinate governors were in with respect to that single person, we will say, who was the supreme governor of the whole, is broken off insensibly and by degrees. The old names by which these subordinate governors were characterized, while they were subordinate, are continued now they are supreme. In this case it seems rather difficult to answer.

1st, in case of defection by whole bodies, instance the Dutch provinces.

23. If an example be required, we may take that of the DUTCH provinces with respect to SPAIN. These provinces were once branches of the Spanish monarchy. They have now, for a long time, been universally spoken of as independent states: independent as well of that of Spain as of every other. They are now in a state of nature with respect to Spain. They were once in a state of political union with respect to Spain: namely, in a state of subjection to a single *governor*, a King, who was King of Spain. At what precise juncture did the dissolution of this political union take place? At what precise time did these provinces cease to be subject to the

King of Spain? This, I doubt, will be rather difficult to agree upon.[1]

24. Suppose the defection to have begun, not by entire provinces, as in the instance just mentioned, but by a handful of fugitives, this augmented by the accession of other fugitives, and so, by degrees, to a body of men too strong to be reduced, the difficulty will be increased still farther. At what precise juncture was it that ancient ROME, or that modern VENICE, became an independent state? *2dly, in case of defection by individuals—instances, Rome—Venice:*

25. In general then, at what precise juncture is it, that persons subject to a government, become, by disobedience, with respect to that government, in a state of nature? When is it, in short, that a *revolt* shall be deemed to have taken place; and when, again, is it, that that revolt shall be deemed to such a degree successful, as to have settled into *independence*? *A revolt, at what juncture it can be said to have taken place.*

26. As it is the obedience of individuals that constitutes a state of submission, so is it their disobedience that must constitute a state of revolt. Is it then every act of disobedience that will do as much? The affirmative, certainly, is what can never be maintained: for then would there be no such thing as government to be found anywhere. Here then a distinction or two obviously presents itself. Disobedience may be distinguished into *conscious* or *unconscious*: and that, with respect as well to the *law* as to the *fact*.[2] Disobedience that is unconscious with respect to either, will readily, I suppose, be acknowledged not to be a revolt. Disobedience again that *Disobediences what do not amount to a revolt:*

---

[1] Upon recollection, I have some doubt whether this example would be found historically exact. If not, that of the defection of the Nabobs of Hindostan may answer the purpose. My first choice fell upon the former; supposing it to be rather better known.

[2] 1. Disobedience may be said to be *unconscious with respect to the fact*, when the party is ignorant either of his having done the act itself, which is forbidden by the law, or else of his having done it in those *circumstances*, in which alone it is forbidden. *1. Disobedience unconscious with respect to the fact.*

2. Disobedience may be said to be *unconscious*, with respect to the *law*; when although he may know of his having done the *act* that is in reality forbidden, and that, under the *circumstances* in which it is forbidden, he knows not of its being forbidden in these *circumstances*. *2. Disobedience unconscious with respect to the Law.*

3. So long as the business of spreading abroad the knowledge of the law continues to lie in the neglect in which it has lain hitherto, instances of disobedience *unconscious with respect to the law*, can never be otherwise than abundant. *3. Illustration.*

is conscious with respect to *both*, may be distinguished into *secret* and *open*; or, in other words, into *fraudulent* and *forcible*.[1] Disobedience that is only fraudulent, will likewise, I suppose, be readily acknowledged not to amount to a revolt.

Disobediences what do amount to a revolt.

27. The difficulty that will remain will concern such disobedience only as is both *conscious*, (and that as well with respect to *law* as *fact*,) and *forcible*. This disobedience, it should seem, is to be determined neither by *numbers* altogether (that is of the persons supposed to be disobedient) nor by *acts*, nor by *intentions*: all three may be fit to be taken into consideration. But having brought the difficulty to this point, at this point I must be content to leave it. To proceed any farther in the endeavour to solve it, would be to enter into a discussion of particular local jurisprudence. It would be entering upon the definition of Treason, as distinguished from Murder, Robbery, Riot, and other such crimes, as, in comparison with Treason, are spoken of as being of a more private nature. Suppose the definition of Treason settled, and the commission of an act of Treason is, as far as regards the person committing it, the characteristic mark we are in search of.

Unfinished state of the above hints.

28. These remarks it were easy to extend to a much greater length. Indeed, it is what would be necessary, in order to give them a proper fulness, and method, and precision. But that could not be done without exceeding the limits of the present design. As they are, they may serve as hints to such as shall be disposed to give the subject a more exact and regular examination.

Our Author's proposition, 'That government results of course,' not true.

29. From what has been said, however, we may judge what truth there is in our Author's observation, that 'when society' (understand *natural* society) 'is once formed, government' (that is political society) (whatever quantity or degree of Obedience is necessary to constitute political society) 'results *of course*; as necessary to preserve and to keep that society in order.' By the words, '*of course*,' is meant, I suppose, *constantly* and *immediately*: at least constantly. According to

Disobediences fraudulent and forcible— the difference, illustrated.

[1] If examples be thought necessary, Theft may serve for an example of *fraudulent* disobedience; Robbery of *forcible*. In Theft, the *person* of the disobedient party, and the *act* of disobedience, are both endeavoured to be kept secret. In Robbery, the *act* of disobedience, at least, if not the *person* of him who disobeys, is manifest and avowed.

this, political society, in any sense of it, ought long ago to have been established all the world over. Whether this be the case, let any one judge from the instances of the Hottentots, of the Patagonians, and of so many other barbarous tribes, of which we hear from travellers and navigators.

30. It may be, after all, we have misunderstood his meaning. We have been supposing him to have been meaning to *Ambiguity of the sentence.* assert a *matter of fact*, and to have written, or at least begun, this sentence in the character of an *historical observer*: whereas, all he meant by it, perhaps, was to speak in the character of a *Censor*, and on a case supposed, to express a *sentiment of approbation*. In short, what he meant, perhaps, to persuade us of, was not that 'government' *does actually* 'result' from natural 'society'; but that it were better that it *should*, to wit, as being necessary to 'preserve and keep' men 'in that state of order,' in which it is of advantage to them that they should be. Which of the above-mentioned characters he meant to speak in, is a problem I must leave to be determined. The distinction, perhaps, is what never so much as occurred to him; and indeed the shifting insensibly, and without warning, from one of those characters to the other, is a failing that seems inveterate in our Author; and of which we shall probably have more instances than one to notice.

31. To consider the whole paragraph (with its appendage) *Darkness of the* together, something, it may be seen, our Author struggles *whole paragraph further* to overthrow, and something to establish. But *how* it is *shewn.* he would overthrow, or *what* it is he would establish, are questions I must confess myself unable to resolve. 'The preservation of mankind,' he observes, 'was effected by single families.' This is what upon the authority of the Holy Scriptures, he assumes; and from this it is that he would have us conclude the notion of an original contract (the same notion which he afterwards adopts) to be ridiculous. The force of this conclusion, I must own, I do not see. Mankind was preserved by single families—Be it so. What is there in this to hinder 'individuals' of those families, or of families descended from those families, from meeting together 'afterwards, in a large plain,' or any where else, 'entering into an *original* contract,' or any other contract, 'and choosing the tallest man,' or any other man, 'present,' or absent, to be

their Governor? The 'flat contradiction' our Author finds between this supposed transaction and the 'preservation of mankind by single families,' is what I must own myself unable to discover. As to the 'actually existing unconnected state of nature' he speaks of, 'the notion of which,' he says, 'is too wild to be seriously admitted,' whether this be the case with it, is what, as he has given us no notion of it at all, I cannot judge of.

Farther proofs of the darkness of the whole paragraph.

32. Something positive, however, in one place, we seem to have. These 'single families,' by which the preservation of mankind was effected; these single families, he gives us to understand, 'formed the first society.' This is something to proceed upon. A society then of the one kind or the other; a natural society, or else a political society, was formed. I would here then put a case, and then propose a question. In this society we will say no *contract* had as yet been entered into; no *habit of obedience* as yet formed. Was this then a *natural* society merely, or was it a *political* one? For my part, according to my notion of the two kinds of society as above explained, I can have no difficulty. It was a merely *natural* one. But, according to our Author's notion, which was it? If it *was* already a *political* one, what notion would he give us of such an one as shall have been a *natural* one; and by what change should such precedent natural one have turned into *this* political one? If this was *not* a political one, then what sort of a society are we to understand any one to be which *is* political? By what mark are we to distinguish it from a natural one? To this, it is plain, our Author has not given any answer. At the same time, that to give an answer to it, was, if any thing, the professed purpose of the long paragraph before us.

A general idea of its character.

33. It is time this passage of our Author were dismissed— As among the expressions of it are some of the most striking of those which the vocabulary of the subject furnishes, and these ranged in the most harmonious order, on a distant glance nothing can look fairer: a prettier piece of tinsel-work one shall seldom see exhibited from the show-glass of political erudition. Step close to it, and the delusion vanishes. It is then seen to consist partly of self-evident observations, and partly of contradictions; partly of what every one knows

already, and partly of what no one can understand at
all.

34. Throughout the whole of it, what distresses me is, not *Difficulty*
the meeting with any positions, such as, thinking them false, *attending this*
I find a difficulty in proving so: but the not meeting with any *examination.*
positions, true, or false, (unless it be here and there a self-
evident one,) that I can find a meaning for. If I can find
nothing positive to accede to, no more can I to contradict.
Of this latter kind of work, indeed, there is the less to do for
any one else, our Author himself having executed it, as we
have seen, so amply.

The whole of it is, I must confess, to me a riddle: more
acute, by far, than I am, must be the Oedipus that can solve it.
Happily, it is not necessary, on account of any thing that
follows, that it should be solved. Nothing is concluded from
it. For aught I can find, it has in itself no use, and none is
made of it. There it is, and as well might it be any where
else, or no where.

35. Were it then possible, there would be no use in its *Use that may be*
being solved: but being, as I take it, *really* unsolvable, it were *made of it.*
of use it should *be seen* to be so. Peace may by this means be
restored to the breast of many a desponding student, who,
now prepossessed with the hopes of a rich harvest of instruction, makes a crime to himself of his inability to reap what,
in truth, his Author has not sown.

36. As to the Original Contract, by turns embraced and *Original Con-*
ridiculed by our Author, a few pages, perhaps, may not be *tract, a fiction.*
ill bestowed in endeavouring to come to a precise notion
about its reality and use. The stress laid on it formerly, and
still, perhaps, by some, is such as renders it an object not
undeserving of attention. I was in hopes, however, till I
observed the notice taken of it by our author, that this
chimera had been effectually demolished by Mr. HUME.[1]

---

[1] 1. In the third Volume of his TREATISE *on* HUMAN NATURE.   1. *Notion of the*
Our Author, one would think, had never so much as opened that celebrated *Original Con-*
book: of which the criminality in the eyes of some, and the merits in the eyes *tract overthrown*
of others, have since been almost effaced by the splendour of more recent *by Mr. Hume.*
productions of the same pen. The magnanimity of our Author scorned,
perhaps, or his circumspection feared, to derive instruction from an enemy:
or, what is still more probable, he knew not that the subject had been so much
is touched upon by that penetrating and acute metaphysician, whose works
lie so much out of the beaten track of Academic reading. But here, as it

D

I think we hear not so much of it now as formerly. The indestructible prerogatives of mankind have no need to be supported upon the sandy foundation of a fiction.

happens, there is no matter for such fears. Those men, who are most alarmed at the dangers of a free enquiry; those who are most intimately convinced that the surest way to truth is by hearing nothing but on one side, will, I dare answer almost, find nothing of that which they deem poison in this third volume. I would not wish to send the Reader to any other than this, which, if I recollect aright, stands clear of the objections that have of late been urged with so much vehemence, against the work in general.[a] As to the two first the Author himself, I am inclined to think, is not ill disposed, at present, to join with those who are of opinion, that they might, without any great loss to the science of Human Nature, be dispensed with. The like might be said perhaps, of a considerable part, even of this. But, after all retrenchments, there will still remain enough to have laid mankind under indelible obligations That the foundations of all *virtue* are laid in *utility*, is there demonstrated, after a few exceptions made, with the strongest force of evidence: but I see not any more than Helvetius saw, what need there was for the exceptions.

2. *History of a mind perplexed by fiction.*

2. For my own part, I well remember, no sooner had I read that part of the work which touches on this subject, than I felt as if scales had fallen from my eyes. I then, for the first time, learnt to call the cause of the people the cause of Virtue.

Perhaps a short sketch of the wanderings of a raw but well-intentioned mind, in its researches after moral truth, may, on this occasion, be not unuseful: for the history of one mind is the history of many. The writings of the honest but prejudiced, Earl of Clarendon, to whose integrity nothing was wanting, and to whose wisdom little, but the fortune of living something later; and the contagion of a monkish atmosphere; these, and other concurrent causes, had lifted my infant affections on the side of despotism. The Genius of the place dwelt in, the authority of the state, the voice of the Church in her solemn offices; all these taught me to call Charles a Martyr, and his opponents rebels. I saw innovation, where indeed innovation, but a glorious innovation, was in their efforts to withstand him. I saw falsehood, where indeed falsehood was in their disavowals of innovation. I saw selfishness, and an obedience to the call of passion, in the efforts of the oppressed to rescue themselves from oppression. I saw strong countenance lent in the sacred writings to monarchic government: and none to any other. I saw *passive obedience* deep stamped with the seal of the Christian Virtues of humility and self-denial.

Conversing with Lawyers, I found them full of the virtues of their Original Contract, as a recipe of sovereign efficacy for reconciling the accidental necessity of resistance with the general duty of submission. This drug of theirs they administered to me to calm my scruples. But my unpractised stomach revolted against their opiate. I bid them open to me that page of history in which the solemnization of this important contract was recorded. They shrunk from this challenge; nor could they, when thus pressed, do otherwise than our Author has done, confess the whole to be a fiction. This, methought, looked ill. I seemed to me the acknowledgment of a bad cause, the bringing a fiction to support it. 'To prove fiction, indeed,' said I, 'there is need of fiction; but it is the characteristic of truth to need no proof but truth. Have you then really any such privilege as that of coining facts? You are spending argument to no purpose. Indulge yourselves in the licence of supposing that to be true which is

a By Dr. BEATTIE, in his *Essay on the Immutability of Truth*.

37. With respect to this, and other fictions, there was once *Fictions in* a time, perhaps, when they had their use. With instruments *general mischie-* of this temper, I will not deny but that some political work *present state of* may have been done, and that useful work, which, under the *things.* then circumstances of things, could hardly have been done with any other. But the season of *Fiction* is now over: insomuch, that what formerly might have been tolerated and countenanced under that name, would, if now attempted to be set on foot, be censured and stigmatized under the harsher appellations of *incroachment* or *imposture.* To attempt to introduce any *new* one, would be *now* a crime: for which reason there is much danger, without any use, in vaunting and propagating such as have been introduced already. In point of political discernment, the universal spread of learning has raised mankind in a manner to a level with each other, in comparison of what they have been in any former time: nor is any man now so far elevated above his fellows, as that he should be indulged in the dangerous licence of cheating them for their good.

38. As to the fiction now before us, in the character of an *This had a* *argumentum ad hominem* coming when it did, and managed *momentary use.* as it was, it succeeded to admiration.

That compacts, by whomsoever entered into, *ought* to be kept;—that men are *bound* by compacts, are propositions which men, without knowing or enquiring why, were disposed universally to accede to. The observance of promises they had been accustomed to see pretty constantly enforced. They had been accustomed to see Kings, as well as others, behave themselves as if bound by them. This proposition, then, 'that men are bound by *compacts;*' and this other, 'that, if one party performs not his part, the other is released from his,' being propositions which no man disputed, were propositions which no man had any call to prove. In theory they were assumed for axioms: and in practice they were

not, and as well may you suppose that proposition itself to be true, which you wish to prove, as that other whereby you hope to prove it.' Thus continued I unsatisfying, and unsatisfied, till I learnt to see that *utility* was the test and measure of all virtue; of loyalty as much as any; and that the obligation to minister to general happiness, was an obligation paramount to and inclusive of every other. Having thus got the instruction I stood in need of, I sat down to make my profit of it. I bid adieu to the original contract: and I left it to those to amuse themselves with this rattle, who could think they needed it.

observed as rules.[1] If, on any occasion, it was thought proper to make a show of proving them, it was rather for form's sake than for any thing else: and that, rather in the way of memento or instruction to acquiescing auditors, than in the way of proof against opponents. On such an occasion the common place retinue of phrases was at hand; *Justice, Right Reason* required it, the *Law* of *Nature* commanded it, and so forth; all which are but so many ways of intimating that a man is firmly persuaded of the truth of this or that moral proposition, though he either thinks he *need not*, or finds he *can't*, tell *why*. Men were too obviously and too generally interested in the observance of these rules to entertain doubts concerning the force of any arguments they saw employed in their support.—It is an old observation how Interest smooths the road to Faith.

Terms of the supposed contract stated.

39. A compact, then, it was said, was made by the King and people: the terms of it were to this effect. The people, on their part, promised to the King a *general obedience*. The King, on his part, promised to *govern* the people in such a *particular* manner always, as should be *subservient* to their happiness. I insist not on the words: I undertake only for the sense; as far as an imaginary engagement, so loosely and so variously worded by those who have imagined it, is capable of any decided signification. Assuming then, as a general rule, that promises, when made, ought to be observed; and, as a point of fact, that a promise to this effect in particular had been made by the party in question, men were more ready to deem themselves qualified to judge when it was such a promise was *broken*, than to decide directly and avowedly on the delicate question, when it was that a King acted so far in *opposition* to the happiness of his people, that it were better no longer to obey him.

Stated thus generally, it could not dispense men from entering into the question of utility, as was intended.

40. It is manifest, on a very little consideration, that nothing was gained by this manœuvre after all: no difficulty removed by it. It was still necessary, and that as much as ever, that the question men studied to avoid should be determined, in order to determine the question they thought to

A compact, or contract.

---

[1] A *compact* or *contract* (for the two words on this occasion, at least, are used in the same sense) may, I think, be defined, a pair of promises, by two persons reciprocally given, the one promise in consideration of the other.

substitute in its room. It was still necessary to determine, whether the King in question had, or had not acted so far in *opposition* to the happiness of his people, that it were better no longer to obey him; in order to determine, whether the promise he was supposed to have made, had, or had not been broken. For what was the supposed purport of this promise? It was no other than what has just been mentioned.

41. Let it be said, that part at least of this promise was to govern in *subservience to Law*: that hereby a more precise rule was laid down for his conduct, by means of this supposal of a promise, than that other loose and general rule to govern in subservience to the *happiness of his people*: and that, by this means, it is the letter of the *Law* that forms the tenor of the rule. *Nor, if stated more particularly, could it answer what was designed by it.*

Now true it is, that the governing in opposition to Law, is *one* way of governing in opposition to the happiness of the people: the natural effect of such a contempt of the Law being, if not actually to destroy, at least to threaten with destruction, all those rights and privileges that are founded on it: rights and privileges on the enjoyment of which that happiness depends. But still it is not this that can be safely taken for the entire purport of the promise here in question: and that for several reasons. *First*, Because the most mischievous, and under certain constitutions the most feasible, method of governing in opposition to the happiness of the people, is, by setting the Law itself in opposition to their happiness. *Secondly*, Because it is a case very conceivable, that a King may, to a great degree, impair the happiness of his people without violating the letter of any single Law. *Thirdly*, Because extraordinary occasions may now and then occur, in which the happiness of the people may be better promoted by acting, for the moment, in *opposition* to the Law, than in *subservience* to it. *Fourthly*, Because it is not any single violation of the Law, as such, that can properly be taken for a breach of his part of the contract, so as to be understood to have released the people from the obligation of performing theirs. For, to quit the fiction, and resume the language of plain truth, it is scarce ever any single violation of the Law that, by being *submitted to*, can produce so much mischief as shall surpass the probable mischief of *resisting* it. If every single instance whatever of such a violation were to be deemed an entire dissolution of the contract, a man who reflects at all would scarce find anywhere, I believe, under the sun, that Government which he could allow to subsist for twenty years together. It is plain, therefore, that to pass any sound decision upon the question which the inventors of this fiction substituted instead of the true one, the latter was still necessary to be decided. All they gained by their contrivance was, the convenience of deciding it obliquely, as it were, and by a side wind—that is, in a crude and hasty way, without any direct and steady examination.

Nor is it an original independent principle.

42. But, after all, for what *reason* is it, that men *ought* to keep their promises? The moment any intelligible reason is given, it is this: that it is for the *advantage* of society they should keep them; and if they do not, that, as far as *punishment* will go, they should be *made* to keep them. It is for the advantage of the whole number that the promises of each individual should be kept: and, rather than they should not be kept, that such individuals as fail to keep them should be punished. If it be asked, how this appears? the answer is at hand:—Such is the benefit to gain, and mischief to avoid, by keeping them, as much more than compensates the mischief of so much punishment as is requisite to oblige men to it. Whether the dependence of *benefit* and *mischief* (that is, of *pleasure* and *pain*) upon men's conduct in this behalf, be as here stated, is a question of *fact*, to be decided, in the same manner that all other questions of fact are to be decided, by testimony, observation, and experience.[1]

Nor can it serve to prove anything, but what may be better proved without it.

43. This then, and no other, being the *reason* why men should be made to keep their promises, viz., that it is for the advantage of society that they should, is a reason that may

[1] The importance which the observance of promises is of to the happiness of society, is placed in a very striking and satisfactory point of view, in a little apologue of MONTESQUIEU, entitled *The History of the Troglodytes.*[a] The Troglodytes are a people who pay no regard to promises. By the natural consequences of this disposition, they fall from one scene of misery into another; and are at last exterminated. The same Philosopher, in his *Spirit of Laws,* copying and refining upon the current jargon, feigns a LAW for this and other purposes, after defining a Law to be a *relation.* How much more instructive on this head is the fable of the Troglodytes than the pseudo-metaphysical sophistry of the *Esprit des Loix* !

[a] See the Collection of his Works.

as well be given at once, why *Kings*, on the one hand, in governing, should in general keep within established Laws, and (to speak universally) abstain from all such measures as tend to the unhappiness of their subjects: and, on the other hand, why *subjects* should obey Kings as long as they so conduct themselves, and no longer; why they should obey in short *so long as the probable mischiefs of obedience are less than the probable mischiefs of resistance*: why, in a word, taking the whole body together, it is their *duty* to obey, just so long as it is their *interest*, and no longer.   This being the case, what need of saying of the one, that he PROMISED so to *govern*; of the other, that they PROMISED so to *obey*, when the fact is otherwise?

44. True it is, that, in this country, according to ancient *The Corona-* forms, some sort of vague promise of *good government* is made *tion-oath does* by Kings at the ceremony of their coronation: and let the *not come up to* acclamations, perhaps given, perhaps not given, by chance *the notion of it.* persons out of the surrounding multitude, be construed into a promise of *obedience* on the part of the *whole* multitude: that whole multitude itself, a small drop collected together by chance out of the ocean of the state: and let the two promises thus made be deemed to have formed a perfect *compact*:— not that either of them is declared to be the *consideration* of the other.[1]

45. Make the most of this concession, one experiment *The obligation* there is, by which every reflecting man may satisfy himself, *of a promise will* I think, beyond a doubt, that it is the consideration of *utility*, *not stand against* and no other, that, secretly but unavoidably, has governed his *while that of* judgment upon all these matters.   The experiment is easy and *utility will* decisive.   It is but to reverse, in supposition, in the first place *against that of a* the import of the *particular* promise thus feigned; in the next *promise.* place, the effect in point of *utility* of the observance of promises *in general*.—Suppose the King to promise that he would govern his subjects *not* according to Law; *not* in the view to promote their happiness:—would this be binding upon *him*?   Suppose the people to promise they would obey him *at all events*, let him govern as he will; let him govern to their destruction.   Would this be binding upon *them*? Suppose the constant and universal effect of an observance

[1] V. supra, par. 38, note, p. 52.

of promises were to produce *mischief*, would it *then* be men's *duty* to observe them? Would it *then* be *right* to make Laws, and apply punishment to *oblige* men to observe them?

A fallacy obviated.

46. 'No;' (it may perhaps be replied) 'but for this reason; among promises, some there are that, as every one allows, are void: now these you have been supposing, are unquestionably of the number. A promise that is in itself *void*, cannot, it is true, create any obligation. But allow the promise to be *valid*, and it is the promise itself that creates the obligation, and nothing else.' The fallacy of this argument it is easy to perceive. For what is it then that the promise depends on for its *validity*? what is it that being *present* makes it *valid*? what is it that being *wanting* makes it *void*? To acknowledge that any *one* promise may be void, is to acknowledge that if any *other* is *binding*, it is not merely because it is a promise. That circumstance then, whatever it be, on which the validity of a promise depends, that circumstance, I say, and not the promise itself must, it is plain, be the cause of the obligation on which a promise is apt in general to carry with it.

The obligation of a promise, were it even independent, would not be extensive enough for the purpose.

47. But farther. Allow, for argument sake, what we have disproved: allow that the obligation of a promise is independent of every other: allow that a promise is binding *propriâ vi*—Binding then on whom? On him certainly who makes it. Admit this: For what reason is the same individual promise to be binding on those who *never* made it? The King, *fifty years ago*, promised my *Great-Grandfather* to govern him according to Law: my Great-Grandfather, *fifty years ago*, promised the King to obey him according to Law. The King, *just now*, promised my *neighbour* to govern him according to Law: my neighbour, *just now*, promised the King to obey him according to Law.—Be it so—What are these promises, all or any of them, to *me*? To make answer to this question, some other principle, it is manifest, must be resorted to, than that of the *intrinsic* obligation of promises upon those who make them.

But the principle of UTILITY *is all-sufficient.*

48. Now this *other* principle that still recurs upon us, what other can it be than the *principle of* UTILITY? The principle which furnishes us with that *reason*, which alone depends not upon any higher reason, but which is itself the sole and all-sufficient reason for every point of practice whatsoever.

CHAPTER II

FORMS OF GOVERNMENT

1. THE contents of the whole digression we are examining, *Subject of the* *present chapter.* were distributed, we may remember, at the outset of this Essay, into five divisions. The first, relative to the manner in which Government in general was formed, has already been examined in the preceding chapter. The next, relative to the different *species* or *forms* it may assume, comes now to be considered.

2. The first object that strikes us in this division of our *Theological* *flourish of our* subject is the theological flourish it sets out with. In God *Author.* may be said, though in a peculiar sense, to be our Author's strength. In theology he has found a not unfrequent source, of ornament to divert us, of authority to overawe us, from sounding into the shallowness of his doctrine.[1]

3. That governors, of some sort of other, we must have, *Governors:* is what he has been shewing in the manner we have seen in *celestial endow-* *ments found for* the last chapter. Now for *endowments* to qualify them for the *them.* exercise of their function. These endowments then, as if it were to make them shew the brighter, and to keep them, as much as possible, from being soiled by the rough hands of impertinent speculators, he has chosen should be of æthereal texture, and has fetched them from the clouds.

'All mankind,'[2] he says, 'will agree that government should be reposed in such persons in whom those qualities are most likely to be found, the perfection of which are among the attributes of Him who is emphatically styled the Supreme Being: the three great requisites, I mean, of wisdom, of goodness, and of power.'

But let us see the whole passage as it stands—

4. 'But as all the members of Society,' (meaning *natural* *The passage* Society) 'are naturally EQUAL,' (i.e. I suppose, with respect to *recited.*

---

[1] This is what there would be occasion to shew at large, were what he says of LAW in *general*, and of the LAWS of *nature*, and *revelation* in particular, to be examined.
[2] 1 Comm., p. 48.

political power, of which none of them as yet have any) 'it may be asked,' (continues he) 'in whose hands are the reins of government to be intrusted? To this the general answer is easy; but the application of it to particular cases, has occasioned one half of those mischiefs which are apt to proceed from misguided political zeal. In general, all mankind will agree that government should be reposed in such persons in whom those qualities are most likely to be found, the perfection of which are among the attributes of Him who is emphatically styled the Supreme Being; the three grand requisites, I mean, of wisdom, goodness, and of power: wisdom, to discern the real interest of the community; goodness, to endeavour always to pursue that real interest; and strength or power, to carry this knowledge and intention into action. These are the natural foundations of sovereignty, and these are the requisites that ought to be found in every well-constituted frame of government.'

Theology on such an occasion as this impertinent. 5. Every thing in its place. Theology in a sermon, or a catechism. But in this place, the flourish we have seen, might, for every purpose of instruction, have much better, it should seem, been spared. What purpose the idea of that tremendous and incomprehensible Being thus unnecessarily introduced can answer, I cannot see, unless it were to bewilder and entrance the reader; as it seems to have bewildered and entranced the writer. Beginning thus, is beginning at the wrong end: it is explaining *ignotum per ignotius*. It is not from the attributes of the Deity, that an idea is to be had of any qualities in men: on the contrary, it is from what we see of the qualities of men, that we obtain the feeble idea we can frame to ourselves, of the attributes of the Deity.

Difficulty it leads him into. 6. We shall soon see whether it be light or darkness our Author has brought back from this excursion to the clouds. The qualifications he has pitched upon for those in whose hands Government is to be reposed we see are *three*: wisdom, goodness, and power. Now of these three, one there is which, I doubt, will give him some trouble to know what to do with. I mean that of *Power*: which, looking upon it as a jewel, it should seem, that would give a lustre to the royal diadem, he was for importing from the celestial regions. In heaven, indeed, we shall not dispute its being to be found; and that at all junctures alike. But the parallel, I doubt, already fails. In the earthly governors in question, or, to speak more properly, candidates for government, by the very supposition there can not, at the juncture he supposes, be any such thing. *Power* is that very quality which, in consideration of these other qualities, which, it is supposed, are possessed by them already, they are now waiting to receive.

7. By Power in this place, I, for my part, mean *political* power: the only sort of power our Author could mean: the only sort of power that is here in question. A little farther on we shall find him speaking of this endowment as being possessed, and that in the highest degree, by a King, a single person. *Natural* power therefore, mere organical power, the faculty of giving the hardest blows, can never, it is plain, be that which he meant to number among the attributes of this godlike personage. *Power, either natural or political.*

8. We see then the dilemma our Author's theology has brought him into, by putting him upon reckoning *power* among the qualifications of his candidates. Power is either *natural* or *political*. *Political* power is what they cannot have by the supposition: for that is the very thing that is to be created, and which, by the establishment of Government, men are going to confer on them. If any, then, it must be *natural* power; the natural strength that a man possesses of himself without the help of Government. But of this, then, if this be it, there is more, if we may believe our Author, in a single member of a society, than in that member and all the rest of the society put together.[1] *In neither sense can it be attributed as he attributes it.*

9. This difficulty, if possible, one should be glad to see cleared up. The truth is, I take it, that in what our Author has said of power, he has been speaking, as it were, by anticipation: and that what he means by it, is not any power of either kind actually possessed by any man, or body of men, at the juncture he supposes, but only a *capacity*, if one may call it so, of *retaining* and *putting* into action political power, whensoever it shall have been conferred. Now, of actual power, the quantity that is possessed is, in every case, one and the *What it is that may.*

---

[1] V. infra, par. 32, p. 66. Monarchy, which is the government of *one*, 'is the most powerful form of government,' he says, 'of any:' more so than Democracy, which he describes as being the Government of *all*.

same: for it is neither more nor less than the supreme power. But as to the capacity above spoken of, there do seem, indeed, to be good grounds for supposing it to subsist in a higher degree in a *single* man than in a *body*.

And for what reason.

10. These grounds it will not be expected that I should display at large: a slight sketch will be sufficient.—The efficacy of power is, in part at least, in proportion to the promptitude of obedience: the promptitude of obedience is, in part, in proportion to the promptitude of command:—command is an expression of will: a will is sooner formed by one than many. And this, or something like it, I take to be the plain English of our Author's metaphor, where he tells us,[1] as we shall see a little farther on,[2] that 'a monarchy is the most powerful' [form of government] 'of any, all the sinews of government being knit together, and united in the hands of the prince.'

Heterogeneous contents of the next paragraph.

11. The next paragraph, short as it is, contains variety of matter. The first two sentences of it are to let us know, that with regard to the manner in which each of the *particular* governments that we know of have been formed, he thinks proper to pass it by. A third is to intimate, for the second time, that all governments must be absolute in some hands or other. In the fourth and last, he favours us with a very comfortable piece of intelligence; the truth of which, but for his averment, few of us perhaps would have suspected. This is, that the qualifications mentioned by the last paragraph as *requisite* to be possessed by all Governors of states are, or at least once upon a time were, *actually* possessed by them: i.e. according to the opinion of somebody; but of what somebody is not altogether clear: whether in the opinion of these Governors themselves, or of the persons governed by them.

The paragraph recited.

12. 'How the several forms of government we now see in the world at first actually began,' says our Author, is matter of great uncertainty, and has occasioned infinite disputes. It is not my business or intention to enter into any of them. However they began, or by what right soever they subsist, there is and must be in all of them a supreme, irresistible, absolute, uncontrolled authority, in which the *jura summi imperii*, or the rights of sovereignty, reside. And this authority

[1] Comm., p. 50.   [2] Par. 32.

is placed in those hands, wherein (according to the OPINION of the FOUNDERS of such respective states, either expressly given or collected from their *tacit* APPROBATION) the qualities requisite for supremacy, wisdom, goodness, and power, are the most likely to be found.'

13. Who those persons are whom our Author means here *Paradoxical* by the word *founders*; whether those who became the *assertion in the* Governors of the states in question, or those who became the *latter part of it,* governed, or both together, is what I would not take upon me *as if all govern-* to determine. For aught I know he may have meant neither *ments were the* the one nor the other, but some third person. And, indeed, *result of a free* what I am vehemently inclined to suspect is, that, in our *preference.* Author's large conception, the mighty and extensive domains of ATHENS and SPARTA, of which we read so much at school and at college, consisting each of several score of miles square, represented, at the time this paragraph was writing, the whole universe: and the respective æras of *Solon* and *Lycurgus,* the whole period of the history of those states.

14. The words 'founders,'—'opinion,'—'approbation,'— *Reasons for sup-* in short the whole complexion of the sentence is such as *posing this to* brings to one's view a system of government utterly different *have been the* from the generality of those we have before our eyes; a *meaning of it.* system in which one would think neither caprice, nor violence, nor accident, nor prejudice, nor passion, had any share: a system uniform, comprehensive, and simultaneous; planned with phlegmatic deliberation; established by full and general assent: such, in short, as, according to common imagination, were the systems laid down by the two sages above-mentioned. If this be the case, the object he had in mind when he said *Founders,* might be neither Governors nor governed, but some *neutral* person: such as those sages, chosen as they were in a manner as umpires, might be considered with regard to the persons who, under the prior constitution, whatever it was, had stood respectively in those two relations.

15. All this, however, is but conjecture: In the proposition *The doctrine of* itself neither this, nor any other restriction is expressed. It is *it applied to* delivered explicitly and emphatically in the character of an *particular in-* universal one. 'In ALL OF THEM,' he assures us, 'this authority,' *stances.* (the supreme authority) '*is* placed in those hands, wherein, according to the *opinion* of the *founders* of such respective

states, these 'qualities of wisdom, goodness, and power,' are the most likely to be found.' In this character it cannot but throw a singular light on history. I can see no end, indeed, to the discoveries it leads to, all of them equally new and edifying. When the Spaniards, for example, became masters of the empire of Mexico, a vulgar politician might suppose it was because such of the Mexicans as remained unexterminated, could not help it. No such thing—It was because the *Applied to par-* Spaniards were of 'opinion' or the Mexicans themselves were *ticular instances.* of 'opinion' (which of the two is not altogether clear) that in Charles V, and his successors, more goodness (of which they had such abundant proofs) as well as wisdom, was likely to be found, than in all the Mexicans put together. The same persuasion obtained between Charlemagne and the German Saxons with respect to the goodness and wisdom of Charlemagne:—between William the Norman and the English Saxons:—between Mahomet II and the subjects of John Paleologus:—between Odoacer and those of Augustulus:—between the Tartar Gingiskan and the Chinese of his time:—between the Tartars Chang-ti and Cam-ghi, and the Chinese of their times:—between the Protector Cromwell and the Scotch:—between Cæsar and the Gauls:—in short, between the Thirty Tyrants, so called, and the Athenians, whom our Author seems to have had in view:—to mention these examples only, out of as many hundred as might be required. All this, if we may trust our Author, he has the '*goodness*' to believe: and by such lessons is the penetration of *General contents* students to be sharpened for piercing into the depths of *of the six remain-* politics.

ing paragraphs 16. So much for the introductory paragraph.—The main *relating to the* part of the subject is treated of in six others: the general *subject of this* *chapter.* contents of which are as follow.

Of the first 17. In the first he tells us how many different forms of *paragraph.* government there are according to the division of the ancients: which division he adopts. These are three: Monarchy, Aristocracy, and Democracy.

Second. 18. The next is to tell us, that by the *sovereign* POWER he means that of '*making laws*.'

Third. 19. In a third he gives us the advantages and disadvantages of these three different forms of government.

20. In a fourth he tells us that these are all the ancients *Fourth.* would allow of.

21. A fifth is to tell us that the British form of government *Fifth.* is different from each of them; being a combination of all, and possessing the advantages of all.

22. In the sixth, and last, he shews us that it could not *Sixth.* possess these advantages, if, instead of being what it is, it were either of those others: and tells us what it is that may destroy it. These two last it will be sufficient here to mention: to examine them will be the task of our next chapter.

23. Monarchy is that form of Government in which the *Definitions of* power of making Laws is lodged in the hands of a *single the three sorts of* member of the state in question. Aristocracy is that form of *governments* Government in which the power of making laws is lodged *according to our* in the hands of *several* members. Democracy is that form of *Author.* government in which the power of making laws is lodged in the hands of '*all*' of them put together. These, according to our Author, are the definitions of the ancients; and these, therefore, without difficulty, are the definitions of our Author.

24. 'The political writers of antiquity,' says he, 'will not *The paragraph* allow more than three regular forms of government; the *recited.* first, when the sovereign power is lodged in an aggregate assembly, consisting of all the members of a community, which is called a Democracy; the second, when it is lodged in a council composed of select members, and then it is styled an Aristocracy; the last, when it is entrusted in the hands of a single person, and then it takes the name of a Monarchy. All other species of governments they say are either corruptions of, or reducible to these three.'

25. 'By the sovereign power, as was before observed, is *And the next.* meant the making of laws; for wherever that power resides, all others must conform to, and be directed by it, whatever appearance the outward form and administration of the government may put on. For it is at any time in the option of the legislature to alter that form and administration by a new edict or rule, and to put the execution of the laws into whatever hands it pleases; and all the other powers of the state must obey the legislative power in the execution of their several functions, or else the constitution is at an end.'

26. Having thus got three regular simple forms of Government (this anomalous complex one of our own out of the question) and just as many qualifications to divide among them; of each of which, by what he told us a while ago, each form of Government must have some share, it is easy to see how their allotments will be made out. Each form of Government will possess one of these qualities in perfection, taking its chance, if one may say so, for its share in the two others.

27. Among these three different forms of Government then, it should seem according to our Author's account of them, there is not much to choose. Each of them has a *qualification*, an *endowment*, to itself. Each of them is completely characterized by this qualification. No intimation is given of any pre-eminence among these qualifications, one above another. Should there be any dispute concerning the preference to be given to any of these forms of government, as proper a method as any of settling it, to judge from this view of them, is that of cross and pile. Hence we may infer, that all the governments that ever were, or will be (except a very particular one that we shall come to presently, that is to say our own) are upon a par: that of ATHENS with that of PERSIA; that of GENEVA with that of MOROCCO: since they are all of them, he tells us, 'corruptions of, or reducible to,' one of these. This is happy. A legislator cannot do amiss. He may save himself the expense of thinking. The choice of a king was once determined, we are told, by the neighing of a horse. The choice of a form of Government might be determined so as well.

28. As to our own form of government, however, this, it is plain, being that which it seemed good to take for the theme of his panegyric, and being made out of the other three, will possess the advantages of all of them put together; and that without any of the disadvantages; the disadvantages vanishing at the word of command, or even without it, as not being suitable to the purpose.

29. At the end of the paragraph which gives us the above definitions, one observation there is that is a little puzzling. 'Other species of government,' we are given to understand, there are besides these; but then those others, if not 'reducible

to,' are but 'corruptions of these.' Now, what there is in any *three, described* of these to be corrupted, is not so easy to understand. The *as they are by him.* essence of these several forms of government, we must always remember, is placed by him, solely and entirely, in the article of *number*: in the ratio of the number of the Govern*ors*, (for so for shortness we will style those in whose hands is lodged this 'power of making laws') to that of the govern*ed*. If the number of the former be, to that of the latter, as *one* to *all*, then is the form of Government a Monarchy: if as *all* to *all*, then is it a Democracy: if as some number *between one and all* to *all*, then is it an Aristocracy. Now then, if we can conceive a fourth number, which not being more than all, is neither one nor all, nor anything between one and all, we can conceive a form of Government, which, upon due proof, may appear to be a corruption of some one or other of these three.[1] If not, we must look for the corruption somewhere else: Suppose it were in our Author's *reason*.[2]

30. Not but that we may meet, indeed, with several other *Governments* hard-worded names for forms of Government: but these *the same as these* names were only so many names for one or other of those *under other* three. We hear often of a *Tyranny*: but this is neither more *names.* nor less than the name a man gives to our Author's Monarchy, when out of humour with it. It is still the government of number *one*. We hear now and then, too, of a sort of Government called an *Oligarchy*: but this is neither more nor less than the name a man gives to our Author's Aristocracy, in the same case. It is still the Government of some number or other, *between one and all*. In fine, we hear now and then of a sort of government fit to break one's teeth, called an *Ochlocracy*: but this is neither more nor less than the name a

---

[1] By the laws of GERMANY, such and such states are to furnish so many men to the general army of the empire: some of them so many men and one half; others, so many and one third; others again, if I mistake not, so many and one fourth. One of these half, third-part, or quarter-men, suppose, possesses himself of the Government: here then we have a kind of corruption of a Monarchy. Is this what our Author had in view?

[2] A more suitable place to look for *corruption* in, if we may take his own word for it, there cannot be. 'Every man's reason,' he assures us,[a] 'is corrupt;' and not only that, but 'his understanding full of ignorance and error.' With regard to others, it were as well not to be too positive: but with regard to a man's self, what he tells us from experience, it would be ill manners to dispute with him.

[a] 1 Comm., p. 41.

E

man gives to a Democracy in the same case. It is still that sort of government, which, according to our Author, is the Government of *all*.

Qualifications of the three forms, how allotted—the subject resumed.   31. Let us now see how he has disposed of his three qualifications among his three sorts or forms of Government. Upon Monarchy, we shall find, he has bestowed the perfection of power; on Aristocracy, of wisdom; on Democracy, of goodness; each of these forms having just enough, we may suppose, of the two remaining qualifications besides its own peculiar one to make up the necessary complement of 'qualities requisite for supremacy.' Kings are, (nay *were* before they were Kings, since it was this qualification determined their subjects to make them Kings,[1]) as strong as so many Hercules's; but then, as to their wisdom, or their goodness, there is not much to say. The members of an Aristocracy are so many Solomons; but then they are not such sturdy folks as your Kings; nor, if the truth is to be spoken, have they much more honesty than their neighbours. As to the members of a Democracy, they are the best sort of people in the world; but then they are but a puny sort of gentry, as to strength, put them all together; and are apt to be a little defective in point of understanding.

The paragraph recited.   32. 'In a democracy,' says he, 'where the right of making laws resides in the people at large, public virtue or goodness of intention, is more likely to be found, than either of the other qualities of government. Popular assemblies are frequently foolish in their contrivance, and weak in their execution; but generally mean to do the thing that is right and just, and have always a degree of patriotism or public spirit. In aristocracies there is more wisdom to be found than in the other frames of Government; being composed, or intended to be composed, of the most experienced citizens; but there is less honesty than in a republic, and less strength than in a monarchy. A monarchy is indeed the most powerful of any, all the sinews of government being knit together and united in the hand of the prince; but then there is imminent danger of his employing that strength to improvident or oppressive purposes.'

[1] 1 Comm., p. 48.

33. 'Thus these three species of government have all of *And the next.*
them their several perfections and imperfections. Democracies
are usually the best calculated to direct the end of a law;
aristocracies to invent the means by which that end shall be
obtained; and monarchies to carry those means into execution. And the ancients, as was observed, had in general no
idea of any other permanent form of government but these
three; for though Cicero declares himself of opinion, *esse
optimé constitutam rempublicam, quae ex tribus generibus illis,
regali, optimo, et populari sit modicé confusa*; yet Tacitus treats
this notion of a mixed government, formed out of them all,
and partaking of the advantages of each, as a visionary whim;
and one, that if effected, could never be lasting or secure.'

34. In the midst of this fine-spun ratiocination, an accident *Democracy, as*
has happened, of which our Author seems not to be aware. *described by him,*
One of his *accidents*, as a logician would say, has lost its *no Government*
at all.
subject: one of the *qualifications* he has been telling us of, is,
somehow or other, become vacant: the form of Government
he designed it for, having unluckily slipped through his
fingers in the handling. I mean Democracy; which he, and,
according to him, the Ancients, make out to be the Government of *all*. Now '*all*' is a great many; so many that, I much
doubt, it will be rather a difficult matter to find these high and
mighty personages power enough, so much as to make a
decent figure with. The members of this redoubtable
Commonwealth will be still worse off, I doubt, in point of
subjects, than *Trinculo* in the play, or than the potentates,
whom some late navigators found lording it, with might
and main, 'κρατέρηφι βίηφι,' over a Spanish settlement: there
were three members of the Government; and they had one
subject among them all.[1] Let him examine it a little, and it
will turn out, I take it, to be precisely that sort of Government, and no other, which one can conceive to obtain,
where there is no Government at all. Our Author, we may

[1] See HAWKESWORTH'S *Voyages*.
The condition of these imaginary sovereigns puts one in mind of the story
of, I forget what King's Fool. The Fool had stuck himself up one day, with
great gravity, in the King's throne, with a stick, by way of a sceptre, in one
hand, and a ball in the other: being asked what he was doing, he answered
'reigning.' Much the same sort of reign, I take it, would be that of the members
of our Author's Democracy.

remember, had shrewd doubts about the existence of a *state of nature*:[1] grant him his Democracy, and it exists in his Democracy.[2]

The qualification designed for it become vacant.

35. The qualification of *goodness*, I think it was, that belonged to the Government of *all*, while there was such a Government. This having taken its flight, as we have seen, to the region of nonentities, the qualification that was designed for it remains upon his hands: he is at liberty, therefore, to make a compliment of it to Aristocracy or to Monarchy, which best suits him. Perhaps it were as well to give it to Monarchy; the title of that form of Government to its own peculiar qualification, *power*, being, as we have seen, rather an equivocal one: or else, which, perhaps, is as good a way of settling matters as any, he may set them to cast lots.

[1] V. supra, ch. I, par. 6.

[2] What is curious is, that the same persons who tell you (having read as much) that Democracy is a form of Government under which the supreme power is vested in all the members of a state, will also tell you (having also read as much) that the Athenian Commonwealth was a Democracy. Now the truth is, that in the Athenian Commonwealth, upon the most moderate computation, it is not one tenth part of the inhabitants of the Athenian state that ever at a time partook of the supreme power: women, children, and slaves, being taken into the account.[a] Civil Lawyers, indeed, will tell you, with a grave face, that a slave is *nobody*; as Common Lawyers will, that a bastard is the *son* of *nobody*. But, to an unprejudiced eye, the condition of a state is the condition of all the individuals, without distinction, that compose it.

[a] See, among Mr. HUME's *Essays*, that *on the populousness of ancient nations*.

CHAPTER III

BRITISH CONSTITUTION

1. With a set of *data*, such as we have seen in the last chapter, *Our Author's panegyric on the British Constitution.* we may judge whether our Author can meet with any difficulty in proving the British Constitution to be the best of all possible governments, or indeed any thing else that he has a mind. In his paragraph on this subject there are several things that lay claim to our attention. But it is necessary we should have it under our eye.

2. 'But happily for us in this island the British Constitution *The paragraph recited.* has long remained, and I trust will long continue, a standing exception to the truth of this observation. For, as with us the executive power of the laws is lodged in a single person, they have all the advantages of strength and dispatch that are to be found in the most absolute monarchy: and, as the legislature of the kingdom is entrusted to three distinct powers entirely independent of each other; first, the King; secondly, the Lords Spiritual and Temporal, which is an aristocratical assembly of persons selected for their piety, their birth, their wisdom, their valour, or their property; and thirdly, the House of Commons, freely chosen by the people from among themselves, which makes it a kind of democracy; as this aggregate body, actuated by different springs, and attentive to different interests, composes the British Parliament, and has the supreme disposal of every thing; there can no inconvenience be attempted by either of the three branches, but will be withstood by one of the other two; each branch being armed with a negative power sufficient to repel any innovation which it shall think inexpedient or dangerous.'

3. 'Here then is lodged the sovereignty of the British *And that which follows it.* Constitution; and lodged as beneficially as is possible for society. For in no other shape could we be so certain of finding the three great qualities of Government so well and so happily united. If the supreme power were lodged in any one of the three branches separately, we must be exposed to

the inconveniencies of either absolute monarchy, aristocracy, or democracy; and so want two of the principal ingredients of good polity, either virtue, wisdom, or power. If it were lodged in any two of the branches; for instance, in the King and House of Lords, our laws might be providently made and well executed, but they might not always have the good of the people in view: if lodged in the King and Commons, we should want that circumspection and mediatory caution, which the wisdom of the Peers is to afford: if the supreme rights of legislature were lodged in the two Houses only, and the King had no negative upon their proceedings, they might be tempted to encroach upon the royal prerogative, or perhaps to abolish the kingly office, and thereby weaken (if not totally destroy) the strength of the executive power. But the constitutional government of this island is so admirably tempered and compounded, that nothing can endanger or hurt it, but destroying the equilibrium of power between one branch of the legislature and the rest. For if ever it should happen that the independence of any one of the three should be lost, or that it should become subservient to the views of either of the other two, there would soon be an end of our constitution. The legislature would be changed from that which was originally set up by the general consent and fundamental act of the society; and such a change, however effected, is, according to Mr. Locke (who perhaps carries his theory too far) at once an entire dissolution of the bands of Government, and the people would be reduced to a state of anarchy, with liberty to constitute to themselves a new legislative power.'

Executive power—the mention of it incongruously introduced.

4. In considering the first of these two paragraphs, in the first place, the phenomenon we should little expect to see from any thing that goes before, is a certain *executive power*, that now, for the first time, bolts out upon us without warning or introduction.

The power, the only power our Author has been speaking of all along till now, is the *legislative*. 'Tis to this, and this alone, that he has given the name of 'sovereign power.' 'Tis this power, the different distributions of which he makes the characteristics of his three different forms of government. 'Tis with these different distributions, distributions made of

the legislative power, that, according to his account, are
connected the several qualifications laid down by him, 'as
requisites for supremacy:' qualifications in the possession of
which consist all the advantages which can belong to any
form of Government. Coming now then to the British
Constitution, it is in the superior degree in which these
qualifications of the legislative body are possessed by it, that
its peculiar excellence is to consist. It is by possessing the
qualification of strength, that it possesses the advantage of a
monarchy. But how is it then that, by his account, it possesses
the qualification of strength? By any disposition made of the
legislative power? By the legislative power's being lodged in
the hands of a single person, as in the case of a monarchy?
No; but to a disposition made of a new power, which comes
in, as it were, in a parenthesis, a new power which we now
hear of for the first time, a power which has not, by any
description given of it, been distinguished from the legislative,
an *executive*.

5. What then is this same executive power? I doubt our *Difficulty of*
Author would not find it a very easy matter to inform us. *determining*
'Why not?' says an objector—'is it not that power which in *what it is as*
this country the King has in addition to his share in the *contra-distinct to*
legislative?' Be it so: the difficulty for a moment is staved off. *legislative.*
But that it is far enough from being solved, a few questions
will soon show us. This power, is it that only which the
King really *has*, or is it all that he is said to have? Is it that only
which he really has, and which he exercises, or is it that also,
which although he be said to have it, he neither does exercise,
nor may exercise? Does it include judiciary power or not?
If it does, does it include the power of making as well
particular decisions and orders, as *general*, *permanent*, *spontaneous* regulations of procedure, such as are some of those we
see made by judges? Doth it include supreme military power
and that as well in ordinary as in a time of martial law? Doth
it include the supreme *fiscal* power;[1] and, in general, that
power which, extending as well over the public money as
over every other article of public property, may be styled

---

[1] By *fiscal* power I mean that which in this country is exercised by what is
called the Board of Treasury.

the *dispensatorial*[1]? Doth it include the power of granting patents for inventions, and charters of incorporation? Doth it include the right of making bye-laws in corporations? And is the right of making bye-laws in corporations the superior right to that of conferring the power to make them, or is it that there is an executive power that is superior to a legislative? This *executive* again, doth it include the right of substituting the laws of war to the laws of peace; and *vice versa*, the laws of peace to the laws of war? Doth it include the right of restraining the trade of subjects by treaties with foreign powers? Doth it include the right of delivering over, by virtue of the like treaties, large bodies of subjects to foreign laws?—He that would understand what power is executive and not legislative, and what legislative and not executive, he that would mark out and delineate the different species of constitutional powers, he that would describe either what *is*, or what *ought to be* the constitution of a country, and particularly of this country, let him *think of these things*.

Independence inaccurately attributed to the three branches of the Government.

6. In the next place we are told in a parenthesis (it being a matter so plain as to be taken for granted) that 'each of these branches of the Legislature is *independent*,'—yes, '*entirely independent*,' of the two others.—Is this then really the case? Those who consider the influence which the King and so many of the Lords have in the election of members of the House of Commons; the power which the King has, at a minute's warning, of putting an end to the existence of any House of Commons, those who consider the influence which the King has over both Houses, by offices of dignity and profit given and taken away again at pleasure; those who consider

---

[1] By *dispensatorial* power I mean as well that which is exercised by the Board of Treasury, as those others which are executed in the several offices styled with us the War Office, Admiralty Board, Navy Board, Board of Ordnance, and Board of Works: excepting from the business of all these offices, the power of appointing persons to fill other subordinate offices: a power which seems to be of a distinct nature from that of making disposition of any article of public property.

Power, political power, is either over *persons* or over *things*. The powers, then, that have been mentioned above, in as far as they concern *things*, are powers over such *things* as are the property of the public: powers which differ in this from those which constitute private ownership, in that the former are, in the main, not *beneficial* (that is, to the possessors themselves) and *indiscriminate*; but *fiduciary*, and *limited* in their exercise to such *acts* as are conducive to the *special* purposes of *public* benefit and security.

that the King, on the other hand, depends for his daily bread on both Houses, but more particularly on the House of Commons; not to mention a variety of other circumstances that might be noticed in the same view, will judge what degree of precision there was in our Author's meaning, when he so roundly asserted the affirmative.

7. One parenthesis more: for this sentence teems with parenthesis within parenthesis. To this we are indebted for a very interesting piece of intelligence: nothing less than a full and true account of the personal merits of the members of the House of Lords for the time being. This he is enabled to do by means of a contrivance of his own, no less simple than it is ingenious: to wit, that of looking at their titles. It is by looking at men's titles that he perceives, not merely that they *ought* to possess certain merits, not that there is reason to *wish* they may possess them, but that they do *actually* possess them, and that it is by possessing those merits that they came to possess these titles. Seeing that some are bishops, he knows that they are pious: seeing that some are peers, he knows that they are wise, rich, valiant.[1]

A happy discovery: merit inseparable from high station.

---

[1] 'The Lords spiritual and temporal, [p. 50] which, says our Author, '*is* an aristocratical assembly of persons selected for their piety, their birth, their wisdom, their valour, or their property.'

I have distributed, I think, these endowments, as our Author could but intend they should be distributed. Birth, to such of the members of that assembly as have their seat in it by *descent*: and, as to those who may chance from time to time to sit there by *creation*, wisdom, valour, and property in *common* among the temporal peers; and piety, singly but entirely, among my Lords the Bishops. As to the other three endowments, if there were any of them to which these right reverend persons could lay any decent claim, it would be wisdom: but since worldly wisdom is what it would be an ill compliment to attribute to them, and the wisdom which is from above is fairly included under piety, I conclude that, when secured in the exclusive possession of this grand virtue, they have all that was intended them. There is a remarkable period in our history, at which, measuring by our Author's scale, these three virtues seem to have been at the boiling point. It was in Queen Anne's reign, not long after the time of the hard frost. I mean in the year 1711. In that auspicious year, these three virtues issued forth, it seems, with such exuberance, as to furnish merit enough to stock no fewer than a dozen respectable persons, who, upon the strength of it, were all made Barons in a day. Unhappily indeed, so little read was a right reverend and contemporary historian,[a] in our Author's method of 'discerning of spirits,' as to fancy, it was neither more nor less than the necessity of making a majority that introduced so large a body of new members thus suddenly into the house. But I leave it to those who are read in the history of that time, to judge of the ground there

[a] See Bishop Burnet's History of his own Times. Vol. 2.

Supposed quali-
ties of the three
pretended forms
of Government
not applicable to
our own.

8. The more we consider the application he makes of the common-place notions concerning the three forms of Government to our own, the more we shall see the wide difference there is between reading and reflecting. Our own he finds to be a combination of these three. It has a Monarchical branch, an Aristocratical, and a Democratical. The Aristocratical is the House of Lords; the Democratical is the House of Commons. Much had our Author read, at school, doubtless, and at college, of the wisdom and gravity of the Spartan senate: something, probably, in Montesquieu, and elsewhere, about the Venetian. He had read of the turbulence and extravagance of the Athenian mob. Full of these ideas, the House of Lords were to be our Spartans or Venetians; the House of Commons, our Athenians. With respect then to the point of wisdom, (for that of honesty we will pass by) the consequence is obvious. The House of Commons, however excellent in point of honesty, is an assembly of less *wisdom* than that of the House of Lords. This is what our Author makes no scruple of assuring us. A Duke's son gets a seat in the House of Commons. There needs no more to make him the very model of an Athenian cobbler.

Wisdom: why
likely to be
wanting in the
members of a
Democracy—

9. Let us find out, if we can, whence this notion of the want of wisdom in the members of a Democracy, and of the abundance of it in those of an Aristocracy, could have had its rise. We shall then see with what degree of propriety such a notion can be transferred to *our* Houses of Lords and Commons.

In the members of a Democracy in particular, there is likely to be a want of wisdom—Why? The greater part being poor, are, when they begin to take upon them the management of affairs, uneducated: being uneducated, they are illiterate: being illiterate, they are ignorant. Ignorant, therefore, and *unwise*, if that be what is meant by ignorant, they *begin*. Depending for their daily bread on the profits of some

can be for so romantic an imagination. As to piety, the peculiar endowment of the mitre, the stock there is of that virtue, should, to judge by the like standard, be, at all times, pretty much upon a level: at all times, without question, at a *maximum*. This is what we can make the less doubt of, since, with regard to ecclesiastical matters, in general, our Author, as in another place he assures us, has had the happiness to find, that 'every thing is as it should be.'[b]

petty traffic, or the labour of some manual occupation, they are nailed to the work-board, or the counter. In the business of Government, it is only by fits and starts that they have leisure so much as to *act*: they have no leisure to *reflect*. Ignorant therefore they *continue*.—But in what degree is this the case with the members of our House of Commons?

10. On the other hand, the members of an Aristocracy, *—and present* being few, are rich: either they are members of the Aristo- *in those of an* cracy, because they are rich; or they are rich, because they *Aristocracy.* are members of the Aristocracy. Being rich, they are educated: being educated, they are learned: being learned, they are knowing. They are at leisure to *reflect*, as well as *act*. They may therefore naturally be expected to become more knowing, that is more wise, as they persevere. In what degree is this the case with the members of the House of Lords more than with those of the House of Commons? The fact is, as every body sees, that either the members of the House of Commons are as much at leisure as those of the House of Lords; or, if occupied, occupied in such a way as tends to give them a more than ordinary insight into some particular department of Government. In whom shall we expect to find so much knowledge of Law as in a professed Lawyer? of Trade, as in a Merchant?

11. But hold—Our Author, when he attributes to the *Why, according* members of an Aristocracy more wisdom than to those of a *to our Author.* Democracy, has a reason of his own. Let us endeavour to understand it, and then apply it, as we have applied the others. In Aristocratical bodies, we are to understand there is more *experience*; at least it is intended by some body or other there *should be*: which, it seems, answers the same purpose as if there *was*. 'In Aristocracies,' says our Author, 'there is more wisdom to be found, than in the other frames of Government; being composed,' continues he, 'or intended to be composed, of the most experienced citizens.'[1] On this ground then it is, that we are to take for granted, that the members of the House of Lords have more wisdom among them, than those of the House of Commons. It is this article of *experience* that, being a qualification possessed by the members of an Aristocratical body, as such, in a superior degree to that in which it

[1] p. 50.

can be possessed by a democratical body, is to afford us a particular ground for attributing a greater share of wisdom to the members of the upper house, than to those of the lower.

Superiority of 'experience,' how far a proof of superiority of wisdom.

12. How is it that a member of an aristocracy, as such, is, of all things, to have attained more *experience* than the member of a democracy, our Author has not told us; nor what it is this experience is to consist of. Is it experience of things *preparatory* to, but different from, the business of governing? This should rather go by the name of *knowledge*. Is it experience of the business itself of governing? Let us see. For the member of the one body, as of the other, there must be a time when he first enters, upon this business. They both enter upon it, suppose, on the same day. Now then is it on that same day that one is more experienced in it than the other? or is it on that day ten years?

How far attributable to aristocracies in general.

13. Those indeed who recollect what we observed but now,[1] may answer without hesitation,—on that day ten years. The reason was there given. It is neither more nor less, than that want of leisure which the bulk of the numerous members of a Democracy must necessarily labour under, more than those of an Aristocracy. But of this, what intimation is there to be collected, from any thing that has been suggested by our Author?

How far to our House of Lords in particular.

14. So much with respect to Aristocracies in general. It happens also by accident, that that particular branch of our *own* government to which he has given the name of the Aristocratical,—the House of Lords,—has actually greater opportunities of acquiring the qualification of experience, than that other branch, the House of Commons, to which he has given the name of the democratical. But to what is this owing? not to any thing in the characteristic natures of those two bodies, not to the one's being Aristocratical, and the other Democratical; but to a circumstance, entirely foreign and accidental, which we shall see presently. But let us observe his reasoning. The House of Lords, he says, is an assembly that behoves to have more wisdom in it, than the House of Commons. This is the proposition. Now for the proof. The first is an Aristocratical assembly; the second a

---

[1] V. supra, par. 9.

Democratical. An Aristocratical assembly has more experience than a Democratical; and on that account more wisdom. Therefore the House of Lords, as was to be proved, has more wisdom than the House of Commons. Now, what the whole of the argument rests upon, we may observe, is this fact, that an Aristocratical assembly, as such, has more experience than a Democratical one; but this, with Aristocratical assemblies in general, we see, is not, for any reason that our Author has given us, the case. At the same time with respect to our House of Lords in particular, in comparison with the House of Commons, it does happen to be the case, owing to this simple circumstance: the members of the House of Lords, when once they begin to sit, sit on for life: those of the House of Commons only from seven years to seven years, or it may happen, less.

15. In speaking, however, in this place, of experience, I would rather be understood to mean opportunity of acquiring experience, than experience itself. For actual experience depends upon other concurrent causes.

What is to be understood by the word 'experience.'

16. It is, however, from superiority of experience alone, that our Author derives superiority of wisdom. He has, indeed, the proverb in his favour: 'Experience,' it has been said of old, 'is the Mother of Wisdom:' be it so;—but then Interest is the Father. There is even an Interest that is the Father of Experience. Among the members of the House of Commons, though none so poor as to be illiterate, are many whose fortunes, according to the common phrase, are yet to make. The fortunes of those of the House of Lords (I speak in general) are made already. The members of the House of Commons may hope to be members of the House of Lords. The members of the House of Lords have no higher House of Lords to rise to. Is it natural for those to be most active who have the *least*, or those who have the *most* interest to be so? Are the experienced those who are the least, or those who are the most active? Does experience come to men when asleep, or when awake? Is it the members of the House of Lords that are the most active, or of the House of Commons? To speak plain, is it in the House of Lords that there is most business done, or in the House of Commons? Was it *after* the *fish* was caught that the successor of St. Peter used the

Opportunity of experience not the sole cause of wisdom.

net, or was it *before*?[1] In a word is there most wisdom ordinarily where there is least, or where there is most to gain by being wise.[2]

17. A word or two more with respect to the characteristic qualifications, as our Author states them, of the higher assembly of our legislature. Experience is, in virtue of their being an aristocratical assembly, to afford them wisdom: thus far we were arrived before. But he now pushes the deduction a step farther.—Wisdom is to afford them 'circumspection and mediatory caution'; qualifications which it seems as if we should see nothing of, were it not for them. Let us now put a case. The business, indeed, that originates in the House of Lords is, as things stand, so little, that our Author seems to forget that there is any. However, some there is. A bill then originates with the Lords, and is sent down to the Commons.—As to 'circumspection' I say nothing: *that*, let us hope, is not wanting to either House. But whose province is 'mediatory caution,' now?

18. Thus much concerning these two branches of our legislature, so long as they continue what, according to our Author's principles, they are at present: the House of Lords the Aristocratical branch: the House of Commons the Democratical. A little while and we shall see them so; but again a little while, perhaps, and we shall not see them so. By what characteristic does our Author distinguish an Aristocratical legislative body from a Democratical one? By that of *number*: by the number of the persons that compose them: by that, and that alone: for no other has he given.

---

[1] Every body has heard the story of him who, from a fisherman, was made Archbishop, and then Pope. While Archbishop, it was his custom every day, after dinner, to have a fishing net spread upon his table, by way of a memento, as he used to say, of the meanness of his original. This farcical ostentation of humility was what, in those days, contributed not a little to the increase of his reputation. Soon after his exaltation to St. Peter's chair, one of his intimates was taking notice to him, one day when dinner was over, of the table's not being decked as usual. 'Peace,' answered the Holy Father, 'when the fish is caught, there is no occasion for the net.'

[2] In the House of Commons itself, is it by the opulent and independent Country gentlemen that the chief business of the House is transacted, or by aspiring, and perhaps needy Courtiers? The man who would persevere in the toil of Government, without any other reward than the favour of the people, is certainly the man for the people to make choice of. But such men are at best but rare. Were it not for those children of Corruption we have been speaking of, the business of the state, I doubt, would stagnate.

Now, therefore, to judge by that, the House of Lords, at present, indeed, *is* the Aristocratical branch: the House of Commons in comparison at least with the other, the Democratical. Thus far is well. But should the list of nobility swell at the rate we have sometimes seen it, there is an assignable period, and that, perhaps, at no very enormous distance, at which the assembly of the Lords will be more numerous than that of the Commons. Which will *then* be the Aristocratical branch of our Legislature? Upon our Author's principles, the House of Commons. Which the Democratical? The House of Lords.

19. The final cause we are to observe, and finishing exploit, *All-perfection of the British Constitution mathematically demonstrated.* the '*portus et sabbatum*,' as Lord Bacon might perhaps have called it,[1] of this sublime and edifying dissertation, is this demonstration, he has been giving us, of the perfection of the British Form of Government. This demonstration (for by no less a title ought it to be called) is founded, we may have observed, altogether upon the properties of *numbers*: properties, newly discovered indeed, and of an extraordinary complexion, *moral* properties; but properties, however, so it seems, of numbers.[2] 'Tis in the nature then of numbers we shall find these characteristic properties of the three Forms of Government, if anywhere. Now the properties of numbers are universally allowed to be the proper subject of that mode of demonstration which is called *mathematical*. The proof our Author has given has therefore already in it the *essence* of such a demonstration. To be complete at all points, it wants nothing but the *form*. This deficiency is no other than what an under-rate workman might easily supply. A mere technical operation does the business. That humble task it shall be my endeavour to perform. The substantial honour I ascribe wholly to our Author, to whom only it is most due.

[1] It is what he says of Theology with respect to the Sciences.—V. Augm. Scient. L. VIII. c. III. p. 97.
[2] V. supra, ch. II. pars. 24, 32, pp. 63, 66.

The demonstra- 20. PROPOSITION.   *THEOREM.*
tion drawn up in
form.   The British Government is all-perfect.

DEMONSTRATION

By definition,	1	The British Government=Monarchy+ Aristocracy+Democracy.
Again, by definition,	2	Monarchy=the Government of 1.
Also,	3	Democracy=the Government of *all.*
Also,	4	Aristocracy=the Government of some number between 1 and *all.*
Put	5	*All*=1,000,000.
Put also	6	The number of governors in an Aristocracy=1,000.
Now then, by assumption,	7	1 has +strength—wisdom—honesty.
Also,	8	1,000 has +wisdom—strength— honesty.
Also,	9	1,000,000 has +honesty—strength— wisdom.
Rejecting—wisdom—honesty[1] in [7]	10	1 has +strength.
Also rejecting— strength—wisdom in [8]	11	1,000 has +wisdom.
Also rejecting — strength—wisdom in [9]	12	1,000,000 has +honesty.
Putting together the expressions [10], [11], and [12],	13	1+1,000+1,000,000 has strength+ wisdom+honesty.
But by the definitions [1], [2], [3], [4], and the suppositions [5] [6],	14	The British Government=1+1,000+ 1,000,000.

[1] Which is done without any sort of ceremony, the quantities marked in the step with the negative sign, being as so many *fluents,* which are at a *maximum,* or a *minimum,* just as happens to be most convenient.

Therefore, by [13]	15	The British Government has+strength +wisdom+honesty.
Changing the ex-pression	16	The British Government is all-power-ful+all-wise+all-honest.
But by definition	17	All-powerful+all-wise+all-honest= all-perfect.
Therefore, by [16] and [17]	18	The British Government is all-perfect, Q.E.D.

☞ SCHOLIUM. After the same manner it may be proved to be *all-weak*, *all-foolish*, and *all-knavish*.

21. Thus much for the British Constitution; and for the *Conclusion of* grounds of that pre-eminence which it boasts, I trust, indeed, *the Chapter.* not without reason, above all others that are known: Such is the idea our Author gives us of those grounds.—'You are not satisfied with it then,' says some one.—Not perfectly.— 'What is then your own?'—In truth this is more than I have yet quite settled. I may have settled it with myself, and not think it worth the giving: but if ever I do think it worth the giving, it will hardly be in the form of a comment on a digres-sion stuffed into the belly of a definition. At any rate it is not likely to be much wished for, by those, who have read what has been given us on this subject by an ingenious foreigner: since it is to a foreigner we were destined to owe the best idea that has yet been given of a subject so much our own. Our Author has copied: but Mr. DE LOLME has thought.

The topic which our Author has thus brought upon the carpet (let any one judge with what necessity) is in respect to some parts of it that we have seen, rather of an invidious nature. Since, however, it *has* been brought upon the carpet, I have treated it with that plainness with which an Englishman of all others is bound to treat it, because an Englishman may thus treat it and be safe. I have said what the subject seemed to demand, without any fear indeed, but without any wish, to give offence: resolving not to permit myself to consider how this or that man might chance to take it. I have spoken with-out sycophantical respects indeed, yet I hope not without decency: certainly without any party spleen. I chose rather to leave it to our Author to compliment men in the lump:

F

and to stand aghast with admiration at the virtues of men unknown.[1] Our Author will do as shall seem meet to him. For my part, if ever I stand forth and sing the song of eulogy to great men, it shall be not because they *occupy* their station, but because they *deserve* it.

[1] V. supra, par. 7.

CHAPTER IV

RIGHT OF THE SUPREME POWER TO MAKE LAWS

1. WE now come to the third topic touched upon in the *Subject of the* digression; namely, the *right*, as our Author phrases it, which *paragraph in question as* the Supreme Power has of making laws. And this topic *stated by our* occupies one pretty long paragraph. The title here given to it *Author.* is the same which in the next succeeding paragraph he has found for it himself. This is fortunate: for, to have been obliged to find a title for it myself, is what would have been to the last degree distressing. To *entitle* a discourse, is to represent the drift of it. But, to represent the drift of this, is a task which, so long at least as I confine my consideration to the paragraph itself, bids defiance to my utmost efforts.

2. 'Tis to another passage or two, a passage or two that we *Drift of it,* have already seen starting up in distant parts of this digression, *conjectured.* that I am indebted for such conjectures as I have been able to make up.

These conjectures, however, I could not have ventured so far to rely on, as on the strength of them to have furnished the paragraph with a title of my own framing. The danger of misrepresentation was too great; a kind of danger which a man cannot but lie imminently exposed to, who ventures to put a precise meaning upon a discourse which in itself has none. That I may just mention, however, in this place, the result of them; what he is really aiming at, I take it, is, to inculcate a persuasion that in every state there must subsist, in some hands or other, a power that is *absolute*. I mention it thus prematurely, that the reader may have some clue to guide him in his progress through the paragraph; which it is now time I should recite.

3. 'Having,' says our Author, 'thus cursorily considered *The paragraph* the three usual species of government, and our own singular *recited.* constitution, selected and compounded from them all, I proceed to observe, that, as the power of making laws constitutes the supreme authority, so wherever the supreme authority in any state resides, it is the right of that authority

to make laws; that is, in the words of our definition, to
prescribe the rule of civil action. And this may be discovered
from the very end and institution of civil states. For a state
is a collective body, composed of a multitude of individuals,
united for their safety and convenience, and intending to act
together as one man. If it therefore is to act as one man, it
ought to act by one uniform will. But in as much as political
communities are made up of many natural persons, each of
whom has his particular will and inclination, these several
wills cannot by any *natural* union be joined together, or tempered and disposed into a lasting harmony, so as to constitute
and produce that one uniform will of the whole. It can
therefore be no otherwise produced than by a *political* union,
by the consent of all persons to submit their own private
wills to the will of one man, or of one, or more assemblies of
men, to whom the supreme authority is entrusted: and this
will of that one man, or assemblage of men is, in different
states, according to their different constitutions, understood
to be law.'

The sense of it considered in itself.

4. The other passages which suggested to me the construction I have ventured to put upon this, shall be mentioned by
and by. First, let us try what is to be made of it by itself.

The leading argument in it nugatory.

5. The obscurity in which the first sentence of this paragraph is enveloped, is such, that I know not how to go about
bringing it to light, without borrowing a word or two of
logicians. Laying aside the preamble, the body of it, viz. 'as
the power of making laws constitutes the supreme authority,
so wherever the supreme authority in any state resides, it is
the right of that authority to make laws,' may be considered
as constituting that sort of syllogism which logicians call an
enthymeme. An *enthymeme* consists of two *propositions*; a
consequent and an *antecedent*. 'The power of making laws,' say
our Author, 'constitutes the supreme authority.' This is his
antecedent. From hence it is he concludes, that 'wherever the
supreme authority in any state resides, it is the right of that
authority to make laws.' This then is his *consequent*.

Now so it is, that this *antecedent*, and this *consequent*, for any
difference at least that I can possibly perceive in them, would
turn out, were they but correctly worded, to mean precisely
the same thing: for, after saying that 'the power of making

aws constitutes the supreme authority,' to tell us that, for
hat reason, 'the supreme authority' is (or has) the power (or
he right) of making laws, is giving us, I take it, much the
ame sort of information, as it would be to us to be told that
a thing is so, *because* it is so: a sort of a truth which there seems
to be no very great occasion to send us upon 'discovering, in
he end and institution of civil states.' That by the 'sovereign
power,' he meant 'the power of making laws;' this, or some-
hing like it, is no more indeed than what he had told us over
and over, and over again, with singular energy and anxiety,
in his 46th page, in his 49th, and in, I know not how many,
pages besides: always taking care, for precision's sake, to give
a little variety to the expression: the words *'power'* and
authority', sometimes, seemingly put for the same idea;
sometimes seemingly opposed to each other: both of them
sometimes denoting the *fictitious* being, the *abstract quality*;
sometimes the *real* being or beings, the *person* or *persons*
supposed to *possess* that *quality*.—Let us disentangle the sense
from these ambiguities; let us learn to speak distinctly of the
persons, and of the *quality* we attribute to them; and then let us
make another effort to find a meaning for this perplexing
passage.

6. By the 'supreme authority' then, (we may suppose our *The antecedent*
Author to say) 'I mean the same thing as when I say the power *stated anew.*
of making laws.' This is the proposition we took notice of
above, under the name of the *antecedent*. This antecedent then,
we may observe, is a definition: a definition, to wit, of the
phrase 'supreme authority.' Now to define a phrase is, to
translate it into another phrase, supposed to be better understood, and expressive of the same ideas. The supposition here
then is, that the reader was already, of himself, tolerably well
acquainted with the import of the phrase 'power of making
laws:' that he was not at all, or was however less acquainted
with the import of the phrase 'supreme authority.' Upon this
supposition then, it is, that in order to his being made clearly
to understand the latter, he is informed of its being synonymous to the former. Let us now introduce the mention of the
person: let us add the word *'person'* to the definition; it will be
the same definition still in substance, only a little more fully
and precisely worded. *For a person to possess* the supreme

authority, is *for a person to possess* the power of making laws. This then is what in substance has been already laid down in the *antecedent*.

The consequent new stated.

7. Now let us consider the *consequent*; which, when detached from the context, may be spoken of as making a sentence of itself. 'Wherever,' says he, 'the supreme authority in any state resides, it is the *right* of that authority to make Laws.'— By '*wherever*' I take it for granted, he means, '*in whatever persons:*' by '*authority*,' in the former part of the sentence,— *power*; by the same word, '*authority*,' in the latter part of the sentence,—*persons*. Corrected therefore, the sentence will stand thus: *In whatever persons in any state the supreme power resides, it is the right of those persons to make Laws.*

That it is identical with the antecedent:

8. The only word now remaining undisposed of, is the word '*right*.' And what to think of this, indeed I know not: whether our Author had a meaning in it, or whether he had none. It is inserted, we may observe, in the latter part only of the sentence: it appears not in the former. Concerning this omission, two conjectures here present themselves: it may have happened by accident; or it may have been made by design. If by accident, then the case is, that the idea annexed to the word '*right*' is no other than what was meant to be included in the former part of the sentence, in which it is *not* expressed, as well as in the latter, in which it *is*. In this case it may, without any change in the signification, be expressed in both. Let it then be expressed, and the sentence, take it altogether, will stand thus: *In whatever persons the right of exercising supreme power in any state resides, it is the right of those persons to make Laws.* If this conjecture be the true one, and I am apt to think it is, we see once more, and, I trust beyond all doubt, that the *consequent* in this *enthymeme* is but a repetition of the *antecedent*. We may judge then, whether it is from any such consideration as that of 'the end and institution of civil states,' or any other consideration that we are likely to gain any further conviction of the truth of this *conclusion*, than it presents us of itself. We may also form some judgment beforehand, what use or meaning there is likely to be in the assemblage of words that is to follow.

—or else nothing to the purpose.

9. What is possible, notwithstanding, however improbable is, that the omission we have been speaking of was *designed*

In this case, what we are to understand is, that the word *'right' was* meant to introduce a new idea into this latter part of the sentence, over and above any that was meant to be suggested by the former. *'Right'* then, according to this construction, in the one place, is to be considered as put in contradistinction to *fact* in the other. The sense is then, that *whatever persons* do actually *exercise supreme power*, (or what, according to the *antecedent* of the *enthymeme*, is the same thing, *the power of making laws*) *those persons* have the right to *exercise it*. But, in this case, neither does what is given as a *consequence* in any respect follow from the *antecedent*, nor can *any thing be* made of it, but what is altogether foreign to the rest of the discourse. So much indeed, that it seems more consonant to probability, as well as more favourable to our Author, to conclude that he had no meaning at all, than that he had this.

10. Let us now try what we can make of the remainder of the paragraph. Being ushered in by the word *'for,'* it seems to lay claim to the appellation of an argument. This argument, setting out, as we have seen, without an object, seems however to have found something like one at last, as if it had picked it up by the way. This object, if I mistake it not, is to persuade men, that the *supreme power*, (that is the *person* or *persons* in use to exercise the supreme power in a state) ought, in all points without exception, to be obeyed. What men intend, he says, to do when they are in a state, is to act, as if they were but 'one man.' But one man has but one will belonging to him. What they intend therefore, or what they *ought* to intend, (a slight difference which our Author seems not to be well aware of) is, to act as if they had but one will. To act as if they had but one will, the way is, for them to 'join' all their wills 'together.' To do this, the most obvious way would be to join them *'naturally'*: but, as *wills* will not splice and dovetail like deal boards, the only feasible way is to join them *'politically.'* Now the only way for men to join their wills together *politically*, is for them all to consent to submit their wills to the will of one. This one will, to which all others are to be submitted, is the will of those persons who are in use to exercise the supreme power; whose wills again, when there happens to be many of them, have, by a process

The rest of the paragraph new stated—supposed drift of it.

of which our Author has said nothing, been reduced (as we must suppose) into *one* already. So far our Author's argument. The above is the substance of it fairly given; not altogether with so much ornament, indeed, as he has given it, but, I trust, with somewhat more precision. The whole concludes, we may observe, with our Author's favourite identical proposition, or something like it, now for the twentieth time repeated.

Weakness of it as a persuasive to obedience. 11. Taking it altogether, it is, without question, a very ingenious argument: nor can any thing in the world answer the purpose better, except just in the case where it happens to be wanted. Not but that a veteran antagonist, trained up in the regular and accustomed discipline of legal fencing, such an one, indeed, *might* contrive perhaps, with due management, to give our Author the honour of the field. But should some undisciplined blunderer, like the Commissary's landlady, thrust in *quart*, when he should have thrust in *tierce*, I doubt much whether he might not get within our Author's guard.—I 'intend?'—'I consent?'—I 'submit' myself?—'Who are you, I wonder, that should know what I do better than I do myself? As to "*submitting my will*" to the wills of the people who made this law you are speaking of,—what I know is, that I never "intended" any such thing: I abominate them, I tell you, and all they ever did, and have always *said* so: and as to my 'consent,' so far have I been from giving it to their law, that from the first to the last, I have protested against it with all my might.' So much for our refractory disputant.—What I should say to him I know: but what our Author could find to answer to him, is more than I can imagine.[1]

A prior paragraph supposed to be relative to the object of this. 12. Let us now return and pick up those other passages which we supposed to have a respect to the same design that seems to be in view in this. First comes the short introductory

[1] One thing in the paragraph we are considering is observable; it is the concluding sentence, in which he brings together the ideas of *law* and *will*. Here then, in the tail of a digression, he comes nearer in fact, though without being aware of it, to the giving a just and precise idea of a law, than in any part of the definition itself from whence he is digressing. If, instead of saying that a law is a *will*, he had called it the *expression* of a *will*, and that sort of expression of a will which goes by the name of a *command*, his definition would, so far as this goes, have been clear as well as right. As it is, it is neither the one nor the other. But of this more, if at all, in another place. The definition of law is a matter of too much nicety and importance to be dispatched in a note.

paragraph that ushers in the whole digression: a paragraph which, however short, and however imperfect with respect to the purpose of giving a general view of the contents of those which follow it, was, in despite of method, to expatiate upon this subject. Upon this subject, indeed, he does expatiate with a force of argument and energy of expression which nothing can withstand. 'This, 'it begins, 'will necessarily lead us into a short enquiry concerning the nature of society and civil government.'[1]—This is all the intimation it gives of the contents of those paragraphs we have examined. Upon *this* before us it touches in energetic terms; but more energetic than precise.—'And the *natural*' (it continues) 'and *inherent* right that belongs to the sovereignty of a state,' (*natural* right, observe, that belongs to the sovereignty of a *political* society) 'wherever that sovereignty be lodged, of making and enforcing laws.'

13. This is not all. The most emphatical passage is yet *Another.* behind. It is a passage in that short paragraph[2] which we found to contain such a variety of matter. He is there speaking of the several forms of government now in being. 'However they began,' says he, 'or by what right soever they subsist, there *is* and *must be* in all of them a *supreme, irresistible, absolute, uncontrolled* authority, in which the *jura summi imperii*, or the rights of sovereignty, reside.'

14. The vehemence, the δεινότης, of this passage is re- *Agitation he* markable. He ransacks the language: he piles up, one upon *betrays.* another, four of the most tremendous epithets he can find; he heaps Ossa upon Pelion: and, as if the English tongue did not furnish expressions strong or imposing enough, he tops the whole with a piece of formidable Latinity. From all this agitation, it is plain, I think, there is a something which he has very much at heart; which he wishes, but fears, perhaps, to bring out undisguised; which in several places, notwithstanding, bursts out involuntarily, as it were, before he is well ready for it; and which, a certain discretion, getting at last the upper hand of propensity, forces, as we have seen, to dribble away in a string of obscure sophisms. Thus oddly enough it happens, that that passage of them all, which, if I

[1] 1 Comm., p. 47.   [2] 1 Comm., p. 48, supra, ch. II, par. 11.

mistake not, is the only one that was meant to be dedicated expressly to the subject, is the least explicit on it.[1]

Cause of it.

15. A courage much stauncher than our Author's might have wavered here. A task of no less intricacy was here to be travelled through, than that of adjusting the claims of those two jealous antagonists, Liberty and Government. A more invidious ground is scarcely to be found any where within the field of politics. Enemies encompass the traveller on every side. He can scarce stir but he must expect to be assaulted with the war-whoop of political heresy from one quarter or another. Difficult enough is the situation of him, who, in these defiles, feels himself impelled one way by fear, and another by affection.

Resource he finds in obscurity.

16. To return to the paragraph which it was the more immediate business of this chapter to examine:—Were the path of obscurity less familiar to our Author, one should be tempted to imagine he had struck into it on the particular occasion before us, in the view of extricating himself from this dilemma. A discourse thus prudently indeterminate might express enough to keep fair with the rulers of the earth, without setting itself in direct array against the prejudices of the people. Viewed by different persons, it might present different aspects: to men in power it might recommend itself, and that from the first, under the character of a practical lesson of obedience for the use of the people; while among the people themselves it might pass muster, for a time at least, in quality of a string of abstract scientific propositions of jurisprudence. It is not till some occasion for making application of it should occur, that its true use and efficacy would be brought to light. The people, no matter on what occasion, begin to murmur, and concert measures of resistance. Now then is the time for the latent virtues of this passage to be called forth. The book is to be opened to them, and in this passage they are to be shewn, what of themselves, perhaps, they would never have observed, a set of arguments curiously strung together and wrapped up, in proof of the universal expedience, or rather *necessity*, of submission: a necessity which is to arise, not out of the reflection that *the probable*

[1] Another passage or two there is which might seem to glance the same way: but these I pass over as less material, after those which we have seen.

RIGHT OF SUPREME POWER TO MAKE LAWS   91

mischiefs of resistance are greater than the probable mischiefs of obedience; not out of any such debatable consideration; but out of a something that is to be much more cogent and effectual: to wit, a certain *metaphysico-legal* impotence, which is to beget in them the sentiment, and answer all the purposes of a natural one. Armed, and full of indignation, our malcontents are making their way to the royal palace. In vain. A certain *estoppel* being made to bolt out upon them, in the manner we have seen, by the force of our Author's legal engineering, their arms are to fall, as it were by enchantment, from their hands. To disagree, to clamour, to oppose, to take back, in short, their wills again, is now, they are told, too late: it is what *can*not be done: their wills have been put in *hotchpot* along with the rest: they *have* 'united',—they *have* 'consented,'—they *have* 'submitted.'—Our Author having thus *put his hook into their nose*, they are to go back as they came, and all is peace. An ingenious contrivance this enough: but popular passion is not to be fooled, I doubt, so easily. Now and then, it is true, one error may be driven out, for a time, by an opposite error: one piece of nonsense by another piece of nonsense: but for barring the door effectually and for ever against all error and all nonsense, there is nothing like the simple truth.

17. After all these pains taken to inculcate unreserved submission, would any one have expected to see our Author himself among the most eager to excite men to disobedience? and that, perhaps, upon the most frivolous pretences? in short, upon any pretence whatsoever? Such, however, upon looking back a little, we shall find him. I say, among the most eager; for other men, at least the most enlightened advocates for liberty, are content with leaving it to subjects to resist, for their own sakes, on the footing of *permission*: this will not content our Author, but he must be forcing it upon them as a point of *duty*. *Inconsistency of the present passage with a former.*

18. 'Tis in a passage antecedent to the digression we are examining, but in the same section, that, speaking of the pretended law of Nature, and of the law of revelation, 'no human laws,' he says, 'should be *suffered* to contradict these.'[1] The expression is remarkable. It is not that no human laws *The former passage recited.*

---
[1] 1 Comm., p. 42.

should contradict them: but that no human laws should be SUFFERED to contradict them. He then proceeds to give us an example. This example, one might think, would be such as should have the effect of softening the dangerous tendency of the rule:—on the contrary, it is such as cannot but enhance it;[1] and, in the application of it to the rule, the substance of the latter is again repeated in still more explicit and energetic terms. 'Nay,' says he, speaking of the act he instances, 'if any human law should allow or enjoin us to commit it, we are BOUND TO TRANSGRESS that human law, or else we must offend both the natural and the divine.'

*Dangerous ten-
dency of it.*

19. The propriety of this dangerous maxim, so far as the Divine Law is concerned, is what I must refer to a future occasion for more particular consideration.[2] As to the LAW *of Nature*, if (as I trust it will appear) it be nothing but a phrase;[3] if there be no other medium for proving any act to be an offence against it, than the mischievous tendency of such act; if there be no other medium for proving a law of the *state* to be contrary to it, than the *inexpediency* of such law, unless the bare unfounded disapprobation of any one who thinks of it be called a proof; if a test for distinguishing such laws as would be *contrary* to the LAW *of Nature* from such as, *without* being contrary to it, are simply *inexpedient*, be that which neither our Author, nor any man else, so much as pretended ever to give; if, in a word, there be scarce any law

[1] It is that of murder. In the word here chosen there lurks a fallacy which makes the proposition the more dangerous as it is the more plausible. It is too important to be altogether past over; at the same time that a slight hint of it, in this place, is all that can be given. Murder is *killing* under certain *circumstances*. —Is the human law then to be allowed to define, in *dernier ressort*, what shall be those *circumstances*, or is it not? If yes, the case of a 'human law allowing or enjoining us to commit it,' is a case that is not so much as supposable: if *no*, adieu to all human laws: to the fire with our Statutes at large, our Reports, our Institutes, and all that we have hitherto been used to call our law books; our law books, the only law books we can be safe in trusting to, are Puffendorf and the Bible.

[2] According to our Author, indeed, it should be to no purpose to make any separate mention of the two laws; since the Divine Law, he tells us, is but 'a part of' that of Nature.[a] Of consequence, with respect to that part, at least, which is common to both, to be contrary to the one, is, of course, to be contrary to the other.

[3] This is what there would be occasion to shew more at large in examining some former parts of this section.

[a] 1 Comm., p. 42.

whatever but what those who have not liked it have found, on some account or another, to be repugnant to some text of scripture; I see no remedy but that the natural tendency of such doctrine is to impel a man, by the force of conscience, to rise up in arms against any law whatever that he happens not to like. What sort of government it is that can consist with such a disposition, I must leave to our Author to inform us.

20. It is the principle of *utility*, accurately apprehended and steadily applied, that affords the only clue to guide a man through these straits. It is for that, if any, and for that alone to furnish a decision which neither party shall dare in *theory* to disavow. It is something to reconcile men even in theory. They are at least, *something* nearer to an effectual union, than when at variance as well in respect of theory as of practice. *The principle of* UTILITY *the only guide under these difficulties.*

21. In speaking of the supposed contract between King and people,[1] I have already had occasion to give the description, and, as it appears to me, the only *general* description that *can* be given, of that juncture at which, and not before, resistance to government becomes *commendable*; or, in other words, reconcilable to just notions, whether of *legal* or not, at least of *moral*, and, if there be any difference, *religious* duty.[2] What was there said was spoken, at the time, with reference to that particular branch of government which was then in question; the branch that in this country is administered by the King. But if it was just, as applied to *that* branch of government, and in *this* country, it could only be for the same reason that it is so when applied to the *whole* of government, and that in *any* country whatsoever. It is *then*, we may say, and not till then, allowable to, if not incumbent on, every man, as well on the score of *duty* as of *interest*, to enter into measures of resistance; when, according to the best calculation he is able to make, *the probable mischiefs of resistance (speaking with respect to the community in general) appear less to him than the probable mischiefs of submission.* This then is to him, that is to each man in particular, the *juncture for resistance*. *Juncture for resistance.*

22. A natural question here is—by what *sign* shall this juncture be known? By what *common* signal alike conspicuous *Not characterizable by any common sign.*

[1] Ch. I.   [2] See Ch. V. par. 7, note 1.

and perceptible to all? A question which is readily enough started, but to which, I hope, it will be almost as readily perceived that it is impossible to find an answer. *Common* sign for such a purpose, I, for my part, know of none: he must be more than a prophet, I think, that can shew us one. For that which shall serve a particular person, I have already given one—his own internal persuasion of a balance of *utility* on the side of resistance.

Freedom in a government depends not upon any limitation to the Supreme Power.

23. Unless such a sign then, which I think impossible, can he shewn, the *field*, if one may say so, of the supreme governor's authority, though not *infinite*, must unavoidably, I think, *unless where limited by express convention*,[1] be allowed to be *indefinite*. Nor can I see any narrower, or other bounds to it, under this constitution, or under any other yet *freer* constitution, if there be one, than under the most *despotic*. *Before* the juncture I have been describing were arrived, resistance, even in a country like this, would come too soon: were the juncture arrived *already*, the time for resistance would be come already, under such a government even as any one should call *despotic*.

Principal circumstances on which it does depend.

24. In regard to a government that is *free*, and one that is *despotic*, wherein is it then that the difference consists? Is it that those persons in whose hands that power is lodged which is acknowledged to be supreme, have less power in the one than in the other, when it is from custom that they derive it? By no means. It is not that the power of one any more than of the other has any certain bounds to it. The distinction turns upon circumstances of a very different complexion:— on the *manner* in which that whole mass of power, which, taken together, is supreme, is, in a free state, *distributed* among the several ranks of persons that are sharers in it:—on the *source* from whence their titles to it are successively derived:— on the frequent and easy *changes* of condition between goverors and governed; whereby the interests of the one class are more or less indistinguishably blended with those of the other:—on the *responsibility* of the governors; or the right which a subject has of having the reasons publicly assigned

[1] This respects the case where one state, has, upon *terms*, submitted itself to the government of another: or where the governing bodies of a number of states agree to take directions in certain specified cases, from some *body* or other that is distinct from all of them: consisting of members, for instance, appointed out of each.

and canvassed of every act of power that is exerted over him:
—on the *liberty of the press*; or the security with which every
man, be he of the one class or the other, may make known
his complaints and remonstrances to the whole community:—
on the *liberty of public association*; or the security with which
malcontents may communicate their sentiments, concert
their plans, and practise every mode of opposition short of
actual revolt, before the executive power can be legally
justified in disturbing them.

25. True then, it may be, that, owing to this last circum- *Freedom in a*
stance in particular, in a state thus circumstanced, the road *government—*
to a revolution, if a revolution be necessary, is to appearance *how far favour-*
shorter; certainly more smooth and easy. More likelihood, *ance.*
certainly there is of its being such a revolution as shall be the
work of a number; and in which, therefore, the interests of
a number are likely to be consulted. Grant then, that by
reason of these facilitating circumstances, the juncture itself
may arrive sooner, and upon less provocation, under what is
called a *free* government, than under what is called an *absolute*
one: grant this;—yet till it *be* arrived, resistance is as much too
soon under one of them as under the other.

26. Let us avow then, in short, steadily but calmly, what *The supreme*
our Author hazards with anxiety and agitation, that the *power not*
authority of the supreme body cannot, *unless where limited by* *limited in itself.*
express convention, be said to have any assignable, any certain
bounds.—That to say there is any act they *cannot* do,—to
speak of any thing of their's as being *illegal*,—as being *void*;—
to speak of their exceeding their *authority* (whatever be the
phrase)—their *power*, their *right*, —is, however common, an
abuse of language.

27. The legislature *cannot* do it? The legislature *cannot* *Arguments that*
make a law to this effect? Why cannot? What is there that *suppose it to be*
should hinder them? Why not this, as well as so many other *so unsatisfac-*
laws murmured at, perhaps, as inexpedient, yet submitted to *tory—*
without any question of the *right*? With men of the same
party, with men whose affections are already lifted against
the law in question, any thing will go down: any rubbish
is good that will add fuel to the flame. But with regard to
an impartial bystander, it is plain that it is not denying the
right of the legislature, their *authority*, their *power*, or whatever

be the word—it is not denying that they *can* do what is in question—it is not that, I say, or any discourse verging that way that can tend to give *him* the smallest satisfaction.

—and inapplicable to particulars.

28. Grant even the proposition in general:—What are we the nearer? Grant that there *are* certain bounds to the *authority* of the legislature:—Of what use is it to say so, when these bounds are what no body has ever attempted to mark out to any useful purpose; that is, in any such manner whereby it might be known beforehand what description a law must be of to fall *within*, and what to fall *beyond* them? Grant that there *are* things which the legislature *can*not do;—grant that there *are* laws which exceed the *power* of the legislature to establish. What rule does this sort of discourse furnish us for determining whether any one that is in question is, or is not of the number? As far as I can discover, none. Either the discourse goes on in the confusion it began; either all rests in vague assertions, and no intelligible argument at all is offered; or if any, such arguments as are drawn from the principle of *utility*: arguments which, in whatever variety of words expressed, come at last to neither more nor less than this: that the tendency of the law is, to a greater or a less degree, pernicious. If this then be the result of the argument, why not come home to it at once? Why turn aside into a wilderness of sophistry, when the path of plain reason is straight before us?

What they lead to is either an appeal to the body of the people—

29. What practical inferences those who maintain this language mean should be deduced from it, is not altogether clear; nor, perhaps, does every one mean the same. Some who speak of a law as being *void* (for to this expression, not to travel through the whole list, I shall confine myself) would persuade us to look upon the authors of it as having thereby *forfeited*, as the phrase is, their *whole* power: as well that of giving force to the particular law in question, as to any other. These are they who, had they arrived at the same practical conclusion through the principle of utility, would have spoken of the law as being to such a degree pernicious, as that, were the bulk of the community to see it in its true light, *the probable mischief of resisting it would be less than the probable mischief of submitting to it.* These point, in the first instance, at *hostile* opposition.

30. Those who say nothing about forfeiture are commonly *—or to the judi-* less violent in their views. These are they who, were they to *cial power.* ground themselves on the principle of utility, and, to use our language, would have spoken of the law as being mischievous indeed, but without speaking of it as being mischievous to the degree that has been just mentioned. The mode of opposition which they point to is one which passes under the appellation of a *legal* one.

31. Admit then the law to be void in their sense, and mark *Which tends to* the consequences. The idea annexed to the epithet *void* is *give it a control* obtained from those instances in which we see it applied *over the legisla-* to a private instrument. The consequence of a *private* *tive.* instrument's being void is, that all persons concerned are to act as if no such instrument had existed. The consequence, accordingly, of a *law's* being void must be, that people shall act as if there were no such law about the matter: and there-fore that if any person in virtue of the mandate of the law should do anything in coercion of another person, which without such law he would be punishable for doing, he would still be punishable; to wit, by appointment of the judicial power. Let the law for instance, be a law imposing a tax: a man who should go about to levy the tax by force would be punishable as a trespasser: should he chance to be killed in the attempt, the person killing him would *not* be punishable as for murder: should he kill, he himself *would*, perhaps, be punishable as for murder. To whose office does it appertain to do those acts in virtue of which such punishments would be inflicted? To that of the Judges. Applied to practice then, the effect of this language is, by an appeal made to the Judges, to confer on those magistrates a controlling power over the acts of the legislature.

32. By this management a *particular* purpose might perhaps, *Remedy worse* by chance be answered: and let this be supposed a good one. *than the disease.* Still what benefit would, from the *general* tendency of such a doctrine, and such a practice in conformity to it, accrue to the body of the people is more than I can conceive. A Parlia-ment, let it be supposed, is too much under the influence of the Crown: pays too little regard to the sentiments and the interests of the people. Be it so. The people at any rate, if not so great a share as they might and ought to have, have

G

had, at least, *some* share in choosing it. Give to the Judges a power of annulling its acts; and you transfer a portion of the supreme power from an assembly which the people have had *some* share, at least, in choosing, to a set of men in the choice of whom they have not the least imaginable share: to a set of men appointed solely by the Crown: appointed *solely*, and avowedly and *constantly*, by that very magistrate whose partial and occasional influence is the very grievance you seek to remedy.

But not so bad as some might represent it.

33. In the heat of debate, some, perhaps, would be for saying of this management that it was transferring at once the supreme authority from the legislative power to the judicial. But this would be going too far on the other side. There is a wide difference between a *positive* and a *negative* part in legislation. There is a wide difference again between a negative upon *reasons* given, and a negative without any. The power of *repealing* a law even for reasons given is a great power: too great indeed for Judges: but still very distinguishable from, and much inferior to that of *making* one.[1]

The supreme power limitable by convention.

34. Let us now go back a little. In denying the existence of any assignable bounds to the supreme power, I added,[2] 'unless where limited by express convention:' for this exception I could not but subjoin. Our Author indeed, in that passage in which, short as it is, he is the most explicit, leaves, we may observe, no room for it. 'However they began,' says he (speaking of the several forms of government) 'however they began, and by what right soever they subsist, there is and must be in ALL of them an authority that is absolute.'— To say this, however, of *all* governments without exception; —to say that *no* assemblage of men can subsist in a state of government, without being subject to some *one* body whose

[1] Notwithstanding what has been said, it would be in vain to dissemble, but that, upon occasion, an appeal of this sort may very well answer, and has, indeed, in general, a tendency to answer, in some sort, the purposes of those who espouse, or profess to espouse, the interests of the people. A public and authorised debate on the propriety of the law is by this means brought on. The artillery of the tongue is played off against the law, under cover of the law itself. An opportunity is gained of impressing sentiments unfavourable to it, upon a numerous and attentive audience. As to any other effects from such an appeal, let us believe that in the instances in which we have seen it made, it is the certainty of miscarriage that has been the encouragement to the attempt.

[2] V. supra, par. 26.

authority stands unlimited so much as by convention; to say, in short, that not even by convention can any limitation be made to the power of that body in a state which in other respects is supreme, would be saying, I take it, rather too much: it would be saying that there is no such thing as government in the German Empire; nor in the Dutch Provinces; nor in the Swiss Cantons; nor was of old in the Achaean league.

35. In this mode of limitation I see not what there is that *—So as the term of it be explicit.* need surprise us. By what is it that any degree of *power* (meaning *political power*) is established? It is neither more nor less, as we have already had occasion to observe,[1] than a habit of, and disposition to obedience: *habit*, speaking with respect to *past* acts; *disposition*, with respect to *future*. This disposition it is as easy, or I am much mistaken, to conceive as being absent with regard to one sort of acts; as present with regard to other. For a body then, which is in other respects supreme, to be conceived as being with respect to a certain sort of acts, limited, all that is necessary is, that this sort of acts be in its description distinguishable from every other.

36. By means of a convention then we are furnished with *Which furnishes what may be taken for a common signal of resistance.* that common signal which, in other cases, we despaired of finding.[2] A certain act is in the instrument of convention specified, with respect to which the government is therein precluded from issuing a law to a certain effect: whether to the effect of commanding the act, of permitting it, or of forbidding it. A law is issued to that effect notwithstanding. The issuing then of such a law (the sense of it, and likewise the sense of that part of the convention which provides against it being supposed clear) is a fact notorious and visible to all: in the issuing then of such a law we have a fact which is *capable* of being taken for that common signal we have been speaking of. These bounds the supreme body in question has marked out to its authority: of such a demarcation then what is the effect? either none at all, or this: that the disposition to obedience confines itself within these bounds. Beyond them the disposition is stopped from extending: beyond them the subject is no more prepared to obey the governing body of his own state, than that of any other. What difficulty, I

[1] V. supra, ch. I. par. 13, note.   [2] V. supra, par. 22.

say, there should be in conceiving a state of things to subsist in which the supreme authority is thus limited,—what greater difficulty in conceiving it with this limitation, than without any, I cannot see. The two states are, I must confess, to me alike conceivable: whether alike expedient,—alike conducive to the happiness of the people, is another question.

A salvo for reformation.

37. God forbid, that from any thing here said it should be concluded that in any society any convention is or can be made, which shall have the effect of setting up an insuperable bar to that which the parties affected shall deem a reformation:—God forbid that any disease in the constitution of a state should be without its remedy. Such might by some be thought to be the case, where that supreme body which in such a convention, was one of the contracting parties, having incorporated itself with that which was the other, no longer subsists to give any new modification to the engagement. Many ways might however be found to make the requisite alteration, without any departure from the spirit of the engagement. Although that body itself which contracted the engagement be no more, a *larger body*, from whence the first is understood to have derived its title, may still subsist. Let this larger body be consulted. Various are the ways that might be conceived of doing this, and that without any disparagement to the dignity of the subsisting legislature: of doing it, I mean to such effect, as that, should the sense of such *larger body* be favourable to the alteration, it may be made by a law, which, in this case, neither ought to be, nor probably would be, regarded by the body of the people as a breach of the convention.[1]

---

[1] In Great Britain, for instance, suppose it were deemed necessary to make an alteration in the Act of Union. If in an article stipulated in favour of England, there need be no difficulty; so that there were a majority for the alteration among the English members, without reckoning the Scotch. The only difficulty would be with respect to an article stipulated in favour of Scotland; on account, to wit, of the small number of the Scotch members, in comparison with the English. In such a case, it would be highly expedient, to say no more, for the sake of preserving the public faith, and to avoid irritating the body of the nation, to take some method for making the establishment of the new law, depend upon their sentiments. One such method might be as follows. Let the new law in question be enacted in the common form. But let its commencement be deferred to a distant period, suppose a year or two: let it then, at the end of that period, be in force, unless petitioned against, by persons of such a description, and in such a number as might be supposed

38. To return for a moment to the language used by those *Notion of a* who speak of the supreme power as being limited in its own *natural limit to* nature. One thing I would wish to have remembered. What *the supreme* is here said of the impropriety, and evil influence of that kind *power, difficult* *to eradicate.* of discourse, is not intended to convey the smallest censure on those who use it, as if intentionally accessory to the ill effects it has a tendency to produce. It is rather a misfortune in the language, than a fault of any person in particular. The original of it is lost in the darkness of antiquity. We inherited it from our fathers, and, maugre all its inconveniencies, are likely, I doubt, to transmit it to our children.

39. I cannot look upon this as a mere dispute of words. *This not a mere* I cannot help persuading myself, that the disputes between *affair of words.* contending parties—between the defenders of a law and the opposers of it, would stand a much better chance of being adjusted than at present, were they but explicitly and constantly referred at once to the principle of UTILITY. The footing on which this principle rests every dispute is that of matter of fact; that is, future fact—the probability of certain future contingencies. Were the debate then conducted under the auspices of this principle, one of two things would happen: either men would come to an agreement concerning that probability, or they would see at length, after due discussion of the real grounds of the dispute, that no agreement was to be hoped for. They would at any rate see clearly and explicitly, the point on which the disagreement turned. The discontented party would then take their resolution to resist or to submit, upon just grounds, according as it should appear to them worth their while—according to what should appear to them, the importance of the matter in dispute—according to what should appear to them the probability or improbability of success—*according*, in short, *as the mischiefs of sub-*

fairly to represent the sentiments of the people in general: persons, for instance, of the description of those who at the time of the Union, constituted the body of electors. To put the validity of the law out of dispute, it would be necessary the fact upon which it was made ultimately to depend, should be in its nature too notorious to be controverted. To determine therefore, whether the conditions upon which the invalidation of it was made to depend, had been complied with, is what must be left to the simple declaration of some person or persons; for instance the King. I offer this only as a general idea: and as one amongst many that perhaps might be offered in the same view. It will not be expected that I should here answer objections, or enter into details.

mission should appear to bear a less, or a greater ratio to the mischiefs of resistance. But the door to reconcilement would be much more open, when they saw that it might be not a mere affair of passion, but a difference of judgment, and that, for any thing they could know to the contrary, a sincere one, that was the ground of quarrel.

The above notion perpetuates wrangling. 40. All else is but womanish scolding and childish altercation, which is sure to irritate, and which never can persuade.— 'I say, the legislature can*not* do this—I say, that it *can*. I say, that to do this, *exceeds* the bounds of its *authority*—I say, it does *not*.'—It is evident, that a pair of disputants setting out in this manner, may go on irritating and perplexing one another for everlasting, without the smallest chance of ever coming to an agreement. It is no more than announcing, and that in an obscure and at the same time, a peremptory and captious manner, their opposite persuasions, or rather affections, on a question of which neither of them sets himself to discuss the grounds. The question of utility, all this while, most probably, is never so much as at all brought upon the carpet: if it be, the language in which it is discussed is sure to be warped and clouded to make it match with the obscure and entangled pattern we have seen.

The principle of UTILITY *puts an end to it.* 41. On the other hand, had the debate been originally and avowedly instituted on the footing of utility, the parties might at length have come to an agreement; or at least to a visible and explicit issue.—'I say, that the mischiefs of the measure in question are to *such* an amount.—*I* say, *not* so, but to a *less*.— *I* say, the benefits of it are only to *such* an amount.—*I* say, *not* so, but to a *greater*.'—This, we see, is a ground of controversy very different from the former. The question is now manifestly a question of conjecture concerning so many future contingent matters of fact: to solve it, both parties then are naturally directed to support their respective persuasions by the only evidence the nature of the case admits of;—the evidence of such *past* matters of fact as appear to be analogous to those contingent *future* ones. Now these *past* facts are almost always numerous: so numerous, that till brought into view for the purpose of the debate, a great proportion of them are what may very fairly have escaped the observation of one of the parties: and it is owing, perhaps, to this and nothing else, that that party is of the persuasion which sets it at variance with the other. Here then, we have a plain and open road, perhaps, to present reconcilement: at the worst to an intelligible and explicit issue,—that is, to such a ground of difference as may, when thoroughly trodden and explored, be found to lead on to reconcilement at the last. Men, let them but once clearly understand one another, will not be long ere they agree. It is the perplexity of ambiguous and sophistical discourse that, while it distracts and eludes the apprehension, stimulates and inflames the passions.

But it is now high time we should return to our Author, from whose text we have been insensibly led astray, by the nicety and intricacy of the question it seemed to offer to our view.

CHAPTER V

DUTY OF THE SUPREME POWER TO MAKE LAWS

Subject of the paragraph examined in the present chapter.

1. WE now come to the last topic touched upon in this digression: a certain *'duty,'* which, according to our Author's account, the supreme power lies under:—the *duty of making laws.*

The paragraph recited.

2. 'Thus far,' says he, 'as to the *right* of the supreme power to make laws; but farther, it is its *duty* likewise. *For since* the respective members are bound to conform themselves to the will of the state, it is expedient that they *receive directions* from the state declaratory of that its will. *But since* it is impossible, in so great a multitude, to give injunctions to every particular man, relative to each particular action, therefore the state establishes general rules for the perpetual information and direction of all persons, in all points, whether of positive or negative duty. And this, in order that every man may know what to look upon as his own, what as another's; what absolute and what relative duties are required at his hands; what is to be esteemed honest, dishonest, or indifferent; what degree every man retains of his natural liberty; what he has given up as the price of the benefits of society; and after what manner each person is to moderate the use and exercise of those rights which the state assigns him, in order to promote and secure the public tranquillity.'

The first sentence examined. The most obvious sense of it nugatory.

3. Still as obscure, still as ambiguous as ever. The *'supreme power'* we may remember, according to the definition so lately given of it by our Author, and so often spoken of, is neither more nor less than the *power to make laws.* Of this power we are now told that it is its *'duty'* to make laws. Hence we learn—what?—that it is its *'duty'* to do what it does; to be, in short, what it is. This then is what the paragraph now before us, with its apparatus of *'fors,'* and *'buts,'* and *'sinces,'* is designed to prove to us. Of this stamp is that meaning, at least, of the initial sentence, which is apparent upon the face of it.

4. Complete the sense of the phrase, 'to make laws;' add to *The next most* it, in this place, what it wants in order to be an adequate *obvious extravagant.* expression of the import which the preceding paragraph seemed to annex to it; you have now, for what is mentioned as the object of the 'duty,' another sense indeed, but a sense still more untenable than the foregoing. 'Thus far,' says our Author (recapitulating what he had been saying before) 'as to the *right*' of the supreme power to make laws.'—By this '*right*' we saw, in the preceding chapter, was meant, a right to make laws *in all cases whatsoever.* 'But further,' he now adds, 'it is its *duty* likewise.' Its *duty* then to do—what? to do the same thing that it was before asserted to be its *right* to do—to make laws in all cases whatsoever: or (to use another word, and that our Author's own, and that applied to the same purpose) that it is its duty to be '*absolute.*'[1] A sort of duty this which will probably be thought rather a singular one.

5. Meantime the observation which, if I conjecture right, *A third sense* he really had in view to make, is one which seems very just *proposed.* indeed, and of no mean importance, but which is very obscurely expressed, and not very obviously connected with the purport of what goes before. The duty he here means is a duty, which respects, I take it, not so much the actual *making* of laws, as the taking of proper measures to *spread abroad* the knowledge of whatever laws happen to *have been* made: a duty which (to adopt some of our Author's own words) is conversant, not so much about *issuing* 'directions' as about providing that such as *are* issued shall be 'received.'

6. Meantime to speak of the *duties* of a supreme power;— *Objection to the* of a *legislature*, meaning a *supreme* legislature;—of a set of *use of the word* men acknowledged to be absolute;—is what, I must own, I *'duty' on this* am not very fond of. Not that I would wish the subordinate *occasion.* part of the community to be a whit less watchful over their governors, or more disposed to unlimited submission in point of *conduct*, than if I were to talk with ever so much peremptoriness of the '*duties*' of these latter, and of the *rights*

---

[1] 1 Comm., p. 49.

which the former have against them:[1] what I am afraid of is, running into solecism and confusion in *discourse*.

[1] With this note let no man trouble himself who is not used, or does not intend to use himself, to what are called *metaphysical* speculations: in whose estimation the benefit of understanding clearly what he is speaking of, is not worth the labour.

1. *Duty* (*political*).

1. That may be said to be my *duty* to do (understand political duty) which you (or some other person or persons) have a *right* to have me made to do. I then have a DUTY *towards* you: you have a RIGHT as *against* me.

2. *Right* (*political*).

2. What you have a right to have me made to do (understand a political right) is that which I am liable, according to law, upon a requisition made on your behalf, to be *punished* for not doing.

3. *Punishment a fundamental idea.*

3. I say *punished*: for without the notion of punishment (that is of *pain* annexed to an act, and accruing on a certain *account*, and from a certain *source*) no notion can we have of either *right* or *duty*.

4. *To define or* expound.

4. Now the idea belonging to the word *pain* is a simple one. To *define* or rather (to speak more generally) to *expound* a word, is to resolve, or to make a progress towards resolving, the idea belonging to it into simple ones.

5. *Words not to be expounded but by* paraphrasis.

5. For expounding the words *duty*, *right*, *power*, *title*, and those other terms of the same stamp that abound so much in ethics and jurisprudence, either I am much deceived, or the only method by which any instruction can be conveyed, is that which is here exemplified. An exposition framed after this method I would term *paraphrasis*.

6. Paraphrasis *what*.

6. A word may be said to be expounded by *paraphrasis*, when not that *word* alone is translated into other *words*, but some whole *sentence* of which it forms a part is translated into another *sentence*; the words of which latter are expressive of such ideas as are *simple*, or are more immediately resolvable into simple ones than those of the former. Such are those expressive of *substances* and *simple modes*, in respect of such *abstract* terms as are expressive of what LOCKE has called *mixed modes*. This, in short, is the only method in which any abstract terms can, at the long run, be expounded to any instructive purpose: that is in terms calculated to raise *images* either of *substances* perceived, or of *emotions*;—sources, one or other of which every idea must be drawn from, to be a clear one.

7. *Definition* per genus et differentiam, not universally applicable.

7. The common method of defining—the method *per genus et differentiam*, as logicians call it, will, in many cases, not at all answer the purpose. Among abstract terms we soon come to such as have no *superior genus*. A definition, *per genus et differentiam*, when applied to these, it is manifest, can make no advance: it must either stop short, or turn back, as it were, upon itself, in a *circulate* or a *repented*.

8. *Further examples;*— disposition, —estate,— interest, — power.

8. 'Fortitude is a virtue:'—Very well:—but what is a virtue? 'A virtue is a disposition:'—Good again:—but what is a *disposition*? 'A *disposition* is a . . .;' and there we stop. The fact is, a *disposition* has no *superior genus*: a *disposition* is not a . . ., any thing:—this is not the way to give us any notion of what is meant by it. 'A *power*,' again 'is a *right*:' and what is a *right*? It is *power*.—An *estate* is an *interest*, says our Author somewhere; where he begins defining an estate:—as well might he have said an *interest* was an *estate*. As well, in short, were it to define in this manner, a conjunction or a preposition. As well were it to say of the preposition *through*, or the conjunction *because*; a *through* is a . . ., or a *because* is a . . ., and so go on defining them.

7. I understand, I think, pretty well, what is meant by the *The* proper *sense of it.* word *duty* (political duty) when applied to myself; and I could not persuade myself, I think, to apply it in the same sense in a regular didactic discourse to those whom I am speaking of as my supreme governors. That is my *duty* to do, which I am liable to be *punished*, according to law, if I do not do: this is the original, ordinary, and proper sense of the word *duty*.[1] Have these supreme governors any such

9. Of this stamp, by the bye, are some of his most fundamental definitions: of consequence they must leave the reader where they found him. But of this, perhaps, more fully and methodically on some future occasion. In the meantime I have thrown out these loose hints for the consideration of the curious.

9. An imperfection frequent in our Author's method.

[1] 1. One may conceive three sorts of duties: *political, moral,* and *religious;* correspondent to the three sorts of *sanctions* by which they are enforced: or the same point of conduct may be a man's duty on these three several accounts. After speaking of the one of these to put the change upon the reader, and without warning begin speaking of another, or not to let it be seen from the first which of them one is speaking of, cannot but be productive of confusion.

1. Duties, three sorts.

2. Political duty is created by punishment: or at least by the will of persons who have punishment in their hands; persons stated and *certain,*—political superiors.

2. Political duty.

3. Religious duty is also created by punishment: by punishment expected at the hands of a person *certain,*—the Supreme Being.

3. Religious duty.

4. Moral duty is created by a kind of motive, which from the *uncertainty* of the *persons* to apply it, and of the *species* and *degree* in which it will be applied, has hardly yet got the name of punishment: by various mortifications resulting from the ill-will of persons *uncertain* and variable,—the community in general: that is, such individuals of that community as he, whose duty is in question, shall happen to be connected with.

4. Moral duty —the proper sense of it.

5. When in any of these three senses a man asserts a point of conduct to be a duty, what he asserts is the existence, actual or probable, of an *external* event: viz. of a punishment issuing from one or other of these sources in consequence of a contravention of the duty: an event *extrinsic* to, and distinct from, as well the conduct of the party spoken of, as the sentiment of him who speaks. If he persists in asserting it to be a duty, but without meaning it should be understood that it is on any one of these three accounts that he looks upon it as such; all he then asserts is his own internal *sentiment*: all he means then is, that he feels himself *pleased* or *displeased* at the thoughts of the point of conduct in question, but without being able to tell *why*. In this case he should e'en say so: and not seek to give an undue influence to his own single suffrage, by delivering it in terms that purport to declare the voice either of God, or of the law, or of the people.

5. Difference between these senses and a fourth which is figurative and improper.

6. Now which of all these senses of the word our Author had in mind; in which of them all he meant to assert that it was the duty of supreme governors to make laws, I know not. *Political* duty is what they cannot be subject to[a]: and to say that a duty even of the *moral* or *religious* kind to this effect is incumbent on them, seems rather a precipitate assertion.

6. Duty not applicable here in any proper sense.

In truth what he meant was neither more nor less, I suppose, than that he

[a] See the note following.

duty? No: for if they are at all liable to punishment according to law, whether it be for *not* doing any thing, or for *doing*, then are they not, what they are supposed to be, supreme governors:[1] those are the supreme governors, by whose appointment the former are liable to be punished.

That in which it is here used figurative. 8. The word duty, then, if applied to persons spoken of as supreme governors, is evidently applied to them in a sense which is figurative and improper: nor therefore are the same conclusions to be drawn from any propositions in which it is used in this sense, as might be drawn from them if it were used in the other sense, which is its proper one.

The proposition acceded to in this last sense. 9. This explanation, then, being premised;—understanding myself to be using the word *duty* in its improper sense, the proposition that it is the duty of the legislature to spread abroad, as much as possible, the knowledge of their will

should be glad to see them do what he is speaking of; to wit, 'make laws:' that is, as he explains himself, spread abroad the knowledge of them. Would he so? So indeed should I; and if asked why, what answer our Author would give I know not; but I, for my part, have no difficulty. I answer,—because I am persuaded that it is for the benefit of the community that they (its governors) should do so. This would be enough to warrant me in my own opinion for saying that they *ought* to do it. For all this, I should not at any rate say that it was their *duty* in a *political* sense. No more should I venture to say it was in a *moral* or *religious* sense, till I were satisfied whether they themselves *thought* the measures useful and feasible, and whether they were generally *supposed* to think so.

Were I satisfied that they *themselves* thought so, God then, I might say, knows they do. God, we are to suppose, will punish them if they neglect pursuing it. It is then their *religious* duty. Were I satisfied that the *people* supposed they thought so: the people, I might say, in case of such neglect,—the people, by various manifestations of its ill-will, will also punish them. It is then their *moral* duty.

In any of these senses it must be observed, there can be no more propriety in averring it to be the duty of the supreme power to pursue the measure in question, than in averring it to be their duty to pursue any other supposeable measure equally beneficial to the community. To usher in the proposal of a measure in this peremptory and assuming guise, may be pardonable in a loose rhetorical harangue, but can never be justifiable in an exact didactic composition. Modes of *private moral* conduct there are indeed many, the tendency whereof is so well known and so generally acknowledged, that the observance of them may well be styled a duty. But to apply the same term to the particular details of *legislative* conduct, especially newly proposed ones, is going, I think, too far, and tends only to confusion.

Governors in what way subject to political duties notwithstanding their being supreme. [1] I mean for what they do, or omit to do, when *acting in a body*: in that body in which, when acting, they are supreme. Because for any thing any of them do separately, or acting in bodies that are subordinate, they may any of them be punished without any disparagement to their supremacy. Not only any *may* be, but many *are*: it is what we see examples of every day.

among the people, is a proposition I am disposed most un-
reservedly to accede to. If this be our Author's meaning, I
join myself to him heart and voice.

10. What particular institutions our Author wished to see
established in this view—what *particular* duties he would have
found for the legislature under this *general* head of duty, is
not very apparent: though it is what should have appeared
more precisely than it does, ere his meaning could be apprehended to any purpose. What increases still the difficulty of
apprehending it, is a practice which we have already had more
than once occasion to detect him in,[1]—a kind of versatility,
than which nothing can be more vexatious to a reader who
makes a point of entering into the sentiments of his Author.
He sets out with the word *duty* in his mouth; and, in the
character of a *Censor*, with all due gravity begins talking to us
of what *ought* to be. 'Tis in the midst of this lecture that our
Proteus slips aside; puts on the *historian*; gives an insensible
turn to the discourse; and, without any warning of the change,
finishes with telling us what *is*. Between these two points,
indeed, the *is*, and the *ought to be*, so opposite as they frequently
are in the eyes of other men, that spirit of obsequious *quietism*
that seems constitutional in our Author, will scarce ever let
him recognize a difference. 'Tis in the second sentence of
the paragraph that he observes that 'it is *expedient* that they'
(the people) 'receive directions from the state' (meaning the
governing body) 'declaratory of that its will.' 'Tis in the very
next sentence that we learn from him, that what it is thus
'*expedient*' that the state *should* do, it *does* do. 'But since it is
impossible in so great a multitude, to give particular injunctions to every particular man relative to each particular action,
therefore,' says he 'the state establishes' (does *actually* establish)
'general rules' (*the* state generally, *any* state, that is to say,
that one can mention, all states, in short, whatever *do* establish)
'general rules for the perpetual information and direction of
all persons in *all* points, whether of positive or of negative
duty.' Thus far our Author; so that, for aught appears,
whatever he could *wish* to see done in this view *is* done.
Neither this state of our own, nor any other, does he wish to

Obscured again by the next sentence—the Censor's part confounded with that of the Historian.

[1] V. supra, ch. II. par. 11, ch. III. par. 7, ch. IV. par 10.

see do any thing more in the matter than he sees done already; nay, nor than what is sure to be done at all events: so that happily the duty he is here so forward to lay on his superiors will not sit on them very heavy. Thus far is he from having any determinate instructive meaning in that part of the paragraph in which, to appearance, and by accident, he comes nearest to it.

Fixed and particularised. Promulgation recommended.

11. Not that the passage however is absolutely so remote from meaning, but that the inventive complaisance of a commentator of the admiring breed might find it pregnant with a good deal of useful matter. The design of disseminating the knowledge of the laws is glanced at by it at least, with a show of approbation. Were our Author's writings then as sacred as they are mysterious; and were they in the number of those which stamp the seal of authority on whatever doctrines can be fastened on them; what we have read might serve as a text, from which the obligation of adopting as many measures as a man should deem subservient to that design, might, without any unexampled violence, be deduced. In this oracular passage I might find inculcated, if not *totidem syllabis*, at least *totidem literis*, as many points of legislative duty as should seem subservient to the purposes of *digestion* and *promulgation*. Thus fortified, I might press upon the legislature, and that on the score of '*duty*,' to carry into execution, and that without delay, many a busy project as yet either unthought of or unheeded. I might call them with a tone of authority to their work: I might bid them go make provision forthwith for the bringing to light such scattered materials as can be found of the judicial decisions of time past,—sole and neglected materials of common law;—for the registering and publishing of all future ones as they arise;—for transforming, by a digest, the body of the common law thus completed, into statute-law;—for breaking down the whole together into *codes* or parcels, as many as there are classes of persons distinguishably concerned in it;—for introducing to the notice and possession of every person his respective code:—works which public necessity cries aloud for, at which professional interest shudders, and at which legislative indolence stands aghast.

12. All these leading points, I say, of legislative economy, *The recommen-dation enforced by our Author's concluding sen-tence.* with as many points of detail subservient to each as a medita- tion not unassiduous has suggested, I might enforce, were it necessary, by our Author's oracular authority. For nothing less than what has been mentioned, I trust, is necessary, in order that every man may be made to know, in the degree in which he *might* and *ought* to be made to know, what (in our Author's words) 'to look upon as his own, what as another's; what absolute and what relative duties are required at his hands; what is to be esteemed honest, dishonest, or indifferent; what degree every man retains of his natural liberty; what he has given up as the price of the benefits of society; and after what manner each person is to moderate the use and exercise of those rights which the state assigns him, in order to promote and secure the public tranquillity.' In taking my leave of our Author, I finish gladly with this pleasing peroration: a scru- tinizing judgment, perhaps, would not be altogether satisfied with it; but the ear is soothed by it, and the heart is warmed.

13. I now put an end to the tedious and intricate war of *Necessity and use of these ver-bal criticisms.* words that has subsisted, in a more particular manner during the course of these two last chapters: a logomachy, wearisome enough, perhaps, and insipid to the reader, but beyond description laborious and irksome to the writer. What remedy? Had there been sense, I should have attached myself to the sense: finding nothing but words; to the words I was to attach myself, or to nothing. Had the doctrine been but *false*, the task of exposing it would have been comparatively an easy one: but it was what is worse, *unmeaning*; and thence it came to require all these pains which I have been here bestowing on it: to what profit let the reader judge.

'Well then,'—(cries an objector)—'the task you have set yourself is at an end; and the subject of it after all, according to your own representation, teaches nothing;—according to your own shewing it is not worth attending to.—Why then bestow on it so much attention?'

In this view—To do something to instruct, but more to undeceive, the timid and admiring student:—to excite him to place more confidence in his own strength, and less in the infallibility of great names: —to help him to emancipate his judgment from the shackles of authority;—to let him see that the not understanding a discourse may as well be the writer's fault as the reader's:—to teach him to distinguish between showy language and sound sense:—to warn him not to pay himself with words:—to shew him that what may tickle the ear, or dazzle the imagination, will not always inform the judgment:—to shew him what it is our Author can do, and has done: and what it is he has not done, and cannot do:—to dispose him rather to fast on ignorance than feed himself with error: to let him see that with regard to an expositor of the law, our Author is not *he that should come,* but that we may be still *looking for another.*—'Who then,' says my objector, 'shall be that other? Yourself?'—No verily. My mission is at an end, when I have *prepared the way before* *him.*

AN INTRODUCTION TO THE

PRINCIPLES OF
MORALS AND LEGISLATION

PREFACE

1. THE following sheets were, as the title-page expresses,[1] printed so long ago as the year 1780. The design, in pursuance of which they were written, was not so extensive as that announced by the present title. They had at that time no other destination than that of serving as an introduction to a plan of a penal code *in terminis*, designed to follow them, in the same volume.

2. The body of the work had received its completion according to the then present extent of the author's views, when, in the investigation of some flaws he had discovered, he found himself unexpectedly entangled in an unsuspected corner of the metaphysical maze. A suspension, at first not apprehended to be more than a temporary one, necessarily ensued: suspension brought on coolness, and coolness, aided by other concurrent causes, ripened into disgust.

3. Imperfections pervading the whole mass had already been pointed out by the sincerity of severe and discerning friends; and conscience had certified the justness of their censure. The inordinate length of some of the chapters, the apparent inutility of others, and the dry and metaphysical turn of the whole, suggested an apprehension, that, if published in its present form, the work would contend under great disadvantages for any chance, it might on other accounts possess, of being read, and consequently of being of use.

4. But, though in this manner the idea of completing the present work slid insensibly aside, that was not by any means the case with the considerations which had led him to engage in it. Every opening, which promised to afford the lights he stood in need of, was still pursued: as occasion arose, the several departments connected with that in which he had at first engaged, were successively explored; insomuch that, in one branch or other of the pursuit, his researches have nearly embraced the whole field of legislation.

5. Several causes have conspired at present to bring to light, under this new title, a work which under its original one had been imperceptibly, but as it had seemed irrevocably, doomed

---

[1] The title-page of the 1789 edition reads, after the title—'printed in the year 1780, and now first published.' W. H.

to oblivion. In the course of eight years, materials for various works, corresponding to the different branches of the subject of legislation, had been produced, and some nearly reduced to shape: and, in every one of those works, the principles exhibited in the present publication had been found so necessary, that, either to transcribe them piece-meal, or to exhibit them somewhere where they could be referred to in the lump, was found unavoidable. The former course would have occasioned repetitions too bulky to be employed without necessity in the execution of a plan unavoidably so voluminous: the latter was therefore indisputably the preferable one.

6. To publish the materials in the form in which they were already printed, or to work them up into a new one, was therefore the only alternative: the latter had all along been his wish, and, had time and the requisite degree of alacrity been at command, it would as certainly have been realised. Cogent considerations, however, concur, with the irksomeness of the task, in placing the accomplishment of it at present at an unfathomable distance.

7. Another consideration is, that the suppression of the present work, had it been ever so decidedly wished, is no longer altogether in his power. In the course of so long an interval, various incidents have introduced copies into various hands, from some of which they have been transferred, by deaths and other accidents, into others that are unknown to him. Detached, but considerable extracts, have even been published, without any dishonourable views, (for the name of the author was very honestly subjoined to them,) but without his privity, and in publications undertaken without his knowledge.

8. It may perhaps be necessary to add, to complete his excuse for offering to the public a work pervaded by blemishes, which have not escaped even the author's partial eye, that the censure, so justly bestowed upon the form, did not extend itself to the matter.

9. In sending it thus abroad into the world with all its imperfections upon its head, he thinks it may be of assistance to the few readers he can expect, to receive a short intimation of the chief particulars, in respect of which it fails of corresponding with his maturer views. It will thence be observed how

in some respects it fails of quadrating with the design announced by its original title, as in others it does with that announced by the one it bears at present.

10. An introduction to a work which takes for its subject the totality of any science, ought to contain all such matters, and such matters only, as belong in common to every particular branch of that science, or at least to more branches of it than one. Compared with its present title, the present work fails in both ways of being conformable to that rule.

11. As an introduction to the principles of *morals*, in addition to the analysis it contains of the extensive ideas signified by the terms *pleasure*, *pain*, *motive*, and *disposition*, it ought to have given a similar analysis of the not less extensive, though much less determinate, ideas annexed to the terms *emotion*, *passion*, *appetite*, *virtue*, *vice*, and some others, including the names of the particular *virtues* and *vices*. But as the true, and, if he conceives right, the only true ground-work for the development of the latter set of terms, has been laid by the explanation of the former, the completion of such a dictionary, so to style it, would, in comparison of the commencement, be little more than a mechanical operation.

12. Again, as an introduction to the principles of *legislation in general*, it ought rather to have included matters belonging exclusively to the *civil* branch, than matters more particularly applicable to the *penal*: the latter being but a means of compassing the ends proposed by the former. In preference therefore, or at least in priority, to the several chapters which will be found relative to *punishment*, it ought to have exhibited a set of propositions which have since presented themselves to him as affording a standard for the operations performed by government, in the creation and distribution of proprietary and other civil rights. He means certain axioms of what may be termed *mental pathology*, expressive of the connection betwixt the feelings of the parties concerned, and the several classes of incidents, which either call for, or are produced by, operations of the nature above mentioned.[1]

---

[1] For example.—*It is worse to lose than simply not to gain.—A loss falls the lighter by being divided.—The suffering of a person hurt in gratification of enmity, is greater than the gratification produced by the same cause.*—These, and a few others which he will have occasion to exhibit at the head of another publication, have the same claim to the appellation of axioms, as those given by

13. The consideration of the division of offences, and every thing else that belongs to offences, ought, besides, to have preceded the consideration of punishment: for the idea of *punishment* presupposes the idea of *offence*: punishment, as such, not being inflicted but in consideration of offence.

14. Lastly, the analytical discussions relative to the classification of offences would, according to his present views, be transferred to a separate treatise, in which the system of legislation is considered solely in respect of its form: in other words, in respect of its *method* and *terminology*.

15. In these respects the performance fails of coming up to the author's own ideas of what should have been exhibited in a work, bearing the title he has now given it, viz., that of an *Introduction to the Principles of Morals and Legislation*. He knows however of no other that would be less unsuitable: nor in particular would so adequate an intimation of its actual contents have been given, by a title corresponding to the more limited design, with which it was written: viz., that of serving as an *introduction to a penal code*.

16. Yet more. Dry and tedious as a great part of the discussions it contains must unavoidably be found by the bulk of readers, he knows not how to regret the having written them, nor even the having made them public. Under every head, the practical uses, to which the discussions contained under that head appeared applicable, are indicated: nor is there, he believes, a single proposition that he has not found occasion to build upon in the penning of some article or other of those provisions of detail, of which a body of law, authoritative or unauthoritative, must be composed. He will venture to specify particularly, in this view, the several chapters shortly characterized by the words *Sensibility, Actions, Intentionality, Consciousness, Motives, Dispositions, Consequences*. Even in the enormous chapter on the division of offences, which, notwithstanding the forced compression the plan has undergone in several of its parts, in manner there mentioned, occupies no fewer than one hundred and four closely printed quarto pages, the ten concluding ones are employed in a statement of the

mathematicians under that name; since, referring to universal experience as their immediate basis, they are incapable of demonstration, and require only to be developed and illustrated, in order to be recognized as incontestable.

practical advantages that may be reaped from the plan of
classification which it exhibits. Those in whose sight the
Defence of Usury has been fortunate enough to find favour,
may reckon as one instance of those advantages the discovery
of the principles developed in that little treatise. In the preface
to an anonymous tract published so long ago as in 1776,[1] he
had hinted at the utility of a natural classification of offences,
in the character of a test for distinguishing genuine from
spurious ones. The case of usury is one among a number of
instances of the truth of that observation. A note at the end
of Sect. XXXV, Chap. XVI. of the present publication, may
serve to show how the opinions, developed in that tract,
owed their origin to the difficulty experienced in the attempt
to find a place in his system for that imaginary offence. To
some readers, as a means of helping them to support the fatigue
of wading through an analysis of such enormous length, he
would almost recommend the beginning with those concluding pages.

17. One good at least may result from the present publication; viz., that the more he has trespassed on the patience of
the reader on this occasion, the less need he will have so to do
on future ones: so that this may do to those, the office which
is done, by books of pure mathematics, to books of mixed
mathematics and natural philosophy. The narrower the
circle of readers is, within which the present work may be
condemned to confine itself, the less limited may be the
number of those to whom the fruits of his succeeding labours
may be found accessible. He may therefore in this respect find
himself in the condition of those philosophers of antiquity,
who are represented as having held two bodies of doctrine,
a popular and an occult one: but, with this difference, that in
his instance the occult and the popular will, he hopes, be
found as consistent as in those they were contradictory; and
that in his production whatever there is of occultness has been
the pure result of sad necessity, and in no respect of choice.

18. Having, in the course of this advertisement, had such
frequent occasion to allude to different arrangements, as
having been suggested by more extensive and maturer views,
it may perhaps contribute to the satisfaction of the reader, to

[1] A Fragment on Government.

receive a short intimation of their nature: the rather, as, without such explanation, references, made here and there to unpublished works, might be productive of perplexity and mistake. The following then are the titles of the works by the publication of which his present designs would be completed. They are exhibited in the order which seemed to him best fitted for apprehension, and in which they would stand disposed, were the whole assemblage ready to come out at once: but the order, in which they will eventually appear, may probably enough be influenced in some degree by collateral and temporary considerations.

19. Part the 1st. Principles of legislation in matters of *civil*, more distinctively termed *private distributive*, or for shortness, *distributive*, *law*.

20. Part the 2nd. Principles of legislation in matters of *penal law*.

21. Part the 3rd. Principles of legislation in matters of *procedure*: uniting in one view the *criminal* and *civil* branches, between which no line can be drawn, but a very indistinct one, and that continually liable to variation.

22. Part the 4th. Principles of legislation in matters of *reward*.

23. Part the 5th. Principles of legislation in matters of *public distributive*, more concisely as well as familiarly termed *constitutional*, law.

24. Part the 6th. Principles of legislation in matters of *political tactics*: or of the art of maintaining *order* in the proceedings of political assemblies, so as to direct them to the end of their institution: viz., by a system of rules, which are to the constitutional branch, in some respects, what the law of procedure is to the civil and the penal.

25. Part the 7th. Principles of legislation in matters betwixt nation and nation, or, to use a new though not inexpressive appellation, in matters of *international* law.

26. Part the 8th. Principles of legislation in matters of *finance*.

27. Part the 9th. Principles of legislation in matters of *political economy*.

28. Part the 10th. Plan of a body of law, complete in all its branches, considered in respect of its *form*; in other words, in

respect of its method and terminology; including a view of the origination and connexion of the ideas expressed by the short list of terms, the exposition of which contains all that can be said with propriety to belong to the head of *universal jurisprudence*.[1]

29. The use of the principles laid down under the above several heads is to prepare the way for the body of law itself exhibited *in terminis*; and which to be complete, with reference to any political state, must consequently be calculated for the meridian, and adapted to the circumstances, of some one such state in particular.

30. Had he an unlimited power of drawing upon *time*, and every other condition necessary, it would be his wish to postpone the publication of each part to the completion of the whole. In particular, the use of the ten parts, which exhibit what appear to him the dictates of utility in every line, being no other than to furnish reasons for the several corresponding provisions contained in the body of law itself, the exact truth of the former can never be precisely ascertained, till the provisions, to which they are destined to apply, are themselves ascertained, and that *in terminis*. But as the infirmity of human nature renders all plans precarious in the execution, in proportion as they are extensive in the design, and as he has already made considerable advances in several branches of the theory, without having made correspondent advances in the practical applications, he deems it more than probable, that the eventual order of publication will not correspond exactly with that which, had it been equally practicable, would have appeared most eligible. Of this irregularity the unavoidable result will be, a multitude of imperfections, which, if the execution of the body of law *in terminis* had kept pace with the development of the principles, so that each part had been adjusted and corrected by the other, might have been avoided. His conduct however will be the less swayed by this inconvenience, from his suspecting it to be of the number of those in which the personal vanity of the author is much more concerned, than the instruction of the public: since whatever amendments may be suggested in the detail

---

[1] Such as obligation, right, power, possession, title, exemption, immunity, franchise, privilege, nullity, validity, and the like.

of the principles, by the literal fixation of the provisions to which they are relative, may easily be made in a corrected edition of the former, succeeding upon the publication of the latter.

31. In the course of the ensuing pages, references will be found, as already intimated, some to the plan of a penal code to which this work was meant as an introduction, some to other branches of the above-mentioned general plan, under titles somewhat different from those, by which they have been mentioned here. The giving this warning is all which it is in the author's power to do, to save the reader from the perplexity of looking out for what has not as yet any existence. The recollection of the change of plan will in like manner account for several similar incongruities not worth particularising.

32. Allusion was made, at the outset of this advertisement, to some unspecified difficulties, as the causes of the original suspension, and unfinished complexion, of the present work. Ashamed of his defeat, and unable to dissemble it, he knows not how to refuse himself the benefit of such an apology as a slight sketch of the nature of those difficulties may afford.

33. The discovery of them was produced by the attempt to solve the questions that will be found at the conclusion of the volume: *Wherein consisted the identity and* completeness *of a law*? *What the distinction, and where the separation, between* a penal *and a* civil *law*? *What the distinction, and where the separation, between the* penal *and* other branches *of* the law?

34. To give a complete and correct answer to these questions, it is but too evident that the relations and dependencies of every part of the legislative system, with respect to every other, must have been comprehended and ascertained. But it is only upon a view of these parts themselves, that such an operation could have been performed. To the accuracy of such a survey one necessary condition would therefore be, the complete existence of the fabric to be surveyed. Of the performance of this condition no example is as yet to be met with any where. *Common* law, as it styles itself in England, *judiciary* law, as it might more aptly be styled every where, that fictitious composition which has no known person for

its author, no known assemblage of words for its substance, forms every where the main body of the legal fabric: like that fancied ether, which, in default of sensible matter, fills up the measure of the universe. Shreds and scraps of real law, stuck on upon that imaginary ground, compose the furniture of every national code. What follows?—that he who, for the purpose just mentioned or for any other, wants an example of a complete body of law to refer to, must begin with making one.

35. There is, or rather there ought to be, a *logic* of the *will*, as well as of the *understanding*: the operations of the former faculty, are neither less susceptible, nor less worthy, than those of the latter, of being delineated by rules. Of these two branches of that recondite art, Aristotle saw only the latter: succeeding logicians, treading the steps of their great founder, have concurred in seeing with no other eyes. Yet so far as a difference can be assigned between branches so intimately connected, whatever difference there is, in point of importance, is in favour of the logic of the will. Since it is only by their capacity of directing the operations of this faculty, that the operations of the understanding are of any consequence.

36. Of this logic of the will, the science of *law*, considered in respect of its *form*, is the most considerable branch,—the most important application. It is, to the art of legislation, what the science of anatomy is to the art of medicine: with this difference, that the subject of it is what the artist has to work *with*, instead of being what he has to operate *upon*. Nor is the body politic less in danger from a want of acquaintance with the one science, than the body natural from ignorance in the other. One example, amongst a thousand that might be adduced in proof of this assertion, may be seen in the note which terminates this volume.

37. Such then were the difficulties: such the preliminaries: —an unexampled work to achieve, and then a new science to create: a new branch to add to one of the most abstruse of sciences.

38. Yet more: a body of proposed law, how complete soever, would be comparatively useless and uninstructive, unless explained and justified, and that in every tittle, by a continued

accompaniment, a perpetual commentary of *reasons*:[1] which reasons, that the comparative value of such as point in opposite directions may be estimated, and the conjunct force, of such as point in the same direction, may be felt, must be marshalled, and put under subordination to such extensive and leading ones as are termed *principles*. There must be therefore, not one system only, but two parallel and connected systems, running on together, the one of legislative provisions, the other of political reasons, each affording to the other correction and support.

39. Are enterprises like these achievable? He knows not. This only he knows, that they have been undertaken, proceeded in, and that some progress has been made in all of them. He will venture to add, if at all achievable, never at least by one, to whom the fatigue of attending to discussions, as arid as those which occupy the ensuing pages, would either appear useless, or feel intolerable. He will repeat it boldly (for it has been said before him), truths that form the basis of political and moral science are not to be discovered but by investigations as severe as mathematical ones, and beyond all comparison more intricate and extensive. The familiarity of the terms is a presumption, but it is a most fallacious one, of the facility of the matter. Truths in general have been called stubborn things: the truths just mentioned are so in their own way. They are not to be forced into detached and general propositions, unincumbered with explanations and exceptions. They will not compress themselves into epigrams. They recoil from the tongue and the pen of the declaimer. They flourish not in the same soil with sentiment. They grow among thorns; and are not to be plucked, like daisies, by infants as they run. Labour, the inevitable lot of humanity, is in no track more inevitable than here. In vain would an Alexander bespeak a peculiar road for royal vanity, or a Ptolemy, a smoother one, for royal indolence. There is no *King's Road*, no *Stadtholder's Gate*, to legislative, any more than to mathematic science.

[1] To the aggregate of them a common denomination has since been allotted—*the rationale*. [1823.]

AN INTRODUCTION TO THE PRINCIPLES OF MORALS AND LEGISLATION

CHAPTER I

OF THE PRINCIPLE OF UTILITY

1. NATURE has placed mankind under the governance of two sovereign masters, *pain* and *pleasure*. It is for them alone to point out what we ought to do, as well as to determine what we shall do. On the one hand the standard of right and wrong, on the other the chain of causes and effects, are fastened to their throne. They govern us in all we do, in all we say, in all we think: every effort we can make to throw off our subjection, will serve but to demonstrate and confirm it. In words a man may pretend to abjure their empire: but in reality he will remain subject to it all the while. The *principle of utility*[1] recognizes this subjection, and assumes it for the foundation of that system, the object of which is to rear the fabric of felicity by the hands of reason and of law. Systems which attempt to question it, deal in sounds instead of senses, in caprice instead of reason, in darkness instead of light.

Mankind governed by pain and pleasure.

[1] Note by the Author, July 1822.

To this denomination has of late been added, or substituted, the *greatest happiness* or *greatest felicity* principle: this for shortness, instead of saying at length *that principle* which states the greatest happiness of all those whose interest is in question, as being the right and proper, and only right and proper and universally desirable, end of human action: of human action in every situation, and in particular in that of a functionary or set of functionaries exercising the powers of Government. The word *utility* does not so clearly point to the ideas of *pleasure* and *pain* as the words *happiness* and *felicity* do: nor does it lead us to the consideration of the *number*, of the interests affected; to the *number*, as being the circumstance, which contributes, in the largest proportion, to the formation of the standard here in question; the *standard of right and wrong*, by which alone the propriety of human conduct, in every situation, can with propriety be tried. This want of a sufficiently manifest connexion between the ideas of *happiness* and *pleasure* on the one hand, and the idea of *utility* on the other, I have every now and then found operating, and with but too much efficiency, as a bar to the acceptance, that might otherwise have been given, to this principle.

But enough of metaphor and declamation: it is not by such means that moral science is to be improved.

2. The principle of utility is the foundation of the present work: it will be proper therefore at the outset to give an explicit and determinate account of what is meant by it. By the principle[1] of utility is meant that principle which approves or disapproves of every action whatsoever, according to the tendency which it appears to have to augment or diminish the happiness of the party whose interest is in question: or, what is the same thing in other words, to promote or to oppose that happiness. I say of every action whatsoever; and therefore not only of every action of a private individual, but of every measure of government.

Principle of utility, what.

3. By utility is meant that property in any object, whereby it tends to produce benefit, advantage, pleasure, good, or happiness, (all this in the present case comes to the same thing) or (what comes again to the same thing) to prevent the happening of mischief, pain, evil, or unhappiness to the party whose interest is considered: if that party be the community in general, then the happiness of the community: if a particular individual, then the happiness of that individual.

Utility what.

4. The interest of the community is one of the most general expressions that can occur in the phraseology of morals: no wonder that the meaning of it is often lost. When it has a meaning, it is this. The community is a fictitious *body*, composed of the individual persons who are considered as constituting as it were its *members*. The interest of the community then is, what?—the sum of the interests of the several members who compose it.

Interest of the community, what.

5. It is in vain to talk of the interest of the community,

A principle, what.

[1] The word principle is derived from the Latin principium: which seems to be compounded of the two words *primus*, first, or chief, and *cipium*, a termination which seems to be derived from *capio*, to take, as in *mancipium, municipium*; to which are analogous, *auceps, forceps*, and others. It is a term of very vague and very extensive signification: it is applied to any thing which is conceived to serve as a foundation or beginning to any series of operations: in some cases, of physical operations; but of mental operations in the present case.

The principle here in question may be taken for an act of the mind; a sentiment; a sentiment of approbation; a sentiment which, when applied to an action, approves of its utility, as that quality of it by which the measure of approbation or disapprobation bestowed upon it ought to be governed.

OF THE PRINCIPLE OF UTILITY 127

without understanding what is the interest of the individual.[1]
A thing is said to promote the interest, or to be *for* the interest,
of an individual, when it tends to add to the sum total of his
pleasures: or, what comes to the same thing, to diminish the
sum total of his pains.

6. An action then may be said to be conformable to the
principle of utility, or, for shortness sake, to utility, (meaning
with respect to the community at large) when the tendency
it has to augment the happiness of the community is greater
than any it has to diminish it.

An action conformable to the principle of utility, what.

7. A measure of government (which is but a particular
kind of action, performed by a particular person or persons)
may be said to be conformable to or dictated by the principle
of utility, when in like manner the tendency which it has to
augment the happiness of the community is greater than any
which it has to diminish it.

A measure of government conformable to the principle of utility, what.

8. When an action, or in particular a measure of government, is supposed by a man to be conformable to the principle
of utility, it may be convenient, for the purposes of discourse,
to imagine a kind of law or dictate, called a law or dictate of
utility; and to speak of the action in question, as being conformable to such law or dictate.

Laws or dictates of utility, what.

9. A man may be said to be a partizan of the principle of
utility, when the approbation or disapprobation he annexes
to any action, or to any measure, is determined by and
proportioned to the tendency which he conceives it to have
to augment or to diminish the happiness of the community: or
in other words, to its conformity or unconformity to the
laws or dictates of utility.

A partizan of the principle of utility, who.

10. Of an action that is conformable to the principle of
utility one may always say either that it is one that ought to
be done, or at least that it is not one that ought not to be done.
One may say also, that it is right it should be done; at least
that it is not wrong it should be done: that it is a right action;
at least that it is not a wrong action. When thus interpreted,
the words *ought*, and *right* and *wrong*, and others of that stamp,
have a meaning: when otherwise, they have none.

Ought, ought not, right and wrong, etc. how to be understood.

---

[1] Interest is one of those words, which not having any superior *genus*,
cannot in the ordinary way be defined.

To prove the rectitude of this principle is at once unnecessary and impossible.

11. Has the rectitude of this principle been ever formally contested? It should seem that it had, by those who have not known what they have been meaning. Is it susceptible of any direct proof? it should seem not: for that which is used to prove every thing else, cannot itself be proved: a chain of proofs must have their commencement somewhere. To give such proof is as impossible as it is needless.

It has seldom, however, as yet been consistently pursued.

12. Not that there is or ever has been that human creature breathing, however stupid or perverse, who has not on many perhaps on most occasions of his life, deferred to it. By the natural constitution of the human frame, on most occasions of their lives men in general embrace this principle, without thinking of it: if not for the ordering of their own actions, yet for the trying of their own actions, as well as of those of other men. There have been, at the same time, not many, perhaps even of the most intelligent, who have been disposed to embrace it purely and without reserve   There are even few who have not taken some occasion or other to quarrel with it, either on account of their not understanding always how to apply it, or on account of some prejudice or other which they were afraid to examine into, or could not bear to part with For such is the stuff that man is made of: in principle and in practice, in a right track and in a wrong one, the rarest of all human qualities is consistency.

It can never be consistently combated.

13. When a man attempts to combat the principle of utility it is with reasons drawn, without his being aware of it, from that very principle itself.[1] His arguments, if they prove any

---

[1] 'The principle of utility, (I have heard it said) is a dangerous principle it is dangerous on certain occasions to consult it.' This is as much as to say what? that it is not consonant to utility, to consult utility: in short, that it i *not* consulting it, to consult it.

Addition by the Author, July 1822.

Not long after the publication of the Fragment on Government, anno 1776, in which, in the character of an all-comprehensive and all-commanding principle, the principle of *utility* was brought to view, one person by whom observation to the above effect was made was *Alexander Wedderburn*, at that time Attorney or Solicitor General, afterwards successively Chief Justice of the Common Pleas, and Chancellor of England, under the successive title of Lord Loughborough and Earl of Rosslyn,. It was made—not indeed in my hearing, but in the hearing of a person by whom it was almost immediately communicated to me. So far from being self-contradictory, it was a shrewd and perfectly true one. By that distinguished functionary, the state of the Government was thoroughly understood: by the obscure individual, at that time not so much as supposed to be so: his disquisitions had not been as yet

thing, prove not that the principle is *wrong*, but that, according to the applications he supposes to be made of it, it is *misapplied*. Is it possible for a man to move the earth? Yes; but he must first find out another earth to stand upon.

14. To disprove the propriety of it by arguments is imposs-ible; but, from the causes that have been mentioned, or from some confused or partial view of it, a man may happen to be disposed not to relish it. Where this is the case, if he thinks the settling of his opinions on such a subject worth the trouble, let him take the following steps and at length, perhaps, he may come to reconcile himself to it. *Course to be taken for surmounting prejudices that may have been entertained against it.*

1. Let him settle with himself, whether he would wish to discard this principle altogether; if so, let him consider what it is that all his reasonings (in matters of politics especially) can amount to?

2. If he would, let him settle with himself, whether he would judge and act without any principle, or whether there is any other he would judge and act by?

3. If there be, let him examine and satisfy himself whether the principle he thinks he has found is really any separate intelligible principle; or whether it be not a mere principle

applied, with any thing like a comprehensive view, to the field of Constitutional Law, nor therefore to those features of the English Government, by which the greatest happiness of the ruling *one* with or without that of a favoured few, are now so plainly seen to be the only ends to which the course of it has at any time been directed. The *principle of utility* was an appellative, at that time employed—employed by me, as it had been by others, to designate that which in a more perspicuous and instructive manner, may, as above, be designated by the name of the *greatest happiness principle*. 'This principle (said Wedderburn) is a dangerous one.' Saying so, he said that which, to a certain extent, is strictly true: a principle, which lays down, as the only *right* and justifiable end of Government, the greatest happiness of the greatest number— how can it be denied to be a dangerous one? dangerous it unquestionably is, to every government which has for its *actual* end or object, the greatest happiness of a certain *one*, with or without the addition of some comparatively small number of others, whom it is a matter of pleasure or accommodation to him to admit, each of them, to a share in the concern, on the footing of so many junior partners. *Dangerous* it therefore really was, to the interest—the sinister interest—of all those functionaries, himself included, whose interest it was, to maximize delay, vexation, and expense, in judicial and other modes of procedure, for the sake of the profit, extractible out of the expense. In a Government which had for its end in view the greatest happiness of the greatest number, Alexander Wedderburn might have been Attorney General and then Chancellor: but he would not have been Attorney General with £15,000 a year, nor Chancellor, with a peerage with a veto upon all justice, with £25,000 a year, and with 500 sinecures at his disposal, under the name of Ecclesiastical Benefices, besides *et cæteras*.

I

in words, a kind of phrase, which at bottom expresses neither more nor less than the mere averment of his own unfounded sentiments; that is, what in another person he might be apt to call caprice?

4. If he is inclined to think that his own approbation or disapprobation, annexed to the idea of an act, without any regard to its consequences, is a sufficient foundation for him to judge and act upon, let him ask himself whether his sentiment is to be a standard of right and wrong, with respect to every other man, or whether every man's sentiment has the same privilege of being a standard to itself?

5. In the first case, let him ask himself whether his principle is not despotical, and hostile to all the rest of human race?

6. In the second case, whether it is not anarchical, and whether at this rate there are not as many different standards of right and wrong as there are men? and whether even to the sane man, the same thing, which is right to-day, may not (without the least change in its nature) be wrong to-morrow? and whether the same thing is not right and wrong in the same place at the same time? and in either case, whether all argument is not at an end? and whether, when two men have said, 'I like this,' and 'I don't like it,' they can (upon such a principle) have any thing more to say?

7. If he should have said to himself, No: for that the sentiment which he proposes as a standard must be grounded on reflection, let him say on what particulars the reflection is to turn? if on particulars having relation to the utility of the act, then let him say whether this is not deserting his own principle, and borrowing assistance from that very one in opposition to which he sets it up: or if not on those particulars, on what other particulars?

8. If he should be for compounding the matter, and adopting his own principle in part, and the principle of utility in part, let him say how far he will adopt it?

9. When he has settled with himself where he will stop, then let him ask himself how he justifies to himself the adopting it so far? and why he will not adopt it any farther?

10. Admitting any other principle than the principle of utility to be a right principle, a principle that it is right for a man to pursue; admitting (what is not true) that the word

right can have a meaning without reference to utility, let him say whether there is any such thing as a *motive* that a man can have to pursue the dictates of it: if there is, let him say what that motive is, and how it is to be distinguished from those which enforce the dictates of utility: if not, then lastly let him say what it is this other principle can be good for?

CHAPTER II

OF PRINCIPLES ADVERSE TO THAT OF UTILITY

All other
principles than
that of utility
must be wrong.

1. If the principle of utility be a right principle to be governed by, and that in all cases, it follows from what has been just observed, that whatever principle differs from it in any case must necessarily be a wrong one. To prove any other principle, therefore, to be a wrong one, there needs no more than just to show it to be what it is, a principle of which the dictates are in some point or other different from those of the principle of utility: to state it is to confute it.

Ways in which
a principle may
be wrong.

2. A principle may be different from that of utility in two ways: 1. By being constantly opposed to it: this is the case with a principle which may be termed the principle of *asceticism*.[1] 2. By being sometimes opposed to it, and sometimes not, as it may happen: this is the case with another, which may be termed the principle of *sympathy* and *antipathy*.

Principle of
asceticism,
what.

3. By the principle of asceticism I mean that principle, which, like the principle of utility, approves or disapproves of any action, according to the tendency which it appears to have to augment or diminish the happiness of the party whose interest is in question; but in an inverse manner: approving

Asceticism,
origin of the
word.
Principles of the
Monks.

[1] Ascetic is a term that has been sometimes applied to Monks. It comes from a Greek word which signifies *exercise*. The practices by which Monks sought to distinguish themselves from other men were called their Exercises. These exercises consisted in so many contrivances they had for tormenting themselves. By this they thought to ingratiate themselves with the Deity. For the Deity, said they, is a Being of infinite benevolence: now a Being of the most ordinary benevolence is pleased to see others make themselves as happy as they can: therefore to make ourselves as unhappy as we can is the way to please the Deity. If any body asked them, what motive they could find for doing all this? Oh! said they, you are not to imagine that we are punishing ourselves for nothing: we know very well what we are about. You are to know, that for every grain of pain it costs us now, we are to have a hundred grains of pleasure by and by. The case is, that God loves to see us torment ourselves at present: indeed he has as good as told us so. But this is done only to try us, in order just to see how we should behave: which it is plain he could not know, without making the experiment. Now then, from the satisfaction it gives him to see us make ourselves as unhappy as we can make ourselves in this present life, we have a sure proof of the satisfaction it will give him to see us as happy as he can make us in a life to come.

of actions in as far as they tend to diminish his happiness; disapproving of them in as far as they tend to augment it.

4. It is evident that any one who reprobates any the least particle of pleasure, as such, from whatever source derived, is *pro tanto* a partizan of the principle of asceticism. It is only upon that principle, and not from the principle of utility, that the most abominable pleasure which the vilest of malefactors ever reaped from his crime would be reprobated, if it stood alone. The case is, that it never does stand alone; but is necessarily followed by such a quantity of pain (or, what comes to the same thing, such a chance for a certain quantity of pain) that the pleasure in comparison of it, is as nothing: and this is the true and sole, but perfectly sufficient, reason for making it a ground for punishment. *A partizan of the principle of asceticism, who.*

5. There are two classes of men of very different complexions, by whom the principle of asceticism appears to have been embraced; the one a set of moralists, the other a set of religionists. Different accordingly have been the motives which appear to have recommended it to the notice of these different parties. Hope, that is the prospect of pleasure, seems to have animated the former: hope, the aliment of philosophic pride: the hope of honour and reputation at the hands of men. Fear, that is the prospect of pain, the latter: fear the offspring of superstitious fancy: the fear of future punishment at the hands of a splenetic and revengeful Deity. I say in this case fear: for of the invisible future, fear is more powerful than hope. These circumstances characterize the two different parties among the partizans of the principle of asceticism; the parties and their motives different, the principle the same. *This principle has had in some a philosophical, in others a religious origin.*

6. The religious party, however, appear to have carried it farther than the philosophical: they have acted more consistently and less wisely. The philosophical party have scarcely gone farther than to reprobate pleasure: the religious party have frequently gone so far as to make it a matter of merit and of duty to court pain. The philosophical party have hardly gone farther than the making pain a matter of indifference. It is no evil, they have said: they have not said, it is a good. They have not so much as reprobated all pleasure in the lump. They have discarded only what they have called *It has been carried farther by the religious party than by the philosophical.*

the gross; that is, such as are organical, or of which the origin is easily traced up to such as are organical: they have even cherished and magnified the refined. Yet this, however, not under the name of pleasure: to cleanse itself from the sordes of its impure original, it was necessary it should change its name: the honourable, the glorious, the reputable, the becoming, the *honestum*, the *decorum*, it was to be called: in short, any thing but pleasure.

The philosophi-cal branch of it has had most influence among persons of education, the religious among the vulgar.

7. From these two sources have flowed the doctrines from which the sentiments of the bulk of mankind have all along received a tincture of this principle; some from the philosophical, some from the religious, some from both. Men of education more frequently from the philosophical, as more suited to the elevation of their sentiments: the vulgar more frequently from the superstitious, as more suited to the narrowness of their intellect, undilated by knowledge: and to the abjectness of their condition, continually open to the attacks of fear. The tinctures, however, derived from the two sources, would naturally intermingle, insomuch that a man would not always know by which of them he was most influenced: and they would often serve to corroborate and enliven one another. It was this conformity that made a kind of alliance between parties of a complexion otherwise so dissimilar: and disposed them to unite upon various occasions against the common enemy, the partizan of the principle of utility, whom they joined in branding with the odious name of Epicurean.

The principle of asceticism has never been steadily applied by either party to the Business of Government.

8. The principle of asceticism, however, with whatever warmth it may have been embraced by its partizans as a rule of private conduct, seems not to have been carried to any considerable length, when applied to the business of government. In a few instances it has been carried a little way by the philosophical party: witness the Spartan regimen. Though then, perhaps, it may be considered as having been a measure of security: and an application, though a precipitate and perverse application, of the principle of utility. Scarcely in any instances, to any considerable length, by the religious: for the various monastic orders, and the societies of the Quakers, Dumplers, Moravians, and other religionists, have been free societies, whose regimen no man has been astricted to without

the intervention of his own consent. Whatever merit a man may have thought there would be in making himself miserable, no such notion seems ever to have occurred to any of them, that it may be a merit, much less a duty, to make others miserable: although it should seem, that if a certain quantity of misery were a thing so desirable, it would not matter much whether it were brought by each man upon himself, or by one man upon another. It is true, that from the same source from whence, among the religionists, the attachment to the principle of asceticism took its rise, flowed other doctrines and practices, from which misery in abundance was produced in one man by the instrumentality of another: witness the holy wars, and the persecutions for religion. But the passion for producing misery in these cases proceeded upon some special ground: the exercise of it was confined to persons of particular descriptions: they were tormented, not as men, but as heretics and infidels. To have inflicted the same miseries on their fellow-believers and fellow-sectaries, would have been as blameable in the eyes even of these religionists, as in those of a partizan of the principle of utility. For a man to give himself a certain number of stripes was indeed meritorious: but to give the same number of stripes to another man, not consenting, would have been a sin. We read of saints, who for the good of their souls, and the mortification of their bodies, have voluntarily yielded themselves a prey to vermin: but though many persons of this class have wielded the reins of empire, we read of none who have set themselves to work, and made laws on purpose, with a view of stocking the body politic with the breed of high-waymen, housebreakers, or incendiaries. If at any time they have suffered the nation to be preyed upon by swarms of idle pensioners, or useless placemen, it has rather been from negligence and imbecility, than from any settled plan for oppressing and plundering of the people. If at any time they have sapped the sources of national wealth, by cramping commerce, and driving the inhabitants into emigration, it has been with other views, and in pursuit of other ends. If they have declaimed against the pursuit of pleasure, and the use of wealth, they have commonly stopped at declamation: they have not, like Lycurgus, made express ordinances for the purpose of banishing the precious metals. If they have established idleness by a law, it has been not because idleness, the mother of vice and misery, is itself a virtue, but because idleness (say they) is the road to holiness. If under the notion of fasting, they have joined in the plan of confining their subjects to a diet, thought by some to be of the most nourishing and prolific nature, it has been not for the sake of making them tributaries to the nations by whom that diet was to be supplied, but for the sake of manifesting their own power, and exercising the obedience of the people. If they have established, or suffered to be established, punishments for the breach of celibacy, they have done no more than comply with the petitions of those deluded rigorists, who, dupes to the ambitious and deep-laid policy of their rulers, first laid themselves under that idle obligation by a vow.

The principle of asceticism, in its origin, was but that of utility misapplied.   9. The principle of asceticism seems originally to have been the reverie of certain hasty speculators, who having perceived, or fancied, that certain pleasures, when reaped in certain circumstances, have, at the long run, been attended with pains more than equivalent to them, took occasion to quarrel with every thing that offered itself under the name of pleasure. Having then got thus far, and having forgot the point which they set out from, they pushed on, and went so much further as to think it meritorious to fall in love with pain. Even this, we see, is at bottom but the principle of utility misapplied.

It can never be consistently pursued.   10. The principle of utility is capable of being consistently pursued; and it is but tautology to say, that the more consistently it is pursued, the better it must ever be for humankind. The principle of asceticism never was, nor ever can be, consistently pursued by any living creature. Let but one tenth part of the inhabitants of this earth pursue it consistently, and in a day's time they will have turned it into a hell.

The principle of sympathy and antipathy, what.   11. Among principles adverse[1] to that of utility, that which

---

[1] The following Note was first printed in January 1789.

It ought rather to have been styled, more extensively, the principle of *caprice*. Where it applies to the choice of actions to be marked out for injunction or prohibition, for reward or punishment, (to stand, in a word, as subjects for *obligations* to be imposed,) it may indeed with propriety be termed, as in the text, the principle of *sympathy* and *antipathy*. But this appellative does not so well apply to it, when occupied in the choice of the *events* which are to serve as sources of *title* with respect to *rights*: where the actions prohibited and allowed, the obligations and rights, being already fixed, the only question at this day seems to have most influence in matters of government, is what may be called the principle of sympathy and

is, under what circumstances a man is to be invested with the one or subjected to the other? from what incidents occasion is to be taken to invest a man, or to refuse to invest him, with the one, or to subject him to the other? In the latter case it may more appositely be characterized by the name of the *phantastic principle*. Sympathy and antipathy are affections of the *sensible* faculty. But the choice of *titles* with respect to *rights*, especially with respect to proprietary rights, upon grounds unconnected with utility, has been in many instances the work, not of the affections but of the imagination.

When, in justification of an article of English Common Law, calling uncles to succeed in certain cases in preference to fathers, Lord Coke produced a sort of ponderosity he had discovered in rights, disqualifying them from ascending in a straight line, it was not that he *loved* uncles particularly, or *hated* fathers, but because the analogy, such as it was, was what his imagination presented him with, instead of a reason, and because, to a judgment unobservant of the standard of utility, or unacquainted with the art of consulting it, where affection is out of the way, imagination is the only guide.

When I know not what ingenious grammarian invented the proposition *Delegatus non potest delegare*, to serve as a rule of law, it was not surely that he had any antipathy to delegates of the second order, or that it was any pleasure to him to think of the ruin which, for want of a manager at home, may befal the affairs of a traveller, whom an unforeseen accident has deprived of the object of his choice: it was, that the incongruity, of giving the same law to objects so contrasted as *active* and *passive* are, was not to be surmounted; and that *-atus* chimes, as well as it contrasts, with *-are*.

When that inexorable maxim, (of which the dominion is no more to be defined, than the date of its birth, or the name of its father, is to be found,) was imported from England for the government of Bengal, and the whole fabric of judicature was crushed by the thunders of *ex post facto* justice, it was not surely that the prospect of a blameless magistracy perishing in prison afforded any enjoyment to the unoffended authors of their misery; but that the music of the maxim, absorbing the whole imagination, had drowned the cries of humanity along with the dictates of common sense.[a]   *Fiat Justitia,*

[a]   Additional Note by the Author, July 1822.

Add, and that the bad system, of Mahometan and other native law was to be put down at all events, to make way for the inapplicable and still more mischievous system of English Judge-made law, and, by the hand of his accomplice Hastings, was to be put into the pocket of Impey—Importer of this instrument of subversion, £8,000 a-year contrary to law, in addition to the £8,000 a-year lavished upon him, with the customary profusion, by the hand of law.—See the Account of this transaction in *Mill's British India.*

To this Governor a statue is erecting by a vote of East India Directors and Proprietors: on it should be inscribed—*Let it but put money into our pockets no tyranny too flagitious to be worshipped by us.*

To this statue of the Arch-malefactor should be added, for a companion, that of the long-robed accomplice: the one lodging the bribe in the hand of the other. The hundred millions of plundered and oppressed Hindoos and Mahometans pay for the one; a Westminster Hall subscription might pay for the other.

What they have done for Ireland with her seven millions of souls, the authorised dealers and perverters of justice have done for Hindostan with her hundred millions. In this there is nothing wonderful. The wonder is—that,

antipathy. By the principle of sympathy and antipathy, I mean that principle which approves or disapproves of certain

ruat cælum, says another maxim, as full of extravagance as it is of harmony: Go heaven to wreck—so justice be but done:—and what is the ruin of kingdoms, in comparison of the wreck of heaven?

So again, when the Prussian chancellor, inspired with the wisdom of I know not what Roman sage, proclaimed in good Latin, for the edification of German ears, *Servitus servitutis non datur*, [Cod. Fred. tom. ii. par. 2. liv. 2. tit. x. § 6. p. 308.] it was not that he had conceived any aversion to the life-holder who, during the continuance of his term, should wish to gratify a neighbour with a right of way or water, or to the neighbour who should wish to accept of the indulgence; but that, to a jurisprudential ear, *-tus -tutis* sound little less melodius than *-atus -are*. Whether the melody of the maxim was the real reason of the rule, is not left open to dispute: for it is ushered in by the conjunction *quia*, reason's appointed harbinger: *quia servitus servitutis non datur.*

Neither would equal melody have been produced, nor indeed could similar melody have been called for, in either of these instances, by the opposite provision: it is only when they are opposed to general rules, and not when by their conformity they are absorbed in them, that more specific ones can obtain a separate existence. *Delegatus potest delegare*, and *Servitus servitutis datur*, provisions already included under the general adoption of contracts, would have been as unnecessary to the apprehension and the memory, as, in comparison of their energetic negatives, they are insipid to the ear.

Were the inquiry diligently made, it would be found that the goddess of harmony has exercised more influence, however latent, over the dispensations of Themis, than her most diligent historiographers, or even her most passionate panegyrists, seem to have been aware of. Every one knows, how, by the ministry of Orpheus, it was she who first collected the sons of men beneath the shadow of the sceptre: yet, in the midst of continual experience, men seem yet to learn, with what successful diligence she has laboured to guide it in its course. Every one knows, that measured numbers were the language of the infancy of law: none seem to have observed, with what imperious sway they have governed her maturer age. In English jurisprudence in particular, the connexion betwixt law and music, however less perceived than in Spartan legislation, is not perhaps real nor less close. The music of the Office, though not of the same kind, is not less musical in its kind, than the music of the Theatre; that which hardens the heart, than that which softens it:—sostenutos as long, cadences as sonorous; and those governed by rules, though not yet promulgated, not less determinate. Search indictments, pleadings, proceedings in chancery, conveyances: whatever trespasses you may find against truth or common sense, you will find none against the laws of harmony. The English Liturgy, just as this quality has been extolled in that sacred office, possesses not a greater measure of it, than is commonly to be found in an English Act of Parliament. Dignity, simplicity, brevity, precision, intelligibility, possibility of being retained or so much as apprehended, every thing yields to Harmony. Volumes might be filled, shelves loaded, with the sacrifices that are made to

---

under such institutions, men, though in ever such small number, should be found, whom the view of the injustices which, by *English Judge-made law*, they are compelled to commit, and the miseries they are thus compelled to produce, deprive of health and rest. Witness the Letter of an English Hindostan Judge, Sept. 1, 1819, which lies before me. I will not make so cruel a requital for his honesty, as to put his name in print: indeed the House of Commons' Documents already published leave little need of it.

actions, not on account of their tending to augment the happiness, nor yet on account of their tending to diminish the happiness of the party whose interest is in question, but merely because a man finds himself disposed to approve or disapprove of them: holding up that approbation or disapprobation as a sufficient reason for itself, and disclaiming the necessity of looking out for any extrinsic ground. Thus far in the general department of morals: and in the particular department of politics, measuring out the quantum (as well as determining the ground) of punishment, by the degree of the disapprobation.

this insatiate power. Expletives, her ministers in Grecian poetry are not less busy, though in different shape and bulk, in English legislation: in the former, they are monosyllables[a]: in the latter, they are whole lines.[b]

To return to the *principle of sympathy and antipathy*: a term preferred at first, on account of its impartiality, to the *principle of caprice*. The choice of an appellative, in the above respects too narrow, was owing to my not having, at that time, extended my views over the civil branch of law, any otherwise than as I had found it inseparably involved in the penal. But when we come to the former branch, we shall see the *phantastic* principle making at least as great a figure there, as the principle of *sympathy and antipathy* in the latter.

In the days of Lord Coke, the light of utility can scarcely be said to have as yet shone upon the face of Common Law. If a faint ray of it, under the name of the *argumentum ab inconvenienti*, is to be found in a list of about twenty topics exhibited by that great lawyer as the co-ordinate leaders of that all-perfect system, the admission, so circumstanced, is as sure a proof of neglect, as, to the status of Brutus and Cassius, exclusion was a cause of notice. It stands, neither in the front, nor in the rear, nor in any post of honour; but huddled in towards the middle, without the smallest mark of preference. [Coke, Littleton, 11. a.] Nor is this Latin *inconvenience* by any means the same thing with the English one. It stands distinguished from *mischief*: and because by the vulgar it is taken for something less bad, it is given by the learned as something worse. *The law prefers a mischief to an inconvenience*, says an admired maxim, and the more admired because as nothing is expressed by it, the more is supposed to be understood.

Not that there is any avowed, much less a constant opposition, between the prescriptions of utility and the operations of the common law: such constancy we have seen to be too much even for ascetic fervor. [Supra, par. x.] From time to time instinct would unavoidably betray them into the paths of reason: instinct which, however it may be cramped, can never be killed by education. The cobwebs spun out of the materials brought together by 'the competition of opposite analogies,' can never have ceased being warped by the silent attraction of the rational principle: though it should have been, as the needle is by the magnet, without the privity of conscience.

[a] Μεν, τοι, γε, νυν, &c.
[b] And be it further enacted by the authority aforesaid, that—Provided always, and it is hereby further enacted and declared that—&c. &c.

This is rather the negation of all principle, than any thing positive.

12. It is manifest, that this is rather a principle in name than in reality: it is not a positive principle of itself, so much as a term employed to signify the negation of all principle. What one expects to find in a principle is something that points out some external consideration, as a means of warranting and guiding the internal sentiments of approbation and disapprobation: this expectation is but ill fulfilled by a proposition, which does neither more nor less than hold up each of those sentiments as a ground and standard for itself.

Sentiments of a partizan of the principle of antipathy.

13. In looking over the catalogue of human actions (says a partizan of this principle) in order to determine which of them are to be marked with the seal of disapprobation, you need but to take counsel of your own feelings: whatever you find in yourself a propensity to condemn, is wrong for that very reason. For the same reason it is also meet for punishment: in what proportion it is adverse to utility, or whether it be adverse to utility at all, is a matter that makes no difference. In that same *proportion* also is it meet for punishment: if you hate much, punish much: if you hate little, punish little: punish as you hate. If you hate not at all, punish not at all: the fine feelings of the soul are not to be overborne and tyrannized by the harsh and rugged dictates of political utility.

The systems that have been formed concerning the standard of right and wrong, are all reducible to this principle.

14. The various systems that have been formed concerning the standard of right and wrong, may all be reduced to the principle of sympathy and antipathy. One account may serve for all of them. They consist all of them in so many contrivances for avoiding the obligation of appealing to any external standard, and for prevailing upon the reader to accept of the author's sentiment or opinion as a reason for itself. The phrases different, but the principle the same.[1]

Various phrases that have served as the characteristic marks of so many pretended systems.
1. *Moral Sense.*
2. *Common Sense.*

[1] It is curious enough to observe the variety of inventions men have hit upon, and the variety of phrases they have brought forward, in order to conceal from the world, and, if possible, from themselves, this very general and therefore very pardonable self-sufficiency.

1. One man says, he has a thing made on purpose to tell him what is right and what is wrong; and that it is called a *moral sense*: and then he goes to work at his ease, and says, such a thing is right, and such a thing is wrong—why? 'because my moral sense tells me it is.'

2. Another man comes and alters the phrase: leaving out *moral*, and putting in *common*, in the room of it. He then tells you, that his common sense teaches him what is right and wrong, as surely as the other's moral sense did: meaning by common sense, a sense of some kind or other, which, he says, is possessed by all mankind: the sense of those, whose sense is not the same as the author's,

15. It is manifest, that the dictates of this principle will *This principle* frequently coincide with those of utility, though perhaps *will frequently* without intending any such thing. Probably more frequently *coincide with* *that of utility.* than not: and hence it is that the business of penal justice is

being struck out of the account as not worth taking. This contrivance does better than the other; for a moral sense, being a new thing, a man may feel about him a good while without being able to find it out: but common sense is as old as the creation; and there is no man but would be ashamed to be thought not to have as much of it as his neighbours. It has another great advantage: by appearing to share power, it lessens envy: for when a man gets up upon this ground, in order to anathematize those who differ from him, it is not by a *sic volo sic jubeo*, but by a *velitis jubeatis*,

3. Another man comes, and says, that as to a moral sense indeed, he cannot 3. *Understand-* find that he has any such thing: that however he has an *understanding*, which *ing.* will do quite as well. This understanding, he says, is the standard of right and wrong: it tells him so and so. All good and wise men understand as he does: if other men's understandings differ in any point from his, so much the worse for them: it is a sure sign they are either defective or corrupt.

4. Another man says, that there is an eternal and immutable Rule of Right: 4. *Rule of* that the rule of right dictates so and so: and then he begins giving you his *Right.* sentiments upon any thing that comes uppermost: and these sentiments (you are to take for granted) are so many branches of the eternal rule of right.

5. Another man, or perhaps the same man (it's no matter) says, that there 5. *Fitness of* are certain practices conformable, and others repugnant, to the Fitness of *Things.* Things; and then he tells you, at his leisure, what practices are conformable and what repugnant: just as he happens to like a practice or dislike it.

6. A great multitude of people are continually talking of the Law of Nature; 6. *Law of* and then they go on giving you their sentiments about what is right and what *Nature.* is wrong: and these sentiments, you are to understand, are so many chapters and sections of the Law of Nature.

7. Instead of the phrase, Law of Nature, you have sometimes, Law of 7. *Law of* Reason, Right Reason, Natural Justice, Natural Equity, Good Order. Any *Reason, Right* of them will do equally well. This latter is most used in politics. The three *Reason,* last are much more tolerable than the others, because they do not very *Natural Justice,* explicitly claim to be any thing more than phrases: they insist but feebly upon *Natural Equity,* the being looked upon as so many positive standards of themselves, and seem *Good Order.* content to be taken, upon occasion, for phrases expressive of the conformity of the thing in question to the proper standard, whatever that may be. On most occasions, however, it will be better to say *utility*: *utility* is clearer, as referring more explicitly to pain and pleasure.

8. We have one philosopher, who says, there is no harm in any thing in 8. *Truth.* the world but in telling a lie: and that if, for example, you were to murder your own father, this would only be a particular way of saying, he was not your father. Of course, when this philosopher sees any thing that he does not like, he says, it is a particular way of telling a lie. It is saying, that the act ought to be done, or may be done, when, *in truth*, it ought not to be done.

9. The fairest and openest of them all is that sort of man who speaks out, 9. *Doctrine of* and says, I am of the number of the Elect: now God himself takes care to inform *Election.* the Elect what is right: and that with so good effect, and let them strive ever so, they cannot help not only knowing it but practising it. If therefore a man wants to know what is right and what is wrong, he has nothing to do but to come to me.

carried on upon that tolerable sort of footing upon which we see it carried on in common at this day. For what more

Repugnancy to Nature.

It is upon the principle of antipathy that such and such acts are often reprobated on the score of their being *unnatural*: the practice of exposing children, established among the Greeks and Romans, was an unnatural practice. Unnatural, when it means any thing, means unfrequent: and there it means something; although nothing to the present purpose. But here it means no such thing: for the frequency of such acts is perhaps the great complaint. It therefore means nothing; nothing, I mean which there is in the act itself. All it can serve to express is, the disposition of the person who is talking of it: the disposition he is in to be angry at the thoughts of it. Does it merit his anger? Very likely it may: but whether it does or no is a question, which, to be answered rightly, can only be answered upon the principle of utility.

Unnatural, is as good a word as moral sense, or common sense; and would be as good a foundation for a system. Such an act is unnatural; that is, repugnant to nature: for I do not like to practise it: and, consequently, do not practise it. It is therefore repugnant to what ought to be the nature of every body else.

Mischief they produce.

The mischief common to all these ways of thinking and arguing (which, in truth, as we have seen, are but one and the same method, couched in different forms of words) is their serving as a cloke, and pretence, and aliment, to despotism: if not a despotism in practice, a despotism however in disposition: which is but too apt, when pretence and power offer, to show itself in practice. The consequence is, that with intentions very commonly of the purest kind, a man becomes a torment either to himself or his fellow-creatures. If he be of the melancholy cast, he sits in silent grief, bewailing their blindness and depravity: if of the irascible, he declaims with fury and virulence against all who differ from him; blowing up the coals of fanaticism, and branding with the charge of corruption and insincerity, every man who does not think, or profess to think, as he does.

If such a man happens to possess the advantages of style, his book may do a considerable deal of mischief before the nothingness of it is understood.

These principles, if such they can be called, it is more frequent to see applied to morals than to politics: but their influence extends itself to both. In politics, as well as morals, a man will be at least equally glad of a pretence for deciding any question in the manner that best pleases him, without the trouble of inquiry. If a man is an infallible judge of what is right and wrong in the actions of private individuals, why not in the measures to be observed by public men in the direction of those actions? accordingly (not to mention other chimeras) I have more than once known the pretended law of nature set up in legislative debates, in opposition to arguments derived from the principle of utility.

Whether utility is actually the sole ground of all the approbation we ever bestow, is a different consideration.

'But is it never, then, from any other considerations than those of utility, that we derive our notions of right and wrong?' I do not know: I do not care. Whether a moral sentiment can be originally conceived from any other source than a view of utility, is one question: whether upon examination and reflection it can, in point of fact, be actually persisted in and justified on any other ground, by a person reflecting within himself, is another: whether in point of right it can properly be justified on any other ground, by a person addressing himself to the community, is a third. The two first are questions of speculation: it matters not, comparatively speaking, how they are decided. The last is a question of practice: the decision of it is of as much importance as that of any can be.

natural or more general ground of hatred to a practice can
there be, than the mischievousness of such practice? What
all men are exposed to suffer by, all men will be disposed to
hate. It is far yet, however, from being a constant ground:
for when a man suffers, it is not always that he knows what
it is he suffers by. A man may suffer grievously, for instance,
by a new tax, without being able to trace up the cause of his
sufferings to the injustice of some neighbour, who has eluded
the payment of an old one.

16. The principle of sympathy and antipathy is most apt
to err on the side of severity. It is for applying punishment in
many cases which deserve none: in many cases which deserve
some, it is for applying more than they deserve. There is no
incident imaginable, be it ever so trivial, and so remote from
mischief, from which this principle may not extract a ground
of punishment. Any difference in taste: any difference in
opinion: upon one subject as well as upon another. No disagreement so trifling which perseverance and altercation will

This principle is most apt to err on the side of severity.

'I feel in myself,' (say you) 'a disposition to approve of such or such an action
in a moral view: but this is not owing to any notions I have of its being a
useful one to the community. I do not pretend to know whether it be an
useful one or not: it may be, for aught I know, a mischievous one.' 'But is it
then,' (say I) 'a mischievous one? examine; and if you can make yourself
sensible that it is so, then, if duty means any thing, that is, moral duty, it is
your *duty* at least to abstain from it: and more than that, if it is what lies in
your power, and can be done without too great a sacrifice, to endeavour to
prevent it. It is not your cherishing the notion of it in your bosom, and giving
it the name of virtue, that will excuse you.'

'I feel in myself,' (say you again) 'a disposition to detest such or such an
action in a moral view; but this is not owing to any notions I have of its
being a mischievous one to the community. I do not pretend to know
whether it be a mischievous one or not: it may be not a mischievous one:
it may be, for aught I know, an useful one.'—'May it indeed,' (say I) 'an
useful one? but let me tell you then, that unless duty, and right and wrong,
be just what you please to make them, if it really be not a mischievous one,
and any body has a mind to do it, it is no duty of yours, but, on the contrary,
it would be very wrong in you, to take upon you to prevent him: detest it
within yourself as much as you please; that it may be a very good reason
(unless it be also a useful one) for your not doing it yourself: but if you go
about, by word or deed, to do any thing to hinder him, or make him suffer
for it, it is you, and not he, that have done wrong: it is not your setting yourself to blame his conduct, or branding it with the name of vice, that will
make him culpable, or you blameless. Therefore, if you can make yourself
content that he shall be of one mind, and you of another, about this matter,
and so continue, it is well: but if nothing will serve you, but that you and he
must needs be of the same mind, I'll tell you what you have to do: it is for you
to get the better of your antipathy, not for him to truckle to it.'

not render serious. Each becomes in the other's eyes an enemy, and, if laws permit, a criminal.[1] This is one of the circumstances by which the human race is distinguished (not much indeed to its advantage) from the brute creation.

But errs, in some instances, on the side of lenity.

17. It is not, however, by any means unexampled for this principle to err on the side of lenity. A near and perceptible mischief moves antipathy. A remote and imperceptible mischief, though not less real, has no effect. Instances in proof of this will occur in numbers in the course of the work.[2] It would be breaking in upon the order of it to give them here.

The theological principle, what —not a separate principle.

18. It may be wondered, perhaps, that in all this while no mention has been made of the *theological* principle; meaning that principle which professes to recur for the standard of right and wrong to the will of God. But the case is, this is not in fact a distinct principle. It is never any thing more or less than one or other of the three before-mentioned principles presenting itself under another shape. The *will* of God here meant cannot be his revealed will, as contained in the sacred writings: for that is a system which nobody ever thinks of

[1] King James the First of England had conceived a violent antipathy against Arians: two of whom he burnt.[a] This gratification he procured himself without much difficulty: the notions of the times were favourable to it. He wrote a furious book against Vorstius, for being what was called an Arminian: for Vorstius was at a distance. He also wrote a furious book, called 'A Counterblast to Tobacco,' against the use of that drug, which Sir Walter Raleigh had then lately introduced. Had the notions of the times co-operated with him, he would have burnt the Anabaptist and the smoke of tobacco in the same fire. However, he had the satisfaction of putting Raleigh to death afterwards, though for another crime.

Disputes concerning the comparative excellence of French and Italian music have occasioned very serious bickerings at Paris. One of the parties would not have been sorry (says Mr. D'Alembert[b]) to have brought government into the quarrel. Pretences were sought after and urged. Long before that, a dispute of like nature, and of at least equal warmth, had been kindled at London upon the comparative merits of two composers at London; where riots between the approvers and disapprovers of a new play are, at this day, not unfrequent. The ground of quarrel between the Bigendians and the Little-endians in the fable, was not more frivolous than many an one which has laid empires desolate. In Russia, it is said, there was a time when some thousands of persons lost their lives in a quarrel, in which the government had taken part, about the number of fingers to be used in making the sign of the cross. This was in days of yore: the ministers of Catherine II. are better *instructed*[c] than to take any other part in such disputes, than that of preventing the parties concerned from doing one another a mischief.

[2] See ch. xvi [Division], par. 42, 44.

[a] Hume's Hist. vol. 6.   [b] Melanges Essai sur la Liberté de la Musique.
[c] Instruct. art. 474, 475, 476.

recurring to at this time of day, for the details of political administration: and even before it can be applied to the details of private conduct, it is universally allowed, by the most eminent divines of all persuasions, to stand in need of pretty ample interpretations; else to what use are the works of those divines? And for the guidance of these interpretations, it is also allowed, that some other standard must be assumed. The will then which is meant on this occasion, is that which may be called the *presumptive* will: that is to say, that which is presumed to be his will on account of the conformity of its dictates to those of some other principle. What then may be this other principle? it must be one or other of the three mentioned above: for there cannot, as we have seen, be any more. It is plain, therefore, that setting revelation out of the question, no light can ever be thrown upon the standard of right and wrong, by any thing that can be said upon the question, what is God's will. We may be perfectly sure, indeed, that whatever is right is conformable to the will of God: but so far is that from answering the purpose of showing us what is right, that it is necessary to know first whether a thing is right, in order to know from thence whether it be conformable to the will of God.[1]

19. There are two things which are very apt to be con- *Antipathy, let* founded, but which it imports us carefully to distinguish:— *the actions it* the motive or cause, which, by operating on the mind of an *dictates be ever* individual, is productive of any act: and the ground or reason *of itself a right* which warrants a legislator, or other by-stander, in regarding *ground of action.*

so right, is never

[1] The principle of theology refers every thing to God's pleasure. But *The principle of* what is God's pleasure? God does not, he confessedly does not now, either *theology how* speak or write to us. How then are we to know what is his pleasure? By *reducible to one* observing what is our own pleasure, and pronouncing it to be his. Accordingly *or another of the* what is called the pleasure of God, is and must necessarily be (revelation *three principles.* apart) neither more nor less than the good pleasure of the person, whoever he be, who is pronouncing what he believes, or pretends, to be God's pleasure. How know you it to be God's pleasure that such or such an act should be abstained from? whence come you even to suppose as much? 'Because the engaging in it would, I imagine, be prejudicial upon the whole to the happiness of mankind;' says the partizan of the principle of utility: 'Because the commission of it is attended with a gross and sensual, or at least with a trifling and transient satisfaction;' says the partizan of the principle of asceticism: 'Because I detest the thought of it; and I cannot, neither ought I to be called upon to tell why;' says he who proceeds upon the principle of antipathy. In the words of one or other of these must that person necessarily answer (revelation apart) who professes to take for his standard the will of God.

K

that act with an eye of approbation. When the act happens, in the particular instance in question, to be productive of effects which we approve of, much more if we happen to observe that the same motive may frequently be productive, in other instances, of the like effects, we are apt to transfer our approbation to the motive itself, and to assume, as the just ground for the approbation we bestow on the act, the circumstance of its originating from that motive. It is in this way that the sentiment of antipathy has often been considered as a just ground of action. Antipathy, for instance, in such or such a case, is the cause of an action which is attended with good effects: but this does not make it a right ground of action in that case, any more than in any other. Still farther. Not only the effects are good, but the agent sees beforehand that they will be so. This may make the action indeed a perfectly right action: but it does not make antipathy a right ground of action. For the same sentiment of antipathy, if implicitly deferred to, may be, and very frequently is, productive of the very worst effects. Antipathy, therefore, can never be a right ground of action. No more, therefore, can resentment, which, as will be seen more particularly hereafter, is but a modification of antipathy. The only right ground of action, that can possibly subsist, is, after all, the consideration of utility, which if it is a right principle of action, and of approbation, in any one case, is so in every other. Other principles in abundance, that is, other motives, may be the reasons why such and such an act *has* been done: that is, the reasons or causes of its being done: but it is this alone that can be the reason why it might or ought to have been done. Antipathy or resentment requires always to be regulated, to prevent its doing mischief: to be regulated by what? always by the principle of utility. The principle of utility neither requires nor admits of any other regulator than itself.

CHAPTER III

1. It has been shown that the happiness of the individuals, *Connexion of* of whom a community is composed, that is their pleasures and *this chapter* their security, is the end and the sole end which the legislator *ceding.* ought to have in view: the sole standard, in conformity to which each individual ought, as far as depends upon the legislator, to be *made* to fashion his behaviour. But whether it be this or any thing else that is to be *done*, there is nothing by which a man can ultimately be *made* to do it, but either pain or pleasure. Having taken a general view of these two grand objects (*viz.*, pleasure, and what comes to the same thing, immunity from pain) in the character of *final* causes; it will be necessary to take a view of pleasure and pain itself, in the character of *efficient* causes or means.

2. There are four distinguishable sources from which *Four sanctions* pleasure and pain are in use to flow: considered separately, *or sources of* they may be termed the *physical*, the *political*, the *moral*, and *pain.* the *religious:* and inasmuch as the pleasures and pains belonging to each of them are capable of giving a binding force to any law or rule of conduct, they may all of them be termed *sanctions.*[1]

[1] Sanctio, in Latin, was used to signify the *act of binding*, and, by a common grammatical transition, *any thing which serves to bind a man:* to wit, to the observance of such or such a mode of conduct. According to a Latin grammarian,[a] the import of the word is derived by rather a far-fetched process (such as those commonly are, and in a great measure indeed must be, by which intellectual ideas are derived from sensible ones) from the word *sanguis*, blood: because, among the Romans, with a view to inculcate into the people a persuasion that such or such a mode of conduct would be rendered obligatory upon a man by the force of which I call the religious sanction (that is, that he would be made to suffer by the extraordinary interposition of some superior being, if he failed to observe the mode of conduct in question) certain ceremonies were contrived by the priests: in the course of which ceremonies the blood of victims was made use of.

A Sanction then is a source of obligatory powers or *motives*: that is, of *pains*

[a] Servius. See Ainsworth's Dict. ad verbum *Sanctio.*

1. The physical sanction.

3. If it be in the present life, and from the ordinary course of nature, not purposely modified by the interposition of the will of any human being, nor by any extraordinary interposition of any superior invisible being, that the pleasure or the pain takes place or is expected, it may be said to issue from or to belong to the *physical sanction*.

2. The political.

4. If at the hands of a *particular* person or set of persons in the community, who under names correspondent to that of *judge*, are chosen for the particular purpose of dispensing it, according to the will of the sovereign or supreme ruling power in the state, it may be said to issue from the *political sanction*.

3. The moral or popular.

5. If at the hands of such *chance* persons in the community, as the party in question may happen in the course of his life to have concerns with, according to each man's spontaneous disposition, and not according to any settled or concerted rule, it may be said to issue from the *moral* or *popular sanction*.[1]

4. The religious.

6. If from the immediate hand of a superior invisible being, either in the present life, or in a future, it may be said to issue from the *religious sanction*.

The pleasures and pains which belong to the religious sanction, may regard either the present life or a future.

7. Pleasures or pains which may be expected to issue from the *physical,* *political,* or *moral* sanctions, must all of them be expected to be experienced, if ever, in the *present* life: those which may be expected to issue from the *religious* sanction, may be expected to be experienced either in the *present* life or in a *future*.

Those which regard the present life, from which soever source they flow, differ only in the circumstances of their production.

8. Those which can be experienced in the present life, can of course be no others than such as human nature in the course of the present life is susceptible of: and from each of these sources may flow all the pleasures or pains of which, in the course of the present life, human nature is susceptible. With regard to these then (with which alone we have in this place

and *pleasures*; which, according as they are connected with such or such modes of conduct, operate, and are indeed the only things which can operate, as *motives*. See Chap. x. [Motives].

[1] Better termed *popular*, as more directly indicative of its constituent cause; as likewise of its relation to the more common phrase *public opinion*, in French *opinion publique*, the name there given to that tutelary power, of which of late so much is said, and by which so much is done. The latter appellation is however unhappy and inexpressive; since if *opinion* is material, it is only in virtue of the influence it exercises over action, through the medium of the affection and the will.

any concern) those of them which belong to any one of those sanctions, differ not ultimately in kind from those which belong to any one of the other three: the only difference there is among them lies in the circumstances that accompany their production. A suffering which befalls a man in the natural and spontaneous course of things, shall be styled, for instance, a *calamity*; in which case, if it be supposed to befall him through any imprudence of his, it may be styled a punishment issuing from the physical sanction. Now this same suffering, if inflicted by the law, will be what is commonly called a *punishment*; if incurred for want of any friendly assistance, which the misconduct, or supposed misconduct, of the sufferer has occasioned to be withholden, a punishment issuing from the *moral* sanction; if through the immediate interposition of a particular providence, a punishment issuing from the religious sanction.

9. A man's goods, or his person, are consumed by fire. *Example.* If this happened to him by what is called an accident, it was a calamity: if by reason of his own imprudence (for instance, from his neglecting to put his candle out) it may be styled a punishment of the physical sanction: if it happened to him by the sentence of the political magistrate, a punishment belonging to the political sanction; that is, what is commonly called a punishment: if for want of any assistance which his *neighbour* withheld from him out of some dislike to his *moral* character, a punishment of the *moral* sanction: if by an immediate act of *God's* displeasure, manifested on account of some *sin* committed by him, or through any distraction of mind, occasioned by the dread of such displeasure, a punishment of the *religious* sanction.[1]

10. As to such of the pleasures and pains belonging to the religious sanction, as regard a future life, of what kind these may be we cannot know. These lie not open to our observation. During the present life they are matter only of expectation: and, whether that expectation be derived from natural or revealed religion, the particular kind of pleasure or pain, if it be different from all those which lie open to our observa- *Those which regard a future life are not specifically known.*

---

[1] A suffering conceived to befall a man by the immediate act of God, as above, is often, for shortness' sake, called a *judgment*: instead of saying, a suffering inflicted on him in consequence of a special judgment formed, and resolution thereupon taken, by the Deity.

tion, is what we can have no idea of. The best ideas we can obtain of such pains and pleasures are altogether unliquidated in point of quality. In what other respects our ideas of them *may* be liquidated will be considered in another place.[1]

The physical sanction included in each of the other three.
11. Of these four sanctions the physical is altogether, we may observe, the ground-work of the political and the moral: so is it also of the religious, in as far as the latter bears relation to the present life. It is included in each of those other three. This may operate in any case, (that is, any of the pains or pleasures belonging to it may operate) independently of *them*: none of *them* can operate but by means of this. In a word, the powers of nature may operate of themselves; but neither the magistrate, nor men at large, *can* operate, nor is God in the case in question *supposed* to operate, but through the powers of nature.

Use of this chapter.
12. For these four objects, which in their nature have so much in common, it seemed of use to find a common name. It seemed of use, in the first place, for the convenience of giving a name to certain pleasures and pains, for which a name equally characteristic could hardly otherwise have been found: in the second place, for the sake of holding up the efficacy of certain moral forces, the influence of which is apt not to be sufficiently attended to. Does the political sanction exert an influence over the conduct of mankind? The moral, the religious sanctions do so too. In every inch of his career are the operations of the political magistrate liable to be aided or impeded by these two foreign powers: who, one or other of them, or both, are sure to be either his rivals or his allies. Does it happen to him to leave them out of his calculations? he will be sure almost to find himself mistaken in the result. Of all this we shall find abundant proofs in the sequel of this work. It behoves him, therefore, to have them continually before his eyes; and that under such a name as exhibits the relation they bear to his own purposes and designs.

[1] See ch. xiii. [Cases unmeet] par. 2. note.

CHAPTER IV

VALUE OF A LOT OF PLEASURE OR PAIN, HOW TO BE MEASURED

1. PLEASURES then, and the avoidance of pains, are the *ends* Use *of this* which the legislator has in view: it behoves him therefore to *chapter.* understand their *value.* Pleasures and pains are the *instruments* he has to work with: it behoves him therefore to understand their force, which is again, in other words, their value.

2. To a person considered *by himself,* the value of a pleasure Circumstances or pain considered *by itself,* will be greater or less, according to *to be taken into* the four following circumstances[1]: *the account in estimating the*

1. Its *intensity.* *value of a plea-*
2. Its *duration.* *sure or pain con-*
3. Its *certainty* or *uncertainty.* *sidered with*
4. Its *propinquity* or *remoteness.* *reference to a single person,*

3. These are the circumstances which are to be considered *and by itself.* in estimating a pleasure or a pain considered each of them by *—considered as* itself. But when the value of any pleasure or pain is considered *connected with* for the purpose of estimating the tendency of any *act* by which *or pains.* it is produced, there are two other circumstances to be taken into account; these are,

5. Its *fecundity,* or the chance it has of being followed by sensations of the *same* kind: that is, pleasures, if it be a pleasure: pains, if it be a pain.

6. Its *purity,* or the chance it has of *not* being followed by

---

[1] These circumstances have since been dominated *elements* or *dimensions* of *value* in a pleasure or a pain.

Not long after the publication of the first edition, the following memoriter verses were framed, in the view of lodging more effectually, in the memory, these points, on which the whole fabric of morals and legislation may be seen to rest.

> *Intense, long, certain, speedy, fruitful, pure—*
> Such marks in *pleasures* and in *pains* endure.
> Such pleasures seek if *private* be thy end:
> If it be *public,* wide let them *extend.*
> Such *pains* avoid, whichever be thy view:
> If pains *must* come, let them *extend* to few.

sensations of the *opposite* kind: that is, pains, if it be a pleasure: pleasures, if it be a pain.

These two last, however, are in strictness scarcely to be deemed properties of the pleasure or the pain itself; they are not, therefore, in strictness to be taken into the account of the value of that pleasure or that pain. They are in strictness to be deemed properties only of the act, or other event, by which such pleasure or pain has been produced; and accordingly are only to be taken into the account of the tendency of such act or such event.

—considered with reference to a number of persons.

4. To a *number* of persons, with reference to each of whom the value of a pleasure or a pain is considered, it will be greater or less, according to seven circumstances: to wit, the six preceding ones; *viz.*

1. Its *intensity*.
2. Its *duration*.
3. Its *certainty* or *uncertainty*.
4. Its *propinquity* or *remoteness*.
5. Its *fecundity*.
6. Its *purity*.

And one other; to wit:

7. Its *extent*; that is, the number of persons to whom it *extends*; or (in other words) who are affected by it.

Process for estimating the tendency of any act or event.

5. To take an exact account then of the general tendency of any act, by which the interests of a community are affected, proceed as follows. Begin with any one person of those whose interests seem most immediately to be affected by it: and take an account,

1. Of the value of each distinguishable *pleasure* which appears to be produced by it in the *first* instance.
2. Of the value of each *pain* which appears to be produced by it in the *first* instance.
3. Of the value of each pleasure which appears to be produced by it *after* the first. This constitutes the *fecundity* of the first *pleasure* and the *impurity* of the first *pain*.
4. Of the value of each *pain* which appears to be produced by it after the first. This constitutes the *fecundity* of the first *pain*, and the *impurity* of the first pleasure.
5. Sum up all the values of all the *pleasures* on the one side, and those of all the pains on the other. The balance, if it be on

the side of pleasure, will give the *good* tendency of the act upon the whole, with respect to the interests of that *individual* person; if on the side of pain, the *bad* tendency of it upon the whole.

6. Take an account of the *number* of persons whose interests appear to be concerned; and repeat the above process with respect to each. *Sum up* the numbers expressive of the degrees of *good* tendency, which the act has, with respect to each individual, in regard to whom the tendency of it is *good* upon the whole: do this again with respect to each individual, in regard to whom the tendency of it is *good* upon the whole: do this again with respect to each individual, in regard to whom the tendency of it is *bad* upon the whole. Take the *balance*; which, if on the side of *pleasure*, will give the general *good tendency* of the act, with respect to the total number or community of individuals concerned; if on the side of pain, the general *evil tendency*, with respect to the same community.

6. It is not to be expected that this process should be strictly *Use of the fore-* pursued previously to every moral judgment, or to every *going process.* legislative or judicial operation. It may, however, be always kept in view: and as near as the process actually pursued on these occasions approaches to it, so near will such process approach to the character of an exact one.

7. The same process is alike applicable to pleasure and pain, *The same pro-* in whatever shape they appear: and by whatever denomina- *cess applicable* tion they are distinguished: to pleasure, whether it be called *to good and evil,* *profit and mis-* *good* (which is properly the cause or instrument of pleasure) *chief, and all* or *profit* (which is distant pleasure, or the cause or instrument *other modifica-* of distant pleasure,) or *convenience*, or *advantage*, *benefit*, *tions of pleasure* *and pain.* *emolument, happiness,* and so forth: to pain, whether it be called *evil*, (which corresponds to *good*) or *mischief*, or *inconvenience*, or *disadvantage*, or *loss*, or *unhappiness*, and so forth.

8. Nor is this a novel and unwarranted, any more than it *Conformity of* is a useless theory. In all this there is nothing but what the *men's practice to* *this theory.* practice of mankind, wheresoever they have a clear view of their own interest, is perfectly conformable to. An article of property, an estate in land, for instance, is valuable, on what account? On account of the pleasures of all kinds which it enables a man to produce, and what comes to the same thing the pains of all kinds which it enables him to avert.

But the value of such an article of property is universally understood to rise or fall according to the length or shortness of the time which a man has in it: the certainty or uncertainty of its coming into possession: and the nearness or remoteness of the time at which, if at all, it is to come into possession. As to the *intensity* of the pleasures which a man may derive from it, this is never thought of, because it depends upon the use which each particular person may come to make of it; which cannot be estimated till the particular pleasures he may come to derive from it, or the particular pains he may come to exclude by means of it, are brought to view. For the same reason, neither does he think of the *fecundity* or *purity* of those pleasures.

Thus much for pleasure and pain, happiness and unhappiness, in *general*. We come now to consider the several particular kinds of pain and pleasure.

CHAPTER V

PLEASURES AND PAINS, THEIR KINDS

1. HAVING represented what belongs to all sorts of pleasures and pains alike, we come now to exhibit, each by itself, the several sorts of pains and pleasures. Pains and pleasures may be called by one general word, interesting perceptions. Interesting perceptions are either simple or complex. The simple ones are those which cannot any one of them be resolved into more: complex are those which are resolvable into divers simple ones. A complex interesting perception may accordingly be composed either, 1. Of pleasures alone: 2. Of pains alone: or, 3. Of a pleasure or pleasures, and a pain or pains together. What determines a lot of pleasure, for example, to be regarded as one complex pleasure, rather than as divers simple ones, is the nature of the exciting cause. Whatever pleasures are excited all at once by the action of the same cause, are apt to be looked upon as constituting all together but one pleasure. *Pleasures and pains are either 1. Simple: or, 2. Complex.*

2. The several simple pleasures of which human nature is susceptible, seem to be as follows: 1. The pleasures of sense. 2. The pleasures of wealth. 3. The pleasures of skill. 4. The pleasures of amity. 5. The pleasures of a good name. 6. The pleasures of power. 7. The pleasures of piety. 8. The pleasures of benevolence. 9. The pleasures of malevolence. 10. The pleasures of memory. 11. The pleasures of imagination. 12. The pleasures of expectation. 13. The pleasures dependent on association. 14. The pleasures of relief. *The simple pleasures enumerated.*

3. The several simple pains seem to be as follows: 1. The pains of privation. 2. The pains of the senses. 3. The pains of awkwardness. 4. The pains of enmity. 5. The pains of an ill name. 6. The pains of piety. 7, The pains of benevolence. 8. The pains of malevolence. 9. The pains of the memory. 10. The pains of the imagination. 11. The pains of expectation. 12. The pains dependent on association.[1] *The simple pains enumerated.*

[1] The catalogue here given, is what seemed to be a complete list of the several simple pleasures and pains of which human nature is susceptible: *Analytical view, why none given.*

1. Pleasures of sense enumerated. 4. 1. The pleasures of sense seem to be as follows: 1. The pleasures of the taste or palate; including whatever pleasures are experienced in satisfying the appetites of hunger and thirst. 2. The pleasure of intoxication. 3. The pleasures of the organ of smelling. 4. The pleasures of the touch. 5. The simple pleasures of the ear; independent of association. 6. The simple pleasures of the eye; independent of association. 7. The pleasure of the sexual sense. 8. The pleasure of health: or, the internal pleasurable feeling or flow of spirits (as it is called) which accompanies a state of full health and vigour; especially at times of moderate bodily exertion. 9. The pleasures of novelty: or, the pleasures derived from the gratification of the appetite of curiosity, by the application of new objects to any of the senses.[1]

2. Pleasures of wealth, which are either of acquisition or of possession. 5. 2. By the pleasures of wealth may be meant those pleasures which a man is apt to derive from the consciousness of possessing any article or articles which stand in the list of instruments of enjoyment or security, and more particularly at the time of his first acquiring them; at which time the pleasure may be styled a pleasure of gain or a pleasure of acquisition: at other times a pleasure of possession.

3. Pleasures of skill. 3. The pleasures of skill, as exercised upon particular objects, are those which accompany the application of such particular instruments of enjoyment to their uses, as cannot be so applied without a greater or less share of difficulty or exertion.[2]

4. Pleasures of amity. 6. 4. The pleasures of amity, or self-recommendation, are the pleasures that may accompany the persuasion of a man's

insomuch, that if, upon any occasion whatsoever, a man feels pleasure or pain, it is either referable at once to some one or other of these kinds, or resolvable into such as are. It might perhaps have been a satisfaction to the reader, to have seen an analytical view of the subject, taken upon an exhaustive plan, for the purpose of demonstrating the catalogue to be what it purports to be, a complete one. The catalogue is in fact the result of such an analysis; which, however, I thought it better to discard at present, as being of too metaphysical a cast, and not strictly within the limits of this design. See Chap. xiii. [Cases unmeet], par. 2. Note.

[1] There are also pleasures of novelty, excited by the appearance of new ideas: these are pleasures of the imagination. See infra 13.

[2] For instance, the pleasure of being able to gratify the sense of hearing, by singing, or performing upon any musical instrument. The pleasure thus obtained, is a thing superadded to, and perfectly distinguishable from, that which a man enjoys from hearing another person perform in the same manner.

being in the acquisition or the possession of the good-will of such or such assignable person or persons in particular: or, as the phrase is, of being upon good terms with him or them: and as a fruit of it, of his being in a way to have the benefit of their spontaneous and gratuitous services.

7. 5. The pleasures of a good name are the pleasures that *5. Pleasures of* accompany the persuasion of a man's being in the acquisition *a good name.* or the possession of the good-will of the world about him; that is, of such members of society as he is likely to have concerns with; and as a means of it, either their love or their esteem, or both: and as a fruit of it, of his being in the way to have the benefit of their spontaneous and gratuitous services. These may likewise be called the pleasures of good repute, the pleasures of honour, or the pleasures of the moral sanction.[1]

8. 6. The pleasures of power are the pleasures that accom- *6. Pleasures of* pany the persuasion of a man's being in a condition to dispose *power.* people, by means of their hopes and fears, to give him the benefit of their services: that is, by the hope of some service, or by the fear of some disservice, that he may be in the way to render them.

9. 7. The pleasures of piety are the pleasures that accom- *7. Pleasures of* pany the belief of a man's being in the acquisition or in posses- *piety.* sion of the good-will or favour of the Supreme Being: and as a fruit of it, of his being in a way of enjoying pleasures to be received by God's special appointment, either in this life, or in a life to come. These may also be called the pleasures of religion, the pleasures of a religious disposition, or the pleasures of the religious sanction.[2]

10. 8. The pleasures of benevolence are the pleasures *8. Pleasures of* resulting from the view of any pleasures supposed to be *benevolence or good-will.* possessed by the beings who may be the objects of benevo- lence; to wit, the sensitive beings we are acquainted with; under which are commonly included, 1. The Supreme Being. 2. Human beings. 3. Other animals. These may also be called the pleasures of good-will, the pleasures of sympathy, or the pleasures of the benevolent or social affections.

11. 9. The pleasures of malevolence are the pleasures *9. Pleasures of* resulting from the view of any pain supposed to be suffered *malevolence or ill-will.* by the beings who may become the objects of malevolence:

---

[1] See Chap. iii. [Sanctions].   [2] See Chap. iii. [Sanctions].

to wit, 1. Human beings. 2. Other animals. These may also be styled the pleasures of ill-will, the pleasures of the irascible appetite, the pleasures of antipathy, or the pleasures of the malevolent or dissocial affections.

10. Pleasures of the memory.

12. 10. The pleasures of the memory are the pleasures which after having enjoyed such and such pleasures, or even in some case after having suffered such and such pains, a man will now and then experience, at recollecting them exactly in the order and in the circumstances in which they were actually enjoyed or suffered. These derivative pleasures may of course be distinguished into as many species as there are of original perceptions, from whence they may be copied. They may also be styled pleasures of simple recollection.

11. Pleasures of the imagination.

13. 11. The pleasures of the imagination are the pleasures which may be derived from the contemplation of any such pleasures as may happen to be suggested by the memory, but in a different order, and accompanied by different groups of circumstances. These may accordingly be referred to any one of the three cardinal points of time, present, past, or future. It is evident they may admit of as many distinctions as those of the former class.

12. Pleasures of expectation.

14. 12. The pleasures of expectation are the pleasures that result from the contemplation of any sort of pleasure, referred to time *future*, and accompanied with the sentiment of *belief*. These also may admit of the same distinctions.[1]

13. Pleasures depending on association.

15. 13. The pleasures of association are the pleasures which certain objects or incidents may happen to afford, not of themselves, but merely in virtue of some association they have contracted in the mind with certain objects or incidents which are in themselves pleasurable. Such is the case, for instance, with the pleasure of skill, when afforded by such a set of incidents as compose a game of chess. This derives its pleasurable quality from its association partly with the pleasure of skill, as exercised in the production of incidents pleasurable of themselves: partly from its association with the pleasures of power. Such is the case also with the pleasure of good luck, when afforded by such incidents as compose the game of hazard, or any other game of chance, when played at for

[1] In contradistinction to these, all other pleasures may be termed pleasures of *enjoyment*.

nothing. This derives its pleasurable quality from its association with one of the pleasures of wealth; to wit, with the pleasure of acquiring it.

16. 14. Farther on we shall see pains grounded upon pleasures; in like manner may we now see pleasures grounded upon pains. To the catalogue of pleasures may accordingly be added the pleasures of *relief*: or, the pleasures which a man experiences when, after he has been enduring a pain of any kind for a certain time, it comes to cease, or to abate. These may of course be distinguished into as many species as there are of pains: and may give rise to so many pleasures of memory, of imagination, and of expectation. *14. Pleasures of relief.*

17. 1. Pains of privation are the pains that may result from the thought of not possessing in the time present any of the several kinds of pleasures. Pains of privation may accordingly be resolved into as many kinds as there are of pleasures to which they may correspond, and from the absence whereof they may be derived. *1. Pains of privation.*

18. There are three sorts of pains which are only so many modifications of the several pains of privation. When the enjoyment of any particular pleasure happens to be particularly desired, but without any expectation approaching to assurance, the pain of privation which thereupon results takes a particular name, and is called the pain of *desire*, or of unsatisfied desire. *These include, 1. Pains of desire.*

19. Where the enjoyment happens to have been looked for with a degree of expectation approaching to assurance, and that expectation is made suddenly to cease, it is called a pain of disappointment. *2. Pains of disappointment.*

20. A pain of privation takes the name of a pain of regret in two cases: 1. Where it is grounded on the memory of a pleasure, which having been once enjoyed, appears not likely to be enjoyed again: 2. Where it is grounded on the idea of a pleasure, which was never actually enjoyed, nor perhaps so much as expected, but which might have been enjoyed (it is supposed), had such or such a contingency happened, which, in fact, did not happen. *3. Pains of regret.*

21. 2. The several pains of the senses seem to be as follows: 1. The pains of hunger and thirst: or the disagreeable sensations produced by the want of suitable substances which *2. Pains of the senses.*

need at times to be applied to the alimentary canal. 2. The pains of the taste: or the disagreeable sensations produced by the application of various substances to the palate, and other superior parts of the same canal. 3. The pains of the organ of smell: or the disagreeable sensations produced by the effluvia of various substances when applied to that organ. 4. The pains of the touch: or the disagreeable sensations produced by the application of various substances to the skin. 5. The simple pains of the hearing: or the disagreeable sensations excited in the organ of that sense by various kinds of sounds: independently (as before), of association. 6. The simple pains of the sight: or the disagreeable sensations if any such there be, that may be excited in the organ of that sense by visible images, independent of the principle of association. 7[1]. The pains resulting from excessive heat or cold, unless these be referable to the touch. 8. The pains of disease: or the acute and uneasy sensations resulting from the several diseases and indispositions to which human nature is liable. 9. The pain of exertion, whether bodily or mental: or the uneasy sensation which is apt to accompany any intense effort, whether of mind or body.

3. Pains of awkwardness.

22. 3[2]. The pains of awkwardness are the pains which sometimes result from the unsuccessful endeavour to apply any particular instruments of enjoyment or security to their uses, or from the difficulty a man experiences in applying them.[3]

No positive pains correspond to the pleasure of the sexual sense.

No positive pains correspond to the pleasure of novelty.

—nor to those of wealth.

Is this a distinct positive pain or only a pain of privation?

[1] The pleasure of the sexual sense seems to have no positive pain to correspond to it: it has only a pain of privation, or pain of the mental class, the pain of unsatisfied desire. If any positive pain of body result from the want of such indulgence, it belongs to the head of pains of disease.

[2] The pleasures of novelty have no positive pains corresponding to them. The pain which a man experiences when he is in the condition of not knowing what to do with himself, that pain, which in French is expressed by a single word *ennui*, is a pain of privation: a pain resulting from the absence, not only of all the pleasures of novelty, but of all kinds of pleasure whatsoever.

The pleasures of wealth have also no positive pains corresponding to them: the only pains opposed to them are pains of privation. If any positive pains result from the want of wealth, they are referable to some other class of positive pains; principally to those of the senses. From the want of food, for instance, result the pains of hunger; from the want of clothing, the pains of cold; and so forth.

[3] It may be a question, perhaps, whether this be a positive pain of itself, or whether it be nothing more than a pain of privation, resulting from the consciousness of a want of skill. It is, however, but a question of words, nor does it matter which way it be determined.

23. 4. The pains of enmity are the pains that may accompany the persuasion of a man's being obnoxious to the
ill-will of such or such an assignable person or persons in
particular: or, as the phrase is, of being upon ill terms with him
or them: and, in consequence, of being obnoxious to certain
pains of some sort or other, of which he may be the cause.

4. Pains of enmity.

24. 5. The pains of an ill-name, are the pains that accompany the persuasion of a man's being obnoxious, or in a way
to be obnoxious to the ill-will of the world about him. These
may likewise be called the pains of ill-repute, the pains of dishonour, or the pains of the moral sanction.[1]

5. Pains of an ill-name.

25. 6.[2] The pains of piety are the pains that accompany the
belief of a man's being obnoxious to the displeasure of the
Supreme Being: and in consequence to certain pains to be
inflicted by his especial appointment, either in this life or in a
life to come. These may also be called the pains of religion;
the pains of a religious disposition; or the pains of the religious
sanction. When the belief is looked upon as well-grounded,
these pains are commonly called religious terrors; when looked
upon as ill-grounded, superstitious terrors.[3]

6. Pains of piety.

26. 7. The pains of benevolence are the pains resulting from
the view of any pains supposed to be endured by other beings.
These may also be called the pains of good-will, of sympathy,
or the pains of the benevolent or social affections.

7. Pains of benevolence.

[1] In as far as a man's fellow-creatures are supposed to be determined by
any event not to regard him with any degree of esteem or good will, or to
regard him with a less degree of esteem or good will than they would otherwise; not to do him any sorts of good offices, or not to do him so many good
offices as they would otherwise; the pain resulting from such consideration may
be reckoned a pain of privation: as far as they are supposed to regard him with
such a degree of aversion or disesteem as to be disposed to do him positive ill
offices, it may be reckoned a positive pain. The pain of privation, and the
positive pain, in this case run one into another indistinguishably.

The positive pains of an ill-name, and the pains of priva-tion, opposed to the pleasures of a good name, run into one another.

[2] There seem to be no positive pains to correspond to the pleasures of
power. The pains that a man may feel from the want or the loss of power,
in as far as power is distinguished from all other sources of pleasure, seem
to be nothing more than pains of privation.

No positive pains correspond to the pleasures of power.

[3] The positive pains of piety, and the pains of privation, opposed to the
pleasures of piety, run one into another in the same manner as the positive
pains of enmity, or of an ill name, do with respect to the pains of privation,
opposed to the pleasures of amity, and those of a good name. If what is
apprehended at the hands of God is barely the not receiving pleasure, the pain
is of the privative class: if, moreover, actual pain be apprehended, it is of the
class of positive pains.

The positive pains of piety, and the pains of privation, opposed to the pleasures of piety, run into one another.

L

8. *Pains of malevolence.*

27. 8. The pains of malevolence are the pains resulting from the view of any pleasures supposed to be enjoyed by any beings who happen to be the objects of a man's displeasure. These may also be styled the pains of ill-will, of antipathy, or the pains of the malevolent or dissocial affections.

9. *Pains of the memory.*

28. 9. The pains of the memory may be grounded on every one of the above kinds, as well of pains of privation as of positive pains. These correspond exactly to the pleasures of the memory.

10. *Pains of the imagination.*

29. 10. The pains of the imagination may also be grounded on any one of the above kinds, as well of pains of privation as of positive pains; in other respects they correspond exactly to the pleasures of the imagination.

11. *Pains of expectation.*

30. 11. The pains of expectation may be grounded on each one of the above kinds, as well of pains of privation as of positive pains. These may be also termed pains of apprehension.[1]

12. *Pains of association.*

31. 12. The pains of association correspond exactly to the pleasures of association.

Pleasures and pains are either self-regarding or extra-regarding.

32. Of the above list there are certain pleasures and pains which suppose the existence of some pleasure or pain of some other person, to which the pleasure or pain of the person in question has regard: such pleasures and pains may be termed *extra-regarding.* Others do not suppose any such thing: these may be termed *self-regarding.*[2] The only pleasures and pains of the extra-regarding class are those of benevolence and those of malevolence: all the rest are self-regarding.[3]

In what ways the law is concerned with the above pains and pleasures.

33. Of all these several sorts of pleasures and pains, there is scarce any one which is not liable, on more accounts than one, to come under the consideration of the law. Is an offence committed? It is the tendency which it has to destroy, in such or such persons, some of these pleasures, or to produce some of these pains, that constitutes the mischief of it, and the

---

[1] In contradistinction to these, all other pains may be termed pains of *sufferance.*

[2] See Chap. x. [Motives].

Pleasures and pains of amity and enmity distinguished from those of benevolence and malevolence.

[3] By this means the pleasures and pains of amity may be the more clearly distinguished from those of benevolence: and on the other hand, those of enmity from those of malevolence. The pleasures and pains of amity and enmity are of the self-regarding cast: those of benevolence and malevolence of the extra-regarding.

ground for punishing it. It is the prospect of some of these
pleasures, or of security from some of these pains, that constitutes the motive or temptation, it is the attainment of them
that constitutes the profit of the offence. Is the offender to be
punished? It can be only by the production of one or more of
these pains, that the punishment can be inflicted.[1]

[1] It would be a matter not only of curiosity, but of some use, to exhibit a *Complex*
catalogue of the several complex pleasures and pains, analyzing them at the *pleasures and*
same time into the several simple ones, of which they are respectively com- *pains omitted,*
posed. But such a disquisition would take up too much room to be admitted *why.*
here. A short specimen, however, for the purpose of illustration, can hardly
be dispensed with.

The pleasures taken in at the eye and ear are generally very complex. The *Specimen.*
pleasures of a country scene, for instance, consist commonly, amongst others, *Pleasures of a*
of the following pleasures: *country pros-*
                                                                              pect.

I. Pleasures of the senses.

1. The simple pleasures of sight, excited by the perception of agreeable
colours and figures, green fields, waving foliage, glistening water, and the
like.
2. The simple pleasure of the ears, excited by the perceptions of the chirping
of birds, the murmuring of waters, the rustling of the wind among the trees.
3. The pleasures of the smell, excited by the perceptions of the fragrance of
flowers, of new-mown hay, or other vegetable substances, in the first stages of
fermentation.
4. The agreeable inward sensation, produced by a brisk circulation of the
blood, and the ventilation of it in the lungs by a pure air, such as that in the
country frequently is in comparison of that which is breathed in towns.

II. Pleasures of the imagination produced by association.

1. The idea of the plenty, resulting from the possession of the objects that
are in view, and of the happiness arising from it.
2. The idea of the innocence and happiness of the birds, sheep, cattle, dogs,
and other gentle or domestic animals.
3. The idea of the constant flow of health, supposed to be enjoyed by all
these creatures: a notion which is apt to result from the occasional flow of
health enjoyed by the supposed spectator.
4. The idea of gratitude, excited by the contemplation of the all-powerful
and beneficent Being, who is looked up to as the author of these blessings.
These four last are all of them, in some measure at least, pleasures of
sympathy.
The depriving a man of this group of pleasures is one of the evils apt to
result from imprisonment: whether produced by illegal violence, or in the
way of punishment, by appointment of the laws.

CHAPTER VI

OF CIRCUMSTANCES INFLUENCING SENSIBILITY

Pain and pleasure not uniformly proportioned to their causes.

1. PAIN and pleasure are produced in men's minds by the action of certain causes. But the quantity of pleasure and pain runs not uniformly in proportion to the cause; in other words, to the quantity of force exerted by such cause. The truth of this observation rests not upon any metaphysical nicety in the import given to the terms *cause*, *quantity*, and *force*: it will be equally true in whatsoever manner such force be measured.

Degree or quantum of sensibility, what.

2. The disposition which any one has to feel such or such a quantity of pleasure or pain, upon the application of a cause of given force, is what we term the degree or *quantum* of his sensibility. This may be either *general*, referring to the sum of the causes that act upon him during a given period: or *particular*, referring to the action of any one particular cause, or sort of cause.

Bias or quality of sensibility, what.

3. But in the same mind such and such causes of pain or pleasure will produce more pain or pleasure than such or such other causes of pain or pleasure: and this proportion will in different minds be different. The disposition which any one has to have the proportion in which he is affected by two such causes, different from that in which another man is affected by the same two causes, may be termed the quality or *bias* of his sensibility. One man, for instance, may be most affected by the pleasures of the taste; another by those of the ear. So also, if there be a difference in the nature or proportion of two pains or pleasures which they respectively experience from the same cause; a case not so frequent as the former. From the same injury, for instance, one man may feel the same quantity of grief and resentment together as another man; but one of them shall feel a greater share of grief than of resentment: the other, a greater share of resentment than of grief.

Exciting causes pleasurable and dolorific.

4. Any incident which serves as a cause, either of pleasure or of pain, may be termed an *exciting* cause: if of pleasure,

pleasurable cause: if of pain, a painful, afflictive, or dolorific cause.[1]

5. Now the quantity of pleasure, or of pain, which a man is liable to experience upon the application of an exciting cause, since they will not depend altogether upon that cause, will depend in some measure upon some other circumstance or circumstances: these circumstances, whatsoever they be, may be termed *circumstances influencing sensibility*.[2] *Circumstances influencing sensibility, what.*

6. These circumstances will apply differently to different exciting causes; insomuch that to a certain exciting cause, a certain circumstance shall not apply at all, which shall apply with great force to another exciting cause. But without entering for the present into these distinctions, it may be of use to sum up all the circumstances which can be found to influence the effect of *any* exciting cause. These, as on a former occasion, it may be as well first to sum up together in the concisest manner possible, and afterwards to allot a few words to the separate explanation of each article. They seem to be as follows: 1. Health. 2. Strength. 3. Hardiness. 4. Bodily imperfection. 5. Quantity and quality of knowledge. 6. Strength of intellectual powers. 7. Firmness of mind. 8. Steadiness of mind. 9. Bent of inclination. 10. Moral sensibility. 11. Moral biases. 12. Religious sensibility. 13. Religious biases. 14. Sympathetic sensibility. 15. Sympathetic biases. 16. Antipathetic sensibility. 17. Antipathetic biases. 18. Insanity. 19. Habitual occupations. 20. Pecuniary circumstances. 21. Connexions in the way of sympathy. 22. Connexions in the way of antipathy. 23. Radical frame of body. 24. Radical frame of mind. 25. Sex. 26. Age. *Circumstances influencing sensibility enumerated.*

[1] The exciting cause, the pleasure or pain produced by it, and the intention produced by such pleasure or pain in the character of a motive, are objects so intimately connected, that, in what follows, I fear I have not, on every occasion, been able to keep them sufficiently distinct. I thought it necessary to give the reader this warning; after which, should there be found any such mistakes, it is to be hoped they will not be productive of much confusion.

[2] Thus, in physical bodies, the momentum of a ball put in motion by impulse, will be influenced by the circumstance of gravity: being in some directions increased, in others diminished by it. So in a ship, put in motion by the wind, the momentum and direction will be influenced not only by the attraction of gravity, but by the motion and resistance of the water, and several other circumstances.

27. Rank. 28. Education. 29. Climate. 30. Lineage. 31. Government. 32. Religious profession.[1]

1. Health.

7. 1. Health is the absence of disease, and consequently of all those kinds of pain which are among the symptoms of disease. A man may be said to be in a state of health when he is not conscious of any uneasy sensations, the primary seat of which can be perceived to be anywhere in his body.[2] In point of general sensibility, a man who is under the pressure of any bodily indisposition, or, as the phrase is, is in an ill state of health, is less sensible to the influence of any pleasurable cause, and more so to that of any afflictive one, than if he were *well*.

Extent and intricacy of this subject.

[1] An analytical view of all these circumstances will be given at the conclusion of the chapter: to which place it was necessary to refer it, as it could not well have been understood, till some of them had been previously explained.

To search out the vast variety of exciting or moderating causes, by which the degree or bias of a man's sensibility may be influenced, to define the boundaries of each, to extricate them from the entanglements in which they are involved, to lay the effect of each article distinctly before the reader's eye, is, perhaps, if not absolutely the most difficult task, at least one of the most difficult tasks, within the compass of moral physiology. Disquisitions on this head can never be completely satisfactory without examples. To provide a sufficient collection of such examples, would be a work of great labour as well as nicety: history and biography would need to be ransacked: a vast course of reading would need to be travelled through on purpose. By such a process the present work would doubtless have been rendered more amusing; but in point of bulk, so enormous, that this single chapter would have been swelled into a considerable volume. Feigned cases, although they may upon occasion serve to render the general matter tolerably intelligible, can never be sufficient to render it palatable. On this therefore, as on so many other occasion, I must confine myself to dry and general instruction: discarding illustration, although sensible that without it instruction cannot manifest half its efficacy. The subject, however, is so difficult, and so new, that I shall think I have not ill succeeded, if, without pretending to exhaust it, I shall have been able to mark out the principal points of view, and to put the matter in such a method as may facilitate the researches of happier inquirers.

The great difficulty lies in the nature of the words; which are not, like pain and pleasure, names of homogeneous real entities, but names of various fictitious entities, for which no common genus is to be found: and which therefore, without a vast and roundabout chain of investigation, can never be brought under any exhaustive plan of arrangement, but must be picked up here and there as they happen to occur.

[2] It may be thought, that in a certain degree of health, this negative account of the matter hardly comes up to the case. In a certain degree of health, there is often such a kind of feeling diffused over the whole frame, such a comfortable feel, or flow of spirits, as it is called, as may with propriety come under the head of positive pleasure. But without experiencing any such pleasurable feeling, if a man experience no painful one, he may be well enough said to be in health.

8. 2. The circumstance of strength, though in point of 2. *Strength.* causality closely connected with that of health, is perfectly distinguishable from it. The same man will indeed generally be stronger in a good state of health than in a bad one. But one man, even in a bad state of health, may be stronger than another even in a good one. Weakness is a common concomitant of disease: but in consequence of his radical frame of body, a man may be weak all his life long, without experiencing any disease. Health, as we have observed, is principally a negative circumstance: strength a positive one. The degree of a man's strength can be measured with tolerable accuracy.[1]

9. 3. Hardiness is a circumstance which, though closely 3. *Hardiness.* connected with that of strength, is distinguishable from it. Hardiness is the absence of irritability. Irritability respects either pain, resulting from the action of mechanical causes; or disease, resulting from the action of causes purely physiological. Irritability, in the former sense, is the disposition to undergo a greater or less degree of pain upon the application of a mechanical cause; such as are most of those applications by which simple afflictive punishments are inflicted, as whipping, beating, and the like. In the latter sense, it is the disposition to contract disease with greater or less facility, upon the application of any instrument acting on the body by its physiological properties; as in the case of fevers, or of colds, or other inflammatory diseases, produced by the application of damp air: or to experience immediate uneasiness, as in the case of relaxation or chilliness produced by an over or under proportion of the matter of heat.

---

[1] The most accurate measure that can be given of a man's strength, seems to *Measure of* be that which is taken from the weight or number of pounds and ounces he *strength, the* can lift with his hands in a given attitude. This indeed relates immediately *weight a man* only to his arms: but these are the organs of strength which are most em- *can lift.* ployed; of which the strength corresponds with most exactness to the general state of the body with regard to strength; and in which the quantum of strength is easiest measured. Strength may accordingly be distinguished into *general* and *particular*.

Weakness is a negative term, and imports the absence of strength. It is, *Weakness,* besides, a relative term, and accordingly imports the absence of such a quantity *what.* of strength as makes the share, possessed by the person in question, less than that of some person he is compared to. Weakness, when it is at such a degree as to make it painful for a man to perform the motions necessary to the going through the ordinary functions of life, such as to get up, to walk, to dress one's self, and so forth, brings the circumstance of health into question, and puts a man into that sort of condition in which he is said to be in ill health.

Difference between strength and hardiness.

Hardiness, even in the sense in which it is opposed to the action of mechanical causes, is distinguishable from strength. The external indications of strength are the abundance and firmness of the muscular fibres: those of hardiness, in this sense, are the firmness of the muscular fibres, and the callosity of the skin. Strength is more peculiarly the gift of nature: hardiness, of education. Of two persons who have had, the one the education of a gentleman, the other, that of a common sailor, the first may be the stronger, at the same time that the other is the hardier.

4. Bodily imperfection.

10. 4. By bodily imperfection may be understood that condition which a person is in, who either stands distinguished by any remarkable deformity, or wants any of those parts or faculties, which the ordinary run of persons of the same sex and age are furnished with: who, for instance, has a hare-lip, is deaf, or has lost a hand. This circumstance, like that of ill-health, tends in general to diminish more or less the effect of any pleasurable circumstance, and to increase that of any afflictive one. The effect of this circumstance, however, admits of great variety: inasmuch as there are a great variety of ways in which a man may suffer in his personal appearance, and in his bodily organs and faculties: all which differences will be taken notice of in their proper places.[1]

5. Quantity and quality of knowledge.

11. 5. So much for circumstances belonging to the condition of the body: we come now to those which concern the condition of the mind: the use of mentioning these will be seen hereafter. In the first place may be reckoned the quantity and quality of the knowledge the person in question happens to possess: that is, of the ideas which he has actually in store, ready upon occasion to call to mind: meaning such ideas as are in some way or other of an interesting nature: that is, of a nature in some way or other to influence his happiness, or that of other men. When these ideas are many, and of importance, a man is said to be a man of knowledge; when few, or not of importance, *ignorant*.

6. Strength of intellectual powers.

12. 6. By strength of intellectual powers may be understood the degree of facility which a man experiences in his endeavours to call to mind as well such ideas as have been

[1] See B. I. Tit. [Irrep. corp. Injuries].

already aggregated to his stock of knowledge, as any others, which, upon any occasion that may happen, he may conceive a desire to place there. It seems to be on some such occasion as this that the words *parts* and *talents* are commonly employed. To this head may be referred the several qualities of readiness of apprehension, accuracy and tenacity of memory, strength of attention, clearness of discernment, amplitude of comprehension, vividity and rapidity of imagination. Strength of intellectual powers, in general, seems to correspond pretty exactly to general strength of body: as any of these qualities in particular does to particular strength.

13. 7. Firmness of mind on the one hand, and irritability on the other, regard the proportion between the degrees of efficacy with which a man is acted upon by an exciting cause, of which the value lies chiefly in magnitude, and one of which the value lies chiefly in propinquity.[1] A man may be said to be of a firm mind, when small pleasures or pains, which are present or near, do not affect him, in a greater proportion to their value, than greater pleasures or pains, which are uncertain or remote[2]; of an irritable mind, when the contrary is the case. *7. Firmness of mind.*

14. 8. Steadiness regards the time during which a given exciting cause of a given value continues to affect a man in nearly the same manner and degree as at first, no assignable external event or change of circumstances intervening to make an alteration in its force.[3] *8. Steadiness.*

15. 9. By the bent of a man's inclinations may be understood the propensity he has to expect pleasure or pain from certain objects, rather than from others. A man's inclinations may be said to have such or such a bent, when, amongst the *9. Bent of inclinations.*

---

[1] See Chap. iv. [Value].

[2] When, for instance, having been determined, by the prospect of some inconvenience, not to disclose a fact, although he should be put to the rack, he perseveres in such resolution after the rack is brought into his presence, and even applied to him.

[3] The facility with which children grow tired of their play-things, and throw them away, is an instance of unsteadiness: the perseverance with which a merchant applies himself to his traffic, or an author to his book, may be taken for an instance of the contrary. It is difficult to judge of the quantity of pleasure or pain in these cases, but from the effects which it produces in the character of a motive: and even then it is difficult to pronounce, whether the change of conduct happens by the extinction of the old pleasure or pain, or by the intervention of a new one.

several sorts of objects which afford pleasure in some degree
to all men, he is apt to expect more pleasure from one particular sort, than from another particular sort, or more from
any given particular sort, than another man would expect
from that sort; or when, amongst the several sorts of objects,
which to one man afford pleasure, whilst to another they
afford none, he is apt to expect, or not to expect, pleasure
from an object of such or such a sort: so also with regard to
pains. This circumstance, though intimately connected with
that of the bias of a man's sensibility, is not undistinguishable
from it. The quantity of pleasure or pain, which on any
given occasion a man may experience from an application of
any sort, may be greatly influenced by the expectations he
has been used to entertain of pleasure or pain from that
quarter; but it will not be absolutely determined by them:
for pleasure or pain may come upon him from a quarter from
which he was not accustomed to expect it.

10. *Moral sensibility.*

16. 10. The circumstances of *moral, religious, sympathetic,*
and *antipathetic sensibility,* when closely considered, will appear
to be included in some sort under that of *bent of inclination.* On
account of their particular importance they may, however,
be worth mentioning apart. A man's moral sensibility may
be said to be strong, when the pains and pleasures of the moral
sanction[1] show greater in his eyes, in comparison with other
pleasures and pains (and consequently exert a stronger
influence) than in the eyes of the persons he is compared with;
in other words, when he is acted on with more than ordinary
efficacy by the sense of honour: it may be said to be weak,
when the contrary is the case.

11. *Moral biases.*

17. 11. Moral sensibility seems to regard the average effect
or influence of the pains and pleasures of the moral sanction,
upon all sorts of occasions to which it is applicable, or happens
to be applied. It regards the average force or *quantity* of the
impulses the mind receives from that source during a given
period. Moral *bias* regards the particular acts on which, upon
so many particular occasions, the force of that sanction is
looked upon as attaching. It regards the *quality* or direction
of those impulses. It admits of as many varieties, therefore, as
there are dictates which the moral sanction may be conceived

[1] See Chap. v. [Pleasures and Pains].

to issue forth. A man may be said to have such or such a *moral bias*, or to have a moral bias in favour of such or such an action, when he looks upon it as being of the number of those of which the performance is dictated by the moral sanction.

18. 12. What has been said with regard to moral sensibility, may be applied, *mutatis mutandis*, to religious. 12. *Religious sensibility.*

19. 13. What has been said with regard to moral biases, may also be applied, *mutatis mutandis*, to religious biases. 13. *Religious biases.*

20. 14. By sympathetic sensibility is to be understood the propensity that a man has to derive pleasure from the happiness, and pain from the unhappiness, of other sensitive beings. It is the stronger, the greater the ratio of the pleasure or pain he feels on their account is to that of the pleasure or pain which (according to what appears to him) they feel for themselves. 14. *Sympathetic sensibility.*

21. 15. Sympathetic bias regards the description of the parties who are the objects of a man's sympathy: and of the acts or other circumstances of or belonging to those persons, by which the sympathy is excited. These parties may be, 1. Certain individuals. 2. Any subordinate class of individuals. 3. The whole nation. 4. Human kind in general. 5. The whole sensitive creation. According as these objects of sympathy are more numerous, the *affection*, by which the man is biased, may be said to be the more *enlarged*. 15. *Sympathetic biases.*

22. 16, 17. Antipathetic sensibility and antipathetic biases are just the reverse of sympathetic sensibility and sympathetic biases. By antipathetic sensibility is to be understood the propensity that a man has to derive pain from the happiness, and pleasure from the unhappiness, of other sensitive beings. 16, 17. *Antipathetic sensibility and biases.*

23. 18. The circumstance of insanity of mind corresponds to that of bodily imperfection. It admits, however, of much less variety, inasmuch as the soul is (for aught we can perceive) one indivisible thing, not distinguishable, like the body, into parts. What lesser degrees of imperfection the mind may be susceptible of, seem to be comprisable under the already-mentioned heads of ignorance, weakness of mind, irritability, or unsteadiness; or under such others as are reducible to them. Those which are here in view are those extraordinary species and degrees of mental imperfection, which, wherever they take place, are as conspicuous and as unquestionable as lameness or blindness in the body: operating partly, it should seem, 18. *Insanity.*

by inducing an extraordinary degree of the imperfections above mentioned, partly by giving an extraordinary and preposterous bent to the inclinations.

19. *Habitual occupations.*

24. 19. Under the head of a man's habitual occupations, are to be understood, on this occasion, as well those which he pursues for the sake of profit, as those which he pursues for the sake of present pleasure. The consideration of the profit itself belongs to the head of a man's pecuniary circumstances. It is evident, that if by any means a punishment, or any other exciting cause, has the effect of putting it out of his power to continue in the pursuit of any such occupation, it must on that account be so much the more distressing. A man's habitual occupations, though intimately connected in point of causality with the bent of his inclinations, are not to be looked upon as precisely the same circumstance. An amusement, or channel of profit, may be the object of a man's *inclinations*, which has never been the subject of his *habitual occupations*: for it may be, that though he wished to betake himself to it, he never did, it not being in his power: a circumstance which may make a good deal of difference in the effect of any incident by which he happens to be debarred from it.

20. *Pecuniary circumstances.*

25. 20. Under the head of pecuniary circumstances, I mean to bring to view the proportion which a man's *means* bear to his *wants*: the sum total of his means of every kind, to the sum total of his wants of every kind. A man's means depend upon three circumstances: 1. His property. 2. The profit of his labour. 3. His connexions in the way of support. His wants seem to depend upon four circumstances. 1. His habits of expense. 2. His connexions in the way of burthen. 3. Any present casual demand he may have. 4. The strength of his expectation. By a man's property is to be understood, whatever he has in store independent of his labour. By the profit of his labour is to be understood the growing profit. As to labour, it may be either of the body principally, or of the mind principally, or of both indifferently: nor does it matter in what manner, nor on what subject, it be applied, so it produce a profit. By a man's connexions in the way of support, are to be understood the pecuniary assistances, of whatever kind, which he is in a way of receiving from any persons who, on whatever account, and in whatever propor-

tion, he has reason to expect should contribute *gratis* to his maintenance: such as his parents, patrons, and relations. It seems manifest, that a man can have no other means than these. What he uses, he must have either of his own, or from other people: if from other people, either *gratis* or for a price. As to habits of expense, it is well known, that a man's desires are governed in a great degree by his habits. Many are the cases in which desire (and consequently the pain of privation connected with it[1]) would not even subsist at all, but for previous enjoyment. By a man's connexions in the way of burthen, are to be understood whatever expense he has reason to look upon himself as bound to be at in the support of those who by law, or the customs of the world, are warranted in looking up to him for assistance; such as children, poor relations, superannuated servants, and any other dependents whatsoever. As to present casual demand, it is manifest, that there are occasions on which a given sum will be worth infinitely more to a man than the same sum would at another time: where, for example, in a case of extremity, a man stands in need of extraordinary medical assistance: or wants money to carry on a law-suit, on which his all depends: or has got a livelihood waiting for him in a distant country, and wants money for the charges of conveyance. In such cases, any piece of good or ill fortune, in the pecuniary way, might have a very different effect from what it would have at any other time. With regard to strength of expectation; when one man expects to gain or to keep a thing which another does not, it is plain the circumstance of not having it will affect the former very differently from the latter; who, indeed, commonly, will not be affected by it at all.

26. 21. Under the head of a man's connexions in the way of sympathy, I would bring to view the number and description of the persons in whose welfare he takes such a concern, as that the idea of their happiness should be productive of pleasure, and that of their unhappiness of pain to him: for instance, a man's wife, his children, his parents, his near relations, and intimate friends. This class of person, it is obvious, will for the most part include the two classes by which his pecuniary circumstances are affected: those, to wit,

21. *Connexions in the way of sympathy.*

---

[1] See Chap. v. [Pleasures and Pains].

from whose means he may expect support, and those whose wants operate on him as a burthen. But it is obvious, that besides these, it may very well include others, with whom he has no such pecuniary connexion: and even with regard to these, it is evident that the pecuniary dependence, and the union of affections, are circumstances perfectly distinguishable. Accordingly, the connexions here in question, independently of any influence they may have on a man's pecuniary circumstances, have an influence on the effect of any exciting causes whatsoever. The tendency of them is to increase a man's general sensibility; to increase, on the one hand, the pleasure produced by all pleasurable causes; on the other, the pain produced by all afflictive ones. When any pleasurable incident happens to a man, he naturally, in the first moment, thinks of the pleasure it will afford immediately to himself: presently afterwards, however (except in a few cases, which is not worth while here to insist on) he begins to think of the pleasure which his friends will feel upon their coming to know of it: and this secondary pleasure is commonly no mean addition to the primary one. First comes the self-regarding pleasure: then comes the idea of the pleasure of sympathy, which you suppose that pleasure of yours will give birth to in the bosom of your friend: and this idea excites again in yours a new pleasure of sympathy, grounded upon his. The first pleasure issuing from your own bosom, as it were from a radiant point, illuminates the bosom of your friend: reverberated from thence, it is reflected with augmented warmth to the point from whence it first proceeded: and so it is with pains.[1]

Nor does this effect depend wholly upon affection. Among near relations, although there should be no kindness, the pleasures and pains of the moral sanction are quickly propagated by a peculiar kind of sympathy: no article, either of honour or disgrace, can well fall upon a man, without extending to a certain distance within the circle of his family. What reflects honour upon the father, reflects honour upon

[1] This is one reason why legislators in general like better to have married people to deal with than single; and people that have children than such as are childless. It is manifest that the stronger and more numerous a man's connexions in the way of sympathy are, the stronger is the hold which the law has upon him. A wife and children are so many pledges a man gives to the world for his good behaviour.

the son: what reflects disgrace, disgrace. The *cause* of this singular and seemingly unreasonable circumstance (that is, its analogy to the rest of the phenomena of the human mind,) belongs not to the present purpose. It is sufficient if the effect be beyond dispute.

27. 22. Of a man's connexions in the way of antipathy, there needs not any thing very particular to be observed. Happily there is no primeval and constant source of antipathy in human nature, as there is of sympathy. There are no permanent sets of persons who are naturally and of course the objects of antipathy to a man, as there are who are the objects of the contrary affection. Sources, however, but too many, of antipathy, are apt to spring up upon various occasions during the course of a man's life: and whenever they do, this circumstance may have a very considerable influence on the effects of various exciting causes. As on the one hand, a punishment, for instance, which tends to separate a man from those with whom he is connected in the way of sympathy, so on the other hand, one which tends to force him into the company of those with whom he is connected in the way of antipathy, will, on that account, be so much the more distressing. It is to be observed, that sympathy itself multiplies the sources of antipathy. Sympathy for your friend gives birth to antipathy on *your* part against all those who are objects of antipathy, as well as to sympathy for those who are objects of sympathy to *him*. In the same manner does antipathy multiply the sources of sympathy; though commonly perhaps with rather a less degree of efficacy. Antipathy against your enemy is apt to give birth to sympathy on *your* part towards those who are objects of antipathy, as well as to antipathy against those who are objects of sympathy, to *him*.

22. *Connexions in the way of antipathy.*

28. 23. Thus much for the circumstances by which the effect of any exciting cause may be influenced, when applied upon any given occasion, at any given period. But besides these supervening incidents, there are other circumstances relative to a man, that may have their influence, and which are co-eval to his birth. In the first place, it seems to be universally agreed, that in the original frame or texture of every man's body, there is a something which, independently of all subsequently intervening circumstances, renders him liable

23. *Radical frame of body.*

to be affected by causes producing bodily pleasure or pain, in a manner different from that in which another man would be affected by the same causes. To the catalogue of circumstances influencing a man's sensibility, we may therefore add his original or radical frame, texture, constitution, or temperament of body.

24. Radical frame of mind.

29. 24. In the next place, it seems to be pretty well agreed, that there is something also in the original frame or texture of every man's mind, which, independently of all exterior and subsequently intervening circumstances, and even of his radical frame of body, makes him liable to be differently affected by the same exciting causes, from what another man would be. To the catalogue of circumstances influencing a man's sensibility, we may therefore further add his original or radical frame, texture, constitution or temperament of mind.[1]

This distinct from the circumstance of frame of body:

30. It seems pretty certain, all this while, that a man's sensibility to causes producing pleasure or pain, even of mind, may depend in a considerable degree upon his original and acquired frame of body. But we have no reason to think that it can depend altogether upon that frame: since, on the one hand, we see persons whose frame of body is as much alike as can be conceived, differing very considerably in respect of their mental frame: and, on the other hand, persons whose frame of mind is as much alike as can be conceived, differing very conspicuously in regard to their bodily frame.[2]

—and from all others.

31. It seems indisputable also, that the different sets of external occurrences that may befall a man in the course of

Idiosyncrasy, what.

[1] The characteristic circumstances whereby one man's frame of body or mind, considered at any given period, stands distinguished from that of another, have been comprised by metaphysicians and physiologists under the name *idiosyncrasy*, from ιδιος, peculiar, and συνκρασις, composition.

Whether the soul be material or immaterial makes no difference.

[2] Those who maintain, that the mind and the body are one substance, may here object, that upon that supposition the distinction between frame of mind and frame of body is but nominal, and that accordingly there is no such thing as a frame of mind distinct from the frame of body. But granting, for argument-sake, the antecedent, we may dispute the consequence. For if the mind be but a part of the body, it is at any rate of a nature very different from the other parts of the body.

A man's frame of body cannot in any part of it undergo any considerable alteration without its being immediately indicated by phænomena discernible by the senses. A man's frame of mind may undergo very considerable alterations, his frame of body remaining the same to all appearance; that is, for any thing that is indicated to the contrary by phænomena cognizable to the senses: meaning those of other men.

his life, will make great differences in the subsequent texture of his mind at any given period: yet still those differences are not solely to be attributed to such occurrences. Equally far from the truth seems that opinion to be (if any such be maintained) which attributes all to nature, and that which attributes all to education. The two circumstances will therefore still remain distinct, as well from one another, as from all others.

32. Distinct however as they are, it is manifest, that at no period in the active part of a man's life can they either of them make their appearance by themselves. All they do is to constitute the latent ground-work which the other supervening circumstances have to work upon: and whatever influence those original principles may have, is so changed and modified, and covered over, as it were, by those other circumstances, as never to be separately discernible. The effects of the one influence are indistinguishably blended with those of the other. *Yet the result of them is not separately discernible.*

33. The emotions of the body are received, and with reason, as probable indications of the temperature of the mind. But they are far enough from conclusive. A man may exhibit, for instance, the exterior appearances of grief, without really grieving at all, or at least in any thing near the proportion in which he appears to grieve. Oliver Cromwell, whose conduct indicated a heart more than ordinarily callous, was as remarkably profuse in tears.[1] Many men can command the external appearances of sensibility with very little real feeling.[2] The female sex commonly with greater facility *Frame of body indicates, but not certainly, that of mind.*

---

[1] Hume's Hist.

[2] The quantity of the sort of pain, which is called grief, is indeed hardly to be measured by any external indications. It is neither to be measured, for instance, by the quantity of the tears, nor by the number of moments spent in crying. Indications rather less equivocal may, perhaps, be afforded by the pulse. A man has not the motions of his heart at command as he has those of the muscles of his face. But the particular significancy of these indications is still very uncertain. All they can express is, that the man is affected; they cannot express in what manner, nor from what cause. To an affection resulting from such or such a cause, he may give an artificial colouring, and attribute it to such or such another cause. To an affection directed in reality to such or such a person as its object, he may give an artificial bias, and represent it as if directed to such or such another object. Tears of rage he may attribute to contrition. The concern he feels at the thoughts of a punishment that awaits him, he may impute to a sympathetic concern for the mischief produced by his offence. A very tolerable judgment, however, may commonly be formed by a dis-

M

than the male: hence the proverbial expression of a woman's tears. To have this kind of command over one's self, was the characteristic excellence of the orator of ancient times, and is still that of the player in our own.

Secondary influencing circumstances.

34. The remaining circumstances may, with reference to those already mentioned, be termed *secondary* influencing circumstances. These have an influence, it is true, on the quantum or bias of a man's sensibility, but it is only by means of the other primary ones. The manner in which these two sets of circumstances are concerned, is such that the primary ones do the business, while the secondary ones lie most open to observation. The secondary ones, therefore, are those those which are most heard of; on which account it will be necessary to take notice of them: at the same time that it is only by means of the primary ones that their influence can be explained; whereas the influence of the primary ones will be apparent enough, without any mention of the secondary ones.

25. Sex.

35. 25. Among such of the primitive modifications of the corporeal frame as may appear to influence the quantum and bias of sensibility, the most obvious and conspicuous are those which constitute the *sex*. In point of quantity, the sensibility of the female sex appears in general to be greater than that of the male. The health of the female is more delicate than that of the male: in point of strength and hardiness of body, in point of quantity and quality of knowledge, in point of strength of intellectual powers, and firmness of mind, she is commonly inferior: moral, religious, sympathetic, and antipathetic sensibility are commonly stronger in her than in the male. The quality of her knowledge, and the bent of her inclinations, are commonly in many respects different. Her moral biases are also, in certain respects, remarkably different: chastity, modesty, and delicacy, for instance, are prized more than courage in a woman: courage, more than any of those qualities, in a man. The religious biases in the two sexes are not apt to be remarkably different; except that the female is

cerning mind, upon laying all the external indications exhibited by a man together, and at the same time comparing them with his actions.

A remarkable instance of the power of the will, over the external indications of sensibility, is to be found in Tacitus's story of the Roman soldier, who raised a mutiny in the camp, pretending to have lost a brother by the lawless cruelty of the General. The truth was, he never had had a brother.

rather more inclined than the male to superstition; that is, to observances not dictated by the principle of utility; a difference that may be pretty well accounted for by some of the before-mentioned circumstances. Her sympathetic biases are in many respects different; for her own offspring all their lives long, and for children in general while young, her affection is commonly stronger than that of the male. Her affections are apt to be less enlarged: seldom expanding themselves so much as to take in the welfare of her country in general, much less that of mankind, or the whole sensitive creation: seldom embracing any extensive class or division, even of her own countrymen, unless it be in virtue of her sympathy for some particular individuals that belong to it. In general, her antipathetic, as well as sympathetic biases, are apt to be less conformable to the principle of utility than those of the male; owing chiefly to some deficiency in point of knowledge, discernment, and comprehension. Her habitual occupations of the amusing kind are apt to be in many respects different from those of the male. With regard to her connexions in the way of sympathy, there can be no difference. In point of pecuniary circumstances, according to the customs of perhaps all countries, she is in general less independent.

36. 26. Age is of course divided into divers periods, of which the number and limits are by no means uniformly ascertained. One might distinguish it, for the present purpose, into, 1. Infancy. 2. Adolescence. 3. Youth. 4. Maturity. 5. Decline. 6. Decrepitude. It were lost time to stop on the present occasion to examine it at each period, and to observe the indications it gives, with respect to the several primary circumstances just reviewed. Infancy and decrepitude are commonly inferior to the other periods, in point of health, strength, hardiness, and so forth. In infancy, on the part of the female, the imperfections of that sex are enhanced: on the part of the male, imperfections take place mostly similar in quality, but greater in quantity, to those attending the states of adolescence, youth, and maturity in the female. In the stage of decrepitude both sexes relapse into many of the imperfections of infancy. The generality of these observations may easily be corrected upon a particular review. *26. Age.*

37. 27. Station, or rank in life, is a circumstance, that, *27. Rank.*

among a civilized people, will commonly undergo a multi-plicity of variations. *Cæteris paribus*, the quantum of sensibility appears to be greater in the higher ranks of men than in the lower. The primary circumstances in respect of which this secondary circumstance is apt to induce or indicate a difference, seem principally to be as follows: 1. Quantity and Quality of knowledge. 2. Strength of mind. 3. Bent of inclination. 4. Moral sensibility. 5. Moral biases. 6. Religious sensibility. 7. Religious biases. 8. Sympathetic sensibility. 9. Sympa-thetic biases. 10. Antipathetic sensibility. 11. Antipathetic biases. 12. Habitual occupations. 13. Nature and pro-ductiveness of a man's means of livelihood. 14. Connexions importing profit. 15. Habit of expense. 16. Connexions importing burthen. A man of a certain rank will frequently have a number of dependents besides those whose dependency is the result of natural relationship. As to health, strength, and hardiness, if rank has any influence on these circumstances, it is but in a remote way, chiefly by the influence it may have on its habitual occupations.

28. *Education.* 38. 28. The influence of education is still more extensive. Education stands upon a footing somewhat different from that of the circumstances of age, sex, and rank. These words, though the influence of the circumstances they respectively denote exerts itself principally, if not entirely, through the medium of certain of the primary circumstances before men-tioned, present, however, each of them a circumstance which has a separate existence of itself. This is not the case with the word education: which means nothing any farther than as it serves to call up to view some one or more of those primary circumstances. Education may be distinguished into physical and mental; the education of the body and that of the mind: mental, again, into intellectual and moral; the culture of the understanding, and the culture of the affections. The educa-tion a man receives, is given to him partly by others, partly by himself. By education then nothing more can be expressed than the condition a man is in in respect of those primary circumstances, as resulting partly from the management and contrivance of others, principally of those who in the early periods of his life have had dominion over him, partly from his own. To the physical part of his education, belong the circumstances of health, strength, and hardiness: sometimes, by accident, that of bodily imperfection; as where by intemperance or negligence an irreparable mischief happens to his person. To the intellectual part, those of quantity and quality of knowledge, and in some measure perhaps those of firmness of mind and steadiness. To the moral part, the bent of his inclinations, the quantity and quality of his moral, religious, sympathetic, and antipathetic sensibility: to all three branches indiscriminately, but under the superior control of external occurrences, his habitual recreations, his property, his means of livelihood, his connexions in the way of profit and of burthen, and his habits of expense. With respect indeed to all these points, the influence of education is modified, in a manner more or less apparent, by that of exterior occurrences; and in a manner scarcely at all apparent, and altogether out of the reach of calculation, by the original texture and constitution as well of his body as of his mind.

39. 29. Among the external circumstances by which the influence of education is modified, the principal are those which come under the head of *climate*. This circumstance places itself in front, and demands a separate denomination, not merely on account of the magnitude of its influence, but also on account of its being conspicuous to every body, and of its applying indiscriminately to great numbers at a time. This circumstance depends for its *essence* upon the situation of that part of the earth which is in question, with respect to the course taken by the whole planet in its revolution round the sun: but for its *influence* it depends upon the condition of the bodies which compose the earth's surface at that part, principally upon the quantities of sensible heat at different periods, and upon the density, and purity, and dryness or moisture of the circumambient air. Of the so often mentioned primary circumstances, there are few of which the production is not influenced by this secondary one; partly by its manifest effects upon the body; partly by its less perceptible effects upon the mind. In hot climates men's health is apt to be more precarious than in cold: their strength and hardiness less: their vigour, firmness, and steadiness of mind less: and thence indirectly their quantity of knowledge: the bent of their inclinations different: most remarkably so in respect of their

29. *Climate.*

superior propensity to sexual enjoyments, and in respect
of the earliness of the period at which that propensity begins
to manifest itself: their sensibilities of all kinds more intense:
their habitual occupations savouring more of sloth than of
activity: their radical frame of body less strong, probably,
and less hardy: their radical frame of mind less vigorous,
less firm, less steady.

30. Lineage.

40. 30. Another article in the catalogue of secondary
circumstances, is that of *race* or *lineage*: the national race or
lineage a man issues from. This circumstance, independently
of that of climate, will commonly make some difference in
point of radical frame of mind and body. A man of negro
race, born in France or England, is a very different being, in
many respects, from a man of French or English race. A man
of Spanish race, born in Mexico or Peru, is at the hour of his
birth a different sort of being, in many respects, from a man
of the original Mexican or Peruvian race. This circumstance,
as far as it is distinct from climate, rank, and education, and
from the two just mentioned, operates chiefly through the
medium of moral, religious, sympathetic, and antipathetic
biases.

**31. Govern-
ment.**

41. 31. The last circumstance but one, is that of government: the government a man lives under at the time in
question; or rather that under which he has been accustomed
most to live. This circumstance operates principally through
the medium of education: the magistrate operating in the
character of a tutor upon all the members of the state, by
the direction he gives to their hopes and to their fears. Indeed
under a solicitous and attentive government, the ordinary
preceptor, nay even the parent himself, is but a deputy, as
it were, to the magistrate: whose controlling influence,
different in this respect from that of the ordinary preceptor,
dwells with a man to his life's end. The effects of the peculiar
power of the magistrate are seen more particularly in the
influence it exerts over the quantum and bias of men's moral,
religious, sympathetic, and antipathetic sensibilities. Under a
well-constituted, or even under a well-administered though
ill-constituted government, men's moral sensibility is commonly stronger, and their moral biases more conformable
to the dictates of utility: their religious sensibility frequently

weaker, but their religious biases less unconformable to the dictates of utility: their sympathetic affections more enlarged, directed to the magistrate more than to small parties or to individuals, and more to the whole community than to either: their antipathetic sensibilities less violent, as being more obsequious to the influence of well-directed moral biases, and less apt to be excited by that of ill-directed religious ones: their antipathetic biases more conformable to well-directed moral ones, more apt (in proportion) to be grounded on enlarged and sympathetic than on narrow and self-regarding affections, and accordingly, upon the whole, more conformable to the dictates of utility.

42. 32. The last circumstance is that of religious profession: 32. *Religiou* the religious profession a man is of: the religious fraternity *profession.* of which he is a member. This circumstance operates principally through the medium of religious sensibility and religious biases. It operates, however, as an indication more or less conclusive, with respect to several other circumstances. With respect to some, scarcely but through the medium of the two just mentioned: this is the case with regard to the quantum and bias of a man's moral, sympathetic, and antipathetic sensibility: perhaps in some cases with regard to quantity and quality of knowledge, strength of intellectual powers, and bent of inclination. With respect to others, it may operate immediately of itself: this seems to be the case with regard to a man's habitual occupations, pecuniary circumstances, and connexions in the way of sympathy and antipathy. A man who pays very little inward regard to the dictates of the religion which he finds it necessary to profess, may find it difficult to avoid joining in the ceremonies of it, and bearing a part in the pecuniary burthens it imposes.[1] By the force of habit and example he may even be led to entertain a partiality for persons of the same profession, and a proportionable antipathy against those of a rival one. In

---

[1] The ways in which a religion may lessen a man's means, or augment his wants, are various. Sometimes it will prevent him from making a profit of his money: sometimes from setting his hand to labour. Sometimes it will oblige him to buy dearer food instead of cheaper: sometimes to purchase useless labour: sometimes to pay men for not labouring: sometimes to purchase trinkets, on which imagination alone has set a value: sometimes to purchase exemptions from punishment, or titles to felicity in the world to come.

particular, the antipathy against persons of different persuasions is one of the last points of religion which men part with. Lastly, it is obvious, that the religious profession a man is of cannot but have a considerable influence on his education. But, considering the import of the term education, to say this is perhaps no more than saying in other words what has been said already.

Use of the preceding observations.

43. These circumstances, all or many of them, will need to be attended to as often as upon any occasion any account is taken of any quantity of pain or pleasure, as resulting from any cause. Has any person sustained an injury? they will need to be considered in estimating the mischief of the offence. Is satisfaction to be made to him? they will need to be attended to in adjusting the *quantum* of that satisfaction. Is the injurer to be punished? they will need to be attended to in estimating the force of the impression that will be made on him by any given punishment.

How far the circumstances in question can be taken into account.

44. It is to be observed, that though they seem all of them, on some account or other, to merit a place in the catalogue, they are not all of equal use in practice. Different articles among them are applicable to different causes. Of those that may influence the effect of the same exciting cause, some apply indiscriminately to whole classes of persons together; being applicable to all, without any remarkable difference in degree: these may be directly and pretty fully provided for by the legislator. This is the case, for instance, with the primary circumstances of bodily imperfection, and insanity: with the secondary circumstance of sex: perhaps with that of age: at any rate with those of rank, of climate, of lineage, and of religious profession. Others, however they may apply to whole classes of persons, yet in their application to different individuals are susceptible of perhaps an indefinite variety of degrees. These cannot be fully provided for by the legislator; but, as the existence of them, in every sort of case, is capable of being ascertained, and the degree in which they take place is capable of being measured, provision may be made for them by the judge, or other executive magistrate, to whom the several individuals that happen to be concerned may be made known. This is the case, 1. With the circumstance of health. 2. In some sort with that of strength. 3. Scarcely with that of

hardiness: still less with those of quantity and quality of knowledge, strength of intellectual powers, firmness or steadiness of mind; except in as far as a man's condition, in respect of those circumstances, may be indicated by the secondary circumstances of sex, age, or rank: hardly with that of bent of inclination, except in as far as that latent circumstance is indicated by the more manifest one of habitual occupations: hardly with that of a man's moral sensibility or biases, except in as far as they may be indicated by his sex, age, rank, and education: not at all with his religious sensibility and religious biases, except in as far as they may be indicated by the religious profession he belongs to: not at all with the quantity or quality of his sympathetic or antipathetic sensibilities, except in as far as they may be presumed from his sex, age, rank, education, lineage, or religious profession. It is the case, however, with his habitual occupations, with his pecuniary circumstances, and with his connexions in the way of sympathy. Of others, again, either the existence cannot be ascertained, or the degree cannot be measured. These, therefore, cannot be taken into account, either by the legislator or the executive magistrate. Accordingly, they would have no claim to be taken notice of, were it not for those secondary circumstances by which they are indicated, and whose influence could not well be understood without them. What these are has been already mentioned.

45. It has already been observed, that different articles in *To what excit-* this list of circumstances apply to different exciting causes: the *ing causes there* circumstance of bodily strength, for instance, has scarcely any *is most occasion* influence of itself (whatever it may have in a roundabout *to apply them.* way, and by accident) on the effect of an incident which should increase or diminish the quantum of a man's property. It remains to be considered, what the exciting causes are with which the legislator has to do. These may, by some accident or other, be any whatsoever: but those which he has principally to do, are those of the painful or afflictive kind. With pleasurable ones he has little to do, except now and then by accident: the reasons of which may be easily enough perceived, at the same time that it would take up too much room to unfold them here. The exciting causes with which he has principally to do, are, on the one hand, the mischievous acts,

which it is his business to prevent; on the other hand, the punishments, by the terror of which it is his endeavour to prevent them. Now of these two sets of exciting causes, the latter only is of his production: being produced partly by his own special appointment, partly in conformity to his general appointment, by the special appointment of the judge. For the legislator, therefore, as well as for the judge, it is necessary (if they would know what it is they are doing when they are appointing punishment) to have an eye to all these circumstances. For the legislator, lest, meaning to apply a certain quantity of punishment to all persons who shall put themselves in a given predicament, he should unawares apply to some of those persons much more or much less than he himself intended: for the judge, lest, in applying to a particular person a particular measure of punishment, he should apply much more or much less than was intended, perhaps by himself, and at any rate by the legislator. They ought each of them, therefore, to have before him, on the one hand, a list of the several circumstances by which sensibility may be influenced; on the other hand, a list of the several species and degrees of punishment which they purpose to make use of: and then, by making a comparison between the two, to form a detailed estimate of the influence of each of the circumstances in question, upon the effect of each species and degree of punishment.

There are two plans or orders of distribution, either of which might be pursued in the drawing up this estimate. The one is to make the name of the circumstance take the lead, and under it to represent the different influences it exerts over the effects of the several modes of punishment: the other is to make the name of the punishment take the lead, and under it to represent the different influences which are exerted over the effects of it by the several circumstances above mentioned. Now of these two sorts of objects, the punishment is that to which the intention of the legislator is directed in the first instance. This is of his own creation, and will be whatsoever he thinks fit to make it: the influencing circumstance exists independently of him, and is what it is whether he will or no. What he has occasion to do is to establish a certain species and degree of punishment: and it is only with reference to that punishment that he has occasion to make any inquiry concerning any of the circumstances here in question. The latter of the two plans therefore is that which appears by far the most useful and commodious. But neither upon the one nor the other plan can any such estimate be delivered here.[1]

46. Of the several circumstances contained in this catalogue, it may be of use to give some sort of analytic view; in order that it may be the more easily discovered if any which ought to have been inserted are omitted; and that, with regard to those which are inserted, it may be seen how they differ and agree. *Analytical view of the circumstances influencing sensibility.*

In the first place, they may be distinguished into *primary* and *secondary*: those may be termed primary, which operate immediately of themselves: those secondary, which operate not but by the medium of the former. To this latter head belong the circumstances of sex, age, station in life, education, climate, lineage, government, and religious profession: the rest are primary. These again are either *connate* or *adventitious*: those which are connate, are radical frame of body and radical frame of mind. Those which are adventitious, are either *personal*, or *exterior*. The personal, again, concern either a man's *dispositions*, or his *actions*. Those which concern his dispositions, concern either his *body* or his *mind*. Those which concern his body are health, strength, hardiness, and bodily imperfection. Those which concern his mind, again, concern either his *understanding* or his *affections*. To the former head belong the circumstances of quantity and quality of knowledge, strength of understanding, and insanity. To the latter belong the circumstances of firmness of mind, steadiness, bent

---

[1] This is far from being a visionary proposal, not reducible to practice. I speak from experience, having actually drawn up such an estimate, though upon the least commodious of the two plans, and before the several circumstances in question had been reduced to the precise number and order in which they are here enumerated. This is a part of the matter destined for another work. See Chap. xiii. [Cases unmeet], par. 2. Note. There are some of these circumstances that bestow particular denominations on the persons they relate to: thus, from the circumstance of bodily imperfections, persons are denominated, deaf, dumb, blind, and so forth: from the circumstance of insanity, idiots, and maniacs: from the circumstance of age, infants: for all which classes of persons particular provision is made in the Code. See B. I. tit. [Exemptions]. Persons thus distinguished will form so many articles in the *catalogus personarum privilegiatarum*. See Appendix tit. [Composition].

of inclination, moral sensibility, moral biases, religious sensibility, religious biases, sympathetic sensibility, sympathetic biases, antipathetic sensibility, and antipathetic biases. Those which regard his actions, are his habitual occupations. Those which are exterior to him, regard either the *things* or the *persons* which he is concerned with; under the former head come his pecuniary circumstances;[1] under the latter, his connexions in the way of sympathy and antipathy.

Analytical view of the constituent articles in a man's pecuniary circumstances.

[1] As to man's pecuniary circumstances, the causes on which those circumstances depend, do not come all of them under the same class. The absolute quantum of a man's property does indeed come under the same class with his pecuniary circumstances in general: so does the profit he makes from the occupation which furnishes him with the means of livelihood. But the occupation itself concerns his own person, and comes under the same head as his habitual amusements: as likewise his habits of expense: his connexions in the ways of profit and of burthen, under the same head as his connexions in the way of sympathy: and the circumstances of his present demand for money, and strength of expectation, come under the head of those circumstances relative to his person which regard his affections.

CHAPTER VII

OF HUMAN ACTIONS IN GENERAL

1. THE business of government is to promote the happiness *The demand for* of the society, by punishing and rewarding. That part of its *punishment depends in part* business which consists in punishing, is more particularly *upon the* the subject of penal law. In proportion as an act tends to *tendency of the* disturb that happiness, in proportion as the tendency of it is *act.* pernicious, will be the demand it creates for punishment. What happiness consists of we have already seen: enjoyment of pleasures, security from pains.

2. The general tendency of an act is more or less pernicious, *Tendency of an* according to the sum total of its consequences: that is, accord- *act determined* ing to the difference between the sum of such as are good, and *by its conse-* the sum of such as are evil. *quences.*

3. It is to be observed, that here, as well as henceforward, *Material con-* wherever consequences are spoken of, such only are meant *sequences only* as are *material*. Of the consequences of any act, the multitude *are to be* and variety must needs be infinite: but such of them only as *regarded.* are material are worth regarding. Now among the consequences of an act, be they what they may, such only, by one who views them in the capacity of a legislator, can be said to be material,[1] as either consist of pain or pleasure, or have an influence in the production of pain or pleasure.[2]

4. It is also to be observed, that into the account of the *These depend in* consequences of the act, are to be taken not such only as *part upon the* might have ensued, were intention out of the question, but *intention.* such also as depend upon the connexion there may be between these first-mentioned consequences and the intention. The connexion there is between the intention and certain con-

---

[1] Or of *importance*.
[2] In certain cases the consequences of an act may be material by serving as evidences indicating the existence of some other material fact, which is even *antecedent* to the act of which they are the consequences: but even here, they are material only because, in virtue of such their evidentiary quality, they have an influence, at a subsequent period of time, in the production of pain and pleasure: for example, by serving as grounds for conviction, and thence for punishment. See tit. [Simple Falsehoods], *verbo* [material].

sequences is, as we shall see hereafter,[1] a means of producing other consequences. In this lies the difference between rational agency and irrational.

5. Now the intention, with regard to the consequences of an act, will depend upon two things: 1. The state of the will or intention, with respect to the act itself. And, 2, The state of the understanding, or perceptive faculties, with regard to the circumstances which it is, or may appear to be, accompanied with. Now with respect to these circumstances, the perceptive faculty is susceptible of three states: consciousness, unconsciousness, and false consciousness. Consciousness, when the party believes precisely those circumstances, and no others, to subsist, which really do subsist: unconsciousness, when he fails of perceiving certain circumstances to subsist, which, however, do subsist: false consciousness, when he believes or imagines certain circumstances to subsist, which in truth do not subsist.

6. In every transaction, therefore, which is examined with a view to punishment, there are four articles to be considered: 1. The *act* itself, which is done. 2. The *circumstances* in which it is done. 3. The *intentionality* that may have accompanied it. 4. The *consciousness*, unconsciousness, or false consciousness, that may have accompanied it.

What regards the act and the circumstances will be the subject of the present chapter: what regards intention and consciousness, that of the two succeeding.

7. There are also two other articles on which the general tendency of an act depends: and on that, as well as on other accounts, the demand which it creates for punishment. These are, 1. The particular *motive* or motives which gave birth to it. 2. The general *disposition* which it indicates. These articles will be the subject of two other chapters.

8. Acts may be distinguished in several ways, for several purposes.

They may be distinguished, in the first place, into *positive* and *negative*. By positive are meant such as consist in motion or exertion: by negative, such as consist in keeping at rest; that is, in forbearing to move or exert one's self in such and such circumstances. Thus, to strike is a positive act: not to

[1] See B. I. tit. [Exemptions] and tit. [Extenuations].

strike on a certain occasion, a negative one. Positive acts are styled also acts of commission; negative, acts of omission or forbearance.[1]

9. Such acts, again, as are negative, may either be *absolutely* so, or *relatively*: absolutely, when they import the negation of all positive agency whatsoever; for instance, not to strike at all: relatively, when they import the negation of such or such a particular mode of agency; for instance, not to strike such a person or such a thing, or in such a direction. *Negative acts may be so relatively or absolutely.*

10. It is to be observed, that the nature of the act, whether positive or negative, is not to be determined immediately by the form of the discourse made use of to express it. An act which is positive in its nature may be characterized by a negative expression: thus, not to be at rest, is as much as to say to move. So also an act, which is negative in its nature, may be characterized by a positive expression: thus, to forbear or omit to bring food to a person in certain circumstances, is signified by the single and positive term *to starve*. *Negative acts may be expressed positively; and vice versa.*

11. In the second place, acts may be distinguished into *external* and *internal*. By external, are meant corporal acts; acts of the body: by internal, mental acts; acts of the mind. Thus, to strike is an external or exterior[2] act: to intend to strike, an internal or interior one. *Acts external and internal.*

12. Acts of *discourse* are a sort of mixture of the two: external acts, which are no ways material, nor attended with any consequences, any farther than as they serve to express *Acts of discourse, what.*

[1] The distinction between positive and negative acts runs through the whole system of offences, and sometimes makes a material difference with regard to their consequences. To reconcile us the better to the extensive, and, as it may appear on some occasions, the inconsistent signification here given to the word *act*, it may be considered, 1. That in many cases, where no exterior or overt act is exercised, the state which the mind is in at the time when the supposed act is said to happen, is as truly and directly the result of the will, as any exterior act, how plain and conspicuous soever. The not revealing a conspiracy, for instance, may be as perfectly the act of the will, as the joining in it. In the next place, that even though the mind should never have had the incident in question in contemplation (insomuch that the event of its not happening should not have been so much as obliquely intentional) still the state of the person's mind was in at the time when, if he *had* so willed, the incident might have happened, is in many cases productive of as material consequences; and not only as likely, but as fit to call for the interposition of other agents, as the opposite one. Thus, when a tax is imposed, your not paying it is an act which at any rate must be punished in a certain manner, whether you happened to think of paying it or not. *Acts of omission are still acts.*

[2] An exterior act is also called by lawyers *overt*.

the existence of internal ones. To speak to another to strike, to write to him to strike, to make signs to him to strike, are all so many acts of discourse.

External acts may be transitive or intransitive.

13. Third, Acts that are external may be distinguished into *transitive* and *intransitive*. Acts may be called transitive, when the motion is communicated from the person of the agent to some foreign body: that is, to such a foreign body on which the effects of it are considered as being *material*; as where a man runs against you, or throws water in your face. Acts may be called intransitive, when the motion is communicated to no other body, on which the effects of it are regarded as material, than some part of the same person in whom it originated: as where a man runs, or washes himself.[1]

A transitive act, its commencement, termination, and intermediate progress.

14. An act of the transitive kind may be said to be in its *commencement*, or in the *first* stage of its progress, while the motion is confined to the person of the agent, and has not yet been communicated to any foreign body, on which the effects of it can be material. It may be said to be in its *termination*, or to be in the last stage of its progress, as soon as the motion or impulse has been communicated to some such foreign body. It may be said to be in the *middle* or intermediate stage or stages of its progress, while the motion, having passed from the person of the agent, has not yet been communicated to any such foreign body. Thus, as soon as a man has lifted up his hand to strike, the act he performs in striking you is in its commencement: as soon as his hand has reached you, it is in its termination. If the act be the motion of a body which is separated from the person of the agent before it reaches the object, it may be said, during that interval, to be in its intermediate progress,[2] or in *gradu mediativo*: as in the case where a man throws a stone or fires a bullet at you.

Distinction between transitive acts and intransitive, recognized by grammarians.

[1] The distinction is well known to the latter grammarians: it is with them indeed that it took its rise: though by them it has been applied rather to the names than to the things themselves. To verbs, signifying transitive acts, as here described, they have given the name of transitive verbs: those significative of intransitive acts they have termed intransitive. These last are still more frequently called *neuter*; that is, *neither* active nor passive. The appellation seems improper: since, instead of their being *neither*, they are both in one.

To the class of acts that are here termed intransitive, belong those which constitute the 3rd class in the system of offences. See Chap. [Division] and B. I. tit. [Self regarding Offences].

[2] Or *in its migration*, or *in transitu*.

15. An act of the *in*transitive kind may be said to be in its *An intransitive*
commencement, when the motion or impulse is as yet con- *act, its com-*
fined to the member or organ in which it originated; and has *mencement, and*
not yet been communicated to any member or organ that is *termination.*
distinguishable from the former. It may be said to be in its
termination, as soon as it has been applied to any other part
of the same person. Thus, where a man poisons himself,
while he is lifting up the poison to his mouth, the act is in its
commencement: as soon as it has reached his lips, it is in its
termination.[1]

16. In the third place, acts may be distinguished into *tran-* *Acts transient*
sient and *continued*. Thus, to strike is a transient act: to lean, *and continued.*
a continued one. To buy, a transient act: to keep in one's
possession, a continued one.

17. In strictness of speech there is a difference between a *Difference*
continued act and a *repetition* of acts. It is a repetition of acts, *between a con-*
tinued act and a
when there are intervals filled up by acts of different natures: *repetition of*
a continued act, when there are no such intervals. Thus, to *acts.*
lean, is one continued act: to keep striking, a repetition of acts.

18. There is a difference, again, between a *repetition* of *Difference*
acts, and a *habit* or *practice*. The term repetition of acts may *between a repeti-*
tion of acts and
be employed, let the acts in question be separated by ever such *a habit.*
short intervals, and let the sum total of them occupy ever so
short a space of time. The term habit is not employed but
when the acts in question are supposed to be separated by
long-continued intervals, and the sum total of them to occupy
a considerable space of time. It is not (for instance) the drinking ever so many times, nor ever so much at a time, in the
course of the same sitting, that will constitute a habit of
drunkenness: it is necessary that such sittings themselves be
frequently repeated. Every habit is a repetition of acts; or,
to speak more strictly, when a man has frequently repeated
such and such acts after considerable intervals, he is said to
have persevered in or contracted a habit: but every repetition
of acts is not a habit.[2]

[1] These distinctions will be referred to in the next chapter: Chap. viii.
[Intentionality]: and applied to practice in B. I. tit. [Extenuations].
[2] A habit, it should seem, can hardly in strictness be termed an aggregate
of acts: acts being a sort of real archetypal entities, and habits a kind of fictitious
entities or imaginary beings, supposed to be constituted by, or to result as it
were out of, the former.

N

19. Fourth, acts may be distinguished into *indivisible* and *divisible*. Indivisible acts are merely imaginary: they may be easily conceived, but can never be known to be exemplified. Such as are divisible may be so, with regard either to matter or to motion. An act indivisible with regard to matter, is the motion or rest of one single atom of matter. An act indivisible, with regard to motion, is the motion of any body, from one single atom of space to the next to it.

Fifth, acts may be distinguished into *simple* and *complex*: simple, such as the act of striking, the act of leaning, or the act of drinking, above instanced: complex, consisting each of a multitude of simple acts, which, though numerous and heterogeneous, derive a sort of unity from the relation they bear to some common design or end; such as the act of giving a dinner, the act of maintaining a child, the act of exhibiting a triumph, the act of bearing arms, the act of holding a court, and so forth.

20. It has been every now and then made a question, what it is in such a case that constitutes *one* act: where one act has ended, and another act has begun: whether what has happened has been one act or many.[1] These questions, it is now evident, may frequently be answered, with equal propriety, in opposite ways: and if there be any occasion on which they can be answered only in one way, the answer will depend upon the nature of the occasion, and the purpose for which the question is proposed. A man is wounded in two fingers at one stroke— Is it one wound or several? A man is beaten at 12 o'clock, and again at 8 minutes after 12—Is it one beating or several? You beat one man, and instantly in the same breath you beat another—Is this one beating or several? In any of these cases it may be *one*, perhaps, as to some purposes, and *several* as to others. These examples are given, that men may be aware of the ambiguity of language: and neither harass themselves with unsolvable doubts, nor one another with interminable disputes.

21. So much with regard to acts considered in themselves: we come now to speak of the *circumstances* with which they may have been accompanied. These must necessarily be taken

---

[1] Distinctions like these come frequently in question in the course of Procedure.

into the account before any thing can be determined relative to the consequences. What the consequences of an act may be upon the whole can never otherwise be ascertained: it can never be known whether it is beneficial, or indifferent, or mischievous. In some circumstances even to kill a man may be a beneficial act: in others, to set food before him may be a pernicious one.

22. Now the circumstances of an act, are, what? Any *Circumstances,* objects[1] whatsoever. Take any act whatsoever, there is nothing *what.* in the nature of things that excludes any imaginable object from being a circumstance to it. Any given object may be a circumstance to any other.[2]

23. We have already had occasion to make mention for *Circumstances* a moment of the *consequences* of an act: these were distin- *material and* guished into material and immaterial. In like manner may *immaterial.* the circumstances of it be distinguished. Now *materiality* is a relative term: applied to the consequences of an act, it bore relation to pain and pleasure: applied to the circumstances, it bears relation to the consequences. A circumstance may be said to be material, when it bears a visible relation in point of causality to the consequences: immaterial, when it bears no such visible relation.

24. The consequences of an act are events.[3] A circumstance *A circumstance* may be related to an event in point of causality in any one of *may be related* four ways: 1. In the way of causation or production. 2. In *to an event in* the way of derivation. 3. In the way of collateral connexion. *ity, in four* 4. In the way of conjunct influence. It may be said to be *ways, viz.:* related to the event in the way of causation, when it is of the *1. Production.* number of those that contribute to the production of such *2. Derivation.* event: in the way of derivation, when it is of the number of *3. Collateral* the events to the production of which that in question has *connexion.* *fluence.*

---

[1] Or entities. See B. II. tit. [Evidence], § [Facts].

[2] The etymology of the word circumstance is perfectly characteristic of its *Circumstance* import: *circum stantia,* things standing round: objects standing round a given *archetypation* object. I forget what mathematician it was that defined God to be a circle, *of the word.* of which the centre is every where, but the circumference no where. In like manner the field of circumstances, belonging to any act, may be defined a circle, of which the circumference is no where, but of which the act in question is the centre. Now then, as any act may, for the purpose of discourse, be considered as a centre, any other act or object whatsoever may be considered as of the number of those that are standing round it.

[3] See B. II. tit. [Evidence], § [Facts].

been contributory: in the way of collateral connexion, where the circumstance in question, and the event in question, without being either of them instrumental in the production of the other, are related, each of them, to some common object, which has been concerned in the production of them both: in the way of conjunct influence, when, whether related in any other way or not, they have both of them concurred in the production of some common consequence.

Example.
Assassination of Buckingham.

25. An example may be of use. In the year 1628, Villiers, Duke of Buckingham, favourite and minister of Charles I. of England, received a wound and died. The man who gave it him was one Felton, who, exasperated at the mal-administration of which that minister was accused, went down from London to Portsmouth, where Buckingham happened then to be, made his way into his anti-chamber, and finding him busily engaged in conversation with a number of people round him, got close to him, drew a knife and stabbed him. In the effort, the assassin's hat fell off, which was found soon after, and, upon searching him, the bloody knife. In the crown of the hat were found scraps of papers, with sentences expressive of the purpose he was come upon. Here then, suppose the event in question is the wound received by Buckingham: Felton's drawing out his knife, his making his way into the chamber, his going down to Portsmouth, his conceiving an indignation at the idea of Buckingham's administration, that administration itself, Charles's appointing such a minister, and so on, higher and higher without end, are so many circumstances, related to the event of Buckingham's receiving the wound, in the way of causation or production: the bloodiness of the knife, a circumstance related to the same event in the way of derivation: the finding of the hat upon the ground, the finding the sentences in the hat, and the writing them, so many circumstances related to it in the way of collateral connexion: and the situation and conversations of the people about Buckingham, were circumstances related to the circumstances of Felton's making his way into the room, going down to Portsmouth, and so forth, in the way of conjunct influence; inasmuch as they contributed in common to the event of Buckingham's receiving the wound,

by preventing him from putting himself upon his guard upon the first appearance of the intruder.[1]

26. These several relations do not all of them attach upon an event with equal certainty. In the first place, it is plain, indeed, that every event must have some circumstance or other, and in truth, an indefinite multitude of circumstances, related to it in the way of production: it must of course have a still greater multitude of circumstances related to it in the way of collateral connexion. But it does not appear necessary that every event should have circumstances related to it in the way of derivation: nor therefore that it should have any related to it in the way of conjunct influence. But of the circumstances of all kinds which actually do attach upon an event, it is only a very small number that can be discovered by the utmost exertion of the human faculties: it is a still smaller number that ever actually do attract our notice: when occasion happens, more or fewer of them will be discovered by a man in proportion to the strength, partly of his intellectual powers, partly of his inclination.[2] It appears

It is not every event that has circumstances related to it in all those ways.

---

[1] The division may be farther illustrated and confirmed by the more simple and particular case of animal generation. To production corresponds paternity: to derivation, filiation: to collateral connexion, collateral consanguinity: to conjunct influence, marriage and copulation.

If necessary, it might be again illustrated by the material image of a chain, such as that which, according to the ingenious fiction of the ancients, is attached to the throne of Jupiter. A section of this chain should then be exhibited by way of specimen, in the manner of the *diagram* of a pedigree. Such a figure I should accordingly have exhibited, had it not been for the apprehension that an exhibition of this sort, while it made the subject a small matter clearer to one man out of a hundred, might, like the mathematical formularies we see sometimes employed for the like purpose, make it more obscure and formidable for the other ninety-nine.

[2] The more remote a connexion of this sort is, of course the more obscure. It will often happen that a connexion, the idea of which would at first sight appear extravagant and absurd, shall be rendered highly probable, and indeed indisputable, merely by the suggestion of a few intermediate circumstances. At Rome, 390 years before the Christian æra, a goose sets up a cackling: two thousand years afterwards a king of France is murdered. To consider these two events, and nothing more, what can appear more extravagant than the notion that the former of them should have had any influence on the production of the latter? Fill up the gap, bring to mind a few intermediate circumstances, and nothing can appear more probable. It was the cackling of a parcel of geese, at the time the Gauls had surprised the Capitol, that saved the Roman commonwealth: had it not been for the ascendancy that commonwealth acquired afterwards over most of the nations of Europe, amongst others over France, the Christian religion, humanly speaking, could not have established itself in the manner it did in that country. Grant then, that such a

therefore that the multitude and description of such of the circumstances belonging to an act, as may appear to be material, will be determined by two considerations: 1. By the nature of things themselves. 2. By the strength or weakness of the faculties of those who happen to consider them.

Use of this chapter.

27. Thus much it seemed necessary to premise in general concerning acts, and their circumstances, previously to the consideration of the particular sorts of acts with their particular circumstances, with which we shall have to do in the body of the work. An act of some sort or other is necessarily included in the notion of every offence. Together with this act, under the notion of the same offence, are included certain circumstances: which circumstances enter into the essence of the offence, contribute by their conjunct influence to the production of its consequences, and in conjunction with the act are brought into view by the name by which it stands distinguished. These we shall have occasion to distinguish hereafter by the name of *criminative* circumstances.[1] Other circumstances again entering into combination with the act and the former set of circumstances, are productive of still farther consequences. These additional consequences, if they are of the beneficial kind, bestow, according to the value they bear in that capacity, upon the circumstances to which they owe their birth the appellation of *exculpative*[2] or *extenuative* circumstances[3]: if of the mischievous kind, they bestow on them the appellation of *aggravative* circumstances.[4] Of all these different sets of circumstances, the criminative are connected with the consequences of the original offence, in the way of production; with the act, and with one another, in the way of conjunct influence: the consequences of the original offence with them, and with the act respectively, in the way of derivation: the consequences of the modified offence, with the criminative, exculpative, and extenuative circumstances respectively, in the way also of derivation: these different sets of circumstances, with the consequences of the modified act or offence, in the way of production: and with one another (in

man as Henry IV. would have existed, no man, however, would have had those motives, by which Ravaillac, misled by a mischievous notion concerning the dictates of that religion, was prompted to assassinate him.

[1] See B. I. tit. [Crim. circumstances].   [2] See B. I. tit. [Justifications].
[3] See B. I. tit. [Extenuations].   [4] See B. I. tit. [Aggravations].

respect of the consequences of the modified act or offence) in the way of conjunct influence. Lastly, whatever circumstances can be seen to be connected with the consequences of the offence, whether directly in the way of derivation, or obliquely in the way of collateral affinity (to wit, in virtue of its being connected, in the way of derivation, with some of the circumstances with which they stand connected in the same manner) bear a *material* relation to the offence in the way of evidence, they may accordingly be styled *evidentiary* circumstances, and may become of use, by being held forth upon occasion as so many proofs, indications, or evidences of its having been committed.[1]

[1] See B. I. tit. [Accessory Offences] and B. II. tit. [Evidence].
It is evident that this analysis is equally applicable to incidents of a purely physical nature, as to those in which moral agency is concerned. If therefore it be just and useful here, it might be found not impossible, perhaps, to find some use for it in natural philosophy.

CHAPTER VIII

OF INTENTIONALITY

Recapitulation.

1. So much with regard to the two first of the articles upon which the evil tendency of an action may depend: *viz.,* the act itself, and the general assemblage of the circumstances with which it may have been accompanied. We come now to consider the ways in which the particular circumstance of *intention* may be concerned in it.

The intention may regard, 1. The act: or, 2. The consequences.

2. First, then, the intention or will may regard either of two objects: 1. The act itself: or, 2. Its consequences. Of these objects, that which the intention regards may be styled *intentional*. If it regards the act, then the act may be said to be intentional:[1] if the consequences, so then also may the consequences. If it regards both the act and consequences, the whole *action* may be said to be intentional. Whichever of those articles is not the object of the intention, may of course be said to be *unintentional*.

It may regard the act without any of the consequences.

3. The act may very easily be intentional without the consequences; and often is so. Thus, you may intend to touch a man without intending to hurt him: and yet, as the consequences turn out, you may chance to hurt him.

—or the consequences without regarding the act in all its stages.

4. The consequences of an act may also be intentional, without the act's being intentional throughout; that is, without its being intentional in every stage of it: but this is not so

Ambiguity of the words voluntary *and* involuntary.

[1] On this occasion the words *voluntary* and *involuntary* are commonly employed. These, however, I purposely abstain from, on account of the extreme ambiguity of their signification. By a voluntary act is meant sometimes, any act, in the performance of which the will has had any concern at all; in this sense it is synonymous to *intentional*: sometimes such acts only, in the production of which the will has been determined by motives not of a painful nature; in this sense it is synonymous to unconstrained, or *uncoerced*: sometimes such acts only, in the production of which the will has been determined by motives, which, whether of the pleasurable or painful kind, occurred to a man himself, without being suggested by anybody else; in this sense it is synonymous to *spontaneous*. The sense of the word involuntary does not correspond completely to that of the word voluntary. Involuntary is used in opposition to intentional; and to unconstrained: but not to spontaneous. It might be of use to confine the signification of the words voluntary and involuntary to one single and very narrow case, which will be mentioned in the next note.

200

frequent a case as the former. You intend to hurt a man, suppose, by running against him, and pushing him down: and you run towards him accordingly: but a second man coming in on a sudden between you and the first man, before you can stop yourself, you run against the second man, and by him push down the first.

5. But the consequences of an act cannot be intentional, *—but not with-* without the act's being itself intentional in at least the first *out regarding* stage. If the act be not intentional in the first stage, it is no *the first stage.* act of yours: there is accordingly no intention on your part to produce the consequences: that is to say, the individual consequences. All there can have been on your part is a distant intention to produce other consequences, of the same nature, by some act of yours, at a future time: or else, without any intention, a bare *wish* to see such event take place. The second man, suppose, runs of his own accord against the first, and pushes him down. You had intentions of doing a thing of the same nature: *viz.*, To run against him, and push him down yourself; but you had done nothing in pursuance of those intentions: the individual consequences therefore of the act, which the second man performed in pushing down the first, cannot be said to have been on your part intentional.[1]

[1] To render the analysis here given of the possible states of the mind in *An act uninten-* point of intentionality absolutely complete, it must be pushed to such a farther *tional in its first* degree of minuteness, as to some eyes will be apt to appear trifling. On this *stage, may be so* account it seemed advisable to discard what follows, from the text to a place *with respect to,* where any one who thinks proper may pass by it. An act of the body, when 1. *Quantity of* of the positive kind, is a motion: now in motion there are always three articles *matter moved;* to be considered: 1. The quantity of matter that moves: 2. The direction in 2. *Direction;* which it moves: and, 3. The velocity with which it moves. Correspondent 3. *Velocity.* to these three articles, are so many modes of intentionality, with regard to an act, considered as being only in its first stage. To be completely unintentional, it must be unintentional with respect to every one of these three particulars. This is the case with those acts which alone are properly termed *involuntary*: acts, in the performance of which the will has no sort of share: such as the contraction of the heart and arteries.

Upon this principle, acts that are unintentional in their first stage, may be distinguished into such as are completely unintentional, and such as are incompletely unintentional: and these again may be unintentional, either in point of quantity of matter alone, in point of direction alone, in point of velocity alone, or in any two of these points together.

The example given further on may easily be extended to this part of the analysis, by any one who thinks it worth the whole.

There seem to be occasions in which even these disquisitions, minute as they may appear, may not be without their use in practice. In the case of homicide, for example, and other corporal injuries, all the distinctions here

A consequence, when intentional. may be directly so, or obliquely.

6. Second. A consequence, when it is intentional, may either be *directly* so, or only *obliquely*. It may be said to be directly or lineally intentional, when the prospect of producing it constituted one of the links in the chain of causes by which the person was determined to do the act. It may be said to be obliquely or collaterally intentional, when, although the consequence was in contemplation, and appeared likely to ensue in case of the act's being performed, yet the prospect of producing such consequence did not constitute a link in the aforesaid chain.

When directly, ultimately so, or mediately.

7. Third. An incident, which is directly intentional, may either be *ultimately* so, or only *mediately*. It may be said to be ultimately intentional, when it stands last of all exterior events in the aforesaid chain of motives; insomuch that the prospect of the production of such incident, could there be a certainty of its taking place, would be sufficient to determine the will, without the prospect of its producing any other. It may be said to be mediately intentional, and no more, when there is some other incident, the prospect of producing which forms a subsequent link in the same chain: insomuch that the prospect of producing the former would not have operated as a motive, but for the tendency which it seemed to have towards the production of the latter.

When directly intentional, it may be exclusively so, or inexclusively.

8. Fourth. When an incident is directly intentional, it may either be *exclusively* so, or *inexclusively*. It may be said to be exclusively intentional, when no other but that very individual incident would have answered the purpose, insomuch that no other incident had any share in determining the will to the act in question. It may be said to have been inexclusively[1] intentional, when there was some other incident, the prospect of which was acting upon the will at the same time.

specified may occur, and in the course of trial may, for some purpose or other, require to be brought to mind, and made the subject of discourse. What may contribute to render the mention of them pardonable, is the use that might possibly be made of them in natural philosophy. In the hands of an expert metaphysician, these, together with the foregoing chapter on human actions, and the section on facts in general, in title Evidence of the Book of Procedure, might, perhaps, be made to contribute something towards an exhaustive analysis of the possible varieties of mechanical inventions.

[1] Or concurrently.

9. Fifth. When an incident is inexclusively intentional, it *When inex-* may be either *con*junctively so, *dis*junctively, or *indiscriminately*. *clusively, it may* It may be said to be conjunctively intentional with regard to *disjunctively, or* such other incident, when the intention is to produce both: *indiscriminately* disjunctively, when the intention is to produce either the one *so.* or the other indifferently, but not both: indiscriminately, when the intention is indifferently to produce either the one or the other, or both, as it may happen.

10. Sixth. When two incidents are disjunctively inten- *When disjunc-* tional, they may be so with or without *preference*. They may *tively, it may be* be said to be so with preference, when the intention is, that *with or without preference.* one of them in particular should happen rather than the other: without preference, when the intention is equally fulfilled, whichever of them happens.[1]

11. One example will make all this clear. William II, *Example.* king of England, being out a stag-hunting, received from Sir Walter Tyrrel a wound, of which he died.[2] Let us take this case, and diversify it with a variety of suppositions, correspondent to the distinctions just laid down.

1. First then, Tyrrel did not so much as entertain a thought of the king's death; or, if he did, looked upon it as an event of which there was no danger. In either of these cases the incident of his killing the king was altogether unintentional.

2. He saw a stag running that way, and he saw the king riding that way at the same time: what he aimed at was to kill the stag: he did not wish to kill the king: at the same time he saw, that if he shot, it was as likely he should kill the king as the stag: yet for all that he shot, and killed the king accordingly. In this case the incident of his killing the king was intentional, but obliquely so.

3. He killed the king on account of the hatred he bore him,

---

[1] There is a difference between the case where an incident is altogether *Difference* unintentional, and that in which, it being disjunctively intentional with *between an inci-* reference to another, the preference is in favour of that other. In the first *dent's being* case, it is not the intention of the party that the incident in question should *unintentional,* happen at all: in the latter case, the intention is rather that the other should *and disjunc-* happen: but if that cannot be, then that this in question should happen rather *tively inten-* than that neither should, and that both, at any rate, should not happen. *tional, when*

All these are distinctions to be attended to in the use of the particle *or*: a *the election is in* particle of very ambiguous import, and of great importance in legislation. *favour of the* See Append. tit. [Composition]. *other.*

[2] Hume's Hist.

and for no other reason than the pleasure of destroying him. In this case the accident of the king's death was not only directly but ultimately intentional.

4. He killed the king, intending fully so to do; not for any hatred he bore him, but for the sake of plundering him when dead. In this case the incident of the king's death was directly intentional, but not ultimately: it was mediately intentional.

5. He intended neither more nor less than to kill the king. He had no other aim nor wish. In this case it was exclusively as well as directly intentional: exclusively, to wit, with regard to every other material incident.

6. Sir Walter shot the king in the right leg, as he was plucking a thorn out of it with his left hand. His intention was, by shooting the arrow into his leg through his hand, to cripple him in both those limbs at the same time. In this case the incident of the king's being shot in the leg was intentional: and that conjunctively with another which did not happen; *viz.*, his being shot in the hand.

7. The intention of Tyrrel was to shoot the king either in the hand or in the leg, but not in both; and rather in the hand than in the leg. In this case the intention of shooting in the hand was disjunctively concurrent, with regard to the other incident, and that with preference.

8. His intention was to shoot the king either in the leg or the hand, whichever might happen: but not in both. In this case the intention was inexclusive, but disjunctively so: yet that, however, without preference.

9. His intention was to shoot the king either in the leg or the hand, or in both, as it might happen. In this case the intention was indiscriminately concurrent, with respect to the two incidents.

Intentionality of the act with respect to its different stages, how far material. 12. It is to be observed, that an act may be unintentional in any stage or stages of it, though intentional in the preceding: and, on the other hand, it may be intentional in any stage or stages of it, and yet unintentional in the succeeding.[1] But whether it be intentional or no in any preceding stage, is immaterial, with respect to the consequences, so it be unintentional in the last. The only point, with respect to which it is material, is the proof. The more stages the act is unintentional

[1] See Chap. vii. [Actions], par. 14.

in, the more apparent it will commonly be, that it was unintentional with respect to the last. If a man, intending to strike you on the cheek, strikes you in the eye, and puts it out, it will probably be difficult for him to prove that it was not his intention to strike you in the eye. It will probably be easier, if his intention was really not to strike you, or even not to strike at all.

13. It is frequent to hear men speak of a good intention, of a bad intention; of the goodness and badness of a man's intention: a circumstance on which great stress is generally laid. It *Goodness and badness of intention dismissed.* is indeed of no small importance, when properly understood: but the import of it is to the last degree ambiguous and obscure. Strictly speaking, nothing can be said to be good or bad, but either in itself; which is the case only with pain or pleasure: or on account of its effects; which is the case only with things that are the causes or preventatives of pain and pleasure. But in a figurative and less proper way of speech, a thing may also be, styled good or bad, in consideration of its cause. Now the effects of an intention to do such or such an act, are the same objects which we have been speaking of under the appellation of its *consequences*: and the causes of intention are called *motives*. A man's intention then on any occasion may be styled good or bad with reference either to the consequences of the act, or with reference to his motives. If it be deemed good or bad in any sense, it must be either because it is deemed to be productive of good or of bad consequences, or because it is deemed to originate from a good or from a bad motive. But the goodness or badness of the consequences depend upon the circumstances. Now the circumstances are no objects of the intention. A man intends the act: and by his intention produces the act: but as to the circumstances, he does not intend *them*: he does not, inasmuch as they are circumstances of it, produce them. If by accident there be a few which he has been instrumental in producing, it has been by former intentions, directed to former acts, productive of those circumstances as the consequences: at the time in question he takes them as he finds them. Acts, with their consequences, are objects of the will as well as of the understanding: circumstances, as such, are objects of the understanding only. All he can do with these, as such, is to know or not

to know them: in other words, to be conscious of them, or not conscious. To the title of Consciousness belongs what is to be said of the goodness or badness of a man's intention, as resulting from the consequences of the act: and to the head of Motives, what is to be said of his intention, as resulting from the motive.

CHAPTER IX

OF CONSCIOUSNESS

1. So far with regard to the ways in which the will or in-*Connexion of* tention may be concerned in the production of any incident: *this chapter with the fore-* we come now to consider the part which the understanding or *going.* perceptive faculty may have borne, with relation to such incident.

2. A certain act has been done, and that intentionally: that *Acts advised* act was attended with certain circumstances: upon these cir-*and unadvised; consciousness,* cumstances depended certain of its consequences; and amongst *what.* the rest, all those which were of a nature purely physical. Now then, take any one of these circumstances, it is plain, that a man, at the time of doing the act from whence such consequences ensued, may have been either conscious, with respect to this circumstance, or unconscious. In other words, he may either have been aware of the circumstance, or not aware: it may either have been present to his mind, or not present. In the first case, the act may be said to have been an *advised* act, with respect to that circumstance: in the other case, an *unadvised* one

3. There are two points, with regard to which an act *Unadvisedness* may have ben advised or unadvised: 1. The *existence* of the *may regard either existence,* circumstance itself. 2. The *materiality* of it.[1] *or materiality.*

4. It is manifest, that with reference to the time of the act, *The circum-* such circumstance may have been either *present*, *past*, or *stance may have been present,* future. *past, or future.*

5. An act which is unadvised, is either *heedless*, or not heed-*An unadvised* less. It is termed heedless, when the case is thought to be *act may be heedless, or not* such, that a person of ordinary prudence,[2] if prompted by an *heedless.* ordinary share of benevolence, would have been likely to have bestowed such and so much attention and reflection upon the material circumstances, as would have effectually disposed him to prevent the mischievous incident from taking

[1] See Chap. vii. [Actions], par. 3.   [2] See Chap. vi. [Sensibility], par. 12.

place: not heedless, when the case is not thought to be such as above mentioned.[1]

A mis-advised act, what.— A mis-supposal.

6. Again. Whether a man did or did not suppose the existence or materiality of a given circumstance, it may be that he *did* suppose the existence and materiality of some circumstance, which either did not exist, or which, though existing, was not material. In such case the act may be said to be *mis-advised*, with respect to such imagined circumstance: and it may be said, that there has been an erroneous supposition, or a *mis-supposal* in the case.

The supposed circumstance might have been material in the way either of prevention or of compensation.

7. Now a circumstance, the existence of which is thus erroneously supposed, may be material either, 1. In the way of prevention: or, 2. In that of compensation. It may be said to be material in the way of prevention, when its effect or tendency, had it existed, would have been to prevent the obnoxious consequences: in the way of compensation, when that effect or tendency would have been to produce other consequences, the beneficialness of which would have outweighed the mischievousness of the others.

It may have been supposed present, past, or future.

8. It is manifest that, with reference to the time of the act, such imaginary circumstance may in either case have been supposed either to be *present, past,* or *future.*

Example, continued from the last chapter.

9. To return to the example exhibited in the preceding chapter.

10. Tyrrel intended to shoot in the direction in which he shot; but he did not know that the king was riding so near that way. In this case the act he performed in shooting, the act of shooting, was unadvised, with respect to the *existence* of the circumstance of the king's being so near riding that way.

11. He knew that the king was riding that way: but at the distance at which the king was, he knew not of the probability there was that the arrow would reach him. In this case the act was unadvised, with respect to the *materiality* of the circumstance.

12. Somebody had dipped the arrow in poison, without Tyrrel's knowing of it. In this case the act was unadvised, with respect to the existence of a *past* circumstance.

13. At the very instant that Tyrrel drew the bow, the king, being screened from his view by the foliage of some bushes,

[1] See B. I. tit. [Extenuations].

was riding furiously, in such manner as to meet the arrow in a direct line: which circumstance was also more than Tyrrel knew of. In this case the act was unadvised, with respect to the existence of a *present* circumstance.

14. The king being at a distance from court, could get nobody to dress his wound till the next day; of which circumstance Tyrrel was not aware. In this case the act was unadvised with respect to what was then a *future* circumstance.

15. Tyrrel knew of the king's being riding that way, of his being so near, and so forth; but being deceived by the foliage of the bushes, he thought he saw a bank between the spot from which he shot, and that to which the king was riding. In this case the act was *mis-advised*, proceeding on the *mis-supposal* of a *preventive* circumstance.

16. Tyrrel knew that every thing was as above, nor was he deceived by the supposition of any preventive circumstance. But he believed the king to be an usurper: and supposed he was coming up to attack a person whom Tyrrel believed to be the rightful king, and who was riding by Tyrrel's side. In this case the act was also mis-advised, but proceeded on the mis-supposal of a *compensative* circumstance.

10. Let us observe the connexion there is between inten- *In what case* tionality and consciousness. When the act itself is intentional, *consciousness* and with respect to the existence of all the circumstances *extends the in-* *advised*, as also with respect to the materiality of those cir- *from the act to* cumstances, in relation to a given consequence, and there is *the conse-* no mis-supposal with regard to any preventive circumstance, *quences.* that consequence must also be intentional: in other words, advisedness, with respect to the circumstances, if clear from the mis-supposal of any preventive circumstance, extends the intentionality from the act to the consequences. Those consequences may be either directly intentional, or only obliquely so: but at any rate they cannot but be intentional.

11. To go on with the example. If Tyrrel intended to shoot *Example* in the direction in which the king was riding up, and knew *continued.* that the king was coming to meet the arrow, and knew the probability there was of his being shot in that same part in which he was shot, or in another as dangerous, and with that same degree of force, and so forth, and was not misled by the erroneous supposition of a circumstance by which the shot

o

would have been prevented from taking place, or any such other preventive circumstance, it is plain he could not but have intended the king's death. Perhaps he did not positively wish it; but for all that, in a certain sense he intended it.

A misadvised act may be rash or not rash. 12. What heedlessness is in the case of an unadvised act, rashness is in the case of a misadvised one. A misadvised act then may be either rash or not rash. It may be termed rash, when the case is thought to be such, that a person of ordinary prudence, if prompted by an ordinary share of benevolence, would have employed such and so much attention and reflection to the imagined circumstance, as, by discovering to him the non-existence, improbability, or immateriality of it, would have effectually disposed him to prevent the mischievous incident from taking place.

The intention may be good or bad in itself, independently of the motive as well as the eventual consequences. 13. In ordinary discourse, when a man does an act of which the consequences prove mischievous, it is a common thing to speak of him as having acted with a good intention or with a bad intention, of his intention's being a good one or a bad one. The epithets good and bad are all this while applied, we see, to the intention: but the application of them is most commonly governed by a supposition formed with regard to the nature of the motive. The act, though eventually it prove mischievous, is said to be done with a good intention, when it is supposed to issue from a motive which is looked upon as a good motive: with a bad intention, when it is supposed to be the result of a motive which is looked upon as a bad motive. But the nature of the consequences intended, and the nature of the motive which gave birth to the intention, are objects which, though intimately connected, are perfectly distinguishable. The intention might therefore with perfect propriety be styled a good one, whatever were the motive. It might be styled a good one, when not only the consequences of the act *prove* mischievous, but the motive which gave birth to it *was* what is called a bad one. To warrant the speaking of the intention as being a good one, it is sufficient if the consequences of the act, had they proved what to the agent they seemed likely to be, *would* have been of a beneficial nature. And in the same manner the intention may be bad, when not only the consequences of the act prove beneficial, but the motive which gave birth to it was a good one.

14. Now, when a man has a mind to speak of your *intention* It is better, when the intention is meant to be spoken of as being good or bad, not to say, the motive. as being good or bad, with reference to the consequences, if he speaks of it at all he must use the word intention, for there is no other. But if a man means to speak of the *motive* from which your intention originated, as being a good or a bad one, he is certainly not obliged to use the word intention: it is at least as well to use the word motive. By the supposition he means the motive; and very likely he may *not* mean the intention. For what is true of the one is very often not true of the other. The motive may be good when the intention is bad: the intention may be good when the motive is bad: whether they are both good or both bad, or the one good and the other bad, makes, as we shall see hereafter, a very essential difference with regard to the consequences.[1] It is therefore much better, when motive is meant, never to say intention.

15. An example will make this clear. Out of malice a man *Example.* prosecutes you for a crime of which he believes you to be guilty, but of which in fact you are not guilty. Here the *consequences* of his conduct are mischievous: for they are mischievous to you at any rate, in virtue of the shame and anxiety which you are made to suffer while the prosecution is depending: to which is to be added, in case of your being convicted, the evil of the punishment. To you therefore they are mischievous; nor is there any one to whom they are beneficial. The man's *motive* was also what is called a bad one: for malice will be allowed by every body to be a bad motive. However, the *consequences* of his conduct, had they proved such as he believed them likely to be, would have been good: for in them would have been included the punishment of a criminal, which is a benefit to all who are exposed to suffer by a crime of the like nature. The *intention* therefore, in this case, though not in a common way of speaking the motive, might be styled a *good* one. But of motives more particularly in the next chapter.

16. In the same sense the intention, whether it be positively Intention, in what cases it may be innocent. good or no, so long as it is not bad, may be termed innocent. Accordingly, let the consequences have proved mischievous, and let the motive have been what it will, the intention may be termed innocent in either of two cases: 1. In the case of un-

[1] See Chap. xii. [Consequences].

advisedness with respect to any of the circumstances on which the mischievousness of the consequences depended: 2. In the case of *mis*-advisedness with respect to any circumstance, which, had it been what it appeared to be, would have served either to prevent or to outweigh the mischief.

Intentionality and consciousness, how spoken of in the Roman law.

17. A few words for the purpose of applying what has been said to the Roman law. Unintentionality, and innocence of intention, seem both to be included in the case of *infortunium*, where there is neither *dolus* nor *culpa*. Unadvisedness coupled with heedlessness, and mis-advisedness coupled with rashness, correspond to the *culpa sine dolo*. Direct intentionality corresponds to *dolus*. Oblique intentionality seems hardly to have been distinguished from direct; were it to occur, it would probably be deemed also to correspond to *dolus*. The division into *culpa*, *lata*, *levis*, and *levissima*, is such as nothing certain can correspond to. What is it that it expresses? A distinction, not in the case itself, but only in the sentiments which any person (a judge, for instance) may find himself disposed to entertain with relation to it: supposing it already distinguished into three subordinate cases by other means.

The word *dolus* seems ill enough contrived: the word *culpa* as indifferently. *Dolus*, upon any other occasion, would be understood to imply deceit, concealment,[1] clandestinity[2]; but here it is extended to open force. *Culpa*, upon any other occasion, would be understood to extend to blame of every kind. It would therefore include *dolus*.[3]

---

[1] See B. I. tit. [Theft] *verbo* [amenable].

[2] Dolus, an virtus quis in hoste requirit?—VIRGIL.
—— δόλῳ ἠὲ καὶ ἀμφαδόν.—HOMER.

[3] I pretend not here to give any determinate explanation of a set of words, of which the great misfortune is, that the import of them is confused and indeterminate. I speak only by approximation. To attempt to determine the precise import that has been given them by a hundredth part of the authors that have used them, would be an endless task. Would any one talk intelligibly on this subject in Latin? let him throw out *dolus* altogether: let him keep *culpa*, for the purpose of expressing not the case itself, but the sentiment that is entertained concerning a case described by other means. For intentionality, let him coin a word boldly, and say *intentionalitas*: for unintentionality, *non-intentionalitas*. For unadvisedness, he has already the word *inscitia*; though the words *imprudentia*, *inobservantia*, were it not for the other senses they are used in, would do better: for unadvisedness coupled with heedlessness, let him say *inscitia culpabilis*; for unadvisedness without heedlessness, *inscitia inculpabilis*: for mis-advisedness coupled with rashness, *error culpabilis*, *error temerarius*, or

18. The above-mentioned definitions and distinctions are *Use of this and* far from being mere matters of speculation. They are capable *the preceding* of the most extensive and constant application, as well to *chapter.* moral discourse as to legislative practice. Upon the degree and bias of a man's intention, upon the absence or presence of consciousness or mis-supposal, depend a great part of the good and bad, more especially of the bad consequences of an act; and on this, as well as other grounds, a great part of the demand for punishment.[1] The presence of intention with regard to such or such a consequence, and of consciousness with regard to such or such a circumstance, of the act, will form so many criminative circumstances,[2] or essential ingredients in the composition of this or that offence: applied to other circumstances, consciousness will form a ground of aggravation, annexable to the like offence.[3] In almost all cases, the absence of intention with regard to certain consequences, and the absence of consciousness, or the presence of mis-supposal, with regard to certain circumstances, will constitute so many grounds of extenuation.[4]

error cum temeritate: for mis-advisedness without rashness, *error inculpabilis*, *error non-temerarius*, or *error sine temeritate*.

It is not unfrequent likewise to meet with the phrase, *malo animo*: a phrase still more indeterminate, if possible, than any of the former. It seems to have reference either to intentionality, or to consciousness, or to the motive, or to the disposition, or to any two or more of these taken together; nobody can tell which: these being objects which seem to have never hitherto been properly distinguished and defined.

[1] See Chap. xiii. [Cases unmeet].
[2] See B. I. tit. [Circumstances influencing].
[3] See B. I. tit. [Aggravations].   [4] See B. I. tit. [Extenuations].

CHAPTER X

OF MOTIVES

§ 1. *Different senses of the word motive*[1]

Motives, why considered.

1. IT is an acknowledged truth, that every kind of act whatever, and consequently every kind of offence, is apt to assume a different character, and be attended with different effects, according to the nature of the *motive* which gives birth to it. This makes it requisite to take a view of the several motives by which human conduct is liable to be influenced.

Purely speculative motives have nothing to do here.

2. By a motive, in the most extensive sense in which the word is ever used with reference to a thinking being, is meant any thing that can contribute to give birth to, or even to prevent, any kind of action. Now the action of a thinking being is the act either of the body, or only of the mind: and an act of the mind is an act either of the intellectual faculty, or of the will. Acts of the intellectual faculty will sometimes rest in the understanding merely, without exerting any influence in the production of any acts of the will. Motives, which are not of a nature to influence any other acts than those, may be styled purely *speculative* motives, or motives resting in speculation. But as to these acts, neither do they exercise any influence over external acts, or over their consequences, nor consequently over any pain or any pleasure that may be in the number of such consequences. Now it is only on account of their tendency to produce either pain or pleasure, that any acts can be material. With acts, therefore, that rest purely in the understanding, we have not here any concern: nor therefore with any object, if any such there be, which, in the

---

[1] Note by the author, July, 1822.

For a tabular simultaneous view of the whole list of MOTIVES, in conjunction with the correspondent *pleasures* and *pains*, *interests* and *desires*, see, by the same author, *Table of the Springs of Action*, &c., with Explanatory Notes and Observations. London: 1817, Hunter, St. Paul's Church Yard, 8vo. pp. 32.

The word *inducement* has of late presented itself, as being in its signification more comprehensive than the word *motive*, and on some occasions more apposite.

character of a motive, can have no influence on any other acts
than those.

3. The motives with which alone we have any concern, are *Motives to the*
such as are of a nature to act upon the will. By a motive *will.*
then, in this sense of the word, is to be understood any thing
whatsoever, which, by influencing the will of a sensitive
being, is supposed to serve as a means of determining him
to act, or voluntarily to forbear to act,[1] upon any occasion.
Motives of this sort, in contradistinction to the former, may
be styled *practical* motives, or motives applying to practice.

4. Owing to the poverty and unsettled state of language, *Figurative and*
the word *motive* is employed indiscriminately to denote two *unfigurative senses of the*
kinds of objects, which, for the better understanding of the *word.*
subject, it is necessary should be distinguished. On some
occasions it is employed to denote any of those really existing
incidents from whence the act in question is supposed to take
its rise. The sense it bears on these occasions may be styled its
literal or *unfigurative* sense. On other occasions it is employed
to denote a certain fictitious entity, a passion, an affection of
the mind, an ideal being which upon the happening of any
such incident is considered as operating upon the mind, and
prompting it to take that course, towards which it is impelled
by the influence of such incident. Motives of this class are
Avarice, Indolence, Benevolence, and so forth; as we shall see
more particularly farther on. This latter may be styled the
figurative sense of the term *motive*.

5. As to the real incidents to which the name of motive is *Motives in-*
also given, these too are of two very different kinds. They *terior and exterior.*
may be either, 1. The *internal* perception of any individual
lot of pleasure or pain, the expectation of which is looked
upon as calculated to determine you to act in such or such a
manner; as the pleasure of acquiring such a sum of money,

[1] When the effect or tendency of a motive is to determine a man to forbear
to act, it may seem improper to make use of the term *motive*; since motive,
properly speaking, means that which disposes an object to *move*. We must
however use that improper term, or a term which, though proper enough,
is scarce in use, the word *determinative*. By way of justification, or at least
apology, for the popular usage in this behalf, it may be observed, that even
forbearance to act, or the negation of motion (that is, of bodily motion)
supposes an act done, when such forbearance is voluntary. It supposes, to wit,
an act of the will, which is as much a positive act, as much a motion, as any
other act of the thinking substance.

the pain of exerting yourself on such an occasion, and so forth: or, 2. Any *external* event, the happening whereof is regarded as having a tendency to bring about the perception of such pleasure or such pain; for instance, the coming up of a lottery ticket, by which the possession of the money devolves to you; or the breaking out of a fire in the house you are in, which makes it necessary for you to quit it. The former kind of motives may be termed interior, or internal: the latter exterior, or external.

Motive in prospect—motive in esse.

6. Two other senses of the term *motive* need also to be distinguished. Motive refers necessarily to action. It is a pleasure, pain, or other event, that prompts to action. Motive then, in one sense of the word, must be previous to such event. But, for a man to be governed by any motive, he must in every case look beyond that event which is called his action; he must look to the consequences of it: and it is only in this way that the idea of pleasure, of pain, or of any other event, can give birth to it. He must look, therefore, in every case, to some event posterior to the act in contemplation: an event which as yet exists not, but stands only in prospect. Now, as it is in all cases difficult, and in most cases unnecessary, to distinguish between objects so intimately connected, as the posterior possible object which is thus looked forward to, and the present existing object or event which takes place upon a man's looking forward to the other, they are both of them spoken of under the same appellation, *motive*. To distinguish them, the one first mentioned may be termed a motive in *prospect*, the other a motive in *esse*: and under each of these denominations will come as well exterior as internal motives. A fire breaks out in your neighbour's house: you are under apprehension of its extending to your own: you are apprehensive, that if you stay in it, you will be burnt: you accordingly run out of it. This then is the act: the others are all motives to it. The event of the fire's breaking out in your neighbour's house is an external motive, and that in *esse*: the idea or belief of the probability of the fire's extending to your own house, that of your being burnt if you continue, and the pain you feel at the thought of such a catastrophe, are all so many internal events, but still in *esse*: the event of the fire's actually extending to your own house, and that of your being

actually burnt by it, external motives in prospect: the pain you would feel at seeing your house a burning, and the pain you would feel while you yourself were burning, internal motives in prospect: which events, according as the matter turns out, may come to be in *esse*: but then, of course, they will cease to act as motives.

7. Of all these motives, which stand nearest to the act, to the production of which they all contribute, is that internal motive in *esse* which consists in the expectation of the internal motive in prospect: the pain or uneasiness you feel at the thoughts of being burnt.[1] All other motives are more or less remote: the motives in prospect, in proportion as the period at which they are expected to happen is more distant from the period at which the act takes place, and consequently later in point of time: the motives in *esse*, in proportion as they also are more distant from that period, and consequently earlier in point of time.[2]

Motives immediate and remote.

8. It has already been observed, that with motives of which the influence terminates altogether in the understanding, we have nothing here to do. If then, amongst objects that are spoken of as motives with reference to the understanding, there be any which concern us here, it is only in as far as such objects may, through the medium of the understanding, exercise an influence over the will. It is in this way, and in this way only, that any objects, in virtue of any tendency they may have to influence the sentiment of belief, may in a practical sense act in the character of motives. Any objects, by tending to induce a belief concerning the existence, actual,

Motives to the understanding, how they may influence the will.

[1] Whether it be the expectation of being burnt, or the pain that accompanies that expectation, that is the immediate internal motive spoken of, may be difficult to determine. It may even be questioned, perhaps, whether they are distinct entities. Both questions, however, seem to be mere questions of words, and the solution of them altogether immaterial. Even the other kinds of motives, though for some purposes they demand a separate consideration, are, however, so intimately allied, that it will often be scarce practicable, and not always material, to avoid confounding them, as they have always hitherto been confounded.

[2] Under the term *esse* must be included as well *past* existence, with reference to a given period, as *present*. They are equally real, in comparison with what is as yet but future. Language is materially deficient, in not enabling us to distinguish with precision between *existence* as opposed to *unreality* and *present* existence as opposed to past. The word existence in English, and *esse*, adopted by lawyers from the Latin, have the inconvenience of appearing to confine the existence in question to some single period considered as being present.

or probable, of a practical motive; that is, concerning the probability of a motive in prospect, or the existence of a motive in *esse*; may exercise an influence on the will, and rank with those other motives that have been placed under the name of practical. The pointing out of motives such as these, is what we frequently mean when we talk of giving *reasons*. Your neighbour's house is on fire as before. I observe to you, that at the lower part of your neighbour's house is some wood-work, which joins on to yours; that the flames have caught this wood-work, and so forth; which I do in order to dispose you to believe as I believe, that if you stay in your house much longer you will be burnt. In doing this, then, I suggest motives to your understanding; which motives, by the tendency they have to give birth to or strengthen a pain, which operates upon you in the character of an internal motive in *esse*, join their force, and act as motives upon the will.

§ 2. *No motives either constantly good or constantly bad*

Nothing can act of itself as a motive but the ideas of pleasure or pain. 9. In all this chain of motives, the principal or original link seems to be the last internal motive in prospect: it is to this that all the other motives in prospect owe their materiality: and the immediately acting motive its existence. This motive in prospect, we see, is always some pleasure, or some pain; some pleasure, which the act in question is expected to be a means of continuing or producing: some pain which it is expected to be a means of discontinuing or preventing. A motive is substantially nothing more than pleasure or pain, operating in a certain manner.

No sort of motive is in itself a bad one. 10. Now, pleasure is in *itself* a good: nay, even setting aside immunity from pain, the only good: pain is in itself an evil; and, indeed, without exception, the only evil; or else the words good and evil have no meaning. And this is alike true of every sort of pain, and of every sort of pleasure. It follows, therefore, immediately and incontestibly, that *there is no such thing as any sort of motive that is in itself a bad one.*[1]

[1] Let a man's motive be ill-will; call it even malice, envy, cruelty; it is still a kind of pleasure that is his motive: the pleasure he takes at the thought of the pain which he sees, or expects to see, his adversary undergo. Now even this wretched pleasure, taken by itself, is good: it may be faint; it may be short;

11. It is common, however, to speak of actions as proceed- *Inaccuracy of* ing from *good* or *bad* motives: in which case the motives meant *expressions in which* good *or* are such as are internal. The expression is far from being an *bad are applied* accurate one; and as it is apt to occur in the consideration of *to motives.* almost every kind of offence, it will be requisite to settle the precise meaning of it, and observe how far it quadrates with the truth of things.

12. With respect to goodness and badness, as it is with *Any sort of* everything else that is not itself either pain or pleasure, so is it *motive may give birth to any* with motives. If they are good or bad, it is only on account of *sort of act.* their effects: good, on account of their tendency to produce pleasure, or avert pain: bad, on account of their tendency to produce pain, or avert pleasure. Now the case is, that from one and the same motive, and from every kind of motive, may proceed actions that are good, others that are bad, and others that are indifferent. This we shall proceed to shew with respect to all the different kinds of motives, as determined by the various kinds of pleasures and pains.

13. Such an analysis, useful as it is, will be found to be a *Difficulties* matter of no small difficulty; owing, in great measure, to a *which stand in the way of an* certain perversity of structure which prevails more or less *analysis of this* throughout all languages. To speak of motives, as of any- *sort.* thing else, one must call them by their names. But the misfortune is, that it is rare to meet with a motive of which the name expresses that and nothing more. Commonly along with the very name of the motive, is tacitly involved a proposition imputing to it a certain quality; a quality which, in many cases, will appear to include that very goodness or badness, concerning which we are here inquiring whether, properly speaking, it be or be not imputable to motives. To use the common phrase, in most cases, the name of the motive is a word which is employed either only in a *good sense*, or else only in a *bad sense*. Now, when a word is spoken of as being used in a good sense, all that is necessarily meant is this: that in conjunction with the idea of the object it is put to signify, it conveys an idea of *approbation*: that is, of a pleasure or satisfaction, entertained by the person who employs the term at the thoughts of such object. In like manner,

it must at any rate be impure: yet while it lasts, and before any bad consequences arrive, it is as good as any other that is not more intense. See Chap. iv. [Value].

when a word is spoken of as being used in a bad sense, all that is necessarily meant is this: that, in conjunction with the idea of the object it is put to signify, it conveys an idea of *disapprobation*: that is, of a displeasure entertained by the person who employs the term at the thoughts of such object. Now, the circumstance on which such approbation is grounded will, as naturally as any other, be the opinion of the *goodness* of the object in question, as above explained: such, at least, it must be, upon the principle of utility: so, on the other hand, the circumstance on which any such disapprobation is grounded, will as naturally as any other, be the opinion of the *badness* of the object: such, at least, it must be, in as far as the principle of utility is taken for the standard.

Now there are certain motives which, unless in a few particular cases, have scarcely any other name to be expressed by but such a word as is used only in a good sense. This is the case, for example, with the motives of piety and honour. The consequence of this is, that if, in speaking of such a motive, a man should have occasion to apply the epithet bad to any actions which he mentions as apt to result from it, he must appear to be guilty of a contradiction in terms. But the names of motives which have scarcely any other name to be expressed by, but such a word as is used only in a bad sense, are many more.[1] This is the case, for example, with the motives of lust and avarice. And accordingly, if in speaking of any such motive, a man should have occasion to apply the epithets good or indifferent to any actions which he mentions as apt to result from it, he must here also appear to be guilty of a similar contradiction.[2]

This perverse association of ideas cannot, it is evident, but throw great difficulties in the way of the inquiry now before

---

[1] For the reason, see Chap. xi. [Dispositions], par. xvii. note.

[2] To this imperfection of language, and nothing more, are to be attributed, in great measure, the violent clamours that have from time to time been raised against those ingenious moralists, who, travelling out of the beaten tract of speculation, have found more or less difficulty in disentangling themselves from the shackles of ordinary language: such as Rochefoucault, Mandeville and Helvetius. To the unsoundness of their opinions, and, with still greater injustice, to the corruption of their hearts, was often imputed, what was most commonly owing either to a want of skill, in matters of language on the part of the author, or a want of discernment, possibly now and then in some instances a want of probity, on the part of the commentator.

us. Confining himself to the language most in use, a man can scarce avoid running, in appearance, into perpetual contradictions. His propositions will appear, on the one hand, repugnant to truth; and on the other hand, adverse to utility. As paradoxes, they will excite contempt: as mischievous paradoxes, indignation. For the truths he labours to convey, however important, and however salutary, his reader is never the better: and he himself is much the worse. To obviate this inconvenience, completely, he has but this one unpleasant remedy; to lay aside the old phraseology and invent a new one. Happy the man whose language is ductile enough to permit him this resource. To palliate the inconvenience, where that method of obviating it is impracticable, he has nothing left for it but to enter into a long discussion, to state the whole matter at large, to confess, that for the sake of promoting the purposes, he has violated the established laws of language, and to throw himself upon the mercy of his readers.[1]

§ 3. *Catalogue of motives corresponding to that of Pleasures and Pains*

14. From the pleasures of the senses, considered in the gross, results the motive which, in a neutral sense, may be termed physical desire: in a bad sense, it is termed sensuality. Name used in a good sense it has none. Of this, nothing can be determined, till it be considered separately, with reference to the several species of pleasures to which it corresponds.

Physical desire corresponding to pleasures of sense in general.

---

[1] Happily, language is not always so intractable, but that by making use of two words instead of one, a man may avoid the inconvenience of fabricating words that are absolutely new. Thus instead of the word lust, by putting together two words in common use, he may frame the neutral expression, sexual desire: instead of the word avarice, by putting together two other words also in common use, he may frame the neutral expression, pecuniary interest. This, accordingly, is the course which I have taken. In these instances, indeed, even the combination is not novel: the only novelty there is consists in the steady adherence to the one neutral expression, rejecting altogether the terms, of which the import is infected by adventitious and unsuitable ideas.

In the catalogue of motives, corresponding to the several sorts of pains and pleasures, I have inserted such as have occurred to me. I cannot pretend to warrant it complete. To make sure of rendering it so, the only way would be to turn over the dictionary from beginning to end: an operation which, in a view to perfection, would be necessary for more purposes than this. See B. I. tit. [Defamation]. and Append. tit. [Composition].

The motive corresponding to the pleasures of the palate.

15. In particular, then, to the pleasures of the taste or palate corresponds a motive, which in a neutral sense having received no name that can serve to express it in all cases, can only be termed, by circumlocution, the love of the pleasures of the palate. In particular cases it is styled hunger: in others, thirst.[1] The love of good cheer expresses this motive, but seems to go beyond: intimating, that the pleasure is to be partaken of in company, and involving a kind of sympathy. In a bad sense, it is styled in some cases greediness, voraciousness, gluttony: in others, principally when applied to children, lickerishness. It may in some cases also be represented by the word daintiness. Name used in a good sense it has none. 1. A boy, who does not want for victuals, steals a cake out of a pastry-cook's shop, and eats it. In this case his motive will be universally deemed a bad one: and if it be asked what it is, it may be answered, perhaps, lickerishness. 2. A boy buys a cake out of a pastry-cook's shop, and eats it. In this case his motive can scarcely be looked upon as either good or bad, unless his master should be out of humour with him; and then perhaps he may call it lickerishness, as before. In both cases, however, his motive is the same. It is neither more nor less than the motive corresponding to the pleasures of the palate.[2]

Sexual desires corresponding to the pleasure of the sexual sense.

16. To the pleasures of the sexual sense corresponds the motive which, in a neutral sense, may be termed sexual desire. In a bad sense, it is spoken of under the name of lasciviousness, and a variety of other names of reprobation. Name used in a good sense it has none.[3]

1. A man ravishes a virgin. In this case the motive is, with-

---

[1] Hunger and thirst considered in the light of motives, import not so much the desire of a particular kind of pleasure, as the desire of removing a positive kind of pain. They do not extend to the desire of that kind of pleasure which depends on the choice of foods and liquors.

[2] It will not be worth while, in every case, to give an instance in which the action may be indifferent: if good as well as bad actions may result from the same motive, it is easy to conceive, that also may be indifferent.

[3] Love indeed includes sometimes this idea: but then it can never answer the purpose of exhibiting it separately: since there are three motives, at least, that may all of them be included in it, besides this: the love of beauty corresponding to the pleasures of the eye, and the motives corresponding to those of amity and benevolence. We speak of the love of children, of the love of parents, of the love of God. These pious uses protect the appellation, and preserve it from the ignominy poured forth upon its profane associates. Even sensual love would not answer the purpose; since that would include the love of beauty.

ut scruple, termed by the name of lust, lasciviousness, and so forth; and is universally looked upon as a bad one. 2. The same man, at another time, exercises the rights of marriage with his wife. In this case the motive is accounted, perhaps, a good one, or at least indifferent: and here people would scruple to call it by any of those names. In both cases, however, the motive may be precisely the same. In both cases it may be neither more nor less than sexual desire.

17. To the pleasures of curiosity corresponds the motive known by the same name: and which may be otherwise called the love of novelty, or the love of experiment; and, on particular occasions, sport, and sometimes play. *Curiosity, &c. corresponding to the pleasures of curiosity.*

1. A boy, in order to divert himself, reads an improving book: the motive is accounted, perhaps, a good one: at any rate not a bad one. 2. He sets his top a spinning: the motive is deemed, at any rate, not a bad one. 3. He sets loose a mad ox among a crowd; his motive is now, perhaps, termed an abominable one. Yet in all three cases the motive may be the very same: it may be neither more nor less than curiosity.

18. As to the other pleasures of sense they are of too little consequence to have given any separate denominations to the corresponding motives. *None to pleasures of sense.*

19. To the pleasures of wealth corresponds the sort of motive which, in a neutral sense, may be termed pecuniary interest: in a bad sense, it is termed, in some cases, avarice, covetousness, rapacity, or lucre: in other cases, niggardliness: in a good sense, but only in particular cases, economy and frugality; and in some cases the word industry may be applied to it: in a sense nearly indifferent, but rather bad than otherwise, it is styled, though only in particular cases, parsimony. *Pecuniary interest to the pleasures of wealth.*

1. For money you gratify a man's hatred, by putting his adversary to death. 2. For money you plough his field for him.—In the first case your motive is termed lucre, and is accounted corrupt and abominable: and in the second, for want of a proper appellation, it is styled industry; and is looked upon as innocent at least, if not meritorious. Yet the motive is in both cases precisely the same: it is neither more nor less than pecuniary interest.

None to the pleasures of skill.

20. The pleasures of skill are neither distinct enough, nor of consequence enough, to have given any name to the corresponding motive.

To the pleasures of amity the desire of ingratiating one's self.

21. To the pleasures of amity corresponds a motive which, in a neutral sense, may be termed the desire of ingratiating one's self. In a bad sense it is in certain cases styled servility: in a good sense it has no name that is peculiar to it: in the cases in which it has been looked on with a favourable eye, it has seldom been distinguished from the motive of sympathy or benevolence, with which, in such cases, it is commonly associated.

1. To acquire the affections of a woman before marriage, to preserve them afterwards, you do every thing, that is consistent with other duties, to make her happy: in this case your motive is looked upon as laudable, though there is no name for it. 2. For the same purpose, you poison a woman with whom she is at enmity: in this case your motive is looked upon as abominable, though still there is no name for it. 3. To acquire or preserve the favour of a man who is richer or more powerful than yourself, you make yourself subservient to his pleasures. Let them even be lawful pleasures, if people choose to attribute your behaviour to this motive, you will not get them to find any other name for it than servility. Yet in all three cases the motive is the same: it is neither more nor less than the desire of ingratiating yourself.

To the pleasures of a good name, the love of reputation.

22. To the pleasures of the moral sanction, or, as they may otherwise be called, the pleasures of a good name, corresponds a motive which, in a neutral sense, has scarcely yet obtained any adequate appellative. It may be styled, the love of reputation. It is nearly related to the motive last preceding: being neither more nor less than the desire of ingratiating one's self with, or, as in this case we should rather say, of recommending one's self to, the world at large. In a good sense, it is termed honour, or the sense of honour: or rather, the word honour is introduced somehow or other upon the occasion of its being brought to view: for in strictness the word honour is put rather to signify that imaginary object, which a man is spoken of as possessing upon the occasion of his obtaining a conspicuous share of the pleasures that are in question. In particular cases, it is styled the love of glory. In a bad

sense, it is styled, in some cases, false honour; in others, pride; in others, vanity. In a sense not decidedly bad, but rather bad than otherwise, ambition. In an indifferent sense, in some cases, the love of fame: in others, the sense of shame. And, as the pleasures belonging to the moral sanction run undistinguishably into the pains derived from the same source,[1] it may also be styled, in some cases, the fear of dishonour, the fear of disgrace, the fear of infamy, the fear of ignominy, or the fear of shame.

1. You have received an affront from a man: according to the custom of the country, in order, on the one hand, to save yourself from the shame of being thought to bear it patiently:[2]

[1] See Chap. vi. [Pleasures and Pains], par. 24 note.

[2] A man's bearing an affront patiently, that is, without taking this method of doing what is called wiping it off, is thought to import one or other of two things: either that he does not possess that sensibility to the pleasures and pains of the moral sanction, which, in order to render himself a respectable member of society, a man ought to possess: or, that he does not possess courage enough to stake his life for the chance of gratifying that resentment which a proper sense of the value of those pleasures and those pains it is thought would not fail to inspire. True it is, that there are divers other motives, by any of which the same conduct might equally be produced: the motives corresponding to the religious sanction, and the motives that come under the head of benevolence. Piety towards God, the practice in question being generally looked upon as repugnant to the dictates of the religious sanction: sympathy for your antagonist himself, whose life would be put to hazard at the same time with your own; sympathy for his connexions; the persons who are dependent on him in the way of support, or connected with him in the way of sympathy: sympathy for your own connexions: and even sympathy for the public, in cases where the man is such that the public appears to have a material interest in his life. But in comparison with the love of life, the influence of the religious sanction is known to be in general but weak: especially among people of those classes who are here in question: a sure proof of which is the prevalence of this very custom. Where it is so strong as to preponderate, it is so rare, that, perhaps, it gives a man a place in the calendar: and, at any rate, exalts him to the rank of martyr. Moreover, the instances in which either private benevolence or public spirit predominate over the love of life, will also naturally be but rare: and, owing to the general propensity to detraction, it will also be much rarer for them to be thought to do so. Now, when three or more motives, any one of them capable of producing a given mode of conduct, apply at once, that which appears to be the most powerful, is that which will of course be deemed to have actually done the *most*: and, as the bulk of mankind, on this as on other occasions, are disposed to decide peremptorily upon superficial estimates, it will generally be looked upon as having done the whole.

The consequence is, that when a man of a certain rank forbears to take this chance of revenging an affront, his conduct will, by most people, be imputed to the love of life: which, when it predominates over the love of reputation, is, by a not unsalutary association of ideas, stigmatized with the reproachful name of cowardice.

P

on the other hand, to obtain the reputation of courage; you challenge him to fight with mortal weapons. In this case your motive will by some people be accounted laudable, and styled honour: by others it will be accounted blameable, and these, if they call it honour, will prefix an epithet of improbation to it, and call it false honour. 2. In order to obtain a post of rank and dignity, and thereby to increase the respects paid you by the public, you bribe the electors who are to confer it, or the judge before whom the title to it is in dispute. In this case your motive is commonly accounted corrupt and abominable, and is styled, perhaps, by some such name as dishonest or corrupt ambition, as there is no single name for it. 3. In order to obtain the good-will of the public, you bestow a large sum in works of private charity or public utility. In this case people will be apt not to agree about your motive. Your enemies will put a bad colour upon it, and call it ostentation: your friends, to save you from this reproach, will choose to impute your conduct not to this motive but to some other; such as that of charity (the denomination in this case given to private sympathy) or that of public spirit. 4. A king, for the sake of gaining the admiration annexed to the name of conqueror (we will suppose power and resentment out of the question) engages his kingdom in a bloody war. His motive, by the multitude (whose sympathy for millions is easily overborne by the pleasure which their imagination finds in gaping at any novelty they observe in the conduct of a single person) is deemed an admirable one. Men of feeling and reflection, who disapprove of the dominion exercised by this motive on this occasion, without always perceiving that it is the same motive which in other instances meets with their approbation, deem it an abominable one; and because the multitude, who are the manufacturers of language, have not given them a simple name to call it by, they will call it by some such compound name as the love of false glory or false ambition. Yet in all four cases the motive is the same: it is neither more nor less than the love of reputation.

To the pleasures of power, the love of power. 23. To the pleasures of power corresponds the motive which, in a neutral sense, may be termed the love of power. People, who are out of humour with it sometimes, call it the lust of power. In a good sense, it is scarcely provided with a name. In certain cases this motive, as well as the love of reputation, are confounded under the same name, ambition. This is not to be wondered at, considering the intimate connexion there is between the two motives in many cases: since it commonly happens, that the same object which affords the one sort of pleasure, affords the other sort at the same time: for instance, offices, which are at once posts of honour and places of trust: and since at any rate reputation is the road to power.

1. If, in order to gain a place in administration, you poison the man who occupies it. 2. If, in the same view, you propose a salutary plan for the advancement of the public welfare; your motive is in both cases the same. Yet in the first case it is accounted criminal and abominable: in the second case allowable, and even laudable.

24. To the pleasures as well as to the pains of the religious sanction corresponds a motive which has, strictly speaking, no perfectly neutral name applicable to all cases, unless the word religion be admitted in this character: though the word religion, strictly speaking, seems to mean not so much the motive itself, as a kind of fictitious personage, by whom the motive is supposed to be created, or an assemblage of acts, supposed to be dictated by that personage: nor does it seem to be completely settled into a neutral sense. In the same sense it is also, in some cases, styled religious zeal: in other cases, the fear of God. The love of God, though commonly contrasted with the fear of God, does not come strictly under this head. It coincides properly with a motive of a different denomination; viz., a kind of sympathy or good-will, which has the Deity for its object. In a good sense, it is styled devotion, piety, and pious zeal. In a bad sense, it is styled, in some cases, superstition, or superstitious zeal: in other cases, fanaticism, or fanatic zeal: in a sense not decidedly bad, because not appropriated to this motive, enthusiasm, or enthusiastic zeal.

The motive belonging to the religious sanction.

1. In order to obtain the favour of the Supreme Being, a man assassinates his lawful sovereign. In this case the motive is now almost universally looked upon as abominable, and is termed fanaticism: formerly it was by great numbers

accounted laudable, and was by them called pious zeal.
2. In the same view, a man lashes himself with thongs. In
this case, in yonder house, the motive is accounted laudable,
and is called pious zeal: in the next house it is deemed contemptible, and called superstition. 3. In the same view, a
man eats a piece of bread (or at least what to external appearance is a piece of bread) with certain ceremonies. In this case,
in yonder house, his motive is looked upon as laudable,
and is styled piety and devotion: in the next house it is deemed
abominable, and styled superstition, as before: perhaps even
it is absurdly styled impiety. 4. In the same view, a man holds
a cow by the tail while he is dying. On the Thames the
motive would in this case be deemed contemptible, and called
superstition. On the Ganges it is deemed meritorious, and
called piety. 5. In the same view, a man bestows a large sum
in works of charity, or public utility. In this case the motive
is styled laudable, by those at least to whom the works in
question appear to come under this description: and by these
at least it would be styled piety. Yet in all these cases the
motive is precisely the same: it is neither more nor less than
the motive belonging to the religious sanction.[1]

Good-will, &c.
to the pleasures
of sympathy.

25. To the pleasures of sympathy corresponds the motive
which, in a neutral sense, is termed good-will. The word
sympathy may also be used on this occasion: though the
sense of it seems to be rather more extensive. In a good sense,
it is styled benevolence: and in certain cases, philanthropy;
and, in a figurative way, brotherly love; in others, humanity;
in others, charity; in others, pity and compassion; in others,
mercy; in others, gratitude; in others, tenderness; in others,
patriotism; in others, public spirit. Love is also employed
in this as in so many other senses. In a bad sense, it has no
name applicable to it in all cases: in particular cases it is styled
partiality. The word zeal, with certain epithets prefixed to it,
might also be employed sometimes on this occasion, though

[1] I am aware, or at least I hope, that people in general, when they see the
matter thus stated, will be ready to acknowledge, that the motive in these
cases, whatever be the tendency of the acts which it produces, is not a bad one:
but this will not render it the less true, that hitherto, in popular discourse it
has been common for men to speak of acts, which they could not but acknowledge to have originated from this source, as proceeding from a bad motive.
The same observation will apply to many of the other cases.

the sense of it be more extensive; applying sometimes to ill as well as to good will. It is thus we speak of party zeal, national zeal, and public zeal. The word attachment is also used with the like epithets: we also say family-attachment. The French expression, *esprit de corps*, for which as yet there seems to be scarcely any name in English, might be rendered in some cases, though rather inadequately, by the terms corporation spirit, corporation attachment, or corporation zeal.

1. A man who has set a town on fire is apprehended and committed: out of regard or compassion for him, you help him to break prison. In this case the generality of people will probably scarcely know whether to condemn your motive or to applaud it: those who condemn your conduct, will be disposed rather to impute it to some other motive: if they style it benevolence or compassion, they will be for prefixing an epithet, and calling it false benevolence or false compassion.[1] 2. The man is taken again, and is put upon his trial: to save him you swear falsely in his favour. People, who would not call your motive a bad one before, will perhaps call it so now. 3. A man is at law with you about an estate: he has no right to it: the judge knows this, yet, having an esteem or affection for your adversary, adjudges it to him. In this case the motive is by every body deemed abominable, and is termed injustice and partiality. 4. You detect a states-man in receiving bribes: out of regard to the public interest, you give information of it, and prosecute him. In this case, by all who acknowledge your conduct to have originated from this motive, your motive will be deemed a laudable one, and styled public spirit. But his friends and adherents will not choose to account for your conduct in any such manner: they will rather attribute it to party enmity. 5. You

---

[1] Among the Greeks, perhaps the motive, and the conduct it gave birth to, would, in such a case, have been rather approved than disapproved of. It seems to have been deemed an act of heroism on the part of Hercules, to have delivered his friend Theseus from hell: though divine justice, which held him there, should naturally have been regarded as being at least upon a footing with human justice. But to divine justice, even when acknowledged under that character, the respect paid at that time of day does not seem to have been very profound, or well-settled: at present, the respect paid to it is profound and settled enough, though the name of it is but too often applied to dictates which could have had no other origin than the worst sort of human caprice.

find a man on the point of starving: you relieve him; and save his life. In this case your motive will by every body be accounted laudable, and it will be termed compassion, pity, charity, benevolence. Yet in all these cases the motive is the same: it is neither more nor less than the motive of good-will.

Ill-will, &c. to the pleasures of antipathy.

26. To the pleasures of malevolence, or antipathy, corresponds the motive which, in a neutral sense, is termed antipathy or displeasure: and, in particular cases, dislike, aversion, abhorrence, and indignation: in a neutral sense, or perhaps a sense leaning a little to the bad side, ill-will: and, in particular cases, anger, wrath, and enmity. In a bad sense it is styled, in different cases, wrath, spleen, ill-humour, hatred, malice, rancour, rage, fury, cruelty, tyranny, envy, jealousy, revenge, misanthropy, and by other names, which it is hardly worth while to endeavour to collect.[1] Like good-will, it is used with epithets expressive of the persons who are the objects of the affection. Hence we hear of party enmity, party rage, and so forth. In a good sense there seems to be no single name for it. In compound expressions it may be spoken of in such a sense, by epithets, such as *just* and *laudable*, prefixed to words that are used in a neutral or nearly neutral sense.

1. You rob a man: he prosecutes you, and gets you punished: out of resentment you set upon him, and hang him with your own hands. In this case your motive will universally be deemed detestable, and will be called malice, cruelty, revenge, and so forth. 2. A man has stolen a little money from you: out of resentment you prosecute him, and get him hanged by course of law. In this case people will probably be a little divided in their opinions about your motive: your friends will deem it a laudable one, and call it a just or laudable resentment; your enemies will perhaps be disposed to deem it blameable, and call it cruelty, malice, revenge, and so forth: to obviate which, your friends will try perhaps to change the

---

[1] Here, as elsewhere, it may be observed, that the same words which are mentioned as names of motives, are also many of them names of passions, appetites, and affections; fictitious entities, which are framed only by considering pleasures or pains in some particular point of view. Some of them are also names of moral qualities. This branch of nomenclature is remarkably entangled: to unravel it completely would take up a whole volume; not a syllable of which would belong properly to the present design.

motive, and call it public spirit. 3. A man has murdered your father: out of resentment you prosecute him, and get him put to death in course of law. In this case your motive will be universally deemed a laudable one, and styled, as before, a just or laudable resentment: and your friends, in order to bring forward the more amiable principle from which the malevolent one, which was your immediate motive, took its rise, will be for keeping the latter out of sight, speaking of the former only, under some such name as filial piety. Yet in all these cases the motive is the same: it is neither more nor less than the motive of ill-will.

27. To the several sorts of pains, or at least to all such of *Self-preserva-*
them as are conceived to subsist in an intense degree, and to *tion, to the several kinds of*
death, which, as far as we can perceive, is the termination of all *pains.*
the pleasures, as well as all the pains we are acquainted with, corresponds the motive, which in a neutral sense is styled, in general, self-preservation: the desire of preserving one's self from the pain or evil in question. Now in many instances the desire of pleasure, and the sense of pain, run into one another undistinguishably. Self-preservation, therefore, where the degree of the pain which it corresponds to is but slight will scarcely be distinguishable, by any precise line, from the motives corresponding to the several sorts of pleasures. Thus in the case of the pains of hunger and thirst: physical want will in many cases be scarcely distinguishable from physical desire. In some cases it is styled, still in a neutral sense, self-defence. Between the pleasures and the pains of the moral and religious sanctions, and consequently of the motives that correspond to them, as likewise between the pleasures of amity, and the pains of enmity, this want of boundaries has already been taken notice of.[1] The case is the same between the pleasures of wealth, and the pains of privation corresponding to those pleasures. There are many cases, therefore, in which it will be difficult to distinguish the motive of self-preservation from pecuniary interest, from the desire of ingratiating one's self, from the love of reputation, and from religious hope: in which cases, those more specific and explicit names will naturally be preferred to this general and inexplicit one. There are also a multitude of compound

[1] See Chap. v. [Pleasures and Pains], par. 24, 25.

names, which either are already in use, or might be devised, to distinguish the specific branches of the motive of self-preservation from those several motives of a pleasurable origin: such as the fear of poverty, the fear of losing such or such a man's regard, the fear of shame, and the fear of God. Moreover, to the evil of death corresponds, in a neutral sense, the love of life; in a bad sense, cowardice: which corresponds also to the pains of the senses, at least when considered as subsisting in an acute degree. There seems to be no name for the love of life that has a good sense; unless it be the vague and general name of prudence.

1. To save yourself from being hanged, pilloried, imprisoned, or fined, you poison the only person who can give evidence against you. In this case your motive will universally be styled abominable: but as the term self-preservation has no bad sense, people will not care to make this use of it: they will be apt rather to change the motive, and call it malice. 2. A woman, having been just delivered of an illegitimate child, in order to save herself from shame, destroys the child, or abandons it. In this case, also, people will call the motive a bad one, and, not caring to speak of it under a neutral name, they will be apt to change the motive, and call it by some such name as cruelty. 3. To save the expense of a halfpenny, you suffer a man, whom you could preserve at that expense, to perish with want, before your eyes. In this case your motive will be universally deemed an abominable one; and, to avoid calling it by so indulgent a name as self-preservation, people will be apt to call it avarice and niggardliness, with which indeed in this case it indistinguishably coincides: for the sake of finding a more reproachful appellation, they will be apt likewise to change the motive, and term it cruelty. 4. To put an end to the pain of hunger, you steal a loaf of bread. In this case your motive will scarcely, perhaps, be deemed a very bad one; and, in order to express more indulgence for it, people will be apt to find a stronger name for it than self-preservation, terming it *necessity*. 5. To save yourself from drowning, you beat off an innocent man who has got hold of the same plank. In this case your motive will in general be deemed neither good nor bad, and it will be termed self-preservation, or necessity, or the love of life. 6. To save your

life from a gang of robbers, you kill them in the conflict. In this case the motive may, perhaps, be deemed rather laudable than otherwise, and, besides self-preservation, is styled also self-defence. 7. A soldier is sent out upon a party against a weaker party of the enemy: before he gets up with them, to save his life, he runs away. In this case the motive will universally be deemed a contemptible one, and will be called cowardice. Yet in all these various cases, the motive is still the same. It is neither more nor less than self-preservation.

28. In particular, to the pains of exertion corresponds the motive, which, in a neutral sense, may be termed the love of ease, or by a stronger circumlocution, the desire of avoiding trouble. In a bad sense, it is termed indolence.[1] It seems to have no name that carries with it a good sense. *To the pains of exertion, the love of ease.*

1. To save the trouble of taking care of it, a parent leaves his child to perish. In this case the motive will be deemed an abominable one, and, because indolence will seem too mild a name for it, the motive will, perhaps, be changed, and spoken of under some such term as cruelty. 2. To save yourself from an illegal slavery, you make your escape. In this case the motive will be deemed certainly not a bad one: and, because indolence, or even the love of ease, will be thought too unfavourable a name for it, it will, perhaps, be styled the love of liberty. 3. A mechanic, in order to save his labour, makes an improvement in his machinery. In this case, people will look upon his motive as a good one; and finding no name for it that carries a good sense, they will be disposed to keep the motive out of sight: they will speak rather of his ingenuity, than of the motive which was the means of his manifesting that quality. Yet in all these cases the motive is the same; it is neither more nor less than the love of ease.

29. It appears then that there is no such thing as any sort of motive which is a bad one in itself: nor, consequently, any such thing as a sort of motive, which in itself is exclusively a good one. And as to their effects, it appears too that these are sometimes bad, at other times either indifferent or good: and this appears to be the case with every sort of motive. If *Motives can only be bad with reference to the most frequent complexion of their effects.*

---

[1] It may seem odd at first sight to speak of the love of ease as giving birth to action: but exertion is as natural an effect of the love of ease as inaction is, when a smaller degree of exertion promises to exempt a man from a greater.

any sort of motive then is either good or bad on the score of its effects, this is the case only on individual occasions, and with individual motives; and this is the case with one sort of motive as well as with another. *If any sort of motive then can, in consideration of its effects, be termed with any propriety a bad one,* it can only be with reference to the balance of all the effects it may have had of both kinds within a given period, that is, of its most usual tendency.

How it is that motives, such as lust, avarice, &c. are constantly bad.

30. What then? (it will be said) are not lust, cruelty, avarice, bad motives? Is there so much as any one individual occasion, in which motives like these can be otherwise than bad? No, certainly: and yet the proposition, that there is no one *sort* of motive but what will on many occasions be a good one, is nevertheless true. The fact is, that these are names which, if properly applied, are never applied but in the cases where the motives they signify happen to be bad. The names of these motives, considered apart from their effects, are sexual desire, displeasure, and pecuniary interest. To sexual desire, when the effects of it are looked upon as bad, is given the name of lust. Now lust is always a bad motive. Why? Because if the case be such, that the effects of the motive are not bad, it does not go, or at least ought not to go, by the name of lust. The case is, then, that when I say, 'Lust is a bad motive' it is a proposition that merely concerns the import of the word lust; and which would be false if transferred to the other word used for the same motive, sexual desire. Hence we see the emptiness of all those rhapsodies of common-place morality, which consist in the taking of such names as lust, cruelty, and avarice, and branding them with marks of reprobation: applied to the *thing*, they are false; applied to the *name*, they are true indeed, but nugatory. Would you do a real service to mankind, show them the cases in which sexual desire *merits* the name of lust; displeasure, that of cruelty; and pecuniary interest, that of avarice.

Under the above restrictions, motives may be distinguished into good, bad, and indifferent or neutral.

31. If it were necessary to apply such denominations as good, bad, and indifferent to motives, they might be classed in the following manner, in consideration of the most frequent complexion of their effects. In the class of good motives might be placed the articles of, 1. Good-will. 2. Love of reputation. 3. Desire of amity. And, 4. Religion. In the class

of bad motives, 5. Displeasure. In the class of neutral or in-different motives, 6. Physical desire. 7. Pecuniary interest. 8. Love of power. 9. Self-preservation; as including the fear of the pains of the senses, the love of ease, and the love of life.

32. This method of arrangement, however, cannot but be *Inconveniences* imperfect; and the nomenclature belonging to it is in danger *of this distribu-* of being fallacious. For by what method of investigation can *tion.* a man be assured, that with regard to the motives ranked under the name of good, the good effects they have had, from the beginning of the world, have, in each of the four species comprised under this name, been superior to the bad? still more difficulty would a man find in assuring himself, that with regard to those which are ranked under the name of neutral or indifferent, the effects they have had have exactly balanced each other, the value of the good being neither greater nor less than that of the bad. It is to be considered, that the interests of the person himself can no more be left out of the estimate, than those of the rest of the community. For what would become of the species, if it were not for the motives of hunger and thirst, sexual desire, the fear of pain, and the love of life? Nor in the actual constitution of human nature is the motive of displeasure less necessary, perhaps, than any of the others: although a system, in which the business of life might be carried on without it, might possibly be conceived. It seems, therefore, that they could scarcely, without great danger of mistakes, be distinguished in this manner even with reference to each other.

33. The only way, it should seem, in which a motive can *It is only in* with safety and propriety be styled good or bad, is with *individual* reference to its effects in each individual instance; and prin- *instances that* cipally from the intention it gives birth to: from which arise, *motives can be* as will be shown hereafter, the most material part of its effects. *good or bad.* A motive is good, when the intention it gives birth to is a good one; bad, when the intention is a bad one: and an intention is good or bad, according to the material consequences that are the objects of it. So far is it from the goodness of the inten-tion's being to be known only from the species of the motive. But from one and the same motive, as we have seen, may result intentions of every sort of complexion whatsoever.

This circumstance, therefore, can afford no clue for the arrangement of the several sorts of motives.

Motives distinguished into social, dissocial, and self-regarding.

34. A more commodious method, therefore, it should seem, would be to distribute them according to the influence which they appear to have on the interests of the other members of the community, laying those of the party himself out of the question: to wit, according to the tendency which they appear to have to unite, or disunite, his interests and theirs. On this plan they may be distinguished into *social*, *dissocial*, and *self-regarding*. In the social class may be reckoned, 1. Good-will. 2. Love of reputation. 3. Desire of amity. 4. Religion. In the dissocial may be placed, 5. Displeasure. In the self-regarding class, 6. Physical desire. 7. Pecuniary interest. 8. Love of power. 9. Self-preservation; as including the fear of the pains of the senses, the love of ease, and the love of life.

—social, into purely-social, and semi-social.

35. With respect to the motives that have been termed social, if any farther distinction should be of use, to that of good-will alone may be applied the epithet of *purely-social*; while the love of reputation, the desire of amity, and the motive of religion, may together be comprised under the division of *semi-social*: the social tendency being much more constant and unequivocal in the former than in any of the three latter. Indeed these last, social as they may be termed, are self-regarding at the same time.[1]

§ 4. *Order of pre-eminence among motives*

The dictates of good-will are the surest of coinciding with those of utility.

36. Of all these sorts of motives, good-will is that of which the dictates,[2] taken in a general view, are surest of coinciding with those of the principle of utility. For the dictates of utility are neither more nor less than the dictates of the most extensive[3] and enlightened (that is *well-advised*[4]) benevolence.

Laws and dictates conceived as issuing from motives.

---

[1] 'Religion,' says the pious Addison, somewhere in the Spectator, 'is the highest species of self-love.'

[2] When a man is supposed to be prompted by any motive to engage, or not to engage, in such or such an action, it may be of use, for the convenience of discourse, to speak of such motive as giving birth to an imaginary kind of *law* or *dictate*, injoining him to engage, or not to engage, in it.[a]

[3] See Chap. iv. [Value], and Chap. vi. [Sensibility], par. 21.

[4] See Chap. ix. [Consciousness].

[a] See Chap. i.

The dictates of the other motives may be conformable to those of utility, or repugnant, as it may happen.

37. In this, however, it is taken for granted, that in the case *Yet do not* in question the dictates of benevolence are not contradicted *in all cases.* by those of a more extensive, that is enlarged, benevolence. Now when the dictates of benevolence, as respecting the interests of a certain set of persons, are repugnant to the dictates of the same motive, as respecting the more important[1] interests of another set of persons, the former dictates, it is evident, are repealed, as it were, by the latter: and a man, were he to be governed by the former, could scarcely, with propriety, be said to be governed by the dictates of benevolence. On this account, were the motives on both sides sure to be alike present to a man's mind, the case of such a repugnancy would hardly be worth distinguishing, since the partial benevolence might be considered as swallowed up in the more extensive: if the former prevailed, and governed the action, it must be considered as not owing its birth to benevolence, but to some other motive: if the latter prevailed, the former might be considered as having no effect. But the case is, that a partial benevolence may govern the action, without entering into any direct competition with the more extensive benevolence, which would forbid it; because the interests of the less numerous assemblage of persons may be present to a man's mind, at a time when those of the more numerous are either not present, or, if present, make no impression. It is in this way that the dictates of this motive may be repugnant to utility, yet still be the dictates of benevolence. What makes those of private benevolence conformable upon the whole to the principle of utility, is, that in general they stand unopposed by those of public: if they are repugnant to them, it is only by accident. What makes them the more conformable, is, that in a civilized society, in most of the cases in which they would of themselves be apt to run counter to those of public benevolence, they find themselves opposed by stronger motives of the self-regarding class, which are played off against them by the laws; and that it is only in cases where they stand unopposed by the other more salutary dictates, that they are left free. An act of injustice or cruelty, com-

---

[1] Or valuable. See Chap. iv. [Value].

mitted by a man for the sake of his father or his son, is punished, and with reason, as much as if it were committed for his own.

Next to them come those of the love of reputation.

38. After good-will, the motive of which the dictates seem to have the next best chance for coinciding with those of utility, is that of the love of reputation. There is but one circumstance which prevents the dictates of this motive from coinciding in all cases with those of the former. This is, that men in their likings and dislikings, in the dispositions they manifest to annex to any mode of conduct their approbation or their disapprobation, and in consequence to the person who appears to practise it, their good or their ill will, do not govern themselves exclusively by the principle of utility. Sometimes it is the principle of asceticism they are guided by: sometimes the principle of sympathy and antipathy. There is another circumstance, which diminishes, not their conformity to the principle of utility, but only their efficacy in comparison with the dictates of the motive of benevolence. The dictates of this motive will operate as strongly in secret as in public: whether it appears likely that the conduct which they recommend will be known or not: those of the love of reputation will coincide with those of benevolence only in proportion as a man's conduct seems likely to be known. This circumstance, however, does not make so much difference as at first sight might appear. Acts, in proportion as they are material, are apt to become known:[1] and in point of reputation, the slightest suspicion often serves for proof. Besides, if an act be a disreputable one, it is not any assurance a man can have of the secrecy of the particular act in question, that will of course surmount the objections he may have against engaging in it. Though the act in question should remain secret, it will go towards forming a habit, which may give birth to other acts, that may not meet with the same good fortune. There is no human being, perhaps, who is at years of discretion, on whom considerations of this sort have not some weight: and they have the more weight upon a man, in proportion to the strength of his intellectual powers, and the firmness of his mind.[2] Add to this, the influence which habit itself, when once formed, has in restraining a man from acts

---

[1] See B. II. tit. [Evidence].   [2] See Chap. vi. [Sensibility], par. 12, 13.

towards which, from the view of the disrepute annexed to them, as well as from any other cause, he has contracted an aversion. The influence of habit, in such cases, is a matter of fact, which, though not readily accounted for, is acknowledged and indubitable.[1]

39. After the dictates of the love of reputation come, as it should seem, those of the desire of amity. The former are disposed to coincide with those of utility, inasmuch as they are disposed to coincide with those of benevolence. Now those of the desire of amity are apt also to coincide, in a certain sort, with those of benevolence. But the sort of benevolence with the dictates of which the love of reputation coincides, is the more extensive; that with which those of the desire of amity coincide, the less extensive. Those of the love of amity have still, however, the advantage of those of the self-regarding motives. The former, at one period or other of his life, dispose a man to contribute to the happiness of a considerable number of persons: the latter, from the beginning of life to the end of it, confine themselves to the care of that single individual. The dictates of the desire of amity, it is plain, will approach nearer to a coincidence with those of the love of reputation, and thence with those of utility, in proportion, *cæteris paribus*, to the number of the persons whose amity a man has occasion to desire: and hence it is, for example, that an English member of parliament, with all his own weaknesses, and all the follies of the people whose amity he has to cultivate, is probably, in general, a better character than the secretary of a visier at Constantinople, or of a naïb in Indostan.

Next those of the desire of amity.

40. The dictates of religion are, under the infinite diversity of religions, so extremely variable, that it is difficult to know what general account to give of them, or in what rank to place the motive they belong to. Upon the mention of religion, people's first thoughts turn naturally to the religion they themselves profess. This is a great source of miscalculation, and has a tendency to place this sort of motive in a

Difficulty of placing those of religion.

[1] Strictly speaking, habit, being but a fictitious entity, and not really any thing distinct from the acts or perceptions by which it is said to be formed, cannot be the cause of any thing. The enigma, however, may be satisfactorily solved upon the principle of association, of the nature and force of which a very satisfactory account may be seen in Dr. Priestley's edition of Hartley on Man.

higher rank than it deserves. The dictates of religion would coincide, in all cases, with those of utility, were the Being, who is the object of religion, universally supposed to be as benevolent as he is supposed to be wise and powerful; and were the notions entertained of his benevolence, at the same time, as correct as those which are entertained of his wisdom and his power. Unhappily, however, neither of these is the case. He is universally supposed to be all-powerful: for by the Deity, what else does any man mean than the Being, whatever he be, by whom every thing is done? And as to knowledge, by the same rule that he should know one thing he should know another. These notions seem to be as correct, for all material purposes, as they are universal. But among the votaries of religion (of which number the multifarious fraternity of Christians is but a small part) there seem to be but few (I will not say how few) who are real believers in his benevolence. They call him benevolent in words, but they do not mean that he is so in reality. They do not mean, that he is benevolent as man is conceived to be benevolent: they do not mean that he is benevolent in the only sense in which benevolence has a meaning. For if they did, they would recognise that the dictates of religion could be neither more nor less than the dictates of utility: not a tittle different: not a tittle less or more. But the case is, that on a thousand occasions they turn their backs on the principle of utility. They go astray after the strange principles its antagonists: sometimes it is the principle of asceticism: sometimes the principle of sympathy and antipathy.[1] Accordingly, the idea they bear in their minds, on such occasions, is but too often the idea of malevolence; to which idea, stripping it of its own proper name, they bestow the specious appellation of the social motive.[2] The dictates of religion, in short, are no other

---

[1] Chap. ii. [Principles Adverse], par. 18.

[2] Sometimes, in order the better to conceal the cheat (from their own eyes doubtless as well as from others) they set up a phantom of their own, which they call Justice: whose dictates are to modify (which being explained, means to oppose) the dictates of benevolence. But justice, in the only sense in which it has a meaning, is an imaginary personage, feigned for the convenience of discourse, whose dictates are the dictates of utility, applied to certain particular cases. Justice, then, is nothing more than an imaginary instrument, employed to forward on certain occasions, and by certain means, the purposes of benevo-

than the dictates of that principle which has been already mentioned under the name of the theological principle.[1] These, as has been observed, are just as it may happen, according to the biases of the person in question, copies of the dictates of one or other of the three original principles: sometimes, indeed, of the dictates of utility: but frequently of those of asceticism, or those of sympathy and antipathy. In this respect they are only on a par with the dictates of the love of reputation: in another they are below it. The dictates of religion are in all places intermixed more or less with dictates unconformable to those of utility, deduced from texts, well or ill interpreted, of the writings held for sacred by each sect: unconformable, by imposing practices sometimes inconvenient to a man's self, sometimes pernicious to the rest of the community. The sufferings of uncalled martyrs, the calamities of holy wars and religious persecutions, the mischiefs of intolerant laws, (objects which can here only be glanced at, not detailed) are so many additional mischiefs over and above the number of those which were ever brought into the world by the love of reputation. On the other hand, it is manifest, that with respect to the power of operating in secret, the dictates of religion have the same advantage over those of the love of reputation, and the desire of amity, as is possessed by the dictates of benevolence.

41. Happily, the dictates of religion seem to approach nearer and nearer to a coincidence with those of utility every day. But why? Because the dictates of the moral sanction do so: and those coincide with or are influenced by these. Men of the worst religions, influenced by the voice and practice of the surrounding world, borrow continually a new and a new leaf out of the book of utility: and with these, in order not to break with their religion, they endeavour, sometimes with violence enough, to patch together and adorn the repositories of their faith. *Tendency they have to improve.*

42. As to the self-regarding and dissocial motives, the order that takes place among these, and the preceding one, in point of extra-regarding influence, is too evident to need insisting *Afterwards come the self-regarding motives: and,* lence. The dictates of justice are nothing more than a part of the dictates of *lastly, that of* benevolence, which, on certain occasions, are applied to certain subjects; to wit, *displeasure.* to certain actions.

[1] See Chap. ii. [Principles Adverse, &c.]

Q

on. As to the order that takes place among the motives of the self-regarding class, considered in comparison with one another, there seems to be no difference which on this occasion would be worth mentioning. With respect to the dissocial motive, it makes a difference (with regard to its extra-regarding effects) from which of two sources it originates; whether from self-regarding or from social considerations. The displeasure you conceive against a man may be founded either on some act which offends you in the first instance, or on an act which offends you no otherwise than because you look upon it as being prejudicial to some other party on whose behalf you interest yourself: which other party may be of course either a determinate individual, or any assemblage of individuals, determinate or indeterminate.[1] It is obvious enough, that a motive, though in itself dissocial, may, by issuing from a social origin, possess a social tendency; and that its tendency, in this case, is likely to be the more social, the more enlarged the description is of the persons whose interests you espouse. Displeasure, venting itself against a man, on account of a mischief supposed to be done by him to the public, may be more social in its effects than any goodwill, the exertions of which are confined to an individual.[2]

§ 5. Conflict among motives

Motives impelling and restraining, what.

43. When a man has it in contemplation to engage in any action, he is frequently acted upon at the same time by the force of divers motives: one motive, or set of motives, acting in one direction; another motive, or set of motives, acting as it were in an opposite direction. The motives on one side disposing him to engage in the action: those on the other, disposing him not to engage in it. Now, any motive, the influence of which tends to dispose him to engage in the action in question, may be termed an *impelling* motive: any motive, the influence of which tends to dispose him not to engage in it, a *restraining* motive. But these appellations may of course be interchanged, according as the act is of the positive kind, or the negative.[3]

---

[1] See Chap. vi. [Sensibility], par. 21.   [2] See *supra*, par. 37.
[3] See Chap. vii. [Actions], par. 8.

44. It has been shown, that there is no sort of motive but *What are the* may give birth to any sort of action. It follows, therefore, *motives most* that there are no two motives but may come to be opposed *frequently at variance.* to one another. Where the tendency of the act is bad, the most common case is for it to have been dictated by a motive either of the self-regarding, or of the dissocial class. In such case the motive of benevolence has commonly been acting, though ineffectually, in the character of a restraining motive. *Example to*

45. An example may be of use, to show the variety of con- *illustrate a* tending motives, by which a man may be acted upon at the *struggle* same time. Crillon, a Catholic (at a time when it was generally *among contend-ing motives.* thought meritorious among Catholics to extirpate Protestants), was ordered by his king, Charles IX of France, to fall privately upon Coligny, a Protestant, and assassinate him: his answer was, 'Excuse me, Sire; but I'll fight him with all my heart.'[1] Here, then, were all the three forces above mentioned, including that of the political sanction, acting upon him at once. By the political sanction, or at least so much of the force of it as such a mandate, from such a sovereign, issued on such an occasion, might be supposed to carry with it, he was enjoined to put Coligny to death in the way of assassination: by the religious sanction, that is, by the dictates of religious zeal, he was enjoined to put him to death in any way: by the moral sanction, or in other words, by the dictates of honour, that is, of the love of reputation, he was permitted (which permission, when coupled with the mandates of his sovereign, operated, he conceived, as an injunction) to fight the adversary upon equal terms: by the dictates of enlarged benevolence (supposing the mandate to be unjustifiable) he was enjoined not to attempt his life in any way, but to remain at peace with him: supposing the mandate to be unjustifiable, by the dictates of private benevolence he was enjoined not to meddle with him at any rate. Among this confusion of repugnant dictates, Crillon, it seems, gave the preference, in the first place, to those of honour: in the next place, to those of benevolence. He would have fought, had his offer been accepted; as it was not, he remained at peace.

Here a multitude of questions might arise. Supposing the

[1] The idea of the case here supposed is taken from an anecdote in real history, but varies from it in several particulars.

dictates of the political sanction to follow the mandate of the sovereign, of what kind were the motives which they afforded him for compliance? The answer is, of the self-regarding kind at any rate: inasmuch as, by the supposition, it was in the power of the sovereign to punish him for non-compliance or reward him for compliance. Did they afford him the motive of religion? (I mean independently of the circumstance of heresy above mentioned) the answer is, Yes, if his notion was, that it was God's pleasure he should comply with them; No, if it was not. Did they afford him the motive of the love of reputation? Yes, if it was his notion that the world would expect and require that he should comply with them: No, if it was not. Did they afford him that of benevolence? Yes, if it was his notion that the community would upon the whole be the better for his complying with them: No, if it was not. But did the dictates of the political sanction, in the case in question, actually follow the mandates of the sovereign: in other words, was such a mandate legal? This we see is a mere question of local jurisprudence, altogether foreign to the present purpose.

Practical use of the above disquisitions relative to motives.

46. What is here said about the goodness and badness of motives, is far from being a mere matter of words. There will be occasion to make use of it hereafter for various important purposes. I shall have need of it for the sake of dissipating various prejudices, which are of disservice to the community, sometimes by cherishing the flame of civil dissensions,[1] at other times, by obstructing the course of justice. It will be shown, that in the case of many offences,[2] the consideration of the motive is a most material one: for that in the first place it makes a very material difference in the magnitude of the mischief:[3] in the next place, that it is easy to be ascertained; and thence may be made a ground for a difference in the demand for punishment: but that in other cases it is altogether incapable of being ascertained; and that, were it capable of being ever so well ascertained, good or bad, it could make no difference in the demand for punishment: that in all cases, the motive that may happen to govern a prosecutor, is a con-

---

[1] See B. I. tit. [Rebellion].
[2] See B. I. tit. [Simp. corp. injuries]. Ib. tit. [Homicide].
[3] See Chap. xi. [Dispositions].

sideration totally immaterial: whence may be seen the mischievousness of the prejudice that is so apt to be entertained against informers; and the consequence it is of that the judge, in particular, should be proof against the influence of such delusions.

Lastly, The subject of motives is one with which it is necessary to be acquainted, in order to pass a judgment on any means that may be proposed for combating offences in their source.[1]

But before the theoretical foundation for these practical observations can be completely laid, it is necessary we should say something on the subject of *disposition*: which, accordingly, will furnish matter for the ensuing chapter.

[1] See Append. tit. [Preventive Institutions].

CHAPTER XI

OF HUMAN DISPOSITIONS IN GENERAL

Disposition what.

1. IN the foregoing chapter it has been shown at large, that goodness or badness cannot, with any propriety, be predicated of motives. Is there nothing then about a man that can properly be termed good or bad, when, on such or such an occasion, he suffers himself to be governed by such or such a motive? Yes, certainly: his *disposition*. Now disposition is a kind of fictitious entity, feigned for the convenience of discourse, in order to express what there is supposed to be *permanent* in a man's frame of mind, where, on such or such an occasion, he has been influenced by such or such a motive, to engage in an act, which, as it appeared to him, was of such or such a tendency.

—how far it belongs to the present subject.

2. It is with disposition as with every thing else: it will be good or bad according to its effects: according to the effects it has in augmenting or diminishing the happiness of the community. A man's disposition may accordingly be considered in two points of view: according to the influence it has, either, 1. on his own happiness: or, 2. on the happiness of others. Viewed in both these lights together, or in either of them indiscriminately, it may be termed, on the one hand, good; on the other, bad; or, in flagrant cases, depraved.[1] Viewed in the former of these lights, it has scarcely any peculiar name, which has as yet been appropriated to it. It might be termed, though but inexpressively, frail or infirm, on the one hand: sound or firm, on the other. Viewed in the other light, it

---

[1] It might also be termed virtuous, or vicious. The only objection to the use of those terms on the present occasion is, the great quantity of good and bad repute that respectively stand annexed to them. The inconvenience of this is, their being apt to annex an ill-proportioned measure of disrepute to dispositions which are ill-constituted only with respect to the party himself: involving them in such a degree of ignominy as should be appropriated to such dispositions only as are mischievous with regard to others. To exalt weaknesses to a level with crimes, is a way to diminish the abhorrence which ought to be reserved for crimes. To exalt small evils to a level with great ones, is the way to diminish the share of attention which ought to be paid to great ones.

might be termed beneficent, or meritorious, on the one hand: pernicious or mischievous, on the other. Now of that branch of a man's disposition, the effects of which regard in the first instance only himself, there needs not much to be said here. To reform it when bad, is the business rather of the moralist than the legislator: nor is it susceptible of those various modifications which make so material a difference in the effects of the other. Again, with respect to that part of it, the effects whereof regard others in the first instance, it is only in as far as it is of a mischievous nature that the penal branch of law has any immediate concern with it: in as far as it may be of a beneficent nature, it belongs to a hitherto but little cultivated, and as yet unnamed branch of law, which might be styled the remuneratory.

3. A man then is said to be of a mischievous disposition, *A mischievous* when, by the influence of no matter what motives, he is *pre-* *disposition; a* *sumed* to be more apt to engage, or form intentions of engag- *meritorious* ing, in acts which are *apparently* of a pernicious tendency, *what.* than in such as are apparently of a beneficial tendency: of a *disposition;* meritorious or beneficent disposition in the opposite case.

4. I say presumed: for, by the supposition, all that appears *What a man's* is one single action, attended with one single train of circum- *disposition is,* stances: but from that degree of consistency and uniformity *matter of pre-* which experience has shown to be observable in the different *sumption.* actions of the same person, the probable existence (past or future) of a number of acts of a similar nature, is naturally and justly inferred from the observation of one single one. Under such circumstances, such as the motive proves to be in one instance, such is the disposition to be presumed to be in others.

5. I say *apparently* mischievous: that is, apparently with *It depends upon* regard to him: such as to him appear to possess that tendency: *what the act* for from the mere event, independent of what to him it *appears to be to* appears beforehand likely to be, nothing can be inferred on *him.* either side. If to him it appears likely to be mischievous, in such case, though in the upshot it should prove innocent, or even beneficial, it makes no difference; there is not the less reason for presuming his disposition to be a bad one: if to him it appears likely to be beneficial or innocent, in such case, though in the upshot it should prove pernicious, there is not

the more reason on that account for presuming his disposition to be a good one. And here we see the importance of the circumstances of intentionality,[1] consciousness,[2] unconsciousness,[2] and mis-supposal.[2]

Which position is grounded on two facts: 1. The correspondence between intentions and consequences:

6. The truth of these positions depends upon two others, both of them sufficiently verified by experience: The one is, that in the ordinary course of things the consequences of actions commonly turn out conformable to intentions. A man who sets up a butcher's shop, and deals in beef, when he intends to knock down an ox, commonly does knock down an ox; though by some unlucky accident he may chance to miss his blow and knock down a man: he who sets up a grocer's shop, and deals in sugar, when he intends to sell sugar, commonly does sell sugar: though by some unlucky accident he may chance to sell arsenic in the room of it.

2. Between the intentions of the same person at different times. The disposition is to be inferred: 1. From the apparent tendency of the act: 2. From the nature of the motive.

7. The other is, that a man who entertains intentions of doing mischief at one time is apt to entertain the like intentions at another.[3]

8. There are two circumstances upon which the nature of the disposition, as indicated by any act, is liable to depend: 1. The apparent tendency of the act: 2. The nature of the motive which gave birth to it. This dependency is subject to different rules, according to the nature of the motive. In stating them, I suppose all along the apparent tendency of the act to be, as it commonly is, the same as the real.

Case 1. Tendency, good—motive, self-regarding.

9. 1. Where the tendency of the act is *good*, and the motive is of the *self-regarding* kind. In this case the motive affords no inference on either side. It affords no indication of a good disposition: but neither does it afford any indication of a bad one.

A baker sells his bread to a hungry man who asks for it. This, we see, is one of those acts of which, in ordinary cases,

---

A disposition, from which proceeds a habit of doing mischief, cannot be a good one.

[1] See Chap. viii.   [2] See Chap. ix.

[3] To suppose a man to be of a good disposition, and at the same time likely, in virtue of that very disposition, to engage in an habitual train of mischievous actions, is a contradiction in terms: nor could such a proposition ever be advanced, but from the giving, to the thing which the word disposition is put for, a reality which does *not* belong to it. If then, for example, a man of religious disposition should, in virtue of that very disposition, be in the habit of doing mischief, for instance, by persecuting his neighbours, the case must be, either that his disposition, though good in certain respects, is not good upon the whole: or that a religious disposition is not in general a good one.

the tendency is unquestionably good. The baker's motive is the ordinary commercial motive of pecuniary interest. It is plain, that there is nothing in the transaction, thus stated, that can afford the least ground for presuming that the baker is a better or a worse man than any of his neighbours.

10. 2. Where the tendency of the act is *bad*, and the motive, as before, is of the *self-regarding* kind. In this case the disposition indicated is a michievous one.   *Case 2.*
Tendency, bad *—motive, self-regarding.*

A man steals bread out of a baker's shop: this is one of those acts of which the tendency will readily be acknowledged to be bad. Why, and in what respects it is so, will be stated farther on.[1] His motive, we will say, is that of pecuniary interest; the desire of getting the value of the bread for nothing. His disposition, accordingly, appears to be a bad one: for every one will allow a thievish disposition to be a bad one.

11. 3. Where the tendency of the act is *good*, and the motive is the purely social one of *good-will*. In this case the disposition indicated is a beneficent one.   *Case 3.*
Tendency, good*—motive, goodwill.*

A baker gives a poor man a loaf of bread. His motive is compassion; a name given to the motive of benevolence, in particular cases of its operation. The disposition indicated by the baker, in this case, is such as every man will be ready enough to acknowledge to be a good one.

12. 4. Where the tendency of the act is *bad*, and the motive is the purely social one of good-will. Even in this case the disposition which the motive indicates is dubious: it may be a mischievous or a meritorious one, as it happens; according as the mischievousness of the act is more or less apparent.   *Case 4.*
Tendency, bad *—motive good-will.*

13. It may be thought, that a case of this sort cannot exist; and that to suppose it, is a contradiction in terms. For the act is one, which, by the supposition, the agent knows to be a mischievous one. How then can it be, that good-will, that is, the desire of doing good, could have been the motive that led him into it? To reconcile this, we must advert to the distinction between enlarged benevolence and confined.[2] The motive that led him into it, was that of confined benevolence. Had he followed the dictates of enlarged benevolence, he   *This case not an impossible one.*

[1] See Chap. xii. [Consequences], and Code, B. I. tit. [Theft].
[2] See Chap. x. [Motives].

would not have done what he did. Now, although he followed the dictates of that branch of benevolence, which in any single instance of its exertion is mischievous, when opposed to the other, yet, as the cases which call for the exertion of the former are, beyond comparison, more numerous than those which call for the exertion of the latter, the disposition indicated by him, in following the impulse of the former, will often be such as in a man, of the common run of men, may be allowed to be a good one upon the whole.

Example I.
14. A man with a numerous family of children, on the point of starving, goes into a baker's shop, steals a loaf, divides it all among the children, reserving none of it for himself. It will be hard to infer that that man's disposition is a mischievous one upon the whole. Alter the case, give him but one child, and that hungry perhaps, but in no imminent danger of starving: and now let the man set fire to a house full of people, for the sake of stealing money out of it to buy the bread with. The disposition here indicated will hardly be looked upon as a good one.

Example II.
15. Another case will appear more difficult to decide than either. Ravaillac assassinated one of the best and wisest of sovereigns, at a time when a good and wise sovereign, a blessing at all times so valuable to a state, was particularly precious: and that to the inhabitants of a populous and extensive empire. He is taken, and doomed to the most excruciating tortures. His son, well persuaded of his being a sincere penitent, and that mankind, in case of his being at large, would have nothing more to fear from him, effectuates his escape. Is this then a sign of a good disposition in the son, or of a bad one? Perhaps some will answer, of a bad one; for, besides the interest which the nation has in the sufferings of such a criminal, on the score of the example, the future good behaviour of such a criminal is more than any one can have sufficient ground to be persuaded of.

Example III.
16. Well then, let Ravaillac, the son, not facilitate his father's escape; but content himself with conveying poison to him, that at the price of an easier death he may escape his torments. The decision will now, perhaps, be more difficult. The *act* is a wrong one, let it be allowed, and such as ought by all means to be punished: but is the *disposition* manifested by it

a bad one? Because the young man breaks the laws in this one instance, is it probable, that if let alone, he would break the laws in ordinary instances, for the satisfaction of any inordinate desires of his own? The answer of most men would probably be in the negative.

17. 5. Where the tendency of the act is *good*, and the motive is a semi-social one, the *love of reputation*. In this case the disposition indicated is a good one.

Case 5.
Tendency, good—motive, love of reputation.

In a time of scarcity, a baker, for the sake of gaining the esteem of the neighbourhood, distributes bread *gratis* among the industrious poor. Let this be taken for granted: and let it be allowed to be a matter of uncertainty, whether he had any real feeling for the sufferings of those whom he has relieved, or no. His disposition, for all that, cannot, with any pretence of reason, be termed otherwise than a good and beneficent one. It can only be in consequence of some very idle prejudice, if it receives a different name.[1]

18. 6. Where the tendency of the act is *bad*, and the motive, as before, is a semi-social one, the love of reputation. In this case, the disposition which it indicates is more or less good or bad: in the first place, according as the tendency of the act is more or less mischievous: in the next place according

Case 6.
Tendency, bad—motive, honour.

[1] The bulk of mankind, ever ready to depreciate the character of their neighbours, in order, indirectly, to exalt their own, will take occasion to refer a motive to the class of bad ones as often as they can find one still better, to which the act might have owed its birth. Conscious that his own motives are not of the best class, or persuaded that if they be, they will not be referred to that class by others; afraid of being taken for a dupe, and anxious to show the reach of his penetration; each man takes care, in the first place, to impute the conduct of every other man to the least laudable of the motives that can account for it: in the next place, when he has gone as far that way as he can, and cannot drive down the individual motive to any lower class, he changes his battery, and attacks the very class itself. To the love of reputation he will accordingly give a bad name upon every occasion, calling it ostentation, vanity, or vain-glory.

The bulk of mankind apt to depreciate this motive.

Partly to the same spirit of detraction, the natural consequence of the sensibility of men to the force of the moral sanction, partly to the influence of the principle of asceticism, may, perhaps, be imputed the great abundance of bad names of motives, in comparison of such as are good or neutral: and, in particular, the total want of neutral names for the motives of sexual desire, physical desire in general, and pecuniary interest. The superior abundance, even of good names, in comparison of neutral ones, would, if examined, be found rather to confirm than disprove the above remark. The language of a people on these points may, perhaps, serve in some measure as a key to their moral sentiments. But such speculative disquisitions are foreign to the purpose of the present work.

as the dictates of the moral sanction, in the society in question, approach more or less to a coincidence with those of utility. It does not seem probable, that in any nation, which is in a state of tolerable civilization, in short, in any nation in which such rules as these can come to be consulted, the dictates of the moral sanction will so far recede from a coincidence with those of utility (that is, of enlightened benevolence) that the disposition indicated in this case can be otherwise than a good one upon the whole.

Example I.   19. An Indian receives an injury, real or imaginary, from an Indian of another tribe. He revenges it upon the person of his antagonist with the most excruciating torments: the case being, that cruelties inflicted on such an occasion, gain him reputation in his own tribe. The disposition manifested in such a case can never be deemed a good one, among a people ever so few degrees advanced, in point of civilization, above the Indians.

Example II.   20. A nobleman (to come back to Europe) contracts a debt with a poor tradesman. The same nobleman, presently afterwards, contracts a debt, to the same amount, to another nobleman, at play. He is unable to pay both: but he pays the whole debt to the companion of his amusements, and no part of it to the tradesman. The disposition manifested in this case can scarcely be termed otherwise than a bad one. It is certainly, however, not so bad as if he had paid neither. The principle of love of reputation, or (as it is called in the case of this partial application of it) honour, is here opposed to the worthier principle of benevolence, and gets the better of it. But it gets the better also of the self-regarding principle of pecuniary interest. The disposition, therefore, which it indicates, although not so good a one as that in which the principle of benevolence predominates, is better than one in which the principle of self-interest predominates. He would be the better for having more benevolence: but would he be the better for having no honour? This seems to admit of great dispute.[1]

Case 7.
Tendency,
good—motive,
piety.
   21. 7. Where the tendency of the act is *good*, and the motive is the semi-social one of *religion*. In this case, the disposition indicated by it (considered with respect to the influence of it

---

[1] See the case of Duels discussed in B. I. tit. [Homicide].

on the man's conduct towards others) is manifestly a beneficent and meritorious one.

A baker distributes bread *gratis* among the industrious poor.
It is not that he feels for their distresses: nor is it for the sake
of gaining reputation among his neighbours. It is for the sake
of gaining the favour of the Deity: to whom, he takes for
granted, such conduct will be acceptable. The disposition
manifested by such conduct is plainly what every man would
call a good one.

22. 8. Where the tendency of the act is *bad*, and the motive
is that of religion, as before. In this case the disposition is
dubious. It is good or bad, and more or less good or bad, in
the first place, as the tendency of the act is more or less mischievous; in the next place, according as the religious tenets of
the person in question approach more or less to a coincidence
with the dictates of utility.

*Case 8.
Tendency, bad—
motive, religion.*

23. It should seem from history, that even in nations in a
tolerable state of civilization in other respects, the dictates of
religion have been found so far to recede from a coincidence
with those of utility; in other words, from those of enlightened
benevolence; that the disposition indicated in this case may
even be a bad one upon the whole. This however is no objection to the inference which it affords of a good disposition
in those countries (such as perhaps are most of the countries of
Europe at present) in which its dictates respecting the conduct
of a man towards other men approach very nearly to a
coincidence with those of utility. The dictates of religion,
in their application to the conduct of a man in what concerns
himself alone, seem in most European nations to savour a
good deal of the ascetic principle: but the obedience to such
mistaken dictates indicates not any such disposition as is
likely to break out into acts of pernicious tendency with respect to others. Instances in which the dictates of religion lead
a man into acts which are pernicious in this latter view, seem
at present to be but rare: unless it be acts of persecution, or
impolitic measures on the part of government, where the
law itself is either the principal actor or an accomplice in the
mischief. Ravaillac, instigated by no other motive than this,
gave his country one of the most fatal stabs that a country
ever received from a single hand: but happily the Ravaillacs

*The disposition
may be bad in
this case.*

254 PRINCIPLES OF MORALS AND LEGISLATION

are but rare. They have been more frequent, however, in France than in any other country during the same period: and it is remarkable, that in every instance it is this motive that has produced them. When they do appear, however, nobody, I suppose, but such as themselves, will be for terming a disposition, such as they manifest, a good one. It seems hardly to be denied, but that they are just so much the worse for their notions of religion; and that had they been left to the sole guidance of benevolence, and the love of reputation, without any religion at all, it would have been but so much the better for mankind. One may say nearly the same thing, perhaps, of those persons who, without any particular obligation, have taken an active part in the execution of laws made for the punishment of those who have the misfortune to differ with the magistrate in matters of religion, much more of the legislator himself, who has put it in their power. If Louis XIV had had no religion, France would not have lost 800,000 of its most valuable subjects. The same thing may be said of the authors of the wars called holy ones; whether waged against persons called Infidels, or persons branded with the still more odious name of Heretics. In Denmark, not a great many years ago, a sect is said to have arisen, who, by a strange perversion of reason, took it into their heads, that, by leading to repentance, murder, or any other horrid crime, might be made the road to heaven. It should all along, however, be observed, that instances of this latter kind were always rare: and that in almost all the countries of Europe, instances of the former kind, though once abundantly frequent, have for some time ceased. In certain countries, however, persecution at home, or (what produces a degree of restraint, which is one part of the mischiefs of persecution) I mean the *disposition* to persecute, whensoever occasion happens, is not yet at an end: insomuch that if there is no *actual* persecution, it is only because there are no heretics; and if there are no heretics, it is only because there are no thinkers.[1]

Case 9.
Tendency,
good—motive,
malevolence.

24. 9. Where the tendency of the act is *good*, and the motive (as before) is the dissocial one of ill-will. In this case the motive seems not to afford any indication on either side.

[1] See B. I. tit. [Offences against Religion].

It is no indication of a good disposition; but neither is it any indication of a bad one.

You have detected a baker in selling short weight: you *Example.* prosecute him for the cheat. It is not for the sake of gain that you engaged in the prosecution; for there is nothing to be got by it: it is not from public spirit: it is not for the sake of reputation; for there is no reputation to be got by it: it is not in the view of pleasing the Deity: it is merely on account of a quarrel you have with the man you prosecute. From the transaction, as thus stated, there does not seem to be anything to be said either in favour of your disposition or against it. The tendency of the act is good: but you would not have engaged in it, had it not been from a motive which there seems no particular reason to conclude will ever prompt you to engage in an act of the same kind again. Your motive is of that sort which may, with least impropriety, be termed a bad one: but the act is of that sort, which, were it engaged in ever so often, could never have any evil tendency; nor indeed any other tendency than a good one. By the supposition, the motive it happened to be dictated by was that of ill-will: but the act itself is of such a nature as to have wanted nothing but sufficient discernment on your part in order to have been dictated by the most enlarged benevolence. Now, from a man's having suffered himself to be induced to gratify his resentment by means of an act of which the tendency is good, it by no means follows that he would be ready on another occasion, through the influence of the same sort of motive, to engage in any act of which the tendency is a bad one. The motive that impelled you was a dissocial one: but what social motive could there have been to restrain you? None, but what might have been outweighed by a more enlarged motive of the same kind. Now, because the dissocial motive prevailed when it stood alone, it by no means follows that it would prevail when it had a social one to combat it.

25. 10. Where the tendency of the act is *bad*, and the motive is the dissocial one of malevolence. In this case the disposition it indicates is of course a mischievous one. *Case* 10. *Tendency*, bad —*motive*, *malevolence*.

The man who stole the bread from the baker, as before, *Example.* did it with no other view than merely to impoverish and afflict him: accordingly, when he had got the bread, he did not eat, or sell it; but destroyed it. That the disposition, evidenced by such a transaction, is a bad one, is what every body must perceive immediately.

Problem—to measure the depravity in a man's disposition.

26. Thus much with respect to the circumstances from which the mischievousness or meritoriousness of a man's disposition is to be inferred in the gross: we come now to the *measure* of that mischievousness or meritoriousness, as resulting from those circumstances. Now with meritorious acts and dispositions we have no direct concern in the present work. All that penal law is concerned to do, is to measure the depravity of the disposition where the act is mischievous. To this object, therefore, we shall here confine ourselves.

A man's disposition is constituted by the sum of his intentions:

27. It is evident, that the nature of a man's disposition must depend upon the nature of the motives he is apt to be influenced by: in other words, upon the degree of his sensibility to the force of such and such motives. For his disposition is, as it were, the sum of his intentions: the disposition he is of during a certain period, the sum or result of his intentions during that period. If, of the acts he has been intending to engage in during the supposed period, those which are apparently of a mischievous tendency, bear a large proportion to those which appear to him to be of the contrary tendency, his disposition will be of the mischievous cast: if but a small proportion, of the innocent or upright.

—which owe their birth to motives.

28. Now intentions, like every thing else, are produced by the things that are their causes: and the causes of intentions are motives. If, on any occasion, a man forms either a good or a bad intention, it must be by the influence of some motive.

A seducing or corrupting motive, what— a tutelary or preservatory motive.

29. When the act, which a motive prompts a man to engage in, is of a mischievous nature, it may, for distinction's sake, be termed a *seducing* or corrupting motive: in which case also any motive which, in opposition to the former, acts in the character of a restraining motive, may be styled a *tutelary*, preservatory, or preserving motive.

Tutelary motives are either standing or occasional.

30. Tutelary motives may again be distinguished into *standing* or constant, and *occasional*. By standing tutelary motives, I mean such as act with more or less force in all, or at least in most cases, tending to restrain a man from *any* mis-

chievous acts he may be prompted to engage in; and that with
a force which depends upon the general nature of the act,
rather than upon any accidental circumstance with which
any individual act of that sort may happen to be accompanied. By occasional tutelary motives, I mean such motives
as may chance to act in this direction or not, according to the
nature of the act, and of the particular occasion on which
the engaging in it is brought into contemplation.

31. Now it has been shown, that there is no sort of motive *Standing tute-*
by which a man may not be prompted to engage in acts *lary motives*
that are of a mischievous nature; that is, which may not come *are,*
to act in the capacity of a seducing motive. It has been shown, *1. Good-will.*
on the other hand, that there are some motives which are
remarkably less likely to operate in this way than others.
It has also been shown, that the least likely of all is that of
benevolence or good-will: the most common tendency of
which, it has been shown, is to act in the character of a tutelary
motive. It has also been shown, that even when by accident
it acts in one way in the character of a seducing motive, still
in another way it acts in the opposite character of a tutelary
one. The motive of good-will, in as far as it respects the
interests of one set of persons, may prompt a man to engage in
acts which are productive of mischief to another and more
extensive set: but this is only because his good-will is imperfect and confined: not taking into contemplation the interests
of all the persons whose interests are at stake. The same
motive, were the affection it issued from more enlarged,
would operate effectually, in the character of a constraining
motive, against that very act to which, by the supposition,
it gives birth. This same sort of motive may therefore,
without any real contradiction or deviation from truth,
be ranked in the number of standing tutelary motives, notwithstanding the occasions in which it may act at the same
time in the character of a seducing one.

32. The same observation, nearly, may be applied to the *2. The love of*
semi-social motive of love of reputation. The force of this, *reputation.*
like that of the former, is liable to be divided against itself.
As in the case of good-will, the interests of some of the
persons, who may be the objects of that sentiment, are liable
to be at variance with those of others: so in the case of love of

R

reputation, the sentiments of some of the persons, whose good opinion is desired, may be at variance with the sentiments of other persons of that number. Now in the case of an act, which is really of a mischievous nature, it can scarcely happen that there shall be no persons whatever who will look upon it with an eye of disapprobation. It can scarcely ever happen, therefore, that an act really mischievous shall not have some part at least, if not the whole, of the force of this motive to oppose it; nor, therefore, that this motive should not act with some degree of force in the character of a tutelary motive. This, therefore, may be set down as another article in the catalogue of standing tutelary motives.

3. The desire of amity.   33. The same observation may be applied to the desire of amity, though not in altogether equal measure. For, notwithstanding the mischievousness of an act, it may happen without much difficulty, that all the persons for whose amity a man entertains any particular present desire which is accompanied with expectation, may concur in regarding it with an eye rather of approbation than the contrary. This is but too apt to be the case among such fraternities as those of thieves, smugglers, and many other denominations of offenders. This, however, is not constantly, nor indeed most commonly the case: insomuch, that the desire of amity may still be regarded, upon the whole, as a tutelary motive, were it only from the closeness of its connexion with the love of reputation. And it may be ranked among standing tutelary motives; since, where it does apply, the force with which it acts depends not upon the occasional circumstances of the act which it opposes, but upon principles as general as those upon which depend the action of the other semi-social motives.

4. The motive of religion.   34. The motive of religion is not altogether in the same case with the three former. The force of it is not, like theirs, liable to be divided against itself. I mean in the civilized nations of modern times, among whom the notion of the unity of the Godhead is universal. In times of classical antiquity it was otherwise. If a man got Venus on his side, Pallas was on the other: if Æolus was for him, Neptune was against him. Æneas, with all his pity, had but a partial interest at the court of heaven. That matter stands upon different footing now-a-days. In any given person, the force of religion, whatever it be, is now all of it on one side. It may balance, indeed, on which side it shall declare itself: and it may declare itself, as we have seen already in but too many instances, on the wrong as well as on the right. It has been, at least till lately, perhaps is still, accustomed so much to declare itself on the wrong side, and that in such material instances, that on that account it seemed not proper to place it, in point of social tendency, on a level altogether with the motive of benevolence. Where it does act, however, as it does in by far the greatest number of cases, in opposition to the ordinary seducing motives, it acts, like the motive of benevolence, in an uniform manner, not depending upon the particular circumstances that may attend the commission of the act; but tending to oppose it, merely on account of its mischievousness; and therefore, with equal force, in whatsoever circumstances it may be proposed to be committed. This, therefore, may also be added to the catalogue of standing tutelary motives.

35. As to the motives which may operate occasionally *Occasional* in the character of tutelary motives, these, it has been already *tutelary* intimated, are of various sorts, and various degrees of strength *motives may be any whatsoever.* in various offences: depending not only upon the nature of the offence, but upon the accidental circumstances in which the idea of engaging in it may come in contemplation. Nor is there any sort of motive which may not come to operate in this character; as may be easily conceived. A thief, for instance, may be prevented from engaging in a projected scheme of house-breaking, by sitting too long over his bottle,[1] by a visit from his doxy, by the occasion he may have to go elsewhere, in order to receive his dividend of a former booty;[2] and so on.

36. There are some motives, however, which seem more *Motives that* apt to act in this character than others; especially as things are *are particularly* now constituted, now that the law has every where opposed *apt to act in this* to the force of the principal seducing motives, artificial *1. Love of ease.* tutelary motives of its own creation. Of the motives here *2. Self-preser-* meant it will be necessary to take a general view. They seem *vation.* to be reducible to two heads; viz. 1. The love of ease; a motive put into action by the prospect of the trouble of the

---

[1] Love of the pleasures of the palate.   [2] Pecuniary interest.

attempt; that is, the trouble which it may be necessary to bestow, in overcoming the physical difficulties that may accompany it. 2. Self-preservation, as opposed to the dangers to which a man may be exposed in the prosecution of it.

Dangers to which self preservation is most apt in this case to have respect, are, 1. Dangers purely physical. 2. Dangers depending on detection.

37. These dangers may be either, 1. Of a purely physical nature: or, 2. Dangers resulting from moral agency; in other words, from the conduct of any such persons to whom the act, if known, may be expected to prove obnoxious. But moral agency supposes knowledge with respect to the circumstances that are to have the effect of external motives in giving birth to it. Now the obtaining such knowledge, with respect to the commission of any obnoxious act, on the part of any persons who may be disposed to make the agent suffer for it, is called *detection*; and the agent concerning whom such knowledge is obtained, is said to be detected. The dangers, therefore, which may threaten an offender from this quarter, depend, whatever they may be, on the event of his detection; and may, therefore, be all of them comprised under the article of the *danger of detection.*

Danger depending on detection may result from, 1. Opposition on the spot: 2. Subsequent punishment.

38. The danger depending upon detection may be divided again into two branches: 1. That which may result from any opposition that may be made to the enterprise by persons on the spot; that is, at the very time the enterprise is carrying on: 2. That which respects the legal punishment, or other suffering, that may await at a distance upon the issue of the enterprise.

The force of the two standing tutelary motives of love of reputation, and desire of amity, depends upon detection.

39. It may be worth calling to mind on this occasion, that among the tutelary motives, which have been styled constant ones, there are two of which the force depends (though not so entirely as the force of the occasional ones which have been just mentioned, yet in a great measure) upon the circumstance of detection. These, it may be remembered, are, the love of reputation, and the desire of amity. In proportion, therefore, as the chance of being detected appears greater, these motives will apply with the greater force: with the less force, as it appears less. This is not the case with the two other standing tutelary motives, that of benevolence, and that of religion.

Strength of a temptation, what is meant by it.

40. We are now in a condition to determine, with some degree of precision, what is to be understood by the *strength of a temptation*, and what indication it may give of the degree

of mischievousness in a man's disposition in the case of any offence. When a man is prompted to engage in any mischievous act, we will say, for shortness, in an offence, the strength of the temptation depends upon the ratio between the force of the seducing motives on the one hand, and such of the occasional tutelary ones, as the circumstances of the case call forth into action, on the other. The temptation, then, may be said to be strong, when the pleasure or advantage to be got from the crime is such as in the eyes of the offender must appear great in comparison of the trouble and danger that appear to him to accompany the enterprise: slight or weak, when that pleasure or advantage is such as must appear small in comparison of such trouble and such danger. It is plain the strength of the temptation depends not upon the force of the impelling (that is of the seducing) motives altogether: for let the opportunity be more favourable, that is, let the trouble, or any branch of the danger, be made less than before, it will be acknowledged, that the temptation is made so much the stronger: and on the other hand, let the opportunity become less favourable, or, in other words, let the trouble, or any branch of the danger, be made greater than before, the temptation will be so much the weaker.

Now, after taking account of such tutelary motives as have been styled occasional, the only tutelary motives that can remain are those which have been termed standing ones. But those which have been termed the standing tutelary motives, are the same that we have been styling social. It follows, therefore, that the strength of the temptation, in any case, after deducting the force of the social motives, is as the sum of the forces of the seducing, to the sum of the forces of the occasional tutelary motives.

41. It remains to be inquired, what indication concerning *Indications* the mischievousness or depravity of a man's disposition is *afforded by this and other* afforded by the strength of the temptation, in the case where *circumstances* any offence happens to have been committed. It appears, *respecting the depravity of an* then, that the weaker the temptation is, by which a man has *offender's dispo-* been overcome, the more depraved and mischievous it shows *sition.* his disposition to have been. For the goodness of his disposition is measured by the degree of his sensibility to the action

of the social motives:[1] in other words, by the strength of the influence which those motives have over him: now, the less considerable the force is by which their influence on him has been overcome, the more convincing is the proof that has been given of the weakness of that influence.

Again, The degree of a man's sensibility to the force of the social motives being given, it is plain that the force with which those motives tend to restrain him from engaging in any mischievous enterprise, will be as the apparent mischievousness of such enterprise, that is, as the degree of mischief with which it appears to *him* likely to be attended. In other words, the less mischievous the offence appears to him to be, the less averse he will be, as far as he is guided by social considerations, to engage in it; the more mischievous, the more averse. If then the nature of the offence is such as must appear to him highly mischievous, and yet he engages in it notwithstanding, it shows, that the degree of his sensibility to the force of the social motives is but slight; and consequently that his disposition is proportionately depraved. Moreover, the less the strength of the temptation was, the more pernicious and depraved does it show his disposition to have been. For the less the strength of the temptation was, the less was the force which the influence of those motives had to overcome: the clearer therefore is the proof that has been given of the weakness of that influence.

Rules for measuring the depravity of disposition indicated by an offence.

42. From what has been said, it seems, that, for judging of the indication that is afforded concerning the depravity of a man's disposition by the strength of the temptation, compared with the mischievousness of the enterprise, the following rules may be laid down.

Rule I. *The strength of the temptation being given, the mischievousness of the disposition manifested by the enterprise, is as the apparent mischievousness of the act.*

Thus, it would show a more depraved disposition, to murder a man for a reward of a guinea, or falsely to charge him with a robbery for the same reward, than to obtain the same sum from him by simple theft: the trouble he would have to take, and the risk he would have to run, being supposed to stand on the same footing in the one case as in the other.

[1] *Supra,* par. 27, 28.

Rule 2. *The apparent mischievousness of the act being given, a man's disposition is the more depraved, the slighter the temptation is by which he has been overcome.*

Thus, it shows a more depraved and dangerous disposition, if a man kill another out of mere sport, as the Emperor of Morocco, Muley Mahomet, is said to have done great numbers, than out of revenge, as Sylla and Marius did thousands, or in the view of self-preservation, as Augustus killed many, or even for lucre, as the same Emperor is said to have killed some. And the effects of such a depravity, on that part of the public which is apprized of it, run in the same proportion. From Augustus, some persons only had to fear, under some particular circumstances. From Muley Mahomet, every man had to fear at all times.

Rule 3. *The apparent mischievousness of the act being given, the evidence which it affords of the depravity of a man's disposition is the less conclusive, the stronger the temptation is by which he has been overcome.*

Thus, if a poor man, who is ready to die with hunger, steal a loaf of bread, it is a less explicit sign of depravity, than if a rich man were to commit a theft to the same amount. It will be observed, that in this rule all that is said is, that the evidence of depravity is in this case the less conclusive: it is not said that the depravity is positively the less. For in this case it is possible, for any thing that appears to the contrary, that the theft might have been committed, even had the temptation been not so strong. In this case, the alleviating circumstance is only a matter of presumption; in the former, the aggravating circumstance is a matter of certainty.

Rule 4. *Where the motive is of the dissocial kind, the apparent mischievousness of the act, and the strength of the temptation, being given, the depravity is as the degree of deliberation with which it is accompanied.*

For in every man, be his disposition ever so depraved, the social motives are those which, wherever the self-regarding ones stand neuter, regulate and determine the general tenor of his life. If the dissocial motives are put in action, it is only in particular circumstances, and on particular occasions; the gentle but constant force of the social motives being for a while subdued. The general and standing bias of every man's nature is, therefore, towards that side to which the force of the social motives would determine him to adhere. This being the case, the force of the social motives tends continually to put an end to that of the dissocial ones; as, in natural bodies, the force of friction tends to put an end to that which is generated by impulse. Time, then, which wears away the force of the dissocial motives, adds to that of the social. The longer, therefore, a man continues, on a given occasion, under the dominion of the dissocial motives, the more convincing is the proof that has been given of his insensibility to the force of the social ones.

Thus, it shows a worse disposition, where a man lays a deliberate plan for beating his antagonist, and beats him accordingly, than if he were to beat him upon the spot, in consequence of a sudden quarrel: and worse again, if, after having had him a long while together in his power, he beats him at intervals, and at his leisure.[1]

Use of this chapter.

43. The depravity of disposition, indicated by an act, is a material consideration in several respects. Any mark of extraordinary depravity, by adding to the terror already inspired by the crime, and by holding up the offender as a person from whom there may be more mischief to be apprehended in future, adds in that way to the demand for punishment. By indicating a general want of sensibility on the part of the offender, it may add in another way also to the demand for punishment. The article of disposition is of the more importance, inasmuch as, in measuring out the quantum of punishment, the principle of sympathy and antipathy is apt to look at nothing else. A man who punishes because he hates, and only because he hates, such a man, when he does not find any thing odious in the disposition, is not for punishing at all; and when he does, he is not for carrying the punishment further than his hatred carries him. Hence the aversion we find so frequently expressed against the maxim, that the punishment must rise with the strength of the temptation; a maxim, the contrary of which, as we shall see, would be as cruel to offenders themselves, as it would be subversive of the purposes of punishment.

[1] See B. I. tit. [Confinement].

CHAPTER XII

OF THE CONSEQUENCES OF A MISCHIEVOUS ACT

§ 1. *Shapes in which the mischief of an act may show itself*

1. HITHERTO we have been speaking of the various articles *Recapitulation.* or objects on which the consequences or tendency of an act may depend: of the bare *act* itself: of the *circumstances* it may have been, or may have been supposed to be, accompanied with: of the *consciousness* a man may have had with respect to any such circumstances: of the *intentions* that may have preceded the act: of the *motives* that may have given birth to those intentions: and of the *disposition* that may have been indicated by the connexion between such intentions and such motives. We now come to speak of *consequences* or tendency: an article which forms the concluding link in all this chain of causes and effects, involving in it the materiality of the whole. Now, such part of this tendency as is of a mischievous nature, is all that we have any direct concern with; to that, therefore, we shall here confine ourselves.

2. The tendency of an act is mischievous when the *Mischief of an* consequences of it are mischievous; that is to say, either the *act, the aggregate of its* certain consequences or the probable. The consequences, *mischievous* how many and whatsoever they may be, of an act, of which *consequences.* the tendency is mischievous, may, such of them as are mischievous, be conceived to constitute one aggregate body, which may be termed the mischief of the act.

3. This mischief may frequently be distinguished, as it were, *The mischief of* into two shares or parcels: the one containing what may be *an act, primary* called the primary mischief; the other, what may be called *or secondary.* the secondary. That share may be termed the *primary*, which it sustained by an assignable individual, or a multitude of assignable individuals. That share may be termed the *secondary*, which, taking its origin from the former, extends itself either over the whole community, or over some other multitude of unassignable individuals.

Primary—
original, or
derivative.

4. The primary mischief of an act may again be distinguished into two branches: 1. The *original*: and, 2. The *derivative*. By the original branch, I mean that which alights upon and is confined to any person who is a sufferer in the first instance, and on his own account: the person, for instance, who is beaten, robbed, or murdered. By the derivative branch, I mean any share of mischief which may befall any other assignable persons in consequence of his being a sufferer, and no otherwise. These persons must, of course, be persons who in some way or other are connected with him. Now the ways in which one person may be connected with another, have been already seen: they may be connected in the way of *interest* (meaning self-regarding interest) or merely in the way of *sympathy*. And again, persons connected with a given person, in the way of interest, may be connected with him either by affording *support* to him, or by deriving it from him.[1]

The secondary—
1. Alarm; or,
2. Danger.

5. The secondary mischief, again, may frequently be seen to consist of two other shares or parcels: the first consisting of *pain*; the other of *danger*. The pain which it produces is a pain of apprehension: a pain grounded on the apprehension of suffering such mischiefs or inconveniences, whatever they may be, as it is the nature of the primary mischief to produce. It may be styled, in one word, the *alarm*. The danger is the *chance*, whatever it may be, which the multitude it concerns may in consequence of the primary mischief stand exposed to, of suffering such mischiefs or inconveniences. For danger is nothing but the chance of pain, or, what comes to the same thing, of loss of pleasure.

Example.

6. An example may serve to make this clear. A man attacks you on the road, and robs you. You suffer a pain on the occasion of losing so much money:[2] you also suffered a pain at the thoughts of the personal ill-treatment you apprehended he might give you, in case of your not happening to satisfy his demands.[3] These together constitute the original branch of the primary mischief, resulting from the act of

---

[1] See Chap. vi. [Sensibility].

[2] Viz., a *pain of privation.* See Chap. v. [Pleasures and Pains], 17.

[3] Viz., a *pain of apprehension*, grounded on the prospect of organical pain, or whatever other mischiefs might have ensued from the ill treatment. Ib. 30.

robbery. A creditor of yours, who expected you to pay him with part of that money, and a son of yours, who expected you to have given him another part, are in consequence disappointed. You are obliged to have recourse to the bounty of your father, to make good part of the deficiency. These mischiefs together make up the derivative branch. The report of this robbery circulates from hand to hand, and spreads itself in the neighbourhood. It finds its way into the newspapers, and is propagated over the whole country. Various people, on this occasion, call to mind the danger which they and their friends, as it appears from this example, stand exposed to in travelling; especially such as may have occasion to travel the same road. On this occasion they naturally feel a certain degree of pain: slighter or heavier, according to the degree of ill-treatment they may understand you to have received; the frequency of the occasion each person may have to travel in that same road, or its neighbourhood; the vicinity of each person to the spot; his personal courage; the quantity of money he may have occasion to carry about with him; and a variety of other circumstances. This constitutes the first part of the secondary mischief, resulting from the act of robbery; viz., the alarm. But people of one description or other, not only are disposed to conceive themselves to incur a chance of being robbed, in consequence of the robbery committed upon you, but (as will be shown presently) they do really incur such a chance. And it is this chance which constitutes the remaining part of the secondary mischief of the act of robbery; viz., the danger.

7. Let us see what this chance amounts to; and whence it comes. How is it, for instance, that one robbery can con-tribute to produce another? In the first place, it is certain that it cannot create any direct motive. A motive must be the prospect of some pleasure, or other advantage, to be enjoyed in future: but the robbery in question is past: nor would it furnish any such prospect were it to come: for it is not one robbery that will furnish pleasure to him who may be about to commit another robbery. The consideration that is to operate upon a man, as a motive or inducement to commit a robbery, must be the idea of the pleasure he expects to derive

The danger, whence it arises —a past offence affords no direct motive to a future.

from the fruits of that very robbery: but this pleasure exists independently of any other robbery.

But it suggests feasibility, and weakens the force of restraining motives;

8. The means, then, by which one robbery tends, as it should seem, to produce another robbery, are two. 1. By suggesting to a person exposed to the temptation, the idea of committing such another robbery (accompanied, perhaps, with the belief of its facility). In this case the influence it exerts applies itself, in the first place, to the understanding. 2. By weakening the force of the tutelary motives which tend to restrain him from such an action, and thereby adding to the strength of the temptation.[1] In this case the influence applies itself to the will. These forces are, 1. The motive of benevolence, which acts as a branch of the physical sanction.[2] 2. The motive of self-preservation, as against the punishment that may stand provided by the political sanction. 3. The fear of shame; a motive belonging to the moral sanction. 4. The fear of the divine displeasure; a motive belonging to the religious sanction. On the first and last of these forces it has, perhaps, no influence worth insisting on: but it has on the other two.

viz.
1. Those issuing from the political sanction.

9. The way in which a past robbery may weaken the force with which the *political* sanction tends to prevent a future robbery, may be thus conceived. The way in which this sanction tends to prevent a robbery, is by denouncing some particular kind of punishment against any who shall be guilty of it: the *real* value of which punishment will of course be diminished by the *real* uncertainty: as also, if there be any difference, the *apparent* value by the *apparent* uncertainty. Now this uncertainty is proportionably increased by every instance in which a man is known to commit the offence, without undergoing the punishment. This, of course, will be the case with every offence for a certain time; in short, until the punishment allotted to it takes place. If punishment takes place at last, this branch of the mischief of the offence is then at last, but not till then, put a stop to.

---

[1] See Chap. xi. [Dispositions], 40.
[2] To wit, in virtue of the pain it may give a man to be a witness to, or otherwise conscious of, the sufferings of a fellow-creature: especially when he is himself the cause of them: in a word, the pain of sympathy. See Chap. v. [Pleasures and Pains], 26.

10. The way in which a past robbery may weaken the force *2. Those issuing* with which the *moral* sanction tends to prevent a future *from the moral.* robbery, may be thus conceived. The way in which the moral sanction tends to prevent a robbery, is by holding forth the indignation of mankind as ready to fall upon him who shall be guilty of it. Now this indignation will be the more formidable, according to the number of those who join in it: it will be the less so, the fewer they are who join in it. But there cannot be a stronger way of showing that a man does not join in whatever indignation may be entertained against a practice, than the engaging in it himself. It shows not only that he himself feels no indignation against it, but that it seems to him there is no sufficient reason for apprehending what indignation may be felt against it by others. Accordingly, where robberies are frequent, and unpunished, robberies are committed without shame. It was thus amongst the Grecians formerly.[1] It is thus among the Arabs still.

11. In whichever way then a past offence tends to pave the *It is said to* way for the commission of a future offence, whether by *operate by the influence of* suggesting the idea of committing it, or by adding to the *example.* strength of the temptation, in both cases it may be said to operate by the force or *influence of example.*

12. The two branches of the secondary mischief of an act, *The alarm and* the alarm and the danger, must not be confounded: though *the danger, though connect-* intimately connected, they are perfectly distinct: either may *ed, are distin-* subsist without the other. The neighbourhood may be *guishable.* alarmed with the report of a robbery, when, in fact, no robbery either has been committed or is in a way to be committed: a neighbourhood may be on the point of being disturbed by robberies, without knowing any thing of the matter. Accordingly, we shall soon perceive, that some acts produce alarm without danger: others, danger without alarm.

13. As well the danger as the alarm may again be divided, *Both may have* each of them, into two branches: the first, consisting of so *respect to the same person, or* much of the alarm or danger as may be apt to result from the *to others.* future behaviour of the same agent: the second, consisting of so much as may be apt to result from the behaviour of other

[1] See Hom. Odyss. L. xix. l. 395; ib. L. iii. l. 71. Plato de Rep. L. i. p. 576, edit. Ficin. Thucyd. L. i.—and see B. I. tit. [Offences against external security].

persons: such others, to wit, as may come to engage in acts of the same sort and tendency.[1]

The primary consequences of an act may be mischievous, and the secondary beneficial.

14. The distinction between the primary and the secondary consequences of an act must be carefully attended to. It is so just, that the latter may often be of a directly opposite nature to the former. In some cases, where the primary consequences of the act are attended with a mischief, the secondary consequences may be beneficial, and that to such a degree, as even greatly to outweigh the mischief of the primary. This is the case, for instance, with all acts of punishment, when properly applied. Of these, the primary mischief being never intended to fall but upon such persons as may happen to have committed some act which it is expedient to prevent, the secondary mischief, that is, the alarm and the danger, extends no farther than to such persons as are under temptation to commit it: in which case, in as far as it tends to restrain them from committing such acts, it is of a beneficial nature.

Analysis of the different shapes in which the mischief of an act may show itself.

15. Thus much with regard to acts that produce positive pain, and that immediately. This case, by reason of its simplicity, seemed the fittest to take the lead. But acts may produce mischief in various other ways; which, together with those already specified, may all be comprised by the following abridged analysis.

Mischief may admit of a division in any one of three points of view. 1. According to its own *nature*. 2. According to its *cause*. 3. According to the person, or other party, who is the *object* of it.[2] With regard to its nature, it may be either *simple* or *complex*[3]: when simple, it may either be *positive* or *negative*: positive, consisting of actual pain: negative, consisting of the loss of pleasure. Whether simple or complex, and whether positive or negative, it may be either *certain* or *contingent*. When it is negative, it consists of the loss of some benefit

---

[1] To the former of these branches is opposed so much of the force of any punishment, as is said to operate in the way of *reformation*: to the latter, so much as is said to operate in the way of *example*. See Chap. xiii. [Cases unmeet], par. 2. note.

[2] There may be other points of view, according to which mischief might be divided, besides these: but this does not prevent the division here given from being an exhaustive one. A line may be divided in any one of an infinity of ways, and yet without leaving in any one of those cases any remainder. See Chap. xvi. [Division] 1. note.

[3] Chap. v. [Pleasures and Pains] 1.

or advantage: this benefit may be material in both or either of two ways: 1. By affording actual pleasure: or, 2. By averting pain or *danger*, which is the chance of pain: that is, by affording *security*. In as far, then, as the benefit which a mischief tends to avert, is productive of security, the tendency of such mischief is to produce *insecurity*. 2. With regard to its *cause*, mischief may be produced either by one *single* action, or not without the *concurrence* of other actions: if not without the concurrence of other actions, these others may be the actions either of the *same person*, or of *other* persons: in either case, they may be either acts of the *same kind* as that in question, or of *other* kinds. 3. Lastly, with regard to the party who is the *object* of the mischief, or, in other words, who is in a way to be affected by it, such party may be either an *assignable*[1] individual, or assemblage of individuals, or else a multitude of *unassignable* individuals. When the object is an assignable individual, this individual may either be the person *himself* who is the author of the mischief, or some *other* person. When the individuals who are the objects of it, are an unassignable multitude, this multitude may be either the *whole* political community or state, or some *subordinate* division of it. Now when the object of the mischief is the author himself, it may be styled *self-regarding*: when any other party is the object, *extra-regarding*: when such other party is an individual, it may be styled *private*: when a subordinate branch of the community, *semi-public*: when the whole community, *public*. Here, for the present, we must stop. To pursue the subject through its inferior distinctions, will be the business of the chapter which exhibits the division of offences.[2]

The cases which have been already illustrated, are those in which the primary mischief is not necessarily otherwise than a *—applied to the preceding cases.* simple one, and that positive: present, and therefore certain: producible by a single action, without any necessity of the concurrence of any other action, either on the part of the same agent, or of others; and having for its object an assignable individual, or, by accident, an assemblage of assignable individuals: extra-regarding therefore, and private. This primary mischief is accompanied by a secondary: the first branch of which is sometimes contingent and sometimes

---

[1] See Chap. xvi. [Division] 4. note. [2] Chap. xvi.

certain, the other never otherwise than contingent: both extra-regarding and semi-public: in other respects, pretty much upon a par with the primary mischief: except that the first branch, viz. the alarm, though inferior in magnitude to the primary, is, in point of extent, and therefore, upon the whole, in point of magnitude, much superior.

—to examples of other cases where the mischief is less conspicuous. Example I. An act of self-intoxication.

16. Two instances more will be sufficient to illustrate the most material of the modifications above exhibited.

A man drinks a certain quantity of liquor, and intoxicates himself. The intoxication in this particular instance does him no sort of harm: or, what comes to the same thing, none that is perceptible. But it is probable, and indeed next to certain, that a given number of acts of the same kind would do him a very considerable degree of harm: more or less according to his constitution and other circumstances: for this is no more than what experience manifests every day. It is also certain, that one act of this sort, by one means or other, tends considerably to increase the disposition a man may be in to practise other acts of the same sort: for this also is verified by experience. This, therefore, is one instance where the mischief producible by the act is contingent; in other words, in which the tendency of the act is no otherwise mischievous than in virtue of its producing a *chance* of mischief. This chance depends upon the concurrence of other acts of the same kind; and those such as must be practised by the same person. The object of the mischief is that very person himself who is the author of it, and he only, unless by accident. The mischief is therefore private and self-regarding.

As to its secondary mischief, alarm, it produces none: it produces indeed a certain quantity of danger by the influence of example: but it is not often that this danger will amount to a quantity worth regarding.

Example II. Non-payment of a tax.

17. Again. A man omits paying his share to a public tax. This we see is an act of the negative kind.[1] Is this then to be placed upon the list of mischievous acts? Yes, certainly. Upon what grounds? Upon the following. To defend the community against its external as well as its internal adversaries, are tasks, not to mention others of a less indispensable nature, which cannot be fulfilled but at a considerable expense.

[1] See Chap. vii. [Actions] 8.

But whence is the money for defraying this expense to come? It can be obtained in no other manner than by contributions to be collected from individuals; in a word, by taxes. The produce then of these taxes is to be looked upon as a kind of *benefit* which it is necessary the governing part of the community should receive for the use of the whole. This produce, before it can be applied to its destination, requires that there should be certain persons commissioned to receive and to apply it. Now if these persons, had they received it, would have applied it to its proper destination, it would have been a benefit: the not putting them in a way to receive it, is then a mischief. But it is possible, that if received, it might not have been applied to its proper destination; or that the services, in consideration of which it was bestowed, might not have been performed. It is possible, that the under-officer, who collected the produce of the tax, might not have paid it over to his principal: it is possible that the principal might not have forwarded it on according to its farther destination; to the judge, for instance, who is to protect the community against its clandestine enemies from within, or the soldier, who is to protect it against its open enemies from without: it is possible that the judge, or the soldier, had they received it, would not however have been induced by it to fulfil their respective duties: it is possible, that the judge would not have sat for the punishment of criminals, and the decision of controversies: it is possible that the soldier would not have drawn his sword in the defence of the community. These, together with an infinity of other intermediate acts, which for the sake of brevity I pass over, form a connected chain of duties, the discharge of which is necessary to the preservation of the community. They must every one of them be discharged, ere the benefit to which they are contributory can be produced. If they are all discharged, in that case the benefit subsists, and any act, by tending to intercept that benefit, may produce a mischief. But if any of them are not, the benefit fails: it fails of itself: it would not have subsisted, although the act in question (the act of non-payment) had not been committed. The benefit is therefore contingent; and, accordingly, upon a certain supposition,

S

the act which consists in the averting of it is not a mischievous one. But this supposition, in any tolerably-ordered government, will rarely indeed be verified. In the very worst-ordered government that exists, the greatest part of the duties that are levied are paid over according to their destination: and, with regard to any particular sum, that is attempted to be levied upon any particular person upon any particular occasion, it is therefore manifest, that, unless it be certain that it will not be so disposed of, the act of withholding it is a mischievous one.

The act of payment, when referable to any particular sum, especially if it be a small one, might also have failed of proving beneficial on another ground: and, consequently, the act of non-payment, of proving mischievous. It is possible that the same services, precisely, might have been rendered without the money as with it. If, then, speaking of any small limited sum, such as the greatest which any one person is called upon to pay at a time, a man were to say, that the non-payment of it would be attended with mischievous consequences; this would be far from certain: but what comes to the same thing as if it were, it is perfectly certain when applied to the whole. It is certain, that if all of a sudden the payment of all taxes was to cease, there would no longer be any thing effectual done, either for the maintenance of justice, or for the defence of the community against its foreign adversaries: that therefore the weak would presently be oppressed and injured in all manner of ways, by the strong at home, and both together overwhelmed by oppressors from abroad. Upon the whole, therefore, it is manifest, that in this case though the mischief is remote and contingent, though in it first appearance it consists of nothing more than the interception of a *benefit*, and though the individuals, in whose favour that benefit would have been reduced into the explicit form of pleasure or security, are altogether unassignable, yet the mischievous tendency of the act is not on all these accounts the less indisputable. The mischief, in point of *intensity* and *duration*, is indeed unknown: it is *uncertain*: it is *remote*. But in point of *extent* it is immense; and in point of *fecundity*, pregnant to a degree that baffles calculation.

18. It may now be time to observe, that it is only in the case where the mischief is extra-regarding, and has an assignable person or persons for its object, that so much of the secondary branch of it as consists in *alarm* can have place. When the individuals it affects are uncertain, and altogether out of sight, no alarm can be produced: as there is nobody whose sufferings you can see, there is nobody whose sufferings you can be alarmed at. No alarm, for instance, is produced by non-payment to a tax. If at any distant and uncertain period of time such offence should chance to be productive of any kind of alarm, it would appear to proceed, as indeed immediately it would proceed, from a very different cause. It might be immediately referable, for example, to the act of a legislator, who should deem it necessary to lay on a new tax, in order to make up for the deficiency occasioned in the produce of the old one. Or it might be referable to the act of an enemy, who, under favour of a deficiency thus created in the fund allotted for defence, might invade the country, and exact from it much heavier contributions than those which had been thus withholden from the sovereign.[1]

No alarm, when no assignable person is the object.

As to any alarm which such an offence might raise among the few who might chance to regard the matter with the eyes of statesmen, it is of too slight and uncertain a nature to be worth taking into the account.

§ 2. *How Intentionality, &c. may influence the mischief of an act.*

19. We have seen the nature of the secondary mischief, which is apt to be reflected, as it were, from the primary, in the cases where the individuals who are the objects of the mischief are assignable. It is now time to examine into the

Secondary mischief influenced by the state of the agent's mind.

---

[1] The investigation might, by a process rendered obvious by analogy, be extended to the consequences of an act of a beneficial nature. In both instances *third* order of consequences may be reckoned to have taken place, when the influence of the act, through the medium of the passive faculty of the patient, has come to affect his active faculty. In this way, 1. Evil may flow out of *evil*:—instance; the exertions of industry put a stop to by the extinction of inducement, resulting from a continued chain of acts of robbery or extortion. 2. *Good out of evil*:—instance; habits of depredation put a stop to by a steady course of punishment. 3. *Evil out of good*:—instance; habits of industry put a stop to by an excessive course of gratuitous bounty. 4. *Good out of good*:—instance; a constant and increasing course of industry, excited and kept up by the rewards afforded by a regular and increasing market for the fruits of it.

circumstances upon which the production of such secondary mischief depends. These circumstances are no others than the four articles which have formed the subjects of the four last preceding chapters: viz. 1. The intentionality. 2. The consciousness. 3. The motive. 4. The disposition. It is to be observed all along, that it is only the *danger* that is immediately governed by the *real* state of the mind in respect to those articles: it is by the *apparent* state of it that the *alarm* is governed. It is governed by the real only in as far as the apparent happens, as in most cases it may be expected to do, to quadrate with the real. The different influences of the articles of intentionality and consciousness may be represented in the several cases following.

Case 1.
Involuntariness.

20. Case 1. Where the act is so completely unintentional, as to be altogether *involuntary*. In this case it is attended with no secondary mischief at all.

A bricklayer is at work upon a house: a passenger is walking in the street below. A fellow-workman comes and gives the bricklayer a violent push, in consequence of which he falls upon the passenger, and hurts him. It is plain there is nothing in this event that can give other people, who may happen to be in the street, the least reason to apprehend any thing in future on the part of the man who fell, whatever there may be with regard to the man who pushed him.

Case 2.
Unintentional-
ity with heed-
lessness.

21. Case 2. Where the act, though not unintentional, is *unadvised*, insomuch that the mischievous part of the consequences is unintentional, but the unadvisedness is attended with *heedlessness*. In this case the act is attended with some small degree of secondary mischief, in proportion to the degree of heedlessness.

A groom being on horseback, and riding through a frequented street, turns a corner at a full pace, and rides over a passenger, who happens to be going by. It is plain, by this behaviour of the groom, some degree of alarm may be produced, less or greater, according to the degree of heedlessness betrayed by him: according to the quickness of his pace the fulness of the street, and so forth. He has done mischief it may be said, by his carelessness, already: who knows but that on other occasions the like cause may produce the like effect?

22. Case 3. Where the act is *misadvised* with respect to a *Case 3.* circumstance, which, had it existed, would *fully* have excluded *Missupposal of* or (what comes to the same thing) outweighed the primary *a complete justi- fication, with-* mischief: and there is no rashness in the case. In this case the *out rashness.* act is attended with no secondary mischief at all.

It is needless to multiply examples any farther.

23. Case 4. Where the act is misadvised with respect to a *Case 4.* circumstance which would have excluded or counter- *Missupposal of* balanced the primary mischief *in part*, but not entirely: and *a partial justifi- cation, without* still there is no rashness. In this case the act is attended with *rashness.* some degree of secondary mischief, in proportion to that part of the primary which remains unexcluded or uncounter- balanced.

24. Case 5. Where the act is misadvised with respect to a *Case 5.* circumstance, which, had it existed, would have excluded or *Missupposal,* counterbalanced the primary mischief entirely, or in part: and *with rashness.* there is a degree of *rashness* in the supposal. In this case, the act is also attended with a farther degree of secondary mischief, in proportion to the degree of rashness.

25. Case 6. Where the consequences are *completely* inten- *Case 6.* tional, and there is no missupposal in the case. In this case the *Consequences completely in-* secondary mischief is at the highest. *tentional, and*

26. Thus much with regard to intentionality and con- *free from mis-* sciousness. We now come to consider in what manner the *supposal.* secondary mischief is affected by the nature of the *motive*. *The nature of a motives takes*

Where an act is pernicious in its primary consequences, the *not away the* secondary mischief is not obliterated by the *goodness* of the *mischief of the* motive; though the motive be of the best kind. For, not- *secondary con- sequences.* withstanding the goodness of the motive, an act of which the primary consequences are pernicious, is produced by it in the instance in question, by the supposition. It may, there- fore, in other instances: although this is not so likely to happen from a good motive as from a bad one.[1]

---

[1] An act of homicide, for instance, is not rendered innocent, much less beneficial, merely by its proceeding from a principle of religion, of honour (that is, of love of reputation) or even of benevolence. When Ravaillac assassinated Henry IV. it was from a principle of religion. But this did not so much as abate from the mischief of the act. It even rendered the act still more mischievous, for a reason that we shall see presently, than if it had originated from a principle of revenge. When the conspirators against the late king of Portugal attempted to assassinate him, it is said to have been from a principle of honour. But this, whether it abated or no, will certainly not be

Nor the benefi-
cialness.

27. An act, which, though pernicious in its primary consequences, is rendered in other respects beneficial upon the whole, by virtue of its secondary consequences, is not changed back again and rendered pernicious upon the whole by the *badness* of the motive: although the motive be of the worst kind.[1]

But it may
aggravate the
mischievousness,
where they are
mischievous.

28. But when not only the primary consequences of an act are pernicious, but, in other respects, the secondary likewise, the secondary mischief may be *aggravated* by the nature of the motive: so much of that mischief, to wit, as respects the future behaviour of the same person.

But not the most
in the case of the
worst motives.

29. It is not from the worst kind of motive, however, that the secondary mischief of an act receives its greatest aggravation.

It does the more,
the more con-
siderable the
tendency of the
motive to pro-
duce such acts.

30. The aggravation which the secondary mischief of an act, in as far as it respects the future behaviour of the same person, receives from the nature of a motive in an individual case, is as the tendency of the motive to produce, on the part of the same person, acts of the like bad tendency with that of the act in question.

—which is as
its strength and
constancy.

31. The tendency of a motive to produce acts of the like kind, on the part of any given person, is as the *strength* and

thought to have outweighed, the mischief of the act. Had a son of Ravaillac's, as in the case before supposed,[a] merely on the score of filial affection, and not in consequence of any participation in his crime, put him to death in order to rescue him from the severer hands of justice, the motive, although it should not be thought to afford any proof of a mischievous disposition, and should, even in case of punishment, have made such rescuer an object of pity, would hardly have made the act of rescue a beneficial one.

[1] The prosecution of offences, for instance, proceeds most commonly from one or other, or both together, of two motives, the one of which is of the self-regarding, the other of the dissocial kind: viz. pecuniary interest, and ill-will: from pecuniary interest, for instance, whenever the obtaining pecuniary amends for damage suffered is one end of the prosecution. It is common enough indeed to hear men speak of prosecutions undertaken from *public spirit*; which is a branch, as we have seen,[b] of the principle of benevolence. Far be it from me to deny but that such a principle may very frequently be an ingredient in the sum of motives, by which men are engaged in a proceeding of this nature. But whenever such a proceeding is engaged in from the sole influence of public spirit, uncombined with the least tincture of self-interest, or ill-will, it must be acknowledged to be a proceeding of the heroic kind. Now acts of heroism are, in the very essence of them, but rare: for if they were common, they would not be acts of heroism. But prosecutions for crimes are very frequent, and yet, unless in very particular circumstances indeed, they are never otherwise than beneficial.

[a] Chap. xi. [Disposition] 15.   [b] See Chap. x. [Motives] 25.

constancy of its influence on that person, as applied to the production of such effects.

32. The tendency of a species of motive to give birth to acts of any kind, among persons in general, is as the *strength*, *constancy*, and *extensiveness*[1] of its influence, as applied to the production of such effects.

General efficacy of a species of motive, how measured.

33. Now the motives, whereof the influence is at once most powerful, most constant, and most extensive, are the motives of physical desire, the love of wealth, the love of ease, the love of life, and the fear of pain: all of them self-regarding motives. The motive of displeasure, whatever it may be in point of strength and extensiveness, is not near so constant in its influence (the case of mere antipathy excepted) as any of the other three. A pernicious act, therefore, when committed through vengeance, or otherwise through displeasure, is not near so mischievous as the same pernicious act, when committed by force of any one of those other motives.[2]

A mischievous act is more so, when issuing from a self-regarding than when from a dissocial motive.

34. As to the motive of religion, whatever it may sometimes prove to be in point of strength and constancy, it is not in point of extent so universal, especially in its application to acts of a mischievous nature, as any of the three preceding motives. It may, however, be as universal in a particular state, or in a particular district of a particular state. It is liable indeed to be very irregular in its operations. It is apt, however, to be infrequently as powerful as the motive of vengeance,

—so even when issuing from the motive of religion.

---

[1] Chap. iv. [Value].

[2] It is for this reason that a threat, or other personal outrage, when committed on a stranger, in pursuance of a scheme of robbery, is productive of more mischief in society, and accordingly is, perhaps, every where more severely punished, than an outrage of the same kind offered to an acquaintance, in prosecution of a scheme of vengeance. No man is always in a rage. But, at all times, every man, more or less, loves money. Accordingly, although a man by his quarrelsomeness should for once have been engaged in a bad action, he may nevertheless remain a long while, or even his whole life-time, without engaging in another bad action of the same kind: for he may very well remain his whole life-time without engaging in so violent a quarrel: nor at any rate will he quarrel with more than one, or a few people at a time. But if a man, by his love of money, has once been engaged in a bad action, such as a scheme of robbery, he may at any time, by the influence of the same motive, be engaged in acts of the same degree of enormity. For take men throughout, if a man loves money to a certain degree to-day, it is probable that he will love it, at least in equal degree, to-morrow. And if a man is disposed to acquire it in that way, he will find inducement to rob, wheresoever and whensoever there are people to be robbed.

or indeed any other motive whatsoever. It will sometimes even be more powerful than any other motive. It is, at any rate, much more constant.[1] A pernicious act, therefore, when committed through the motive of religion, is more mischievous than when committed though the motive of ill-will.

How the secondary mischief is influenced by disposition.

35. Lastly, The secondary mischief, to wit, so much of it as hath respect to the future behaviour of the same person, is aggravated or lessened by the apparent depravity or beneficence of his disposition: and that in the proportion of such apparent depravity or beneficence.

Connexion of this with the succeeding chapter.

36. The consequences we have hitherto been speaking of, are the *natural* consequences, of which the act, and the other articles we have been considering, are the causes: consequences that result from the behaviour of the individual, who is the offending agent, without the interference of political authority. We now come to speak of *punishment*: which, in the sense in which it is here considered, is an *artificial* consequence, annexed by political authority to an offensive act, in one instance; in the view of putting a stop to the production of events similar to the obnoxious part of its natural consequences, in other instances.

---

[1] If a man happen to take it into his head to assassinate with his own hands, or with the sword of justice, those whom he calls heretics, that is, people who think, or perhaps only speak, differently upon a subject which neither party understands, he will be as much inclined to do this at one time as at another. Fanaticism never sleeps: it is never glutted: it is never stopped by philanthropy; for it makes a merit of trampling on philanthropy: it is never stopped by conscience; for it has pressed conscience into its service. Avarice, lust, and vengeance, have piety, benevolence, honour; fanaticism has nothing to oppose it.

CHAPTER XIII

CASES UNMEET FOR PUNISHMENT

§ 1. *General view of cases unmeet for punishment*

1. THE general object which all laws have, or ought to *The end of law* have, in common, is to augment the total happiness of the *is, to augment* community; and therefore, in the first place, to exclude, as *happiness.* far as may be, every thing that tends to subtract from that happiness: in other words, to exclude mischief.

2. But all punishment is mischief: all punishment in itself *But punishment* is evil. Upon the principle of utility, if it ought at all to be *is an evil.* admitted, it ought only to be admitted in as far as it promises to exclude some greater evil.[1]

---

[1] What follows, relative to the subject of punishment, ought regularly to be *What concerns* preceded by a distinct chapter on the ends of punishment. But having little *the end, and* to say on that particular branch of the subject, which has not been said before, *several other* it seemed better, in a work, which will at any rate be but too voluminous, *topics relative to* to omit this title, reserving it for another, hereafter to be published, intituled *punishment, dis-* *The Theory of Punishment.*[a] To the same work I must refer the analysis of the *missed to an-* several possible modes of punishment, a particular and minute examination *other work.* of the nature of each, and of its advantages and disadvantages, and various other disquisitions, which did not seem absolutely necessary to be inserted here. A very few words, however, concerning the *ends* of punishment, can scarcely be dispensed with.

The immediate principal end of punishment is to control action. This *Concise view of* action is either that of the offender, or of others: that of the offender it controls *the ends of pun-* by its influence, either on his will, in which case it is said to operate in the *ishment.* way of *reformation*; or on his physical power, in which case it is said to operate by *disablement*: that of others it can influence no otherwise than by its influence over their wills; in which case it is said to operate in the way of *example*. A kind of collateral end, which it has a natural tendency to answer, is that of affording a pleasure or satisfaction to the party injured, where there is one, and, in general, to parties whose ill-will, whether on a self-regarding account, or on the account of sympathy or antipathy, has been excited by the offence. This purpose, as far as it can be answered *gratis*, is a beneficial one. But no punishment ought to be allotted merely to this purpose, because (setting aside

---

[a] This is the work which, from the Author's papers, has since been published by Mr. Dumont in French, in company with *The Theory of Reward* added to it, for the purpose of mutual illustration. It is in contemplation to publish them both in English, from the Author's manuscripts, with the benefit of any amendments that have been made by Mr. Dumont. [*Note to Edition of* 1823.]

Therefore ought not to be admitted:
1. Where groundless.

3. It is plain, therefore, that in the following cases punishment ought not to be inflicted.

1. Where it is *groundless*: where there is no mischief for it to prevent: the act not being mischievous upon the whole.

2. Inefficacious.

2. Where it must be *inefficacious*: where it cannot act so as to prevent the mischief.

3. Unprofitable.

3. Where it is *unprofitable*, or too *expensive*: where the mischief it would produce would be greater than what it prevented.

4. Or needless.

4. Where it is *needless*: where the mischief may be prevented, or cease of itself, without it: that is, at a cheaper rate.

§ 2. *Cases in which punishment is groundless*

These are,

1. Where there has never been any mischief: as in the case of consent.

4. 1. Where there has never been any mischief: where no mischief has been produced to any body by the act in question. Of this number are those in which the act was such as might, on some occasions, be mischievous or disagreeable, but the person whose interest it concerns gave his *consent* to the performance of it.[1] This consent, provided it be free, and fairly obtained,[1] is the best proof that can be produced, that, to the person who gives it, no mischief, at least no immediate mischief, upon the whole, is done. For no man can be so good a judge as the man himself, what it is gives him pleasure or displeasure.

2. Where the mischief was outweighed: as in precaution against calamity, and the exercise of powers.

5. 2. Where the mischief was *outweighed*: although a mischief was produced by that act, yet the same act was necessary to the production of a benefit which was of greater value[2] than the mischief. This may be the case with any thing that is done in the way of precaution against instant calamity, as

its effects in the way of control) no such pleasure is ever produced by punishment as can be equivalent to the pain. The punishment, however, which is allotted to the other purpose, ought, as far as it can be done without expense, to be accommodated to this. Satisfaction thus administered to a party injured, in the shape of a dissocial pleasure,[a] may be styled a vindictive satisfaction or compensation: as a compensation, administered in the shape of a self-regarding profit, or stock of pleasure, may be styled a lucrative one. See B. I. tit. vi. [Compensation]. Example is the most important end of all, in proportion as the *number* of the persons under temptation to offend is to *one*.

[1] See B. I. tit. [Justifications].   [2] See supra, Chap. iv. [Value].

[a] See Chap. x. [Motives].

also with any thing that is done in the exercise of the several sorts of powers necessary to be established in every community, to wit, domestic, judicial, military, and supreme.[1]

6. 3. Where there is a certainty of an adequate compensation: and that in all cases where the offence can be committed. This supposes two things: 1. That the offence is such as admits of an adequate compensation: 2. That such a compensation is sure to be forthcoming. Of these suppositions, the latter will be found to be a merely ideal one: a supposition that cannot, in the universality here given to it, be verified by fact. It cannot, therefore, in practice, be numbered amongst the grounds of absolute impunity. It may, however, be admitted as a ground for an abatement of that punishment, which other considerations, standing by themselves, would seem to dictate.[2]

3.—or will, for a certainty be cured by compensation.

§ 3. *Cases in which punishment must be inefficacious.*

These are,

7. 1. Where the penal provision is *not established* until after the act is done. Such are the cases, 1. Of an *ex-post facto law*; where the legislator himself appoints not a punishment till after the act is done. 2. Of a sentence beyond the law; where the judge, of his own authority, appoints a punishment which the legislator had not appointed.

1. Where the penal provision comes too late: as in,
1. An ex-post-facto law,
2. An ultra-legal sentence.

8. 2. Where the penal provision, though established, is *not conveyed* to the notice of the person on whom it seems intended that it should operate. Such is the case where the law has omitted to employ any of the expedients which are necessary, to make sure that every person whatsoever, who is within the reach of the law, be apprized of all the cases whatsoever, in which (being in the station of life he is in) he can be subjected to the penalties of the law.[3]

2. Or is not made known: as in a law not sufficiently promulgated.

[1] See Book I. tit. [Justifications].

[2] This, for example, seems to have been one ground, at least, of the favour shown by perhaps all systems of laws, to such offenders as stand upon a footing of responsibility: shown, not directly indeed to the persons themselves; but to such offences as none but responsible persons are likely to have the opportunity of engaging in. In particular, this seems to be the reason why embezzlement, in certain cases, has not commonly been punished upon the footing of theft: nor mercantile frauds upon that of common sharping.[a]

Hence the favour shown to the offences of responsible offenders: such as simple mercantile frauds.

[3] See B. II. Appendix, tit. iii. [Promulgation].

[a] See tit. [Simple merc. Defraudment].

3. *Where the will cannot be deterred from any act: as in,*

[a] *Infancy.*

9. 3. Where the penal provision, though it were conveyed to a man's notice, *could produce no effect* on him, with respect to the preventing him from engaging in any act of the *sort* in question. Such is the case, 1. In extreme *infancy*; where a man has not yet attained that state or disposition of mind in which the prospect of evils so distant as those which are held forth by the law, has the effect of influencing his conduct. 2. In *insanity*;

[b] *Insanity.*

where the person, if he has attained to that disposition, has since been deprived of it through the influence of some permanent though unseen cause. 3. In *intoxication*; where he has

[c] *Intoxication.*

been deprived of it by the transient influence of a visible cause: such as the use of wine, or opium, or other drugs, that act in this manner on the nervous system: which condition is indeed neither more nor less than a temporary insanity produced by an assignable cause.[1]

4. *Or not from the individual act in question, as in,*

10. 4. Where the penal provision (although, being conveyed to the party's notice, it might very well prevent his engaging in acts of the sort in question, provided he knew that it related to those acts) could not have this effect, with regard to the *individual* act he is about to engage in: to wit, because he knows not that it is of the number of those to which the penal provision relates. This may happen, 1. In the

[a] *Unintentionality.*

case of *unintentionality*; where he intends not to engage, and thereby knows not that he is about to engage, in the *act* in which eventually he is about to engage.[2] 2. In the case of

---

In infancy and intoxication the case can hardly be proved to come under the rule.

[1] Notwithstanding what is here said, the cases of infancy and intoxication (as we shall see hereafter) cannot be looked upon in practice as affording sufficient grounds for absolute impunity. But this exception in point of practice is no objection to the propriety of the rule in point of theory. The ground of the exception is neither more nor less than the difficulty there is of ascertaining the matter of fact: viz. whether at the requisite point of time the party was actually in the state in question; that is, whether a given case comes really under the rule. Suppose the matter of fact capable of being perfectly ascertained, without danger or mistake, the impropriety of punishment would be as indubitable in these cases as in any other.[a]

The reason for not punishing in these three cases is commonly put upon a wrong footing.

The reason that is commonly assigned for the establishing an exemption from punishment in favour of infants, insane persons, and persons under intoxication, is either false in fact, or confusedly expressed. The phrase is, that the will of these persons concurs not with the act; that they have no vicious will; or, that they have not the free use of their will. But suppose all this to be true? What is it to the purpose? Nothing: except in as far as it implies the reason given in the text.

[2] See Chap. viii. [Intentionality].

[a] See B.I. tit. iv. [Exemptions], and tit. vii. [Extenuations].

unconsciousness; where, although he may know that he is about to engage in the *act* itself, yet, from not knowing all the material *circumstances* attending it, he knows not of the *tendency* it has to produce that mischief, in contemplation of which it has been made penal in most instances. 3. In the case of *missupposal*; where, although he may know of the tendency the act has to produce that degree of mischief, he supposes it, though mistakenly, to be attended with some circumstance, or set of circumstances, which, if it had been attended with, it would either not have been productive of that mischief, or have been productive of such a greater degree of good, as has determined the legislator in such a case not to make it penal.[1] *[b] Unconsciousness.*

[c] Missupposal.

11. 5. Where, though the penal clause might exercise a full and prevailing influence, were it to act alone, yet by the *predominant* influence of some opposite cause upon the will, it must necessarily be ineffectual; because the evil which he sets himself about to undergo, in the case of his *not* engaging in the act, is so great, that the evil denounced by the penal clause, in case of his engaging in it, cannot appear greater. This may happen, 1. In the case of *physical danger*; where the evil is such as appears likely to be brought about by the unassisted powers of *nature*. 2. In the case of a *threatened mischief*; where it is such as appears likely to be brought about through the intentional and conscious agency of *man*.[2] *5. Or is acted on by an opposite superior force: as by,*

[a] Physical danger.

[b] Threatened mischief.

12. 6. Where (though the penal clause may exert a full and prevailing influence over the *will* of the party) yet his *physical faculties* (owing to the predominant influence of some physical cause) are not in a condition to follow the determination of the will: insomuch that the act is absolutely *involuntary*. Such is the case of physical *compulsion* or *restraint*, by whatever *6.— or the bodily organs cannot follow its determination: as under Physical compulsion or restraint.*

---

[1] See Chap. ix. [Consciousness].

[2] The influences of the *moral* and *religious* sanctions, or, in other words, of the motives of *love of reputation* and *religion*, are other causes, the force of which may, upon particular occasions, come to be greater than that of any punishment which the legislator is *able*, or at least which he will *think proper*, to apply. These, therefore, it will be proper for him to have his eye upon. But the force of these influences is variable and different in different times and places: the force of the foregoing influences is constant and the same, at all times and every where. These, therefore, it can never be proper to look upon as safe grounds for establishing absolute impunity: owing (as in the above-mentioned cases of infancy and intoxication) to the impracticability of ascertaining the matter of fact. *Why the influence of the moral and religious sanctions is not mentioned in the same view.*

means brought about; where the man's hand, for instance, is pushed against some object which his will disposes him *not* to touch; or tied down from touching some object which his will disposes him to touch.

§ 4. *Cases where punishment is unprofitable*

These are,

1. *Where, in the sort of case in question, the punishment would produce more evil than the offence would.*

13. 1. Where, on the one hand, the nature of the offence, on the other hand, that of the punishment, are, *in the ordinary state of things*, such, that when compared together, the evil of the latter will turn out to be greater than that of the former.

Evil producible by a punishment—its four branches—viz.

14. Now the evil of the punishment divides itself into four branches, by which so many different sets of persons are affected. 1. The evil of *coercion* or *restraint*: or the pain which it gives a man not to be able to do the act, whatever it be, which by the apprehension of the punishment he is deterred from doing. This is felt by those by whom the law is *observed*.

[a] Restraint.

[b] Apprehension.

2. The evil of *apprehension*: or the pain which a man, who has exposed himself to punishment, feels at the thoughts of undergoing it. This is felt by those by whom the law has been *broken*, and who feel themselves in *danger* of its being executed

[c] Sufferance.

upon them. 3. The evil of *sufferance*[1]: or the pain which a man feels, in virtue of the punishment itself, from the time when he begins to undergo it. This is felt by those by whom the law is broken, and upon whom it comes actually to be

[d] Derivative evils.

executed. 4. The pain of sympathy, and the other *derivative* evils resulting to the persons who are in *connection* with the several classes of original sufferers just mentioned.[2] Now of these four lots of evil, the first will be greater or less, according to the nature of the act from which the party is restrained: the second and third according to the nature of the punishment which stands annexed to that offence.

(The evil of the offence being different, according to the nature of the offence, cannot be represented here.)

15. On the other hand, as to the evil of the offence, this will also, of course, be greater or less, according to the nature of each offence. The proportion between the one evil and the other will therefore be different in the case of each particular offence. The cases, therefore, where punishment is unprofit-

---

[1] See Chap. v. [Pleasures and Pains].
[2] See Chap. xii. [Consequences] 4.

able on this ground, can by no other means be discovered, than by an examination of each particular offence; which is what will be the business of the body of the work.

16. 2. Where, although in the *ordinary state* of things, the evil resulting from the punishment is not greater than the benefit which is likely to result from the force with which it operates, during the same space of time, towards the excluding the evil of the offences, yet it may have been rendered so by the influence of some *occasional circumstances*. In the number of these circumstances may be, 1. The multitude of delinquents at a particular juncture; being such as would increase, beyond the ordinary measure, the *quantum* of the second and third lots, and thereby also of a part of the fourth lot, in the evil of the punishment. 2. The extraordinary value of the services of some one delinquent; in the case where the effect of the punishment would be to deprive the community of the benefit of those services. 3. The displeasure of the *people*; that is, of an indefinite number of the members of the *same* community, in cases where (owing to the influences of some occasional incident) they happen to conceive, that the offence or the offender ought not to be punished at all, or at least ought not to be punished in the way in question. 4. The displeasure of *foreign powers*; that is, of the governing body, or a considerable number of the members of some *foreign* community or communities, with which the community in question is connected.

2.—Or in the individual case in question: by reason of

[a] The multitude of delinquents.

[b] The value of a delinquent's service.

[c] The displeasure of the people.

[d] The displeasure of foreign powers.

§ 5. *Cases where punishment is needless.*

These are,

17. 1. Where the purpose of putting an end to the practice may be attained as effectually at a cheaper rate: by instruction, for instance, as well as by terror: by informing the understanding, as well as by exercising an immediate influence on the will. This seems to be the case with respect to all those offences which consist in the disseminating pernicious principles in matters of *duty*; of whatever kind the duty be; whether political, or moral, or religious. And this, whether such principles be disseminated *under*, or even *without*, a sincere persuasion of their being beneficial. I say, even *without*:

1. Where the mischief is to be prevented at a cheaper rate; as,

By instruction.

for though in such a case it is not instruction that can prevent the writer from endeavouring to inculcate his principles, yet it may the readers from adopting them: without which, his endeavouring to inculcate them will do no harm. In such a case, the sovereign will commonly have little need to take an active part: if it be the interest of *one* individual to inculcate principles that are pernicious, it will as surely be the interest of *other* individuals to expose them. But if the sovereign must needs take a part in the controversy, the pen is the proper weapon to combat error with, not the sword.

CHAPTER XIV

OF THE PROPORTION BETWEEN PUNISHMENTS AND OFFENCES

1. WE have seen that the general object of all laws is to prevent mischief; that is to say, when it is worth while; but that, where there are no other means of doing this than punishment, there are four cases in which it is *not* worth while. *Recapitulation.*

2. When it *is* worth while, there are four subordinate designs or objects, which, in the course of his endeavours to compass, as far as may be, that one general object, a legislator, whose views are governed by the principle of utility, comes naturally to propose to himself. *Four objects of punishment.*

3. 1. His first, most extensive, and most eligible object, is to prevent, in as far as it is possible, and worth while, all sorts of offences whatsoever:[1] in other words, so to manage, that no offence whatsoever may be committed. *1st Object—to prevent all offences.*

4. 2. But if a man must needs commit an offence of some kind or other, the next object is to induce him to commit an offence *less* mischievous, *rather* than one *more* mischievous, of two offences that will either of them suit his purpose. *2nd Object—to prevent the worst.*

5. 3. When a man has resolved upon a particular offence, the next object is to dispose him to do *no more* mischief than is *necessary* to his purpose: in other words, to do as little mischief as is consistent with the benefit he has in view. *3rd Object—to keep down the mischief.*

6. 4. The last object is, whatever the mischief be, which it is proposed to prevent, to prevent it at as *cheap* a rate as possible. *4th Object—to act at the least expense.*

7. Subservient to these four objects, or purposes, must be the rules or canons by which the proportion of punishments[2] to offences is to be governed. *Rules of proportion between punishments and offences.*

---

[1] By *offences* I mean, at present, acts which appear to him to have a tendency to produce mischief.

[2] The same rules (it is to be observed) may be applied, with little variation, to rewards as well as punishment: in short, to motives in general, which, *The same rule applicable to*

**Rule 1.
Outweigh the
profit of the
offence.**

8. Rule 1. The first object, it has been seen, is to prevent, in as far as it is worth while, all sorts of offences; therefore, *The value of the punishment must not be less in any case than what is sufficient to outweigh that of the profit[1] of the offence.[2]*

If it be, the offence (unless some other considerations, independent of the punishment, should intervene and operate efficaciously in the character of tutelary motives[3]) will be sure to be committed notwithstanding[4]: the whole lot of

**motives in
general.**

according as they are of the pleasurable or painful kind, are of the nature of *reward* or *punishment*: and, according as the act they are applied to produce is of the positive or negative kind, are styled impelling or restraining. See Chap. x. [Motives] 47.

**Profit may be of
any other kind
as well as
pecuniary.**

[1] By the profit of an offence, is to be understood, not merely the pecuniary profit, but the pleasure or advantage, of whatever kind it be, which a man reaps, or expects to reap, from the gratification of the desire which prompted him to engage in the offence.[a]

**Impropriety of
the notion that
the punishment
ought not to in-
crease with the
temptation.**

It is the profit (that is, the expectation of the profit) of the offence that constitutes the *impelling* motive, or, where there are several, the sum of the impelling motives, by which a man is prompted to engage in the offence. It is the punishment, that is, the expectation of the punishment, that constitutes the *restraining* motive, which, either by itself, or in conjunction with others, is to act upon him in a *contrary* direction, so as to induce him to abstain from engaging in the offence. Accidental circumstances apart, the strength of the temptation is as the force of the seducing, that is, of the impelling motive or motives. To say then, as authors of great merit and great name have said, that the punishment ought not to increase with the strength of the temptation, is as much as to say in mechanics, that the moving force or *momentum* of the *power* need not increase in proportion to the momentum of the *burthen*.

[2] Beccaria, dei diletti, § 6, id. trad. par. Morellet, § 23.

[3] See Chap. xi. [Dispositions] 29.

[4] It is a well-known adage, though it is to be hoped not a true one, that every man has his price. It is commonly meant of a man's virtue. This saying, though in a very different sense, was strictly verified by some of the Anglo-Saxon laws: by which a fixed price was set, not upon a man's virtue indeed, but upon his life: that of the sovereign himself among the rest. For 200 shillings you might have killed a peasant: for six times as much, a nobleman: for six-and-thirty times as much you might have killed the king.[b] A king in those days was worth exactly 7,200 shillings. If then the heir to the throne, for example, grew weary of waiting for it, he had a secure and legal way of gratifying his impatience: he had but to kill the king with one hand, and pay himself with the other, and all was right. An earl Godwin, or a duke Streon, could have bought the lives of a whole dynasty. It is plain, that if ever a king in those days died in his bed, he must have had something else, besides this law, to thank for it. This being the production of a remote and barbarous age, the absurdity of it is presently recognized: but, upon examination, it would be found, that the freshest laws of the most civilized nations are continually

[a] See Chap. x. [Motives] § 1.
[b] Wilkins' Leg. Anglo-Sax. p. 71, 72. See Hume, Vol. I, App. I. p. 219.

unishment will be thrown away: it will be altogether *in-fficacious*.[1]

9. The above rule has been often objected to, on account *The propriety of* f its seeming harshness: but this can only have happened *taking the* or want of its being properly understood. The strength of *strength of the* he temptation, *cæteris parubis*, is as the profit of the offence: *ground of abate-* ne quantum of the punishment must rise with the profit *ment, no objec-* f the offence: *cæteris paribus*, it must therefore rise with the *tion to this rule.* rength of the temptation. This there is no disputing. True . is, that the stronger the temptation, the less conclusive is ne indication which the act of delinquency affords of the epravity of the offender's disposition.[2] So far then as the bsence of any aggravation, arising from extraordinary epravity of disposition, may operate, or at the utmost, so ar as the presence of a ground of extenuation, resulting from ne innocence or beneficence of the offender's disposition, an operate, the strength of the temptation may operate in batement of the demand for punishment. But it can never perate so far as to indicate the propriety of making the unishment ineffectual, which it is sure to be when brought elow the level of the apparent profit of the offence.

The partial benevolence which should prevail for the eduction of it below this level, would counteract as well nose purposes which such a motive would actually have in iew, as those more extensive purposes which benevolence ught to have in view: it would be cruelty not only to the ublic, but to the very persons in whose behalf it pleads: in s effects, I mean, however opposite in its intention. Cruelty › the public, that is cruelty to the innocent, by suffering iem, for want of an adequate protection, to lie exposed › the mischief of the offence: cruelty even to the offender mself, by punishing him to no purpose, and without the

ling into the same error.[a] This, in short, is the case wheresoever the punish-ent is fixed while the profit of delinquency is indefinite: or, to speak more ecisely, where the punishment is limited to such a mark, that the profit of linquency may reach beyond it.
[1] See Chap. xiii. [Cases unmeet], § 1.
[2] See Chap. xi. [Dispositions], 42.

[a] See in particular the *English Statute laws* throughout, *Bonaparte's* Penal ode, and the recently enacted or not enacted *Spanish* Penal Code.—*Note by* Author, July 1822.

chance of compassing that beneficial end, by which alone
the introduction of the evil of punishment is to be justified.

Rule 2.
Venture more
against a great
offence than a
small one.

10. Rule 2. But whether a given offence shall be prevented
in a given degree by a given quantity of punishment, is never
any thing better than a chance; for the purchasing of which
whatever punishment is employed, is so much expended in
advance. However, for the sake of giving it the better
chance of outweighing the profit of the offence,

The greater the mischief of the offence, the greater is the expense
which it may be worth while to be at, in the way of punishment.

Rule 3.
Cause the least
of two offences
to be preferred.

11. Rule 3. The next object is, to induce a man to choose
always the least mischievous of two offences; therefore

Where two offences come in competition, the punishment for the
greater offence must be sufficient to induce a man to prefer the less.

Rule 4.
Punish for each
particle of the
mischief.

12. Rule 4. When a man has resolved upon a particular
offence, the next object is, to induce him to do no more
mischief than what is necessary for his purpose: therefore

The punishment should be adjusted in such manner to each
particular offence, that for every part of the mischief there may be a
motive to restrain the offender from giving birth to it.[3]

Rule 5.
Punish in no
degree without
special reason.

13. Rule 5. The last object is, whatever mischief is guarded
against, to guard against it at as cheap a rate as possible:
therefore

Example—In-
cendiarism and
coining.

[1] For example, if it can ever be worth while to be at the expense of so
horrible a punishment as that of burning alive, it will be more so in the view
of preventing such a crime as that of murder or incendiarism, than in the view
of preventing the uttering of a piece of bad money. See B. I. tit. [Defraud-
ment touching the Coin] and [Incendiarism].

[2] Espr. des Loix, L. vi. c. 16.

Example.—In
blows given and
money stolen.

[3] If any one have any doubt of this, let him conceive the offence to be
divided into as many separate offences as there are distinguishable parcels of
mischief that result from it. Let it consist, for example, in a man's giving you
ten blows, or stealing from you ten shillings. If then, for giving you ten blows
he is punished no more than for giving you five, the giving you five of the
ten blows is an offence for which there is no punishment at all: which being
understood, as often as a man gives you five blows, he will be sure to give
you five more, since he may have the pleasure of giving you these five for
nothing. In like manner, if for stealing from you ten shillings, he is punished
no more than for stealing five, the stealing of the remaining five of those ten
shillings is an offence for which there is no punishment at all. This rule is
violated in almost every page of every body of laws I have ever seen.

The profit, it is to be observed, though frequently, is not constantly, proportioned to the mischief: for example, where a thief, along with the things he
covets, steals others which are of no use to him. This may happen through
wantonness, indolence, precipitation, &c. &c.

The punishment ought in no case to be more than what is necessary to bring it into conformity with the rules here given.

14. Rule 6. It is further to be observed, that owing to the different manners and degrees in which persons under different circumstances are affected by the same exciting cause, a punishment which is the same in name will not always either really produce, or even so much as appear to others to produce, in two different persons the same degree of pain: therefore

Rule 6. Attend to circumstances influencing sensibility.

That the quantity actually inflicted on each individual offender may correspond to the quantity intended for similar offenders in general, the several circumstances influencing sensibility ought always to be taken into account.[1]

15. Of the above rules of proportion, the four first, we may perceive, serve to mark out the limits on the side of diminution; the limits *below* which a punishment ought not to be *diminished*: the fifth, the limits on the side of increase; the limits *above* which it ought not to be *increased*. The five first are calculated to serve as guides to the legislator: the sixth is calculated, in some measure, indeed, for the same purpose; but principally for guiding the judge in his endeavours to conform, on both sides, to the intentions of the legislator.

Comparative view of the above rules.

16. Let us look back a little. The first rule, in order to render it more conveniently applicable to practice, may need perhaps to be a little more particularly unfolded. It is to be observed, then, that for the sake of accuracy, it was necessary, instead of the word *quantity* to make use of the less perspicuous term *value*. For the word *quantity* will not properly include the circumstances either of certainty or proximity: circumstances which, in estimating the value of a lot of pain or pleasure, must always be taken into the account.[2] Now, on the one hand, a lot of punishment is a lot of pain; on the other hand, the profit of an offence is a lot of pleasure, or what is equivalent to it. But the profit of the offence is commonly more *certain* than the punishment, or, what comes to the same thing, *appears* so at least to the offender. It is at any rate commonly more *immediate*. It follows, therefore, that, in order to maintain its superiority over the profit of the offence, the punishment must have its value made up in some

Into the account of the value of a punishment, must be taken its deficiency in point of certainty and proximity.

[1] See Chap. vi. [Sensibility].   [2] See Chap. iv. [Value].

other way, in proportion to that whereby it falls short in the two points of *certainty* and *proximity*. Now there is no other way in which it can receive any addition to its *value*, but by receiving an addition in point of *magnitude*. Wherever then the value of the punishment falls short, either in point of *certainty*, or of *proximity*, of that of the profit of the offence, it must receive a proportionable addition in point of *magnitude*.[1]

Also, into the account of the mischief, and profit of the offence, the mischief and profit of other offences of the same habit.

17. Yet farther. To make sure of giving the value of the punishment the superiority over that of the offence, it may be necessary, in some cases, to take into the account the profit not only of the *individual* offence to which the punishment is to be annexed, but also of such *other* offences of the *same sort* as the offender is likely to have already committed without detection. This random mode of calculation, severe as it is, it will be impossible to avoid having recourse to, in certain cases: in such, to wit, in which the profit is pecuniary, the chance of detection very small, and the obnoxious act of such a nature as indicates a habit: for example, in the case of frauds against the coin. If it be *not* recurred to, the practice of committing the offence will be sure to be, upon the balance of the account, a gainful practice. That being the case, the legislator will be absolutely sure of *not* being able to suppress it, and the whole punishment that is bestowed upon it will be thrown away. In a word (to keep to the same expressions we set out with) that whole quantity of punishment will be *inefficacious*.

Rule 7. Want of certainty must be made up in magnitude.

18. Rule 7. These things being considered, the three following rules may be laid down by way of supplement and explanation to Rule 1.

To enable the value of the punishment to outweigh that of the profit of the offence, it must be increased, in point of magnitude, in proportion as it falls short in point of certainty,

Rule 8. So also want of proximity.

19. Rule 8. *Punishment must be further increased in point of magnitude, in proportion as it falls short in point of proximity.*

Rule 9. For acts indicative of a habit punish as for the habit.

20. Rule 9. *Where the act is conclusively indicative of a habit such an increase must be given to the punishment as may enable it to outweigh the profit not only of the individual offence, but of such*

[1] It is for this reason, for example, that simple compensation is never looked upon as sufficient punishment for theft or robbery.

other like offences as are likely to have been committed with impunity by the same offender.

21. There may be a few other circumstances or considera- *The remaining* tions which may influence, in some small degree, the demand *rules are of less importance.* for punishment: but as the propriety of these is either not so demonstrable, or not so constant, or the application of them not so determinate, as that of the foregoing, it may be doubted whether they be worth putting on a level with the others.

22. Rule 10. *When a punishment, which in point of quality* *Rule 10.* *is particularly well calculated to answer its intention, cannot exist* *For the sake of in less than a certain quantity, it may sometimes be of use, for the* *quality, increase in quantity. sake of employing it, to stretch a little beyond that quantity which, on other accounts, would be strictly necessary.*

23. Rule 11. *In particular, this may sometimes be the case,* *Rule 11.* *where the punishment proposed is of such a nature as to be par-* *Particularly for ticularly well calculated to answer the purpose of a moral lesson.*[1] *a moral lesson.*

24. Rule 12. The tendency of the above considerations is *Rule 12.* to dictate an augmentation in the punishment: the following *Attend to cir- cumstances rule operates in the way of diminution. There are certain *which may ren- cases (it has been seen[2]) in which, by the influence of accidental *der punishment circumstances, punishment may be rendered unprofitable *unprofitable.* in the whole: in the same cases it may chance to be rendered unprofitable as to a part only. Accordingly,

In adjusting the quantum of punishment, the circumstances, by which all punishment may be rendered unprofitable, ought to be attended to.

25. Rule 13. It is to be observed, that the more various *Rule 13.* and minute any set of provisions are, the greater the chance is *For simplicity's sake, small dis- that any article in them will not be borne in mind: without *proportions may which, no benefit can ensue from it. Distinctions, which are *be neglected.*

---

[1] A punishment may be said to be calculated to answer the purpose of a *A punishment* moral lesson, when, by reason of the ignominy it stamps upon the offence, it *applied by way* is calculated to inspire the public with sentiments of aversion towards those *of moral lesson,* pernicious habits and dispositions with which the offence appears to be con- *what.* nected; and thereby to inculcate the opposite beneficial habits and dispositions.

It is this, for example, if any thing, that must justify the application of so *Example.—In* severe a punishment as the infamy of a public exhibition, hereinafter proposed, *simple corporal* for him who lifts up his hand against a woman, or against his father. See *injuries.* B. I. tit. [Simp. corporal injuries].

It is partly on this principle, I suppose, that military legislators have justified *Example.—In* to themselves the inflicting death on the soldier who lifts up his hand against *military laws.* his superior officer.

[2] See Chap. xiii. [Cases unmeet], § 4.

more complex than what the conceptions of those whose conduct it is designed to influence can take in, will even be worse than useless. The whole system will present a confused appearance: and thus the effect, not only of the proportions established by the articles in question, but of whatever is connected with them, will be destroyed.[1] To draw a precise line of direction in such case seems impossible. However, by way of memento, it may be of some use to subjoin the following rule.

Among provisions designed to perfect the proportion between punishments and offences, if any occur, which, by their own particular good effects, would not make up for the harm they would do by adding to the intricacy of the Code, they should be omitted.[2]

Auxiliary force of the physical, moral, and religious sanction, not here allowed for— why.

26. It may be remembered, that the political sanction, being that to which the sort of punishment belongs, which in this chapter is all along in view, is but one of four sanctions, which may all of them contribute their share towards producing the same effects. It may be expected, therefore, that in adjusting the quantity of political punishment, allowance should be made for the assistance it may meet with from those other controlling powers. True it is, that from each of these several sources a very powerful assistance may sometimes be derived. But the case is, that (setting aside the moral sanction, in the case where the force of it is expressly adopted into and modified by the political[3]) the force of those other powers is never determinate enough to be depended upon. It can never be reduced, like political punishment, into exact lots, nor meted out in number, quantity, and value. The legislator is therefore obliged to provide the full complement of punishment, as if he were sure of not receiving any assistance whatever from any of those quarters. If he does, so much the better: but lest he should not, it is necessary he should, at all events, make that provision which depends upon himself.

[1] See B. II. tit. [Purposes], Append. tit. [Composition].

Proportionality carried very far in the present work—why.

[2] Notwithstanding this rule, my fear is, that in the ensuing model, I may be thought to have carried my endeavours at proportionality too far. Hitherto scarce any attention has been paid to it. Montesquieu seems to have been almost the first who has had the least idea of any such thing. In such a matter, therefore, excess seemed more eligible than defect. The difficulty is to invent: that done, if any thing seems superfluous, it is easy to retrench.

[3] See B. I. tit. [Punishments].

27. It may be of use, in this place, to recapitulate the *Recapitulation.*
several circumstances, which, in establishing the proportion
betwixt punishments and offences, are to be attended to.
These seem to be as follows:

1. *On the part of the offence:*
    1. The profit of the offence;
    2. The mischief of the offence;
    3. The profit and mischief of other greater or lesser
       offences, of different sorts, which the offender may
       have to choose out of;
    4. The profit and mischief of other offences, of the same
       sort, which the same offender may probably have
       been guilty of already.

2. *On the part of the punishment:*
    5. The magnitude of the punishment: composed of its
       intensity and duration;
    6. The deficiency of the punishment in point of cer-
       tainty;
    7. The deficiency of the punishment in point of prox-
       imity;
    8. The quality of the punishment;
    9. The accidental advantage in point of quality of a
       punishment, not strictly needed in point of quan-
       tity;
    10. The use of a punishment of a particular quality, in the
        character of a moral lesson.

3. *On the part of the offender:*
    11. The responsibility of the class of persons in a way to
        offend;
    12. The sensibility of each particular offender;
    13. The particular merits or useful qualities of any par-
        ticular offender, in case of a punishment which
        might deprive the community of the benefit of
        them;
    14. The multitude of offenders on any particular occa-
        sion.

4. *On the part of the public,* at any particular conjuncture:
    15. The inclinations of the people, for or against any
        quantity or mode of punishment;
    16. The inclinations of foreign powers.

5. *On the part of the law;* that is, of the public for a continuance:

17. The necessity of making small sacrifices, in point of proportionality, for the sake of simplicity.

The nicety here observed vindicated from the charge of inutility.

28. There are some, perhaps, who, at first sight, may look upon the nicety employed in the adjustment of such rules, as so much labour lost: for gross ignorance, they will say, never troubles itself about laws, and passion does not calculate. But the evil of ignorance admits of cure[1]: and as to the proposition that passion does not calculate this, like most of these very general and oracular propositions, is not true. When matters of such importance as pain and pleasure are at stake, and these in the highest degree (the only matters, in short, that can be of importance) who is there that does not calculate? Men calculate, some with less exactness, indeed, some with more: but all men calculate. I would not say, that even a madman does not calculate.[2] Passion calculates, more or less, in every man: in different men, according to the warmth or coolness of their dispositions: according to the firmness or irritability of their minds: according to the nature of the motives by which they are acted upon. Happily, of all passions, that is the most given to calculation, from the excesses of which, by reason of its strength, constancy, and universality, society has most to apprehend:[3] I mean that which corresponds to the motive of pecuniary interest: so that these niceties, if such they are to be called, have the best chance of being efficacious, where efficacy is of the most importance.

[1] See Append. tit. [Promulgation].
[2] There are few madmen but what are observed to be afraid of the strait waistcoat.
[3] See Chap. xii. [Consequences], 33.

CHAPTER XV

OF THE PROPERTIES TO BE GIVEN TO A LOT OF PUNISHMENT

1. It has been shown what the rules are, which ought to be *Properties are to* observed in adjusting the proportion between the punishment *be governed by* and the offence. The properties to be given to a lot of punish- *proportion.* ment, in every instance, will of course be such as it stands in need of, in order to be capable of being applied, in conformity to those rules: the *quality* will be regulated by the *quantity*.

2. The first of those rules, we may remember, was, that *Property 1.* the quantity of punishment must not be less, in any case, than *Variability.* what is sufficient to outweigh the profit of the offence: since, as often as it is less, the whole lot (unless by accident the deficiency should be supplied from some of the other sanctions) is thrown away: it is *inefficacious*. The fifth was, that the punishment ought in no case to be more than what is required by the several other rules: since, if it be, all that is above that quantity is *needless*. The fourth was, that the punishment should be adjusted in such manner to each individual offence, that every part of the mischief of that offence may have a penalty (that is, a tutelary motive) to encounter it: otherwise, with respect to so much of the offence as has not a penalty to correspond to it, it is as if there were no punishment in the case. Now to none of those rules can a lot of punishment be conformable, unless, for every variation in point of quantity, in the mischief of the species of offences to which it is annexed, such lot of punishment admits of a correspondent variation. To prove this, let the profit of the offence admit of a multitude of degrees. Suppose it, then, at any one of these degrees: if the punishment be less than what is suitable to that degree, it will be *inefficacious*; it will be so much thrown away: if it be more, as far as the difference extends, it will be *needless*; it will therefore be thrown away also in that case.

The first property, therefore, that ought to be given to a

lot of punishment, is that of being variable in point of quantity, in conformity to every variation which can take place in either the profit or mischief of the offence. This property might, perhaps, be termed, in a single word, *variability*.

Property 2. Equability.

3. A second property, intimately connected with the former, may be styled *equability*. It will avail but little, that a mode of punishment (proper in all other respects) has been established by the legislator; and that capable of being screwed up or let down to any degree that can be required; if, after all, whatever degree of it be pitched upon, that same degree shall be liable, according to circumstances, to produce a very heavy degree of pain, or a very slight one, or even none at all. In this case, as in the former, if circumstances happen one way, there will be a great deal of pain produced which will be *needless*: if the other way, there will be no pain at all applied, or none that will be *efficacious*. A punishment, when liable to this irregularity, may be styled an unequable one: when free from it, an equable one. The quantity of pain produced by the punishment will, it is true, depend in a considerable degree upon circumstances distinct from the nature of the punishment itself: upon the condition which the offender is in, with respect to the circumstances by which a man's sensibility is liable to be influenced. But the influence of these very circumstances will in many cases be reciprocally influenced by the nature of the punishment: in other words, the pain which is produced by any mode of punishment, will be the joint effect of the punishment which is applied to him, and the circumstances in which he is exposed to it. Now there are some punishments, of which the effect may be liable to undergo a greater alteration by the influence of such foreign circumstances, than the effect of other punishments is liable to undergo. So far, then, as this is the case, equability or unequability may be regarded as properties belonging to the punishment itself.

Punishments which are apt to be deficient in this respect.

4. An example of a mode of punishment which is apt to be unequable, is that of *banishment*, when the *locus a quo* (or place the party is banished from) is some determinate place appointed by the law, which perhaps the offender cares not whether he ever see or no. This is also the case with *pecuniary*, or

quasi-pecuniary punishment, when it respects some particular species of property, which the offender may have been possessed of, or not, as it may happen. All these punishments may be split down into parcels, and measured out with the utmost nicety: being divisible by time, at least, if by nothing else. They are not, therefore, any of them defective in point of variability: and yet, in many cases, this defect in point of equability may make them as unfit for use as if they were.[1]

5. The third rule of proportion was, that where two offences come in competition, the punishment for the greater offence must be sufficient to induce a man to prefer the less. *Property 3. Commensurability to other punishments.* Now, to be sufficient for this purpose, it must be evidently and uniformly greater: greater, not in the eyes of some men only, but of all men who are liable to be in a situation to take their choice between the two offences; that is, in effect, of all mankind. In other words, the two punishments must be perfectly *commensurable*. Hence arises a third property, which may be termed *commensurability*: to wit, with reference to other punishments.[2]

6. But punishments of different kinds are in very few instances uniformly greater one than another; especially when the lowest degrees of that which is ordinarily the greater, are compared with the highest degrees of that which is ordinarily the less; in other words, punishments of different kinds are in few instances uniformly commensurable. The only certain and universal means of making two lots of punishment perfectly commensurable, is by making the lesser an ingredient in the composition of the greater. This may be done in either of two ways. 1. By adding to the lesser punishment another quantity of punishment of the same kind. 2. By adding to it *How two lots of punishment may be rendered perfectly commensurable.*

---

[1] By the English law, there are several offences which are punished by a total forfeiture of moveables, not extending to immoveables. This is the case with suicide, and with certain species of theft and homicide. In some cases, this is the principal punishment: in others, even the only one. The consequence is, that if a man's fortune happens to consist in moveables, he is ruined; if in immoveables, he suffers nothing.

[2] See *View of the Hard-Labour Bill*, Lond. 1778, p. 100.

For the idea of this property, I must acknowledge myself indebted to an anonymous letter in the St. James's Chronicle, of the 27th of September, 1777; the author of which is totally unknown to me. If any one should be disposed to think lightly of the instruction, on account of the channel by which it was first communicated, let him tell me where I can find an idea more ingenious or original.

another quantity of a different kind. The latter mode is not less certain than the former: for though one cannot always be absolutely sure, that to the same person a given punishment will appear greater than another given punishment; yet one may be always absolutely sure, that any given punishment, so as it does but come into contemplation, will appear greater than none at all.

Property 4.
Character-
isticalness.

7. Again: Punishment cannot act any farther than in as far as the idea of it, and of its connection with the offence, is present in the mind. The idea of it, if not present, cannot act at all; and then the punishment itself must be *inefficacious.* Now, to be present, it must be remembered, and to be remembered it must have been learnt. But of all punishments that can be imagined, there are none of which the connection with the offence is either so easily learnt, or so efficaciously remembered, as those of which the idea is already in part associated with some part of the idea of the offence: which is the case when the one and the other have some circumstance that belongs to them in common. When this is the case with a punishment and an offence, the punishment is said to bear an *analogy* to, or to be *characteristic* of, the offence.[1] *Characteristicalness* is, therefore, a fourth property, which on this account ought to be given, whenever it can conveniently be given, to a lot of punishment.

The mode of
punishment the
most eminently
characteristic, is
that of retalia-
tion.

8. It is obvious, that the effect of this contrivance will be the greater, as the analogy is the closer. The analogy will be the closer, the more *material*[2] that circumstance is, which is in common. Now the most material circumstance that can belong to an offence and a punishment in common, is the hurt or damage which they produce. The closest analogy, therefore, that can subsist between an offence and the punishment annexed to it, is that which subsists between them when the hurt or damage they produce is of the same nature: in other words, that which is constituted by the circumstance of identity in point of damage.[3] Accordingly, the mode of

[1] See Montesq. Esp. des Loix, L. xii, chap. iv. He seems to have the property of characteristicalness in view; but that the idea he had of it was very indistinct, appears from the extravagant advantages he attributes to it.

[2] See Chap. vii [Actions], 3.

[3] Besides this, there are a variety of other ways in which the punishment may bear an analogy to the offence. This will be seen by looking over the table of punishments.

punishment, which of all others bears the closest analogy to the offence, is that which in the proper and exact sense of the word is termed *retaliation*. Retaliation, therefore, in the few cases in which it is practicable, and not too expensive, will have one great advantage over every other mode of punishment.

9. Again: It is the idea only of the punishment (or, in other words, the *apparent* punishment) that really acts upon the mind; the punishment itself (the *real* punishment) acts not any farther than as giving rise to that idea. It is the apparent punishment, therefore, that does all the service, I mean in the way of example, which is the principal object.[1] It is the real punishment that does all the mischief.[2] Now the ordinary and obvious way of increasing the magnitude of the apparent punishment, is by increasing the magnitude of the real. The apparent magnitude, however, may to a certain degree be increased by other less expensive means: whenever, therefore, at the same time that these less expensive means would have answered that purpose, an additional real punishment is employed, this additional real punishment is *needless*. As to these less expensive means, they consist, 1. In the choice of a particular mode of punishment, a punishment of a particular quality, independent of the quantity.[3] 2. In a particular set of *solemnities* distinct from the punishment itself, and accompanying the execution of it.[4]

Property 5. Exemplarity.

10. A mode of punishment, according as the appearance of it bears a greater proportion to the reality, may be said to be the more *exemplary*. Now as to what concerns the choice of the punishment itself, there is not any means by which a given quantity of punishment can be rendered more exemplary, than by choosing it of such a sort as shall bear an *analogy* to the offence. Hence another reason for rendering the punishment analogous to, or in other words characteristic of, the offence.

The most effectual way of rendering a punishment exemplary is by means of analogy.

11. Punishment, it is still to be remembered, is in itself an expense: it is in itself an evil.[5] Accordingly the fifth rule of proportion is, not to produce more of it than what is demanded by the other rules. But this is the case as often as

Property 6. Frugality.

---

[1] See Chap. xiii. [Cases unmeet], § 1, 2. note.   [2] Ib. § 4. par. iii.
[3] See B. I. tit. [Punishments].   [4] See B. II. tit. [Execution].
[5] Ch. xiii. [Cases unmeet], par. iii.

any particle of pain is produced, which contributes nothing to the effect proposed. Now if any mode of punishment is more apt than another to produce any such superfluous and needless pain, it may be styled *unfrugal*; if less, it may be styled *frugal*. *Frugality*, therefore, is a sixth property to be wished for in a mode of punishment.

Frugality belongs in perfection to pecuniary punishment.

12. The perfection of frugality, in a mode of punishment, is where not only no superfluous pain is produced on the part of the person punished, but even that same operation, by which he is subjected to pain, is made to answer the purpose of producing pleasure on the part of some other person. Understand a profit or stock of pleasure of the self-regarding kind: for a pleasure of the dissocial kind is produced almost of course, on the part of all persons in whose breasts the offence has excited the sentiment of ill-will. Now this is the case with pecuniary punishment, as also with such punishments of the *quasi-pecuniary* kind as consist in the subtraction of such a species of possession as is transferable from one party to another. The pleasure, indeed, produced by such an operation, is not in general equal to the pain[1]: it may, however, be so in particular circumstances, as where he, from whom the thing is taken, is very rich, and he, to whom it is given, very poor: and, be it what it will, it is always so much more than can be produced by any other mode of punishment.

Exemplarity and frugality, in what they differ and agree.

13. The properties of exemplarity and frugality seem to pursue the same immediate end, though by different courses. Both are occupied in diminishing the ratio of the real suffering to the apparent: but exemplarity tends to increase the apparent; frugality to reduce the real.

Other properties of inferior importance.

14. Thus much concerning the properties to be given to punishments in general, to whatsoever offences they are to be applied. Those which follow are of less importance, either as referring only to certain offences in particular, or depending upon the influence of transitory and local circumstances.

In the first place, the four distinct ends into which the main and general end of punishment is divisible,[2] may give rise to so many distinct properties, according as any particular mode of punishment appears to be more particularly adapted to the compassing of one or of another of those ends. To that

---

[1] Ib. note.   [2] See Chap. xiii. [Cases unmeet], par. 2. note.

of *example*, as being the principal one, a particular property has already been adapted. There remains the three inferior ones of *reformation, disablement,* and *compensation.*

15. A seventh property, therefore, to be wished for in a mode of punishment, is that of *subserviency to reformation*, or *reforming tendency*. Now any punishment is subservient to reformation in proportion to its *quantity*: since the greater the punishment a man has experienced, the stronger is the tendency it has to create in him an aversion towards the offence which was the cause of it: and that with respect to all offences alike. But there are certain punishments which, with regard to certain offences, have a particular tendency to produce that effect by reason of their *quality*: and where this is the case, the punishments in question, as applied to the offences in question, will *pro tanto* have the advantage over all others. This influence will depend upon the nature of the motive which is the cause of the offence: the punishment most subservient to reformation will be the sort of punishment that is best calculated to invalidate the force of that motive.

Property 7. Subserviency to reformation.

16. Thus, in offences originating from the motive of ill-will,[1] that punishment has the strongest reforming tendency, which is best calculated to weaken the force of the irascible affections. And more particularly, in that sort of offence which consists in an obstinate refusal, on the part of the offender, to do something which is lawfully required of him,[2] and in which the obstinacy is in great measure kept up by his resentment against those who have an interest in forcing him to compliance, the most efficacious punishment seems to be that of confinement to spare diet.

—applied to offences originating in ill-will.

17. Thus, also, in offences which owe their birth to the joint influence of indolence and pecuniary interest, that punishment seems to possess the strongest reforming tendency, which is best calculated to weaken the force of the former of those dispositions. And more particularly, in the cases of theft, embezzlement, and every species of defraudment, the mode of punishment best adapted to this purpose seems, in most cases, to be that of penal labour.

—to offences originating in indolence joined to pecuniary interest.

18. An eighth property to be given to a lot of punishment in certain cases, is that of *efficacy with respect to disablement*, or,

Property 8. Efficacy with respect to disablement.

[1] See Chap. x. [Motives].   [2] See B. I. tit. [Offences against Justice].

U

as it might be styled more briefly, *disabling efficacy*. This is a property which may be given in perfection to a lot of punishment; and that with much greater certainty than the property of subserviency to reformation. The inconvenience is, that this property is apt, in general, to run counter to that of frugality: there being, in most cases, no certain way of disabling a man from doing mischief, without, at the same time, disabling him, in a great measure, from doing good, either to himself or others. The mischief therefore of the offence must be so great as to demand a very considerable lot of punishment, for the purpose of example, before it can warrant the application of a punishment equal to that which is necessary for the purpose of disablement.

—is most con-
spicuous in
capital punish-
ment.

19. The punishment, of which the efficacy in this way is the greatest, is evidently that of death. In this case the efficacy of it is certain. This accordingly is the punishment peculiarly adapted to those cases in which the name of the offender, so long as he lives, may be sufficient to keep a whole nation in a flame. This will now and then be the case with competitors for the sovereignty, and leaders of the factions in civil wars: though, when applied to offences of so questionable a nature, in which the question concerning criminality turns more upon success than any thing else; an infliction of this sort may seem more to savour of hostility than punishment. At the same time this punishment, it is evident, is in an eminent degree *unfrugal*; which forms one among the many objections there are against the use of it, in any but very extraordinary cases.[1]

Other punish-
ments in which
it is to be found.

20. In ordinary cases the purpose may be sufficiently answered by one or other of the various kinds of confinement and banishment: of which, imprisonment is the most strict and efficacious. For when an offence is so circumstanced that it cannot be committed but in a certain place, as is the case, for the most part, with offences against the person, all the law has to do, in order to disable the offender from committing it, is to prevent his being in that place. In any of the offences which consist in the breach or the abuse of any kind of trust, the purpose may be compassed at a still cheaper rate, merely by forfeiture of the trust; and in general, in an

[1] See B. I. tit. [Punishments].

of those offences which can only be committed under favour of some relation in which the offender stands with reference to any person, or sets of persons, merely by forfeiture of that relation: that is, of the right of continuing to reap the advantages belonging to it. This is the case, for instance, with any of those offences which consist in an abuse of the privileges of marriage, or of the liberty of carrying on any lucrative or other occupation.

21. The *ninth* property is that of *subserviency to compensa-* tion. This property of punishment, if it be *vindictive* com- pensation that is in view, will, with little variation, be in proportion to the quantity: if *lucrative*, it is the peculiar and characteristic property of pecuniary punishment.

Property 9. Subserviency to compensation.

22. In the rear of all these properties may be introduced that of *popularity*; a very fleeting and indeterminate kind of property, which may belong to a lot of punishment one moment, and be lost by it the next. By popularity is meant the property of being acceptable, or rather not unacceptable, to the bulk of the people, among whom it is proposed to be established. In strictness of speech, it should rather be called *absence of unpopularity*: for it cannot be expected, in regard to such a matter as punishment, that any species or lot of it should be positively acceptable and grateful to the people: it is sufficient, for the most part, if they have no decided aversion to the thoughts of it. Now the property of characteristicalness, above noticed, seems to go as far towards conciliating the approbation of the people to a mode of punishment, as any: insomuch that popularity may be regarded as a kind of secondary quality, depending upon that of characteristicalness.[1] The use of inserting this property in the catalogue, is chiefly to make it serve by way of memento to the legislator not to introduce, without a cogent necessity, any mode or lot of punishment, towards which he happens to perceive any violent aversion entertained by the body of the people.

Property 10. Popularity.

23. The effects of unpopularity in a mode of punishment are analogous to those of unfrugality. The unnecessary pain,

Mischiefs resulting from the

---

[1] The property of characteristicalness, therefore, is useful in a mode of punishment in three different ways: 1. It renders a mode of punishment, before infliction, more easy to be borne in mind: 2. It enables it, especially after infliction, to make the stronger impression, when it is there; that is, renders it more *exemplary*; 3. It tends to render it more acceptable to the people, that is, it renders it the more *popular*.

Characteristicalness renders a punishment,
1. memorable:
2. exemplary:
3. popular.

unpopularity of which denominates punishment unfrugal, is most apt to be
a punishment— that which is produced on the part of the offender. A portion
—discontent of superfluous pain is in like manner produced when the
among the punishment is unpopular: but in this case it is produced on
people, and the part of persons altogether innocent, the people at large.
weakness in the This is already one mischief; and another is, the weakness
law. which it is apt to introduce into the law. When the people
are satisfied with the law, they voluntarily lend their assistance
in the execution: when they are dissatisfied, they will naturally
withhold that assistance; it is well if they do not take a positive
part in raising impediments. This contributes greatly to the
uncertainty of the punishment; by which, in the first instance,
the frequency of the offence receives an increase. In process
of time that deficiency, as usual, is apt to draw on an increase
in magnitude: an addition of a certain quantity which otherwise would be *needless.*[1]

This property 24. This property, it is to be observed, necessarily supposes,
supposes a pre- on the part of the people, some prejudice or other, which
judice which the it is the business of the legislator to endeavour to correct. For
legislator ought if the aversion to the punishment in question were grounded
to cure. on the principle of utility, the punishment would be such as,
on other accounts, ought not to be employed: in which case
its popularity or unpopularity would never be worth drawing
into question. It is properly therefore a property not so much
of the punishment as of the people: a disposition to entertain
an unreasonable dislike against an object which merits their
approbation. It is the sign also of another property, to wit,
indolence or weakness, on the part of the legislator: in suffering the people, for the want of some instruction, which ought
to be and might be given them, to quarrel with their own
interest. Be this as it may, so long as any such dissatisfaction
subsists, it behoves the legislator to have an eye to it, as much
as if it were ever so well grounded. Every nation is liable
to have its prejudices and its caprices, which it is the business
of the legislator to look out for, to study, and to cure.[2]

Property 11. 25. The eleventh and last of all the properties that seem
Remissibility. to be requisite in a lot of punishment, is that of *remissibility.*[3]

---

[1] See Chap. xiii. [Cases unmeet], § v.
[2] See Chap. xiii. [Cases unmeet], § iv. par. iv.
[3] See View of the Hard Labour Bill, p. 109.

The general presumption is, that when punishment is applied, punishment is needful: that it ought to be applied, and therefore cannot want to be *remitted*. But in very particular, and those always very deplorable cases, it may by accident happen otherwise. It may happen that punishment shall have been inflicted, where, according to the intention of the law itself, it ought not to have been inflicted: that is, where the sufferer is innocent of the offence. At the time of the sentence passed he appeared guilty: but since then, accident has brought his innocence to light. This being the case, so much of the destined punishment as he has suffered already, there is no help for. The business is then to free him from as much as is yet to come. But *is* there any yet to come? There is very little chance of there being any, unless it be so much as consists of *chronical* punishment: such as imprisonment, banishment, penal labour, and the like. So much as consists of *acute* punishment, to wit where the penal process itself is over presently, however permanent the punishment may be in its effects, may be considered as *ir*remissible. This is the case, for example, with whipping, branding, mutilation, and capital punishment. The most perfectly irremissible of any is capital punishment. For though other punishments cannot, when they are over, be remitted, they may be compensated for; and although the unfortunate victim cannot be put into the same condition, yet possibly means may be found of putting him into as good a condition, as he would have been in if he had never suffered. This may in general be done very effectually where the punishment has been no other than pecuniary.

There is another case in which the property of remissibility may appear to be of use: this is, where, although the offender has been justly punished, yet on account of some good behaviour of his, displayed at a time subsequent to that of the commencement of the punishment, it may seem expedient to remit a part of it. But this it can scarcely be, if the proportion of the punishment is, in other respects, what it ought to be. The purpose of example is the more important object, in comparison of that of reformation.[1] It is not very likely, that less punishment should be required for the former purpose

---

[1] See Chap. xiii. [Cases unmeet], 2. note.

than for the latter. For it must be rather an extraordinary case, if a punishment, which is sufficient to deter a man who has only thought of it for a few moments, should not be sufficient to deter a man who has been feeling it all the time. Whatever, then, is required for the purpose of example, must abide at all events: it is not any reformation on the part of the offender, that can warrant the remitting of any part of it: if it could, a man would have nothing to do but to reform immediately, and so free himself from the greatest part of that punishment which was deemed necessary. In order, then, to warrant the remitting of any part of a punishment upon this ground, it must first be supposed that the punishment at first appointed was more than was necessary for the purpose of example, and consequently that a part of it was *needless* upon the whole. This indeed, is apt enough to be the case, under the imperfect systems that are as yet on foot: and therefore, during the continuance of those systems, the property of remissibility may, on this second ground likewise, as well as on the former, be deemed a useful one. But this would not be the case in any new-constructed system, in which the rule of proportion above laid down should be observed. In such a system, therefore, the utility of this property would rest solely on the former ground.

To obtain all these properties, punishments must be mixed. 26. Upon taking a survey of the various possible modes of punishment, it will appear evidently, that there is not any one of them that possesses all the above properties in perfection. To do the best that can be done in the way of punishment, it will therefore be necessary, upon most occasions, to compound them, and make them into complex lots, each consisting of a number of different modes of punishment put together: the nature and proportions of the constituent parts of each lot being different, according to the nature of the offence which it is designed to combat.

The foregoing properties re-capitulated. 27. It may not be amiss to bring together, and exhibit in one view, the eleven properties above established. They are as follows:

Two of them are concerned in establishing a proper proportion between a single offence and its punishment; viz.

1. Variability.
2. Equability.

One, in establishing a proportion, between more offences than one, and more punishments than one; viz.

3. Commensurability.

A fourth contributes to place the punishment in that situation in which alone it can be efficacious; and at the same time to be bestowing on it the two farther properties of exemplarity and popularity; viz.

4. Characteristicalness.

Two others are concerned in excluding all useless punishment; the one indirectly, by heightening the efficacy of what is useful; the other in a direct way; viz.

5. Exemplarity.

6. Frugality.

Three others contribute severally to the three inferior ends of punishment; viz.

7. Subserviency to reformation.

8. Efficacy in disabling.

9. Subserviency to compensation.

Another property tends to exclude a collateral mischief, which a particular mode of punishment is liable accidentally to produce; viz.

10. Popularity.

The remaining property tends to palliate a mischief, which all punishment, as such, is liable accidentally to produce; viz.

11. Remissibility.

The properties of commensurability, characteristicalness, exemplarity, subserviency to reformation, and efficacy in disabling, are more particularly calculated to augment the *profit* which is to be made by punishment: frugality, subserviency to compensation, popularity, and remissibility, to diminish the *expense*: variability and equability are alike subservient to both those purposes.

28. We now come to take a general survey of the system *Connection of* of *offences*: that is, of such *acts* to which, on account of the *this with the en-suing chapter.* mischievous *consequences* they have a *natural* tendency to produce, and in the view of putting a stop to those consequences, it may be proper to annex a certain *artificial* consequence, consisting of punishment, to be inflicted on the authors of such acts, according to the principles just established.

CHAPTER XVI

DIVISION OF OFFENCES

§ 1. *Classes of Offences.*

Distinction be-tween what are offences and

Method pur-sued in the following divisions.

[1] IT is necessary, at the outset, to make a distinction between such acts as *are* or *may* be, and such as *ought* to be offences.

[1] This chapter is an attempt to put our ideas of offences into an exact method. The particular uses of *method* are various: but the general one is, to enable men to understand the things that are the subjects of it. To understand a thing, is to be acquainted with its qualities or properties. Of these properties, some are common to it with other things; the rest, peculiar. But the qualities which are peculiar to any one sort of thing are few indeed, in comparison with those which are common to it with other things. To make it known in respect of its *difference*, would therefore be doing little, unless it were made known also by its *genus*. To understand it perfectly, a man must therefore be informed of the points in which it agrees, as well as of those in which it disagrees, with all other things. When a number of objects, composing a logical whole, are to be considered together, all of these possessing with respect to one another a certain congruency or agreement denoted by a certain name, there is but one way of giving a perfect knowledge of their nature; and that is, by distributing them into a system of parcels, each of them a part, either of some other parcel, or, at any rate, of the common whole. This can only be done in the way of *bipartition*, dividing each superior branch into two, and but two, immediately subordinate ones; beginning with the logical whole, dividing that into two parts, then each of those parts into two others; and so on. These first distinguished parts agree in respect of those properties which belong to the whole: they differ in respect of those properties which are peculiar to each. To divide the whole into more than two parcels at once, for example into three, would not answer the purpose; for, in fact, it is but two objects that the mind can compare together exactly at the same time. Thus then, let us endeavour to deal with offences; or rather, strictly speaking, with acts which possess such properties as seem to indicate them fit to be constituted offences. The task is arduous; and, as *yet* at least, perhaps *for ever*, above our force. There is no speaking of objects but by their names: but the business of giving them names has always been prior to the true and perfect knowledge of their natures. Objects the most dissimilar have been spoken of and treated as if their properties were the same. Objects the most similar have been spoken of and treated as if they had scarce anything in common. Whatever discoveries may be made concerning them, how different soever their congruencies and disagreements may be found to be from those which are indicated by their names, it is not without the utmost difficulty that any means can be found out of expressing these discoveries by a conformable set of names. Change the import of the old names, and you are in perpetual danger of being misunderstood: introduce an entire new set of names, and you are sure not to be understood at all. Complete success, then, is, as yet at least, unattainable. But an attempt, though imperfect, may have its use: and, at the worst, it may

Any act *may* be an offence, which they whom the community *what ought* are in the habit of obeying shall be pleased to make one: that *to be.* is, any act which they shall be pleased to prohibit or to punish. But, upon the principle of utility, such acts alone *ought* to be made offences, as the good of the community requires should be made so.

2. The good of the community cannot require, that any act *No act ought to* should be made an offence, which is not liable, in some way *be an offence* or other, to be detrimental to the community. For in the case *detrimental to* of such an act, all punishment is *groundless*.[1] *the community.*

3. But if the whole assemblage of any number of indivi- *To be so, it must* duals be considered as constituting an imaginary compound *be detrimental to* *body*, a community or political state; any act that is detrimental *more of its* to any one or more of those *members* is, as to so much of its *members.* effects, detrimental to the *state*.

4. An act cannot be detrimental to a *state*, but by being *These may be* detrimental to some one or more of the *individuals* that com- *assignable or* pose it. But those individuals may either be *assignable*[2] or *not.* *unassignable*.

5. When there is any assignable individual to whom an *If assignable,* offence is detrimental, that person may either be a person *other* *the offender* than the offender, or the offender *himself*. *himself, or* *others.*

6. Offences that are detrimental, in the first instance, to *Class 1.* assignable persons other than the offender, may be termed by *Private offences.* one common name, *offences against individuals*. And of these may be composed the 1st class of offences. To contrast them with offences of the 2nd and 4th classes, it may also sometimes be convenient to style them *private* offences. To contrast them at the same time with offences of the 3rd class, they may be styled *private extra-regarding* offences.

7. When it appears, in general, that there are persons to *Class 2.* whom the act in question may be detrimental, but such *Semi-public* persons cannot be individually assigned, the circle within *offences.*

accelerate the arrival of that perfect system, the possession of which will be the happiness of some maturer age. Gross ignorance descries no difficulties; imperfect knowledge finds them out, and struggles with them: it must be perfect knowledge that overcomes them.

[1] See Chap. xiii. [Cases unmeet], § ii. 1.

[2] That is, either by name, or at least by description, in such manner as to *Persons assign-* be sufficiently distinguished from all others; for instance, by the circumstance *able, how.* of being the owner or occupier of such and such goods. See B. I. tit. [Personation], supra, Chap. xii. [Consequences], 15.

which it appears that they may be found, is either of less extent than that which comprises the whole community, or not. If of less, the persons comprised within this lesser circle may be considered for this purpose as composing a body of themselves; comprised within, but distinguishable from, the greater body of the whole community. The circumstance that constitutes the union between the members of this lesser body, may be either their residence within a particular place, or, in short, any other less explicit principle of union, which may serve to distinguish them from the remaining members of the community. In the first case, the act may be styled an *offence against a neighbourhood*: in the second, an offence against a particular *class* of persons in the community. Offences, then, against a class or neighbourhood, may, together, constitute the 2nd class of offences.[1] To contrast them with private offences on the one hand, and public on the other, they may also be styled *semi-public* offences.

Class 3.
Self-regarding
offences.

8. Offences, which in the first instance are detrimental to the offender himself, and to no one else, unless it be by their being detrimental to himself, may serve to compose a third class. To contrast them the better with offences of the first, second, and fourth classes, all which are of a *transitive* nature, they might be styled *intransitive*[2] offences; but still better, *self-regarding*.

Class 4.
Public offences.

9. The fourth class may be composed of such acts as ought to be made offences, on account of the distant mischief which they threaten to bring upon an unassignable indefinite multitude of the whole number of individuals, of which the community is composed; although no particular individual should appear more likely to be a sufferer by them than

Limits between
private, semi-
public, and
public offences,
are, strictly
speaking, un-
distinguishable.

[1] With regard to offences against a class or neighbourhood, it is evident, that the fewer the individuals are, of which such class is composed, and the narrower that neighbourhood is, the more likely are the persons, to whom the offence is detrimental, to become assignable; insomuch that, in some cases, it may be difficult to determine concerning a given offence, whether it be an offence against individuals, or against a class or neighbourhood. It is evident also, that the larger the class or neighbourhood is, the more it approaches to a coincidence with the great body of the state. The three classes, therefore, are liable to a certain degree, to run into one another, and be confounded. But this is no more than what is the case, more or less, with all those ideal compartments under which men are wont to distribute objects for the convenience of discourse.

[2] See Chap. vii. [Actions], 13.

another. These may be called *public* offences, or offences against the *state*.

10. A fifth class, or appendix, may be composed of such acts as, according to the circumstances in which they are committed, and more particularly according to the purposes to which they are applied, may be detrimental in any one of the ways in which the act of one man can be detrimental to another. These may be termed *multiform*, or *heterogeneous* offences.[1] Offences that are in this case may be reduced to two

Class 5. Multiform *offences, viz.* 1. *Offences by falsehood.* 2. *Offences against trust.*

---

[1] 1. Offences by *falsehood*: 2. Offences against *trust*. See also par. xx. to xxx. and par. lxvi. Maturer views have suggested the feasibility, and the means, of ridding the system of this anomalous excrescence. Instead of considering these as so many *divisions* of offences, divided into *genera*, correspondent and collateral to the several *genera* distinguished by other appellations, they may be considered as so many specific differences, respectively applicable to those *genera*. Thus, in the case of a *simple personal injury*, in the operation of which a plan of falsehood has been employed: it seems more simple and more natural, to consider the offence thus committed as a particular *species* or *modification* of the *genus* of offence termed a *simple personal injury*, than to consider the simple personal injury, when effected by such means, as a modification of the *division* of offences entitled *Offences through falsehood.* By this means the circumstances of the intervention of falsehood as an instrument, and of the existence of a particular obligation of the nature of a trust, will be reduced to a par with various other classes of circumstances capable of affording grounds of modification, commonly of *aggravation* or *extenuation*, to various genera of offences: instance, *Premeditation*, and *conspiracy*, on the one hand; *Provocation received*, and *intoxication*, on the other. This class will appear, but too plainly, as a kind of botch in comparison of the rest. But such is the fate of science, and more particularly of the moral branch; the distribution of things must in a great measure be dependent on their names: arrangement, the work of mature reflection, must be ruled by nomenclature, the work of popular caprice.

In the book of the laws, offences must therefore be treated of as much as possible under their accustomed names. Generical terms, which are in continual use, and which express ideas for which there are no other terms in use, cannot safely be discarded. When any such occur, which cannot be brought to quadrate with such a plan of classification as appears to be most convenient upon the whole, what then is to be done? There seems to be but one thing; which is, to retain them, and annex them to the regular part of the system in the form of an appendix. Though they cannot, when entire, be made to rank under any of the classes established in the rest of the system, the divisions to which they give title may be broken down into lesser divisions, which may not be alike intractable. By this means, how discordant soever with the rest of the system they may appear to be at first sight, on a closer inspection they may be found conformable.

This must inevitably be the case with the names of offences, which are so various and universal in their nature, as to be capable, each of them, of doing whatever mischief can be done by any other kind or kinds of offences whatsoever. Offences of this description may well be called anomalous.

Such offences, it is plain, cannot but show themselves equally intractable under every kind of system. Upon whatever principle the system be con-

The imperfections of language an obstacle to arrangement.

Irregularity of this class.

—which could not be avoided

great heads: 1. Offences by *falsehood*: and 2. Offences against *trust*.

§ 2. Divisions and sub-divisions

Divisions of Class 1. (1) Offences against person; (2) Property; (3) Reputation; (4) Condition; (5) Person and property; (6) Person and reputation.

11. Let us see by what method these classes may be farther sub-divided. First, then, with regard to offences against individuals.

In the present period of existence, a man's being and well-being, his happiness and his security; in a word, his pleasures and his immunity from pains, are all dependent, more or less, in the first place, upon his *own person*; in the next place, upon the *exterior objects* that surround him. These objects are either *things*, or other *persons*. Under one or other of these classes must evidently be comprised every sort of exterior object, by means of which his interest can be affected. If then, by means of any offence, a man should on any occasion become a sufferer, it must be in one or other of two ways: 1. *absolutely*, to wit, immediately in his own person; in which case the offence may be said to be an offence against his person; or, 2. *relatively*, by reason of some *material* relation[1] which the

on any other plan.

structed, they cannot, any of them, with any degree of propriety, be confined to any one division. If, therefore, they constitute a blemish in the present system, it is such a blemish as could not be avoided but at the expense of a greater. The class they are here thrown into will traverse, in its subordinate ramifications, the other classes and divisions of the present system: true, but so would they of any other. An irregularity, and that but a superficial one, is a less evil than continual error and contradiction. But even this slight deviation, which the fashion of language seemed to render unavoidable at the outset, we shall soon find occasion to correct as we advance. For though the first great parcels into which the offences of this class are divided are not referable, any of them, to any of the former classes, yet the subsequent lesser subdivisions *are*.

[1] See Chap. vii. [Actions], 3 and 24.

In what manner pleasure and pain depend upon the relation a man bears to exterior objects.

If, by reason of the word *relation*, this part of the division should appear obscure, the unknown term may be got rid of in the following manner. Our ideas are derived, all of them, from the senses; pleasurable and painful ones, therefore, among the rest: consequently, from the operation of sensible objects upon our senses. A man's happiness, then, may be said to depend more or less upon the *relation* he bears to any sensible object, when such object is in a way that stands a chance, greater or less, of producing to him, or averting from him, pain or pleasure. Now this, if at all, it must do in one or other of two ways; 1. In an *active* way, properly so called; viz. by motion: or, 2. In a *passive* or quiescent way, by being moved to, or acted upon: and in either case, either, 1. in an *immediate* way, by acting upon, or being acted on by, the organs of sense, without the intervention of any other external object: or, 2. in a more or less *remote* way, by acting upon, or being acted on by, some other external object, which (with the intervention of a greater or less number of such objects, and at the end of more or less considerable intervals

before mentioned exterior objects may happen to bear, in the way of *causality* (see chap. vii. Actions, par. 24) to his happiness. Now in as far as a man is in a way to derive either happiness or security from any object which belongs to the class of *things*, such thing is said to be his *property*, or at least he is said to have a *property* or an *interest* therein: an offence, therefore, which tends to lessen the facility he might otherwise have of deriving happiness or security from an object which belongs to the class of things, may be styled an offence against his property. With regard to persons, in as far as, from objects of this class, a man is in a way to derive happiness or security, it is in virtue of their *services*: in virtue of some services, which, by one sort of inducement or another, they may be disposed to render him.[1] Now, then, take any man, by way of example, and the disposition whatever it may be, which he may be in to render you service, either has no other connection to give birth or support to it, than the general one which binds him to the whole species, or it has some other connection more particular. In the latter case, such a connection may be spoken of as constituting, in your favour, a kind of fictitious or incorporeal object of property, which is styled your *condition*. An offence, therefore, the tendency of which is to lessen the facility you might otherwise have of deriving happiness from the services of a person thus specially connected with you, may be styled an offence against your condition in life, or simply against your condition. Conditions in life must evidently be as various as the relations by which they are constituted. This will be seen more particularly farther on. In the mean time those of husband, wife, parent, child, master, servant, citizen of such or such a city, natural-

of time) will come at length to act upon, or be acted upon by, those organs. And this is equally true, whether the external objects in question be things or persons. It is also equally true of pains and pleasures of the mind, as of those of the body: all the difference is, that in the production of these, the pleasure or pain may result immediately from the perception which it accompanies: in the production of those of the mind, it cannot result from the action of an object of sense, any otherwise than by *association*; to wit, by means of some connection which the perception has contracted with certain prior ones, lodged already in the memory.[a]

[1] See Chap. x. [Motives].

[a] See Chap. v. [Pleasures and Pains] 15, 31. Chap. x. [Motives], 39, note.

born subject of such or such a country, may answer the purpose of examples.

Where there is no such particular connection, or (what comes to the same thing) where the disposition, whatever it may be, which a man is in to render you service, is not considered as depending upon such connection, but simply upon the good-will he bears to you; in such case, in order to express what chance you have of deriving a benefit from his services, a kind of fictitious object of property is spoken of, as being constituted in your favour, and is called your *reputation*. An offence, therefore, the tendency of which is to lessen the facility you might otherwise have had of deriving happiness or security from the services of persons at large, whether connected with you or not by any special tie, may be styled an offence against your *reputation*. It appears, therefore, that if by any offence an individual becomes a sufferer, it must be in one or other of the four points above mentioned; viz. his person, his property, his condition in life, or his reputation. These sources of distinction, then, may serve to form so many subordinate divisions. If any offences should be found to affect a person in more than one of these points at the same time, such offences may respectively be put under so many separate divisions; and such compound divisions may be sub-joined to the preceding simple ones. The several divisions (simple and compound together) which are hereinafter established, stand as follows: 1. Offences against person. 2. Offences against reputation. 3. Offences against property. 4. Offences against condition. 5. Offences against person and property together. 6. Offences against person and reputation together.[1]

Divisions of Class 2. 1. Offences through calamity.

12. Next with regard to semi-public offences. Pain, considered with reference to the time of the act from which it is liable to issue, must, it is evident, be either present, past, or future. In as far as it is either present or past, it cannot be the

[1] Subsequent consideration has here suggested several alterations. The necessity of adding to *property, power,* in the character of a distinguishable as well as valuable object or subject-matter of possession, has presented itself to view: and in regard to the fictitious entity here termed *condition* (for shortness instead of saying *condition in life*), it has been observed to be a sort of composite object, compounded of *property, reputation, power,* and *right to services.* For this *composite* object the more proper place was therefore at the tail of the several *simple* ones.—*Note by the Editor, July,* 1822.

result of any act which comes under the description of a semi-public offence: for if it be present or past, the individuals who experience, or who have experienced, it are *assignable*.[1] There remains that sort of mischief, which, if it ever come to exist at all, is as yet but future: mischief, thus circumstanced, takes the name of *danger*.[2] Now, then, when by means of the act of any person a whole neighbourhood, or other class of persons, are exposed to danger, this danger must either be *intentional* on his part, or *unintentional*.[3] If unintentional, such danger, when it is converted into actual mischief, takes the name of a *calamity*: offences, productive of such danger, may be styled *semi-public offences operating through calamity*; or, more briefly, *offences through calamity*. If the danger be intentional, insomuch that it might be produced, and might convert itself into actual mischief, without the concurrence of any calamity, it may be said to originate in *mere delinquency*: offences, then, which, without the concurrence of any calamity, tend to produce such danger as disturbs the security of a local, or other subordinate class of persons, may be styled *semi-public offences operating merely by delinquency*, or more briefly, *offences of mere delinquency*.

13. With regard to any farther sub-divisions, offences through calamity will depend upon the nature of the several calamities to which man, and the several things that are of use to him, stand exposed. These will be considered in another place.[4] *Sub-divisions of offences through calamity, dismissed.*

14. Semi-public offences of mere delinquency will follow the method of division applied to offences against individuals. It will easily be conceived, that whatever pain or inconvenience any given individual may be made to suffer, to the danger of that pain or inconvenience may any number of individuals, assignable or not assignable, be exposed. Now there are four points or articles, as we have seen, in respect to which an individual may be made to suffer pain or *2. Offences of mere delinquency, how they correspond with the divisions of private offences.*

---

[1] Supra, iv. note.   [2] See Chap. xii. [Consequences].
[3] See Chap. viii. [Intentionality].
[4] See B. I. tit. [Semi-public offences]. In the mean time that of *pestilence* may serve as an example. A man, without any intention of giving birth to such a calamity, may expose a neighbourhood to the danger of it, by breaking *quarantine* or violating any of those other preventive regulations which governments, at certain conjunctures, may find it expedient to have recourse to, for the purpose of guarding against such danger.

inconvenience. If then, with respect to any one of them, the connection of causes and effects is such, that to the danger of suffering in that article a number of persons, who individually are not assignable, may, by the delinquency of one person, be exposed, such article will form a ground of distinction on which a particular sub-division of semi-public offences may be established: if, with respect to any such article, no such effect can take place, that ground of distinction will lie for the present unoccupied: ready, however, upon any change of circumstances, or in the manner of viewing the subject, to receive a correspondent subdivision of offences, if ever it should seem necessary that any such offences should be created.

Divisions of Class 3 co-incide with those of Class 1.

15. We come next to self-regarding offences; or, more properly, to acts productive in the first instance of no other than a self-regarding mischief: acts which, if in any instance it be thought fit to constitute them offences, will come under the denomination of offences against one's self. This class will not for the present give us much trouble. For it is evident, that in whatever points a man is vulnerable by the hand of another, in the same points may he be conceived to be vulnerable by his own. Whatever divisions therefore will serve for the first class, the same will serve for this. As to the questions, What acts are productive of a mischief of this stamp? and, among such as *are*, which it may, and which it may not, be *worth while*[1] to treat upon the footing of offences? these are points, the latter of which at least is too unsettled, and too open to controversy, to be laid down with that degree of confidence which is implied in the exhibition of properties which are made use of as the groundwork of an arrangement. Properties for this purpose ought to be such as show themselves at first glance, and appear to belong to the subject beyond dispute.

Divisions of Class 4.

16. Public offences may be distributed under eleven divisions.[2] 1. Offences against *external* security. 2. Offences

Exhaustive method departed froui.

---

[1] See Chap. xiii. [Cases unmeet], § iv.

[2] In this part of the analysis, I have found it necessary to deviate in some degree from the rigid rules of the exhaustive method I set out with. By me, or by some one else, this method may, perhaps, be more strictly pursued at some maturer period of the science. At present, the benefit that might result from the unrelaxed observance of it, seemed so precarious, that I could not

against *justice*. 3. Offences against the *preventive* branch of the *police*. 4. Offences against the public *force*. 5. Offences against the *positive* increase of the national *felicity*. 6. Offences against the public *wealth*. 7. Offences against *population*. 8. Offences against the *national wealth*. 9. Offences against the *sovereignty*. 10. Offences against *religion*. 11. Offences against the national *interest* in general. The way in which these several sorts of offences connect with one another, and with the interest of the public, that is, of an unassignable multitude of the individuals of which that body is composed, may be thus conceived.

17. Mischief by which the interest of the public as above *Connection of* defined may be affected, must, if produced at all, be produced *the nine first* either by means of an influence exerted on the operations of *with another.* *divisions one* government, or by other means, without the exertion of such influence.[1] To begin with the latter case: mischief, be it what it will, and let it happen to whom it will, must be produced either by the unassisted powers of the agent in question, or by the instrumentality of some other agents. In the latter case, these agents will be either persons or things. Persons again must be either not members of the community in question, or members. Mischief produced by the instrumen-

help doubting whether it would pay for the delay and trouble. Doubtless such a method is eminently instructive: but the fatigue of following it out is so great, not only to the author, but probably also to the reader, that if carried to its utmost length at the first attempt, it might perhaps do more disservice in the way of disgust, than service in the way of information. For knowledge, like physic, how salutary soever in itself, becomes no longer of any use, when made too unpalatable to be swallowed. Mean time, it cannot but be a mortifying circumstance to a writer, who is sensible of the importance of his subject, and anxious to do it justice, to find himself obliged to exhibit what he perceives to be faulty, with any view, how indistinct soever, of something more perfect before his eyes. If there be any thing new and original in this work, it is to the exhaustive method so often aimed at that I am indebted for it. It will, therefore, be no great wonder if I should not be able to quit it without reluctance. On the other hand, the marks of stiffness which will doubtless be perceived in a multitude of places, are chiefly owing to a solicitous, and not perfectly successful, pursuit of this same method. New instruments are seldom handled at first with perfect ease.

[1] The idea of government, it may be observed, is introduced here without any preparation. The fact of its being established, I assume as notorious, and the necessity of it as alike obvious and incontestable. Observations indicating that necessity, if any such should be thought worth looking at in this view, may be found by turning to a passage in a former chapter, where they were incidentally adduced for the purpose of illustration. See Chap. xii. [Consequences], § xvii.

X

tality of persons, may accordingly be produced by the instrumentality either of *external* or of *internal* adversaries. Now when it is produced by the agent's own unassisted powers, or by the instrumentality of internal adversaries, or only by the instrumentality of things, it is seldom that it can show itself in any other shape (setting aside any influence it may exert on the operations of government) than either that of an offence against assignable individuals, or that of an offence against a local or other subordinate class of persons. If there should be a way in which mischief can be produced, by any of these means, to individuals altogether unassignable, it will scarcely be found conspicuous or important enough to occupy a title by itself: it may accordingly be referred to the miscellaneous head of *offences against the national interest in general*.[1] The only mischief, of any considerable account, which can be made to impend indiscriminately over the whole number of members in the community, is that complex kind of mischief which results from a state of war, and is produced by the instrumentality of external adversaries; by their being provoked, for instance, or invited, or encouraged to invasion. In this way may a man very well bring down a mischief, and that a very heavy one, upon the whole community in general, and that without taking a part in any of the injuries which came in consequence to be offered to particular individuals.

Next with regard to the mischief which an offence may bring upon the public by its influence on the operations of the government. This it may occasion either, 1. In a more immediate way, by its influence on those *operations* themselves: 2. In a more remote way, by its influence on the *instruments* by or by the help of which those operations should be performed: or 3. In a more remote way still, by its influence on the *sources* from whence such instruments are to be derived. First then, as to the operations of government, the tendency of these, in as far as it is conformable to what on the principle

---

[1] See infra, liv. note. Even this head, ample as it is, and vague as it may seem to be, will not, when examined by the principle of utility, serve, any more than another, to secrete any offence which has no title to be placed there. To show the pain or loss of pleasure which is likely to ensue, is a problem, which before a legislator can justify himself in adding the act to the catalogue of offences, he may in this case, as in every other, be called upon to solve.

of utility it ought to be, is in every case either to avert mischief from the community, or to make an addition to the sum of positive good.[1] Now mischief, we have seen, must come either from external adversaries, from internal adversaries, or from calamities. With regard to mischief from external adversaries, there requires no further division. As to mischief from internal adversaries, the expedients employed for averting it may be distinguished into such as may be applied *before* the discovery of any mischievous design in particular, and such as cannot be employed but in consequence of the discovery of some such design: the former of these are commonly referred to a branch which may be styled the *preventive* branch of the *police*: the latter to that of justice.[2] Secondly, As to the *instruments* which government, whether in the averting of evil or in the producing of positive good,

---

[1] For examples, see infra, liv. note. This branch of the business of government, a sort of work of supererogation, as it may be called, in the calendar of political duty, is comparatively but of recent date. It is not for this that the untutored many could have originally submitted themselves to the dominion of the few. It was the dread of evil, not the hope of good, that first cemented societies together. Necessaries come always before luxuries. The state of language marks the progress of ideas. Time out of mind the military department has had a name: so has that of justice: the power which occupies itself in preventing mischief, not till lately, and that but a loose one, the police: for the power which takes for its object the introduction of positive good, no peculiar name, however inadequate, seems yet to have been devised.

[2] The functions of justice, and those of the police, must be apt in many points to run one into another: especially as the business would be very badly managed if the same persons, whose more particular duty it is to act as officers of the police, were not upon occasion to act in the capacity of officers of justice. The ideas, however, of the two functions may still be kept distinct: and I see not where the line of separation can be drawn, unless it be as above.

As to the word *police*, though of Greek extraction, it seems to be of French growth: it is from France, at least, that it has been imported into Great Britain, where it still retains its foreign garb: in Germany, if it did not originate there, it has at least been naturalized. Taken all together, the idea belonging to it seems to be too multifarious to be susceptible of any single definition. Want of words obliged me to reduce the two branches here specified into one. Who would have endured in this place to have seen two such words as the *phthano-paranomic* or *crime-preventing*, and the *phthano-symphoric* or *calamity-preventing*, branches of the police? the inconveniences of uniting the two branches under the same denomination, are, however, the less, inasmuch as the operations requisite to be performed for the two purposes will in many cases be the same. Other functions, commonly referred to the head of police, may be referred either to the head of that power which occupies itself in promoting in a positive way the increase of the national felicity, or of that which employs itself in the management of the public wealth. See infra, liv. note.

can have to work with, these must be either *persons* or *things*. Those which are destined to the particular function of guarding against mischief from adversaries in general, but more particularly from external adversaries,[1] may be distinguished from the rest under the collective appellation of the *public military force*, and, for conciseness' sake, the *military force*. The rest may be characterised by the collective appellation of the *public wealth*. Thirdly, with regard to the sources or funds from whence these instruments, howsoever applied, must be derived, such of them as come under the denomination of *persons* must be taken out of the whole number of persons that are in the community, that is, out of the total *population* of the state: so that the greater the population, the greater may *cæteris paribus* be this branch of the public wealth; and the less, the less. In like manner, such as come under the denomination of *things* may be, and most of them commonly are, taken out of the sum total of those things which are the separate properties of the several members of the community: the sum of which properties may be termed *the national wealth*:[2] so that the greater the national wealth, the greater *cæteris paribus* may be this remaining branch of the public wealth; and the less, the less. It is here to be observed, that if the influence exerted on any occasion by any individual over the operations of the government be pernicious, it must

---

[1] It is from abroad that those pernicious enterprises are most apt to originate, which come backed with a greater quantity of physical force than the persons who are in a more particular sense the officers of justice are wont to have at their command. Mischief, the perpetration of which is ensured by a force of such magnitude, may therefore be looked upon in general as the work of *external* adversaries. Accordingly, when the persons by whom it is perpetrated are in such force as to bid defiance to the ordinary efforts of justice, they loosen themselves from their original denomination in proportion as they increase in force, till at length they are looked upon as being no longer members of the state, but as standing altogether upon a footing with external adversaries. Give force enough to robbery, and it swells into rebellion: give permanence enough to rebellion, and it settles into hostility.

[2] It must be confessed, that in common speech the distinction here established between the public wealth and the national wealth is but indifferently settled: nor is this to be wondered at; the ideas themselves, though here necessary to be distinguished, being so frequently convertible. But I am mistaken if the language will furnish any other two words that would express the distinction better. Those in question will, I imagine, be allowed to be thus far well chosen, that if they were made to change their places, the import given to them would not appear to be quite so proper as that which is given to them as they stand at present.

be in one or other of two ways: 1. By causing, or tending to cause, operations *not* to be performed which *ought* to be performed; in other words, by *impeding* the operations of government. Or, 2. By causing operations to *be* performed which ought *not* to be performed; in other words, by *misdirecting* them. Lastly, to the total assemblage of the persons by whom the several political operations above mentioned come to be performed, we set out with applying the collective appellation of *the government*. Among these persons there *commonly*[1] is some one person, or body of persons whose office it is to assign and distribute to the rest their several departments, to determine the conduct to be pursued by each in the performance of the particular set of operations that belongs to him, and even upon occasion to exercise his function in his stead. Where there is any such person, or body of persons, *he* or *it* may, according as the turn of the phrase requires, be termed *the sovereign*, or the *sovereignty*. Now it is evident, that to impede or misdirect the operations of the sovereign, as here described, may be to impede or misdirect the operations of the several departments of government as described above.

From this analysis, by which the connection between the several above-mentioned heads of offences is exhibited, we may now collect a definition for each article. By *offences against external security*, we may understand such offences whereof the tendency is to bring upon the public a mischief resulting from the hostilities of foreign adversaries. By *offences against justice*, such offences whereof the tendency is to impede or misdirect the operations of that power which is employed in the business of guarding the public against the mischiefs resulting from the delinquency of internal adversaries, as far as it is to be done by expedients, which do not come to be applied in any case till *after* the discovery of some particular design of the sort of those which they are calculated to prevent. By *offences against the preventive branch of the police*, such offences whereof the tendency is to impede or misdirect

---

[1] I should have been afraid to have said *necessarily*. In the United Provinces, in the Helvetic, or even in the Germanic body, where is that one assembly in which an absolute power over the whole resides? where was there in the Roman Commonwealth? I would not undertake for certain to find an answer to all these questions.

the operations of that power which is employed in guarding against mischiefs resulting from the delinquency of internal adversaries, by expedients that come to be applied *beforehand*; or of that which is employed in guarding against the mischiefs that might be occasioned by physical calamities. By *offences against the public force*, such offences whereof the tendency is to impede or misdirect the operations of that power which is destined to guard the public from the mischiefs which may result from the hostility of foreign adversaries, and, in case of necessity, in the capacity of ministers of justice, from mischiefs of the number of those which result from the delinquency of internal adversaries.

By *offences against the increase of the national felicity*, such offences whereof the tendency is to impede or misapply the operations of those powers that are employed in the conducting of various establishments, which are calculated to make, in so many different ways, a positive addition to the stock of public happiness. By *offences against the public wealth*, such offences whereof the tendency is to diminish the amount or misdirect the application of the money, and other articles of wealth, which the government reserves as a fund, out of which the stock of instruments employed in the service above mentioned may be kept up. By *offences against population*, such offences whereof the tendency is to diminish the numbers or impair the political value of the sum total of the members of the community. By *offences against the national wealth*, such offences whereof the tendency is to diminish the quantity, or impair the value, of the things which compose the separate properties or estates of the several members of the community.

Connection of offences against religion with the foregoing ones.

18. In this deduction, it may be asked, what place is left for *religion*? This we shall see presently. For combating the various kinds of offences above enumerated, that is, for combating all the offences (those not excepted which we are now about considering) which it is in man's nature to commit, the state has two great engines, *punishment* and *reward*: punishment, to be applied to all, and upon all ordinary occasions: reward, to be applied to a few, for particular purposes, and upon extraordinary occasions. But whether or no a man has done the act which renders him an object meet for punish-

ment or reward, the eyes of those, whosoever they be, to whom the management of these engines is entrusted cannot always see, nor, where it is punishment that is to be administered, can their hands be always sure to reach him. To supply these deficiencies in point of power, it is thought necessary, or at least *useful* (without which the *truth* of the doctrine would be nothing to the purpose), to inculcate into the minds of the people the belief of the existence of a power applicable to the same purposes, and not liable to the same deficiencies: the power of a supreme invisible being, to whom a disposition of contributing to the same ends to which the several institutions already mentioned are calculated to contribute, must for this purpose be ascribed. It is of course expected that this power will, at one time or other, be employed in the promoting of those ends: and to keep up and strengthen this expectation among men, is spoken of as being the employment of a kind of allegorical personage, feigned, as before,[1] for convenience of discourse, and styled *religion*. To diminish, then, or misapply the influence of religion, is *pro tanto* to diminish or misapply what power the state has of combating with effect any of the before-enumerated kinds of offences; that is, all kinds of offences whatsoever. Acts that appear to have this tendency may be styled *offences against religion*. Of these then may be composed the tenth division of the class of offences against the state.[2]

---

[1] See par. xvii. with regard to *justice*.

[2] It may be observed, that upon this occasion I consider religion in no other light, than in respect of the influence it may have on the happiness of the *present* life. As to the effects it may have in assuring us of and preparing us for a better life to come, this is a matter which comes not within the cognizance of the legislator. See tit. [Offences against religion].

I say offences against *religion*, the fictitious entity: not offences against God, the real being. For, what sort of pain should the act of a feeble mortal occasion to a being unsusceptible of pain? How should an offence affect him? Should it be an offence against his person, his property, his reputation, or his condition?

It has commonly been the way to put offences against religion foremost. The idea of precedence is naturally enough connected with that of reverence. Ἐκ Διὸς ἀρχώμεσθα. But for expressing reverence, there are other methods enough that are less equivocal. And in point of method and perspicuity, it is evident, that with regard to offences against religion, neither the nature of the mischief which it is their tendency to produce, nor the reason there may be for punishing them, can be understood, but from the consideration of the several mischiefs which result from the several other sorts of offences. In a political view, it is only because those others are mischievous, that offences against religion are so too.

Connection of offences against the national interest in general with the rest.

19. If there be any acts which appear liable to affect the state in any one or more of the above ways, by operating in prejudice of the external security of the state, or of its internal security; of the public force; of the increase of the national felicity; of the public wealth; of the national population; of the national wealth; of the sovereignty; or of religion; at the same time that it is not clear in which of all these ways they will affect it most, nor but that, according to contingencies, they may affect it in one of these ways only or in another; such acts may be collected together under a miscellaneous division by themselves, and styled *offences against the national interest in general*. Of these then may be composed the eleventh and last division of the class of offences against the state.

Sub-divisions of Class 5 enumerated. Divisions of offences by falsehood.

20. We come now to class the fifth: consisting of *multiform* offences. These, as has been already intimated, are either offences by *falsehood*, or offences concerning *trust*. Under the head of offences by falsehood, may be comprehended, 1. Simple falsehoods. 2. Forgery. 3. Personation. 4. Perjury.[1] Let us observe in what particulars these four kinds of falsehood agree, and in what they differ.

Offences by falsehood, in what they agree with one another.

21. Offences by falsehood, however diversified in other particulars, have this in common, that they consist in some abuse of the faculty of discourse, or rather, as we shall see hereafter, of the faculty of influencing the sentiment of belief in other men,[2] whether by discourse or otherwise. The use of discourse is to influence belief, and that in such manner as to give other men to understand that things are as they are

---

[1] This division of falsehoods, it is to be observed, is not regularly drawn out: that being what the nature of the case will not here admit of. Falsehood may be infinitely diversified in other ways than these. In a particular case, for instance, simple falsehood when uttered by writing, is distinguished from the same falsehood when uttered by word of mouth; and has had a particular name given to it accordingly. I mean, where it strikes against reputation; in which case, the instrument it has been uttered by has been called a *libel*. Now it is obvious, that in the same manner it might have received a distinct name in all other cases where it is uttered by writing. But there has not happened to be any thing in particular that has disposed mankind in those cases to give it such a name. The case is, that among the infinity of circumstances by which it might have been diversified, those which constitute it a libel, happen to have engaged a peculiar share of attention on the part of the institutors of language: either in virtue of the influence which these circumstances have on the tendency of the act, or in virtue of any particular degree of force with which on any other account they may have disposed it to strike upon the imagination.

[2] See B. I. tit. [Falsehoods].

really. Falsehoods, of whatever kind they be, agree in this: that they give men to understand that things are otherwise than as in reality they are.

22. Personation, forgery, and perjury, are each of them —*in what they distinguished from other modes of uttering falsehood by* differ. certain special circumstances. When a falsehood is not accompanied by any of those circumstances, it may be styled simple falsehood. These circumstances are, 1. The *form* in which the falsehood is uttered. 2. The circumstance of its relating or not to the identity of the *person* of him who utters it. 3. The solemnity of the *occasion* on which it is uttered.[1] The particular application of these distinctive characters may more commodiously be reserved for another place.[2]

23. We come now to the sub-divisions of offences by *Sub-divisions of* falsehood. These will bring us back into the regular track of *offences by falsehood are* analysis, pursued, without deviation, through the four pre- *determined by* ceding classes. *the divisions of the preceding* By whatever means a mischief is brought about, whether *classes.* falsehood be or be not of the number, the individuals liable to be affected by it must either be assignable or unassignable. If assignable, there are but four material articles in respect to which they can be affected: to wit, their persons, their properties, their reputations, and their conditions in life. The case is the same, if, though unassignable, they are comprisable in any class subordinate to that which is composed of the whole number of members of the state. If the falsehood tend to the detriment of the whole state, it can only be by operating in one or other of the characters, which every act that is an offence against the state must assume; viz., that of an offence against external security, against justice, against the preventive branch of the police, against the public force, against the increase of the national felicity, against the public wealth, against the national population, against the national wealth, against the sovereignty of the state, or against its religion.

[1] There are two other circumstances still more material; viz., 1. The parties whose interest is affected by the falsehood: 2. The point or article in which that interest is affected. These circumstances, however, enter not into the composition of the generical character. Their use is, as we shall see, to characterize the several species of each genus. See B. I. tit. [Falsehoods]
[2] Ibid.

Offences of this class in some instances change their names; others not.

24. It is the common property, then, of the offences that belong to this division, to run over the same ground that is occupied by those of the preceding classes. But some of them, as we shall see, are apt, on various occasions, to drop or change the names which bring them under this division: this is chiefly the case with regard to simple falsehoods. Others retain their names unchanged; and even thereby supersede the names which would otherwise belong to the offences which they denominate: this is chiefly the case with regard to personation, forgery, and perjury. When this circumstance then, the circumstance of falsehood, intervenes, in some cases the name which takes the lead is that which indicates the offence by its effect; in other cases, it is that which indicates the expedient or instrument as it were by the help of which the offence is committed. Falsehood, take it by itself, consider it as not being accompanied by any other material circumstances, nor therefore productive of any material effects, can never, upon the principle of utility, constitute any offence at all. Combined with other circumstances, there is scarce any sort of pernicious effect which it may not be instrumental in producing. It is therefore rather in compliance with the laws of language, than in consideration of the nature of the things themselves, that falsehoods are made separate mention of under the name and in the character of distinct offences. All this would appear plain enough, if it were now a time for entering into particulars: but that is what cannot be done, consistently with any principle of order or convenience, until the inferior divisions of those other classes shall have been previously exhibited.

A trust—what.

25. We come now to offences against trust. A trust is, where there is any particular act which one party, in the exercise of some *power*, or some *right*,[1] which is conferred on

---

Power and right, why no complete definition is here given of them.

[1] Powers, though not a species of rights (for the two sorts of fictitious entities, termed a *power* and a *right*, are altogether disparate) are yet so far included under rights, that wherever the word *power* may be employed, the word *right* may also be employed: The reason is, that wherever you may speak of a person as having a power, you may also speak of him as having a right to such power: but the converse of this proposition does not hold good: there are cases in which, though you may speak of a man as having a right, you cannot speak of him as having a power, or in any other way make any mention of that word. On various occasions you have a *right*, for instance, to the services of the magistrate: but if you are a private person, you have no

him, is bound to perform for the benefit of another. Or,
more fully, thus: A party is said to be invested with a trust,

power over him: all the power is on his side. This being the case, as the word
right was employed, the word *power* might perhaps, without any deficiency
in the sense, have been omitted. On the present occasion however, as in speaking of trusts this word is commonly made more use of than the word *right*,
it seemed most eligible, for the sake of perspicuity, to insert them both.

It may be expected that, since the word *trust* has been here expounded, the
words *power* and *right*, upon the meaning of which the exposition of the word
trust is made to depend, should be expounded also: and certain it is, that no
two words can stand more in need of it than these do. Such exposition I
accordingly set about to give, and indeed have actually drawn up: but the
details into which I found it necessary to enter for this purpose, were of such
length as to take up more room than could consistently be allotted to them in
this place. With respect to these words, therefore, and a number of others,
such as *possession*, *title*, and the like, which in point of import are inseparably
connected with them, instead of exhibiting the exposition itself, I must content
myself with giving a general idea of the plan which I have pursued in framing
it: and as to every thing else, I must leave the import of them to rest upon
whatever footing it may happen to stand upon in the apprehension of each
reader. Power and right, and the whole tribe of fictitious entities of this stamp,
are all of them, in the sense which belongs to them in a book of jurisprudence,
the results of some manifestation or other of the legislator's will with respect
to such or such an act. Now every such manifestation is either a prohibition,
a command, or their respective negations; viz. a permission, and the declaration which the legislator makes of his will when on any occasion he leaves
an act uncommanded. Now, to render the expression of the rule more concise, the commanding of a positive act may be represented by the prohibition
of the negative act which is opposed to it. To know then how to expound a
right, carry your eye to the act which, in the circumstances in question, would
be a violation of that right: the law creates the right by prohibiting that act.
Power, whether over a man's own person, or over other persons, or over
things, is constituted in the first instance by permission: but in as far as the law
takes an active part in corroborating it, it is created by prohibition, and by
command: by prohibition of such acts (on the part of other persons) as are
judged incompatible with the exercise of it; and upon occasion, by command
of such acts as are judged to be necessary for the removal of such or such
obstacles of the number of those which may occur to impede the exercise of it.
For every right which the law confers on one party, whether that party be
an individual, a subordinate class of individuals, or the public, it thereby imposes
on some other party *a duty* or *obligation*. But there may be laws which command or prohibit acts, that is, impose duties, without any other view than the
benefit of the agent: these generate no rights: duties, therefore, may be either
extra-regarding or *self-regarding*: extra-regarding have rights to correspond to
them: self-regarding, none.

That the exposition of the words *power* and *right* must, in order to be correct,
enter into a great variety of details, may be presently made appear. One
branch of the system of rights and powers, and but one, are those of which
property is composed: to be correct, then, it must, among other things, be
applicable to the whole tribe of modifications of which property is susceptible.
But the commands and prohibitions, by which the *powers* and *rights* that compose those several modifications are created, are of many different forms:
to comprise the exposition in question within the compass of a single para-

when, being invested with a *power*, or with a *right*, there is a certain behaviour which, in the exercise of that power, or of that right, he is bound to maintain for the benefit of some other party. In such case, the party first mentioned is styled a trustee; for the other party, no name has ever yet been found: for want of a name, there seems to be no other resource than to give a new and more extensive sense to the word *beneficiary*, or to say at length *the party to be benefited*.[1]

graph, would therefore be impossible: to take as many paragraphs for it as would be necessary, in order to exhibit these different forms, would be to engage in a detail so ample, that the analysis of the several possible species of property would compose only a part of it. This labour, uninviting as it was, I have accordingly undergone: but the result of it, as may well be imagined, seemed too voluminous and minute to be exhibited in an outline like the present. Happily it is not necessary, except only for the scientific purpose of arrangement, to the understanding of any thing that need be said on the penal branch of the art of legislation. In a work which should treat of the civil branch of that art, it would find its proper place: and in such a work, if conducted upon the plan of the present one, it would be indispensable. Of the limits which seem to separate the one of these branches from the other, a pretty ample description will be found in the next chapter: from which some further lights respecting the course to be taken for developing the notions to be annexed to the words *right* and *power*, may incidentally be collected. See in particular, § 3 and 4. See also par. 55 of the present chapter.

I might have cut this matter very short, by proceeding in the usual strain, and saying, that a power was a faculty, and that a right was a privilege, and so on, following the beaten track of definition. But the inanity of such a method, in cases like the present, has been already pointed out[a]: a power is not a—any thing: neither is a right a—any thing: the case is, they have neither of them any superior genus: these, together with *duty*, *obligation*, and a multitude of others of the same stamp, being of the number of those fictitious entities, of which the import can by no other means be illustrated than by showing the relation which they bear to real ones.

[1] The first of these parties is styled in the law language, as well as in common speech, by the name here given to him. The other is styled, in the technical language of the English law, a *cestuy que trust*: in common speech, as we have observed, there is, unfortunately, no name for him. As to the law phrase, it is antiquated French, and though complex, it is still elliptical, and to the highest degree obscure. The phrase in full length would run in some such manner as this: *cestuy al use de qui le trust est créé*: he to whose use the trust or benefit is created. In a particular case, a *cestuy que trust* is called by the Roman law, *fidei-commissarius*. In imitation of this, I have seen him somewhere or other called in English a *fide-committee*. This term, however, seems not very expressive. A *fide-committee*, or, as it should have been, a *fidei*-committee, seems, literally speaking, to mean one who is committed to the good faith of another. Good faith seems to consist in the keeping of a promise. But a trust may be created without any promise in the case. It is indeed common enough to exact a promise, in order the more effectually to oblige a man to do that which he is made to promise he will do. But this is merely an accidental

[a] See Fragment of Government, Chap. v. § 6, note.

The trustee is also said to have a trust *conferred* or *imposed* upon him, to be *invested* with a trust, to have had a trust given him to execute, to perform, to discharge, or to fulfil. The party to be benefited, is said to have a trust established or created in his favour: and so on through a variety of other phrases.

26. Now it may occur, that a *trust* is oftentimes spoken of as a species of *condition*:[1] that a trust is also spoken of as a species of *property*: and that a condition itself is also spoken of in the same light. It may be thought, therefore, that in the first class, the division of offences against condition should *Offences against trust, condition, and property, why ranked under separate divisions.* have been included under that of the offences against property: and that at any rate, so much of the fifth class now before us as contains offences against trust, should have been included under one or other of those two divisions of the first class. But upon examination it will appear, that no one of these divisions could with convenience, nor even perhaps with propriety, have been included under either of the other two. It will appear at the same time, that there is an intimate connection subsisting amongst them all: insomuch that of the lists of the offences to which they are respectively exposed, any one may serve in great measure as a model for any other. There are certain offences to which all trusts as such are exposed: to all these offences every sort of condition will be

circumstance. A trust may be created without any such thing. What is it that constitutes a legal obligation in any case? A command, express or virtual, together with punishment appointed for the breach of it. By the same means may an obligation be constituted in this case as well as any other. Instead of the word *beneficiary*, which I found it necessary to adopt, the sense would be better expressed by some such word as *beneficiendary* (a word analagous in its formation to *referendary*), were it such an one as the ear could bring itself to endure. This would put it more effectually out of doubt, that the party meant was the party who *ought* to receive the benefit, whether he actually receives it or no: whereas the word *beneficiary* might be understood to intimate, that the benefit was *actually* received: while in offences against trust the mischief commonly is, that such benefit is reaped not by the person it was designed for, but by some other: for instance, the trustee.

[1] It is for shortness' sake that the proposition is stated as it stands in the text. If critically examined, it might be found, perhaps, to be scarcely justifiable by the laws of language. For the fictitious entities, characterized by the two abstract terms, *trust* and *condition*, are not subalternate but disparate. To speak with perfect precision, we should say that he who is invested with a trust is, on that account, spoken of as being invested with a condition: viz. the condition of a trustee. We speak of the condition of a trustee as we speak of the condition of a husband or a father.

found exposed: at the same time that particular species of the offences against trust will, upon their application to particular conditions, receive different particular denominations. It will appear also, that of the two groups of offences into which the list of those against trust will be found naturally to divide itself, there is one, and but one, to which property, taken in its proper and more confined sense, stands exposed: and that these, in their application to the subject of property, will be found susceptible of distinct modifications, to which the usage of language, and the occasion there is for distinguishing them in point of treatment, make it necessary to find names.

In the first place, as there are, or at least may be (as we shall see) conditions which are not trusts,[1] so there are trusts of which the idea would not be readily and naturally understood to be included under the word *condition*: add to which, that of those conditions which do include a trust, the greater number include other ingredients along with it: so that the idea of a condition, if on the one hand it stretches beyond the idea of a trust, does on the other hand fall short of it. Of the several sorts of trusts, by far the most important are those in which it is the public that stands in the relation of *beneficiary*. Now these trusts, it should seem, would hardly present themselves at first view upon the mention of the word *condition*. At any rate, what is more material, the most important of the offences against these kinds of trust would not seem to be included under the denomination of offences against condition. The offences which by this latter appellation would be brought to view, would be such only as seemed to affect the interests of an individual: of him, for example, who is considered as being invested with that condition. But in offences against public trust, it is the influence they have on the interests of the public that constitutes by much the most material part of their pernicious tendency: the influence they have on the interests of any individual, the only part of their influence which would be readily brought to view by the appellation of offences against condition, is comparatively as nothing. The word trust directs the attention at once to the interests of that party for whom the person in question is trustee: which party, upon the addition of the epithet public, is

[1] Infra, 55.

immediately understood to be the body composed of the whole assemblage, or an indefinite portion of the whole assemblage of the members of the state. The idea presented by the words *public trust* is clear and unambiguous: it is but an obscure and ambiguous garb that that idea could be expressed in by the words *public condition*. It appears, therefore, that the principal part of the offences, included under the denomination of offences against trust, could not, commodiously at least, have been included under the head of offences against condition.

It is evident enough, that for the same reasons neither could they have been included under the head of offences against property. It would have appeared preposterous, and would have argued a total inattention to the leading principle of the whole work, the principle of utility, to have taken the most mischievous and alarming part of the offences to which the public stands exposed, and forced them into the list of offences against the property of an individual: of that individual, to wit, who in that case would be considered as having in him the property of that public trust, which by the offences in question is affected.

Nor would it have been less improper to have included conditions, all of them, under the head of property: and thereby the whole catalogue of offences against condition, under the catalogue of offences against property. True it is, that there are offences against condition, which perhaps with equal propriety, and without any change in their nature, might be considered in the light of offences against property: so extensive and so vague are the ideas that are wont to be annexed to both these objects. But there are other offences which though with unquestionable propriety they might be referred to the head of offences against condition, could not, without the utmost violence done to language, be forced under the appellation of offences against property. Property, considered with respect to the proprietor, implies invariably a benefit, and nothing else: whatever obligations or burthens may, by accident, stand annexed to it, yet in itself it can never be otherwise than beneficial. On the part of the proprietor it is created not by any commands that are laid on him, but by his being left free to do with such or such an article as he likes. The obligations it is created by, are in every instance laid upon other people. On the other hand, as to conditions, there are several which are of a mixed nature, importing as well a burthen to him who stands invested with them as a benefit: which indeed is the case with those conditions which we hear most of under that name, and which make the greatest figure.

There are even conditions which import nothing but burthen, without any spark of benefit. Accordingly, when between two parties there is such a relation, that one of them stands in the place of an object of property with respect to the other; the word *property* is applied only on one side; but the word *condition* is applied alike to both: it is but one of them that is said on that account to be possessed of a property; but both of them are alike spoken of as being possessed of or being invested with a condition: it is the master alone that is considered as possessing a property, of which the servant, in virtue of the services he is bound to render, is the object: but the servant, not less than the master, is spoken of as possessing or being invested with a condition.

The case is, that if a man's condition is ever spoken of as constituting an article of his *property*, it is in the same loose and indefinite sense of the word in which almost every other offence that could be imagined might be reckoned into the list of offences against property. If the language indeed were in every instance, in which it made use of the phrase, *object of property*, perspicuous enough to point out under that appellation the material and really existent body, the *person* or the *thing* in which those acts terminate, by the performance of which the property is said to be *enjoyed*; if, in short, in the import given to the phrase *object of property*, it made no other use of it than the putting it to signify what is now called a corporeal *object*, this difficulty and this confusion would not have occurred. But the import of the phrase *object of property*, and in consequence the import of the word *property*, has been made to take a much wider range. In almost every case in which the law does any thing for a man's benefit or advantage, men are apt to speak of it, on some occasion or other, as conferring on him a sort of property. At the same time, for one reason or other, it has in several cases been not practicable, or not agreeable, to bring to view, under the appellation of *the object of his property*, the thing in which the acts, by the performance of which the property is said to be enjoyed, have their termination, or the person in whom they have their commencement. Yet something which could be spoken of under that appellation was absolutely requisite.[1] The expedient then has been to create, as it were, on every occasion, an ideal being, and to assign to a man this ideal being for the object of his property: and these are the sort of objects to which men of science, in taking a view of the operations of the law in this behalf, came, in process of time, to give the name of *incorporeal*. Now of these incorporeal objects of property the variety is prodigious. Fictitious entities of this kind have been fabricated almost out of every thing: not *conditions* only (that of a trustee included), but even *reputation* have been of the number. Even *liberty* has been considered in this same point of view: and though on so many occasions it is contrasted with *property*, yet on other occasions, being reckoned into the catalogue of possessions, it seems to have

---

[1] It is to be observed, that in common speech, in the phrase *the object of a man's property*, the words *the object of* are commonly left out; and by an ellipsis, which, violent as it is, is now become more familiar than the phrase at length, they have made that part of it which consists of the words *a man's property* perform the office of the whole. In some cases then it was only on a *part* of the object that the acts in question might be performed: and to say, on this account, that the object was a man's property, was as much as to intimate that they might be performed on any part. In other cases it was only certain particular acts that might be exercised on the object: and to say of the object that it was his property, was as much as to intimate that any acts whatever might be exercised on it. Sometimes the acts in question were not to be exercised but at a future *time*, nor then, perhaps, but in the case of the happening of a particular event, of which the happening was *uncertain*: and to say of an object that it was his property, was as much as to intimate that the acts in question might be exercised on it at any time. Sometimes the object on which the acts in question were to have their termination, or their commencement, was a human creature: and to speak of one human creature as being the property of another is what would shock the ear every where but where slavery is established, and even there, when applied to persons in any other condition than that of slaves. Among the first Romans, indeed, the wife herself was the property of her husband; the child, of his father; the servant, of his master. In the civilized nations of modern times, the two first kinds of property are altogether at an end: and the last, unhappily not yet at an end, but however verging, it is to be hoped, towards extinction. The husband's property is now the company[a] of his wife; the father's the guardianship and service of his child; the master's, the service of his servant.

[a] The *consortium*, says the English Law.

been considered as a branch of property. Some of these applications of the words *property, object of property* (the last, for instance), are looked upon, indeed, as more figurative, and less proper than the rest: but since the truth is, that where the immediate object is incorporeal, they are all of them improper, it is scarce practicable any where to draw the line.

Notwithstanding all this latitude, yet, among the relations in virtue of which you are said to be possessed of a condition, there is one at least which can scarcely, by the most forced construction, be said to render any other man, or any other thing, the object of your property This is the right of persevering in a certain course of action; for instance, in the exercising of a certain trade. Now to confer on you this right, in a certain degree at least, the law has nothing more to do than barely to abstain from forbidding you to exercise it. Were it to go farther, and, for the sake of enabling you to exercise your trade to the greater advantage, prohibit others from exercising the like, then, indeed, persons might be found, who in a certain sense, and by a construction rather forced than otherwise, might be spoken of as being the objects of your property: viz. by being made to render you that sort of negative service which consists in the forbearing to do those acts which would lessen the profits of your trade. But the ordinary right of exercising any such trade or profession, as is not the object of a monopoly, imports no such thing; and yet, by possessing this right, a man is said to possess a condition: and by forfeiting it, to forfeit his condition.

After all, it will be seen, that there must be cases in which, according to the usage of language, the same offence may, with more or less appearance of propriety, be referred to the head of offences against condition, or that of offences against property, indifferently. In such cases the following rule may serve for drawing the line. Wherever, in virtue of your possessing a property, or being the object of a property possessed by another, you are characterised, according to the usage of language, by a particular name, such as master, servant, husband, wife, steward, agent, attorney, or the like, there the word *condition* may be employed in exclusion of the word *property*: and an offence in which, in virtue of your bearing such relation, you are concerned, either in the capacity of an offender, or in that of a party injured, may be referred to the head of offences against condition, and not to that of offences against property. To give an example: Being bound, in the capacity of land steward to a certain person, to oversee the repairing of a certain bridge, you forbear to do so; in this case, as the services you are bound to render are of the number of those which give occasion to the party, from whom they are due, to be spoken of under a certain generical name, viz. that of land steward, the offence of withholding them may be referred to the class of offences against condition. But suppose that, without being engaged in that general and miscellaneous course of service, which with reference to a particular person would denominate you his land steward, you were bound, whether by usage or by contract, to render him that single sort of service which consists in the providing, by yourself or by others, for the repairing of that bridge: in this case, as there is not any such current denomination to which, in virtue of your being bound to render this service, you stand aggregated (for that of architect, mason, or the like, is not here in question), the offence you commit by withholding such service cannot with propriety be referred to the class of offences against condition: it can only therefore be referred to the class of offences against property.

By way of further distinction, it may be remarked, that where a man, in virtue of his being bound to render, or of others being bound to render him, certain services, is spoken of as possessing a condition, the assemblage of services is generally so considerable, in point of duration, as to constitute a course of considerable length, so as on a variety of occasions to come to be varied and repeated: and in most cases, when the condition is not of a domestic nature, sometimes for the benefit of one person, sometimes for that of another. Services which come to be rendered to a particular person on a particular occasion, especially if they be of short duration, have seldom the effect of occasioning either party to be spoken of as being invested with a condition. The particular occasional services which one man may come, by contract or otherwise, to be bound to render to another, are innumerably various: but the number of conditions which have names may be counted, and are, comparatively, but few.

If after all, notwithstanding the rule here given for separating conditions from articles of property, any object should present itself which should appear to be referable, with equal propriety, to either head, the inconvenience would not be material; since in such cases, as will be seen a little farther on, which ever appellation were adopted, the list of the offences, to which the object stands exposed, would be substantially the same.

These difficulties being cleared up, we now proceed to exhibit an analytical view of the several possible offences against trust.

Offences against trust—their connection with each other.

27. Offences against trust may be distinguished, in the first place, into such as concern the existence of the trust in the hands of such or such a person, and such as concern the *exercise* of the functions that belong to it.[1] First then, with regard to such as relate to its existence. An offence of this description, like one of any other description, if an offence it ought to be, must to some person or other import a preju-

---

[1] We shall have occasion, a little farther on, to speak of the person in whose hands the trust exists, under the description of the person who possesses, or is in possession of it, and thence of the possession of the trust abstracted from the consideration of the possessor. However different the expression, the import is in both cases the same. So irregular and imperfect is the structure of language on this head, that no one phrase can be made to suit the idea on all the occasions on which it is requisite it should be brought to view: the phrase must be continually shifted, or new modified: so likewise in regard to conditions, and in regard to property. The being invested with, or possessing a condition; the being in possession of an article of property, that is, if the object of the property be corporeal; the having a legal title (defeasible or indefeasible) to the physical possession of it, answers to the being in possession of a trust, or the being the person in whose hands a trust exists. In like manner, to the *exercise* of the *functions* belonging to a trust, or to a condition, corresponds the *enjoyment* of an article of property; that is, if the object of it be corporeal, the *occupation*. These verbal discussions are equally tedious and indispensable. Striving to cut a new road through the wilds of jurisprudence, I find myself continually distressed, for want of tools that are fit to work with. To frame a complete set of new ones is impossible. All that can be done is, to make here and there a new one in cases of absolute necessity, and for the rest, to patch up from time to time the imperfections of the old.

As to the bipartition which this paragraph sets out with, it must be acknowledged not to be of the nature of those which to a first glance afford a sort of intuitive proof of their being exhaustive. There is not that marked connection and opposition between the terms of it, which subsists between contradictory terms and between terms that have the same common genus. I imagine, however, that upon examination it would be found to be exhaustive notwithstanding: and that it might even be demonstrated so to be. But the demonstration would lead us too far out of the ordinary track of language.

dice. This prejudice may be distinguished into two branches: 1. That which may fall on such persons as are or should be invested with the trust: 2. That which may fall on the persons for whose sake it is or should be instituted, or on other persons at large. To begin with the former of these branches. Let any trust be conceived. The consequences which it is in the nature of it to be productive of to the possessor, must, in as far as they are *material*,[1] be either of an advantageous or of a disadvantageous nature: in as far as they are advantageous, the trust may be considered as a *benefit* or privilege: in as far as they are disadvantageous, it may be considered as a *burthen*.[2] To consider it then upon the footing of a benefit. The trust either is of the number of those which ought by law to subsist;[3] that is, which the legislator meant should be

[1] See Chap. vii. [Actions], 3.

[2] If advantageous, it will naturally be on account of the *powers* or rights that are annexed to the trust: if disadvantageous, on account of the *duties*.

[3] It may seem a sort of anachronism to speak on the present occasion of a trust, condition, or other possession, as one of which it may happen that a man ought or ought not to have had possession given him by the law, for, the plan here set out upon is to give such a view all along of the laws that are proposed, as shall be taken from the reasons which there are for making them: the reason then it would seem should subsist before the law: not the law before the reason. Nor is this to be denied: for, unquestionably, upon the principle of utility, it may be said with equal truth of those operations by which a trust, or any other article of property, is instituted, as of any other operations of the law, that it never can be expedient they should be performed, unless some reason for performing them, deduced from that principle, can be assigned. To give property to one man, you must impose obligation on another: you must oblige him to do something which he may have a mind not to do, or to abstain from doing something which he may have a mind to do: in a word, you must in some way or other expose him to inconvenience. Every such law, therefore, must at any rate be mischievous in the first instance; and if no good effects can be produced to set against the bad, it must be mischievous upon the whole. Some reasons, therefore, in this case, as in every other, there ought to be. The truth is, that in the case before us, the reasons are of too various and complicated a nature to be brought to view in an analytical outline like the present. Where the offence is of the number of those by which *person* or *reputation* are affected, the reasons for prohibiting it lie on the surface, and apply to every man alike. But *property*, before it can be offended against, must be created, and at the instant of its creation distributed, as it were, into parcels of different sorts and sizes, which require to be assigned, some to one man and some to another, for reasons, of which many lie a little out of sight, and which being different in different cases, would take up more room than could consistently be allotted to them here. For the present purpose, it is sufficient if it appear, that for the carrying on of the several purposes of life, there are trusts, and conditions, and other articles of property, which must be possessed by somebody: and that it is not every article that can, nor every article that ought, to be possessed by every body. What articles ought to be

established; or is not. If it is, the possession which at any time you may be deprived of, with respect to it, must at that time be either present or to come: if to come (in which case it may be regarded either as certain or as contingent), the investitive event, or event from whence your possession of it should have taken its commencement, was either an event in the production of which the will of the offender should have been instrumental, or any other event at large: in the former case, the offence may be termed *wrongful non-investment of trust*: in the latter case, *wrongful interception of trust*.[1] If at the time of the offence whereby you are deprived of it, you were already in possession of it, the offence may be styled *wrongful divestment of trust*. In any of these cases, the effect of the offence is either to put somebody else into the trust, or not: if not, it is wrongful divestment, wrongful interception, or wrongful divestment, and nothing more: if it be, the person put in possession is either the wrong-doer himself, in which case it may be styled *usurpation of trust*; or some other person, in which case it may be styled *wrongful investment*, or attribution, *of trust*. If the trust in question is *not* of the number of those which ought to subsist, it depends upon the manner in which one man deprives another of it, whether such deprivation shall or shall not be an offence, and, accordingly, whether non-investment, interception, or divestment, shall or shall not be wrongful. But the putting any body into it must at any rate be an offence: and this offence may be either usurpation or wrongful investment, as before.

created, and to what persons, and in what cases they ought to be respectively assigned, are questions which cannot be settled here. Nor is there any reason for wishing that they could, since the settling them one way or another is what would make no difference in the nature of any offence whereby any party may be exposed, on the occasion of any such institution, to sustain a detriment.

[1] In the former case, it may be observed, the act is of the negative kind: in the latter, it will commonly be of the positive kind.

As to the expression *non-investment of trust*, I am sensible that it is not perfectly consonant to the idiom of the language: the usage is to speak of a person as being invested (that is clothed) with a trust, not of a trust as of a thing that is itself *invested* or *put on*. The phrase at length would be, *the non-investment of a person with a trust;* but this phrase is by much too long-winded to answer the purpose of an appellative. I saw, therefore, no other resource than to venture upon the ellipsis here employed. The ancient lawyers, in the construction of their appellatives, have indulged themselves in much harsher ellipsises without scruple. See above, 25. note. It is already the usage to speak of a trust as a thing that *vests*, and as a thing that may be *divested*.

In the next place, to consider it upon the footing of a burthen. In this point of view, if no other interest than that of the persons liable to be invested with it were considered, it is what ought not, upon the principle of utility, to subsist: if it ought, it can only be for the sake of the persons in whose favour it is established. If then it ought *not* on any account to subsist, neither non-investment, interception, nor divestment, can be wrongful with relation to the persons first mentioned, whatever they may be on any other account, in respect of the manner in which they happen to be performed: for usurpation, though not likely to be committed, there is the same room as before: so likewise is there for wrongful investment; which, in as far as the trust is considered as a burthen, may be styled *wrongful imposition of trust*. If the trust, being still of the burthensome kind, is of the number of those which *ought* to subsist, any offence that can be committed, with relation to the existence of it, must consist either in causing a person to *be* in possession of it, who ought *not* to be, or in causing a person *not* to be in possession of it who *ought* to be: in the former case, it must be either usurpation or wrongful divestment, as before: in the latter case, the person who is caused to be not in possession, is either the wrong-doer himself, or some other: if the wrong-doer himself, either at the time of the offence he was in possession of it, or he was not: if he was, it may be termed *wrongful abdication* of trust; if not, *wrongful detrectation*[1] or *non-assumption*: if the person, whom the offence causes not to be in the trust, is any other person, the offence must be either wrongful divestment, wrongful non-investment, or wrongful interception, as before: in any of which cases to consider the trust in the light of a burthen, it might also be styled *wrongful exemption from trust*.

Lastly, with regard to the prejudice which the persons for whose benefit the trust is instituted, or any other persons whose interests may come to be affected by its existing or not existing in such or such hands, are liable to sustain. Upon

---

[1] I do not find that this word has yet been received into the English language. In the Latin, however, it is very expressive, and is used in a sense exactly suitable to the sense here given to it. *Militiam detrectare*, to endeavour to avoid serving in the army, is a phrase not unfrequently met with in the Roman writers.

examination it will appear, that by every sort of offence whereby the persons who are or should be in possession of it are liable, in that respect, to sustain a prejudice, the persons now in question are also liable to sustain a prejudice. The prejudice, in this case, is evidently of a very different nature from what it was of in the other: but the same general names will be applicable in this case as in that. If the beneficiaries, or persons whose interests are at stake upon the exercise of the trust, or any of them, are liable to sustain a prejudice, resulting from the quality of the person by whom it may be filled, such prejudice must result from the one or the other of two causes: 1. From a person's having the possession of it who ought not to have it: or 2. From a person's not having it who ought: whether it be a benefit or burthen to the possessor, is a circumstance that to this purpose makes no difference. In the first of these cases the offences from which the prejudice takes its rise are those of usurpation of trust, wrongful attribution of trust, and wrongful imposition of trust: in the latter, wrongful non-investment of trust, wrongful interception of trust, wrongful divestment of trust, wrongful abdication of trust, and wrongful detrectation of trust.

So much for the offences which concern the existence or possession of a trust: those which concern the exercise of the functions that belong to it may be thus conceived. You are in possession of a trust: the time then for your acting in it must, on any given occasion, (neglecting for simplicity's sake, the then present instant) be either past or yet to come. If past, your conduct on that occasion must have been either conformable to the purposes for which the trust was instituted, or unconformable: if conformable, there has been no mischief in the case: if unconformable, the fault has been either in yourself alone, or in some other person, or in both: in as far as it has lain in yourself, it has consisted either in your *not* doing something which you ought to do, in which case it may be styled *negative breach of trust;* or in your *doing* something which you ought *not* to do: if in the doing something which you ought not to do, the party to whom the prejudice has accrued is either the same for whose benefit the trust was instituted, or some other party at large: in the former of these cases, the offence may be styled *positive breach of trust*; in the other, *abuse of trust*.[1] In as far as the fault lies in another person, the offence on his part may be styled *disturbance of trust*. Supposing the time for your acting in the trust to be yet to come, the effect of any act which tends to render your conduct unconformable to the purposes of the trust, may be either to render it actually and eventually unconformable, or to produce a chance of its being so. In the former of these cases, it can do no otherwise than take one or other of the shapes that have just been mentioned. In the latter case, the blame must lie either in yourself alone, or in some other person, or in both together, as before. If in another person, the acts whereby he may tend to render your conduct unconformable, must be exercised either on yourself, or on other objects at large. If exercised on yourself, the influence they possess must either be such as operates immediately on your body, or such as operates immediately on your mind. In the latter case, again, the tendency of them must be to deprive you either of the knowledge, or of the power, or of the inclination,[2] which would be necessary to your maintaining such a conduct as shall be conformable to the purposes in question. If they be such, of which the tendency is to deprive you of the inclination in question, it must be by applying to your will the force of some *seducing* motive.[3] Lastly, This motive must be either of the *coercive*, or of the *alluring* kind; in other words, it must present itself either in the shape of a mischief or of an advantage. Now in none of all the cases that have been mentioned, except the last, does the offence

---

[1] What is here meant by abuse of trust, is the exercise of a power usurped over strangers, under favour of the powers properly belonging to the trust. The distinction between what is here meant by breach of trust, and what is here meant by abuse of trust, is not very steadily observed in common speech: and in regard to public trusts, it will even in many cases be imperceptible. The two offences are, however, in themselves perfectly distinct: since the persons, by whom the prejudice is suffered, are in many cases altogether different. It may be observed, perhaps, that with regard to abuse of trust, there is but one species here mentioned; viz. that which corresponds to positive breach of trust: none being mentioned as corresponding to negative breach of trust. The reason of this distinction will presently appear. In favour of the parties, for whose benefit the trust was created, the trustee is bound to act; and therefore merely by his doing nothing they may receive a prejudice: but in favour of other persons at large he is not bound to act: and therefore it is only from some positive act on his part that any prejudice can ensue to them.

[2] See infra, 54 note; and Chap. xviii. [Indirect Legislation].

[3] See Chap. xi. [Dispositions], 29.

receive any new denomination; according to the event it is either a disturbance of trust, or an abortive attempt to be guilty of that offence. In this last it is termed *bribery;* and it is that particular species of it which may be termed *active* bribery, or *bribe-giving.* In this case, to consider the matter on your part, either you accept of the bribe, or you do not: if not, and you do not afterwards commit, or go about to commit, either a breach or an abuse of trust, there is no offence, on your part, in the case: if you do accept it, whether you eventually do or do not commit the breach or the abuse which it is the bribe-giver's intention you should commit, you at any rate commit an offence which is also termed bribery: and which, for distinction sake, may be termed *passive* bribery, or *bribe-taking.*[1] As to any farther distinctions, they will depend upon the nature of the particular sort of trust in question, and therefore belong not to the present place. And thus we have thirteen sub-divisions of offences against trust: viz. 1. Wrongful non-investment of trust. 2. Wrongful interception of trust. 3. Wrongful divestment of trust. 4. Usurpation of trust. 5. Wrongful investment or attribution of trust. 6. Wrongful abdication of trust. 7. Wrongful detrectation of trust. 8. Wrongful imposition of trust. 9. Negative breach of trust. 10. Positive breach of trust. 11. Abuse of trust. 12. Disturbance of trust. 13. Bribery.

Prodigality in trustees dismissed to Class 3.

28. From what has been said, it appears that there cannot be any other offences, on the part of a trustee, by which a *beneficiary* can receive on any particular occasion any assignable specific prejudice. One sort of acts, however, there are by which a trustee may be put in some *danger* of receiving a prejudice, although neither the nature of the prejudice, nor the occasion on which he is in danger of receiving it, should be assignable. These can be no other than such acts, whatever they may be, as dispose the trustee to be acted upon by a

[1] To bribe a trustee, as such, is in fact neither more nor less than to *suborn* him to be guilty of a breach or an abuse of trust. Now subornation is of the number of those *accessory* offences which every principal offence, one as well as another, is liable to be attended with. See infra, 31. note; and B. I. tit [Accessory offences]. This particular species of subornation however being one that, besides its having a specific name framed to express it, is apt to engage a peculiar share of attention, and to present itself to view in company with other offences against trust, it would have seemed an omission not to have included it in that catalogue.

given bribe with greater effect than any with which he could otherwise be acted upon: or in other words, which place him in such circumstances as have a tendency to increase the quantum of his sensibility to the action of any motive of the sort in question.[1] Of these acts, there seem to be no others, that will admit of a description applicable to all places and times alike, than acts of *prodigality* on the part of the trustee. But in acts of this nature the prejudice to the *beneficiary* is contingent only and unliquidated; while the prejudice to the trustee himself is certain and liquidated. If therefore on any occasion it should be found advisable to treat it on the footing of an offence, it will find its place more naturally in the class of self-regarding ones.

29. As to the subdivisions of offences against trust, these are perfectly analogous to those of offences by falsehood. The trust may be private, semi-public, or public: it may concern property, person, reputation, or condition; or any two or more of those articles at a time: as will be more particularly explained in another place. Here too the offence, in running over the ground occupied by the three prior classes, will in some instances change its name, while in others it will not. *The subdivisions of offences against trust are also determined by the divisions of the preceding classes.*

30. Lastly, if it be asked, What sort of relation there subsists between falsehoods on one hand, and offences concerning trust on the other hand; the answer is, they are altogether disparate. Falsehood is a circumstance that may enter into the composition of any sort of offence, those concerning trust, as well as any other: in some as an accidental, in others as an essential instrument. Breach or abuse of trust are circumstances which, in the character of accidental concomitants, may enter into the composition of any other offences (those against falsehood included) besides those to which they respectively give name. *Connection between offences by falsehood and offences against trust.*

§ 3. *Genera of Class I.*

31. Returning now to class the first, let us pursue the distribution a step farther, and branch out the several divisions of that class, as above exhibited, into their respective *genera*, that is, into such minuter divisions as are capable of being *Analysis into genera pursued no farther than Class 1.*

[1] See Chap. vi. [Sensibility] 2.

characterised by denominations of which a great part are already current among the people.[1] In this place the analysis must stop. To apply it in the same regular form to any of the other classes seems scarcely practicable: to semi-public, as also to public offences, on account of the interference of local circumstances: to self-regarding ones, on account of the necessity it would create of deciding prematurely upon points which may appear liable to controversy: to offences by false-hood, and offences against trust, on account of the dependence there is between this class and the three former. What remains to be done in this way, with reference to these four classes, will require discussion, and will therefore be introduced with more propriety in the body of the work, than in a preliminary part, of which the business is only to draw outlines.

Offences against an individual may be simple in their effects, or complex.

32. An act, by which the happiness of an individual is disturbed, is either *simple* in its effects or *complex*. It may be styled simple in its effects, when it affects him in one only of the articles or points in which his interest, as we have seen, is liable to be affected: complex, when it affects him in several of those points at once. Such as are simple in their effects must of course be first considered.

Offences against person—their genera.

33. In a simple way, that is in one way at a time, a man's happiness is liable to be disturbed either 1. By actions referring to his own person itself; or 2. By actions referring to such external objects on which his happiness is more or less dependent. As to his own person, it is composed of two different parts, or reputed parts, his body and his mind. Acts which exert a pernicious influence on his person, whether it be on the corporeal or on the mental part of it, will operate thereon either immediately, and without affecting his will, or mediately, through the intervention of that faculty: viz. by means of the influence which they cause his will to exercise over his body. If with the intervention of his will, it must be by *mental coercion*: that is, by causing him to *will* to maintain,

---

[1] In the enumeration of these genera, it is all along to be observed, that offences of an accessory nature are not mentioned; unless it be here and there where they have obtained current names which seemed too much in vogue to be omitted. Accessory offences are those which, without being the very acts from which the mischief in question takes its immediate rise, are, in the way of causality, connected with those acts. See Chap. vii. [Actions] 24. and B. I. tit. [Accessory offences].

and thence actually to maintain, a certain conduct which it is disagreeable, or in any other way pernicious, to him to maintain. This conduct may either be positive or negative:[1] when positive, the coercion is styled *compulsion* or *constraint*: when negative, *restraint*. Now the way in which the coercion is disagreeable to him, may be by producing either pain of body, or only pain of mind. If pain of body is produced by it, the offence will come as well under this as under other denominations, which we shall come to presently. Moreover, the conduct which a man, by means of the coercion, is forced to maintain, will be determined either specifically and originally, by the determination of the particular acts themselves which he is forced to perform or to abstain from, or generally and incidentally, by means of his being forced to be or not to be in such or such a place. But if he is prevented from being in one place, he is confined thereby to another. For the whole surface of the earth, like the surface of any greater or lesser body, may be conceived to be divided into two, as well as into any other number of parts or spots. If the spot then, which he is confined to, be smaller than the spot which he is excluded from, his condition may be called *confinement*: if larger, *banishment*.[2] Whether an act, the effect of which is to exert a pernicious influence on the person of him who suffers by it, operates with or without the intervention of an act of his will, the mischief it produces will either be *mortal* or *not mortal*. If not mortal, it will either be *reparable*, that is temporary; or *irreparable*, that is perpetual. If reparable, the mischievous act may be termed a *simple corporal injury*; if irreparable, an *irreparable corporal injury*. Lastly, a pain that a man experiences in his mind will either be a pain of actual *sufferance*, or a pain of *apprehension*. If a pain of apprehension, either the offender himself is represented as intending to bear a part in the production of it, or he is not. In the former case the offence may be styled *menacement*: in the latter case, as also where the pain is a pain of actual sufferance, a *simple mental*

---

[1] Chap. vii. [Actions], 8.
[2] Of these, and the several other leading expressions which there is occasion to bring to view in the remaining part of this analysis, ample definitions will be found in the body of the work, conceived in *terminis legis*. To give particular references to these definitions, would be encumbering the page to little purpose.

injury. And thus we have nine genera or kinds of personal injuries; which, when ranged in the order most commodious for examination, will stand as follows: viz. 1. Simple corporal injuries. 2. Irreparable corporal injuries. 3. Simple injurious restrainment. 4. Simple injurious compulsion.[1] 5. Wrongful confinement. 6. Wrongful banishment. 7. Wrongful homicide. 8. Wrongful menacement.[2] 9. Simple mental injuries.[3]

[1] Injurious restrainment at large, and injurious compulsion at large, are her, styled *simple*, in order to distinguish them from confinement, banishmente robbery, and extortion; all which are, in many cases, but so many modifications of one or other of the two first-mentioned offences.

To constitute an offence an act of simple injurious restrainment, or simple injurious compulsion, it is sufficient if the influence it exerts be, in the first place, pernicious; in the next place, exerted on the person by the medium of the will: it is not necessary that that part of the person on which it is exerted be the part to which it is pernicious: it is not even necessary that it should immediately be pernicious to either of these parts, though to one or other of them it must be pernicious in the long-run, if it be pernicious at all. An act in which the body, for example, is concerned, may be very disagreeable, and thereby pernicious to him who performs it, though neither disagreeable nor pernicious to his body: for instance, to stand or sit in public with a label on his back, or under any other circumstances of ignominy.

[2] It may be observed, that wrongful menacement is included as well in simple injurious restrainment as in simple injurious compulsion, except in the rare case where the motives by which one man is prevented by another from doing a thing that would have been materially to his advantage, or induced to do a thing that is materially to his prejudice, are of the *alluring* kind.

[3] Although, for reasons that have been already given (supra 31), no complete catalogue, nor therefore any exhaustive view, of either semi-public or self-regarding offences, can be exhibited in this chapter, it may be a satisfaction, however, to the reader, to see some sort of list of them, if it were only for the sake of having examples before his eyes. Such lists cannot anywhere be placed to more advantage than under the heads of the several divisions of private extra-regarding offences, to which the semi-public and self-regarding offences in question respectively correspond. Concerning the two latter, however, and the last more particularly, it must be understood that all I mean by inserting them there, is to exhibit the mischief, if any, which it is of the nature of them respectively to produce, without deciding upon the question, whether it would be *worth while* [see Chap. xiii. Cases unmeet] in every instance, for the sake of combating that mischief, to introduce the evil of punishment. In the course of this detail, it will be observed, that there are several heads of extra-regarding private offences, to which the correspondent heads, either of semi-public or self-regarding offences. or of both, are wanting. The reasons of these deficiencies will probably, in most instances, be evident enough upon the face of them. Lest they should not, they are however specified in the body of the work. They would take up too much room were they to be inserted here.

I. SEMI-PUBLIC OFFENCES through calamity. Calamities, by which the persons or properties of men, or both, are liable to be affected, seem to be as follows: 1. Pestilence or contagion. 2. Famine, and other kinds of scarcity. 3. Mischiefs producible by persons deficient in point of understanding, such as infants,

34. We come now to offences against reputation merely. *Offence against* These require but few distinctions. In point of reputation *reputation.* there is but one way of suffering, which is by losing a portion of the good-will of others. Now, in respect of the good-will which others bear you, you may be a loser in either of two ways: 1. By the manner in which you are thought to behave *yourself*; and 2. By the manner in which *others* behave, or are thought to behave, towards you. To cause people to think that you yourself have so behaved, as to have been guilty of any of those acts which cause a man to possess less than he did before of the good-will of the community, is what may be styled *defamation*. But such is the constitution

idiots, and maniacs, for want of their being properly taken care of. 4. Mischief producible by the ravages of noxious animals, such as beasts of prey, locusts, &c. &c. 5. Collapsion, or fall of large masses of solid matter, such as decayed buildings, or rocks, or masses of snow. 6. Inundation or submersion. 7. Tempest. 8. Blight, 9. Conflagration. 10. Explosion. In as far as a man may contribute, by any imprudent act of his, to give birth to any of the above calamities, such act may be an offence. In so far as a man may fail to do what is incumbent on him to do towards preventing them, such failure may be an offence.

II. SEMI-PUBLIC OFFENCES of mere delinquency. A whole neighbourhood may be made to suffer. 1. Simple corporal injuries: in other words, they may be made to suffer in point of health, by offensive or dangerous trades or manufactures: by selling or falsely puffing off unwholesome medicines or provisions: by poisoning or drying up of springs, destroying of aqueducts, destroying woods, walls, or other fences against wind and rain: by any kinds of artificial scarcity; or by any other calamities intentionally produced. 2. and 3. Simple injurious restrainment, and simple injurious compulsion: for instance, by obliging a whole neighbourhood, by dint of threatening hand-bills or threatening discourses, publicly delivered, to join, or forbear to join, in illuminations, acclamations, outcries, invectives, subscriptions, undertakings, processions, or any other mode of expressing joy or grief, displeasure, or approbation; or, in short, in any other course of conduct whatsoever. 4. and 5. Confinement and banishment: by the spoiling of roads, bridges, or ferry-boats: by destroying or unwarrantably pre-occupying public carriages, or houses of accommodation. 6. By menacement: as by incendiary letters, and tumultuous assemblies: by newspapers or handbills, denouncing vengeance against persons of particular denominations: for example, against Jews, Catholics, Protestants, Scotchmen, Gascons, Catalonians, &c. 7. Simple mental injuries: as by distressful, terrifying, obscene, or irreligious exhibitions; such as exposure of sores by beggars, exposure of dead bodies, exhibitions or reports of counterfeit witchcrafts or apparitions. exhibition of obscene or blasphemous prints: obscene or blasphemous discourses held in public: spreading false news of public defeats in battle, or of other misfortunes.

III. Self-regarding offences against person. 1. Fasting. Abstinence from venery, self-flagellation, self-mutilation, and other self-denying and self-tormenting practices. 2. Gluttony, drunkenness, excessive venery, and other species of intemperance. 3. Suicide.

of human nature, and such the force of prejudice, that a man merely by manifesting his own want of good-will towards you, though ever so unjust in itself, and ever so unlawfully expressed, may in a manner force others to withdraw from you a part of theirs. When he does this by words, or by such actions as have no other effect than in as far as they stand in the place of words, the offence may be styled *vilification*. When it is done by such actions as, besides their having this effect, are injuries to the person, the offence may be styled a *personal insult*: if it has got the length of reaching the body, a *corporal insult*: if it stopped short before it reached that length, it may be styled *insulting menacement*. And thus we have two *genera* or kinds of offences against reputation merely; to wit, 1 Defamation; and 2. Vilification, or Revilement.[1] As to corporal insults, and insulting menacement, they belong to the compound title of offences against person and reputation both together.

Offences against property. 35. If the property of one man suffers by the delinquency of another, such property either was in trust with the offender, or it was not: if it was in trust, the offence is a breach of trust, and of whatever nature it may be in other respects, may be styled *dissipation in breach of trust*, or *dissipation of property in trust*. This is a particular case: the opposite one is the more common: in such case the several ways in which property may, by possibility, become the object of an offence, may be thus conceived. Offences against property, of whatever kind it be, may be distinguished, as hath been already intimated,[2] into such as concern the legal possession of it, or right to it, and such as concern only the enjoyment of it, or, what is the same thing, the exercise of that right. Under the former of these heads come, as hath been already intimated,[3] the several offences of *wrongful non-investment*, *wrongful interception*, *wrongful divestment*, *usurpation*, and *wrongful attribution*. When in the commission of any of these offences a falsehood has served as an instrument, and that, as it is commonly called, a *wilful*, or as it might more properly be termed, an *advised*[4] one, the epithet *fraudulent* may be prefixed to the name of the

---

[1] I. SEMI-PUBLIC OFFENCES. 1. Calumniation and vilification of particular denominations of persons; such as Jews, Catholics, &c.

II. SELF-REGARDING OFFENCES. 1. Incontinence in females. 2. Incest.

[2] Supra 27.   [3] Ib.   [4] See Chap. ix. [Consciousness], 2.

offence, or substituted in the room of the word *wrongful*. The circumstance of fraudulency then may serve to characterise a particular species, comprisable under each of those generic heads: in like manner the circumstance of *force*, of which more a little farther on, may serve to characterise another. With respect to wrongful interception in particular, the *investitive event* by which the title to the thing in question should have accrued to you, and for want of which such title is, through the delinquency of the offender, as it were, *intercepted*, is either an act of his own, expressing it as his will, that you should be considered by the law as the person who is legally in possession of it, or it is any other event at large: in the former case, if the thing, of which you should have been put into possession, is a sum of money to a certain amount, the offence is that which has received the name of *insolvency*; which branch of delinquency, in consideration of the importance and extent of it, may be treated on the footing of a distinct genus of itself.[1]

[1] The light in which the offence of insolvency is here exhibited, may *Payment, what.* perhaps at first consideration be apt to appear not only novel but improper. It may naturally enough appear, that when a man owes you a sum of money, for instance, the right to the money is yours already, and that what he withholds from you by not paying you, is not the legal title to it, possession of it, or power over it, but the physical possession of it, or power over it, only. But upon a more accurate examination this will be found not to be the case. What is meant by payment, is always an act of investitive power, as above explained; an expression of an act of the will, and not a physical act: it is an act exercised *with relation* indeed *to* the thing said to be *paid*, but not in a physical sense exercised *upon it*. A man who owes you ten pounds, takes up a handful of silver to that amount, and lays it down on a table at which you are sitting. If then by words, or gestures, or any means whatsoever, addressing himself to you, he intimates it is to be his will that you should take up the money, and do with it as you please, he is said to have *paid* you: but if the case was, that he laid it down not for that purpose, but for some other, for instance, to count it and examine it, meaning to take it up again himself or leave it for somebody else, he has *not* paid you: yet the physical acts, exercised upon the pieces of money in question, are in both cases the same. Till he does express a will to that purport, what you have is not, properly speaking, the legal possession of the money, or a right to the money, but only a right to have him, or in his default perhaps a minister of justice, compelled to render you that sort of service, by the rendering of which he is said to pay you: that is, to express such will as above-mentioned, with regard to some corporeal article, or other of a certain species, and of value equal to the amount of what he owes you: or, in other words, to exercise in your favour an act of investitive power with relation to some such article.

True it is, that in certain cases a man may perhaps not be deemed, according to common acceptation, to have *paid* you, without rendering you a further

Z

Next, with regard to such of the offences against property as concern only the enjoyment of the object in question. This object must be either a service, or set of services,[1] which should have been rendered by some *person*, or else an article belonging to the class of *things*. In the former case, the offence may be styled *wrongful withholding of services*.[2] In the latter case it may admit of farther modifications, which may be thus conceived: When any object which you have had the physical occupation or enjoyment of, ceases, in any degree, in consequence of the act of another man, and without any change made in so much of that power as depends upon the intrinsic physical condition of your person, to be subject to that power; this cessation is either owing to change in the intrinsic condition of the thing itself, or in its exterior situation with respect to you, that is, to its being situated out of your reach. In the former case, the nature of the change is either such as to put it out of your power to make any use of it at all, in which case the thing is said to be *destroyed*, and the offence whereby it is so treated may be termed *wrongful destruction*: or such only as to render the uses it is capable of being put to

set of services, and those of another sort: a set of services, which are rendered by the exercising of certains acts of a physical nature upon the very thing with which he is said to pay you: to wit, by transferring the thing to a certain place where you may be sure to find it, and where it may be convenient for you to receive it. But these services, although the obligation of rendering them should be annexed by law to the obligation of rendering those other services in the performance of which the operation of payment properly consists, are plainly acts of a distinct nature: nor are they essential to the operation: by themselves they do not constitute it, and it may be performed without them. It *must* be performed without them wherever the thing to be transferred happens to be already as much within the reach, physically speaking, of the creditor, as by any act of the debtor it can be made to be.

This matter would have appeared in a clearer light had it been practicable to enter here into a full examination of the nature of property, and the several modifications of which it is susceptible: but every thing cannot be done at once.

[1] Supra 26.

[2] Under wrongful withholding of services is included *breach of contract:* for the obligation to render services may be grounded either on contract, or upon other titles: in other words, the event of a man's engaging in a contract is one out of many other investitive events from which the right of receiving them may takes its commencement. See Chap. xvii. [Limits], § iv.

Were the word *services* to be taken in its utmost latitude (negative included as well as positive) this one head would cover the whole law. To this place then are to be referred such services only, the withholding of which does not coincide with any of the other offences, for which separate denominations have been provided.

of less value than before, in which case it is said to be *damaged*, or to have sustained damage, and the offence may be termed *wrongful endamagement*. Moreover, in as far as the value which a thing is of to you is considered as being liable to be in some degree impaired, by any act on the part of any other person exercised upon that thing, although on a given occasion no perceptible damage should ensue, the exercise of any such act is commonly treated on the footing of an offence, which may be termed *wrongful using* or *occupation*.

If the cause of the thing's failing in its capacity of being of use to you, lies in the exterior situation of it with relation to you, the offence may be styled *wrongful detainment*.[1] Wrongful detainment, or detention, during any given period of time, may either be accompanied with the intention of detaining the thing for ever (that is for an indefinite time), or not: if it be, and if it be accompanied at the same time with the intention of not being amenable to law for what is done, it seems to answer to the idea commonly annexed to the word *embezzlement*, an offence which is commonly accompanied with breach of trust.[2] In the case of wrongful occupation, the physical faculty of occupying may have been obtained with or without the assistance or consent of the proprietor, or other person appearing to have a right to afford such assistance or consent. If without such assistance or consent, and the occupation be accompanied with the intention of detaining the thing for ever, together with the intention of not being amenable to law for what is done, the offence seems to

---

[1] In the English law, *detinue* and *detainer*: detinue applied chiefly to movables; detainer, to immovables. Under detinue and detainer cases are also comprised, in which the offence consists in forbearing to transfer the legal possession of the thing: such cases may be considered as coming under the head of wrongful non-investment. The distinction between mere physical possession and legal possession, where the latter is short-lived and defeasible, seems scarcely hitherto to have been attended to. In a multitude of instances they are confounded under the same expressions. The cause is, that probably under all laws, and frequently for very good reasons, the legal possession, with whatever certainty defeasible upon the event of a trial, is, down to the time of that event, in many cases annexed to the appearance of the physical.

[2] In attempting to exhibit the import belonging to this and other names of offences in common use, I must be understood to speak all along with the utmost diffidence. The truth is, the import given to them is commonly neither determinate nor uniform: so that in the nature of things, no definition that can be given of them by a private person can be altogether an exact one. To fix the sense of them belongs only to the legislator.

answer to the idea commonly annexed to the word *theft* or *stealing*. If in the same circumstances a force is put upon the body of any person who uses, or appears to be disposed to use, any endeavours to prevent the act, this seems to be one of the cases in which the offence is generally understood to come under the name of *robbery*.

If the physical faculty in question was obtained with the assistance or consent of a proprietor or other person above spoken of, and still the occupation of the thing is an offence, it may have been either because the assistance or consent was not fairly or because it was not freely obtained. If not *fairly* obtained, it was obtained by falsehood, which, if *advised*, is in such a case termed *fraud*: and the offence, if accompanied with the intention of not being amenable to law, may be termed *fraudulent obtainment* or *defraudment*.[1] If not *freely* obtained, it was obtained by *force*: to wit, either by a force put upon the body, which has been already mentioned, or by a force put upon the mind. If by a force put upon the mind, or in other words, by the application of coercive motives,[2] it must be by producing the apprehension of some evil: which evil, if the act is an offence, must be some evil to which on the occasion in question the one person has no right to expose the other. This is one case in which, if the offence be accompanied with the intention of detaining the thing for ever, whether it be or be not accompanied with the intention of not being amenable to law, it seems to agree with the idea of what is commonly meant by *extortion*. Now the part a man takes in exposing another to the evil in question, must be either a positive or a negative part. In the former case, again, the evil must either be present or distant. In the case then where the assistance or consent is obtained by a force put upon the body, or where, if by a force put upon the mind, the part taken in the exposing a man to the apprehension of the evil is positive, the evil present, and the object of it his person, and if at any rate the extortion, thus applied, be

---

[1] The remaining cases comes under the head of usurpation, or wrongful investment of property. The distinction seems hardly hitherto to have been attended to: it turns like another, mentioned above, upon the distinction between legal possession and physical. The same observation may be applied to the case of extortion hereafter following.

[2] Vide supra, 27.

accompanied with the intention of not being amenable to law, it seems to agree with the remaining case of what goes under the name of *robbery*.

As to dissipation in breach of trust, this, when productive of a pecuniary profit to the trustee, seems to be one species of what is commonly meant by *peculation*. Another, and the only remaining one, seems to consist in acts of occupation exercised by the trustee upon the things which are the objects of the fiduciary property, for his own benefit, and to the damage of the beneficiary. As to robbery, this offence, by the manner in which the assistance or consent is obtained, becomes an offence against property and person at the same time. Dissipation in breach of trust, and peculation, may perhaps be more commodiously treated of under the head of offences against trust.[1] After these exceptions, we have thirteen genera or principal kinds of offences against property, which, when ranged in the order most commodious for examination, may stand as follows, viz. 1. Wrongful non-investment of property. 2. Wrongful interception of property. 3. Wrongful divestment of property. 4. Usurpation of property. 5. Wrongful investment of property. 6. Wrongful withholding of services. 7. Wrongful destruction or endamagement. 8. Wrongful occupation. 9. Wrongful detainment. 10. Embezzlement. 11. Theft. 12. Defraudment. 13. Extortion.[2]

We proceed now to consider offences which are complex in their effects. Regularly, indeed, we should come to offences against condition; but it will be more convenient to speak

[1] Usury, which, if it must be an offence, is an offence committed with consent, that is, with the consent of the party supposed to be injured, cannot merit a place in the catalogue of offences, unless the consent were either unfairly obtained or unfreely: in the first case, it coincides with defraudment; in the other, with extortion.

[2] I. SEMI-PUBLIC OFFENCES. 1. Wrongful divestment, interception, usurpation, &c., of valuables, which are the property of a corporate body; or which are in the indiscriminate occupation of a neighbourhood; such as parish churches, altars, relics, and other articles appropriated to the purposes of religion: or things which are in the indiscriminate occupation of the public at large; such as mile-stones, market-houses, exchanges, public gardens, and cathedrals. 2. Setting on foot what have been called *bubbles*, or fraudulent partnership, or gaming adventures; propagating false news, to raise or sink the value of stocks, or of any other denomination of property.
II. SELF-REGARDING OFFENCES. 1. Idleness. 2. Gaming. 3. Other species of prodigality.

first of offences by which a man's interest is affected in two of the preceding points at once.

Offences against person and reputation.

36. First, then, with regard to offences which affect person and reputation together. When any man, by a mode of treatment which affects the person, injures the reputation of another, his end and purpose must have been either his own immediate pleasure, or that sort of reflected pleasure, which in certain circumstances may be reaped from the suffering of another. Now the only immediate pleasure worth regarding, which any one can reap from the person of another, and which at the same time is capable of affecting the reputation of the latter, is the pleasure of the sexual appetite.[1] This pleasure, then, if reaped at all, must have been reaped either against the consent of the party, or with consent. If with consent, the consent must have been obtained either freely and fairly both, or freely but not fairly, or else not even freely; in which case the fairness is out of the question. If the consent be altogether wanting, the offence is called *rape*: if not fairly obtained, *seduction* simply: if not freely, it may be called *forcible seduction*. In any case, either the offence has gone the length of consummation, or has stopped short of that period; if it has gone that length, it takes one or other of the names just mentioned: if not, it may be included alike in all cases under the denomination of a *simple lascivious injury*. Lastly, to take the case where a man injuring you in your reputation, by proceedings that regard your person, does it for the sake of that sort of pleasure which will sometimes result from the contemplation of another's pain. Under these circumstances either the offence has actually gone the length of a corporal injury, or it has rested in menacement: in the first case it may be styled a *corporal insult*; in the other, it may come under the name of *insulting menacement*. And thus we have six genera, or kind of offences, against person and reputation together; which, when ranged in the order most commodious for consideration, will stand thus: 1. Corporal insults. 2. Insulting menacement. 3. Seduction. 4. Rape. 5. Forcible seduction. 6. Simple lascivious injuries.[2]

[1] See Chap. v. [Pleasures and Pains].
[2] I. Semi-public Offences—none.
　II. Self-regarding Offences. 1. Sacrifice of virginity. 2. Indecencies not public.

37. Secondly, with respect to those which affect person *Offences against* and property together. That a force put upon the person of a *person and property.* man may be among the means by which the title to property may be unlawfully taken away or acquired, has been already stated.[1] A force of this sort then is a circumstance which may accompany the offences of wrongful interception, wrongful divestment, usurpation, and wrongful investment. But in these cases the intervention of this circumstance does not happen to have given any new denomination to the offence.[2] In all or any of these cases, however, by prefixing the epithet *forcible*, we may have so many names of offences, which may either be considered as constituting so many species of the genera belonging to the division of offences against property, or as so many genera belonging to the division now before us. Among the offences that concern the enjoyment of the thing, the case is the same with wrongful destruction and wrongful endamagement; as also with wrongful occupation and wrongful detainment. As to the offence of wrongful occupation, it is only in the case where the thing occupied belongs to the class of immovables, that, when accompanied by the kind of force in question, has obtained a particular name which is in common use: in this case it is called *forcible entry*: forcible detainment, as applied also to immovables, but only to immovables, has obtained, among lawyers at least, the name of *forcible detainer*.[3] And thus we may distinguish ten genera, or kinds of offences, against person and property together, which, omitting for conciseness' sake the epithet *wrongful*, will stand thus: 1. Forcible interception of property. 2. Forcible divestment of property. 3. Forcible usurpation. 4. Forcible investment. 5. Forcible destruction or endamagement. 6. Forcible occupation of movables. 7. Forcible entry.

[1] Supra.

[2] In the technical language of the English law, property so acquired is said to be acquired by *duress*.

[3] Applied to movables, the circumstance of force has never, at least by the technical part of the language, been taken into account: no such combination of terms as *forcible occupation* is in current use. The word *detinue* is applied to movables only: and (in the language of the law) the word *forcible* has never been combined with it. The word applied to immovables is *detainer*: this is combined with the word *forcible*: and what is singular, it is scarcely in use without that word. It was impossible to steer altogether clear of this technical nomenclature, on account of the influence which it has on the body of the language.

8. Forcible detainment of movables. 9. Forcible detainment of immovables. 10. Robbery.[1]

Offences against condition.— Conditions domestic or civil.

38. We come now to offences against *condition*. A man's condition or station in life is constituted by the legal relation he bears to the persons who are about him; that is, as we have already had occasion to show,[2] by *duties*, which, by being imposed on one side, give birth to *rights* or *powers* on the other. These relations, it is evident, may be almost infinitely diversified. Some means, however, may be found of circumscribing the field within which the varieties of them are displayed. In the first place, they must either be such as are capable of displaying themselves within the circle of a private family, or such as require a larger space. The conditions constituted by the former sort of relations may be styled *domestic*: those constituted by the latter, *civil*.

Domestic conditions grounded on natural relationships.

39. As to domestic conditions, the legal relations by which they are constituted may be distinguished into 1. Such as are superadded to relations purely natural: and 2. Such as, without any such natural basis, subsist purely by institution. By relations purely natural, I mean those which may be said to subsist between certain persons in virtue of the concern which they themselves, or certain other persons, have had in the process which is necessary to the continuance of the species. These relations may be distinguished, in the first place, into contiguous and uncontiguous. The uncontiguous subsist through the intervention of such as are contiguous. The contiguous may be distinguished, in the first place, into *connubial*, and *post-connubial*.[3] Those which may be termed connubial are two: 1. That which the male bears towards the female: 2. That which the female bears to the male.[4] The post-connubial are either *productive* or *derivative*.

---

[1] I. Semi-public Offences. 1. Incendiarism. 2. Criminal inundation.
    II. Self-regarding Offences—none.

[2] Supra, 25. note.

[3] By the terms *connubial* and *post-connubial*, all I mean at present to bring to view is, the mere physical union, apart from the ceremonies and legal engagements that will afterwards be considered as accompanying it.

Relations— two result from every two objects.

[4] The vague and undetermined nature of the fictitious entity, called a relation, is, on occasions like the present, apt to be productive of a good deal of confusion. A relation is either said to be *borne by* one of the objects which are parties to it, to the other, or to *subsist between* them. The latter mode of phraseology is, perhaps, rather the more common. In such case the idea seems to be,

The productive is that which the male and female above-mentioned bear each of them towards the children who are the immediate fruit of their union; this is termed the relation of *parentality*. Now as the parents must be, so the children may be, of different sexes. Accordingly the relation of parentality may be distinguished into four species: 1. That which a father bears to his son: this is termed *paternity*. 2. That which a father bears to his daughter: this also is termed paternity. 3. That which a mother bears to her son: this is called *maternity*. 4. That which a mother bears to her daughter: this also is termed maternity. Uncontiguous natural relations may be distinguished into *immediate* and *remote*. Such as are immediate, are what one person bears to another in consequence of their bearing each of them one simple relation to some third person. Thus the paternal grandfather is related to the paternal grandson by means of the two different relations, of different kinds, which together they bear to the father: the brother on the father's side, to the brother, by means of the two relations of the same kind, which together they bear to the father. In the same manner we might proceed to find places in the system for the infinitely diversified relations which result from the combinations that may be formed by mixing together the several sorts of relationships by *ascent*, relationships by *descent*, *collateral* relationships, and relationships by *affinity*: which latter, when the union between the two parties through whom the affinity takes place is sanctioned by matrimonial solemnities, are termed relationships by *marriage*. But this, as it would be a most intricate and tedious task, so happily is it, for the present purpose, an

that from the consideration of the two objects there results but one relation, which belongs as it were in common to them both. In some cases, this perhaps may answer the purpose very well: it will not, however, in the present case. For the present purpose it will be necessary we should conceive two relations as resulting from the two objects, and *borne*, since such is the phrase, *by* the one of them to or towards the other: one relation borne by the first object to the second: another relation borne by the second object to the first. This is necessary on two accounts: 1. Because for the relations themselves there are in many instances separate names: for example, the relations of guardianship and wardship: in which case, the speaking of them as if they were but one, may be productive of much confusion. 2. Because the two different relationships give birth to so many conditions: which conditions are so far different, that what is predicated and will hold good of the one, will, in various particulars, as we shall see, not hold good of the other.

unnecessary one. The only natural relations to which it will be necessary to pay any particular attention, are those which, when sanctioned by law, give birth to the conditions of husband and wife, the two relations comprised under the head of parentality, and the corresponding relations comprised under the head of filiality or filiation.

What then are the relations of a legal kind which can be superinduced upon the above-mentioned natural relations? They must be such as it is the nature of law to give birth to and establish. But the relations which subsist purely by institution exhaust, as we shall see, the whole stock of relationships which it is in the nature of the law to give birth to and establish. The relations then which can be superinduced upon those which are purely natural, cannot be in themselves any other than what are of the number of those which subsist purely by institution: so that all the difference there can be between a legal relation of the one sort, and a legal relation of the other sort, is, that in the former case the circumstance which gave birth to the natural relation serves as a mark to indicate where the legal relation is to fix: in the latter case, the place where the legal relation is to attach is determined not by that circumstance but by some other. From these considerations it will appear manifestly enough, that for treating of the several sorts of conditions, as well natural as purely conventional, in the most commodious order, it will be necessary to give the precedence to the latter. Proceeding throughout upon the same principle, we shall all along give the priority, not to those which are first by nature, but to those which are most simple in point of description. There is no other way of avoiding perpetual anticipations and repetitions.

Domestic rela-
tions which are
purely of legal
institution.

40. We come now to consider the domestic or family relations, which are purely of legal institution. It is to these in effect, that both kinds of domestic conditions, considered as the work of law, are indebted for their origin. When the law, no matter for what purpose, takes upon itself to operate, in a matter in which it has not operated before, it can only be by imposing *obligation*.[1] Now when a legal obligation is imposed on any man, there are but two ways in which it can

[1] See Chap. xvii. [Limits], § iii.

in the first instance be enforced. The one is by giving the power of enforcing it to the party in whose favour it is imposed: the other is by reserving that power to certain third persons, who, in virtue of their possessing it, are styled ministers of justice. In the first case, the party favoured is said to possess not only a *right* as against the party obliged, but also a *power* over him: in the second case, a *right* only, uncorroborated by power. In the first case, the party favoured may be styled a *superior*, and as they are both members of the same family, a *domestic superior*, with reference to the party obliged: who, in the same case, may be styled a *domestic inferior*, with reference to the party favoured. Now in point of possibility, it is evident, that domestic conditions, or a kind of fictitious possession analogous to domestic conditions, might have been looked upon as constituted, as well by rights alone, without powers on either side, as by powers. But in point of utility[1]

[1] Two persons, who by any means stand engaged to live together, can never live together long, but one of them will choose that some act or other should be done which the other will choose should not be done. When this is the case, how is the competition to be decided? Laying aside generosity and good-breeding, which are the tardy and uncertain fruits of long-established laws, it is evident that there can be no certain means of deciding it but physical power: which indeed is the very means by which family as well as other competitions must have been decided, long before any such office as that of legislator had existence. This then being the order of things which the legislator finds established by nature, how should he do better than to acquiesce in it? The persons who by the influence of causes that prevail every where, stand engaged to live together, are, 1. Parent and child, during the infancy of the latter: 2. Man and wife: 3. Children of the same parents. Parent and child, by necessity: since, if the child did not live with the parent (or with somebody standing in the place of the parent) it could not live at all: husband and wife, by a choice approaching to necessity: children of the same parents, by the necessity of their living each of them with the parents. As between parent and child, the necessity there is of a power on the part of the parent for the preservation of the child supersedes all farther reasoning. As between man and wife, that necessity does not subsist. The only reason that applies to this case is the necessity of putting an end to competition. The man would have the meat roasted, the woman boiled: shall they both fast till the judge comes in to dress it for them? The woman would have the child dressed in green; the man, in blue: shall the child be naked till the judge comes in to clothe it? This affords a reason for giving a power to one or other of the parties: but it affords none for giving the power to the one rather than to the other. How then shall the legislator determine? Supposing it equally easy to give it to either, let him look ever so long for a reason why he should give it to the one rather than to the other, and he may look in vain. But how does the matter stand already? for there were men and wives (or, what comes to the same thing, male and female living together as man and wife) before there were legislators. Looking round him then, he finds almost every where the male the stronger

it does not seem expedient: and in point of fact, probably owing to the invariable perception which men must have had of the inexpediency, no such conditions seem ever to have been constituted by such feeble hands. Of the legal relationships then, which are capable of being made to subsist within the circle of a family, there remain those only in which the obligation is enforced by power. Now then, wherever any such power is conferred, the end or purpose for which it was conferred (unless the legislator can be supposed to act without a motive) must have been the producing of a benefit to somebody: in other words, it must have been conferred for the *sake* of somebody. The person then, for whose sake it is conferred, must either be one of the two parties just mentioned, or a third party: if one of these two, it must be either the superior or the inferior. If the superior, such superior is commonly called a *master*; and the inferior is termed his *servant*: and the power may be termed a *beneficial* one. If it be for the sake of the inferior that the power is established, the superior is termed a *guardian*; and the inferior his *ward*: and the power, being thereby coupled with a trust, may be termed a *fiduciary* one. If for the sake of a third party, the superior may be termed a *superintendent*; and the inferior his *subordinate*. This third party will either be an assignable individual or set of individuals, or a set of unassignable individuals. In this latter case the trust is either a public or a semi-public one: and the condition which it constitutes is not of the domestic, but of the civil kind. In the former case,

of the two; and therefore possessing already, by purely physical means, that power which he is thinking of bestowing on one of them by means of law. How then can he do so well as by placing the legal power in the same hands which are beyond comparison the more likely to be in possession of the physical? in this way, few transgressions, and few calls for punishment: in the other way, perpetual transgressions, and perpetual calls for punishment. Solon is said to have transferred the same idea to the distribution of state powers. Here then was *generalization*: here was the work of genius. But in the disposal of domestic power, every legislator, without any effort of genius, has been a Solon. So much for *reasons*:[a] add to which, in point of *motives*,[b] that legislators seem all to have been of the male sex, down to the days of Catherine. I speak here of those who frame laws, not of those who touch them with a sceptre.

[a] Social motives: sympathy for the public: love of reputation, &c.

[b] Self-regarding motives: or social motives, which are social in a less extent: sympathy for persons of a particular description: persons of the same sex.

this third party or *principal*, as he may be termed, either has a beneficial power over the superintendent, or he has not: if he has, the superintendent is his servant, and consequently so also is the subordinate: if not, the superintendent is the master of the subordinate; and all the advantage which the principal has over his superintendent, is that of possessing a set of rights, uncorroborated by power; and therefore, as we have seen,[1] not fit to constitute a condition of the domestic kind. But be the condition what it may which is constituted by these rights, of what nature can the obligations be, to which the superintendent is capable of being subjected by means of them? They are neither more nor less than those which a man is capable of being subjected to by powers. It follows, therefore, that the functions of a principal and his superintendent coincide with those of a master and his servant; and consequently that the offences relative to the two former conditions will coincide with the offences relative to the two latter.

41. Offences to which the condition of a master, like any other kind of condition, is exposed, may, as hath been already intimated,[2] be distinguished into such as concern the existence of the condition itself, and such as concern the performance of the functions of it, while subsisting. First then, with regard to such as affect its existence. It is obvious enough that the services of one man may be a benefit to another: the condition of a master may therefore be a beneficial one. It stands exposed, therefore, to the offences of *wrongful non-investment*, *wrongful interception, usurpation, wrongful investment*, and *wrongful divestment*. But how should it stand exposed to the offences of *wrongful abdication, wrongful detrectation*, and *wrongful imposition*? Certainly it cannot of itself; for services, when a man has the power of exacting them or not, as he thinks fit, can never be a burthen. But if to the powers, by which the condition of a master is constituted, the law thinks fit to annex any obligation on the part of the master; for instance, that of affording maintenance, or giving wages, to the servant, or paying money to anybody else; it is evident that in virtue of such obligation the condition *may* become a burthen. In this case, however, the condition possessed by the master will

Offences touching the condition of a master.

---

[1] Supra, note, page 263.   [2] Vide supra, 27.

not, properly speaking, be the pure and simple condition of a master: it will be a kind of complex object, resolvable into the beneficial condition of a master, and the burthensome obligation which is annexed to it. Still however, if the nature of the obligation lies within a narrow compass, and does not, in the manner of that which constitutes a trust, interfere with the exercise of those powers by which the condition of the superior is constituted, the latter, notwithstanding this foreign mixture, will still retain the name of mastership.[1] In this case therefore, but not otherwise, the condition of a master may stand exposed to the offences of *wrongful abdication*, *wrongful detrectation*, and *wrongful imposition*. Next as to the behaviour of persons with reference to this condition, while considered as subsisting. In virtue of its being a benefit, it is exposed to *disturbance*. This disturbance will either be the offence of a stranger, or the offence of the servant himself. Where it is the offence of a stranger, and is committed by taking the person of the servant, in circumstances in which the taking of an object belonging to the class of things would be an act of theft, or (what is scarcely worth distinguishing from theft) an act of embezzlement: it may be termed *servant-stealing*. Where it is the offence of the servant himself, it is styled *breach of duty*. Now the most flagrant species of breach of duty, and that which includes indeed every other, is that which consists in the servant's withdrawing himself from the place in which the duty should be performed. This species of breach of duty is termed *elopement*. Again, in virtue of the power belonging to this condition, it is liable, on the part of the master to *abuse*. But this power is not coupled with a trust. The condition of a master is therefore not exposed to any offence which is analogous to breach of trust. Lastly, on account of its being exposed to abuse, it may be conceived to stand, in point of possibility, exposed to *bribery*. But considering how few, and how insignificant, the persons are who are liable to be subject to the power here in question, this is

[1] In most civilized nations there is a sort of domestic condition, in which the superior is termed a master, while the inferior is termed sometimes indeed a servant, but more particularly and more frequently an *apprentice*. In this case, though the superior is, in point of usage, known by no other name than that of a master, the relationship is in point of fact a mixed one, compounded of that of *master* and that of *guardian*.

an offence which, on account of the want of temptation, there will seldom be any example of in practice. We may therefore reckon thirteen sorts of offences to which the condition of a master is exposed: viz. 1. Wrongful non-investment of mastership. 2. Wrongful interception of mastership. 3. Wrongful divestment of mastership. 4. Usurpation of mastership. 5. Wrongful investment of mastership. 6. Wrongful abdication of mastership. 7. Wrongful detrectation of mastership. 8. Wrongful imposition of mastership. 9. Abuse of mastership. 10. Disturbance of mastership. 11. Breach of duty in servants. 12. Elopement of servants. 13. Servant-stealing.

42. As to the *power* by which the condition of a master is *Various modes* constituted, this may be either *limited* or *unlimited*. When it is *of servitude.* altogether unlimited, the condition of the servant is styled *pure slavery*. But as the rules of language are as far as can be conceived from being steady on this head, the term slavery is commonly made use of wherever the limitations prescribed to the power of the master are looked upon as inconsiderable. Whenever any such limitation is prescribed, a kind of fictitious entity is thereby created, and, in quality of an incorporeal object of possession, is bestowed upon the servant: this object is of the class of those which are called *rights*: and in the present case is termed, in a more particular manner, a *liberty*; and sometimes a *privilege*, an *immunity*, or an *exemption*. Now those limitations on the one hand, and these liberties on the other, may, it is evident, be as various as the acts (positive or negative) which the master may or may not have the power of obliging the servant to submit to or to perform. Correspondent then to the infinitude of these liberties, is the infinitude of the modifications which the condition of mastership (or, as it is more common to say in such a case, that of servitude) admits of. These modifications, it is evident, may, in different countries, be infinitely diversified. In different countries, therefore, the offences characterised by the above names will, if specifically considered, admit of very different descriptions. If there be a spot upon the earth so wretched as to exhibit the spectacle of pure and absolutely unlimited slavery, on that spot there will be no such thing as any abuse of mastership; which means neither more nor less than that

no abuse of mastership will there be treated on the footing of an offence. As to the question, Whether any, and what, modes of servitude ought to be established or kept on foot? this is a question, the solution of which belongs to the civil branch of the art of legislation.

Offences touching the condition of a servant.
43. Next, with regard to the offences that may concern the condition of a servant. It might seem at first sight, that a condition of this kind could not have a spark of benefit belonging to it: that it could not be attended with any other consequences than such as rendered it a mere burthen. But a burthen itself may be a benefit, in comparison of a greater burthen. Conceive a man's situation then to be such, that he must, at any rate, be in a state of pure slavery. Still may it be material to him, and highly material, who the person is whom he has for his master. A state of slavery then, under one master, may be a beneficial state to him, in comparison with a state of slavery under another master. The condition of a servant then is exposed to the several offences to which a condition, in virtue of its being a beneficial one, is exposed.[1] More than this, where the power of the master is limited, and the limitations annexed to it, and thence the liberties of the servant, are considerable, the servitude may even be positively eligible. For amongst those limitations may be such as are sufficient to enable the servant to possess property of his own: being capable then of possessing property of his own, he may be capable of receiving it from his master: in short, he may receive *wages*, or other emoluments, from his master; and the benefit resulting from these wages may be so considerable as to outweigh the burthen of the servitude, and, by that means, render that condition more beneficial upon the whole, and more eligible, than that of one who is not in any respect under the control of any such person as a

---

[1] It may seem at first, that a person who is in the condition of a slave, could not have it in his power to engage in such course of proceeding as would be necessary, in order to give him an apparent title to be reckoned among the slaves of another master. But though a slave in point of *right*, it may happen that he has eloped for instance, and is not a slave in point of *fact*: or, suppose him a slave in point of fact, and ever so vigilantly guarded, still a person connected with him by the ties of sympathy, might do that for him which, though willing and assenting, he might not be able to do for himself: might forge a deed of donation, for example, from the one master to the other.

master. Accordingly, by these means the conditions of the servant may be so eligible, that his entrance into it, and his continuance in it, may have been altogether the result of his own choice. That the nature of the two conditions may be the more clearly understood, it may be of use to show the sort of correspondency there is between the offences which affect the existence of the one, and those which affect the existence of the other. That this correspondency cannot but be very intimate is obvious at first sight. It is not, however, that a given offence in the former catalogue coincides with an offence of the same name in the latter catalogue: usurpation of servantship with usurpation of mastership, for example. But the case is, that an offence of one denomination in the one catalogue coincides with an offence of a different denomination in the other catalogue. Nor is the coincidence constant and certain: but liable to contingencies, as we shall see. First, then, wrongful non-investment of the condition of a servant, if it be the offence of one who should have been the master, coincides with wrongful detrectation of mastership: if it be the offence of a third person, it involves in it non-investment of mastership, which, provided the mastership be in the eyes of him who should have been master a beneficial thing, but not otherwise, is wrongful. 2. Wrongful interception of the condition of a servant, if it be the offence of him who should have been master, coincides with wrongful detrectation of mastership: if it be the offence of a third person, and the mastership be a beneficial thing, it involves in it wrongful interception of mastership. 3. Wrongful divestment of servantship, if it be the offence of the master, but not otherwise, coincides with wrongful abdication of mastership: if it be the offence of a stranger, it involves in it divestment of mastership, which, in as far as the mastership is a beneficial thing, is wrongful. 4. Usurpation of servantship coincides necessarily with wrongful imposition of mastership: it will be apt to involve in it wrongful divestment of mastership: but this only in the case where the usurper, previously to the usurpation, was in a state of servitude under some other master. 5. Wrongful investment of servantship (the servantship being considered as a beneficial thing) coincides with imposition of mastership; which, if in the eyes

2 A

of the pretended master the mastership should chance to be a burthen, will be wrongful. 6. Wrongful abdication of servantship coincides with wrongful divestment of mastership. 7. Wrongful detrectation of servantship, with wrongful non-investment of mastership. 8. Wrongful imposition of servantship, if it be the offence of the pretended master, coincides with usurpation of mastership: if it be the offence of a stranger, it involves in it imposition of mastership, which, if in the eyes of the pretended master the mastership should be a burthen, will be wrongful. As to abuse of mastership, disturbance of mastership, breach of duty in servants, elopement of servants, and servant-stealing, these are offences which, without any change of denomination, bear equal relation to both conditions. And thus we may reckon thirteen sorts of offences to which the condition of a servant stands exposed: viz. 1. Wrongful non-investment of servantship. 2. Wrongful interception of servantship. 3. Wrongful divestment of servantship. 4. Usurpation of servantship. 5. Wrongful investment of servantship. 6. Wrongful abdication of servantship. 7. Wrongful detrectation of servantship. 8. Wrongful imposition of servantship. 9. Abuse of mastership. 10. Disturbance of mastership. 11. Breach of duty in servants. 12. Elopement of servants. 13. Servant-stealing.

Guardianship, what—Necessity of the institution.

44. We now come to the offences to which the condition of a guardian is exposed. A guardian is one who is invested with power over another, living within the compass of the same family, and called a ward; the power being to be exercised for the benefit of the ward. Now then, what are the cases in which it can be for the benefit of one man, that another, living within the compass of the same family, should exercise power over him? Consider either of the parties by himself, and suppose him, in point of understanding, to be on a level with the other, it seems evident enough that no such cases can ever exist.[1] To the production of happiness on the part of any given person (in like manner as to the production of any other effect which is the result of

---

[1] Consider them *together* indeed, take the sum of the two interests, and the case, as we have seen (supra, 40), is then the reverse. That case, it is to be remembered, proceeds only upon the supposition that the two parties are obliged to live together; for suppose it to be at their option to part, the necessity of establishing the power ceases.

human agency) three things it is necessary should concur: knowledge, inclination, and physical power. Now as there is no man who is so sure of being *inclined*, on all occasions, to promote your happiness as you yourself are, so neither is there any man who upon the whole can have had so good opportunities as you must have had of *knowing* what is most conducive to that purpose. For who should know so well as you do what it is that gives you pain or pleasure?[1] Moreover, as to power, it is manifest that no superiority in this respect, on the part of a stranger, could, for a constancy, make up for so great a deficiency as he must lie under in respect of two such material points as knowledge and inclination. If then there be a case where it can be for the advantage of one man to be under the power of another, it must be on account of some palpable and very considerable deficiency, on the part of the former, in point of intellects, or (which is the same thing in other words) in point of knowledge or understanding. Now there are two cases in which such palpable deficiency is known to take place. These are, 1. Where a man's intellect is not yet arrived at that state in which it is capable of directing his own inclination in the pursuit of happiness: this is the case of *infancy*.[2] 2. Where by some particular known or unknown circumstance his intellect has either never arrived at that state, or having arrived at it has fallen from it: which is the case of *insanity*.

By what means then is it to be ascertained whether a man's intellect is in that state or no? For exhibiting the quantity of sensible heat in a human body we have a very tolerable sort of instrument, the thermometer; but for exhibiting the quantity of intelligence, we have no such instrument. It is evident, therefore, that the line which separates the quantity of intelligence which *is* sufficient for the purposes of self-government from that which is *not* sufficient, must be, in a great measure, arbitrary. Where the insufficiency is the result of want of age, the sufficient quantity of intelligence, be it what it may, does not accrue to all at the same period of their lives. It becomes therefore necessary for legislators to cut the gordian knot, and fix upon a particular period, at which and not before, truly or not, every person whatever shall be deemed, as far as depends

---

[1] Chap. xvii. [Limits], § i.   [2] See Chap. xiii. [Cases unmeet], § iii.

upon age, to be in possession of this sufficient quantity.[1] In this case then a line is drawn which may be the same for every man, and in the description of which, such as it is, whatever persons are concerned may be certain of agreeing: the circumstance of time affording a mark by which the line in question may be traced with the utmost degree of nicety. On the other hand, where the insufficiency is the result of insanity, there is not even this resource: so that here the legislator has no other expedient than to appoint some particular person or persons to give a particular determination of the question, in every instance in which it occurs, according to his or their particular and arbitrary discretion. Arbitrary enough it must be at any rate, since the only way in which it can be exercised is by considering whether the share of intelligence possessed by the individual in question does or does not come up to the loose and indeterminate idea which persons so appointed may chance to entertain with respect to the quantity which is deemed sufficient.

Duration to be given to it.

45. The line then being drawn, or supposed to be so, it is expedient to a man who cannot, with safety to himself, be left in his own power, that he should be placed in the power of another. How long then should he remain so? Just so long as his inability is supposed to continue: that is, in the case of infancy, till he arrives at that period at which the law deems him to be of full age: in the case of insanity, till he be of sound mind and understanding. Now it is evident, that this period, in the case of infancy, may not arrive for a considerable time: and in the case of insanity, perhaps never. The duration of the power belonging to this trust must therefore, in the one case, be very considerable; in the other case, be indefinite.

[1] In certain nations, women, whether married or not, have been placed in a state of perpetual wardship: this has been evidently founded on the notion of a decided inferiority in point of intellects on the part of the female sex, analogous to that which is the result of infancy or insanity on the part of the male. This is not the only instance in which tyranny has taken advantage of its own wrong, alleging as a reason for the domination it exercises, an imbecility, which, as far as it has been real, has been produced by the abuse of that very power which it is brought to justify. Aristotle, fascinated by the prejudice of the times, divides mankind into two distinct species, that of freemen, and that of slaves. Certain men were born to be slaves, and ought to be slaves.—Why? Because, they are so.

46. The next point to consider, is what *may* be the extent of *Powers that* it? for as to what *ought* to be, that is a matter to be settled, not *may, and duties that ought to be* in a general analytical sketch, but in a particular and circum- *annexed to it.* stantial dissertation. By possibility, then, this power may possess any extent that can be imagined: it may extend to any acts which, physically speaking, it may be in the power of the ward to perform himself, or be the object of if exercised by the guardian. Conceive the power, for a moment, to stand upon this footing: the condition of the ward stands now exactly upon a footing with pure slavery. Add the obligation by which the power is turned into a trust: the limits of the power are now very considerably narrowed. What then is the purport of this obligation? Of what nature is the course of conduct it prescribes? It is such a course of conduct as shall be best calculated for procuring to the ward the greatest quantity of happiness which his faculties, and the circum-stances he is in, will admit of: saving always, in the first place, the regard which the guardian is permitted to show to his own happiness; and, in the second place, that which he is obliged, as well as permitted, to show to that of other men. This is, in fact, no other than that course of conduct which the ward, did he but know how, ought, in point of *prudence*, to maintain of himself: so that the business of the former is to govern the latter precisely in the manner in which this latter ought to govern himself. Now to instruct each indivi-dual in what manner to govern his own conduct in the details of life, is the particular business of private ethics: to instruct individuals in what manner to govern the conduct of those whose happiness, during nonage, is committed to their charge, is the business of the art of private education. The details therefore, of the rules to be given for that purpose, any more than the acts which are capable of being committed in violation of those rules, belong not to the art of legislation: since, as will be seen more particularly hereafter,[1] such details could not, with any chance of advantage, be provided for by the legislator. Some general outlines might indeed be drawn by his authority: and, in point of fact, some are in every civilized state. But such regulations, it is evident, must be liable to great variation: in the first place, according to the

[1] See Chap. xvii. [Limits], § i.

infinite diversity of civil conditions which a man may stand invested with in any given state: in the next place, according to the diversity of local circumstances that may influence the nature of the conditions which may chance to be established in different states. On this account, the offences which would be constituted by such regulations could not be comprised under any concise and settled denominations, capable of a permanent and extensive application. No place, therefore, can be allotted to them here.

Offences touch-
ing the condition
of a guardian.

47. By what has been said, we are the better prepared for taking an account of the offences to which the condition in question stands exposed. Guardianship being a private trust, is of course exposed to those offences, and no others, by which a private trust is liable to be affected. Some of them, however, on account of the special quality of the trust, will admit of some further particularity of description. In the first place, breach of this species of trust may be termed *mismanagement* of guardianship: in the second place, of whatever nature the duties are which are capable of being annexed to this condition, it must often happen, that in order to fulfil them, it is necessary the guardian should be at a certain particular place. Mismanagement of guardianship, when it consists in the not being, on the occasion in question, at the place in question, may be termed *desertion* of guardianship. Thirdly, It is manifest enough, that the object which the guardian ought to propose to himself, in the exercise of the powers to which those duties are annexed, is to procure for the ward the greatest quantity of happiness which can be procured for him, consistently with the regard which is due to the other interests that have been mentioned: for this is the object which the ward would have proposed to himself, and might and ought to have been allowed to propose to himself, had he been capable of governing his own conduct. Now, in order to procure this happiness, it is necessary that he should possess a certain power over the objects on the use of which such happiness depends. These objects are either the person of the ward himself, or other objects that are extraneous to him. These other objects are either things or persons. As to *things*, then, objects of this class, in as far as a man's happiness depends upon the use of them, are styled his *property*. The

case is the same with the services of any *persons* over whom he may happen to possess a beneficial power, or to whose services he may happen to possess a beneficial right. Now when property of any kind, which is in trust, suffers by the delinquency of him with whom it is in trust, such offence, of whatever nature it is in other respects, may be styled *dissipation* in breach of trust: and if it be attended with a profit to the trustee, it may be styled *peculation*.[1] Fourthly, For one person to exercise a power of any kind over another, it is necessary that the latter should either perform certain acts, upon being commanded so to do by the former, or at least should suffer certain acts to be exercised upon himself. In this respect a ward must stand upon the footing of a servant: and the condition of a ward must, in this respect, stand exposed to the same offences to which that of a servant stands exposed: that is, on the part of a stranger, to *disturbance*, which, in particular circumstances, will amount to *theft*: on the part of the ward, to *breach of duty*: which, in particular circumstances, may be effected by *elopement*. Fifthly, There does not seem to be any offence concerning guardianship that corresponds to *abuse of trust*: I mean in the sense to which the last-mentioned denomination has been here confined.[2] The reason is, that guardianship, being a trust of a private nature, does not, as such, confer upon the trustee any power, either over the persons or over the property of any party, other than the *beneficiary* himself. If by accident it confers on the trustee a power over any persons whose services constitute a part of the property of the beneficiary, the trustee becomes thereby, in certain respects, the master of such servants.[3] Sixthly, Bribery also is a sort of offence to which, in this case, there is not commonly much temptation. It is an offence, however, which by possibility is capable of taking this direction: and must therefore be aggregated to the number of the offences to which the condition of a guardian stands exposed. And thus we have in all seventeen of these offences: viz. 1. Wrongful non-investment of guardianship. 2. Wrongful interception of guardianship. 3. Wrongful divestment of guardianship. 4. Usurpation of guardianship. 5. Wrongful investment of guardianship. 6. Wrongful abdication of guardianship.

---

[1] Supra, 35.   [2] Vide supra, 25.   [3] Vide supra, 40.

7. Detrectation of guardianship. 8. Wrongful imposition of guardianship. 9. Mismanagement of guardianship. 10. Desertion of guardianship. 11. Dissipation in prejudice or wardship. 12. Peculation in prejudice of wardship. 13. Disturbance of guardianship. 14. Breach of duty to guardians. 15. Elopement from guardians. 16. Ward-stealing. 17. Bribery in prejudice of wardship.

Offences touching the condition of a ward. 48. Next, with regard to offences to which the condition of wardship is exposed. Those which first affect the existence of the condition itself are as follows: 1. Wrongful non-investment of the condition of a ward. This, if it be the offence of one who should have been guardian, coincides with wrongful detrectation of guardianship: if it be the offence of a third person, it involves in it non-investment of guardianship, which, provided the guardianship is, in the eyes of him who should have been guardian, a desirable thing, is wrongful. 2. Wrongful interception of wardship. This, if it be the offence of him who should have been guardian, coincides with wrongful detrectation of guardianship: if it be the offence of a third person, it involves in it interception of guardianship, which, provided the guardianship is, in the eyes of him who should have been guardian, a desirable thing, is wrongful. 3. Wrongful divestment of wardship. This, if it be the offence of the guardian, but not otherwise, coincides with wrongful abdication of guardianship: if it be the offence of a third person, it involves in it divestment of guardianship, which, if the guardianship is, in the eyes of the guardian, a desirable thing, is wrongful. 4. Usurpation of the condition of a ward: an offence not very likely to be committed. This coincides at any rate with wrongful imposition of guardianship; and if the usurper were already under the guardianship of another guardian, it will involve in it wrongful divestment of such guardianship.[1] 5. Wrongful investment of wardship (the wardship being considered as a

[1] This effect it may be thought will not necessarily take place: since a ward may have two guardians. One man then is guardian by right: another man comes and makes himself so by usurpation. This may very well be, and yet the former may continue guardian notwithstanding. How then (it may be asked) is he divested of his guardianship?—The answer is—Certainly not of the whole of it: but, however, of a part of it: of such part as is occupied, if one may so say, that is, of such part of the powers and rights belonging to it as are exercised, by the usurper.

beneficial thing): this coincides with imposition of guardian-ship, which, if in the eyes of the pretended guardian the guardianship should be a burthen, will be wrongful. 6. Wrongful abdication of wardship. This coincides with wrongful divestment of guardianship. 7. Wrongful detrectation of wardship. This coincides with wrongful interception of guardianship. 8. Wrongful imposition of wardship. This, if the offender be the pretended guardian, coincides with usurpa-tion of guardianship: if a stranger, it involves in it wrongful imposition of guardianship. As to such of the offences relative to this condition, as concern the consequences of it while subsisting, they are of such a nature that, without any change of denomination, they belong equally to the condition of a guardian and that of a ward. We may therefore reckon seventeen sorts of offences relative to the condition of a ward: 1. Wrongful non-investment of wardship. 2. Wrongful interception of wardship. 3. Wrongful divestment of ward-ship. 4. Usurpation of wardship. 5. Wrongful investment of wardship. 6. Wrongful abdication of wardship. 7. Wrongful detrectation of wardship. 8. Wrongful imposition of ward-ship. 9. Mismanagement of guardianship. 10. Desertion of guardianship. 11. Dissipation in prejudice of wardship. 12. Peculation in prejudice of wardship. 13. Disturbance of guardianship. 14. Breach of duty to guardians. 15. Elope-ment from guardians. 16. Ward-stealing. 17. Bribery in prejudice of wardship.

49. We come now to the offences to which the condition of a parent stands exposed: and first, with regard to those by which the very existence of the condition is affected. On this occasion, in order to see the more clearly into the subject, it will be necessary to distinguish between the natural relation-ship, and the legal relationship which is superinduced as it were upon the natural one. The natural one being constituted by a particular event, which, either on account of its being already past, or on some other account, is equally out of the power of the law neither is, nor can be made, the subject of an offence. *Is* a man your father? It is not any offence of mine that can make you not his son. Is he *not* your father? It is not any offence of mine that can render him so. But although he does in fact bear that relation to you, I, by an

Offences touch-ing the condition of a parent.

offence of mine, may perhaps so manage matters, that he shall not be *thought* to bear it: which, with respect to any legal advantages which either he or you could derive from such relationship, will be the same thing as if he did not. In the capacity of a witness, I may cause the judges to believe that he is not your father, and to decree accordingly: or, in the capacity of a judge, I may myself decree him not to be your father. Leaving then the purely natural relationship as an object equally out of the reach of justice and injustice, the legal condition, it is evident, will stand exposed to the same offences, neither more nor less, as every other condition, that is capable of being either beneficial or burthensome, stands exposed to. Next, with regard to the exercise of the functions belonging to this condition, considered as still subsisting. In parentality there must be two persons concerned, the father and the mother. The condition of a parent includes, therefore, two conditions; that of a father, and that of a mother, with respect to such or such a child. Now it is evident, that between these two parties, whatever beneficiary powers, and other rights, as also whatever obligations, are annexed to the condition of a parent, may be shared in any proportions that can be imagined. But if in these several objects of legal creation, each of these two parties have severally a share, and if the interests of all these parties are in any degree provided for, it is evident that each of the parents will stand, with relation to the child, in two several capacities: that of a master, and that of a guardian. The condition of a parent then, in as far as it is the work of law, may be considered as a complex condition, compounded of that of a guardian, and that of a master. To the parent then, in quality of guardian, results a set of duties, involving, as necessary to the discharge of them, certain powers: to the child, in the character of a ward, a set of rights corresponding to the parent's duties, and a set of duties corresponding to his powers. To the parent again, in quality of master, a set of beneficiary powers, without any other necessary limitation (so long as they last) than what is annexed to them by the duties incumbent on him in quality of a guardian: to the child, in the character of a servant, a set of duties corresponding to the parent's beneficiary powers, and without any other necessary limitation (so long as they last) than what is annexed to them by the rights which belong to the child in his capacity of ward. The condition of a parent will therefore be exposed to all the offences to which either that of a guardian or that of a master are exposed: and, as each of the parents will partake, more or less, of both those characters, the offences to which the two conditions are exposed may be nominally, as they will be substantially, the same. Taking them then all together, the offences to which the condition of a parent is exposed will stand as follows: 1. Wrongful non-investment of parentality.[1] 2. Wrongful interception of parentality. 3. Wrongful divestment of parentality. 4. Usurpation of parentality. 5. Wrongful investment of parentality. 6. Wrongful abdication of parentality. 7. Wrongful detrectation of parentality. 8. Wrongful imposition of parentality. 9. Mismanagement of parental guardianship. 10. Desertion of parental guardianship. 11. Dissipation in prejudice of filial wardship. 12. Peculation in prejudice of filial wardship. 13. Abuse of parental powers. 14. Disturbance of parental guardianship. 15. Breach of duty to parents. 16. Elopement from parents. 17. Child-stealing. 18. Bribery in prejudice of filial wardship.

50. Next with regard to the offences to which the *filial* condition,[2] the condition of a son or daughter, stands exposed.

Offences touching the filial condition.

[1] At first view it may seem a solecism to speak of the condition of parentality as one which a man can have need to be invested with. The reason is, that it is not common for any ceremony to be required as necessary to a man's being deemed in law the father of such or such a child. But the institution of such a ceremony, whether advisable or not, is at least perfectly conceivable. Nor are there wanting cases in which it has actually been exemplified. By an article in the Roman law, adopted by many modern nations, an illegitimate child is rendered legitimate by the subsequent marriage of his parents. If then a priest, or other person whose office it was, were to refuse to join a man and woman in matrimony, such refusal, besides being a wrongful non-investment with respect to the two matrimonial conditions, would be a wrongful non-investment of parentality and filiation, to the prejudice of any children who should have been legitimated.

[2] In English we have no word that will serve to express with propriety the person who bears the relation opposed to that of parent. The word *child* is ambiguous, being employed in another sense, perhaps more frequently than in this: more frequently in opposition to *a person of full age*, an *adult*, than in correlation to a *parent*. For the condition itself we have no other word than *filiation*: an ill-contrived term, not analogous to *paternity* and *maternity*: the proper term would have been *filiality*: the word filiation is as frequently, perhaps, and more consistently, put for the act of establishing a person in the possession of the condition of filiality.

The principles to be pursued in the investigation of offences of this description have already been sufficiently developed. It will be sufficient, therefore, to enumerate them without further discussion. The only peculiarities by which offences relative to the condition in question stand distinguished from the offences relative to all the preceding conditions, depend upon this one circumstance; viz. that it is certain every one must have had a father and a mother: at the same time that it is not certain that every one must have had a master, a servant, a guardian, or a ward. It will be observed all along, that where a person, from whom, if alive, the benefit would be taken, or on whom the burthen would be imposed, be dead, so much of the mischief is extinct along with the object of the offence. There still, however, remains so much of the mischief as depends upon the advantage or disadvantage which might accrue to persons related, or supposed to be related, in the several remoter degrees, to him in question. The catalogue then of these offences stands as follows: 1. Wrongful non investment of filiation. This, if it be the offence of him or her who should have been recognised as the parent, coincides with wrongful detrectation of parentality: if it be the offence of a third person, it involves in it non-investment of parentality, which, provided the parentality is, in the eyes of him or her who should have been recognised as the parent, a desirable thing, is wrongful. 2. Wrongful interception of filiation. This, if it be the offence of him or her who should have been recognised as the parent, coincides with wrongful detrectation of parentality: if it be the offence of a third person, it involves in it interception of parentality, which, provided the parentality is, in the eyes of him or her who should have been recognised as parent, a desirable thing, is wrongful. 3. Wrongful divestment of filiation. This, if it be the offence of him or her who should be recognised as parent, coincides with wrongful abdication of parentality: if it be the offence of a third person, it involves in it divestment of parentality; to wit, of paternity, or of maternity, or of both; which, if the parentality is, in the eyes of him or her who should be recognised as parent, a desirable thing, are respectively wrongful. 4. Usurpation of filiation. This coincides with wrongful imposition of parentality; to wit, either of paternity, or of maternity, or of both: and necessarily involves in it divestment of parentality, which, if the parentality thus divested were, in the eyes of him or her who are thus divested of it, a desirable thing, is wrongful. 5. Wrongful investment of filiation: (the filiation being considered as a beneficial thing). This coincides with imposition of parentality, which, if in the eyes of the pretended father or mother the parentality should be an undesirable thing, will be wrongful. 6. Wrongful abdication of filiation. This necessarily coincides with wrongful divestment of parentality; it also is apt to involve in it wrongful imposition of parentality; though not necessarily either to the advantage or to the prejudice of any certain person. For if a man, supposed at first to be your son, appears afterwards not to be yours, it is certain indeed that he is the son of some other man, but it may not appear who that other man is. 7. Wrongful detrectation of filiation. This coincides with wrongful non-investment or wrongful interception of parentality. 8. Wrongful imposition of filiation. This, if it be the offence of the pretended parent, coincides necessarily with usurpation of parentality: if it be the offence of a third person, it necessarily involves imposition of parentality; as also divestment of parentality: either or both of which, according to the circumstance above mentioned, may or may not be wrongful. 9. Mismanagement of parental guardianship. 10. Desertion of parental guardianship. 11. Dissipation in prejudice of filial wardship. 12. Peculation in prejudice of filial wardship. 13. Abuse of parental power. 14. Disturbance of parental guardianship. 15. Breach of duty to parents. 16. Elopement from parents. 17. Child-stealing. 18. Bribery in prejudice of parental guardianship.

51. We shall now be able to apply ourselves with some advantage to the examination of the several offences to which the marital condition, or condition of a husband, stands exposed. A husband is a man, between whom and a certain woman, who in this case is called his wife, there subsists a legal obligation for the purpose of their living together, and in particular for the purpose of a sexual intercourse to be carried on between them. This obligation will naturally be considered in four points of view: 1. In respect of its commencement. 2. In respect of the placing of it. 3. In respect

Condition of a husband.—Powers, duties, and rights, that may be annexed to it.

of the nature of it. 4. In respect of its duration. First then, it is evident, that in point of possibility, one method of commencement is as conceivable as another: the time of its commencement might have been marked by one sort of event (by one sort of *signal*, as it may here be called) as well as by another. But in practice the signal has usually been, as in point of utility it ought constantly to be, a contract entered into by the parties, that is, a set of signs, pitched upon by the law, as expressive of their *mutual consent*, to take upon them this condition. Secondly, and thirdly, with regard to the placing of the obligations which are the result of the contract, it is evident that they must rest either solely on one side, or mutually on both. On the first supposition, the condition is not to be distinguished from pure slavery. In this case, either the wife must be the slave of the husband, or the husband of the wife. The first of these suppositions has perhaps never been exemplified; the opposing influence of physical causes being too universal to have ever been surmounted: the latter seems to have been exemplified but too often; perhaps among the first Romans; at any rate, in many barbarous nations. Thirdly, with regard to the nature of the obligations. If they are not suffered to rest all on one side, certain rights are thereby given to the other. There must, therefore, be rights on both sides. Now, where there are mutual rights possessed by two persons, as against each other, either there are powers annexed to those rights, or not. But the persons in question are, by the supposition, to live together: in which case we have shown,[1] that it is not only expedient, but in a manner necessary, that on one side there should be powers. Now it is only on one side that powers can be: for suppose them on both sides, and they destroy one another. The question is then, In which of the parties these powers shall be lodged? we have shown, that on the principle of utility they ought to be lodged in the husband. The powers then which subsist being lodged in the husband, the next question is, Shall the interest of one party only, or of both, be consulted in the exercise of them? it is evident, that on the principle of utility the interests of both ought alike to be consulted: since in two persons, taken together, more happiness is producible

[1] Supra, 40 note.

than in one. This being the case, it is manifest, that the legal relation which the husband will bear to the wife will be a complex one: compounded of that of master and that of guardian.

52. The offences then to which the condition of a husband will be exposed, will be the sum of those to which the two conditions of master and guardian are exposed. Thus far the condition of a husband, with respect to the general outlines of it, stands upon the same footing as that of a parent. But there are certain reciprocal services, which being the main subject of the matrimonial contract, constitute the essence of the two matrimonial relations, and which neither a master nor guardian, as such, nor a parent, at any rate, have usually been permitted to receive. These must of course have been distinguished from the indiscriminate train of services at large which the husband in his character of master is empowered to exact, and of those which in his character of guardian he is bound to render. Being thus distinguished, the offences relative to the two conditions have, in many instances, in as far as they have reference to these peculiar services, acquired particular denominations. In the first place, with regard to the contract, from the celebration of which the legal condition dates its existence. It is obvious that in point of possibility, this contract might, on the part of either sex, subsist with respect to several persons of the other sex at the same time: the husband might have any number of wives: the wife might have any number of husbands: the husband might enter into the contract with a number of wives at the same time: or, if with only one at a time, he might reserve to himself a right of engaging in a similar contract with any number, or with only such or such a number of other women afterwards, during the continuance of each former contract. This latter accordingly is the footing upon which, as is well known, marriage is and has been established in many extensive countries: particularly in all those which profess the Mahometan religion. In point of possibility, it is evident that the like liberty might be reserved on the part of the wife: though in point of practice no examples of such an arrangement seem ever to have occurred. Which of all these arrangements is in point of utility the most expedient, is a question which

Offences touching the condition of a husband.

would require too much discussion to answer in the course of an analytical process like the present, and which belongs indeed to the civil branch of legislation, rather than to the penal.[1] In Christian countries, the solemnization of any such contract is made to exclude the solemnization of any subsequent one during the continuance of a former: and the solemnization of any such subsequent contract is accordingly treated as an offence, under the name of *Polygamy*. Polygamy then is at any rate, on the part of the man, a particular modification of that offence which may be styled usurpation of the condition of a husband. As to its other effects, they will be different, according as it was the man only, or the woman only, or both, that were in a state of matrimony at the time of the commission of the offence. If the man only, then his offence involves in it *pro tanto* that of wrongful divestment of the condition of a wife, in prejudice of his prior wife.[2] If the woman only, then it involves in it *pro tanto* that of wrongful divestment of the condition of a husband, in prejudice of her prior husband. If both were already married, it of course involves both the wrongful divestments which have just been mentioned. And on the other hand also, the converse of all this may be observed with regard to polygamy on the part of the woman. Secondly, As the engaging not to enter into any subsequent engagement of the like kind during the continuance of the first, is one of the conditions on which the law lends its sanction to the first; so another is, the inserting as one of the articles of this engagement, an undertaking not to render to, or accept from, any other person the services which form the characteristic object of it: the rendering or acceptance of any such service is accordingly treated as an offence, under the name of *adultery*: under which name is also comprised the offence of the stranger, who, in the commission of the above offence, is the necessary accomplice. Thirdly, Disturbing either of the parties to this engagement, in the possession of these characteristic services, may, in like manner, be distinguished from the offence of disturbing them in the enjoyment of the miscellaneous advantages derivable from the

---

[1] See Chap. xvii. [Limits], § iv.

[2] In this case also, if the woman knew not of the prior marriage, it is besides a species of seduction; and, in as far as it affects her, belongs to another division of the offences of this class. Vide supra, 36.

same condition; and on whichever side the blame rests, whether that of the party, or that of a third person, may be termed *wrongful withholding of connubial services*. And thus we have one-and-twenty sorts of offences to which, as the law stands at present in Christian countries, the condition of a husband stands exposed: viz. 1. Wrongful non-investment of the condition of a husband. 2. Wrongful interception of the condition of a husband. 3. Wrongful divestment of the condition of a husband. 4. Usurpation of the condition of a husband. 5. Polygamy. 6. Wrongful investment of the condition of a husband. 7. Wrongful abdication of the condition of a husband. 8. Wrongful detrectation of the condition of a husband. 9. Wrongful imposition of the condition of a husband. 10. Mismanagement of marital guardianship. 11. Desertion of marital guardianship. 12. Dissipation in prejudice of matrimonial wardship. 13. Peculation in prejudice of matrimonial wardship. 14. Abuse of marital power. 15. Disturbance of marital guardianship. 16. Wrongful withholding of connubial services. 17. Adultery. 18. Breach of duty to husbands. 19. Elopement from husbands. 20. Wife-stealing. 21. Bribery in prejudice of marital guardianship.[1]

53. Next with regard to the offences to which the condition of a wife stands exposed. From the patterns that have been exhibited already, the coincidences and associations that take place between the offences that concern the existence of this condition and those which concern the existence of the condition of a husband, may easily enough be apprehended without farther repetitions. The catalogue of those now under consideration will be precisely the same in every article as the catalogue last exhibited. *Offences touching the condition of a wife.*

54. Thus much for the several sorts of offences relative to the several sorts of domestic conditions: those which are constituted by such natural relations as are contiguous being included. There remain those which are uncontiguous: of which, after so much as has been said of the others, it will

---

[1] I. SEMI-PUBLIC OFFENCES.—Falsehoods contesting, or offences against justice destroying, the validity of the marriages of people of certain descriptions: such as Jews, Quakers, Hugonots, &c. &c.

II. SELF-REGARDING OFFENCES.—Improvident marriage on the part of minors.

2B

naturally be expected that some notice should be taken. These, however, do not afford any of that matter which is necessary to constitute a condition. In point of fact, no power seems ever to be annexed to any of them. A grandfather, perhaps, may be called by the law to take upon him the guardianship of his orphan grandson: but then the power he has belongs to him not as grandfather, but as guardian. In point of possibility, indeed, power might be annexed to these relations, just as it might to any other. But still no new sort of domestic condition would result from it: since it has been shown that there can be no others, that, being constituted by power, shall be distinct from those which have been already mentioned. Such as they are, however, they have this in common with the before-mentioned relations, that they are capable of importing either benefit or burthen: they therefore stand exposed to the several offences whereby those or any other relations are liable to be affected in point of existence. It might be expected, therefore, that in virtue of these offences, they should be added to the list of the relations which are liable to be objects of delinquency. But the fact is, that they already stand included in it: and although not expressly named, yet as effectually as if they were. On the one hand, it is only by affecting such or such a contiguous relation that any offence affecting uncontiguous relations can take place. On the other hand, neither can any offence affecting the existence of the contiguous relations be committed, without affecting the existence of an indefinite multitude of such as are uncontiguous. A false witness comes, and causes it to be believed that you are the son of a woman, who, in truth, is not your mother. What follows? An endless tribe of other false persuasions—that you are the grandson of the father and of the mother of this supposed mother: that you are the son of some husband of hers, or, at least, of some man with whom she has cohabited: the grandson of his father and his mother; and so on: the brother of their other children, if they have any: the brother-in-law of the husbands and wives of those children, if married: the uncle of the children of those children: and so on.—On the other hand, that you are not the son of your real mother, nor of your real father: that you are not the grandson of either of your real grandfathers or grandmothers; and so

on without end: all which persuasions result from, and are
included in, the one original false persuasion of your being the
son of this your pretended mother.

It should seem, therefore, at first sight, that none of the
offences against these uncontiguous relations could ever come
expressly into question: for by the same rule that one ought,
so it might seem ought a thousand others: the offences against
the uncontiguous being merged as it were in those which
affect the contiguous relations. So far, however, is this from
being the case, that in speaking of an offence of this stamp, it
is not uncommon to hear a great deal said of this or that
uncontiguous relationship which it affects, at the same time
that no notice at all shall be taken of any of those which are
contiguous. How happens this? Because, to the uncontiguous
relation are annexed perhaps certain remarkable advantages
or disadvantages, while to all the intermediate relations
none shall be annexed which are in comparison worth
noticing. Suppose Antony or Lepidus to have contested the
relationship of Octavius (afterwards Augustus) to Caius
Julius Cæsar. How could it have been done? It could only
have been by contesting, either Octavius's being the son of
Atia, or Atia's being the daughter of Julia, or Julia's being
the daughter of Lucius Julius Cæsar, or Lucius Julius Cæsar's
being the father of Caius. But to have been the son of Atia,
or the grandson of Julia, or the great grandson of Lucius Julius
Cæsar, was, in comparison, of small importance. Those intervening relationships were, comparatively speaking, of no
other use to him than in virtue of their being so many
necessary links in the genealogical chain which connected
him with the sovereign of the empire.

As to the advantages and disadvantages which may happen
to be annexed to any of those uncontiguous relationships, we
have seen already that no powers over the correlative person,
nor any corresponding obligations, are of the number. Of
what nature then can they be? They are, in truth, no other
than what are the result either of local and accidental institutions, or of some spontaneous bias that has been taken by
the moral sanction. It would, therefore, be to little purpose
to attempt tracing them out *a priori* by any exhaustive process:
all that can be done is, to pick up and lay together some of

the principal articles in each catalogue by way of specimen. The advantages which a given relationship is apt to impart, seem to be referable chiefly to the following heads: 1. Chance of succession to the property, or a part of the property, of the correlative person. 2. Chance of pecuniary support, to be yielded by the correlative person, either by appointment of law, or by spontaneous donation. 3. Accession of legal rank; including any legal privileges which may happen to be annexed to it: such as capacity of holding such and such beneficial offices; exemption from such and such burthensome obligations; for instance, paying taxes, serving burthensome offices, &c. &c. 4. Accession of rank by courtesy; including the sort of reputation which is customarily and spontaneously annexed to distinguished birth and family alliance: whereon may depend the chance of advancement in the way of marriage, or in a thousand other ways less obvious. The disadvantages which a given relation is liable to impart, seem to be referable chiefly to the following heads: 1. Chance of being obliged, either by law, or by force of the moral sanction, to yield pecuniary support to the correlative party. 2. Loss of legal rank: including the legal disabilities, as well as the burthensome obligations, which the law is apt to annex, sometimes with injustice enough, to the lower stations. 3. Loss of rank by courtesy: including the loss of the advantages annexed by custom to such rank. 4. Incapacity of contracting matrimony with the correlative person, where the supposed consanguinity or affinity lies within the prohibited degrees.[1]

---

[1] In pursuance of the plan adopted with relation to semi-public and self-regarding offences, it may here be proper to exhibit such a catalogue as the nature of the design will admit, of the several genera or inferior divisions of public offences.

I. OFFENCES against the EXTERNAL SECURITY of the state. 1. Treason (in favour of foreign enemies). It may be positive or negative (negative consisting for example, in the not opposing the commission of positive). 2. *Espionage* (in favour of foreign rivals not yet enemies). 3. Injuries to foreigners at large (including piracy). 4. Injuries to privileged foreigners (such as ambassadors).

II. OFFENCES AGAINST JUSTICE. Offences against judicial trust: viz. Wrongful non-investment of judicial trust, wrongful interception of judicial trust, wrongful divestment of judicial trust, usurpation of judicial trust, wrongful investment of judicial trust, wrongful abdication of judicial trust, wrongful detrectation of judicial trust, wrongful imposition of judicial trust, breach of judicial trust,

45. We now come to civil conditions: these, it may well *Civil conditions.* be imagined, may be infinitely various: as various as the acts

abuse of judicial trust, disturbance of judicial trust, and bribery in prejudice of judicial trust.

Breach and abuse of judicial trust may be either intentional or unintentional. Intentional is culpable at any rate. Unintentional will proceed either from inadvertence, or from mis-supposal: if the inadvertence be coupled with heedlessness, or the mis-supposal with rashness, it is culpable: if not, blameless. For the particular acts by which the exercise of judicial trust may be *disturbed* see B. i. tit. [Offences against justice]. They are too multifarious, and too ill provided with names, to be exhibited here.

If a man fails in fulfilling the duties of this trust, and thereby comes either to break or to abuse it, it must be through some deficiency in the three requisite and only requisite endowments, of knowledge, inclination, and power. [See supra, 27.] A deficiency in any of those points, if any person be in fault, may proceed either from his own fault, or from the fault of those who should act with or under him. If persons who are in fault are persons invested with judicial trust, the offence comes under the head of breach or abuse of trust: if other persons, under that of disturbance of trust.

The ill effects of any breach, abuse, or disturbance of judicial trust, will consist in the production of some article or articles in the list of the mischiefs which it ought to be the original purpose of judicial procedure to remedy or avert, and of those which it ought to be the incidental purpose of it to avoid producing. These are either primary (that is immediate) or remote: remote are of the 2nd, 3rd, or 4th order, and so on. The primary are those which import actual pain to persons assignable, and are therefore mischievous in themselves: the secondary are mischievous on account of the tendency they have to produce some article or articles in the catalogue of those of the first order; and are therefore mischievous in their effects. Those of the 3rd order are mischievous only on account of the connection they have in the way of productive tendency, as before, with those of the 2nd order: and so on.

Primary inconveniences, which it ought to be the object of procedure to provide against, are, 1. The continuance of the individual offence itself, and thereby the increase as well as continuance of the mischief of it. 2. The continuance of the whole mischief of the individual offence. 3. The continuance of a part of the mischief of the individual offence. 4. Total want of amends on the part of persons injured by the offence. 5. Partial want of amends on the part of persons injured by the offence. 6. Superfluous punishment of delinquents. 7. Unjust punishment of persons accused. 8. Unnecessary labour, expense, or other suffering or danger, on the part of superior judicial officers. 9. Unnecessary labour, expense, or other suffering or danger, on the part of ministerial or other subordinate judicial officers. 10. Unnecessary labour, expense, or other suffering or danger, on the part of persons whose co-operation is requisite *pro re natâ*, in order to make up the necessary complement of knowledge and power on the part of judicial officers, who are such by profession. 11. Unnecessary labour, expense, or other suffering or danger, on the part of persons at large, coming under the sphere of the operations of the persons abovementioned.

Secondary inconveniences are, in the consultative, pre-interpretative (or purely civil) branch of procedure. 1. Misinterpretation or adjudication. In the executive (including the penal) branch. 2. Total impunity of delinquents: (as favouring the production of other offences of the like nature). 3. Partial impunity of delinquents. 4. Application of punishment improper in specie, though perhaps not in degree (this lessening the beneficial efficacy of the

which a man may be either commanded or allowed, whether
for his own benefit, or that of others, to abstain from or to

quantity employed). 5. Uneconomical application of punishment, though
proper, perhaps, as well in specie as in degree. 6. Unnecessary pecuniary
expense on the part of the state.

Inconveniences of the 3rd order are, 1. Unnecessary delay. 2. Unnecessary
intricacy.

Inconveniences of the 4th order are, 1. Breach. 2. Abuse, 3. Disturbance,
of judicial trust, as above: viz. in as far as these offences are preliminary to
and distinct from those of the 2nd and 3rd orders.

Inconveniences of the 5th order are, Breach of the several regulations of
procedure, or other regulations, made in the view of obviating the inconveniences above enumerated: viz. if preliminary and distinct, as before.

III. OFFENCES against the PREVENTIVE branch of the POLICE. 1. Offences
against *phthano–paranomic* trust: (φθάνω, to prevent, παρανομία, an offence).
2. Offences against *phthano–symphoric* trust: (συμφορά, a calamity). The two
trusts may be termed by the common appellation of *prophylactic*: (πρό, beforehand, and φυλάττω, to guard against).

IV. OFFENCES against the PUBLIC FORCE. 1. Offences against military trust,
corresponding to those against judicial trust Military desertion is a breach of
military duty, or of military trust. Favouring desertion is a disturbance of it.
2. Offences against that branch of public trust which consists in the management of the several sorts of things appropriated to the purposes of war:
such as arsenals, fortifications, dock-yards, ships of war, artillery, ammuni-
tion, military magazines, and so forth. It might be termed *polemo–tamieutic*:
from πόλεμος, war; and ταμίευς, a steward.[a]

V. OFFENCES against the POSITIVE INCREASE of the NATIONAL FELICITY. 1.
Offences against *epistemo–threptic* trust: (ἐπιστήμη, knowledge; and τρέφω, to
nourish or promote). 2. Offences against *eupædagogic* trust: (εὖ, well; and
παιδαγωγέω, to educate). 3. Offences against *noso–comial* trust: (νόσος, a disease;
and κομίζω, to take care of). 4. Offences against *moro–comial* trust: (μόρος, an
insane person). 5. Offences against *ptocho–comial* trust: (πτωχοί, the poor).
6. Offences against *antembletic* trust: (ἀντεμβάλλω, to bestow in reparation of a
loss). 7. Offences against *hedonarchic* trust: (ἡδοναί, pleasures; and ἄρχομαι, to
preside over). The above are examples of the principal establishments which
should or might be set on foot for the purpose of making, in so many different
ways, a positive addition to the stock of national felicity. To exhibit an exhaustive analysis of the possible total of these establishments would not be
a very easy task: nor on the present occasion is it a necessary one: for be they
of what nature and in what number they may, the offences to which they
stand exposed will, in as far as they are offences against trust, be in point of
denomination the same: and as to what turns upon the particular nature of
each trust, they will be of too local a nature to come within the present plan.

All these trusts might be comprised under some such general name as that
of *agatho–poieutic* trust: (ἀγαθοποιέω, to do good to any one).

VI. OFFENCES against the PUBLIC WEALTH. 1. Non-payment of forfeitures.
2. Non-payment of taxes, including smuggling. 3. Breach of the several

[a] A number of different branches of public trust, none of which have yet
been provided with appellatives, have here been brought to view: which then
were best? to coin new names for them out of the Greek; or, instead of a word
to make use of a whole sentence? In English, and in French, there is no other
alternative; no more than in any of the other southern languages. It rests with
the reader to determine.

perform. As many different denominations as there are of persons distinguished with a view to such commands and allowances (those denominations only excepted which relate

regulations made to prevent the evasion of taxes. 4. Offences against fiscal trust: the same as offences against judicial and military trusts. Offences against the original revenue, not accruing either from taxes or forfeitures, such as that arising from the public demesnes, stand upon the same footing as offences against private property. 5. Offences against *demosio-tamietuic* trust: (δημοσία, things belonging to the public; and ταμιευς, a steward) viz. against that trust, of which the object is to apply to their several destinations such articles of the public wealth as are provided for the indiscriminate accommodation of individuals: such as public roads and waters, public harbours, post-offices, and packet boats, and the stock belonging to them; market-places, and other such public buildings; race-grounds, public walks and so forth. Offences of this description will be apt to coincide with offences against *agatho-poieutic* trust as above, or with offences against *ethno-plutistic* trust hereafter mentioned, according as the benefit in question is considered in itself, or as resulting from the application of such or such a branch or portion of the public wealth.

VII. OFFENCES against POPULATION. 1. Emigration. 2. Suicide. 3. Procurement of impotence or barrenness. 4. Abortion. 5. Unprolific coition. 6. Celibacy.

VIII. OFFENCES against the NATIONAL WEALTH. 1. Idleness. 2. Breach of the regulations made in the view of preventing the application of industry to purposes less profitable, in prejudice of purposes more profitable. 3. Offences against *ethno-plutistic* trust: (ἔθνος, the nation at large; πλουτίζω, to enrich).

IX. OFFENCES against the SOVEREIGNTY. 1. Offences against sovereign trust: corresponding to those against judicial, prophylactic, military, and fiscal trusts. Offensive rebellion includes wrongful interception, wrongful divestment, usurpation, and wrongful investment, of sovereign trust, with the offences accessory thereto. Where the trust is in a single person, wrongful interception, wrongful divestment, usurpation, and wrongful investment cannot, any of them, be committed without rebellion: abdication and detrectation can never be deemed wrongful: breach and abuse of sovereign trust can scarcely be punished: no more can bribe-taking: wrongful imposition of it is scarce practicable. When the sovereignty is shared among a number, wrongful interception, wrongful divestment, usurpation, and wrongful investment, may be committed without rebellion: none of the offences against this trust are impracticable: nor is there any of them but might be punished. Defensive rebellion is disturbance of this trust. Political tumults, political defamation, and political vilification, are offences accessory to such disturbance.

Sovereign power (which, upon the principle of utility, can never be other than fiduciary) is exercised either by rule or without rule: in the latter case it may be termed *autocratic*: in the former case it is divided into two branches, the *legislative* and the *executive*.[a] In either case, where the designation of the person by whom the power is to be possessed, depends not solely upon mere physical events, such as that of natural succession, but in any sort upon the will of another person, the latter possesses an *investitive* power, or right of investiture, with regard to the power in question: in like manner may any person also possess a *divestitive* power. The powers above enumerated, such as judicial power, military power, and so forth, may therefore be exercisable by a man,

---

[a] See Chap. xvii. [Limits], § iii.

to the conditions above spoken of under the name of domestic ones) so many civil conditions one might enumerate. Means however, more or less explicit, may be found out of circumscribing their infinitude.

What the materials are, if so they may be called, of which conditions, or any other kind of legal possession, can be made up, we have already seen: beneficial powers, fiduciary powers, beneficial rights, fiduciary rights, relative duties, absolute duties. But as many conditions as import a power or right of the fiduciary kind, as possessed by the person whose condition is in question, belong to the head of trusts. The catalogue of the offences to which these conditions are exposed, coincides therefore exactly with the catalogue of offences against trust: under which head they have been considered in a general point of view under the head of offences against trust: and such of them as are of a domestic nature, in a more particular manner in the character of offences against the several domestic conditions. Conditions constituted by such duties of the relative kind, as have for their counterparts trusts constituted by fiduciary powers, as well as rights on the side of the correlative party, and those

---

either directly, *propriâ manu*; or indirectly, *manu alienâ*.[a] Power to be exercised *manu alienâ* is investitive, which may or may not be accompanied by divestitive. Of sovereign power, whether autocratic, legislative, or executive, the several public trusts above mentioned form so many subordinate branches. Any of these powers may be placed, either, 1. in an individual; or, 2. in a body politic: who may be either supreme or subordinate. Subordination on the part of a magistrate may be established, 1. By the person's being punishable: 2. By his being removable: 3. By the orders being reversible.

X. OFFENCES against RELIGION. 1. Offences tending to weaken the force of the religious sanction: including blasphemy and profaneness. 2. Offences tending to misapply the force of the religious sanction: including false prophecies, and other pretended revelations: also heresy, where the doctrine broached is pernicious to the temporal interests of the community. 3. Offences against religious trust, where any such is thought fit to be established.

XI. OFFENCES against the NATIONAL INTEREST in general. 1. Immoral publications. 2. Offences against the trust of an ambassador; or, as it might be termed, *presbeutic* trust. 3. Offences against the trust of a privy-counsellor; or, as it might be termed, *symbouleutic* trust. 4. In pure or mixed monarchies, prodigality on the part of persons who are about the person of the sovereign, though without being invested with any specific trust. 5. Excessive gaming on the part of the same persons. 6. Taking presents from rival powers without leave.

a In the former case, the power might be termed in one word, *autochirous*: in the latter *heterochirous* (αὐτός, a man's own; χείρ, a hand; ἑτέρος, another's).

of a private nature, have also been already discussed under
the appellation of domestic conditions. The same observation may be applied to the conditions constituted by such
powers of the beneficial kind over persons as are of a private
nature: as also to the subordinate correlative conditions
constituted by the duties corresponding to those rights and
powers. As to absolute duties, there is no instance of a
condition thus created, of which the institution is upon the
principle of utility to be justified; unless the several religious
conditions of the monastic kind should be allowed of as
examples. There remain, as the only materials out of which
the conditions which yet remain to be considered can be
composed, conditions constituted by beneficial powers over
things; conditions constituted by beneficial rights to things
(that is, rights to powers over things) or by rights to those
rights, and so on; conditions constituted by rights to services;
and conditions constituted by the duties corresponding to
those respective rights. Out of these are to be taken those
of which the materials are the ingredients of the several
modifications of property, the several conditions of proprietor-
ship. These are the conditions, if such for a moment they may
be styled, which having but here and there any specific
names, are not commonly considered on the footing of
conditions: so that the acts which, if such conditions were
recognised, might be considered as offences against those
conditions, are not wont to be considered in any other light
than that of offences against property.

Now the case is, as hath been already intimated,[1] that of
these civil conditions, those which are wont to be considered
under that name, are not distinguished by any uniform and
explicit line from those of which the materials are wont to be
carried to the head of property: a set of rights shall, in one
instance, be considered as constituting an article of property
rather than a condition: while, in another instance, a set of
rights of the same stamp is considered as constituting rather a
condition than an article of property. This will probably be
found to be the case in all languages: and the usage is different
again in one language from what it is in another. From these
causes it seems to be impracticable to subject the class of civil

[1] Supra, 17.

conditions to any exhaustive method: so that for making a complete collection of them there seems to be no other expedient than that of searching the language through for them, and taking them as they come. To exemplify this observation, it may be of use to lay open the structure as it were of two or three of the principal sorts or classes of conditions, comparing them with two or three articles of property which appear to be nearly of the same complexion: by this means the nature and generation, if one may so call it, of both these classes of ideal objects may be the more clearly understood.

The several sorts of civil conditions that are not fiduciary may all, or at least the greater part of them, be comprehended under the head of *rank*, or that of *profession*; the latter word being taken in its most extensive sense, so as to include not only what are called the liberal professions, but those also which are exercised by the several sorts of traders, artists, manufacturers, and other persons of whatsoever station, who are in the way of making a profit by their labour. Among ranks then, as well as professions, let us, for the sake of perspicuity, take for examples such articles as stand the clearest from any mixture of either fiduciary or beneficial power. The rank of knighthood is constituted, how? by prohibiting all other persons from performing certain acts, the performance of which is the symbol of the order, at the same time that the knight in question, and his companions, are permitted: for instance, to wear a ribbon of a certain colour in a certain manner: to call himself by a certain title: to use an armorial seal with a certain mark on it. By laying all persons but the knight under this prohibition, the law subjects them to a set of duties: and since from the discharge of these duties a benefit results to the person in whose favour they are created, to wit, the benefit of enjoying such a share of extraordinary reputation and respect as men are wont to yield to a person thus distinguished, to discharge them is to render him a service: and the duty being a duty of the negative class, a duty consisting in the performance of certain acts of the negative kind,[1] the service is what may be called *a service of forbearance*. It appears then, that to generate this condition

[1] See Chap. vii. [Actions] 78.

there must be two sorts of services: that which is the immediate cause of it, a service of the negative kind, to be rendered by the community at large: that which is the cause again of this service, a service of the positive kind, to be rendered by the law.

The condition of a professional man stands upon a narrower footing. To constitute this condition there needs nothing more than a permission given him on the part of the legislator to perform those acts, in the performance of which consists the exercise of his profession: to give or sell his advice or assistance in matters of law or physic: to give or sell his services as employed in the executing or overseeing of a manufacture or piece of work of such or such a kind: to sell a commodity of such or such a sort. Here then we see there is but one sort of service requisite; a service which may be merely of the negative kind, to be rendered by the law: the service of permitting him to exercise his profession: a service which, if there has been no prohibition laid on before, is rendered by simply forbearing to prohibit him.

Now the ideal objects, which in the cases above specified are said to be conferred upon a man by the services that are respectively in question, are in both cases not articles of property but conditions. By such a behaviour on the part of the law, as shall be the reverse of that whereby they were respectively produced, a man may be made to forfeit them: and what he is then said to forfeit is in neither case his property; but in one case, his rank or dignity: in the other case, his trade or his profession: and in both cases, his condition.

Other cases there are again in which the law, by a process of the same sort with that by which it constituted the former of the two above-mentioned conditions, confers on him an ideal object, which the laws of language have placed under the head of property. The law permits a man to sell books: that is, all sorts of books in general. Thus far all that it has done is to invest him with a condition: and this condition he would equally possess, although everybody else in the world were to sell books likewise. Let the law now take an active part in his favour, and prohibit all other persons from selling books of a certain description, he remaining at liberty to sell them as before. It therefore confers on him a sort of exclusive privilege or monopoly, which is called a *copy-right*. But by investing him with this right, it is not said to invest him with any new sort of condition: what it invests him with is spoken of as an article of property; to wit, of that sort of property which is termed incorporeal:[1] and so on in the case of an engraving, a mechanical engine, a medicine; or, in short, of a saleable article of any other sort. Yet when it gave him an exclusive right of wearing a particular sort of ribbon, the object which it was then considered as conferring on him was not an article of property but a condition.

By forbearing to subject you to certain disadvantages, to which it subjects an alien, the law confers on you the condition of a natural-born subject: by subjecting him to them, it imposes on him the condition of an alien: by conferring on you certain privileges or rights, which it denies to a *roturier*, the law confers on you the condition of a *gentilhomme*; by forbearing to confer on him those privileges, it imposes on him the condition of a *roturier*.[2] The rights, out of which the two advantageous conditions here exemplified are both of them as it were composed, have for their counterpart a sort of services of forbearance, rendered, as we have seen, not by private individuals, but by the law itself. As to the duties which it creates in rendering you these services, they are to be considered as duties imposed by the legislator on the ministers of justice.

It may be observed, with regard to the greater part of the conditions here comprised under the general appellation of *civil*, that the relations corresponding to those by which they are respectively constituted, are not provided with appellatives. The relation which has a name, is that which is borne by the party favoured to the party bound: that which is borne by the party bound to the party favoured has not any. This is a circumstance that may help to distinguish them from those conditions which we have termed domestic. In the domestic conditions, if on the one side the party *to* whom the power

---

[1] The reason probably why an object of the sort here in question is referred to the head of property, is, that the chief value of it arises from its being capable of being made a source of property in the more ordinary acceptations of the word; that is, of money, consumable commodities, and so forth.

[2] The conditions themselves having nothing that corresponds to them in England, it was necessary to make use of foreign terms.

is given is called a master; on the other side, the party *over* whom that power is given, the party who is the object of that power, is termed a servant. In the civil conditions this is not the case. On the one side, a man, in virtue of certain services of forbearance, which the rest of the community are bound to render him, is denominated a knight of such or such an order: but on the other side, these services do not bestow any particular denomination on the persons from whom such services are due. Another man, in virtue of the legislator's rendering that sort of negative service which consists in the not prohibiting him from exercising a trade, invests him at his option with the condition of a trader: it accordingly denominates him a farmer, a baker, a weaver, and so on: but the ministers of the law do not, in virtue of their rendering the man this sort of negative service, acquire for themselves any particular name. Suppose even that the trade you have the right of exercising happens to be the object of a monopoly, and that the legislator, besides rendering you himself those services which you derive from the permission he bestows on you, obliges other persons to render you those farther services which you receive from their forbearing to follow the same trade; yet neither do they, in virtue of their being thus bound, acquire any particular name.

After what has been said of the nature of the several sorts of civil conditions that have names, the offences to which they are exposed may, without much difficulty, be imagined. Taken by itself, every condition which is thus constituted by a permission granted to the possessor, is of course of a beneficial nature: it is, therefore, exposed to all those offences to which the possession of a benefit is exposed. But either on account of a man's being obliged to persevere when once engaged in it, or on account of such other obligations as may stand annexed to the possession of it, or on account of the comparative degree of disrepute which may stand annexed to it by the moral sanction, it may by accident be a burthen: it is on this account liable to stand exposed to the offences to which, as hath been seen, every thing that partakes of the nature of a burthen stands exposed. As to any offences which may concern the exercise of the functions belonging to it, if it happens to have any duties annexed to it, such as those, for instance, which are constituted by regulations touching the exercise of a trade, it will stand exposed to so many breaches of duty; and lastly, whatsoever are the functions belonging to it, it will stand exposed at any rate to *disturbance*.

In the forming however of the catalogue of these offences, exactness is of the less consequence, inasmuch as an act, if it should happen not to be comprised in this catalogue, and yet is in any respect of a pernicious nature, will be sure to be found in some other division of the system of offences: if a baker sells bad bread for the price of good, it is a kind of fraud upon the buyer; and perhaps an injury of the simple corporal kind done to the health of an individual, or a neighbourhood: if a clothier sells bad cloth for good at home, it is a fraud; if to foreigners abroad, it may, over and above the fraud put upon the foreign purchaser, have pernicious effects perhaps in the prosperity of the trade at home, and become thereby an offence against the national wealth. So again with regard to *disturbance*: if a man be disturbed in the exercise of his trade, the offence will probably be a wrongful *interception of the profit* he might be presumed to have been in a way to make by it: and were it even to appear in any case that a man exercised a trade, or what is less unlikely, a liberal profession, without having profit in his view, the offence will still be reducible to the head of *simple injurious restrainment*, or *simple injurious compulsion*.

§ 4. *Advantages of the present method.*

General idea of the method here pursued.

56. A few words, for the purpose of giving a general view of the method of division here pursued, and of the advantages which it possesses, may have their use. The whole system of offences, we may observe, is branched out into five classes. In the three first, the subordinate divisions are taken from the same source; viz. from the consideration of the different points, in respect whereof the interest of an individual is exposed to suffer. By this uniformity, a considerable degree of light seems to be thrown upon the whole system; particularly upon the offences that come under the third class: objects which have never hitherto been brought into any sort of order. With regard to the fourth class, in settling the precedence between its several subordinate divisions, it seemed

most natural and satisfactory to place those first, the connection whereof with the welfare of individuals seemed most obvious and immediate. The mischievous effects of those offences, which tend in an immediate way to deprive individuals of the protection provided for them against the attacks of one another, and of those which tend to bring down upon them the attacks of foreign assailants, seem alike obvious and palpable. The mischievous quality of such as tend to weaken the force that is provided to combat those attacks, but particularly the latter, though evident enough, is one link farther off in the chain of causes and effects. The ill effects of such offences as are of disservice only by diminishing the particular fund from whence that force is to be extracted, such effects, I say, though indisputable, are still more distant and out of sight. The same thing may be observed with regard to such as are mischievous only by affecting the universal fund. Offences against the sovereignty in general would not be mischievous, if offences of the several descriptions preceding were not mischievous. Nor in a temporal view are offences against religion mischievous, except in as far as, by removing, or weakening, or misapplying one of the three great incentives to virtue, and checks to vice, they tend to open the door to the several mischiefs, which it is the nature of all those other offences to produce. As to the fifth class, this, as hath already been observed, exhibits, at first view, an irregularity, which however seems to be unavoidable. But this irregularity is presently corrected, when the analysis returns back, as it does after a step or two, into the path from which the tyranny of language had forced it a while to deviate.

It was necessary that it should have two purposes in view: the one, to exhibit, upon a scale more or less minute, a systematical enumeration of the several possible modifications of delinquency, denominated or undenominated; the other, to find places in the list for such names of offences as were in current use: for the first purpose, nature was to set the law; for the other, custom. Had the nature of the things themselves been the only guide, every such difference in the manner of perpetration, and such only, should have served as a ground for a different denomination, as was attended with a difference in point of effect. This however of itself would never have been sufficient; for as on one hand the new language, which it would have been necessary to invent, would have been uncouth, and in a manner unintelligible: so on the other hand the names, which were before in current use, and which, in spite of all systems, good or bad, must have remained in current use, would have continued unexplained. To have adhered exclusively to the current language, would have been as bad on the other side; for in that case the catalogue of offences, when compared to that of the mischiefs that are capable of being produced, would have been altogether broken and uncomplete.

To reconcile these two objects, in as far as they seemed to be reconcilable, the following course has therefore been pursued. The logical whole, constituted by the sum total of possible offences, has been bisected in as many different directions as were necessary, and the process in each direction carried down to that stage at which the particular ideas thus divided found names in current use in readiness to receive them. At that period I have stopped; leaving any minuter distinctions to be enumerated in the body of the work, as so many species of the genus characterised by such or such a name. If in the course of any such process I came to a mode of conduct which, though it required to be taken notice of, and perhaps had actually been taken notice of, under all laws, in the character of an offence, had hitherto been expressed under different laws, by different circumlocutions, without ever having received any name capable of occupying the place of a substantive in a sentence, I have frequently ventured so far as to fabricate a new name for it, such an one as the idiom of the language, and the acquaintance I happened to have with it, would admit of. These names consisting in most instances, and that unavoidably, of two or three words brought together, in a language too which admits not, like the German and the Greek, of their being melted into one, can never be upon a par, in point of commodiousness, with those univocal appellatives which make part of the established stock.

In the choice of names in current use, care has been taken to avoid all such as have been grounded on local distinctions, ill founded perhaps in the nation in which they received their birth, and at any rate not applicable to the circumstances of other countries.

The analysis, as far as it goes, is as applicable to the legal concerns of one country as of another: and where, if it had descended into further details, it would have ceased to be so, there I have taken care always to stop: and thence it is that it has come to be so much more particular in the class of offences against individuals, than in any of the other classes. One use then of this arrangement, if it should be found to have been properly conducted, will be its serving to point out in what it is that the legal interests of all countries agree, and in what it is that they are liable to differ: how far a rule that is proper for one, will serve, and how far it will not serve, for another. That the legal interests of different ages and countries have nothing in common, and that they have every thing, are suppositions equally distant from the truth.[1]

57. A natural method, such as it hath been here attempted *Its advantages.* to exhibit, seems to possess four capital advantages; not to *1. It is convenient for the* mention others of inferior note. In the first place, it affords *apprehension* such assistance to the apprehension and to the memory, as *and the memory.* those faculties would in vain look for in any technical arrangement.[2] That arrangement of the objects of any science may, it should seem, be termed a *natural* one, which takes such properties to characterise them by, as men in general are, by the common constitution of man's nature, independently of any accidental impressions they may have received from the influence of any local or other particular causes, accustomed to attend to: such, in a word, as *naturally*, that is readily and at first sight, engage, and firmly fix, the attention of any one to whom they have once been pointed out. Now by what other means should an object engage or fix a man's attention, unless by interesting him? and what circumstance belonging to any action can be more interesting, or rather what other circumstance belonging to it can be at all interesting to him, than that of the influence it promises to have on

---

[1] The above hints are offered to the consideration of the few who may be disposed to bend their minds to disquisitions of this uninviting nature: to sift the matter to the bottom, and engage in the details of illustration, would require more room than could in this place be consistently allowed.

[2] See Fragment on Government, pref. p. xlv. edit. 1776.—pref. p. xlvii. edit. 1823.

2c

his own happiness, and the happiness of those who are about him? By what other mark then should he more easily find the place which any offence occupied in the system, or by what other clue should he more readily recall it?

—2. It gives room for general propositions.

58. In the next place, it not only gives at first glance a general intimation of the nature of each division of offences, in as far as that nature is determined by some one characteristic property, but it gives room for a number of general propositions to be formed concerning the particular offences that come under that division, in such manner as to exhibit a variety of other properties that may belong to them in common. It gives room, therefore, for the framing of a number of propositions concerning them, which, though very general, because predicated of a great number of articles, shall be as generally true.[1]

—3. It points out the reason of the law.

59. In the third place, it is so contrived, that the very place which any offence is made to occupy, suggests the reason of its being put there. It serves to indicate not only that such and such acts *are* made offences, but *why* they *ought* to be. By this means, while it addresses itself to the understanding, it recommends itself in some measure to the affections. By the intimation it gives of the nature and tendency of each obnoxious act, it accounts for, and in some measure vindicates, the treatment which it may be thought proper to bestow upon that

[1] Imagine what a condition a science must be in, when as yet there shall be no such thing as forming any extensive proposition relative to it, that shall be at the same time a true one: where, if the proposition shall be true of some of the particulars contained under it, it shall be false with regard to others. What a state would botany, for example, be in, if the classes were so contrived, that no common characters could be found for them? Yet in this state, and no better, seems every system of penal law to be, authoritative or unauthoritative, that has ever yet appeared. Try if it be otherwise, for instance, with the *delicta privata et publica*, and with the *publica ordinaria*, and *publica extra-ordinaria* of the Roman law.[a] All this for want of method: and hence the necessity of endeavouring to strike out a new one.

Nor is this want of method to be wondered at. A science so new as that of penal legislation, could hardly have been in any better state. Till objects are distinguished, they cannot be arranged. It is thus that *truth* and *order* go on hand in hand. It is only in proportion as the former is discovered, that the latter can be improved. Before a certain order is established, truth can be but imperfectly announced: but until a certain proportion of truth has been developed and brought to light, that order cannot be established. The discovery of truth leads to the establishment of order: and the establishment of order fixes and propagates the discovery of truth.

[a] See Heinecc, Elem. p. vii. § 79, 80.

act in the way of punishment. To the subject then it is a kind of perpetual apology: showing the necessity of every defalcation, which, for the security and prosperity of each individual, it is requisite to make from the liberty of every other. To the legislator it is a kind of perpetual lesson: serving at once as a corrective to his prejudices, and as a check upon his passions. Is there a mischief which has escaped him? in a natural arrangement, if at the same time an exhaustive one, he cannot fail to find it. Is he tempted ever to force innocence within the pale of guilt? the difficulty of finding a place for it advertises him of his error. Such are the uses of a map of universal delinquency, laid down upon the principle of utility: such the advantages, which the legislator as well as the subject may derive from it. Abide by it, and every thing that is arbitrary in legislation vanishes. An evil-intentioned or prejudiced legislator durst not look it in the face. He would proscribe it, and with reason: it would be a satire on his laws.

60. In the fourth place, a natural arrangement, governed as *—4. It is alike* it is by a principle which is recognized by all men, will serve *applicable to the* alike for the jurisprudence of all nations. In a system of *laws of all nations.* proposed law, framed in pursuance of such a method, the language will serve as a glossary by which all systems of positive law might be explained, while the matter serves as a standard by which they might be tried. Thus illustrated, the practice of every nation might be a lesson to every other: and mankind might carry on a mutual interchange of experiences and improvements as easily in this as in every other walk of science. If any one of these objects should in any degree be attained, the labour of this analysis, severe as it has been, will not have been thrown away.

§ 5. *Characters of the five classes.*

61. It has been mentioned[1] as an advantage possessed by *Characters of* this method, and not possessed by any other, that the objects *the classes, how* comprised under it are cast into groups, to which a variety of *deducible from the above* propositions may be applied in common. A collection of *method.* these propositions, as applied to the several classes, may be

[1] Supra, 58.

considered as exhibiting the distinctive characters of each class. So many of these propositions as can be applied to the offences belonging to any given class, so many properties are they found to have in common: so many of these common properties as may respectively be attributed to them, so many properties may be set down to serve as *characters* of the class. A collection of these characters it may here be proper to exhibit. The more of them we can bring together, the more clearly and fully will the nature of the several classes, and of the offences they are composed of, be understood.

Characters of
Class 1.

62. Characters of Class 1; composed of PRIVATE offences, or offences against assignable *individuals*.

1. When arrived at their last stage (the stage of *consummation*[1]) they produce, all of them, a primary mischief as well as a secondary.[2]

2. The individuals whom they affect in the first instance[3] are constantly *assignable*. This extends to all; to *attempts* and *preparations*, as well as to such as have arrived at the stage of consummation.[4]

3. Consequently they admit of *compensation*:[5] in which they differ from the offences of all the other classes, as such.

4. They admit[6] also of *retaliation*;[7] in which also they differ from the offences of all the other classes.

5. There is always some person who has a natural and peculiar interest to prosecute them. In this they differ from self-regarding offences: also from semi-public and public ones; except in as far as the two latter may chance to involve a private mischief.

6. The mischief they produce is obvious: more so than that of semi-public offences: and still more so than that of self-regarding ones, or even public.

7. They are every where, and must ever be, obnoxious to

---

[1] Chap. vii. [Actions], xiv. [2] See Chap. xii. [Consequences], 3.

[3] That is, by their primary mischief.

[4] See supra, 31. note, and B. I. tit. [Accessory offences].

[5] See Chap. xiii. [Cases unmeet], 2, note.

[6] I mean, that retaliation is *capable* of being applied in the cases in question; not that it *ought* always to be employed. Nor is it capable of being applied in every *individual* instance of each offence, but only in some individual instance of each *species* of offence.

[7] See Chap. xv. [Properties], 8.

the censure of the world: more so than semi-public offences as such; and still more so than public ones.

8. They are more *constantly* obnoxious to the censure of the world than self-regarding offences: and would be so universally, were it not for the influence of the two false principles; the principle of asceticism, and the principle of antipathy.[1]

9. They are less apt than semi-public and public offences to require different descriptions[2] in different states and countries: in which respect they are much upon a par with self-regarding ones.

10. By certain circumstances of aggravation, they are liable to be transformed into semi-public offences; and by certain others, into public

11. There can be no ground for punishing them, until they can be proved to have occasioned, or to be about to occasion, some particular mischief to some particular individual. In this they differ from semi-public offences, and from public.

12. In slight cases, *compensation* given to the individual affected by them may be a sufficient ground for remitting punishment: for if the primary mischief has not been sufficient to produce any alarm, the whole of the mischief may be cured by compensation. In this also they differ from semi-public offences, and from public ones.

63. Characters of Class 2; composed of SEMI-PUBLIC *Characters of* offences, or offences affecting a whole subordinate *class* of *Class 2.* persons.

1. As such, they produce no primary mischief. The mischief they produce consists of one or other or both branches of the secondary mischief produced by offences against individuals, without the primary.

2. In as far as they are to be considered as belonging to this class, the persons whom they affect in the first instance are not individually assignable.

3. They are apt, however, to involve or terminate in some

---

[1] Chap. ii. [Principles adverse].

[2] It seems to be from their possessing these three last properties, that the custom has arisen of speaking of them, or at least of many of them, under the name of offences against the *law of nature*: a vague expression, and productive of a multitude of inconveniences. See Chap. ii. [Principles adverse], 14, note.

primary mischief of the first order; which when they do, they advance into the first class, and become private offences.

4. They admit not, as such, of compensation.

5. Nor of retaliation.

6. As such, there is never any one particular individual whose exclusive interest it is to prosecute them: a circle of persons may, however, always be marked out, within which may be found some who have a greater interest to prosecute than any who are out of that circle have.

7. The mischief they produce is in general pretty obvious: not so much so indeed as that of private offences, but more so upon the whole than that of self-regarding and public ones.

8. They are rather less obnoxious to the censure of the world than private offences; but they are more so than public ones: they would also be more so than self-regarding ones, were it not for the influence of the two false principles, the principle of sympathy and antipathy, and that of asceticism.

9. They are more apt than private and self-regarding offences to require different descriptions in different countries: but less so than public ones.

10. There may be ground for punishing them before they have been proved to have occasioned, or to be about to occasion, mischief to any particular individual; which is not the case with private offences.

11. In no cases can satisfaction given to any particular individual affected by them be a sufficient ground for remitting punishment: for by such satisfaction it is but a part of the mischief of them that is cured. In this they differ from private offences; but agree with public.

Characters of Class 3.

64. Characters of Class 3; consisting of SELF REGARDING offences: offences against *one's self*.

1. In individual instances it will often be questionable, whether they are productive of any primary[1] mischief at all: secondary, they produce none.

2. They affect not any other individuals, assignable or not assignable, except in as far as they affect the offender himself;

[1] Because the person, who in general is most likely to be sensible to the mischief (if there is any) of any offence, viz. the person whom it most affects, shows by his conduct that he is not sensible of it.

unless by possibility in particular cases; and in a very slight
and distant manner the whole state

3. They admit not, therefore, of *compensation*.

4. Nor of *retaliation*.

5. No person has naturally any peculiar interest to prosecute them: except in as far as in virtue of some *connection* he
may have with the offender, either in point of *sympathy*
or of *interest*,[1] a mischief of the *derivative* kind[2] may happen to
devolve upon him.[3]

6. The mischief they produce is apt to be unobvious and
in general more questionable than that of any of the other
classes.[4]

7. They are however apt, many of them, to be more
obnoxious to the censure of the world than public offences;
owing to the influence of the two false principles; the
principle of asceticism, and the principle of antipathy. Some
of them more even than semi-public, or even than private
offence.

8. They are less apt than offences of any other class to
require different descriptions in different states and countries.[5]

9. Among the inducements[6] to punish them, antipathy
against the offender is apt to have a greater share than
sympathy for the public.

10. The best plea for punishing them is founded on a faint
probability there may be of their being productive of a
mischief, which, if real, will place them in the class of public
ones: chiefly in those divisions of it which are composed
of offences against population, and offences against the national
wealth.

65. Characters of Class 4; consisting of PUBLIC offences, or *Characters of*
offences against *the state* in general.   *Class 4.*

---

[1] See Chap. vi. [Sensibility], 26, 27.

[2] See Chap. xii. [Consequences], 4.

[3] Among the offences, however, which belong to this class there are some
which in certain countries it is not uncommon for persons to be disposed to
prosecute without any artificial inducement and merely on account of an
antipathy, which such acts are apt to excite. See Chap. ii. [Principles adverse], 11.

[4] See note 1 in the preceding page.

[5] Accordingly, most of them are apt to be ranked among offences against
the law of nature. Vide supra, Characters of the 1st class, 62, note.

[6] I mean the considerations, right or wrong, which induce or dispose the
legislator to treat them on the footing of offences.

1. As such, they produce not any primary mischief; and the secondary mischief they produce, which consists frequently of danger without alarm, though great in *value*, is in *specie* very indeterminate.

2. The individuals whom they affect, in the first instance, are constantly unassignable; except in as far as by accident they happen to involve or terminate in such or such offences against individuals.

3. Consequently they admit not of compensation.

4. Nor of retaliation.

5. Nor is there any person who has naturally any particular interest to prosecute them; except in as far as they appear to affect the power, or in any other manner the private interest, of some person in authority.

6. The mischief they produce, as such, is comparatively unobvious; much more so than that of private offences, and more so likewise, than that of semi-public ones.

7. They are, as such, much less obnoxious to the censure of the world, than private offences; less even than semi-public, or even than self-regarding offences; unless in particular cases, through sympathy to certain persons in authority, whose private interests they may appear to affect.

8. They are more apt than any of the other classes to admit of different descriptions, in different states and countries.

9. They are constituted, in many cases, by some circumstances of aggravation superadded to a private offence: and therefore, in these cases, involve the mischief and exhibit the other characters belonging to both classes. They are however, even in such cases, properly enough ranked in the 4th class, inasmuch as the mischief they produce in virtue of the properties which aggregate them to that class, eclipses and swallows up that which they produce in virtue of those properties which aggegate them to the 1st.

10. There may be sufficient ground for punishing them, without their being proved to have occasioned, or to be about to occasion, any particular mischief to any particular individual. In this they differ from private offences, but agree with semi-public ones. Here, as in semi-public offences, the *extent* of the mischief makes up for the *uncertainty* of it.

11. In no case can satisfaction, given to any particular

individual affected by them, be a sufficient ground for remitting punishment. In this they differ from private offences; but agree with semi-public.

66. Characters of Class 5, or appendix: composed of MULTIFORM or ANOMALOUS offences; and containing offences by FALSEHOOD, and offences concerning TRUST.

Characters of Class 5.

1. Taken collectively, in the parcels marked out by their popular appellations, they are incapable of being aggregated to any systematical method of distribution, grounded upon the mischief of the offence.

2. They may, however, be thrown into sub-divisions, which may be aggregated to such a method of distribution.

3. These sub-divisions will naturally and readily rank under the divisions of the several preceding classes of this system.

4. Each of the two great divisions of this class spreads itself in that manner over all the preceding classes.

5. In some acts of this class, the distinguishing circumstance which constitutes the essential character of the offence, will in some instances enter necessarily, in the character of a criminative circumstance, into the constitution of the offence; insomuch that, without the intervention of this circumstance, no offence at all, of that denomination, can be committed.[1] In other instances, the offence may subsist without it; and where it interferes, it comes in as an accidental independent circumstance, capable of constituting a ground of aggravation.[2]

---

[1] Instance, offences by falsehood, in the case of *defraudment*.
[2] Instance, offences by falsehood, in the case of simple corporal injuries, and other offences against person.

CHAPTER XVII

OF THE LIMITS OF THE PENAL BRANCH OF JURISPRUDENCE

§ 1. *Limits between Private Ethics and the Art of Legislation.*

1. So much for the division of offences in general. Now an offence is an act prohibited, or (what comes to the same thing) an act of which the contrary is commanded, by the law: and what is it that the law can be employed in doing, besides prohibiting and commanding? It should seem then, according to this view of the matter, that were we to have settled what may be proper to be done with relation to offences, we should thereby have settled every thing that may be proper to be done in the way of law. Yet that branch which concerns the method of dealing with offences, and which is termed sometimes the *criminal*, sometimes the *penal*, branch, is universally understood to be but one out of two branches which compose the whole subject of the art of legislation; that which is termed the *civil* being the other.[1] Between these two branches then, it is evident enough, there cannot but be a very intimate connection; so intimate is it indeed, that the limits between them are by no means easy to mark out. The case is the same in some degree between the whole business of legislation (civil and penal branches taken together) and that of private ethics. Of these several limits however it will be in a manner necessary to exhibit some idea: lest, on the one hand, we should seem to leave any part of the subject that *does* belong to us untouched, or,

---

[1] And the *constitutional* branch, what is become of it? Such is the question which many a reader will be apt to put. An answer that might be given is— that the matter of it might without much violence be distributed under the two other heads. But, as far as recollection serves, that branch, notwithstanding its importance, and its capacity of being lodged separately from the other matter, had at that time scarcely presented itself to my view in the character of a distinct one: the thread of my enquiries had not as yet reached it. But in the concluding note of this same chapter, in paragraphs 22. to the end, the omission may be seen in some measure supplied.

on the other hand, to deviate on any side into a track which does not belong to us.

In the course of this enquiry, that part of it I mean which concerns the limits between the civil and the penal branch of law, it will be necessary to settle a number of points, of which the connection with the main question might not at first sight be suspected. To ascertain what sort of a thing *a* law is; what the *parts* are that are to be found in it; what it must contain in order to be *complete*; what the connection is between that part of a body of laws which belongs to the subject of *procedure* and the rest of the law at large:—all these, it will be seen, are so many problems, which must be solved before any satisfactory answer can be given to the main question above mentioned.

Nor is this their only use: for it is evident enough, that the notion of a complete law must first be fixed, before the legislator can in any case know what it is he has to do, or when his work is done.

2. Ethics at large may be defined, the art of directing *Ethics in general, what.* men's actions to the production of the greatest possible quantity of happiness, on the part of those whose interest is in view.

3. What then are the actions which it can be in a man's *Private ethics.* power to direct? They must be either his own actions, or those of other agents. Ethics, in as far as it is the art of directing a man's own actions, may be styled the *art of self-government*, or *private ethics*.

4. What other agents then are there, which, at the same *The art of government:* time that they are under the influence of man's direction, are *that is, of legis-* susceptible of happiness? They are of two sorts: 1. Other *lation and ad-* human beings who are styled persons. 2. Other animals, *ministration.* which, on account of their interests having been neglected by the insensibility of the ancient jurists, stand degraded into the class of *things*.[1] As to other human beings, the art

---

[1] Under the Gentoo and Mahometan religions, the interests of the rest *Interests of the* of the animal creation seem to have met with some attention. Why have *inferior animals* they not, universally, with as much as those of human creatures, allowance *improperly* made for the difference in point of sensibility? Because the laws that are have *neglected in* been the work of mutual fear; a sentiment which the less rational animals *legislation.* have not had the same means as man has of turning to account. Why *ought* they not? No reason can be given. If the being eaten were all, there is very

of directing their actions to the above end is what we mean, or at least the only thing which, upon the principle of utility, we *ought* to mean, by the art of government: which, in as far as the measures it displays itself in are of a permanent nature, is generally distinguished by the name of *legislation*: as it is by that of *administration*, when they are of a temporary nature, determined by the occurrences of the day.

Art of education. 5. Now human creatures, considered with respect to the maturity of their faculties, are either in an *adult*, or in a *non-adult* state. The art of government, in as far as it concerns the direction of the actions of persons in a non-adult state, may be termed the art of *education*. In as far as this business is entrusted with those who, in virtue of some private relationship, are in the main the best disposed to take upon them, and the best able to discharge, this office, it may be termed the art of *private education*: in as far as it is exercised by those whose province it is to superintend the conduct of the whole community, it may be termed the art of *public education*.

good reason why we should be suffered to eat such of them as we like to eat: we are the better for it, and they are never the worse. They have none of those long-protracted anticipations of future misery which we have. The death they suffer in our hands commonly is, and always may be, a speedier, and by that means a less painful one, than that which would await them in the inevitable course of nature. If the being killed were all, there is very good reason why we should be suffered to kill such as molest us: we should be the worse for their living, and they are never the worse for being dead. But is there any reason why we should be suffered to torment them? Not any that I can see. Are there any why we should *not* be suffered to torment them? Yes, several. See B. I. tit. [Cruelty to animals]. The day has been, I grieve to say in many places it is not yet past, in which the greater part of the species, under the denomination of slaves, have been treated by the law exactly upon the same footing as, in England for example, the inferior races of animals are still. The day *may* come, when the rest of the animal creation may acquire those rights which never could have been withholden from them but by the hand of tyranny. The French have already discovered that the blackness of the skin is no reason why a human being should be abandoned without redress to the caprice of a tormentor.[a] It may come one day to be recognized, that the number of the legs, the villosity of the skin, or the termination of the *os sacrum*, are reasons equally insufficient for abandoning a sensitive being to the same fate. What else is it that should trace the insuperable line? Is it the faculty of reason, or, perhaps, the faculty of discourse? But a full-grown horse or dog is beyond comparison a more rational, as well as a more conversable animal, than an infant of a day, or a week, or even a month, old. But suppose the case were otherwise, what would it avail? the question is not, Can they *reason*? nor, Can they *talk*? but, Can they *suffer*?

[a] See Lewis XIVth's Code Noir.

6. As to ethics in general, a man's happiness will depend, *Ethics exhibits* in the first place, upon such parts of his behaviour as none but *the rules of,* himself are interested in; in the next place, upon such parts of *1. Prudence.* it as may affect the happiness of those about him. In as far as *3. Beneficence.* his happiness depends upon the first-mentioned part of his behaviour, it is said to depend upon his *duty to himself.* Ethics then, in as far as it is the art of directing a man's actions in this respect, may be termed the art of discharging one's duty to one's self: and the quality which a man manifests by the discharge of this branch of duty (if duty it is to be called) is that of *prudence.* In as far as his happiness, and that of any other person or persons whose interests are considered, depends upon such parts of his behaviour as may affect the interests of those about him, it may be said to depend upon his *duty to others*; or, to use a phrase now somewhat antiquated, his *duty to his neighbour.* Ethics then, in as far as it is the art of directing a man's actions in this respect, may be termed the art of discharging one's duty to one's neighbour. Now the happiness of one's neighbour may be consulted in two ways: 1. In a negative way, by forbearing to diminish it. 2. In a positive way, by studying to increase it. A man's duty to his neighbour is accordingly partly negative and partly positive: to discharge the negative branch of it, is *probity*: to discharge the positive branch, *beneficence.*

7. It may here be asked, How it is that upon the principle *Probity and* of private ethics, legislation and religion out of the question, *beneficence,* a man's happiness depends upon such parts of his conduct as *nect with* affect, immediately at least, the happiness of no one but him- *prudence.* self: this is as much as to ask, What motives (independent of such as legislation and religion may chance to furnish) can one man have to consult the happiness of another? by what motives, or, which comes to the same thing, by what obligations, can he be bound to obey the dictates of *probity* and *beneficence*? In answer to this, it cannot but be admitted, that the only interests which a man at all times and upon all occasions is sure to find *adequate* motives for consulting, are his own. Notwithstanding this, there are no occasions in which a man has not some motives for consulting the happiness of other men. In the first place, he has, on all occasions, the purely social motive of sympathy or benevolence: in the next place,

he has, on most occasions, the semi-social motives of love of amity and love of reputation. The motive of sympathy will act upon him with more or less effect, according to the *bias* of his sensibility:[1] the two other motives, according to a variety of circumstances, principally according to the strength of his intellectual powers, the firmness and steadiness of his mind, the quantum of his moral sensibility, and the characters of the people he has to deal with.

Every act which is a proper object of ethics is not of legislation.

8. Now private ethics has happiness for its end: and legislation can have no other. Private ethics concerns every member, that is, the happiness and the actions of every member, of any community that can be proposed; and legislation can concern no more. Thus far, then, private ethics and the art of legislation go hand in hand. The end they have, or ought to have, in view, is of the same nature. The persons whose happiness they ought to have in view, as also the persons whose conduct they ought to be occupied in directing, are precisely the same. The very acts they ought to be conversant about, are even in a *great measure* the same. Where then lies the difference? In that the acts which they ought to be conversant about, though in a great measure, are not *perfectly and throughout* the same. There is no case in which a private man ought not to direct his own conduct to the production of his own happiness, and of that of his fellow-creatures: but there are cases in which the legislator ought not (in a direct way at least, and by means of punishment applied immediately to particular *individual* acts) to attempt to direct the conduct of the several other members of the community. Every act which promises to be beneficial upon the whole to the community (himself included) each individual ought to perform of himself: but it is not every such act that the legislator ought to compel him to perform. Every act which promises to be pernicious upon the whole to the community (himself included) each individual ought to abstain from of himself: but it is not every such act that the legislator ought to compel him to abstain from.

The limits between the provinces of private ethics and legislation, marked

9. Where then is the line to be drawn?—We shall not have far to seek for it. The business is to give an idea of the cases in which ethics ought, and in which legislation ought not

---

[1] Chap. vi. [Sensibility], 3.

(in a direct manner at least) to interfere. If legislation inter- *out by the cases* feres in a direct manner, it must be by punishment.[1] Now the *unmeet for punishment.* cases in which punishment, meaning the punishment of the political sanction, ought not to be inflicted, have been already stated.[2] If then there be any of these cases in which, although legislation ought not, private ethics does or ought to interfere, these cases will serve to point out the limits between the two arts or branches of science. These cases, it may be remembered, are of four sorts: 1. Where punishment would be groundless. 2. Where it would be inefficacious. 3. Where it would be unprofitable. 4. Where it would be needless. Let us look over all these cases, and see whether in any of them there is room for the interference of private ethics, at the same time that there is none for the direct interference of legislation.

10. 1. First then, as to the cases where punishment would be 1. *Neither* groundless. In these cases it is evident, that the restrictive *ought to apply* interference of ethics would be groundless too. It is because, *where punish-* upon the whole, there is no evil in the act, that legislation *ment is* ground- ought not to endeavour to prevent it. No more, for the same *less.* reason, ought private ethics.

11. 2. As to the cases in which punishment would be *in-* 2. *How far* efficacious. These, we may observe, may be divided into two *private ethics* sets or classes. The first do not depend at all upon the nature *can apply in the* of the act: they turn only upon a defect in the timing of the *cases where* punishment. The punishment in question is no more than *punishment* what, for any thing that appears, ought to have been applied *would be* ineffi- to the act in question. It ought, however, to have been *cacious.* applied at a different time; viz., not till after it had been properly denounced. These are the cases of an *ex-post-facto* law; of a judicial sentence beyond the law; and of a law not sufficiently promulgated. The acts here in question then might, for anything that appears, come properly under the department even of coercive legislation: of course do they under that of private ethics. As to the other set of cases, in which punishment would be inefficacious; neither do these depend upon the nature of the act, that is, of the *sort* of act:

[1] I say nothing in this place of reward: because it is only in a few extraordinary cases that it can be applied, and because even where it is applied, it may be doubted perhaps whether the application of it can, properly speaking, be termed an act of legislation. See infra, § 3

[2] Chap. xiii. [Cases unmeet].

they turn only upon some extraneous *circumstances*, with which an act of *any* sort may chance to be accompanied. These, however, are of such a nature as not only to exclude the application of legal punishment, but in general to leave little room for the influence of private ethics. These are the cases where the will could not be deterred from any act, even by the extraordinary force of artificial punishment: as in the cases of extreme infancy, insanity, and perfect intoxication: of course, therefore, it could not by such slender and precarious force as could be applied by private ethics. The case is in this respect the same, under the circumstances of unintentionality with respect to the event of the action, unconsciousness with regard to the circumstances, and mis-supposal with regard to the existence of circumstances which have not existed; as also where the force, even of extraordinary punishment, is rendered inoperative by the superior force of a physical danger or threatened mischief. It is evident, that in these cases, if the thunders of the law prove impotent, the whispers of simple morality can have but little influence.

3 *How far, where* it *would be* unprofitable. 12. 3. As to the cases where punishment would be *unprofitable*. These are the cases which constitute the great field for the exclusive interference of private ethics. When a punishment is unprofitable, or in other words too expensive, it is because the evil of the punishment exceeds that of the offence. Now the evil of the punishment, we may remember,[1] is distinguishable into four branches: 1. The evil of coercion, including constraint or restraint, according as the act commanded is of the positive kind or the negative. 2. The evil of apprehension. 3. The evil of sufferance. 4. The derivative evils resulting to persons in *connection* with those by whom the three above-mentioned original evils are sustained. Now with respect to those original evils, the persons who lie exposed to them may be two very different sets of persons. In the first place, persons who may have actually committed, or been prompted to commit, the acts really meant to be prohibited. In the next place, persons who may have performed, or been prompted to perform, such other acts as they fear may be in danger of being involved in the punishment designed only for the former. But of these two sets of

---

[1] See Chap. xiii. [Cases unmeet], § iv.

acts, it is the former only that are pernicious: it is, therefore, the former only that it can be the business of private ethics to endeavour to prevent. The latter being by the supposition not mischievous, to prevent them is what it can no more be the business of ethics to endeavour at, than of legislation. It remains to show how it may happen, that there should be acts really pernicious, which, although they may very properly come under the censure of private ethics, may yet be no fit objects of the legislator to control.

13. Punishment then, as applied to delinquency, may be unprofitable in both or either of two ways: 1. By the expense it would amount to, even supposing the application of it to be confined altogether to delinquency: 2. By the danger there may be of its involving the innocent in the fate designed only for the guilty. First then, with regard to the cases in which the expense of the punishment as applied to the guilty, would outweigh the profit to be made by it. These cases, it is evident, depend upon a certain proportion between the evil of the punishment and the evil of the offence. Now were the offence of such a nature, that a punishment which, in point of *magnitude*, should but just exceed the profit of it, would be sufficient to prevent it, it might be rather difficult perhaps to find an instance in which such punishment would clearly appear to be unprofitable. But the fact is, there are many cases in which a punishment, in order to have any chance of being efficacious, must, in point of magnitude, be raised a great deal above that level. Thus it is, wherever the danger of detection is, or, what comes to the same thing, is likely to appear to be, so small, as to make the punishment appear in a high degree uncertain. In this case it is necessary, as has been shown,[1] if punishment be at all applied, to raise it in point of magnitude as much as it falls short in point of certainty. It is evident, however, that all this can be but guess-work: and that the effect of such a proportion will be rendered precarious, by a variety of circumstances: by the want of sufficient promulgation on the part of the law:[2] by the particular circumstances of the temptation:[3] and by the circumstances

Which it may be, 1. Although confined to the guilty.

---

[1] Chap. xiv. [Proportion], 17, Rule 7.
[2] Chap. xiii. [Cases unmeet], § iii. Append tit. [Promulgation].
[3] Chap. xi. [Disposition], 35, &c.

2D

influencing the sensibility of the several individuals who are exposed to it.[1] Let the *seducing* motives be strong, the offence then will at any rate be frequently committed. Now and then indeed, owing to a coincidence of circumstances more or less extraordinary, it will be detected, and by that means punished. But for the purpose of example, which is the principal one, an act of punishment, considered in itself, is of no use: what use it can be of, depends altogether upon the expectation it raises of similar punishment, in future cases of similar delinquency. But this future punishment, it is evident, must always depend upon detection. If then the want of detection is such as must in general (especially to eyes fascinated by the force of the seducing motives) appear too improbable to be reckoned upon, the punishment, though it should be inflicted, may come to be of no use. Here then will be two opposite evils running on at the same time, yet neither of them reducing the quantum of the other: the evil of the disease and the evil of the painful and inefficacious remedy. It seems to be partly owing to some such considerations, that fornication, for example, or the illicit commerce between the sexes, has commonly either gone altogether unpunished, or been punished in a degree inferior to that in which, on other accounts, legislators might have been disposed to punish it.

2. By enveloping the innocent. 14. Secondly, with regard to the cases in which political punishment, as applied to delinquency, may be unprofitable, in virtue of the danger there may be of its involving the innocent in the fate designed only for the guilty. Whence should this danger then arise? From the difficulty there may be of fixing the idea of the guilty action: that is, of subjecting it to such a definition as shall be clear and precise enough to guard effectually against misapplication. This difficulty may arise from either of two sources: the one permanent, to wit, the nature of the *actions* themselves: the other occasional, I mean the qualities of the *men* who may have to deal with those actions in the way of government. In as far as it arises from the latter of these sources, it may depend partly upon the use which the *legislator* may be *able* to make of language; partly upon the use which, according to the apprehension of

[1] Chap. vi. [Sensibility].

the legislator, the *judge* may be *disposed* to make of it. As far as legislation is concerned, it will depend upon the degree of perfection to which the arts of language may have been carried, in the first place, in the nation in general; in the next place, by the *legislator* in particular. It is to a sense of this difficulty, as it should seem, that we may attribute the caution with which most legislators have abstained from subjecting to censure, on the part of the law, such actions as come under the notion of rudeness, for example, or treachery, or ingratitude. The attempt to bring acts of so vague and questionable a nature under the control of law, will argue either a very immature age, in which the difficulties which give birth to that danger are not descried; or a very enlightened age, in which they are overcome.[1]

15. For the sake of obtaining the clearer idea of the limits between the art of legislation and private ethics, it may now be time to call to mind the distinctions above established with regard to ethics in general. The degree in which private ethics stands in need of the assistance of legislation, is different in the three branches of duty above distinguished. Of the rules of moral duty, those which seem to stand least in need of the assistance of legislation are the rules of *prudence*. It can only be through some defect on the part of the understanding, if a man be ever deficient in point of duty to himself. If he does wrong, there is nothing else that it can be owing to but either some *inadvertence*[2] or some *mis-supposal*[2] with regard to the circumstances on which his happiness depends. It is a standing topic of complaint, that a man knows too little of himself. Be it so: but is it so certain that the legislator must know more[3]? It is plain, that of individuals

Legislation how far necessary for the enforcement of the dictates of prudence.

[1] In certain countries, in which the voice of the people has a more especial control over the hand of the legislator, nothing can exceed the dread which they are under of seeing any effectual provision made against the offences which come under the head of *defamation*, particularly that branch of it which may be styled the *political*. This dread seems to depend partly upon the apprehension they may think it prudent to entertain of a defect in point of ability or integrity on the part of the legislator, partly upon a similar apprehension of a defect in point of integrity on the part of the judge.

[2] See Chap. ix. [Consciousness].

[3] Chap. xvi. [Division], 52.

On occasions like this the legislator should never lose sight of the well-known story of the oculist and the sot. A countryman who had hurt his eyes by drinking, went to a celebrated oculist for advice. He found him at table,

2D*

the legislator can know nothing: concerning those points of conduct which depend upon the particular circumstances of each individual, it is plain, therefore, that he can determine nothing to advantage. It is only with respect to those broad lines of conduct in which all persons, or very large and permanent descriptions of persons, may be in a way to engage, that he can have any pretence for interfering; and even here the propriety of his interference will, in most instances, lie very open to dispute. At any rate, he must never expect to produce a perfect compliance by the mere force of the sanction of which he is himself the author. All he can hope to do, is to increase the efficacy of private ethics, by giving strength and direction to the influence of the moral sanction. With what chance of success, for example, would a legislator go about to extirpate drunkenness and fornication by dint of legal punishment? Not all the tortures which ingenuity could invent would compass it: and, before he had made any progress worth regarding, such a mass of evil would be produced by the punishment, as would exceed, a thousand-fold, the utmost possible mischief of the offence. The great difficulty would be in the procuring evidence; an object which could not be attempted, with any probability of success, without spreading dismay through every family,[1] tearing the bonds of sympathy asunder,[2] and rooting out the influence of all the social motives. All that he can do then, against offences of this nature, with any prospect of advantage, in the way of direct legislation, is to subject them, in cases of notoriety, to a slight censure, so as thereby to cover them with a slight shade of artificial disrepute.

—Apt to go too far in this respect.

16. It may be observed, that with regard to this branch of duty, legislators have, in general, been disposed to carry their interference full as far as is expedient. The great difficulty here is, to persuade them to confine themselves within bounds. A thousand little passions and prejudices have led them to narrow the liberty of the subject in this line, in cases in which

with a glass of wine before him. 'You must leave off drinking,' said the oculist. 'How so?' says the countryman. '*You* don't, and yet methinks your own eyes are none of the best.'—'That's very true, friend,' replied the oculist: 'but you are to know, I love my bottle better than my eyes.'

[1] Evil of apprehension: third branch of the evil of a punishment. Chap. xiii. § iv.

[2] Derivative evils: fourth branch of the evil of a punishment. Ib.

the punishment is either attended with no profit at all, or with none that will make up for the expense.

17. The mischief of this sort of interference is more par- —*Particularly*
ticularly conspicuous in the article of religion. The reasoning, *in matters of*
in this case, is of the following stamp. There are certain *religion.*
errors, in matters of belief, to which all mankind are prone:
and for these errors in judgment, it is the determination
of a Being of infinite benevolence, to punish them with an
infinity of torments. But from these errors the legislator
himself is necessarily free: for the men, who happen to be at
hand for him to consult with, being men perfectly enlightened,
unfettered, and unbiassed, have such advantages over all the
rest of the world, that when they sit down to enquire out the
truth relative to points so plain and so familiar as those in
question, they cannot fail to find it. This being the case,
when the sovereign sees his people ready to plunge headlong
into an abyss of fire, shall he not stretch out a hand to save
them? Such, for example, seems to have been the train of
reasoning, and such the motives, which led Lewis the XIVth
into those coercive measures which he took for the conversion
of heretics and the confirmation of true believers. The
ground-work, pure sympathy and loving-kindness: the
super-structure, all the miseries which the most determined
malevolence could have devised.[1] But of this more fully in
another place.[2]

18. The rules of *probity* are those, which in point of ex- —*How far*
pediency stand most in need of assistance on the part of the *necessary for the*
enforcement of

[1] I do not mean but that other motives of a less social nature might have
introduced themselves, and probably, in point of fact, did introduce themselves, in the progress of the enterprise. But in point of possibility, the motive
above mentioned, when accompanied with such a thread of reasoning, is
sufficient, without any other, to account for all the effects above alluded to. If
any others interfere, their interference, how natural soever, may be looked
upon as an accidental and inessential circumstance, not necessary to the production of the effect. Sympathy, a concern for the danger they appear to be
exposed to, gives birth to the wish of freeing them from it; that wish shows
itself in the shape of a command: this command produces disobedience:
disobedience on the one part produces disappointment on the other: the pain
of disappointment produces ill-will towards those who are the authors of it.
The affections will often make this progress in less time than it would take to
describe it. The sentiment of wounded pride, and other modifications of the
love of reputation and the love of power, add fuel to the flame. A kind of
revenge exasperates the severities of coercive policy.

[2] See B. I. tit. [Self-regarding offences.]

the dictates of probity. legislator, and in which, in point of fact, his interference has been most extensive. There are few cases in which it *would* be expedient to punish a man for hurting *himself*: but there are few cases, if any, in which it would *not* be expedient to punish a man for injuring his neighbour. With regard to that branch of probity which is opposed to offences against property, private ethics depends in a manner for its very existence upon legislation. Legislation must first determine what things are to be regarded as each man's property, before the general rules of ethics, on this head, can have any particular application. The case is the same with regard to offences against the state. Without legislation there would be no such thing as a *state*: no particular persons invested with powers to be exercised for the benefit of the rest. It is plain, therefore, that in this branch the interference of the legislator cannot any where be dispensed with. We must first know what are the dictates of legislation, before we can know what are the dictates of private ethics.[1]

—of the dictates of beneficence. 19. As to the rules of beneficence, these, as far as concerns matters of detail, must necessarily be abandoned in great measure to the jurisdiction of private ethics. In many cases the beneficial quality of the act depends essentially upon the disposition of the agent; that is, upon the motives by which he appears to have been prompted to perform it: upon their belonging to the head of sympathy, love of amity, or love of reputation; and not to any head of self-regarding motives, brought into play by the force of political constraint: in a word, upon their being such as denominate his conduct *free* and *voluntary*, according to one of the many senses given to those ambiguous expressions.[2] The limits of the law on this

---

[1] But suppose the dictates of legislation *are* not what they *ought to be*: what are then, or (what in this case comes to the same thing) what ought to be, the dictates of private ethics? Do they coincide with the dictates of legislation, or do they oppose them, or do they remain neuter? a very interesting question this, but one that belongs not to the present subject. It belongs exclusively to that of private ethics. Principles which may lead to the solution of it may be seen in A Fragment on Government, p. 150, Lond. edit. 1776—and p. 114, edit. 1823.

[2] If we may believe M. Voltaire,[a] there was a time when the French ladies who thought themselves neglected by their husbands, used to petition *pour être embesoignèes*: the technical word which, he says, was appropriated to this

[a] Quest, sur l'Encyclop. tom. 7. art. Impuissance.

head seem, however, to be capable of being extended a good deal farther than they seem ever to have been extended hitherto. In particular, in cases where the person is in danger, why should it not be made the duty of every man to save another from mischief, when it can be done without prejudicing himself, as well as to abstain from bringing it on him? This accordingly is the idea pursued in the body of the work.[1]

20. To conclude this section, let us recapitulate and bring to a point the difference between private ethics, considered as an art or science, on the one hand, and that branch of jurisprudence which contains the art of science of legislation, on the other. Private ethics teaches how each man may dispose himself to pursue the course most conducive to his own happiness, by means of such motives as offer of themselves: the art of legislation (which may be considered as one branch of the science of jurisprudence) teaches how a multitude of men, composing a community, may be disposed to pursue that course which upon the whole is the most conducive to the happiness of the whole community, by means of motives to be applied by the legislator. *Difference between private ethics and the art of legislation recapitulated.*

We come now to exhibit the limits between penal and civil jurisprudence. For this purpose it may be of use to give a distinct though summary view of the principal branches into which jurisprudence, considered in its utmost extent, is wont to be divided.

§ 2. *Jurisprudence, its branches*

21. Jurisprudence is a fictitious entity: nor can any meaning be found for the word, but by placing it in company with some word that shall be significative of a real entity. To know what is meant by jurisprudence, we must know, for example, what is meant by a book of jurisprudence. A book of juris- *Jurisprudence, expository—censorial.*

purpose. This sort of law-proceedings seems not very well calculated to answer the design: accordingly we hear nothing of them now-a-days. The French ladies of the present age seem to be under no such difficulties.

[1] A woman's head-dress catches fire: water is at hand: a man, instead of assisting to quench the fire, looks on, and laughs at it. A drunken man, falling with his face downwards into a puddle, is in danger of suffocation: lifting his head a little on one side would save him: another man sees this and lets him lie. A quantity of gunpowder lies scattered about a room: a man is going into it with a lighted candle: another, knowing this, lets him go in without warning. Who is there that in any of these cases would think punishment misapplied?

prudence can have but one or the other of two objects: 1. To
ascertain what the *law*¹ is: 2. to ascertain what it ought to be.
In the former case it may be styled a book of *expository* jurisprudence; in the latter, a book of *censorial* jurisprudence: or,
in other words, a book on the *art of legislation*.

*Expository
jurisprudence,
authoritative—
unauthoritative.*

22. A book of expository jurisprudence, is either *authoritative* or *unauthoritative*. It is styled authoritative, when it is
composed by him who, by representing the state of the law
to be so and so, causeth it so to be; that is, of the legislator himself: unauthoritative, when it is the work of any other person
at large.

*Sources of the
distinctions yet
remaining.*

23. Now *law*, or *the law*, taken indefinitely, is an abstract
and collective term; which, when it means any thing, can
mean neither more nor less than the sum total of a number of
individual laws taken together.² It follows, that of whatever
other modifications the subject of a book of jurisprudence is
susceptible, they must all of them be taken from some
circumstance or other of which such individual laws, or the
assemblages into which they may be sorted, are susceptible.
The circumstances that have given rise to the principal
branches of jurisprudence we are wont to hear of, seem to be
as follows: 1. The *extent* of the laws in question in point of
dominion. 2. The *political quality* of the persons whose conduct they undertake to regulate. 3. The *time* of their being in
force. 4. The *manner* in which they are *expressed*. 5. The
concern which they have with the article of *punishment*.

*Jurisprudence,
local—univer-
sal.*

24. In the first place, in point of extent, what is delivered
concerning the laws in question, may have reference either to

---

¹ The word *law* itself, which stands so much in need of a definition, must
wait for it awhile (see § 3): for there is no doing every thing at once. In the
mean time every reader will understand it according to the notion he has been
accustomed to annex to it.

² In most of the European languages there are two different words for
distinguishing the abstract and the concrete senses of the word *law*: which
words are so wide asunder as not even to have any etymological affinity.
In Latin, for example, there is *lex* for the concrete sense, *jus* for the abstract:
in Italian, *legge* and *diritto*: in French, *loi* and *droit*: in Spanish, *ley* and *derecho*:
in German, *gesetz* and *recht*. The English is at present destitute of this advantage.

In the Anglo-Saxon, besides *lage*, and several other words, for the concrete
sense, there was the word *right*, answering to the German *recht*, for the abstract
as may be seen in the compound *folc-right*, and in other instances. But the word
right having long ago lost this sense, the modern English no longer possesses
this advantage.

the laws of such or such a nation or nations in particular, or to the laws of all nations whatsoever: in the first case, the book may be said to relate to *local*, in the other, to *universal, jurisprudence*.

Now of the infinite variety of nations there are upon the earth, there are no two which agree exactly in their laws: certainly not in the whole: perhaps not even in any single article: and let them agree to-day, they would disagree to-morrow. This is evident enough with regard to the *substance* of the laws: and it would be still more extraordinary if they agreed in point of *form*; that is, if they were conceived in precisely the same strings of words. What is more, as the languages of nations are commonly different, as well as their laws, it is seldom that, strictly speaking, they have so much as a single *word* in common. However, among the words that are appropriated to the subject of law, there are some that in all languages are pretty exactly correspondent to one another: which comes to the same thing nearly as if they were the same. Of this stamp, for example, are those which correspond to the words *power, right, obligation, liberty*, and many others.

It follows, that if there are any books which can, properly speaking, be styled books of universal jurisprudence, they must be looked for within very narrow limits. Among such as are expository, there can be none that are authoritative: nor even, as far as the *substance* of the laws is concerned, any that are unauthoritative. To be susceptible of an universal application, all that a book of the expository kind can have to treat of, is the import of words: to be, strictly speaking, universal, it must confine itself to terminology. Accordingly the definitions which there has been occasion here and there to intersperse in the course of the present work, and particularly the definition hereafter given of the word *law*, may be considered as matter belonging to the head of universal jurisprudence. Thus far in strictness of speech: though in point of usage, where a man, in laying down what he apprehends to be the law, extends his view to a few of the nations with which his own is most connected, it is common enough to consider what he writes as relating to universal jurisprudence.

It is in the censorial line that there is the greatest room for disquisitions that apply to the circumstances of all nations alike: and in this line what regards the substance of the laws in question is as susceptible of an universal application, as what regards the words. That the laws of all nations, or even of any two nations, should coincide in all points, would be as ineligible as it is impossible: some leading points, however, there seem to be, in respect of which the laws of all civilized nations might, without inconvenience, be the same. To mark out some of these points will, as far as it goes, be the business of the body of this work.

—internal and international.

25. In the second place, with regard to the *political quality* of the persons whose conduct is the object of the law. These may, on any given occasion, be considered either as members of the same state, or as members of different states: in the first case, the law may be referred to the head of *internal*, in the second case, to that of *international*[1] jurisprudence.

Now as to any transactions which may take place between individuals who are subjects of different states, these are regulated by the internal laws, and decided upon by the internal tribunals, of the one or the other of those states: the case is the same where the sovereign of the one has any immediate transactions with a private member of the other: the sovereign reducing himself, *pro re natâ*, to the condition of a private person, as often as he submits his cause to either tribunal; whether by claiming a benefit, or defending himself against a burthen. There remain then the mutual transactions between sovereigns, as such, for the subject of that branch of jurisprudence which may be properly and exclusively termed *international*.[2]

[1] The word *international*, it must be acknowledged, is a new one; though, it is hoped, sufficiently analogous and intelligible. It is calculated to express, in a more significant way, the branch of law which goes commonly under the name of the *law of nations*: an appellation so uncharacteristic, that, were it not for the force of custom, it would seem rather to refer to internal jurisprudence. The chancellor D'Aguesseau has already made, I find, a similar remark: he says that what is commonly called *droit* des *gens*, ought rather to be termed *droit* entre *les gens*.[a]

[2] In the times of James I. of England and Philip III. of Spain, certain merchants at London happened to have a claim upon Philip, which his ambassador Gondemar did not think fit to satisfy. They applied for counsel to Selden, who advised them to sue the Spanish monarch in the court of King's Bench, and prosecute him to an outlawry. They did so: and the sheriffs of London were accordingly commanded, in the usual form, to take the body of the

[a] Œuvres, Tom. ii. p. 337, edit. 1773, 12mo.

With what degree of propriety rules for the conduct of persons of this description can come under the appellation of *laws*, is a question that must rest till the nature of the thing called *a law* shall have been more particularly unfolded.

It is evident enough, that international jurisprudence may, as well as internal, be censorial as well as expository, unauthoritative as well as authoritative.

26. Internal jurisprudence, again, may either concern all the members of a state indiscriminately, or such of them only as are connected in the way of residence, or otherwise, with a particular district. Jurisprudence is accordingly sometimes distinguished into *national* and *provincial*. But as the epithet *provincial* is hardly applicable to districts so small as many of those which have laws of their own are wont to be, such as towns, parishes, and manors; the term *local* (where universal jurisprudence is plainly out of the question) or the term *particular*, though this latter is not very characteristic, might either of them be more commodious.[1]

Internal juris-prudence, national and provincial, local or particular.

27. Thirdly, with respect to *time*. In a work of the expository kind, the laws that are in question may either be such as are still in force at the time when the book is writing, or such as have ceased to be in force. In the latter case the subject of it might be termed *ancient*; in the former, *present* or *living* jurisprudence: that is, if the substantive *jurisprudence*, and no other, must at any rate be employed, and that with an epithet in both cases. But the truth is, that a book of the former kind is rather a book of history than a book of juris-

Jurisprudence, ancient—living.

---

defendant Philip, wherever it was to be found within their bailiwick. As to the sheriffs, Philip, we may believe, was in no great fear of them: but what answered the same purpose, he happened on his part to have demands upon some other merchants, whom, so long as the outlawry remained in force, there was no proceeding against. Gondemar paid the money [a] This was internal jurisprudence: if the dispute had been betwixt Philip and James himself, it would have been international.

As to the word *international*, from this work, or the first of the works edited in French by Mr. Dumont, it has taken root in the language. Witness reviews and newspapers.

[1] The term *municipal* seemed to answer the purpose very well, till it was taken by an English author of the first eminence to signify internal law in general, in contradistinction to international law, and the imaginary law of nature. It might still be used in this sense, without scruple, in any other language.

[a] Selden's Table-Talk, tit. Law.

prudence; and, if the word *jurisprudence* be expressive of the subject, it is only with some such words as *history* or *antiquities* prefixed. And as the laws which are any where in question are supposed, if nothing appears to the contrary, to be those which are in force, no such epithet as that of *present* or *living* commonly appears.

Where a book is so circumstanced, that the laws which form the subject of it, though in force at the time of its being written, are in force no longer, that book is neither a book of living jurisprudence, nor a book on the history of jurisprudence: it is no longer the former, and it never was the latter. It is evident that, owing to the changes which from time to time must take place, in a greater or less degree, in every body of laws, every book of jurisprudence, which is of an expository nature, must in the course of a few years, come to partake more or less of this condition.

The most common and most useful object of a history of jurisprudence, is to exhibit the circumstances that have attended the establishment of laws actually in force. But the exposition of the dead laws which have been superseded, is inseparably interwoven with that of the living ones which have superseded them. The great use of both these branches of *science*, is to furnish examples for the *art* of legislation.[1]

Jurisprudence, statutory— customary.

28. Fourthly, in point of *expression*, the laws in question may subsist either in the form of *statute* or in that of *customary* law.

As to the difference between these two branches (which respects only the article of form or expression) it cannot properly be made appear till some progress has been made in the definition of a law.

[1] Of what stamp are the works of Grotius, Puffendorf, and Burlamaqui? Are they political or ethical, historical or juridical, expository or censorial? —Sometimes one thing, sometimes another: they seem hardly to have settled the matter with themselves. A defect this to which all books must almost unavoidably be liable, which take for their subject the pretended *law of nature*: an obscure phantom, which, in the imaginations of those who go in chase of it, points sometimes to *manners*, sometimes to *laws*; sometimes to what law *is*, sometimes to what it *ought* to be.[a] Montesquieu sets out upon the censorial plan: but long before the conclusion, as if he had forgot his first design, he throws off the censor, and puts on the antiquarian. The Marquis Beccaria's book, the first of any account that is uniformly censorial, concludes as it sets out, with penal jurisprudence.

[a] See Chap. ii. [Principles Adverse], 14.

29. Lastly, The most intricate distinction of all, and that *Jurisprudence,* which comes most frequently on the carpet, is that which is *civil — penal — criminal.* made between the *civil* branch of jurisprudence and the *penal,* which letter is wont, in certain circumstances, to receive the name of *criminal.*

What is a penal code of laws? What a civil code? Of what *Question con-* nature are their contents? Is it that there are two sorts of laws, *cerning the dis-* the one penal the other civil, so that the laws in a penal code *the civil branch* are all penal laws, while the laws in a civil code are all civil *and the penal,* laws? Or is it, that in every law there is some matter which is *stated.* of a penal nature, and which therefore belongs to the penal code; and at the same time other matter which is of a civil nature, and which therefore belongs to the civil code? Or is it, that some laws belong to one code or the other exclusively, while others are divided between the two? To answer these questions in any manner that shall be tolerably satisfactory, it will be necessary to ascertain what a *law* is; meaning one entire but single law: and what are the parts into which a law, as such, is capable of being distinguished: or, in other words, to ascertain what the properties are that are to be found in every object which can with propriety receive the appellation of *a* law. This then will be the business of the third and fourth sections: what concerns the import of the word *criminal,* as applied to law, will be discussed separately in the fifth.[1]

[1] Here ends the original work, in the state into which it was brought in   *I.* November, 1780. What follows is now added in January, 1789.   *Occasion and*

The third, fourth, and fifth sections intended, as expressed in the text, to *purpose of this* have been added to this chapter, will not here, nor now be given; because *concluding note.* to give them in a manner tolerably complete and satisfactory, might require a considerable volume. This volume will form a work of itself, closing the series of works mentioned in the preface.

What follows here may serve to give a slight intimation of the nature of the task, which such a work will have to achieve: it will at the same time furnish, not any thing like a satisfactory answer to the questions mentioned in the text, but a slight and general indication of the course to be taken for giving them such an answer.

What is a law? What the parts of a law? The subject of these questions,   *II.* it is to be observed, is the *logical,* the *ideal,* the *intellectual* whole, not the *By a law here* physical one: the *law,* and not the *statute.* An enquiry, directed to the latter *is not meant a* sort of object, could neither admit of difficulty nor afford instruction. In *statute.* this sense whatever is given for law by the person or persons recognized as possessing the power of making laws, is *law.* The Metamorphoses of Ovid, if thus given, would be law. So much as was embraced by one and the same act of authentication, so much as received the touch of the sceptre at one stroke, is *one* law: a whole law, and nothing more. A statute of George II.

made to substitute an *or* instead of an *and* in a former statute is a complete law; a statute containing an entire body of laws, perfect in all its parts, would not be more so. By the word *law* then, as often as it occurs in the succeeding pages is meant that ideal object, of which the part, the whole, or the multiple, or an assemblage of parts, wholes, and multiples mixed together, is exhibited by a statute; not the statute which exhibits them.

III.
Every law is either a command, or a revocation of one.

Every law, when complete, is either of a *coercive* or an *uncoercive* nature. A coercive law is a *command*.

An uncoercive, or rather a *discoercive*, law is the *revocation*, in whole or in part, of a coercive law.

IV.
A declaratory law is not, properly speaking, a law.

What has been termed a *declaratory* law, so far as it stands distinguished from either a coercive or a discoercive law, is not properly speaking a law. It is not the expression of an act of the will exercised at the time: it is a mere notification of the existence of a law, either of the coercive or the discoercive kind, as already subsisting: of the existence of some document expressive of some act of the will, exercised, not at the time, but at some former period. If it does any thing more than give information of this fact, viz. of the prior existence of a law of either the coercive or the discoercive kind, it ceases *pro tanto* to be what is meant by a declaratory law, and assuming either the coercive or the discoercive quality.

V.
Every coercive law creates an offence.

Every coercive law creates an *offence*, that is, converts an act of some sort, or other into an offence. It is only by so doing that it can *impose obligation*, that it can *produce coercion*.

VI.
A law creating an offence, and one appointing punishment, are distinct laws.

A law confining itself to the creation of an offence, and a law commanding a punishment to be administered in case of the commission of such an offence, are two distinct laws; not parts (as they seem to have been generally accounted hitherto) of one and the same law. The acts they command are altogether different; the persons they are addressed to are altogether different. Instance, *Let no man steal*; and, *Let the judge cause whoever is convicted of stealing to be hanged.*

They might be styled; the former, a *simply imperative* law; the other a *punitory*: but the punitory, if it commands the punishment to be inflicted, and does not merely permit it, is as truly *imperative* as the other: only it is punitory besides, which the other is not.

VII.
A discoercive law can have no punitory one appertaining to it but through the intervention of a coercive one.

A law of the discoercive kind, considered in itself, can have no punitory law belonging to it: to receive the assistance and support of a punitory law, it must first receive that of a simply imperative or coercive law, and it is to this latter that the punitory law will attach itself, and not to the discoercive one. Example; discoercive law. *The sheriff has power to hang all such as the judge, proceeding in due course of law, shall order him to hang.* Example of a coercive law, made in support of the above discoercive one. *Let no man hinder the sheriff from hanging such as the judge, proceeding in due course of law, shall order him to hang.* Example of a punitory law, made in support of the above coercive one. *Let the judge cause to be imprisoned whosoever attempts to hinder the sheriff from hanging one, whom the judge, proceeding in due course of law, has ordered him to hang.*

VIII.
But a punitory law involves the simply imperative one it belongs to.

But though a simply imperative law, and the punitory law attached to it, are so far distinct laws, that the former contains nothing of the latter, and the latter, in its direct tenor, contains nothing of the former; yet by *implication*, and that a necessary one, the punitory does involve and include the import of the simply imperative law to which it is appended. To say to the judge, *Cause to be hanged whoever in due form of law is convicted of stealing*, is, though not a direct, yet as intelligible a way of intimating to men in general that they must not steal, as to say to them directly, *Do not steal*: and one sees, how much more likely to be efficacious.

It should seem then, that, wherever a simply imperative law is to have a punitory one appended to it, the former might be spared altogether: in which case, saving the exception (which naturally should seem not likely to be a frequent one) of a law capable of answering its purpose without such an appendage, there should be no occasion in the whole body of the law for any other than punitory, or in other words than *penal*, laws. And this, perhaps, would be the case, were it not for the necessity of a large quantity of matter of the *expository* kind, of which we come now to speak.

IX.
The simply imperative one be spared, but for its expository matter.

It will happen in the instance of many, probably of most, possibly of all commands endued with the force of a public law, that, in the expression given to such a command, it shall be necessary to have recourse to terms too complex in their signification to exhibit the requisite ideas, without the assistance of a greater or less quantity of matter of an expository nature. Such terms, like the symbols used in algebraical notation, are rather substitutes and indexes to the terms capable of themselves of exhibiting the ideas in question, than the real and immediate representatives of those ideas.

X.
Nature of such expository matter.

Take for instance the law, *Thou shalt not steal.* Such a command, were it to rest there, could never sufficiently answer the purpose of a law. A word of so vague and unexplicit a meaning can no otherwise perform this office, than by giving a general intimation of a variety of propositions, each requiring, to convey it to the apprehension, a more particular and ample assemblage of terms. Stealing, for example, (according to a definition not accurate enough for use, but sufficiently so for the present purpose), is *the taking of a thing which is another's, by one who has no* TITLE *so to do, and is conscious of his having none.* Even after this exposition, supposing it a correct one, can the law be regarded as completely expressed? Certainly not. For what is meant by *a man's having a* TITLE *to take a thing?* To be complete, the law must have exhibited, amongst a multitude of other things, two catalogues: the one of events to which it has given the quality of *conferring title* in such a case; the other of the events to which it has given the quality of *taking it away.* What follows? That for a man to have *stolen*, for a man to *have had no title to what he took*, either no one of the articles contained in the first of those lists must have happened in his favour, or if there has, some one of the number of those contained in the second must have happened to his prejudice.

Such then is the nature of a general law, that while the imperative part of it, the *punctum saliens* as it may be termed, of this artificial body, shall not take up above two or three words, its expository appendage, without which that imperative part could not rightly perform its office, may occupy a considerable volume.

XI.
The vastness of its comparative bulk is not peculiar to legislative commands.

But this may equally be the case with a private order given in a family. Take for instance one from a bookseller to his foreman. *Remove, from this shop to my new one, my whole stock, according to this printed catalogue.—Remove, from this shop to my new one, my whole stock*, is the imperative matter of this order; the catalogue referred to contains the expository appendage.

The same mass of expository matter may serve in common for, may appertain in common to, many commands, many masses of imperative matter. Thus, amongst other things, the catalogue of *collative* and *ablative* events, with respect to *titles* above spoken of (see No. IX. of this note), will belong in common to all or most of the laws constitutive of the various offences against property. Thus, in mathematical diagrams, one and the same base shall serve for a whole cluster of triangles.

XII.
The same mass of expository matter may serve in common for many laws.

Such expository matter, being of a complexion so different from the imperative it would be no wonder if the connection of the former with the latter should escape the observation: which, indeed, is perhaps pretty generally the case. And so long as any mass of legislative matter presents itself, which is

XIII.
The imperative character essential to law, is

apt to be concealed in and by expository matter.

not itself imperative or the contrary, or of which the connection with matter of one of those two descriptions is not apprehended, so long and so far the truth of the proposition, *That every law is a command or its opposite,* may remain unsuspected, or appear questionable; so long also may the incompleteness of the greater part of those masses of legislative matter, which wear the complexion of complete laws upon the face of them, also the method to be taken for rendering them really complete, remain undiscovered.

XIV.
The concealment is favoured by the multitude of indirect forms in which imperative matter is capable of being couched.

A circumstance, that will naturally contribute to increase the difficulty of the discovery, is the great variety of ways in which the imperation of a law may be conveyed—the great variety of forms which the imperative part of a law may indiscriminately assume: some more directly, some less directly expressive of the imperative quality. *Thou shalt not steal. Let no man steal. Whoso stealeth shall be punished so and so. If any man steal, he shall be punished so and so. Stealing is where a man does so and so; the punishment for stealing is so and so. To judges so and so named, and so and so constituted, belong the cognizance of such and such offences; viz. stealing*—and so on. These are but part of a multitude of forms of words, in any of which the command by which stealing is prohibited might equally be couched: and it is manifest to what a degree, in some of them, the imperative quality is clouded and concealed from ordinary apprehension.

XV.
Number and nature of the laws in a code how determined.

After this explanation, a general proposition or two, that may be laid down, may help to afford some little insight into the structure and contents of a complete body of laws.—So many different sorts of *offences* created, so many different laws of the *coercive* kind: so many *exceptions* taken out of the descriptions of those offences, so many laws of the *discoercive* kind.

To class *offences,* as hath been attempted to be done in the preceding chapter, is therefore to class *laws*: to exhibit a complete catalogue of all the offences created by law, including the whole mass of expository matter necessary for fixing and exhibiting the import of the terms contained in the several laws, by which those offences are respectively created, would be to exhibit a complete collection of the laws in force: in a word a complete body of law; a *pannomion,* if so it might be termed.

XVI.
General idea of the limits between a civil and a penal code.

From the obscurity in which the limits of a *law,* and the distinction betwixt a law of the civil or simply imperative kind and a punitory law, are naturally involved, results the obscurity of the limits betwixt a civil and a penal *code,* betwixt a civil branch of the law and the penal.

The question, *What parts of the total mass of legislative matter belong to the civil branch, and what to the penal*? supposes that divers political states, or at least that some one such state, are to be found, having as well a civil code as a penal code, each of them complete in its kind, and marked out by certain limits. But no *one* such state has ever yet existed.

To put a question to which a true answer can be given, we must substitute to the foregoing question some such a one as that which follows:

Suppose two masses of legislative matter to be drawn up at this time of day, the one under the name of a civil code, the other of a penal code, each meant to be complete in its kind—in what general way, is it natural to suppose, that the different sorts of matter, as above distinguished, would be distributed between them?

To this question the following answer seems likely to come as near as any other to the truth.

The *civil* code would not consist of a collection of civil laws, each complete in itself, as well as clear of all penal ones:

Neither would the *penal* code (since we have seen that it *could* not) consist of a collection of punitive laws, each not only complete it itself, but clear of all civil ones. But

The civil code would consist chiefly of mere masses of expository matter. *XVII.*
The imperative matter, to which those masses of expository matter respectively *Contents of a*
appertained, would be found—not in that same code—not in the civil code— *civil code.*
nor in a pure state, free from all admixture of punitory laws; but in the penal
code—in a state of combination—involved, in manner as above explained,
in so many correspondent punitory laws.

The penal code then would consist principally of punitive laws, involving *XVIII.*
the imperative matter of the whole number of civil laws: along with which *Contents of a*
would probably also be found various masses of expository matter, apper- *penal code.*
taining not to the civil, but to the punitory laws. The body of penal law,
enacted by the Empress-Queen Maria Theresa, agrees pretty well with this
account.

The mass of legislative matter published in French as well as German, under *XIX.*
the auspices of Frederic II. of Prussia, by the name of Code Frederic, but never *In the Code*
established with force of law,[1] appears, for example, to be almost wholly *Frederic the im-*
composed of masses of expository matter, the relation of which to any im- *perative char-*
perative matter appears to have been but very imperfectly apprehended. *acter is almost*

In that enormous mass of confusion and inconsistency, the ancient Roman, *lost in the ex-*
or, as it is termed by way of eminence, the *civil* law, the imperative matter, *pository matter.*
and even all traces of the imperative character, seem at last to have been *XX.*
smothered in the expository. *Esto* had been the language of primæval sim- *So in the Roman*
plicity: *esto* had been the language of the twelve tables. By the time of *law.*
Justinian (so thick was the darkness raised by clouds of commentators) the
penal law had been crammed into an odd corner of the civil—the whole
catalogue of offences, and even of crimes, lay buried under a heap of *obligations*
—*will* was hid in *opinion*—and the original *esto* had transformed itself into
videtur, in the mouths even of the most despotic sovereigns.

Among the barbarous nations that grew up out of the ruins of the Roman *XXI.*
Empire, Law, emerging from under the mountain of expository rubbish, *In the barbarian*
reassumed for a while the language of command: and then she had simplicity *codes it stands*
at least, if nothing else, to recommend her. *conspicuous.*

Besides the civil and the penal, every complete body of law must contain *XXII.*
a third branch, the *constitutional*. *Constitutional*

The constitutional branch is chiefly employed in conferring, on particular *code, its con-*
classes of persons, *powers*, to be exercised for the good of the whole society, *nexion with the*
or of considerable parts of it, and prescribing *duties* to the persons invested with *two others.*
those powers.

The powers are principally constituted, in the first instance, by discoercive
or permissive laws, operating as exceptions to certain laws of the coercive
or imperative kind. Instance: *A tax-gatherer, as such, may, on such and such an*
occasion, take such and such things, without any other TITLE.

The duties are created by imperative laws, addressed to the persons on whom
the powers are conferred. Instance: *On such and such an occasion, such and such*
a tax-gatherer shall take such and such things. Such and such a judge shall, in such
and such a case, cause persons so and so offending to be hanged.

The parts which perform the function of indicating who the individuals
are, who, in every case, shall be considered as belonging to those classes, have
neither a permissive complexion, nor an imperative.

They are so many masses of expository matter, appertaining in common
to all laws, into the texture of which, the names of those classes of persons
have occasion to be inserted. Instance: imperative matter:—*Let the judge*
cause whoever, in due course of law, is convicted of stealing, to be hanged. Nature of
the expository matter:—Who is the person meant by the word *judge*? He who
has been *invested* with that office in such a manner: and in respect of whom no

---

[1] Mirabeau sur la Monarchie Prussienne, Tom. v. Liv. 8, p. 215.

event has happened, of the number of those, to which the effect is given, of reducing him to the condition of one *divested* of that office.

XXIII.
Thus the matter of one law may be divided among all three codes.

Thus it is, that one and the same law, one and the same command, will have its matter divided, not only between two great codes, or main branches of the whole body of the laws, the civil and the penal; but amongst three such branches, the civil, the penal, and the constitutional.

XXIV.
Expository matter, a great quantity of it exists everywhere, in no other form than that of common or judiciary law.

In countries, where a great part of the law exists in no other shape, than that of which in England is called *common* law but might be more expressively termed *judiciary*, there must be a great multitude of laws, the import of which cannot be sufficiently made out for practice, without referring to this common law, for more or less of the expository matter belonging to them. Thus in England the exposition of the word *title*, that basis of the whole fabric of the laws of property, is nowhere else to be found. And, as uncertainty is of the very essence of every particle of law so denominated (for the instant it is clothed in a certain authoritative form of words it changes its nature, and passes over to the other denomination) hence it is that a great part of the laws in being in such countries remain uncertain and incomplete. What are those countries? To this hour, every one on the surface of the globe.

XXV.
Hence the deplorable state of the science of legislation, considered in respect of its form.

Had the science of architecture no fixed nomenclature belonging to it— were there no settled names for distinguishing the different sorts of buildings, nor the different parts of the same building from each other—what would it be? It would be what the science of legislation, considered with respect to its *form*, remains at present.

Were there no architects who could distinguish a dwelling-house from a barn, or a side-wall from a ceiling, what would architects be? They would be what all legislators are at present.

XXVI.
Occasions affording an exemplification of the difficulty as well as importance of this branch of science —attempts to limit the power of supreme representative legislatures.

From this very slight and imperfect sketch, may be collated not an answer to the questions in the text but an intimation, and that but an imperfect one, of the course to be taken for giving such an answer; and, at any rate, some idea of the difficulty, as well as of the necessity, of the task.

If it were thought necessary to recur to experience for proofs of this difficulty, and this necessity, they need not be long wanting.

Take, for instance, so many well-meant endeavours on the part of popular bodies, and so many well-meant recommendations in ingenious books, to restrain supreme representative assemblies from making laws in such and such cases, or to such and such an effect. Such laws, to answer the intended purpose, require a perfect mastery in the science of law considered in respect of its form—in the sort of anatomy spoken of in the preface to this work: but a perfect, or even a moderate insight into that science, would prevent their being couched in those loose and inadequate terms, in which they may be observed so frequently to be conceived; as a perfect acquaintance with the dictates of utility on that head would, in many, if not in most, of those instances discounsel the attempt. Keep to the letter, and in attempting to prevent the making of bad laws, you will find them prohibiting the making of the most necessary laws, perhaps even of all laws: quit the letter, and they express no more than if each man were to say, *Your laws shall become ipso facto void, as often as they contain any thing which is not to my mind.*

Of such unhappy attempts, examples may be met with in the legislation of many nations: but in none more frequently than in that newly-created nation, one of the most enlightened, if not the most enlightened, at this day on the globe.

XXVII.
Example: American declarations of rights.

Take for instance the *Declaration of Rights*, enacted by the State of North Carolina, in convention, in or about the month of September, 1788, and said to be copied, with a small exception, from one in like manner enacted by the State of Virginia.[1]

[1] Recherches sur les Etats Unis, 8vo, 1788, vol. i, p. 158.

The following, to go no farther, is the first and fundamental article:

'That there are certain natural rights, of which men, when they form a social compact, cannot deprive or divest their posterity, among which are the enjoyment of life and liberty, with the means of acquiring, possessing, and protecting property, and pursuing and obtaining happiness and safety.'

Not to dwell on the oversight of confining to posterity the benefit of the rights thus declared, what follows? That—as against those whom the protection, thus meant to be afforded, includes—every law, or other order, *divesting* a man of *the enjoyment of life or liberty*, is void.

Therefore this is the case, amongst others, with every coercive law.

Therefore, as against the persons thus protected, every order, for example, to pay money on the score of taxation, or of debt from individual to individual, or otherwise, is void: for the effect of it, if complied with, is 'to *deprive* and *divest him*,' *pro tanto*, of the enjoyment of liberty, viz. the liberty of paying or not paying as he thinks proper: not to mention the species opposed to imprisonment, in the even of such a mode of coercion's being resorted to: likewise of property, which is itself a '*means of acquiring, possessing, and protecting property, and of pursuing and obtaining happiness and safety*.'

Therefore also, as against such persons, every order to attack an armed enemy in time of war, is also void: for, the necessary effect of such an order is 'to *deprive* some of them of *the enjoyment of life*.'

The above-mentioned consequences may suffice for examples, amongst an endless train of similar ones.[1]

Leaning on his elbow, in an attitude of profound and solemn meditation, '*What a multitude of things there are*' (exclaimed the dancing-master Marcel) '*in a minuet!* '—May we now add?—*and in a law*.

[1] The Virginian Declaration of Rights, said, in the French work above quoted, to have been enacted the 1st of June, 1776, is not inserted in the publication entitled '*The Constitutions of the several independent states of America, &c.*' *Published by order of Congress: Philadelphia printed. Reprinted for Stockdale and Walker, London*, 1782: though that publication contains the form of government enacted in the same convention, between the 6th of May and the 5th of July in the same year.

But in that same publication is contained a *Declaration of Rights*, of the province of *Massachusetts*, dated in the years 1779 and 1780, which in its first article is a little similar: also one of the province of *Pennsylvania*, dated between July 15th and September 28th, in which the similarity is rather more considerable.

Moreover, the famous *Declaration of Independence*, published by Congress July 5th, 1776, after a preamble opening, goes on in these words: '*We hold these truths to be self-evident: that all men are created equal: that they are endued* by the creator *with certain unalienable rights:* that *amongst those are life, liberty, and the pursuit of happiness*.'

The Virginian Declaration of Rights is that, it seems, which claims the honour of having served as a model to those of the other Provinces; and in respect of the above leading article, at least, to the above-mentioned general Declaration of Independence. See Recherches, &c. i. 197.

Who can help lamenting, that so rational a cause should be rested upon reasons, so much fitter to beget objections, than to remove them?

But with men, who are unanimous and hearty about *measures*, nothing so weak but may pass in the character of *a reason*: nor is this the first instance in the world, where the conclusion has supported the premises, instead of the premises the conclusion.